The Sword and the Scepter

The Sword and the Scepter

THE PROBLEM OF MILITARISM IN GERMANY

Volume IV:

THE REIGN OF GERMAN MILITARISM AND THE DISASTER OF 1918

By GERHARD RITTER

Translated from the German by HEINZ NORDEN

 University of Miami Press
Coral Gables, Florida

Translated from the first edition published originally under the title *Staatskunst und Kriegshandwerk: Das Problem des Militarismus in Deutschland. Vierter Band: Die Herrschaft des deutschen Militarismus und die Katastrophe von 1918* by R. Oldenbourg Verlag, Munich, Copyright © 1968 by R. Oldenbourg Verlag, Munich.

Copyright © 1973 by University of Miami Press

ISBN 0-87024-235-0

Library of Congress Catalog Card No. 68-31041

Editorial Consultant for this volume:
Dr. H. W. Koch, University of York, England

Designed by Bernard Lipsky

Manufactured in the United States of America

Contents

Foreword

WHEN DEATH came to Gerhard Ritter on July 1, 1967, the present fourth volume of *The Sword and the Scepter* was virtually finished. Thus his last wish, to see this last part completed and published, was at least partly fulfilled. We are grateful on his account. What is left to me is the sorrowful but rewarding duty of transmitting to the world this volume, which concludes the great work of my father's old age.

The third volume ended with the fall of Bethmann Hollweg in July 1917. The present fourth volume leads on to the collapse in November 1918. It embraces a period in which the sinister predominance of the military, already revealed in the opening bars, grew inexorably stronger until internal revolution robbed the civil power of any further capacity for action. In the end there was the grotesque situation that the crucial telegram signifying agreement to the armistice terms of Compiègne was signed *Reichskanzler* (Chancellor), though dispatched by the OHL, the *Oberste Heeresleitung* (supreme army command).

This fourth volume too is based entirely on original documentary research. To the very last Gerhard Ritter was intent on finding additional source material. Intensive work in the archives of the foreign ministry in Bonn in January 1967 was followed by a trip to London in March, where, greatly aided by British colleagues and library heads, he succeeded in gaining access to important new material.

"Nothing could be more precarious than the trade of the historian of the recent past," Gerhard Ritter wrote in his foreword to the third volume of this work. It is his job to give "a lucid, multidimensional projection of events in which light and shade are fairly apportioned." This was his goal in writing this fourth volume as well. It was his constant endeavor to comprehend his source material entirely on his own, without ever submitting to some preconceived opinion. Almost eighty years old, he was, to the last moment of his life, ready to learn, prepared to modify his view of the world, past and present, in the light of new research and new findings. Yet behind everything he has written we sense the warm and living breath of a man who has relived everything, every situation, hence knows how to encompass it in representing it, calmly weighing the facts, yet profoundly *engagé*.

His original design provided for following the present volume with two further long review chapters. They were to be less concerned with documentation but rather were to deal in essay form with the relation of scepter and sword, in the Weimar era, and lastly under Hitler. It was then that a complete reversal took place. As Gerhard Ritter put it in the foreword to his second volume, we witnessed a "totally unique situation unprecedented in history. It was the soldiers who had to oppose the blind militarism of the civilian political leadership." The preliminary studies for these two chapters were virtually finished, and Gerhard Ritter was about to embark on the final version when death plucked the pen from his fingers.

The present volume, nevertheless, is complete in itself and comes to a natural conclusion with the armistice of 1918. Gerhard Ritter himself said on more than one occasion that it was ready for publication as it stood, even if he were not vouchsafed the time to complete the two additional chapters. The only task left to us was to effect that publication, in the measure that we were able to do so without the guidance of his all-embracing scholarship. We must therefore ask for indulgence for any defects that may turn up, especially in the Notes and Bibliographies.

I take pleasure in expressing my warmest appreciation to those who assisted me in seeing the book to press: Dr. Klaus Schwabe, Dr. Karl-Heinrich Oldendorf, Mrs. Uta Oldendorf, and Dr. Siegfried Büttner—all four of them former students of Gerhard Ritter who felt a sense of gratitude and obligation toward their master's final work. They gave generous help not only in reading proof and compiling the German index, but in providing constructive comment. I wish also to thank my dear husband, who gave me loyal advice and support.

October 1967   DR. RENATE VOLZ, née RITTER

The Sword and the Scepter

ONE

The Predominance
of Militarist Thinking
and Its
Political Repercussions

1

The Problem of a Negotiated Peace in the Fall of 1917

Part 1

The World, the German Peace Resolution, and the Chancellorship of Michaelis

A T THE MOMENT when the fall of Bethmann Hollweg swept away the last impediment to the concentration of supreme political power in the hands of the OHL in Germany, spirits in the enemy camp were at the lowest ebb reached at any time in the First World War; and the watchword of "sticking it out at any price" met with greater war-weariness than ever before, indeed with open mass resistance.

Since the failure of its great spring offensive under Nivelle, the French army, a major part of it in a state of mutiny, had neither dared nor been able throughout the year to mount another large-scale attack. The French minister of war Painlevé had stated in May 1917 that between Soissons and Paris only two divisions were left on which complete reliance could be placed, a situation General Pétain was able to improve only slowly by combining the harshest discipline with kid-glove treatment. On June 8, reporting to the British war cabinet, General Henry Wilson, then England's representative at French headquarters, drew an extremely gloomy picture of the state of the French army. He said he did not believe General Pétain capable of holding it together for a fourth war winter, unless morale were once again raised by a great military or political triumph. Since no opening was in sight for a great and successful military strike, all Lloyd George could do was to concentrate every effort on a negotiated peace with Austria, seeking to overcome Italian opposition to such a step.[1]

In the course of midsummer the situation of the Entente grew worse. The last desperate Russian offensive in July failed, and German and Austrian counter-attacks led to the loss of almost all of Galicia and the Bukovina. Late in the summer it became clear that even the British effort to force a breakthrough in Flanders by means of an almost inconceivable concentration of heavy artillery would remain futile in the end—that truly hellish fighting is among the author's most horrible personal memories of the war. Tension between Lloyd George and his General Staff was even then already strained to the limit.[2]

No one was surprised that the unending attacks by the Italians on the Isonzo continued to fail. Far more alarming was the news that reached Paris and London about the demoralization of the Italian troops,[3] horrifyingly confirmed late in October by the disaster at Tolmein, when 300,000 Italians were taken prisoner. Thanks to the commitment of French and British divisions, the tidal flood of German and Austrian attack columns following the rupture of the Italian lines was halted in the end; but to the Allies, the Italian front was henceforth only a worrisome burden rather than a source of relief.

Lloyd George held that for a long time past now only the German and British ranks had any true fighting spirit left.[4] Even at the higher levels of the French officer corps doubts stirred as to whether the time might not have come for a swift and moderate peace.[5] Late in the year, of course, Lenin's November Revolution led to the final and total dissolution of the Russian front. Indeed, the only hope the Western powers had left was America. The struggle against the German U-boats could be won only with the support of the American navy. Even mighty Britain, once so rich, was now lost without powerful financial support by America, particularly since it was compelled to bear a major share of the financial burdens of its continental allies.

This state of dependence was painfully felt in Paris and London during the summer, as the American ambassadors Sharp and Page reported, not without patriotic pride.[6] The appearance of the American general Pershing, of the first few American soldiers and sailors, even of American nurses in uniform—all these aroused new hope and enthusiasm in the two headquarters; but when would the first effective American forces be put together, when would they be shipped to Europe? Even by the winter of 1917-1918 no more than a single American division was in full fighting trim.

And when the Americans did come, would they be more successful than the British in forcing a breakthrough? Ambassador Sharp dreaded the prospect of feeding hundreds of thousands of brave American boys to the hopeless slaughter of the trenches. He advised his president to consider the alternative of building and manning 10,000 airplanes, to provide the Allies with absolute air superiority.[7]

Balfour asked the British generals in the early summer of 1917 when the full effect of American ground participation could be expected. He was told that the war was unlikely to end before the summer or fall of 1919. Would the Allies be able to stick it out that long? It is true that more and more German

U-boats were being sunk, and the scare news that reached the American admiral Sims in April—that Britain had food stocks left for only six weeks—turned out to be exaggerated;[8] but even in July the American ambassador Page seriously feared that the Germans would win the war at sea. He was disturbed not so much by the scarcity of food—that could be partly handled by rationing—as by that of crucial war material; and if the war went on and on, were the Americans, on their part, prepared to "stick it out" indefinitely?

The American ambassador had an even greater worry. What if before winter the Germans were to offer the Allies everything they were bound to be after?— the restoration of Belgium and France; the return of Alsace-Lorraine; and the relinquishment of Germany's colonies, provided only that Austria was not carved up, i.e., that the prospect of a united *Mitteleuropa* was not swept aside. In the light of the general war-weariness in Europe, such an offer might well meet with success; and in that case all hope would be gone for America to gain the goals to which Page so ardently aspired, which he had painted in such glowing colors—America as the leading naval and mercantile power; as the world's spiritual leader; as the liberator of the old Europe from imperialism and the "myth of monarchy" in general, that "queerest thing in the world," from all the ancient "privileges" and nationalist prejudices, from "patriotic" provincialism, in favor of the brotherhood of man.

True, the struggle for such lofty goals—which would gain Britain all the German colonies, as a mere by-product—would exact an immense toll in blood; but were not the nations concerned long since overpopulated? In five to ten years all the misery would be forgotten, all the heaps of rubble cleaned up. As for the American people, they would come out of the war sounder and more virile. There was no danger that the Anglo-Saxon race, with its age-old democracy, would lapse into militarism. On the other hand, the war would almost certainly bring men of a higher type into political life; and liberation would bring to Europe too much more new life than would be killed off. The struggle must not be broken off prematurely![9]

There must be no yielding, no pacifist catchwords! This was also the view of the French premier and foreign minister Ribot. He describes in his memoirs the deep concern with which he followed the political vacillations of his cabinet colleague, the socialist Thomas, and his party, under the impact of the Russian Revolution. Ribot professes to have seen through the efforts of neutral—and especially Scandinavian—socialists to bring about an international socialist conference in Stockholm, to discuss questions of war and peace—it was no more than a German scheme.[10] Bethmann Hollweg's calculation was to exploit the Russian revolutionaries and their sympathizers throughout the world, with the help of Scheidemann, in order to paralyze Allied strategy and escape his responsibility for unleashing the war.

Ribot's reply to the Soviet program of a "peace without annexations and indemnities" was a speech in the French chamber on May 22, in which, with great rhetorical and dialectical skill, he drew an idealized picture of French war aims. No, France did not want a peace of conquest; but for that very reason France condemned the peace of Frankfurt in 1871. For forty years Bismarck had subjected Europe to a regime of force. Now at last the return of the plundered provinces was to restore justice. No, there were to be no reparations, if that meant arbitrary acts of vengeance, in President Wilson's meaning; but restitution for the damage done by those who started the war, i.e,., punishment of the guilty and elimination of military despotism—that was the purest justice rather than vengeance!

No French government, from Ribot to Clémenceau, departed by as much as one jot or tittle from this line of a peace of just atonement. For the French, the political interests of France were identical with the cause of "justice"—what was there to negotiate? Not even the French socialists caused any real trouble for this policy in the chamber. It is true that Ribot and his predecessor Briand were sharply challenged when French socialist deputies learned in St. Petersburg of sweeping annexationist plans which Doumergue had discussed with the czarist government as recently as February (See Vol. III, pp. 248-252); but the two ministers, in a secret session, were soon able to assuage the rising opposition, and subsequently, on June 5, the chamber, by an overwhelming majority (467 to 52), adopted an agenda in which the return of Alsace-Lorraine to France's maternal arms was declared to be a just war aim.[11] The socialist minority, urging a revision of contractual Allied war aims along the lines advocated by the Bolshevists, was either intimidated or voted down; and when the socialists met in convention in Paris on May 28 and, to everyone's surprise, decided by a large majority to send delegates to the Stockholm conference, there was no public outcry when the government refused to issue them passports.

Reason for the refusal was fear of any discussion with the Germans on matters of peace, no matter how informal. The radical left wing of the French socialists, like the Soviets and the German "independent" social democrats, wanted to see the fate of Alsace-Lorraine settled by plebiscite. That was irksome enough, but it was not the crucial point. What mattered was that once it were known that French socialists were discussing peace with Germans, French army morale might completely collapse.

Nowhere else did the notion of a negotiated peace encounter such tenacious opposition—and precisely because France suffered far more severely from exhaustion than any other country. It was the uncertain morale of the army and of the radical left that stiffened the spine of the moderate Ribot government. This went so far that Ribot himself and many other politicians (including the former minister of war Millerand) even shrank from secret negotiations for a separate peace with Austria and Turkey. They feared that these might widen into general peace talks, and at bottom they wanted no peace unless it were preceded by military victory.[12]

This was not true of all the leading men. As we shall see in Part 3 of this chapter, in midsummer, after the failure of the Kerensky offensive and the final defection of Russia as an active force, some serious endeavors were launched from Paris in the direction of breaking up the alliance of the Central Powers and bringing about the kind of understanding with Austria that Ribot had managed to sabotage the preceding spring (see Vol. III, p. 382ff.)—an understanding, by the way, that would have been entirely at Germany's expense; for there was never any wavering on that one point: The main goal of French war policy was the return of the western provinces lost in 1870 (and still not reconquered). By comparison, the liberation of Belgium continued to play a subsidiary role.[13]

The over-all picture, as regards political trends and forces, was similar in Italy. There were widespread war-weariness, peace demonstrations, food riots in the industrial cities (reaching the level of heavy street fighting, especially in Turin), much inflammatory criticism of the government by the socialist opposition, long secret sessions that threatened to bring down the Boselli cabinet—but in the end there were always large "patriotic" majorities that supported the government.

Most surprising, perhaps, in all this was the continuing effect of patriotic oratory, especially from the lips of Foreign Minister Sonnino. Time and again he was able to draw the mantle of moral idealism over his government's massive annexationist policies—they were represented as a crusade to liberate the oppressed, to restore justice that had been trampled underfoot. He skillfully duped the Allied governments by exploiting the allegedly ever-present revolutionary threat to Italy. He rejected any attempt to moderate his war aims as an affront. Indeed, he blackmailed the Allies into ever-greater promises.[14] Thus rising domestic unrest, economic difficulties (caused not least by the activities of German U-boats in the Mediterranean), and war-weariness failed to dampen Italy's territorial ambitions.

Only in October, in the wake of chaotic scenes in the chamber, did the opposition succeed in toppling the Boselli government. They were aided by Catholic voices that were looking to the peace initiative of Pope Benedict XV for salvation. News of the disaster of Tolmein-Karfreit burst upon these sessions and compelled all the parties to agree on a political program.

The British attitude was more equivocal than either the French or the Italian. Since his famous "knockout" interview of September 28, 1916 (see Vol. III, p. 258), Lloyd George had been accounted Britain's strong man, and he deserved this appellation, since he would not hear of peace until "Prussian militarism" had been destroyed. On the other hand, Lloyd George was not at all inclined to see his country's strength sapped merely for the territorial aggrandizement of its allies. We have already seen that he was much firmer than Ribot in seeking to keep Italian territorial ambitions in check. He tried to persuade them to forego Trieste, if that would make possible a separate peace with Austria (see Vol. III, p. 383ff.). We also know that he was ready for talks with Turkey and Austria about a separate peace, and that he persisted with this intention right down to March 1918.[15]

But Lloyd George was in a difficult position in respect of peace efforts. He was publicly committed to a strong-arm policy that employed police power to suppress pacifist demonstrations; and as a former Liberal he was closely watched by the suspicious right extremists, the "die-hards." Even the slightest hint of peace talks was likely to get him into trouble.[16] Yet by rejecting Soviet demands for a peace without annexations he was also likely to clash with Britain's industrial workers on whom everything depended. It was a worrisome dilemma. At times the radical agitation of the Independent Labour party and the Union for Democratic Control seemed to pose a serious threat. At the Leeds Labour Conference of June 3, already discussed (see Vol. III, p. 413), the institution of a workers' and soldiers' council on the Russian model was actually discussed, though only theoretically.

Lloyd George was, nevertheless, initially inclined to allow British delegates to attend the Stockholm conference. In a letter to the French minister of labor Thomas he said that it must be made clear to the world, and especially to the German people, that the cause of the Entente was the cause of democratic freedom. The Russian peace formula of self-determination and no annexations and indemnities would be entirely acceptable unless it were to compel the French and British to redeliver the African colonies to the Germans and Mesopotamia to the Turks "for exploitation" and to forego the return of Alsace-Lorraine, which "Prussian militarism" had wrested from the French. The socialists from the Entente countries might well make the Russian and German delegates understand such an attitude, and the Germans might see that peace was being delayed only by the crimes of their own government, that peace might be much more readily negotiated if Germany and Austria adopted a democratic form of government. If French and British socialists were denied passports it would create the impression that the Entente governments were afraid of open discussions with the Russian revolutionaries.[17]

The British prime minister was clearly toying with the idea of encouraging revolutionary agitation in Germany and Austria with the help of the international socialist conference, thus undermining the rule of Prussian militarism. In that way it might be possible to avoid waging war to the bitter end. For a time he even tied his hopes to the domestic reforms contemplated by Bethmann Hollweg. In April, at the height of the U-boat crisis, he mentioned to Lord Riddell, his close friend and head of the London press association, the possibility that the "constitutional" government Bethmann Hollweg apparently envisaged might be more willing to negotiate moderate peace terms than the present German government which was subservient to the militarists.[18]

In all likelihood Lloyd George was not greatly concerned about German willingness to evacuate Belgium and France at the proper time, even though he never failed to demand clear-cut German declarations about Belgium in his propaganda speeches. Early in September, following the papal peace note still to be discussed, he conjectured at once that the Germans would probably be willing to clear out of these territories if they got back their colonies, but would be unlikely to forego Alsace-Lorraine, which could bring about an awkward situation.[19] It would be awkward because, while he and his foreign secretary Balfour set no great store by the acquisition of the German colonies,[20] the British dominions in Africa strongly insisted on this, and because British pacifists saw no merit whatever in the unyielding French attitude on Alsace-Lorraine. Actually, to Ribot's chagrin, Lloyd George waited until January 1918 before publicly committing himself to the return of Alsace-Lorraine, having entertained intermittent hopes that the Germans might after all console themselves for its loss with major territorial gains in the east.[21]

Of course the idea of undermining German imperial autocracy with the help of the socialist international entailed a considerable gamble. The French cabinet had already barred the way early in June by denying passports to the French socialist delegates; and when Henderson, the moderate socialist in the British cabinet, in concert with French socialists, Russian delegates, and the radical British pacifist Ramsay MacDonald, tried to ram through the dispatch of British delegates, there was a storm of patriotic indignation throughout the land, as well as in the cabinet and the House of Commons. Despite warnings from Lloyd George, Henderson persuaded a great Labour party conference in London on August 10 to come out for participation in the Stockholm meeting with a strong majority.[22] There was an open break and Henderson was obliged to leave the cabinet. The socialists were denied passports and Britain chose the same nakedly nationalist course as France.

But unlike Paris, where a kind of nationalist terror ruled the chamber, there was wide-open discussion on the peace problem in the House of Commons, though only a tiny minority opposed the policy of sticking it out until final victory. Its spokesmen were the Liberals Trevelyan, Lee Smith, and Ponsonby, together with MacDonald and Snowden of the Independent Labour party on the extreme left. They reacted very positively to the peace resolution of the German Reichstag, and a four-hour debate on July 26 provided telling evidence of the impression this resolution made among Germany's enemies.

Thus the insistence of the German opponents of the peace resolution that it would betoken German war-weariness and demoralization abroad was shown to be quite without foundation.[23] Even had there been such an impression, the continuing tremendous achievements of the German armies would have soon served to dispel it. Actually, the Entente countries viewed the German peace resolution as a "trap" rather than a sign of weakness, an attempt to disrupt the united enemy front by hypocritical assurances that the Germans sought reconciliation. Such, at any rate, was the theme of the instant counterpropaganda, which ran along the same lines with which Bethmann Hollweg's peace offer of December 1916 had been impugned and deprecated.

Such imputations, however, were far less plausible in the face of a resolution adopted by a sizable majority of German deputies, predominantly from the parties of the left, than in the case of an initiative by an allegedly "autocratic" imperialist regime. One may well suspect that the Reichstag resolution initially represented an acute embarrassment to anti-German propaganda. In the French chamber it was passed over in silence, in the British press attempts were made to ignore it;[24] but the small group of determined liberal and radical Labour members of the House of Commons saw to it that it was nevertheless made public and debated. This debate is worth a closer look, because it serves to show how hopeless then was the cause of a negotiated peace.

MacDonald read the text of the Reichstag resolution, virtually unknown to the British public, and moved that the House respond with an affirmative declaration.[25] The assertion by the London *Times* that the resolution was only a dramatic gesture was untrue, he said. The German public was widely behind it. It was true that the German Reichstag did not actually govern, but it was all the more free to reflect the views of the German people. Scheidemann had discovered in Stockholm just how precarious was the position of the German people in the eyes of the world. A great process of soul-searching had begun in Germany. It was true that no Englishman could understand how the Germans could still believe that they were engaged in a defensive war; but incidents like Lloyd George's "knockout" speech (see Vol. III, p. 258) and the Paris economic conference with its boycott resolutions for the postwar period merely served to confirm them in their mistaken views, and so did the inflammatory articles in the British press. Modern mass war was no longer purely a government matter. The people must. be won over. The Reichstag resolution clearly betokened a new German willingness for negotiation, and this should be exploited. War aims and the secret treaties in which they were embodied should be revised, for they seemed in ill accord with the moral protestations of the government. Britain would have to wait a long time for help from the United States—or was a war of exhaustion already taken for granted? That would have evil consequences for the Allies too.

The Liberal Charles Philips Trevelyan said that he found British government policy contradictory. At one time the refusal to negotiate with the Germans was based on the contention that the Junkers and militarists were undeserving of trust. Now the refusal was maintained in the face of a declaration backed by representatives of the workers, bourgeois radicals, liberals, and even a generous half of the conservative elements. Was the Reichstag really powerless? Well then, did the House of Commons control British foreign policy? There could be no doubt of a real change in the German people, and Scheidemann had stated that if the House of Commons adopted a similar resolution, peace could come tomorrow. Since the Russian Revolution czarism was no longer a threat to the Germans and propaganda among the workers no longer featured the bogey of "czarist reaction." The workers no longer had any reason to rally behind Prussian militarism. If the war were ended by negotiation and without needless humiliation, German militarism would be finished in any event. That was why the Junkers and reactionaries in Germany feared nothing more than a negotiated peace—and here Trevelyan quoted from the *Kreuzzeitung;* but a negotiated peace meant that the Allied camp too would have to forego grandiose visions of conquest.

These exigencies were also emphasized by the Liberal Lee Smith, who mocked the newly discovered democratic conversion zeal of Messrs. Milner, Curzon, and Bonar Law. "Knockout blows," he said, would never convert the German people to democracy—that would take a reasonable peace which would make militarism seem superfluous to them. If Britain challenged the Germans to forego territorial aggrandizement, why should not the Entente do likewise? Why did it pass up every opportunity for peace talks? The Allies were so inflexible that they were even abandoning Kerensky, and soon they would witness, in Russia, the greatest military disaster of the war. The stupidity of British politicians and their press in dealing with the situation in Russia was almost beyond comprehension. No less grotesque, however—so added the Member R. D. Denman—was the British attitude toward Germany. Did Britain expect the Kaiser's government to abdicate, as a condition for negotiating with it? The Germans would have to be utter fools to bring down their own government in midwar.

Reading these statements today, one can scarcely avoid being startled by their profound and prophetic insight, which rose above current political issues; but they represented the views of only a hopelessly small minority. How much suffering the world would have been spared, had it then been possible to end the war in the spirit of the Reichstag resolution and its British advocates! But we see from these debates also that the fall of Bethmann Hollweg took much of the steam out of the Reichstag resolution. All the arguments marshaled by Asquith, the former prime minister and now leader of the opposition, and the Conservative secretary of war Bonar Law, were the same worn-out war slogans, endlessly repeated.[26] There must be no peace with the Germans until German militarism was crushed and Europe was at last safe. This was coupled with the knowingly mendacious propaganda claim that the free nations were far above any selfish imperialist or annexationist goals;

while restoration of the status quo would represent a continuing threat to the small nations, through "dynastic intrigue" and military coercion.

What was Germany's political position, Asquith asked? What had really happened? For a while it had looked as though the moderates might prevail on the other side. Then, suddenly, the military leaders appeared on the political stage and forced the dismissal of the very Chancellor in whom William II only a few days earlier had expressed absolute trust. What else could this mean but that the extremists had carried the day? The Reichstag was not even consulted in the appointment of the new Chancellor. Yes, he had voted for the resolution, but his support had been lukewarm—he had added the reservation "as I understand it." Well, how did he understand it? Was Germany ready to get out of Belgium and make amends for the destruction it had wrought there, including the enslavement of Belgian workers? Was it prepared to restore full and unlimited sovereignty to Belgium? These were questions to which an unequivocal reply must be given.[27] Bonar Law, the Conservative, evidently regarded even these questions as superfluous. He insisted that the new Chancellor, Michaelis, was no more than a tool of the OHL, just as Haase, the leader of the independent social democrats, had asserted in the Reichstag. What store could be put by fine words, which Michaelis voiced only to please the political parties? Had he not expressly declared that he was determined to retain full control?

This view of what was happening in the Reichstag was indeed in keeping with that of the radical leftist Haase. It meant a one-sided, spiteful rejection. Yet can we claim that it completely distorted the true situation? Had there really been the basic change of heart in Germany which the authors of the Reichstag resolution had hoped for, with which they expected to impress the world? According to a later statement by Riezler, Bethmann Hollweg, just prior to his fall, had planned a major speech in the Reichstag in which he would have proclaimed a radically new domestic policy, defining his prior declarations about Belgium more precisely, and telling the right in no uncertain terms that it would not set German policy.[28] This was meant to be a reply to a very clever speech Lloyd George had delivered in Glasgow, chiding Bethmann Hollweg for "almost" foregoing Belgium, but then giving way again before the Junkers, when they gave him a difficult time. Negotiations with a genuinely democratic German government, Lloyd George had said, might take place in quite a different spirit and with far less distrust than was harbored toward one dominated by the militarists.[29]

There can be little doubt that such a speech by Bethmann Hollweg would have made a strong impression on Lloyd George, who, as late as 1918, told an intimate that he always liked to read Bethmann Hollweg's speeches and regarded them as having considerable stature. They were firm and lucid, every word like the blow of a hammer.[30] Such a public declaration by the Chancellor, coupled with the solemn proclamation of the Reichstag resolution, would at the very least have marked a quite unmistakable turn in German policy that could not have been ignored in the enemy countries.

What happened instead, in the Reichstag session of July 19, stopped at mere half-measures. The very wording of the Reichstag resolution, modified again and again in lengthy debate, had turned vague and pale under pressure of nationalist countercurrents.[31] As had been agreed with the party leaders, the new Chancellor, instead of simply taking it over, presented his own artfully devised program, which he "hoped to achieve within the framework of the resolution." This was intended to emphasize his autonomy and thus also accord with the wishes of the OHL, which avoided any formal statement of approval, indeed forbade publication of any such statement.[32]

Thus the majority parties received the Chancellor's declaration with applause. Only Haase, the radical leftist, at once pilloried as an ominous reservation Michaelis's addendum to the agreed text of his speech—namely that he thought he could reconcile the resolution "as he understood it" with his program. According to Michaelis's memoirs, his intention was merely to reserve to himself a certain reasonable leeway in interpreting the resolution—in other words, if annexations and indemnities were to be had for the asking, he might not forego them in all circumstances.[33]

This, by the way, was how he professed to have understood a statement by Scheidemann in the preliminary discussions; but when his interpretation was challenged late in August in the majority party caucus, in discussions with the party leaders, and before the main committee of the Reichstag, Michaelis got into a serious dilemma. New to the tricks of parliamentary tactics, he involved himself in contradictions and thus soon lost the confidence of the majority parties—or more precisely, despite his best efforts, he never even succeeded in winning their confidence in the first place. This was largely because his appointment, despite the formal agreement on the peace resolution, represented virtually the opposite of what the majority parties had expected from a change in the chancellorship.

True, Michaelis was not a Pan-German, and he was critical of exaggerated war propaganda and territorial aims;[34] nor was he a reactionary, as shown by his appointment of liberal and moderate figures to high office and his attitude toward Prussian electoral reform. Equally, he was not a blind partisan of Ludendorff, whose brusque and imperious manner he always found uncongenial and whose attitude toward the Kaiser he described as "insubordinate"; but Michaelis was an old-style Prussian bureaucrat of strictly monarchist persuasion, who regarded parliamentary intervention into the executive as irksome, if not wholly improper, and who sharply recoiled from giving high office to politicians without expert training.

The parliamentarians soon realized this and they thought that his assurances of close cooperation with them represented merely a tactical move. This also applied to his pledges to consult them in major questions of foreign policy—which was actually done after August 28, through the so-called sevens committee. They distrusted him and were critical of the changes he made at the top—though without putting forward concrete counterproposals. An added factor was that Michaëlis, by the very circumstances of his appointment, had no alternative to trying to avoid clashes with the OHL even more carefully than Bethmann Hollweg had done. Thus by late August the Chancellor's position on the home front was already in a bad way. The democrat Haussmann had no compunction in describing him as "impossible"; and if demands for his prompt dismissal did not find an immediate Reichstag majority, this was mainly because of a reluctance to damage Germany's position abroad by two changes in the chancellorship in swift succession—a reluctance entertained particularly by Erzberger and the centrist party.[35]

In the light of all these events, the peace initiative of the Reichstag, launched with such great hopes, must be considered a failure in every respect. At home too, instead of healing the divisions among the German people, it merely served to deepen them balefully. The foolish slogans about a "peace of victory" and a "peace of compromise," about a "Hindenburg peace" and a "Scheidemann peace," turned more and more into ugly fighting words in the bitter quarrels between the right and the left that split the nation beyond any possibility of reconciliation and poisoned political life in Germany right down to the end of the Weimar Republic.

The opening gun was fired late in August with the formation of the so-called fatherland party, in which Tirpitz once again played a fateful political role, beside a leading agricultural bureaucrat, Kapp, whose inflammatory propensities we have already noted. Their goal was to fight the peace resolution and the sentiments behind it, and by the use of modern propaganda techniques they succeeded in instilling militarist and annexationist ideas widely among the middle class—by July 1918, they had achieved a membership of one and a quarter millions.[36] By contrast, only modest success attended the efforts of a group of liberal professors—Ernst Troeltsch, Friedrich Meinecke, Walter Götz—to found a moderate counterorganization, the people's league for freedom and fatherland. Partly responsible was the fact that the fatherland party received generous support from the OHL, and also through a program of patriotic indoctrination Ludendorff instituted in the army, while military censorship largely suppressed socialist publicity. The stock-in-trade of this patriotic agitation was crude invective against the Reichstag for its "shameful" peace resolution and the "traitorous" deputies who had supported it. Rightist reaction and assertions of patriotism thus became dangerously intermingled. Not the least reason for Michaelis's fall, which soon eventuated, was that he showed himself incapable of dealing vigorously with this spiteful campaign, which War Minister Stein tried to defend and trivialize clumsily in the Reichstag.[37]

Of course there was trouble between extremists and moderates in all the belligerent countries; but only in Germany, unlike the Western countries, did this lead to the formal organization of mutually hostile mass groups, permanently polluting the political atmosphere. One has a choice of viewing this as an expression of either stanch and uncompromising vitality or political immaturity on the part of the German people. Certainly the war, to Germany, was far more a matter of life and death than it was for its Western enemies. National survival and centuries of tradition were at stake. As a result, after the disaster of 1918, mutual recrimination got completely out of hand, leading to deadly hatred and assassinations on the part of nationalist fanatics. Here the dragon seed of the fatherland party with its intemperate charges against the peace resolution and its authors ultimately came to a bloody harvest.

Part 2
The Papal Peace Initiative and the Entente Statesmen

FROM THE EARLY months of the war onward Pope Benedict XV was continually intent on damping down the furies of war as much as possible by the exercise of his spiritual authority. Initially these efforts did meet with some success on the compassionate side. At his suggestion prisoners-of-war no longer fit for military service were exchanged, captured civilians were repatriated, and the sick and wounded were transferred to hospitals in Switzerland. On the other hand an armistice he proposed for Christmas Day 1914 failed because of French and Russian opposition.[38]

As early as January 1915, furthermore, Benedict intervened in political questions by protesting, in the most cautious terms, against the violation of Belgian neutrality—as the only "neutral"! Thenceforth one of the main goals of papal policy was to promote the restoration of the freedom and independence of Catholic Belgium, thus making sure of its loyalty. The Poles too found an advocate in Rome, insofar as papal concern for the Central Powers permitted. Germany and Austria were the only two major powers represented at the Holy See with ambassadors while also having resident papal nuncios. In these two countries the Catholic church enjoyed high political prestige, while the anticlericalism that predominated in Italy and France prevented any closer contact between statesmen and the Holy See. The further fact that the pope feared Russia as a dangerous enemy of the church of Rome and had

opposed Italian entry into the war naturally resulted in closer Vatican relations with Vienna and Berlin—and Munich as well—than with the Entente
countries, despite a strictly preserved neutrality and the close personal connections with French Catholicism cultivated by the papal secretary of state
Gasparri, a former nuncio to Paris.

In December 1916 Emperor Charles of Austria sent the pope a personal
letter asking for a papal manifesto in support of the peace appeal by the
Central Powers. The Prussian envoy at the Vatican transmitted a similar request. This, of course, the Holy See was unwilling to concede. It did, however, press Vienna and Berlin for more concrete peace proposals, especially
for the future of Belgium for which it appended a draft. It also displayed a
willingness to transmit to the Entente governments any confidentially communicated outlines for peace negotiations, but the two countries failed to
respond. Nevertheless, they kept up their diplomatic contacts and repeatedly
(see Vol. III, p. 245f.) tried to use Vatican diplomacy to pave the way for a
separate peace with Belgium, an endeavor in which Erzberger played a zealous
part.

Together with the journalist Viktor Naumann, this resourceful intermediary was a frequent visitor to the papal nunciature in Munich, which gradually
grew into something like a center for the Catholic peace movement, involving
also the Bavarian premier Count Hertling and the Austrian foreign minister
Czernin. At the suggestion of the nuncio Aversa, Naumann drafted a long
memorandum for the pope at the Austrian foreign ministry. This was transmitted to Rome late in April and was also submitted to Bethmann Hollweg.[39] It sharply pointed up the danger to the Catholic church in leaving
peace agitation to international socialism, especially the Soviets. For the sake
of returning peace to the world, the pope, it said, had to accept even the risk
of martyrdom, i.e., of a threat to his personal safety at the hands of "Italian
freemasons and their henchmen." A preliminary program for negotiation was
appended, quite plainly bearing the stamp of Vienna as the place of origin of
the document. It provided for full restoration of Belgium, no large-scale
annexations, an exchange of "land masses," and a fundamental reorganization
in the Balkans. To put over this program, Catholic bishops and organizations
throughout the world were to initiate a peace movement.

Naturally neither the government in Vienna nor that in Berlin could identify itself with this memorandum, and both carefully avoided any direct
approach to the Holy See for negotiation; yet they did clearly let it be known
that they would welcome a papal initiative for peace,[40] and Aversa's successor, the new papal nuncio Pacelli, eagerly tackled such a project. During his
courtesy visits to the Kaiser and the Chancellor late in June he took careful
soundings of German peace intentions (see Vol. III, p. 461f.). As we have
already seen, Bethmann Hollweg gave him considerable encouragement by

showing a willingness to relinquish Belgium and negotiate with France—his statements had been carefully agreed on beforehand with foreign minister Zimmermann, who repeated them to Pacelli. As for the Kaiser, he exhorted the nuncio to launch a major peace initiative in almost the same words as Naumann's.[41] Only a few weeks earlier Emperor Charles had said the same thing in a reply to Pope Benedict, though he virtually rejected the pope's proposal that Austria forego South Tyrol to make possible a separate peace with Italy.

Thus the Central Powers, and especially Germany, were actually behind the decision of the Holy See to launch a great diplomatic peace offensive at the beginning of the fourth year of the war. The papacy correctly discerned that the time was particularly auspicious, following the collapse of the Kerensky offensive, i.e., of the whole eastern Allied front, and publication of the Reichstag resolution. The initial steps were prepared in deepest secrecy, in discussions between Pacelli and the German Chancellor and the German foreign ministry. This time there was to be no mere appeal for peace. Rome hoped for greater success with presentation of a concrete peace program—provided the agreement of the German government could be secured beforehand. Pacelli entertained great hopes in this respect, as a result of his talks with Bethmann Hollweg. The papal "promemoria" which the nuncio presented on July 24 as the draft for a mediation offer was carefully attuned to Bethmann Hollweg's statements in its most important point—Belgium's full military, political, and economic independence was to be secured against Germany, Britain, and France by appropriate guarantees to be agreed on. As a prerequisite, the evacuation of Belgium and France was demanded in return for the German colonies.

President Wilson's wishes were taken into account in the initial statements about freedom of the seas, arms limitation, and an international court of arbitration. In these respects, Gasparri could least expect opposition from the Germans, judging from their attitude thus far; but he dared not offer concrete proposals on the most delicate points—settling postwar economic relations, and Franco-German and Austro-Italian border questions, in other words the problems of Alsace-Lorraine and South Tyrol. This was true also of the future of Poland and the Balkan countries. All that was to be left to the peace conference, which would take account of the wishes of the populations. Even so, the papal secretary of state was apparently hopeful on these matters too, in the light of Bethmann Hollweg's statement to Pacelli on June 26, that peace need not fail over the question of Alsace-Lorraine if France were willing to negotiate. On the question of South Tyrol, Emperor Charles had shown himself not quite so inflexible as before during a discussion with Pacelli on June 30; and as far as territorial questions in the east were concerned, Russia's military impotence gave more hope than ever that an understanding could be reached.

We may indeed assume that this peace program, by and large, accorded with Bethmann Hollweg's views or could have been reconciled with them. There would of course have been the reservation that Germany would evacuate the territories occupied in the west only when an acceptable peace was secured—until then they would have to be kept as "bargaining counters."[42] After all, what Bethmann Hollweg had confidentially told the nuncio on June 24 represented merely an informal view, approved by neither the Kaiser nor the OHL, hence in no way binding. Had Bethmann Hollweg remained in office, he would have had to fight for the Kaiser's assent against the determined opposition of the OHL, or he would have had to outmaneuver the Kaiser in some way. With Bethmann Hollweg gone, neither Zimmermann nor his successor Kühlmann nor the new Chancellor Michaelis could dream of giving immediate assent to the papal peace program.[43] They would first have to gain the approval of headquarters at Kreuznach, and it was a foregone conclusion that the OHL would vigorously oppose the relinquishment of Belgium. Then too, such a program would require consultation with Germany's allies.

Thus, to Pacelli's bitter disappointment, there were reservations, objections, hesitations, and ifs and buts from the very outset. The nuncio soon realized that the new men in Berlin would do nothing without first covering themselves with the OHL. He feared that the program would be badly watered down in consequence and urged Rome to take the initiative promptly without awaiting the official German response he had been promised. In this he succeeded, though not until August 12, when a conference of Entente statesmen in London, which it had been hoped to influence, was already over.

The Holy See was unwilling to let its decisions depend on the German response, which would have put the whole project in the light of being a German-inspired scheme. Even so, in the final version of its peace note Rome went so far as to take into account virtually all the objections Zimmermann had voiced on July 24, when the nuncio had presented the first draft—except his demand that Germany must receive "guarantees of future Belgian neutrality. In this form, accommodated to German desires, the note went to all the belligerent governments in mid-August, though it was dated August 1, the anniversary of the outbreak of the war. In eloquent phraseology it implored them to put an end to the slaughter and seek a reasonable settlement, after three years of bloody struggle.

What was the effect? Let us first consider the reception in the Entente countries, before turning to what happened in Germany.

The message met with unconditional approval, even warm expressions of gratitude, only in Belgium, whose full restoration did after all form the main burden of its demands. King Albert thanked the pope in person.[44] In all the remaining Entente countries the response was compounded of distrust and uncertainty on the one hand and open rejection, indeed resentment and indignation, on the other.

Of all the governments, the Italian took the papal initiative least seriously. It felt secure behind the London pact of 1915, Article 15 of which obliged the Allies to protect Italy against attempted papal intervention in the peace treaties. Sonnino therefore refused to give any reply. Still, in a confidential talk with the American chargé d'affaires he did show concern over the possible effect of the papal note on Italian Catholics and socialists, in whose ranks there were more and more signs of war-weariness and opposition to the government's chauvinist course just then, manifested in threatening demonstrations. He endeavored to throw suspicion on the papal action as an Austrian plot and to persuade President Wilson to give a "sound and firm" reply promptly, thus easing his domestic situation. Not until a stormy chamber session in October did he pluck up the courage to voice open rejection of the papal note–at a time when the whole enterprise had already failed internationally.[45]

The attitude of Russian diplomacy does not seem to have been entirely consistent. The Russian ambassador in Rome, Giers, described as "perfidious" the timing of the papal message at the very moment when Russia was suffering severe defeats; and he also criticized its vague statements on eastern questions. On the other hand the Russian ambassador in Washington confessed to Colonel House his serious concern that brusque rejection of the papal note on the part of the Entente might bring on an ominous split between the Russian government and the Soviets. Unequivocally negative was the attitude of the Russian foreign minister Tereschenko, who was quite unwilling to conclude peace with any imperial government. He did, however, avoid a separate answer to the pope, pressing for a joint Entente reply.[46]

The most hostile response came from France. Paris had long watched the lively traffic between papal and German emissaries in Switzerland with much suspicion, sensing that papal diplomacy was likely to be promoting pacifist tendencies throughout the world. Now these suspicions were thought to be confirmed. The cabinet at once decided that a mere diplomatic acknowledgment be given. If the Allies insisted on a substantive reply, this would have to be concerted.[47]

The Paris press, of course, did not fail to criticize the papal note as "pro-German" for not assuring the French of reparations and the return of Alsace-Lorraine while proposing the return of the German colonies. Ribot almost certainly shared these strictures, but was extremely reserved when he talked to the American ambassador Sharp. He said that the British reaction must be awaited. It would carry much weight with the Allies. He also urged that President Wilson state his position. There were bound to be wide differences of opinion among the European Allies, but a joint reply should nevertheless be found.48 Obviously he was quite uncertain of how the Anglo-Saxon powers would react and felt that he must on no account allow France to appear to foil the work of peace by its obstinacy and greed. Since Sonnino and Tereschenko were also anxious to avoid acquiring such a reputation, everything depended in the end on the attitudes of Britain and America.

French diplomacy did try to influence the Americans as much as possible. Jules Cambon, secretary general of the foreign ministry in Paris, explained to Ambassador Sharp that the pope merely wished to come to the aid of Austria, the country of his special concern, and above all sought to enhance the prestige of the Catholic church in the world by his peace initiative. France could not cooperate in these goals. Simultaneously, on August 23, the French ambassador Jusserand tried to convince Colonel House that the papal note was no more than a German-inspired device, the German peace offer of December warmed up all over again. What it really amounted to was restoration of the status quo. This would mean letting the criminal go scot-free instead of making an example of him. Besides, how could one think of entering into any agreement with these Germans? How could the words of these dangerous gangsters be trusted? France saw no alternative to repeating the Allied answer to President Wilson's January mediation offer, in which the Allies had already set forth their war aims.49

Colonel House on his part did not at all share the view that the papal action represented a German plot and feared that brusque Allied rejection would be a very bad thing. It would discourage the German liberals and convince them that the Allies were out to destroy Germany. It would also accelerate the collapse of Russia, long since weary of the war. He had at once written Wilson on receipt of the papal note that this chance for a swift end to the terrible struggle must not be missed, especially since otherwise democratic government would break down in Russia.50 Total German defeat was not as important as welding Russia into a vigorous republic. A sound and enduring peace might very well be built on the basis of the status quo as envisaged by the pope—House went into detail on this. He proposed that Wilson tell the pope that the door to negotiations remained open. Indeed, Wilson should take over from papal diplomacy as peace mediator, by putting forward a statement of American peace aims that would show the German people that no one was contemplating their destruction or dismemberment. At the same time he should declare that negotiation with the present government, the Prussian autocrats and militarists, was impossible. This would make a very great impression and almost unleash a revolution in Germany—if the Kaiser's government dared oppose negotiations. Once the German people were in a position to have a voice in such negotiations, the overwhelming majority would almost certainly be prepared to accept a peace that other nations in the world could also accept, a peace based on international amity and justice.51

One can scarcely read these sentiments of the American statesman today without emotion. Despite their admixture of wrongheaded and indeed primitive ideas about the attitude of the German people,[52] they were so very close to the desires and hopes of the Reichstag majority that backed the peace resolution of July 19! Had Wilson taken the advice of his friend, he would have given tremendous impetus to the peace movement in the countries of Europe and to the forces of democracy in Germany—though no doubt he would have severely irked the Entente governments, which were waiting with the greatest eagerness for his response. This was precisely what he did not wish or dare to do.

In any event, through House he cabled Balfour on August 18, in reply to Balfour's request for Wilson's views, that he had not yet decided whether to answer the pope at all. If he did so, he would voice serious objections, even though greeting the papal peace action as such with gratitude and sympathy. In the first place it was not at all clear whether the proposed peace terms would meet with approval in any country, hence to debate them would be highly speculative. In the second place they meant a return to the status quo, leaving everything as before, in a state that threatened the peace of Europe. In the third place no durable treaty was possible with the present autocratic German regime, which was morally bankrupt, habitually violated treaties, and made a mockery of all law. This, in fact, already amounted to a rejection; and the situation was not retrieved when Colonel House, clearly taken aback, added on his own that he was opposed to simply slamming the door, which would merely give new impetus to the Prussian militarists.

Actually the Foreign Office in London, unlike the Quai d'Orsay, was initially by no means resolved simply to reject the papal peace note. For that reason Balfour advised Paris to await the German Chancellor's statement in the Reichstag, which was expected on August 21; and in his inquiry to Wilson he said that the papal note carried many difficult questions that must be carefully considered.[53] Receipt of the note was acknowledged to the Vatican on August 16, with courteous assurances that the British government fully appreciated its lofty and well-meant intentions and would study it with the greatest care. The war cabinet did precisely that in an extended consultation on August 20.

But it was at once agreed at this meeting that the kind of complete and mutual pardon proposed by Benedict XV was in no circumstances acceptable. It was impossible to treat the German government as though it were inspired by the same principles as the Allied nations. The Germans, in other words, must not be placed on the same moral plane as their enemies. On the other hand, the cabinet was reluctant simply to point to the Allied peace proposals of January 10. Not that anyone gave any thought to revising the list of peace aims then announced! A request by the Russian government to convene a conference for such a revision was unanimously rejected.

Yet it was also agreed that the January program had made an unfavorable impression in the neutral countries, indeed had served even British antiwar propaganda as proof that the government pursued imperialist and grasping goals. Hence it might be better to allow it to fade in the public memory. Instead, President Wilson might be encouraged to proclaim to the world the moral ideals of the Allies. It should be suggested to him, however, that it would be better to wait until the Central Powers had enough time to reply to the papal note on their part. Much depended on leaving the first step to them, to give them plenty of time to formulate their peace aims. If they included the evacuation of Belgium, this would show noteworthy progress on the part of the Central Powers in the direction of a settlement.[54] If they did not take such a step it would prove that there was no basis whatever for talks. If the Central Powers once again offered to make their terms known only at a conference, they should be advised that Britain would be unable to take part in such a conference unless there were a reasonable basis for negotiations.

The British government was thus very much interested in taking advantage of the occasion of the papal note to learn whether there were any chance of a settlement with the Central Powers, first of all concerning Belgium. Balfour was charged with formulating a directive to this end to Count Salis, the British envoy at the Vatican. This was done the following day in a very cleverly worded telegram that, on the one hand, sought to create an impression of goodwill on the part of the British government,[55] while on the other hand it avoided any commitment and attributed any responsibility for the failure of the peace initiative to the Germans in advance. It said that without first consulting its allies, the British government could not determine whether there were any point in responding to the papal appeal and discussing terms for an enduring peace. In the opinion of the British government it was unlikely that progress could be made until the Central Powers officially stated their war aims, especially the extent of restoration and reparation they were prepared to concede and the effective guarantees they were in a position to offer to protect the world against a repetition of the current horror. Thus far the Germans had not given an unequivocal statement concerning even the restoration of Belgium, though they had confessed themselves guilty of causing Belgium's misery. The Allies, after all, had made their war aims known to President Wilson long since, in January. Neither Germany nor Austria had submitted any such declaration—hence it could not even be established on what points there were differences.[56]

In formal terms this was certainly no more than a delaying action, but it did challenge the German government to set forth its war aims promptly, prior to any negotiations—war aims that meant sweeping concessions: full restoration and indemnification of Belgium, large reparation payments, and effective guarantees of future good conduct. It was quite discernible that for the time being at least the British government clung to the peace terms proclaimed on January 10, even though London knew very well that the general response in Germany had been that these terms were intolerable and humiliating. Did Balfour really believe that noteworthy progress in the direction of a settlement could be made on this basis, in the matter of Belgium if nothing else? Did he really anticipate that the new Chancellor was in a position to give sweeping assurances along the lines of the Reichstag resolution? [57] Judging from the deliberations of the war cabinet on August 20 as we know them, it is hard to stigmatize his policy as a mere tactical maneuver to expose German policy on war aims and Belgium. It is certain that he was unwilling to take any step without the knowledge of Britain's allies, to whom the directive to Count Salis was at once communicated. It is equally certain that neither Wilson nor Ribot was ready for peace talks with the Kaiser's government.

This became immediately plain from the agitated reaction drawn from Paris by the Salis directive. Ribot instantly expressed his regrets at not having been consulted beforehand. He was irked over the fact that Britain had allowed itself to become involved in a discussion with the Vatican on the peace issue in the first place. He requested that Count Salis be advised that the French government supported his verbal communication to Gasparri in such a way as to regard itself as being excused from any further reply of its own to the pope.

Quite evidently this was the easiest way to avoid a separate reply expressing a direct rejection and thus courting adverse world opinion. Astonishingly enough, however, Lord Robert Cecil, Balfour's deputy, on August 23 transmitted the gist of the French communication to Rome in an oversimplified form, as though the government in Paris had agreed with the views contained in the directive of August 21.[58] This led to a grave misunderstanding in the Vatican. Gasparri had already assured Count Salis on August 23 that the Germans stood ready to restore Belgian independence, citing the Reichstag resolution. The skeptical response was that the Reichstag, after all, did not govern Germany; but when Gasparri heard that the French government shared the British views, he thought he had come very close to the realization of his hopes. If only he had official assurance from the German government that Belgian independence would be restored, he was confident of being able to persuade both Western powers to enter into peace talks.

Count Salis, apparently desirous to help mediate peace himself, did not dare encourage these hopes, but was incautious enough to say that a German declaration on Belgium would be welcome. He even left copies of the directives from London of August 21 and 23 in the hands of the papal secretary of state. On August 24 Gasparri promptly asked him to wire London that the Holy See had asked the German government for an official declaration on

Belgium and would reply to the Foreign Office as soon as it had been received. A simultaneous dispatch went to the nuncio Pacelli, with a French translation of the British directive to Salis of August 21 and a statement that the French government had expressed agreement with the British views. Pacelli was asked to make every effort to obtain a precise official statement from the German government concerning its intentions with respect to Belgium. If this were satisfactory it would mark a substantial step forward on the road to peace.[59]

Papal diplomacy, in other words, was doing everything to inject itself at the earliest moment. It was now basing its formal mediation effort on the fact that the British had not rejected the papal appeal outright but were biding their time. The impression was to be created in Berlin—and was indeed created—that the Foreign Office had extended a peace feeler. Yet it is certainly inconceivable that Balfour or Cecil planned for even a moment to commence peace talks with the German government without first obtaining Allied agreement. Domestic considerations were behind the British willingness to allow the Germans ample time for a well-considered reply to the papal note. In the light of the unrest among the working class and the pacifist tendencies that had affected wide circles of the middle class, the British government could not risk a charge of having frivolously rebuffed any possible chance for peace that appeared on the horizon; but this British willingness did not in the least foreshadow the spirit in which Britain might receive a possible German declaration voluntarily foregoing Belgium. There was after all the reference to the Allied war aims statement of January 10, which went far beyond the problem of Belgium.

Even that, however, was too much for the French. The French ambassador in Rome, Barrère, reported to Ribot how Salis had carried out his mission, and a strongly worded wire was instantly dispatched to London, insisting that the Vatican was merely leading the British envoy down a slippery slope. France would under no circumstances follow him there. Ribot urgently requested that Count Salis be instructed to deter Gasparri from any further attempt at "semiofficial" intervention. It was most undesirable for the British government to become involved in any way with the negotiations between the pope and the German government.[60]

Thus both Britain and France studiously avoided a substantive reply to the pope's peace proposal, while at the same time avoiding a formal rejection because of the unfavorable public effect such a step might have had. Instead, they waited for the German reply—and this was very slow in coming. Meanwhile, to the great gratification of most of their politicians, President Wilson made it unnecessary for them to do anything more; for on August 27 he made good Colonel House's earlier prospect of a separate reply to the pope, on the text of which he did not consult the Allies. He rightly anticipated that they would have objected to some of his phraseology, in which he spoke of a peace without vengeance, without economic restrictions and privileges, without reprisal dismemberments and the creation of self-seeking alliances. Such language happened to be part and parcel of the American ideology, and Wilson deemed it essential if he were to convince the Americans of the war's justice.

For the rest, Wilson sharply opposed the papal goal of restoration of the status quo, which would merely expose the world to renewed German threats. More than that, he hurled almost grotesque charges against the bloody and inhuman tyranny of the Kaiser's government, its insensate brutality and designs for world rule. With such a government no treaty could be concluded. By contrast, some friendly words were devoted to the German people, who were challenged to provide an unmistakable token of their will for peace. Since this clearly implied a refusal to acknowledge the Reichstag resolution as such an expression, it virtually amounted to indirect encouragement of revolution, repeated in a number of Wilson's subsequent speeches.

The document was a characteristic Wilsonian product, drafted in the isolation of his study, with only the advice of House. In tone it was essentially directed to the American public, and for that reason it was given to the press even before it was received by the Allies. Ambassador Page's spirits soared. He wrote House that Wilson had scored a direct bull's-eye; and in a message to the president he said that at last the Europeans had been shown a great ideal—the destruction of Prussian autocracy, the liberation of the world from a sinister threat—beside which all other goals faded into insignificance. The effect on Germany would be worth more than a dozen battles. Perhaps it might even lead to a revolution in Germany—at any rate, such an eventuality was brought measurably closer.[61]

A more rational view prevailed in Britain. General Smuts of South Africa, then a member of the war cabinet, thought that the refusal to have anything to do with the Hohenzollerns was downright foolish. The Anglo-Saxons simply failed to understand the German mentality. The Germans worshipped their newly created Reich, and this love could not be simply uprooted. Lloyd George even displayed some understanding of the fact that the OHL exerted such a powerful political influence in Germany. In contrast to their British and French colleagues, the Germans, as it happened, were able to look back on a long series of proud victories.[62] The French ambassador Jusserand put forward a similar argument, but in the opposite direction. It was a mistake to think that the German people were any better than their leaders. They were thoroughly infected with the "Prussian virus." France was far better aware of this than America. All that Wilson could reply was that he had been under the necessity of making rejection of the papal note plausible to the American people.[63]

Despite these reservations, however, there was profound relief in Paris as in London over the fact that the American president had rejected the papal note on his own, finding an effective propaganda line to that end. In the Vatican disappointment was equally profound. It was precisely on account of Wilson that the note had opened with a demand for instrumentalities to secure enduring peace and for a proclamation of freedom of the seas.

Nevertheless, the two Western powers could not simply identify themselves with Wilson's reply, despite House's urgings, if only because it contained so much that they found unwelcome. On the other hand, the British government declined to entertain Ribot's proposal to parallel Wilson's reply with a separate one from the two Western powers that would amount to an outright rejection.[64] Its apparent purpose would have been to remove the Belgian question from the focus of discussion and instead speak of war guilt, reparations, indemnities, and guarantees. In other words, new obstacles to peace talks were to be piled up, if the Germans did agree to relinquish Belgium.

London was reluctant, since this would have given rise at once to a renewed debate on peace terms among the Allies. This would revive suspicion among the British public of their war aims and their basic readiness to consider peace. It was decided to notify the Allied governments formally that the British government regarded the matter of the papal peace note settled with Wilson's reply and that it was now up to the Central Powers to provide their reply. This was done on September 1.[65]

Germany now had the floor.

Part 3

Kühlmann, the OHL, and the Papal Peace Initiative

OUR REVIEW so far points clearly in one direction. It confirms once again the basic theme of our third volume. Calm statesmanship was in an almost hopeless dilemma amid the turbulence of unleashed passions, power drives, and military exigencies of modern total mass war. Numberless people in France, Britain, and Italy yearned for an end to the bloody struggle before the fourth winter of the war set in. They were not interested in victory proper, they wanted peace by compromise and diplomatic negotiation; but the Entente statesmen felt obliged to stick it out to the complete subjugation of the dreaded enemy, since all would have been in vain unless his power were radically broken. It was hard to hold out a hand of reconciliation after years of preaching deadly hatred of the fiendish *boche,* of denouncing him as a war criminal and public enemy. Above all, if they were in earnest in believing in the mortal threat of Prussian militarism and imperial autocracy, how could they dare consider peace unless the claws and fangs of the beast were first drawn? Would that not be an admission of their own impotence? Once again national power and prestige proved to be the strongest political motives. On their behalf no sacrifice of lives and resources was too great.

Were things any different on the German side? One great difference lay in the military-political situation. Now beyond attainment was a full military triumph, the kind of "final victory" Germany's foes expected to be brought on by American intervention, the hunger blockade, and ultimately the inevitable exhaustion of German manpower reserves, even though only by the fall of 1919. Henceforth the curve of the Central Powers pointed visibly downward—indeed, at a steep gradient in Austria and Turkey. Germany faced the danger of fighting on to full exhaustion to no purpose. This, at any rate, was the light in which the situation appeared to many cool and temperate politicians, since hope for a decisive U-boat success had vanished. It was this disillusionment that resulted in the peace resolution of July 19, even though this was not necessarily a symptom of discouragement and resignation. In the minds of most of its authors, at any rate, it was a sincere expression of peaceful intentions, all the more genuine since the Germans, after three years of war, unlike their enemies, were no longer under the necessity of nourishing their political self-assurance and prestige by great military successes. Three years of tremendous military achievement had enabled the Central Powers to resist the joint onslaught of all the great European powers, even though these were being strengthened by large-scale American deliveries of war material while the Germans were cut off from overseas sources. Germany's front lines were still deep in enemy territory; indeed, in the late summer and fall of 1917 they had penetrated even more deeply into Russia and Italy. If Germany were now able to make peace, essentially leaving its old possessions undiminished, that would be "triumph" enough. Great-power status had been preserved, indeed greatly augmented, for the foreseeable future.

Yet this very fact—of which the political leadership was quite well aware even after Bethmann Hollweg's fall—constituted the greatest obstacle to a negotiated peace. We have already seen that neither France and its European allies nor President Wilson wished to hear of restoration of the status quo. They did not believe that the future of Europe could be sufficiently secured against new inroads by "Prussian militarism" without a considerable lessening of German power; and the only differences of opinion among them concerned the precise manner and degree of this reduction. They wanted territorial "guarantees"—but in the end they wanted more, the destruction of Prussian militarism, i.e., a marked weakening if not the destruction of the instrumentalities of German power. Yet unless and until Germany was manifestly defeated, how could any German statesman dream of offering the enemy more than unconditional return of all occupied territory?

We have already heard how the fatherland party ranted and raved against the Reichstag resolution. As we shall see, the all-powerful OHL continued to cling with the utmost tenacity to its annexationist designs; but voluntary surrender of German soil to the enemy would have raised the most profound indignation deep into the ranks of even the social democrats who, earlier in the year, had not even appreciated that there was a "question of Alsace-Lorraine."[66] In the meantime, in discussion with representatives of the second socialist international at Stockholm, they had learned just how serious a question it was; but even by early October, in the Reichstag, they demonstrated by their attitude that they fully shared the patriotic sentiments of most Germans with respect to the "Reich provinces."[67]

Alsace-Lorraine apart, by late summer and fall of 1917 Germany's situation did not appear so hopeless to its people that they were prepared to view and accept a "negotiated peace" in terms of the emasculation of their country and the dismemberment of its allies, proclaimed on January 10 as the Allied war aims. They were even less minded to do so in the light of the current collapse of the Russian front, with the prospect that the two-front war might turn into one with but a single front.

The only valid conclusion is that there was no realistic possibility of a peaceful settlement between the governments of the Entente and those of the Central Powers. Whether Germany agreed to the papal effort or responded with reservations or outright rejection, the idea of peace mediation prior to a conclusive military decision was foredoomed. Indeed, it had actually failed with Wilson's reply, even before Germany took any official position. It is important to clarify this situation, however, to avoid overestimating the negotiations conducted in August and September 1917 with great energy among the Michaelis government, the Reichstag parties, and the papal nuncio— efforts that have been explored and discussed in infinite detail by politicians, publicists, and historians.

It was, nevertheless, no matter of indifference how Germany would react to the papal peace appeal. The war, after all, was not a war of governments but of peoples, and in the wake of the March Revolution in Russia their attitudes had grown more and more important to grand policy. Thus what we have already remarked with respect to the peace calls of the St. Petersburg Soviets in the preceding spring (Vol. III, p. 412ff.) applies equally to the papal peace note. In dealing with it the German government had to be concerned not so much with the immediate foreign policy effect as with the impression made on the war-weary masses, on the advocates of peace throughout the world and not least in Germany itself.

For the second time there was a real chance—a far better one than before—

to demonstrate to the whole world in the most impressive fashion, by immediate and unconditional acceptance of the proposals, that Germany was indeed eager for peace. The impression would be all the greater if the government and the Reichstag were shown to be working hand in hand. This would not have been a diplomatic action in the traditional sense, but a propaganda coup, indeed a moral challenge. It would have confirmed, concretized, and rendered plausible what the Reichstag resolution of July 19 proclaimed. It would have enlisted the special sympathies of loyal Catholics throughout the world, and the enemy governments would have incurred grave moral odium by failing to respond to the challenge. At the same time, such German action would have helped refute Wilson's blanket indictment of German militarism and its dangers or at least weakened it, while reinforcing the conviction of the embattled German people that their government was pursuing peace.

It is impossible to say with any certainty what the practical consequences would have been. Of course the British government was not abjectly dependent on the pressure of public opinion, which it skillfully manipulated, and this was even more true of the French; but from sources accessible to us today we know unequivocally that the British cabinet was not utterly insensitive to such pressures, as maintained by Kühlmann in his memoirs.[68] Swift acceptance of the papal note and its concrete proposals would have greatly eased Germany's political situation while making that of its enemies far more difficult. This was especially true of France, which seemed to be erecting an insurmountable obstacle to peace by calling for the return of Alsace-Lorraine at the very moment when Germany publicly pledged the relinquishment of Belgium.

It did not happen, for two reasons. Foreign Minister von Kühlmann, newly appointed by Chancellor Michaelis, did not want to take the step, nor was he able to take it.

There were many reasons for his unwillingness, and we shall hear of them. One immediate reason was that he regarded the relinquishment of Belgium as a diplomatic bargaining element, in the traditional quid pro quo sense, rather than as a matter of political morality and worldwide peace propaganda. Belgium was to be used as a hostage, much like the other occupied enemy territories. Kühlmann was unwilling to concede to Belgium the unique significance it claimed everywhere, especially in the eyes of the pope. Kühlmann never doubted that Belgian independence would have to be restored, but he would not pledge this publicly until secret diplomacy had established that an acceptable peace could be had for this price.

Kühlmann was a past master of political protocol, and in the years just before the war he had done a great deal to promote an Anglo-German rapprochement, being especially responsible for the understanding on colonial questions that was reached then. He had much confidence in his intimate knowledge of British conditions and personalities. Yet he completely misjudged the scope and possible approaches for an Anglo-German understanding. He staked his policy on the peace sentiments of liberal and moderate conservative figures like Asquith, Balfour, and Lansdowne, unable to appreciate that in wartime they could not prevail against Lloyd George, the popular leader, whose cool statesmanship, moreover, he underestimated.

Kühlmann, nevertheless, was not altogether mistaken in his professed conviction that the British were at bottom interested only in the liberation of Belgium—and especially the coast of Flanders—rather than the return of Alsace-Lorraine; but he was badly deceived in believing that the British were prepared to negotiate with Germany on this question in deepest secrecy, keeping even their allies in the dark. He erred even more badly in assuming that Paris would obediently comply, however grudgingly, with the barest British hint to abandon its "dream" of the return of Alsace-Lorraine.[69]

This airy prediction shows quite clearly that Kühlmann had no real conception of the deep bond which the common war effort had knitted between the Entente powers, a bond that went beyond mere treaty obligations into the moral sphere. He failed to appreciate how deep an abyss had been torn open between the Germans and Britons in every walk of life, including even the upper classes and the Liberals; and he was unaware of the explosive blend of hatred, fear, and admiration engendered by Germany's military achievements and much-decried "atrocities" in Belgium and Northern France.

The only possible immediate approach to an understanding—before it was too late—would have been at least to moderate hatred and distrust by an unmistakable and unequivocal demonstration of peaceful intent that would have been widely recognized. Secret soundings and carefully doled-out partial offers were not the suitable means to such an end. They would have been greeted as either symptoms of weakness or attempts to split the enemy coalition. Yet this was precisely the tortuous course of Kühlmann's program, as he developed it to Michaelis in several memoranda.

To do him justice it must be added that he could not possibly have prevailed, even had he publicly sponsored unconditional acceptance of the papal peace proposals and especially the relinquishment of Belgium, with the payment of indemnities. The OHL would have prevented that as a matter of course. Its blanketing shadow was already cast over Kühlmann's very first memorandum of July 27, in which he set forth his plan to the Chancellor. He was persuaded, "in order to offer at least something to the military,"[70] to accept phraseology that in the anticipated negotiations with Britain, initially sweeping demands about Belgium should be put forward, for tactical reasons, even though "it would be virtually impossible to realize them." In particular, strong pressure was to be exerted for the retention of Liège, without, however, making this an absolute condition. An attempt was also to be made to acquire the Congo colony and the ore basin of Briey, the latter possibly by an exchange of territory. Perhaps it might also be possible to enclose the Grand Duchy of Luxembourg completely with Prussian territory, to be ceded by France, thus bringing it into a "closer relation" with Germany. On the basis of his prewar experiences Kühlmann thought that the French might well calm down over the question of Alsace-Lorraine, if that region were at last granted a proper constitutional status within the Reich, rather than being carved up among the federal states. In the east, improved security for the borders of East Prussia would suffice, possibly by the enlargement of Silesia, in order to take Poland into an even more effective "pincers." Kühlmann was prepared to forego the elevation of Poland to the status of an "autonomous" mon-archy—in other words, turning it into a satellite—if that meant a separate peace with Russia.

This program will be seen to be rather rickety, holding out possibilities of compromise in both directions. At heart Kühlmann was convinced that it was futile to continue the struggle and he prepared to forego all territorial con-quest. It is not clear whether he seriously believed that mere tactical demands could accomplish anything in the Belgian question except to nip negotiations in the bud. If he really hoped to win over the OHL for his program by such demands, he was promptly disillusioned in the talks in which he and Michaelis engaged in Kreuznach on August 9.[71]

Ludendorff served up a long OHL shopping list, which he tried to force on the new Chancellor as a kind of government program—indeed, one might almost say an official directive. It provided for a sharp intensification of domestic controls: a central office for press guidance; a patriotically oriented information service to improve popular morale; military measures to raise productivity in the coal-mining industry; reorganization of food controls; industrial integration for more efficient utilization of manpower; a thorough sifting of industry and government personnel to provide additional army reserves, etc. The "Germanization" of Alsace-Lorraine was to be speeded by economic and police measures like the liquidation of French real property, the settlement of Germans, the purchase of forests by the Prussian govern-ment, and the removal of French influence on the clergy and the teaching and nursing professions. As for carving up the region among the several federal states, a goal pursued by Bavaria for many years, the OHL declared itself opposed. The best solution would be to incorporate it into Prussia. If it were to become a separate federal state, Prussia should retain railway and military sovereignty.

Other points related to the peace program. A few villages in Upper Alsace might be ceded to France, but that was all. "Border rectifications" in Ger-many's favor beyond the ridge of the Vosges were desirable. Courland and Lithuania must be closely tied to Germany—plans to that effect had already been discussed with a representative of the foreign ministry on July 31.[72] Michaelis had expressly agreed to them. In Estonia and Finland the OHL and the Reich chancellery were to join in launching an anti-British, pro-German propaganda campaign. The existing autonomy movement in the Ukraine was to be exploited for tacit, friendly integration with Germany. An agreement should be reached with Austria under which the Ukrainian part of East Galicia could be offered to the Ukrainians. Polish autonomy was to be preserved only if the Austrians agreed to relinquish to Germany the Lublin district which they now administered—otherwise the Germans should drag their feet in further building up a Polish state. If the Poles "failed"—i.e., if they resisted the imposition of a German protectorate—there might well be a fourth partition of Poland. In that event large border territories would have to be annexed, almost to the gates of Warsaw. If Polish integration with Germany came to nothing, this would cancel the conditions for Austrian predominance in Rumania, which had been agreed on in Kreuznach on May 18.[73]

In the matter of greatest urgency, the future of Belgium, the OHL initially clung to its unrealistic demands of April 23 (see Vol. III, p. 418f.) for permanent German rule over that country; but the Chancellor did wring from it an express acknowledgment that this goal was attainable only if Britain were compelled to yield. The OHL insisted, however, that Liège and its northern approaches must remain in German hands under all circumstances.[74] The union of Luxembourg with Germany was to be effected as quietly as possible. Luxembourg must not have a direct border with France; i.e., there must be intervening German territory acquired from France. The coal and ore region of Longwy and Briey was indispensable to Germany. To spare French feelings, however, a "temporary settlement"—i.e., purely economic control—might be effected by private contractual agreements rather than formal acquisition; but a westward expansion of the fortified area around Metz was desirable. Lastly, a Central European economic alliance was to be established, to insure the permanent cohesion of the present Quadruple Alliance.

One has to envisage the totality of this sweeping OHL program to appreciate the hopelessness of reaching agreement with these generals on any basis for peace talks.[75] They did in the end realize that "corseting" Belgium would be possible only if Britain were forced to its knees by the U-boat campaign; but the consequences to be drawn from this realization remained unstated. No formal agreement between the OHL and the political leadership seems, in fact, to have been reached at all. Yet the General Staff shopping list was recorded as embodying the "conclusions of the meeting," and Michaelis accepted them as such. Indeed, he acknowledged their correct formulation by his signature.

It was quickly shown that on this basis no agreement on a common policy was possible with Austria either. The fall of Bethmann Hollweg greatly worried Count Czernin; and ever since the end of July he had been intent on bringing his influence to bear on all the German agencies and personages he could reach, to convince them of the urgent necessity for making peace before the winter set in. He worked on Michaelis, the Kaiser, the crown prince, Crown Prince Rupprecht of Bavaria—and on Ludendorff as well.[76] To all of them he brought home Austria's domestic plight, and also the threatening collapse or defection of Turkey. He renewed his proposals for a territorial exchange, developed in the spring (see Vol. III, pp. 393f., 396f., 440). Germany was to yield at least parts of Alsace-Lorraine to France—Czernin now spoke only of the French-speaking parts of Lorraine, especially Metz and its environs. By way of compensation it would gain the exclusive protectorate over Poland, and Austria was willing to forego, in favor of Poland and in return for Rumania, the province of Galicia, important because of its oil resources.

Unlike Kühlmann, Czernin expected very little of any efforts to reach an understanding with Britain, of whose tenacity and stamina he had rightly formed a high estimate.[77] On the other hand he tended to overestimate French war-weariness and readiness for peace. What he did see correctly was that, at the moment, the question of Alsace-Lorraine was the prime obstacle to a negotiated peace. On this point there was a crucial discussion in Berlin on August 14 with Kühlmann, Michaelis, and the Vice-Chancellor, Helfferich.

One reads the abbreviated minutes of this discussion with a sense of shock.[78] It showed a terrifying gulf between the two allies and took so dramatic a turn that it almost precipitated an open break. Michaelis later reported that Czernin, from sheer frustration, ultimately burst into tears— understandably enough, for he realized again, as he had already in a recent talk with Ludendorff, that the last chance for a swift end to the war was slipping from his hands.[79] Yet the domestic state of his country—and latterly, with the fall of Tisza, of Hungary as well—had grown so ominous that he saw the inevitable approach of disaster. What added to his sense of frustration was that at this very time, August 7 and 8, a former Austrian diplomat, the retired legation councilor Count Revertera, had been meeting in Switzerland with Major Count Armand, representing the former French war minister Painlevé, for top-secret talks that for the first time gave hope of serious peace discussions with French circles. Armand had submitted a formal offer of a separate peace from the two Western powers. Austria was to cede South Tyrol to Italy, together with Trieste, or at least turn the latter into a free port. In return, the Entente powers would support its acquisition of Silesia and the formation of a league that would include Bavaria and Poland, the latter within the borders of 1772. When Revertera balked at a separate peace, he was promised that the Western powers would submit a program for a general peace, which the Austrian foreign ministry might consider and pass on to Berlin.[80]

We do not yet know enough about the backers and the Paris management of these talks, held in Fribourg in Switzerland, to judge their precise political significance. It would appear that they were initiated by the French General Staff and War Minister Painlevé rather than by Ribot. We may be certain, however, that the Entente statesmen were at this time very eager to find a kind of counterpoise for the defection of the Russian ally by disrupting the Quadruple Alliance of the Central Powers. Lloyd George had been briefed about Armand's mission, which he eagerly welcomed.[81] The effort, in other words, carried considerable weight.

Czernin, at any rate, had good reason to believe that the West, especially France, was indeed interested in peace. At the same time he faced a serious quandary. Should he enter into negotiations on a separate Austrian peace treaty, betraying his Germany ally? Or should he accept only the role of mediator between Germany and the Entente? He made it rather clear in the Berlin talks that he was about to become involved in certain negotiations for which he needed a firmly agreed basis of peace terms; and his Berlin ambassador Prince Hohenlohe broadly hinted that Austrian mediation might bring dangerous consequences; but there was a complete unwillingness on the German side to make any concessions in the question of Alsace-Lorraine, such as accepting all or part of Poland and Galicia in return. This would have brought emphatic opposition not only from the OHL—on the demands of which Michaelis reported at length—but also from the entire German people.

Kühlmann shrugged his shoulders and went so far as to say that if worse came to worst, Germany would simply have to fight on alone. And Michaelis, who was trying to be conciliatory, added, "We don't want to tie you to the war." When he urgently warned Czernin against any negotiations on a separate peace, the latter sharply retorted that Austria had not started the war on its own but had been pushed into it by Berlin. In the end there was agreement to accept the status quo as a common basis for peace negotiations, even with respect to Italy—which meant hanging on to South Tyrol. Czernin declared that the Alsace-Galicia exchange was off.

The discussion made a deep impression on Michaelis. A few weeks later, reporting on it to Crown Prince Rupprecht, he backed Czernin completely on the point that the Central Powers would have to agree on a minimum program, showed himself inclined to restore at least complete political autonomy to Belgium, failed to say anything further about "guarantees," and seemed to set little store by the Flemish autonomy movement. In the east he regarded certain border rectifications in Lithuania and Poland as sufficient, was willing to turn Courland into a "neutral state," and was even ready to return Poland to Russia. If Germany insisted on holding on to Belgium, he said, it would never reach peace with Britain.[82]

At heart, therefore, Michaelis was ready for very moderate peace terms in both west and east.[83] Yet his official missive to Czernin of August 17, in which he summarized the results of the Berlin talks, sounded quite different. The painfully agreed status quo peace formula was once again bent in the direction of the OHL—it must on no account bar the way to a peace that would bring Courland, Lithuania, and Poland into a close economic and military connection with Germany; there must be free scope for the economic exploitation of the Longwy-Briey ore basin; and Belgium should be closely integrated with Germany, both economically and militarily, even if the more sweeping demands of the OHL should prove to be beyond attainment.[84]

Thus, although Michaelis offered no objections, Czernin stood little chance to pave the way for a general peace in talks with the French; nor was the nuncio Pacelli able to secure a satisfactory declaration about Belgium. Czernin's limitations became clear as soon as Major Armand, on August 22, submitted the list of general peace terms he had brought from Paris—he is supposed to have described it as a maximum program that was to some extent negotiable. It provided for full restoration of Belgium and evacuation of occupied France; reparations for all damage done, including ships sunk; the cession to France of Alsace-Lorraine within the borders of 1814, together with an agreement covering the left bank of the Rhine that would amount to demilitarization; Luxembourg to remain independent; the cession of Heligoland to Britain, while Trieste and South Tyrol, to the language line, were to become Italian; the restoration of Serbia and Rumania within the borders of 1914 and 1913; Serbia to be joined with Montenegro and given an Adriatic port; creation of a Polish national state within the borders of 1772, i.e., as it was prior to the several partitions; and lastly certain vaguely defined settlements with respect to Turkey. To soften the loss of Alsace-Lorraine, France agreed to back the restoration of a German colonial domain, by the return or exchange of colonies. There was even mention of indemnifying Germany with French Madagascar or Indochina, as well as with regions in the Baltic.

The whole thing was essentially a reiteration of the Allied peace programs of the preceding January—except that scarcely any heed was taken of Russia and once again there was no mention of dissolving the Austrian Empire into its various national components, nor of carving up Turkey. On the contrary, the offer of a separate peace was coupled with an express assurance that the Western powers had no intention of dismembering Austria. They did, however, count on Emperor Charles granting considerable autonomy to his various peoples, in order to bridge the gulf that had opened up between Austria and newly democratic Russia—indeed, the Slavic peoples generally. It was further held out that a newly created Poland, under a Hapsburg sovereign, would undoubtedly wish to join such a Danubian federation, which France and Britain, in a formal note, said they would welcome without prejudice and support economically. They would also assist Austria in any efforts to regain its former influence in Germany, establish neighborly relations with Serbia, and effect border rectifications with Montenegro, specifically the acquisition of Mount Lovchen.

These were indeed tempting prospects for Austria. In fact, this Fribourg program was the only concrete peace offer that was ever made to the Central Powers. It asked much more of Germany than of Austria—not least, the surrender of all formerly Polish territory. Czernin was sufficiently impressed to suggest that Painlevé should meet him in person in Vaduz, Liechtenstein; but he was also sufficiently loyal to inform the German foreign ministry of the two offers immediately, though it had been agreed that in the first instance Vienna alone would come to a decision, i.e., commit itself to acceptance.

Ambassador Prince Hohenlohe transmitted the message in Berlin on August 30, adding that Czernin was minded to reject the proposed peace terms as beyond discussion but wanted to keep the line open and offer a counterproposal. The most important concession in it would be restoration of the status quo in Belgium, to which he hoped Germany would be inclined, if its economic interests there were safeguarded. There would also be mention of "border rectifications" in Alsace, but first it would be necessary to know the precise nature of the concessions that would be offered in return. In the east Germany must without question obtain military border rectifications. All payment of reparations and all cession of Austrian territory to Italy would be rejected outright. Since France demanded Alsatian territory, Austria was entitled to ask Serbia and Montenegro for border rectifications, though it basically accepted the principle of the status quo. Poland and Rumania would be free to determine their own future and political orientation, though a change of dynasty would be necessary in Rumania.[85]

Could Czernin have seriously believed that negotiations with Painlevé were possible on such a basis? Or was he submitting this plan in Berlin solely to learn the maximum concessions Berlin was willing to make in the west, if a prospect of peace opened up there—or if Austria really threatened to defect? The most noteworthy feature of the plan was the outright refusal of any concession to Italy, though the French program demanded the cession of South Tyrol only to the language line. This rejection was quite in keeping with the attitude of Emperor Charles, who during this time had once again become hopelessly obdurate.[86] It naturally made any further negotiations with the Entente impossible from the outset and was bound to create the unfortunate impression in Berlin that Austria expected Germany to make all the concessions.

Kühlmann told Hohenlohe at once that he took a very dim view of Austria accepting any responsibility in acting as a mediator on matters that concerned

Germany exclusively; nor was he swayed when Czernin, during a visit Kühlmann paid to Vienna on September 1, eloquently told him how tempting the Entente offer was for Austria. To enhance his persuasive efforts, Czernin exaggerated the promises of support for a Danubian federation, which he said might include Bavaria, Saxony, and Silesia!

Kühlmann was determined not to lose the initiative in the peace question to the Austrians nor to allow them to dominate the coalition. On the critical Belgian question he obstinately refused to give the Austrian minister a binding declaration that might serve in further talks with Painlevé. On this point he was pursuing his own diplomatic design, of which we will hear. Czernin was left with no alternative to reducing his counterproposals to the Painlevé-Armand program virtually to zero and ultimately dropping the idea altogether. He forewent any continuation of the Fribourg talks, and thus the only halfway tangible chance for peace—or for a separate peace—was allowed to lapse.

It is impossible to establish today—nor is it particularly important—whether the lion's share of this failure must be put at the door of Berlin for its obduracy on the Belgian issue or of Emperor Charles for his on the matter of South Tyrol.[87] That section of the country certainly played the same part in Austrian eyes as did Alsace in Germany's. But these two questions do not exhaust the obstacles to a peaceful understanding. Czernin can have been under no illusions that his "counterproposal" would have had as little practical value in winning over the Entente as did the latter's proposal in appealing to the Central Powers.

And could Austria have seriously thought of a separate peace? It would have amounted to military as well as moral bankruptcy for the monarchy. At this very time the Austrian chief of staff, Baron von Arz, was requesting German support for an ambitiously planned attack to improve the situation on the Isonzo front, which had become urgently necessary after the eleventh battle there.[88] But for German military aid, Austria would have been utterly at the mercy of the Entente powers. Allied support for the establishment of a "Danubian federation," moreover, was quite meaningless in the face of the firm treaty assurances the Western powers had given Italy, Serbia, and Rumania, of which Vienna was well aware. It was inconceivable that such a federation should come into being under the leadership of a country that would have demonstrated its complete impotence by voluntarily withdrawing from the war; and it was equally grotesque to imagine that Austria could regain its former influence in Southern Germany after shamefully betraying the German Reich. No Austrian government would have survived such an act.

Kühlmann was so little afraid of a separate peace with Austria that in the end he was persuaded to withdraw his objections to Czernin traveling to Vaduz. It was Czernin who had last-minute doubts. As he writes in his memoirs, even the faintest whisper of such a meeting might have sounded the alarm, and everyone would have scrambled to save his own hide.[89] This would have been particularly true in Bulgaria and Turkey, where certain forces had long been seeking contact with the enemy and an end to the war. These clandestine activities were being helped by repeated tempting offers of a separate peace that had been reaching Bulgaria and Turkey ever since the preceding February.

There was still another reason why Czernin shunned a personal encounter with Painlevé at this particular time. Vienna had learned in late August that Czernin's memorandum of April 12, in which he had described Austria's plight as hopeless (See Vol. III, pp. 409 and 429f.), had become known to Entente circles in Berne. Czernin's negotiating position would have certainly been very weak, since the French statesmen were able to read in black and white his solemn assurances that Austria was unequal to lasting through a fourth winter, that rumblings of revolution could be distinctly heard, and that unless the heads of the Central Powers managed to make peace within the next few months, their peoples would do so over their heads.

Compared to the Fribourg talks between Armand and Revertera, the treatment of the papal peace effort by the two Central Powers appears almost in the light of a sideshow. Czernin, like Kühlmann, was originally inclined to look on it as completely unpromising and to leave its rejection to the Entente powers, in other words to drag his feet. The two statesmen agreed that any reply they might give should be essentially along the same lines, couched in the vaguest terms, except for welcoming such pacifist notions in the papal note as disarmament, an international court of arbitration, and freedom of the seas.[90]

They were less influenced by the aims of the Holy See than by concern for public opinion, to which they wished to demonstrate the peaceful intentions of the Central Powers, but without committing themselves to concrete peace terms. Czernin did draft a very skillful but ambiguous note of reply, in which Emperor Charles, as a faithful son of the Catholic church, personally thanked the pope for his high-minded efforts and said he stood ready to initiate negotiations with the enemy on a peace that would bring honor to both sides, while insuring the continuance of the Austrian monarchy and its peaceful development. The pope's concrete and practical proposals were described as suitable for initiating talks about disarmament and arbitration, offering precisely the kind of guarantee the Austrian monarchy required for its survival and peaceful development.[91]

This sounded like acceptance of the papal appeal, but actually reserved everything that was in Austrian eyes necessary to an "honorable" peace, with security. It made the success of such negotiations dependent, moreover, on acceptance of the pope's "pacifist" proposals—general disarmament, a court of arbitration, freedom of the seas—which Czernin, as he immediately advised Berlin, thought the Allies quite unlikely to concede. There was not a word about Belgium, Alsace-Lorraine, and South Tyrol—indeed, to the pope's bitter disappointment, Emperor Charles had at once told the nuncio when the note was delivered that cession of South Tyrol to Italy was out of the question. The whole reply was, in other words, no more than a maneuver, as Czernin himself interpreted it in Berlin.[92] Czernin, however, planned to release to the press only that part of the reply that stated that the papal proposals were acknowledged to be a suitable basis for negotiations. Hence the reply might still exert a considerable effect.

This, however, would be true only if it were not delayed too long; and from late August onward Czernin kept pressing Berlin vigorously for dispatch. He objected to any change in his text and threatened otherwise to proceed without regard for the Germans. Kühlmann on his part rebuffed Czernin rather brusquely. He had sent Pacelli a provisional acknowledgment, pledging sympathetic consideration and study of the papal appeal, together with a fuller reply later on. He was unwilling to proceed any further until Germany's enemies had stated their position and all of Germany's allies, i.e., Bulgaria and Turkey as well, were heard from.[93]

Why this procrastination? The reason seems to have been that Kühlmann still hoped for a negative response from the Entente, in which case the Central Powers could have issued a carefully and vaguely formulated statement of assent and got the better of the situation in the eyes of the world. Although there were transparent reservations in the Austrian reply, its blanket acceptance went beyond Kühlmann's liking. The reply note he himself caused to be drafted consisted of a long-winded declamation about the Kaiser's long-demonstrated love of peace and of a rather insincere profession of faith in a new world order of law in place of force, along the lines of the pope's pacifist proposals.[94] This was supplemented by some vague concluding remarks expressing the hope that Germany's enemies too might see in the papal proposals a suitable basis for entering into preparations for a just peace, "appropriate to the European situation." There was not a word of territorial peace terms!

Toward his allies Kühlmann tried to justify his hesitance and this vague and almost empty reply with the argument that he had heard from Pacelli that the pope was in no hurry for a reply, indeed rather preferred a statement couched in vague terms. This was in fact a deliberate distortion of certain of the nuncio's statements which pursued quite a different aim. Pacelli was actually waiting with growing impatience for a clear-cut acceptance and had merely asked that it not be burdened with too many reservations and discussion of detail, as had been the case with Zimmermann's reply to submission on July 28 of a first draft of the papal note.[95]

Kühlmann's real motive was of quite a different order. He wanted no papal mediation at all, regarding it as unpromising and indeed dangerous—principally because it could not be effected without an official and full statement of German peace aims, approved by all of Germany's allies. Here he fared similarly to Bethmann Hollweg in December 1916—actually rather worse, for in the meantime the OHL had grown all-powerful, the war propaganda of the extreme nationalists had become even better organized, and the alliance among the Central Powers had begun to show cracks. Kühlmann was in no position to put forward a moderate war aims program, for there was none. True, he had reached agreement with Czernin on August 14, as we already know, that both powers envisaged restoration of the status quo and were willing to forego annexations; but the OHL could never be won over to complete renunciation, and there would be constant struggle with it over the central problem, the surrender of Belgium—we shall see with what indifferent success this met in September.

As for Bulgaria and Turkey, neither was to be won over to the papal note in any way. They insisted on fulfillment of the many pledges they had received from the Central Powers in the course of the war. Bulgaria continued to pursue the goal of sweeping territorial expansion. Turkey complained bitterly that Czernin was minded to accept the note at all as a basis for negotiation, seeing that the "freedom of the seas" it proclaimed threatened its rule over the Straits, while the clause about Armenia imperiled its possession of that area. Indeed, Turkey insisted that its allies guarantee the maintenance of its full sovereignty over all its provinces.[96]

To evade all these difficulties, Kühlmann thought it wisest not even to touch on territorial peace settlements in the answer to the papal note, not even in the form of acknowledging it generally as a suitable basis for negotiation. Familiar with the facts of political life, he was evidently unworried that in consequence the answer would tend to be lacking in color and propaganda impact. He was considering an altogether different approach.

The talks with Czernin had shown him quite clearly that Germany must now pursue an active policy in the peace question, unless it were willing to risk losing its Austrian ally, but he was reluctant to go ahead without first covering himself on two sides. He wanted formal authority from the Kaiser, with the assent of the OHL; and he desired to take secret soundings in Britain, to establish whether there were any prospect of an acceptable peace, if Germany showed sufficient willingness to make concessions. Both of these goals required careful preparation and several weeks' time; and Kühlmann feared that his British soundings would be rendered ineffective in advance, if there were an immediate German declaration relinquishing Belgium, the very concession he wished to use for bargaining purposes in London. What made him hesitate, in other words, was not an unwillingness to reach an understanding over Belgium but a question of diplomatic tactics.

Meanwhile the Reichstag majority that had supported the peace resolution of July 19 was pressing for a reply to the papal note. The greatest zeal was displayed by the deputy Erzberger who, with bustling optimism, tried to play the role of middleman between papal diplomacy and the German government, hoping to gain a major share in the credit for the great papal peace work. On close terms with a high official in the foreign ministry, the envoy Bergen, he actually submitted two drafts for a reply late in August. Both accepted the main thoughts of the papal appeal, though the second draft included a reservation that details could not be discussed until all the powers had come to an agreement that peace negotiations would be useful.[97]

It was Erzberger too who urged immediate discussion of the papal note before the joint caucus of the Reichstag majority parties.[98] Such a discussion did take place on August 20, but it brought no clear-cut decisions. The Chancellor's worry of being prematurely forced to respond in detail before the Reichstag main committee proved to be unfounded.[99] The party leaders do not seem to have appreciated the great importance of some public display of German peace-willingness in further support of the Reichstag resolution. Then too, they may have been uncertain of what to say about the concrete papal proposals. Some of them felt that at bottom the papal note said nothing that was not already in the resolution, and they wished to see what the enemy would say. Others, like the democrats Haussmann and Gothein, wanted a clear-cut reply, especially in the matter of Belgium, a demand subsequently further emphasized by the social democrat David.

None of them, however, was in any hurry. Even Ebert said that the views of Germany's allies should be awaited. What they were all mainly concerned with was to show the world that the Reichstag now had a voice in foreign affairs. They wished to preclude a reply from the Chancellor in which they had not had a decisive influence. It was agreed in a discussion between Michaelis and the party leaders that the Chancellor should give only a general reply before the main committee. The papal action was to be welcomed with reserve tinged with warmth, but without leaving the impression that Germany urgently wanted peace. In the words of the centrist deputy Mayer-Kaufbeuren, Austria must not agree too vocally either.

Accordingly, the session of the main committee on August 21 passed without a debate on foreign policy.[100] There was, however, as already mentioned (see p. 15), a turbulent debate about the Chancellor's attitude on the Reichstag resolution, with the result that confidence in him was severely shaken. To calm the troubled waters, Michaelis appointed a so-called sevens committee, consisting of seven deputies from all the major parties—not merely the left and center—and another seven members of the federal council. Presided over by the Chancellor himself, it was to advise him in matters of special importance, beginning with the answer to the papal peace note.

This met the clamor on the part of the majority parties for a direct voice in foreign affairs, though the solution actually represented a compromise, since the opponents of the Reichstag resolution also had seats on the new committee—Count Westarp for the conservatives, Stresemann for the national liberals—and seven members of the executive, from the federal council, were included. (Actually, this had virtually no effect in practice.) The entire instrumentality ended with Michaelis's fall and went into action in but two sessions.

By the time the first one took place, on August 28, the situation had already shifted. Erzberger now took the view that while the answer need not deal with every territorial problem, it must include a passage about the unconditional restoration of Belgium. It is perfectly clear what made Erzberger take this step. Czernin had set the Austrian deputy Baron Vassilkov to go to work on Erzberger and the social democrat Südekum (see Vol. III, pp. 429, 471) in that direction. An added factor was news from Switzerland and Holland, circulated in part among German liberals through the German envoy at The Hague, Friedrich Rosen, and going back to pacifist groups abroad. It was to the effect that among British opposition circles there was a movement afoot that was urging a negotiated peace, but that it could gain a hearing only if there were an unequivocal official German pledge to set Belgium free. The rallying point of these circles was said to be Asquith, and there was constant reference to his speech in the House of Commons on July 26, in which he challenged the position of the German Chancellor on the Belgian question.[101]

Apparently this left a deep impression on the parties of the left, and their joint caucus, at a preliminary meeting on August 28, decided unanimously to insist that the Chancellor include a statement on the relinquishment of Belgium in his reply to the papal note. True, there were some differences of opinion on the nature and extent of German indemnities to be paid to Belgium; and even Erzberger was still naive enough to regard demands for certain guarantees as feasible. Belgium was to have neither army nor fortifications, and the Flemish should become independent of the Walloons.

Only the day before, in Vienna, Kühlmann had sharply emphasized that he would not allow Czernin to force him into precipitate peace negotiations but would let the enemy speak first and would limit himself to general agreement with the papal note, without entering into a discussion of details.[102] In accordance with this he told the sevens committee that the Quadruple Alliance would have to give a coordinated reply, that no agreement had yet been reached with Austria, and that only preliminary reactions from Bulgaria and Turkey were at hand so far, both suggesting that differences were likely to arise on such questions as freedom of the seas. He posed the question of whether the reply should not limit itself to major questions, like the rule of law over force.

Following Scheidemann's lead, there was general agreement that "idealistic" considerations should be strongly emphasized; but all the members from the left, most notably Ebert, vigorously supported a declaration concerning Belgium, since otherwise peace talk would never eventuate. The federal council delegates from the Hanseatic cities, Hesse, and Brunswick all put forward diplomatic reservations rather than any clear-cut opinions. Lerchenfeld and Varnbüler, for Bavaria and Württemberg, remained silent, though both had instructions to support any peace effort. As Varnbüler reported to Stuttgart, they were reluctant to aggravate the Chancellor's already badly shaken position by further exposing him to the counterpressures of the OHL —with whose opposition they were familiar—the Reichstag, and the federal council.[103]

Kühlmann unerringly went his own way. In a memorandum of September 3, already discussed[104] and probably intended for the Kaiser and the Chancellor, he explained the need to outmaneuver the Austrians in the peace question by an immediate German initiative, preferably in London, since Germany had nothing to offer to France. Secret soundings in London would constitute an adequate alternative to Reichstag and popular clamor for an official declaration on Belgium and would almost certainly bring a swift and clear-cut diplomatic solution. On September 5 and 6 he persuaded Czernin in personal meetings to change the text of the Austrian reply note radically, bringing it very close to the German draft—though it retained a very carefully formulated concluding phrase generally accepting the papal peace appeal in more clear-cut fashion than did the German document.[105] On September 8 Kühlmann formulated another memorandum, intended solely for the Chancellor, in which he made the relinquishment of Belgium dependent on British acceptance of certain basic principles for the peace to come, even should the' German soundings in London meet with a positive response. German prewar territorial integrity must be maintained; a colonial domain appropriate to Germany's status must be restored by return of the former German colonies or exchange; indemnities to Belgium must take the form of "neighborly aid" rather than atonement of wrongdoing.[106]

What may have stiffened Kühlmann's attitude is that on September 5 he had learned of a letter Pacelli had sent to Michaelis on August 30,[107] reporting on the inconclusive British reply communicated by the British envoy to the Vatican, Count Salis. As we have already seen (see p. 25), Gasparri took this to be a British peace feeler and at once transmitted the message to Michaelis through Pacelli. Yet from the British text Kühlmann can have concluded at best that this was a rather rash interpretation and that for the time being London was still sticking to the peace program of January 10. It was this situation he was seeking to meet. All the same, as we shall see, Kühlmann skillfully exploited Pacelli's letter as a tactical aid to his diplomacy.

With Michaelis, Kühlmann was convinced that he could not venture on secret soundings in London without first securing agreement from the Kaiser and the OHL to relinquish Belgium. This was a difficult task indeed. To secure political backing to that end, Michaelis did what Bethmann Hollweg had been in the habit of doing in such cases. On September 4 he outlined the proposed policy to the Prussian cabinet. He described the papal peace action as a hopeless undertaking, because a general peace conference at this time was out of the question. But by answering the papal note appropriately it might be possible to get individual countries to establish contact with each other thus paving the way for further peace talks.

This was in complete accordance with Kühlmann's plans—first, separate negotiations with Britain, which might then be gradually expanded. Yet Michaelis expressed himself on the Belgian question in a way that showed him to be quite far removed from outright relinquishment—he said that the acquisition of only the Flemish coast was "impossible"—and that clearly indicated his uncertainty of the extent of the concessions he might wrest from the OHL. He did not reject outright the OHL plan to dissolve the Belgian army and raze the Belgian fortifications. He appeared uncertain, however, of whether a deployment area beyond Aachen could be secured, and was reluctant to allow possible negotiations to fail on that account. He insisted on Flemish autonomy, especially in church and school matters, and he had Helfferich draw up sweeping plans for integrating the Belgian economy with the German.[108]

If the Chancellor allowed the Reichstag to commit him to a public statement on the restoration of Belgium, any discussion with the OHL on this subject was bound to fail. Thus everything had to be done, first of all, to get the sevens committee to desist from such a demand. To this end Kühlmann had confidential talks with Erzberger and Scheidemann, and here, as in the ensuing second committee meeting on September 10, he did not shrink from considerable dissimulation. Erzberger knew of Pacelli's letter to Michaelis of August 30, without apparently knowing its content.[109] Kühlmann pretended to appease his curiosity by telling him in deepest secrecy what he subsequently (according to a report by Lerchenfeld) put to the committee in the following terms: The Holy See had privately and confidentially advised the Germans not to enter into detail in their public reply to the papal peace appeal, but to communicate such details confidentially. It was mentioned in this connection that Rome had had hints that certain circles in the German enemy camp were no longer hostile to an exchange of ideas—indeed, that there was hope of coming closer to the goal within a matter of weeks. The old-fashioned style of papal diplomacy, Kühlmann added before the committee, made it advisable to follow these recommendations. Unfortunately, he could not tell everything he knew and must ask the members to trust him and grant him a measure of discretion.[110]

From some notes about the session found among Erzberger's papers, Kühlmann was even more outspoken. He said that the papal secretary of state had asked the Chancellor for his position on Belgium, as the result of an inquiry from an enemy power that desired to know the German war aims, especially with respect to Belgium.[111] Scheidemann reports that on September 9, during a long conversation, Kühlmann told him: "I can assure you with certainty that within three to four weeks negotiations on the Belgian question will be under way between Britain and ourselves. . . . You will admit that in the circumstances it would be utter folly to ruin the chances for such talks by telling the world in our reply to the pope what we propose to discuss." Kühlmann also allegedly assured him that the Holy See had been advised of the proposed German answer, was in complete agreement with it, and in no way insisted that Belgium be publicly discussed in it.[112]

If the minister really made such a statement, he was certainly guilty of considerable distortion. He could have cited nothing more than Pacelli's letter of August 15, addressed to Bergen, in which he pleaded that the German answer not be burdened with too much detail and too many reservations (see p. 41). In later years Kühlmann disputed the accuracy of Scheidemann's report; but even if Scheidemann did misunderstand Kühlmann or distort his words,[113] Kühlmann certainly lulled the delegates into believing that London had already sent out a peace feeler, that agreement had been reached with the Vatican on how to respond, and thus that top-secret negotiations with the enemy were already under way and must on no account be interfered with. Actually such negotiations were at the time only a vague hope; nor did Kühlmann have the slightest intention of letting the Holy See know in confidence about the German position on Belgium—at least not until his London soundings were well under way.

All of Kühlmann's hopes were staked on the peace feeler he himself planned through an old friend of his in Brussels, a neutral diplomat, the Spanish Marqués Villalobar. He wished to keep a free hand until then, rather than going off half-cocked—that was his crucial motive. He put forward still other arguments in the debate with the delegates. He spoke of the extraordinary difficulties he had encountered in agreeing on a text with Germany's allies. The current version—which was read aloud but not distributed—represented a compromise down to the last phrase. Any further change would create new differences. This was simply not true, or at least grossly exaggerated. Much weightier was Kühlmann's concern that a declaration on Belgium would at once unleash a troublesome debate about the territorial aims of the Central Powers. This was true also of his warning against unconditionally turning over Germany's strongest trump card, concessions on Belgium, before negotiations had even begun.

Kühlmann's confidential talk made a very strong impression on Erzberger, if only because the centrist deputy was always eager to be trusted with diplomatic secrets. During the session Erzberger described the note of reply as excellent and agreed that it was necessary to ignore Belgium, in order not to interfere with papal diplomacy.[114] He did say that the Reichstag resolution of July 19 should be approvingly mentioned in the reply. Scheidemann, on the other hand, did not allow the minister's dialectical skill to swerve him from the simple conclusion that without an official declaration on Belgium there would be no bridges to peace—a stand he took at the session as well. But except for Ebert he stood alone in the committee, which allowed the seasoned Kühlmann to carry it along, especially since Kühlmann, like Michaelis, gave eager assurances that substantively there was full agreement on the Belgian question between the government and the Reichstag majority. It was therefore resolved to include in the reply note, in place of a statement about Belgium, a clause that said it had been drafted in close cooperation with representatives of the German people and that expressed an urgent desire to find a useful basis for a just and permanent peace, along the lines of the desires of His Holiness and of the peace message of the German Reichstag of July 19.

Papal diplomats learned of this decision at an early stage and fought almost desperately to secure concrete acceptance of their proposals, at least on the Belgian question, instead of so vague a reply. If that were impossible, they requested that the reply be at least delayed—its transmission had been set for September 20—or if that were not possible, that its proposed publication on September 22 be delayed to gain further time for negotiations with the two contending parties.[115] These alternatives were rejected as impractical, and the German note, dated September 18, was transmitted on the same day as that of the Austrians.

The German government clearly did not wish to commit itself publicly to acceptance of the concrete papal proposals. To do so would have unloosed the strongest OHL opposition, a storm of protest from the Pan-Germans and the fatherland party,[116] and lastly the hostility of the Bulgarian and Turkish governments. There was profound disappointment in Rome, since all further effort on behalf of peace now seemed to have become hopeless, though for the time being Pacelli clung to the hope that a second, confidential reply specifically on the Belgian issue that had been held out to him might bring a turn for the better. On August 18 he had written to the German foreign ministry that acceptance of the pope's mediation proposals would work out very favorably for Germany. In the eyes of the world, he said, responsibility for continuation of the war would rest on those who rejected the proposals. If Germany did the rejecting, everyone would say that the peace offer of December 1916 and the Reichstag resolution were the merest pretense. If, on the other hand, Germany accepted and the Entente did not, the situation would be reversed, and wide and ominous dissatisfaction would arise in some of the Entente countries.[117]

Some of these predictions promptly came true. In a speech of September 26, Asquith jeered at the series of "pious phrases" in which the German government, in its reply to the pope, was merely seeking to cover up its refusal to return Alsace-Lorraine, the brutal seizure of which was the ultimate cause of European strife and of the miseries of the present war. The Germans were as unwilling to atone for the "crime of 1871" as they were to restore and indemnify Belgium unconditionally.[118]

Actually, Wilson had, in the meantime, rejected the papal peace initiative for the Allied side far more unequivocally than the Germans; but Wilson had justified his rejection with the moral inferiority and total unreliability of the Germans. As for the British government, it did no more than tacitly identify itself with Wilson's arguments, preferring to avoid the onus, before the world, of a separate rejection.

Part 4
Futile Peace Feelers in London and Paris

AS WE ALREADY know, it was not at all Kuhlmann's intention that there should be no further attempts to secure a negotiated peace, once the papal peace initiative was swept aside. On the contrary, they were now only to start, by means of secret soundings to be taken in London. To this end he needed, first of all, authority from the Kaiser and the OHL. Michaelis tried very hard to obtain this. What militated in his favor was that during a tour of the western front he had found full agreement on the need for a prompt end to the war among a number of generals, including the Prussian and Bavarian crown princes.[119]

These front-line generals, unlike Ludendorff, were exposed day after day to the steadily growing striking power of their Western foes. What is more, they keenly felt the conversely diminishing resources and reserves on the German side. An added factor was concern over Austrian deficiencies, which Count Czernin managed to drive home on his visits to the front. In a discussion with the Chancellor on August 31, Crown Prince Rupprecht expressed the fullest agreement with Michaelis's and Kühlmann's ideas concerning a negotiated peace, on the basis of restoring the independence of Belgium and foregoing Longwy and Briey. More than that, he voiced doubts concerning the political activities of the OHL.[120]

The German crown prince was curiously inconsistent in his attitude. [121]

During a visit in May Czernin had persuaded him to write Bethmann Hollweg that peace must be concluded at any price by the fall, since things could not long continue as they were. If necessary, there would even have to be cessions in Lorraine. Following Czernin's lead, he had made similar representations to Ludendorff, but had been rebuffed with such vehemence that he gave way, indeed, offered his service to the general in bringing down the "spineless" Chancellor (see Vol. III, p. 478ff.).

Under the influence of his shrewd and politically realistic chief of staff, Count Schulenburg, the crown prince nevertheless seems to have clung to his belief in the need for a prompt end to the war and to his pessimistic evaluation of the chances of military success. Yet when he returned from Berlin to his headquarters, he inveighed bitterly against the Reichstag resolution, even though it was intended to help shorten the war. What probably irked him most was that it represented an effort to intervene in the field of foreign policy, i.e., the privileges of the crown.

Nevertheless, a day before the resolution was debated in the Reichstag on July 18, he wrote an extremely pessimistic memorandum, which he submitted to the Kaiser, the Chancellor, and the OHL—and, unfortunately, soon afterward to Czernin as well, who showed it to Emperor Charles, with the result that a copy got into the hands of the French government, probably by the route of Bourbon family correspondence, with which we are already familiar (see Vol. III, p. 375ff.). It was drafted in close consultation with the Catholic journalist Viktor Naumann, whom we already know and who probably had a hand in its wording. It strongly emphasized the need for a prompt end to the war, to preserve the dynasty and insure the maintenance of the integrity of the German Reich and the survival of the German people. There was no mention of concessions in the west, but an urgent appeal for a separate peace with Russia.

In curious contrast with this policy of moderation was the crown prince's unremitting and impassioned opposition to the imperial cabinet chief Valentini, whom he viewed as heir to the spirit of Bethmann Hollweg and fought to have removed from the court. When Czernin again paid a visit in mid-August, the crown prince seemed to share the Austrian's pessimism to such a degree that Czernin persuaded Emperor Charles to send him a handwritten letter in which the Austrian proposal for German territorial concessions in Alsace in return for compensation in the east was reiterated, with a request that the crown prince support this approach with the Kaiser; but in the meantime the crown prince had clashed with Ludendorff over his memorandum so violently that he was threatened with changes in his personal staff. Hence he gave way and sharply rejected Emperor Charles's importunities, though he had the political sections of his reply drafted by the foreign ministry.[122]

Thus the Chancellor and the foreign minister could count on the crown prince's support in their efforts to enlist the Kaiser for concessions in the Belgian question and for the idea of a negotiated peace. The crown prince, however, entertained serious doubts of the possibility of reaching an understanding with Britain, of all the powers. At a crown council of September 11, to which he was bidden by the Kaiser and which will be discussed shortly, he remained silent, although we may take it virtually for granted that he counseled his father beforehand to support a negotiated peace. In any event, directly following the session he told Helfferich that, in his view, any chance to secure a decent peace should be seized, and that peace must not be allowed to fail over any single demand, however justified.[123]

Michaelis did not neglect to report promptly to Hindenburg about the impressions he had taken away from his own tour of the front. He had found confidence everywhere, but also a receptive attitude to the most serious consideration of any chances for peace that might present themselves. Even Admiral Schröder, in command of the marine corps in Flanders, had shown himself ready to reexamine minimum naval demands, in the event there were a chance of peace before the final success of the U-boat campaign. He had even suggested a prompt meeting on this subject.[124]

At Michaelis's request such a meeting was convened on September 11 in the form of a crown council. By showing him Pacelli's letter of August 30, which was represented as a first British peace feeler, Michaelis had pleasantly surprised the Kaiser and got him to agree in principle to the diplomatic step that Kühlmann contemplated. Thus everything had been carefully prepared.

Yet there was no real hope of persuading the military to forego Belgium altogether, and Michaelis does not even seem to have expected such a thing. In a kind of cabinet session he held with his ministers on September 8— actually a constitutional innovation! he spoke of restoring the territorial integrity of Belgium, with sweeping (but not complete) maintenance of its sovereignty, dependent on partly military, partly economic guarantees, which he hoped to secure in separate negotiations with the Belgian government, in the form of voluntary adherence of Belgium to Germany.

He met with general agreement, though the navy minister objected to handing over the coast of Flanders.[125] At the last moment the Kaiser too seemed to waver, evidently under the influence of naval people. During the night of September 10-11 he sent the Chancellor a long handwritten message (on telegram forms), which quite clearly stated his fears that the naval officers, Tirpitz, and the fatherland party would offer indignant opposition. He seemed to be desperately searching for a compromise that might assuage them—surrender of the Flemish coast but retention of Zeebrugge, which might be leased or used on Belgian suffrance; and as an equivalent for the loss of the coast, increased naval construction and the acquisition of foreign bases like Vlonë and Corfu. Without such a quid pro quo, he said, he could not show his face to the navy. His sense of insecurity showed itself in a ranting tirade against the British, whom he claimed to know better than did the foreign ministry. By reaching out the hand of peace, those "chaps" were merely showing that they considered the war lost. It was essential to show them a "stiff upper lip," so that Germany, in the "Second Punic War" that would undoubtedly come, had a better position than in the first.[126]

Michaelis barely managed to calm down the Kaiser before the meeting, and also to keep Kühlmann from presenting his resignation; but the crown council nevertheless took place in an atmosphere curiously overlaid with illusions. The first of these illusions arose when Michaelis and Kühlmann darkly spoke of a British peace feeler, apparent from neutral communications. In an even greater illusion, the Kaiser immediately described this alleged peace feeler as a great U-boat success and as a sign that Britain regarded its cause as lost. As so often in the presence of high officers and officials, he indulged in braggadocio and drew a picture of Britain in the darkest colors. Playing the role of the magnanimous victor, however, he acceded to Kühlmann's proposal for authority to state that Germany stood ready to restore the integrity and sovereignty of Belgium. Yes, let King Albert return—his, the Kaiser's, monarchist sympathies made it difficult for him to cast a colleague from the throne.

But the Kaiser found it extremely unpalatable to forego the Flemish coast, in the presence of his admirals, as shown by his grotesque compromise proposals that the German heavy guns might be left emplaced there, with the right to inspect them from time to time to see that they were in working condition. Admiral Holtzendorff immediately and vigorously protested against relinquishing the coast; and the Kaiser repeated the demands for "compensation" he had put forward in his nocturnal letter to Michaelis—first of all another naval base, possibly Vlonë or Corfu in the Mediterranean, then complete exclusion of British influence in Belgium, the economy of which must be closely integrated with that of Germany, and lastly a solution to the Flemish question. All this was to be settled in direct negotiations between Belgium and Germany, as was the question of Liège. For the special gratification of the German navy, the Kaiser offered a fantastic proposal he had repeatedly made before. After the end of the war in Europe, the navy was to sail to America, there to collect war indemnities from Cuba, Brazil, and other countries that had joined Germany's enemies.[127]

The demand for close economic integration was to be effected by tying Belgium to Germany in a political sense as well, or at least by keeping it away from military conflict in its own interest. "Military guarantees" probably meant that the country was to be occupied until integration had been achieved, i.e., for a matter of years. For this period Liège was to be held as a temporary hostage—this, at least, was how Michaelis phrased Hindenburg's minimum demand in a letter to him the next day, in order to have a written commitment.

It seems quite unlikely that Michaelis opposed such a demand at the meeting itself. Possibly he even put forward the idea of economic integration himself, for he had allowed Helfferich to offer similar proposals before the Prussian cabinet on September 4, and in the last ministerial conference of September 8 he had spoken of "partly economic, partly military guarantees." [128] Thus even before the crown council, his own Belgian program was limited to a relinquishment hemmed in with major reservations, and naturally the Kaiser did not go beyond it. Apparently Michaelis was concerned with three things. Claims to the Flemish coast were to be unequivocally dropped; the restoration of the Belgian monarchy was to be firmly pledged; and the question of Liège was to be left open—at the very least, its annexation was not to be made an absolute condition for a peace settlement. Here too the Kaiser followed his lead. He did speak of negotiations about Liège between Belgium and Germany but passed over in silence the OHL demand that this fortress and the territory around it be annexed.[129]

What had actually been achieved? Certainly no more than agreement to relinquish Belgium under so many reservations and limitations that Kühlmann's design could be described only as having failed—had he felt obliged to stick strictly to the text of the crown council decisions. Fortunately no proper resolutions were adopted at all, the Kaiser merely summarizing the results of the discussions in rather vague terminology: "The war situation in the fourth year compels us not to allow the question of the Flemish coast to keep us from bringing an honest and decent peace to the German people. Close economic integration with Germany, however, must be demanded." This could be stretched to mean authority for Kühlmann to voice German readiness for the restoration of Belgian integrity and sovereignty, though only with a limitation imposed by the Kaiser—this applied only if peace could be secured before the end of the year. Actually the Kaiser seemed to approve of his statements being interpreted liberally. After the session he jovially shook hands with the foreign minister and said: "Well, Kühlmann, now that you have a free hand show us what you can do and get us peace by Christmas."[130]

The generals and admirals departed in considerable dissatisfaction. They had expected a strong policy of the new Chancellor and were disappointed by his stand. To reassure them, Michaelis wrote long letters to Hindenburg and Holtzendorff, in which he tried to convince them that renunciation of the Flemish coast could still bring Germany an honorable peace rather than one of "hunger and appeasement." He asked Hindenburg to exert a moderating influence on annexationist visitors to headquarters.

Kühlmann thought that Michaelis had gone much too far in adapting himself to the wishes of the OHL; but Hindenburg replied with a letter that was full of resentment, and Ludendorff with a long memorandum in which he went even beyond his earlier sweeping war aims, in east and west. Not only did he insist on the economic and political integration of Belgium, to be enforced by continued occupation, but he demanded integration with Holland too. His only concession was that he did not think outright annexation of Belgium feasible. How completely his determination to win darkened his view of the situation in Germany is seen from this passage: "Our military situation is more favorable than that of the Entente, our alliances are firmer. Our domestic difficulties are less serious than those among our enemies."

Nevertheless Ludendorff admitted that peace before the onset of winter was "desirable"—but only if it brought Germany full security against future Entente attack, which he regarded as inevitable.[131] Tirpitz too did not neglect to commend himself to the new Chancellor as an expert on British questions and to admonish him to remain firm. A protectorate over Belgium was an indispensable element in Germany's entire economic and political position in the world. The fact that Britain was now appealing to the pope for help (!) in gaining freedom for Belgium was, so Tirpitz said, clear proof that both Britain and France were on the brink of yielding. This was not the time for Germany to lose its nerve. Tirpitz insisted that his intelligence proved the great effectiveness of the U-boat campaign. The German workers were not really backing the party leaders of the left. All that they wanted was a sound peace.[132]

Kühlmann was meanwhile going his way, heedless of military displeasure. Directly following the crown council, he visited his Spanish friend, the Marqués Villalobar, at his hotel. Villalobar had come to Berlin in secret and in violation of his solemn obligations as a neutral. The verbal brief Kühlmann gave him for establishing contact in London seems to have run along the following lines: Germany was ready and able to enter into peace talks with Britain on the bas of restoring Belgian integrity and sovereignty. To this end Britain would h. e to acknowledge that Germany's borders would remain unchanged, that its colonies would be returned, that no indemnities would be demanded, and that there would be no economic warfare. It will be noted that, wisely, there was no mention of any limitations on Belgian sovereignty, though minimal German peace terms were set forth, as in Kühlmann's confidential memorandum of September 8 (see p. 45). Restoration of the status quo, i.e., the border of 1914, had after all been agreed between Germany and Austria on August 14 (see p. 36).

Kühlmann thus followed his own very free interpretation of the decision of the crown council in which he had just participated. Evidently he felt entitled to ignore the subject of Belgian integration with Germany, so far as London was concerned, leaving this for the special negotiations proposed at the crown council but for the time being quite out of the question anyway. If Villalobar's soundings resulted in a real opportunity for peace, Kühlmann had reason to hope (as had Bethmann Hollweg in his peace offer of December 1916) that the Kaiser would scarcely withstand such a temptation and in the end would drop all his reservations with respect to Belgium. If it were to transpire that there was a serious possibility of peace talks, the clamor of public opinion would sweep aside all annexationist obstacles.

Of course Kühlmann was not foolish enough to trust blindly to the success of his peace feeler. On the contrary, as he explained more than once subsequently, he could venture it only in deepest secrecy precisely because the issue was so uncertain—for even the news from Rome offered no certainty of a British desire for peace; but if, on the other hand, Germany publicly announced its voluntary relinquishment of Belgium, only to receive "a brusque rebuff and a flood of insults" from the other side, as happened in response to Bethmann Hollweg's peace offer (or Wilson's reply to the papal note), this, in Kühlmann's view, would amount to such a serious setback and loss of prestige for the German government that it would have to resign within twenty-four hours. The latent conflict between government and Reichstag on one side and the OHL on the other, moreover, would then be apparent to all the world.[133]

The objections to this line of reasoning had already been stated by Pacelli on August 18 (see p. 48). The immediate goal was not so much a diplomatic success as the moral effect on worldwide public opinion. Yet from all that we now know of the attitudes of the Kaiser, the OHL, and the navy, can anyone imagine that any Chancellor could have long remained in office, if he had seriously tried to get the Kaiser to publicly forego Belgium without any reservations, thus meeting the wishes of Scheidemann, Ebert, Haussmann, and the left wing of the center party? And suppose he had obtained such agreement, which is almost beyond belief, what if Germany's enemies had then poured scorn on him, pointing to Alsace-Lorraine, South Tyrol, Trieste, and what not? The German political leadership was certainly ready to forego Belgium and reach a negotiated peace—Kühlmann even more so than Michaelis, who kept looking for a compromise with the OHL—but the German generals and admirals were not; and the fall of Bethmann Hollweg had but recently demonstrated that the military held the political whip hand. In the fatherland party they had at their disposal a well-organized propaganda agency for winning over public opinion to their side. They were even able to intimidate the Kaiser.

Thus Kühlmann was taking considerable chances by venturing on such a peace feeler in the existing situation. It was an attempt to outmaneuver the OHL, so to speak, to go far beyond the authority granted by the crown council, in launching a diplomatic peace initiative. It is understandable that in the circumstances Kühlmann hesitated to advise the Holy See of his endeavor. He had little confidence in the discretion of so international a body as the college of cardinals. There had been some very disagreeable experiences, moreover, concerning indiscretions by the deputy Erzberger, who constantly tried to push his way as a middleman into the exchanges between the foreign ministry and the papal nunciature. Erzberger had a remarkably wide intelligence organization of his own, enabling him to stick his nose into many affairs—indeed, sometimes he saw Pacelli's letters to Michaelis even before they reached their addressee. Great caution was certainly in order.

Kühlmann was even less in a position to tell the papal diplomats about the reservations in the Belgian question that had been put forward in the crown council.[134] He actually delayed replying to Pacelli's confidential communication of August 30 until two weeks after the crown council, to allow a proper start to Villalobar's undertaking. Ultimately, on September 24, in a letter signed by Michaelis, he gave so carefully worded a provisional acknowledgment that Rome misinterpreted it as a final rejection.

This letter created a major sensation when it was made public in July 1919. The conservatives under the leadership of Helfferich were then about to mount a sharp attack on Erzberger's earlier activities; and Erzberger used the letter for a counterattack on Michaelis and the parties of the right. He said it proved that the former Chancellor, against assurances Kühlmann had given the sevens committee, instead of promoting a negotiated peace by secretly advising the Holy See of Germany's willingness to relinquish Belgium, had actually sabotaged peace by sending Pacelli a letter of rejection, which was carefully kept secret from the deputies. Erzberger insisted he had learned of the letter only in July 1919. We know beyond doubt today[135] that Erzberger knew about this controversial letter no later than December 1917, indeed, that he then defended Kühlmann's policy to Pacelli and gave an entirely correct interpretation to Michaelis's letter as a merely tentative acknowledgment, pending the result of certain inquiries in Britain, which had to be awaited before a public declaration on Belgium became possible.

Reading the controversial letter today without a preconceived opinion, one can scarcely reach any other conclusion than that it was a very shrewd document—provided, of course, it is agreed that the German foreign ministry could not take the chance of initiating the Holy See into its secrets. The letter expresses warm sympathy for the efforts of Pope Benedict, but calmly and without the slightest rancor notes that peace negotiations between Britain and Germany would promise success, indeed be possible, only if the idea of summoning Germany before some kind of tribunal were dropped in favor of a spirit of reconciliation and mutual respect. The letter further said that the British Foreign Office directive to Count Salis, which had been confidentially communicated to the Vatican on August 30, offered no unequivocal proof that Britain was prepared to take a conciliatory attitude, especially since it clung to the Entente peace terms of January 1917, to which only an utterly vanquished Germany could ever accede. Lastly the letter said that a definite declaration by the German government on its intentions with respect to Belgium and the desired guarantees could not be given until certain prerequisites were sufficiently clarified. Efforts were being made, however, to obtain such clarity, and it was hoped that further information could be supplied in the not too distant future. Assurances were given that this reluctance did not stem from distaste for a declaration on Belgium, nor from an underestimate of its importance, nor from any desire to regard the guarantees as an insurmountable obstacle to the cause of peace.

It was a disagreeable necessity that the upshot of the crown council compelled the writer even to mention "guarantees" for the future conduct of Belgium in such an official document, and to avoid even hinting of the fact that direct contact with Britain had been taken up meanwhile, to clear up the "prerequisites." At the receiving end the letter was bound to create the impression that it was, at bottom, a final rejection, merely couched in pleasant rhetoric. The result was severe disappointment, and even Pacelli now regarded the papal peace initiative as a complete failure.

When it became known in December 1917 that Germany had stretched out a peace feeler to Britain through a Spanish intermediary, resentment was added to disappointment. The Vatican felt that it had been pushed aside in favor of others, indeed that it had been openly deceived. Erzberger was among those who were then trying to help restore Pacelli's shaken faith in the sincerity and goodwill of the German government.

Villalobar's peace mission is still shrouded in almost complete obscurity.[136] The only aspect that is so far documented is that on September 18 the Spanish foreign minister Lema told the British ambassador in Madrid, Sir Arthur Hardinge, that he had heard from one of his diplomats that the German government wished to communicate with the British government concerning the question of peace. Spain itself did not wish to become involved, but the minister would appreciate being told whether the British government was at all interested in receiving the German suggestion, or whether it rejected any form of discussion. He had the news from a highly placed personage.

After lengthy consultations, of which we shall hear, a reply was given on October 8, to the effect that the British government was ready to receive any communication the German government cared to offer concerning peace, and that it would discuss such a communication with its allies. Berlin learned of this reply only in December, from revelations in Bolshevist press dispatches. That was all. What is the explanation?

Lema's statement may be regarded as a kind of shot across the bow of

Villalobar's contemplated endeavor. Evidently the Spaniard failed to secure official permission from his own government to carry out the mission Kühlmann had requested. He had actually met the German minister against its wishes, and he was apparently denied authority to establish contact in London even as a private individual rather than as an official envoy. Lema is said to have been jealous of the marquis, who enjoyed considerable prestige abroad.[137] Villalobar, on his part, was not anxious to have his government see the hand he held, owing to Kühlmann's trust. He wanted to forestall its initiating a mediation effort of its own, which would have been as unwelcome to his ministerial friend as was the papal initiative. It would have probably put more pressure on him to make known the entire war aims program of Germany and its allies immediately, thus either deterring the other side from negotiations and providing it with a propaganda coup or—if the German war aims were sharply cut back—mobilizing the OHL and its henchmen against him. Lema himself knew nothing about Germany's intentions except what he told the British ambassador—he was particularly in the dark about the German position in Belgium. What probably happened was that Lema begrudged Villalobar the credit for transmitting such important news.

Actually, there was so little substance to the new effort that the stir it created within the British Foreign Office comes as a surprise. Balfour immediately circulated Hardinge's wire in the cabinet and on September 20 wrote an extended memorandum for the prime minister on what might be done in response. The existing British documents completely preclude the possibility that he had in the meantime received any direct news from Villalobar on Germany's plans.[138] Balfour, in other words, never knew (and never mentioned) what was known to the Spaniard, namely that the German government was prepared to relinquish Belgium, if it were guaranteed its 1914 borders, the return of its colonies, and freedom from war indemnities and economic warfare. He would have presumably regarded such an offer as beyond discussion. But since he never mentioned it, we cannot assert that Kühlmann's peace feeler failed because the German demands were excessive— to say nothing of the far-reaching limitations on Belgian sovereignty that had been discussed at the crown council in Bellevue palace. Even Villalobar knew nothing of those.

The German peace feeler did not fail, in the proper sense—it never even came off, though it created deep interest within the British Foreign Office and the war cabinet. As is shown in his memorandum of September 20,[139] Balfour immediately sensed that Kühlmann was behind the Spanish inquiry. He also realized that the Germans, for the time being, were interested only in informal discussions on peace terms. He saw clearly that the time for the regular machinery of diplomacy to swing into action on peace talks proper had not yet arrived, since the war was still raging at full fury. He saw further that the German inquiry, officially transmitted through normal diplomatic channels, carried incomparably greater weight than the many familiar peace offers from conspiratorial groups in Turkey, and even the peace feelers from Vienna, since Austria was firmly tied to Germany's apron strings. Of course Balfour allowed for the possibility that Kühlmann was trying to sow discord among the Allies, but Balfour was inclined to believe that he was sincerely searching for a basis for an agreement, which must have seemed more readily attainable to him by initiating a diplomatic dialogue rather than a general debate.

It would have scarcely been possible to read Kühlmann's mind more precisely. Yet what was the response?

Kühlmann's offer must on no account be simply ignored, Balfour said. That would merely strengthen the Pan-German forces, redouble German war zeal, and divide public opinion in Britain by encouraging the suspicion that the war was being continued solely for its own sake. What then was to be done? The greatest danger that could arise from such peace talks as Kühlmann was now proposing was undoubtedly that they might create disunity among Germany's enemies. Balfour apparently feared that Germany might make similar offers to Italy and France, which were fighting only for national goals, not for the general goals of Britain and America. What if Germany now offered these allies everything that they might win in a victorious war, possibly even more? It would then be extremely difficult for those governments to get their countries to fight for goals that were not their own.

There was no certain method of banishing such a danger. The best British policy would be complete frankness. Britain must not take a single step without fully informing France, Italy, America, Russia, and Japan. It was of course possible that in that event the Germans would drop the whole matter; but that was a risk that had to be taken, in the light of the danger that even the most noncommittal talks behind the backs of Britain's friends could lead to misunderstandings. Hence Balfour proposed that the Allied ambassadors be assembled and told of the communication from Madrid. They would be advised that the British government thought it wise to listen to any proposal coming from the German side. Britain would keep its allies currently informed and commit itself to nothing, until they had a chance to consider any proposals. Balfour's memorandum closes with a characteristic remark. If the Germans were to reject the idea of communicating their proposals to Britain's allies, that might be, to put it bluntly, the best thing that could happen at the moment.

This intensely personal reluctance of the Briton to become involved in a diplomatic escapade is as unsurprising as his intense loyalty to Britain's allies. What is surprising is that Balfour did not fear excessive demands from the Germans but sweeping offers to Italy—presumably South Tyrol and Trieste—

and France–Alsace-Lorraine–on a par with any Belgian offer made to Britain, with consequent concern that the entire war alliance might fall apart. As we shall presently see, there was similar concern in France. If this was indeed the prevailing situation–in other words, if a negotiated peace prior to military victory was viewed as a downright danger–then there surely was no prospect of a negotiated peace short of complete German submission to the will of its enemies.

Even so, Lloyd George did not immediately agree. Apparently the burden of responsibility for prolonging the dreadful and so far fruitless war weighed heavily on him. He put off a decision. Bonar Law too thought that Britain should, in the first instance, listen to what the Germans had to say, without immediately consulting its allies. The agreement of Painlevé, however, who had just become premier, would have to be obtained. The British would also have to hear from his lips what the current state of his negotiations with Austria was on the question of peace.[140]

Into the discussions on these matters burst the news that the Germans were, in the meantime, also seeking to negotiate with the French, allegedly making them sweeping offers–the return of Alsace-Lorraine, the restoration of Belgium and Serbia, territorial concessions to Italy, and colonial concessions to Britain. The French ambassador Paul Cambon, who brought this news on September 21, was deeply concerned because it might prove very difficult to persuade the French to fight on, once it were known that Alsace-Lorraine could be secured by negotiation. Russia and Rumania too would then probably seek to make peace separately. Balfour found his worries fully substantiated. All the Germans seemed to want was to split the Entente.

What was behind this alleged offer to the French that so surprised the British? It was actually a myth, though there was a real substrate.

Ever since December 1916 a Belgian notable, the industrialist Coppée, supported by his son, cardinal archbishop Mercier, and by a certain Countess Mérode, who was a friend of the German envoy von der Lancken at the government general in Brussels, had been intent on serving as an intermediary between German diplomats and the Belgian government at Le Havre for purposes of negotiating a separate peace with Belgium. In January 1917, he had submitted such a program to King Albert and Premier de Broqueville at Le Havre. Allegedly carrying Lancken's approval, it provided for full restoration of Belgium. De Broqueville had agreed in principle to a negotiated peace but like King Albert, he did not wish to part company with France. Since then the Belgian negotiators had been intent on expanding the peace talks to include France. The Countess Mérode, in particular, displayed much patriotic zeal and feminine temperament in efforts to win over a leading French politician, the former premier Aristide Briand, to her mediation plans and to elicit from Lancken statements favoring moderate German terms for France as well.

As we have seen (Vol. III, p. 240ff.), Bethmann Hollweg was working toward a Belgo-German understanding in principle, and he both encouraged and authorized Lancken to show himself as conciliatory as possible, though always with the reservation that he might have to disavow Lancken and all his works. He was mainly concerned with learning from the lips of a leading French politician precisely what France's minimum demands were and whether there were any realistic chance for an agreement. Surprisingly enough, he even obtained Ludendorff's consent to Lancken's plans. Lancken himself evidently played the role picked out for him with as much boldness as caution. He made very tempting promises to the Belgians against a separate peace and even agreed to negotiate in person with de Broqueville. In the matter of Alsace he always insisted that Germany was receptive and amenable to concessions, that discussions on this subject would be promising, etc.— without, however, in his own words, ever mentioning outright cession.

After originally resisting the idea, Briand allowed the Countess Mérode to persuade him to agree to a meeting with Lancken in Switzerland, but this was put off again and again. It would seem that he gradually warmed to the idea of once again playing a major political role as peace mediator between Germany and France; and if the Belgian middlemen understood him correctly, he apparently at times ventilated plans for defusing the problem of Alsace. He considered some such solution as neutralizing the region until a plebiscite could be held at a later date, but this was only in the event that it proved impossible to secure outright cession, a demand on which he proposed to insist initially.

By mid-August, after much backing and filling, it seemed that the contemplated meeting between Briand and Lancken might soon take place. Lancken asked the new Chancellor's government to confirm his negotiating authority, and this was done, though only with certain restrictions, since Kühlmann's own designs were based entirely on Britain rather than on France. Lancken was instructed to show himself as receptive as possible, but always to report to Berlin before making any commitments.

The Belgians, on their part, were quite vocal in describing Lancken's good intentions. They assured Briand that they would unquestionably succeed in securing the outright return of Alsace-Lorraine from the German negotiator and insisted that they had reliable indications to that end from Lancken's lips. Presumably their ardent desire first of all to bring about a meeting prompted them to indulge in considerable exaggeration.[141]

In mid-September Briand decided to yield to the Belgian importunities and meet with Lancken in Ouchy on Lake Geneva, obtaining, of course, the agreement of Poincaré, Premier Painlevé, and Foreign Minister Ribot. Only the last made any serious difficulties. In the view of Briand's biographer, personal jealousy may have played a major part, though the crucial element was probably that Ribot thought the whole project a mere German trap. Of course, disastrous consequences both at home and abroad might attend any publicity concerning the very fact that a figure like Briand was engaged in secret talks with a German emissary in Switzerland. After all, when he was still premier in January, he had officially rejected a German peace offer, in the name of the Allies. Briand himself thought that with the onset of official negotiations the soldiers of France might drop their guns.142

Ribot was insistent on asking Allied consent before the Swiss trip and demanded that Briand provide a written statement of his intentions. This was drafted on September 19, in the form of a letter to Ribot, and one has but to glance at this document to see the utter lack of realism of the whole undertaking. Before embarking on negotiations, Briand wanted the following assurances from his opposite number: the Allies to proceed jointly in the peace question—in other words, no separate peace; the occupied territories to be evacuated before peace talks began; the full return of Alsace-Lorraine; full indemnity for all damage done, though not in the form of exemplary atonement; reservation of demands for guarantees in favor of the Entente powers. On the other hand, France would put forward no claim to the left bank of the Rhine, and no economic restrictions would be imposed on Germany.

One can only wonder at the Frenchman's frivolous optimism. Could he have seriously believed—or allowed the Belgian middlemen to persuade him— that any German negotiator would agree to peace talks on such a basis? Jules Cambon, secretary general of the French foreign ministry, wrote his brother Paul, the French ambassador in London, that Briand had simply been taken in. Barthou spoke of delusions of grandeur; and Ribot did not even transmit his rival's letter to London and Rome, but merely a communication regarding it, in which he more than hinted that the Allied governments should take a negative stand. He said Briand had been advised that if the Germans were really of a mind to accept such a peace before the winter set in, it would not require the kind of hazardous preliminary negotiations he contemplated.

The whole thing was in fact no more than a bubble that would have burst at once, had the talks in Ouchy actually taken place. Paul Cambon showed Ribot's letter to the British foreign secretary on September 21, i.e., the day after Balfour's memorandum on Kühlmann, which we already know. The two of them quickly agreed that they were dealing with no more than a German effort to sow discord among the Entente powers.143 The Briton said that the Germans could not possibly be speaking of the restoration of Belgium and the return of Alsace-Lorraine in the same breath, unless they were admitting defeat. Yet the time had not arrived for that. We see that the coincidence of news from both Madrid and Paris resulted in the British foreign secretary conceiving distrust even of a peace feeler sent out by Kühlmann in dead earnest. He immediately notified Cambon, told him what he was recommending in his memorandum, and added that the British government proposed to advise Spain that it saw itself unable to enter into any *conversation séparée.*

For Briand the negative reply from London, soon corroborated by similar advice from Rome, spelled finis to his peace project. Possibly his illusory hopes were also shaken under the impression of the evasive German reply to the papal peace appeal, which became known at that time.[144, 145] In any event, on September 23 he abandoned the idea of going to Ouchy, where Baron Lancken, prematurely summoned by Mme. de Mérode, waited for him in vain.

London did not make up its mind quite so quickly. Lloyd George apparently gave long and careful consideration to the question of whether he could afford to reject out of hand this newly visible German willingness to enter into negotiations, and whether it might not pay to try coming a step closer toward peace by such talks. Unlike Balfour, Lloyd George seemed disinclined to simply put down Lancken's peace feeler as a splitting tactic.[146] When the British war cabinet met on September 24, Balfour found himself at the outset virtually alone in the view that not a step must be taken in the matter without first consulting the major Allied powers. Most of the members would have preferred first to listen discreetly to the German proposals and only then to inform the Allies. There was clearly the fear that such talks would come to nothing if all five Allies immediately had a voice in them.

Most worrying of all was the attitude of Soviet Russia, whose defection from the alliance seemed to impend—it had already virtually ceased to fight. Was it still to be given a voice? From Cambon's communication Lloyd George had gained the impression that while the Germans were prepared to grant major concessions in the west, they wished to compensate themselves with Lithuania and Courland in the east. Was the war to be carried on for the retention of Russia's western provinces, even though the Russians themselves were no longer willing to fight for them and the areas in question were not even Russian, in the ethnic sense?

The prime minister said that if Russia were responsible for ruining the Entente's chances of success, it should pay the penalty. He asked whether the Allies would still be able to force their will on the Germans after the defection of Russia. Would the blockade alone bring them to their knees? This was far from certain, if the Germans prevailed in the east, which would mean that they would emerge from the war stronger than when they went in. There would then be only the great empires left, the British and the German. This prospect alarmed all the participants, and sentiment for holding out at all costs spread. Lloyd George agreed, but only on condition that General Robertson, the chief of staff, could give assurances that the Allies were able to smash Germany even without Russian help and without the powerful effect the blockade had exerted thus far. It was decided in the end that the prime minister would advise Painlevé of the wire from Spain—but for the time being him alone. He would also say that the British government was willing to listen to what the Germans had to say and would discuss the general situation with Painlevé.

This was done on September 26 in Boulogne, and Lloyd George reported to the war cabinet on the following day. Painlevé had described Lancken's initiative as a serious effort. What impressed Lloyd George was that Briand too took it quite seriously, though his reports on what the Germans offered varied somewhat. He had first said that they were willing to give up Belgium and Alsace-Lorraine entirely, and then again that they were merely willing to discuss the question of Alsace-Lorraine.

Lloyd George quite likely concluded that the Germans were prepared to relinquish Belgium in any event and that they were inclined to compromise on Alsace-Lorraine. This should really have been enough for Britain; but as Lloyd George wrote in his memoirs, Painlevé seemed afraid not so much that the German overtures were a ruse as that they were sincere. He seemed to doubt that France would be in a position to fight on, if it became known that the Germans were offering all of Belgium and nine-tenths of Alsace-Lorraine. The French minister, in other words, shared the British view that no talks of any kind were wanted until Germany's military power was broken.[147]

Did Lloyd George really share this view wholeheartedly? Painlevé must have sensed that he was reluctant to commit his country's last resources for reconquering all of Alsace-Lorraine for France. Lloyd George had hitherto avoided any public avowal of such a British obligation; and a recent statement by Balfour in the House of Commons in which he said it was his personal— rather than official—view that the French had a claim to the lost provinces had caused a considerable stir in France, where it was considered far too timid.

Painlevé had pressed Lloyd George strongly to declare publicly that Britain would not down arms until Alsace-Lorraine were once again French. The prime minister balked—difficult times were ahead, and the time had not yet come to accept a solemn obligation that might turn into a heavy burden. In the end he did agree to issue such a declaration, but only on Painlevé's word of honor that France would hold out at all costs.

The cabinet session of September 27, in which Lloyd George reported his latest impressions of France, showed how deeply concerned he was. He said that the French had already virtually stopped fighting. They kept putting off a promised relief offensive, and would probably continue to do so into the winter, which would preclude it. They would certainly not lift a finger to regain any Russian provinces, and in all likelihood, neither would British and American soldiers, if the Russians did not bestir themselves.

Lord Curzon argued that it was not merely a matter of Russia's western provinces, but of not allowing Russia to become a German satellite. The effectiveness of the British blockade, moreover, was not in serious danger, since with the present chaos prevailing in Russia it would take six or seven months before Germany could obtain supplies from there. G. N. Barnes and Balfour insisted that the British would indeed fight on, from fear that there would be another war within a few years if Germany grew stronger. They would simply have to be told what they were fighting for—which was more than conquering a few Adriatic islands for Italy. Lloyd George remained skeptical. He did not wish to be committed in any way, including official speeches,[148] to fighting on for Russia, so long as it did not defend itself.

No final decision was reached at this session. Immediately Lloyd George asked the generals whether they thought Britain had any chance of winning, if the war turned into a single-front war.[149] Robertson, the chief of staff, said no, but the French generalissimo Foch was optimistic, and Haig, the British commander-in-chief, joined him, pointing out that in the wake of the great British offensive scarcely a single German division on the western front was intact. In the end what influenced Lloyd George most—he was always suspicious of his own generals—was Foch's unshakable confidence and the conviction that the U-boat menace was essentially under control.

Thus he was in the end swayed by military rather than political considerations. He yielded to Balfour's proposal and agreed to a meeting of the Allied ambassadors, which was set for October 6. They were advised of the British reply to the Spanish foreign ministry, of which we have already heard (p. 57), to the effect that the British government stood ready to receive peace proposals from Germany and discuss them with its allies.[150] Indirectly this constituted a rejection of separate negotiations and noncommittal preliminary talks, together with a challenge to submit considered peace proposals to the arbitrament of the Entente powers in concert. It was virtually certain that the Central Powers would never accede to such an approach, unless they considered the war a lost cause.

The ambassadors agreed, once Balfour explained to them that the Germans evidently sought to split the Entente, first satisfying Britain and the United States by proposals concerning Belgium, then doing likewise with France over Alsace-Lorraine, and thus winning over power after power to their side. There was also the suspicion that they were merely intent on preliminary talks with at least a few of the enemy governments, without immediately committing themselves to final peace terms. Paul Cambon added that once the parties sat down at the peace table, the war could no longer be vigorously pursued. Negotiations must start only when the Allies had full assurance of attaining their most important goals.

The peace proposals, in other words, were to be given a hearing, but negotiations would be entered into only if the Germans voluntarily submitted to their enemies at the outset. The precise concessions they were prepared to offer were not known—but that did not matter. Even if they were willing to forego Alsace-Lorraine and Belgium, as the British believed, Britain was not minded to enter into secret preliminary talks. They felt too closely tied to their allies to take such a risk. In sum, there was to be no peace for the Germans until they admitted final defeat.

Oddly enough, though the decision of October 6 was transmitted to Villalobar by his minister, Villalobar did not pass it on to Berlin, for reasons that are not entirely clear.[151] Thus Kühlmann was quite unaware of his Spanish friend's failure when, on October 9, he delivered a now-famous speech on Alsace-Lorraine in the Reichstag:

> We have but one answer to the question of whether Germany will make any concessions in the matter of Alsace-Lorraine. That answer is no, no, never! So long as a single German can still lift a gun, the integrity of the Reich territory, handed down to us by our fathers as a glorious heritage, shall never be the subject of any negotiations or concessions. Alsace-Lorraine is Germany's shield, the symbol of German unity.

Kühlmann's words brought a storm of applause from every side of the house; and he himself, in his memoirs, assures us that this extempore speech was to serve as an appeal to patriotic sentiment to restore a sense of unity to a chamber that was torn with passionate divisions.[152] It was in this session, by the way, that Michaelis's doom was sealed, when he incautiously hurled charges at the independent social democrats, without evidence that would stand up in a court of law, accusing them of sharing responsibility for the Kiel naval mutiny.[153] As for Kühlmann, he was far too shrewd a diplomat to be carried away into making so important a foreign policy statement, purely by current domestic considerations. What then was his real motive?

On September 21 Reuters in London had put out a dispatch that evidently emanated from the Foreign Office. It mentioned rumors that were then current in the German press, to the effect that the German government was paving the way for an understanding on the future of Belgium. The London dispatch said that if concessions on the Belgian question were actually in store, this could only mean a confession of German weakness that would not mislead the Entente governments. The object of the war was not merely the liberation of Belgium but the final liquidation of Prussian militarism.[154]

Obviously there was apprehension in Britain at the merest rumor that the Germans would offer concessions in the Belgian question, because of the effect this would have on public opinion. The stories in the German press culminated in an article in the *Münchner Neueste Nachrichten* on September 20, widely considered to have been officially inspired. It said in a tone of authority that both government and Reichstag now acknowledged that rather than conquest, understanding and compromise must be the German goals, even in the Belgian question—provided, of course, that Germany's enemies also unconditionally forewent conquest and sought negotiation.

Before the main committee of the Reichstag on September 28, Kühlmann denied that he was responsible for this article. His hand had been forced by a furious attack on the part of the fatherland party, which actually charged that Britain had been sent a German note on Belgium; this the minister vehemently denounced as "one of the crudest inventions I have ever encountered in political life."[155] It may be conjectured, however, that, at the very least, the Munich article was not unwelcome to him; for it hinted publicly of a willingness to which the foreign ministry, in its official reply to the papal note, had not wished to commit itself.

What was the reaction? The very same Asquith on whose goodwill Kühlmann had staked his hopes declared in a speech on September 26—we have already heard of it (p. 49)—that the German annexation of Alsace-Lorraine in 1871 was a crime that must be atoned for, and jeered at Germany's alleged peacefulness. Kühlmann's Reichstag speech was the counter-reaction. Its purpose was to strip bare before the world as a piece of hypocrisy the French phrase about *désannexion* and to make it clear that, since agreement could certainly be reached on all the other issues, the only thing holding up peace was France's insistence on the reconquest of Alsace-Lorraine.

Kühlmann was well aware that he was doing no harm in France with such a statement. Lancken's mission had failed for the time being, and Lancken himself had advised him to make the German position crystal clear in public now.[156] Did Kühlmann perhaps think he would register an impression in Britain, not taking Balfour's argumentation as the last word? There is no conclusive answer. If he really wished to exert such an effect, it would have been far better to underline Germany's readiness to relinquish Belgium and not to reject outright any compromise in the question of Alsace-Lorraine. Undoubtedly Kühlmann's speech was not only a calculated political act, but also an outburst of passionate and embittered patriotism.

It did not change the situation, for the decision had been taken in London three days earlier; but it did provide the occasion for Lloyd George to redeem his pledge to Painlevé. On October 10 he declared in a public speech that no matter how long the war might last, Britain would stand by its valiant ally France until that country's oppressed children were freed from their humiliating foreign yoke.[157]

The iron ring around Germany had been forged even more firmly.

2

The Dictate of Brest-Litovsk

Part 1
The OHL and Self-Determination

OME TWO WEEKS after Kühlmann's Reichstag speech and Lloyd George's reply, the Italian front on the Isonzo collapsed, and another two weeks later came the Bolshevist coup d'etat in St. Petersburg known as the October Revolution which ushered in a new era of history. The very first manifesto of the first Pan-Russian congress of soviets—at which the coup was effected—proclaimed a "democratic peace and immediate armistice," and the next day saw the issuance by the new rulers of the famous proclamation to the world proletariat to rise and force the governments of the belligerent nations to begin peace negotiations immediately. It called for a "peace without annexations or tribute, on the basis of the self-determination of nations."

The Soviets had called for such a peace ever since the March Revolution; but the new government was a minority regime, formed in the first instance by a tiny group of professional revolutionaries, and its fate depended on turning words into action. It owed its success in achieving power largely to the support of the mutinous soldiers of St. Petersburg and the country's general war-weariness.

A new situation was thus created for the Central Powers, opening up an unprecedented chance for peace, at least on the eastern front, at almost the same time when hope had died for a negotiated peace with the Western powers. This chance grew even greater when the new council of people's commissars on the next day declared all treaties concluded with the Allies null and void, to the extent that they encompassed annexations. To the consternation of the Allied governments it not only announced that it would make them public but immediately did so. In practice this meant that Russia was openly breaking with its quondam friends. The frantic efforts of Western

diplomats, especially the Americans, somehow to continue the war alliance—an alliance between the capitalists and imperialists and the Russian
"proletarians"—were seen to be not only vain but downright absurd.[1]

Germany faced two alternatives. Either it swiftly concluded the kind of
"honest peace without annexations" proposed by the soviets, thereby probably establishing enduring peace and even neighborly relations with Russia; or
it exploited the beaten enemy's total military impotence to expand its own
power, securing "guarantees" against renewed military attack by territorial
acquisitions. Understandably, the first alternative was preeminently demanded and pursued by the German parties of the left, most eagerly by the
social democrats. Scheidemann actually went to Stockholm in December
1917, in hopes of establishing direct contact with the Bolshevists through the
second socialist international, and thus gaining a voice in the course of negotiations. It was soon seen that Lenin and his followers set little store by the
parliamentary efforts of the German social democrats, but did expect them to
stage large-scale strikes and menacing peace demonstrations in order to bring
pressure to bear on militarists at supreme headquarters.

Scheidemann and Ebert, who were patriots rather than revolutionaries,
could not be persuaded. They felt that they shared responsibility for preserving domestic tranquility during the war and were content with peaceful mass
rallies and intensive propaganda in the press directed against the Pan-German
policy of annexation. Throughout the winter, together with the leaders of the
center and progressive parties, they endeavored, in the joint caucus of the
majority parties, to push German diplomacy in the direction of a peaceful
understanding with the Bolshevists and of resisting the policy of brute force
represented by the OHL; but they never went so far as to court open conflict
with the government of the aged Count Hertling, Michaelis's successor,[2] and
were thus denied success. Only revolutionary action could have smashed the
political dominance of the OHL.[3]

Actually, the efforts of the Bolshevist leaders on behalf of an honest peace
without annexations were harmed by their constant harping on the need for
world revolution by the workers and soldiers. Their unbridled hate propaganda against the "capitalists, exploiters, and militarists" terrified and outraged the middle class, but by no means that class alone. This campaign began
on November 11 with an appeal to the German proletariat and had risen by
early February to a radio proclamation addressed to German soldiers, calling
on them to mutiny and to kill their officers and generals, and even the Kaiser.
There was a question in many people's minds as to whether any peaceful and
neighborly relations were still possible with these bloodthirsty fanatics who
swiftly earned hatred within their own country and proceeded to establish a
reign of terror. Everything had to be staked on separating their regime from
Germany by means of a *cordon sanitaire,* a strip of well-protected buffer

states. Was there any other way in which Germany and the free world generally could be guarded against the contagion of Bolshevist ideas?

As we know, this line of reasoning persuaded the Western powers as a whole to intervene politically, economically, and militarily in the Russian civil war that soon ensued, on the side of the enemies of Lenin and Bolshevism. Indeed, in a secret Franco-Russian treaty of December 23 Southern Russia was formally carved up into spheres of interest. From the beginning the question of buffer states was the central problem in the peace talks that began on December 20 at Brest-Litovsk between the Quadruple Alliance and delegates of the Soviet government. It was this question alone that delayed peace for many weeks, for there were scarcely any other major differences between the delegations; indeed, from the outset the Germans endeavored to create an almost friendly atmosphere.

All the same, it proved impossible to reach agreement on this crucial issue, and the negotiations broke up on a shrill note of discord, with a new advance of German troops into the Russian interior becoming necessary to compel the Russians to sign the peace document formally. How did matters reach such a pass? And was it, in the given circumstances, inevitable that such an unfortunate stage should have been reached, seemingly confirming to the world that Wilson was right in holding that there could be no negotiating with the German autocrats and militarists?

It did not seem so in the beginning, for in one of their earliest proclamations, on November 11, the new rulers in St. Petersburg had said: "The Russian Revolution does not reach out for foreign possessions—on the contrary, it grants to all the peoples who were subjugated by czarism the full right to decide freely whether they desire to live with the Russian people or separately from them."[4] This astonishing outgrowth of the revolutionary doctrine of the right of self-determination had a strong impact. It was all the more surprising since at the outset, at least, only the Finns and Poles were striving for complete independence, while all the other non-Russian ethnic groups within the czarist empire went no further than asking for a measure of autonomy.

Indeed, one of the most baffling problems is why Lenin came to offer such seemingly sweeping concessions to the principle of nationalism, which orthodox Marxists and even the most radical socialists of the so-called Zimmerwald school regarded as hopelessly antiquated and part of nineteenth-century bourgeois ideology. Lenin did meet with vehement opposition on this point among his closest associates. Yet here as elsewhere the dominant element of his character came into play, rigid dogmatism combined in mysterious fashion with an infallible sense of political realism, of what would work in practice. Lenin was much more a man of power than an ideologue. Like his comrades, this prophet of proletarian world revolution and international working-class solidarity loathed the ideal of "national culture," which was quite foreign to him and which he thought absurd; yet in proclaiming unlimited "self-determination" he thought he would hold a weapon to change the world—not merely the old European order, particularly multiracial Austria, but also the great colonial empires of the Age of Imperialism.

Marx and Engels had regarded the many petty non-Russian ethnic groups belonging to the czarist empire—the Latvians and Lithuanians, the Georgians, Kirghizes, and Crimean Tartars—as mere "debris" that would be automatically absorbed into Great Russia in the process of Eastern industrialization, since these peoples could not otherwise survive economically. Marxists generally believed that vast centrally directed national economies were superior to the parochialism of smaller states; and Lenin, even though he had preached the doctrine of absolute self-determination ever since 1913, does not seem to have believed this would "Balkanize" Russia in the long run. Caught up in the Marxist historical approach, he was probably convinced that in the end sentimental nationalism and separatism would yield to the workers' economic self-interest, the evident advantages of a large-scale economy and of proletarian class ideology—in other words, the blandishments of a Bolshevist workers' and peasants' society. Once nationalist grievances were appeased, proletarian class interest would outweigh everything else.

Lenin even had the audacity of not shrinking from temporary cooperation with the bourgeois nationalist movements of "backward" peoples. Apparently he greatly underestimated the explosive force of nationalism and separatism, just as he greatly overestimated the attractive force of his new proletarian republicanism; but like his closest associate in nationalist questions, Stalin, he was confident that there would ultimately be sufficient propaganda weapons, methods of systematic infiltration, and if necessary even brute force to push the backward peoples in the direction he wanted. A professional revolutionary and long without a country, Lenin was probably immune to patriotic sentiment. He was not worried that Russia might for a time fall to pieces. To establish the rule of his party over so many disparate elements, it was necessary that life in Russia be kept in the wildest uproar.[5]

Vigorous efforts in that direction were initiated as early as the winter of 1917-1918, especially in the Ukraine, where an autonomous republic had been proclaimed on November 20, though still entirely within an over-all Russian framework; and also in the provinces of Livonia and Estonia, where late in November both the Estonians and Latvians and the German-speaking Balts were threatening to defect from Russia. Here Red Guards and bands of adventurers of every kind collaborated with Bolshevist agitators to mobilize the rural and urban proletariat against the estate owners, wealthy peasants, industrialists, and "capitalist" bourgeoisie, to lay the groundwork for the new-style Soviet state. The "dictatorship of the proletariat" and the expropriation of private property for which the way was being paved here were anything but expressions of "the popular will." It was a new form of rule by force, the one-party state. It soon became clear that "self-determination" for the Latvians and Ukrainians meant the sole choice of the establishment of proletarian Soviet republics.

At the Soviet congress of January 28, 1918, Stalin said so openly, stating that the only reason why the Bolshevists had supported the Ukrainian people's government—the Kiev central "Rada" that came into being in the summer of 1917—was because it opposed the bourgeois government of Kerensky. Once a nationalist state had been created, the class struggle had to begin. Since the Rada, gone bourgeois, tried to prevent that, it had to be fought and destroyed.6 Self-determination, in other words, was the monopoly of the proletariat and had to be exercised exclusively in its interests. The dictatorship of the proletariat was the mortal enemy of bourgeois parliamentary "freedom"; this was made plain to the world on January 19, 1918, when the Soviet government dispersed by force of arms the newly elected national constituent assembly, because its membership was overwhelmingly non-Bolshevist.

Here was a glittering chance for German diplomacy! The victorious eastward advances of the German armies, beginning with the campaign of 1915, not only could have been made to appear as acts of liberation— they could have had such an effect in practice. Had Germany taken the Soviet government at its word and forced it to permit the Poles, Balts, and Ukrainians true self-determination, not only would the *cordon sanitaire* for which the world clamored have been created against the Bolshevist "virus," but German policy would have achieved a moral authority that would have gravely embarrassed the Western Allies and made Wilson's scornful speeches about German autocracy and militarism a mockery.

Of course it would not have been possible to evacuate the occupied eastern territories during the war or until a new order was not only established but militarily secured there; for marauding bands of Russian stragglers, deserters, and criminals made the countryside unsafe, and there was always the danger of Bolshevist attack, which the small Baltic states would have been incapable of repelling on their own. Indeed, the very establishment of these new states was imperiled by the fact that the Bolshevists planned to flood them beforehand with hundreds of thousands of doubtful elements who claimed to have been expelled from those areas, now insisted on a vote, and were expected to weight every plebiscite in favor of the Soviets. This strategy was actually employed in Estonia and Livonia soon after the October Revolution.7

There was much concern over these developments in the Reichstag's joint majority party caucus, but we cannot be certain that the security measures it proposed on Erzberger's initiative would have been adequate: final evacuation only three months after the Russian army was demobilized and the immediate conclusion of military conventions with the buffer states that would make it possible to leave German garrisons behind beyond that deadline, until at least some Baltic regiments had been organized.

Actually, there was not even any serious debate on these proposals. General Hoffmann, Ludendorff's representative at Brest-Litovsk, instantly and indignantly rejected them. Kühlmann, who may have wished he could accept them, said that in the matter of concessions he had already gone to the utmost limits of what could be accepted, in the light of OHL demands.[8]

The military, in other words, stood squarely in the way of any such solution. They never wanted anything but the extension of German power over the entire Baltic region, and to them self-determination was only a thin camouflage for annexation. The quarrel with Austria over Poland continued interminably, as we shall see in Chapter 4. In the event it were knocked down to Austria, the OHL called for border guarantees so massive that they virtually amounted to a fourth partititon. The Polish question, however, did not figure prominently in the negotiations with the Soviet government, for Poland's separation from Russia had been acknowledged by the declaration of the Central Powers of November 5, 1916, and the proclamation of the Russian provisional government of March 29, 1917. The struggle over the future of the Baltic provinces was waged with all the greater ferocity.

We recall the serious reservations Bethmann Hollweg had voiced to Falkenhayn at the first emergence in 1915 of annexationist plans in the Baltic region.[9] He said that in both the military and the political sense the acquisition of Baltic border territories would be highly undesirable. In a military sense their exposed situation made them hard to defend. In a political sense it was an illusion to regard them as essentially German, since the predominantly Latvian population—only about 7 per cent spoke German—represented a very unwelcome element of revolutionary character. Economically speaking, Germany needed neither additional ports in the Baltic nor large agricultural areas. To cut off Russia by force from its ice-free Baltic ports, moreover, would become a source of enduring enmity, since Russia needed these ports for its overseas exports.

By 1917 nothing had altered the cogency of these arguments—except that in the meantime Ludendorff had established his own personal fief in Lithuania and Courland.[10] It had become a domain which he ruled like a dictator, with the help of a purely military administration, permitting no interference by any civilian "government general," as in Brussels and Warsaw. More than that, by means of intensive propaganda he had made recapture of "the ancient territories of the Teutonic Order," the goal of a powerful movement in Germany, which even by the winter of 1915-1916 embraced many intellectuals. The movement was further stimulated by an influx of Baltic Germans that included a remarkably large number of scholars and publicists of stature. The movement found its strongest support, naturally, among the Pan-Germans and rightist parties; but there was much sympathy for the Baltic people among the moderates as well, and at the very least, there was a broad range of political views.[11] In the Bismarckian era and even down to 1914, the Baltic issue had fallen almost into oblivion in German awareness, despite the fact that czarist Russification bore down heavily on that area. Now it suddenly enjoyed a new lease on life.

The sympathies of the intellectuals, however, were not really the deciding factor. What gained such a wide hearing for the annexationism of Ludendorff and the Pan-Germans were simply the experiences of 1914-1915 — the Russian invasion of East Prussia and the fearful losses in the winter Battle of the Masurian Lakes (see Vol. III, p. 55f.). Indeed, the OHL's plans of conquest were directed from the beginning not merely toward "Teutonic" Courland but with equal intensity toward Lithuania, a purely non-German peasant economy in the region between the Dvina and Niemen rivers, of interest as a kind of delaying area in the defense of East Prussia. The generals put forward the need for advancing the German border here and on the Narev with such conviction that they achieved almost a national consensus. In the end even Bethmann Hollweg, in his Reichstag speech of April 5, 1916, proclaimed the separation from Russia of the area between the Baltic Sea and the Volhynian marshes as an essential war aim (see Vol. III, p. 116). Actually, Bethmann Hollweg was always opposed to integrating non-German elements with Germany and tried to keep this to a minimum.[12] On April 21, 1917, he consulted the Prussian cabinet on the question of whether proclaiming autonomy for Courland and Lithuania along the lines of "self-determination" might not avoid the alternatives of annexation and ambiguous "border rectifications" (see Vol. III, p. 418f.). Bethmann Hollweg was clearly thinking in terms of buffer states.

Since the Reichstag resolution of July 19 with its outright renunciation of annexations, the only way for German border guarantees in the east that still remained open was such a proclamation of autonomy for the Baltic countries, which could then act as buffers between Russia and the West. Undoubtedly the Reichstag parties that supported the resolution acted with the utmost sincerity. They could hardly have done otherwise. They would have betrayed their own cause, had they admitted that the war was being continued for eastern conquest. There was rising concern among them, especially in view of the increasingly restive working class in both Germany and Austria, that peace was being delayed by veiled annexationist goals.

Their concern was well-founded. In its war aims program of April 23, 1917, with which we are already familiar, the OHL had not only demanded outright annexation of Courland and Lithuania, but described as desirable the acquisition of parts of other Baltic provinces, including the islands at the mouth of the Bay of Riga.[13] In consequence Riga was taken and occupied on September 5, and in mid-October the islands of Sarema, Khiuma, and Muhu as well, which controlled access to the bay. On July 31, at a conference of his administrative advisers in Lithuania and Courland that met in Bingen, Ludendorff took advantage of the change in the chancellorship to lay down precisely his further tactics in incorporating his Baltic "empire" with Prussia.[14]

The goal was to hand sovereignty over Courland and Lithuania to the king of Prussia in such a form that this appeared to be "the will of the people." To this end the two chiefs of the military administrations were each to convoke a "council of trust" (Vertrauensrat), composed of men of whose German loyalties there could be no doubt. They were to be told nothing of the ultimate goal, but only—in a speech that was laid down in writing to the last word— that there was a prospect of popular participation in the administration. The reply required of the council was also set down verbatim. They were to plead for German protection. Following this, they were to become provisional "provincial councils," representing the people of Courland and Lithuania. The traditional corporate diet of Courland was thereupon to ask "voluntarily" for its dissolution, with the prospect that at a later date another diet composed of "representatives from all walks of life" would be instituted, in such a manner, however, that German elements would control an absolute majority in Courland, Lithuanians in their country.

Although these were all purely political issues, Ludendorff unhesitatingly laid claim to their settlement by the OHL. All that was left to do for the two subaltern representatives of the foreign ministry who were present was to provide their rubber stamp. In the Kreuznach talks of August 9 (see p. 33), Michaelis too gave his approval, and so this travesty of the founding of states took place strictly according to plan from September 18 to 22. The diet of Courland decided to convoke an expanded assembly, following the proposal of the occupation authorities. This met immediately and by a unanimous voice vote adopted the proposed petition to the Kaiser. This was almost certainly not accomplished by coercion but by the fervent assent of the assembled Baltic Germans and pro-German Latvians. The ordained provincial council was chosen—or rather confirmed—by the same method.[15]

The occupation authority was now in possession of an instrumentality that would make both the separation of Courland from Russia and its integration with Germany appear to be an expression of the people's will. The same spectacle was simultaneously enacted in Lithuania. In that country, however, there was no German-speaking upper crust, and even convocation of a council of trust had caused much difficulty. It seemed at first that no one could be found anywhere who would collaborate with the hated German military administration. In the end it did prove possible to assemble an organizing committee, which was immediately subjected to strong pressure. The German military government made it plain that if the Lithuanian representatives refused to incorporate their country in the German Reich, its fate would be determined exclusively by German strategic interest; i.e., it would be annexed in part, while the rest would be left to the Russians and Poles. This threat resulted in a resolution at least mentioning that relations between the autonomous state that was to be established and Germany would be the subject of further discussions. A national council (the Taryba) was to be formed for these discussions and this was managed with the help of a large representative assembly that met in Vilnyus on September 18. The declaration issued by this assembly, however, was very cautiously worded. In view of the fact that the country's interests were directed more toward the West than the East, it said, it was entirely possible that closer relations with Germany might be established.[16]

Actually, no other way of establishing a new state—for example, by the free choice of a national assembly—was available if the Germans insisted on integration. For one thing, they could not very well grant the people of Courland and Lithuania universal suffrage, which not even Prussia enjoyed; and none who knew these countries could have doubted that, given the opportunity, their vote would have been overwhelmingly anti-German.[17] Beyond question the German military administration under Ludendorff did spend much energy, not merely on exploiting the country, but also on rebuilding what had been destroyed—road, railway, and bridge construction, the creation of a large-scale timber industry and others, improvements in agriculture, the organization of schools, courts, and a pro-German press. Ludendorff was very proud of these achievements, which he describes at great length in his memoirs.[18]

But one thing Ludendorff could not accomplish was winning over the hearts of the non-German population. The Baltic Germans scarcely had any choice. Holding aloof from Russia since the fall of czarism, caught in a hopeless dilemma between the Bolshevists and the Latvians, both of whom threatened their political dominance, indeed their property and their very existence, they could only look to the Germans for salvation. All other sections of the population disliked the Germans, if they did not hate them. Perhaps the main cause was the inevitable hardships of a protracted occupation, especially in Lithuania, where the Germans could not understand a word of the language, and of a war that even inside Germany was exhausting all economic and manpower reserves.

It was indeed a great misfortune for the Lithuanians and Latvians that Ludendorff with his iron will insisted on running the whole country by means of his military machine, allowing not the slightest intervention by the Chancellor, the Reich office of the interior, or any other civilian agency. All direct traffic between representatives of the non-German inhabitants and the Chancellor or the Reich office was either prohibited outright or virtually precluded by passport difficulties.[19] That Ludendorff was able to do this throws a surprising and glaring light on power relations in Germany.

To rebuild, with a largely untrained staff, a region the Russians had left an almost hopeless and uninhabited wasteland[20] was an unpromising undertaking from the outset; and since the Germans, for reasons of prestige, were virtually deaf to complaints by the people, especially under the arrogant chief of administration in Lithuania, Prince Isenburg, there was inevitably much abuse of power. The middle and lower "armchair" echelons were customarily guilty of cruel mistreatment in the collection of foodstuffs and livestock and in assembling the so-called labor battalions, and there was no recourse against them.[21]

To avoid or at least mitigate all this would have taken steadily increasing popular participation in running the country. The imperious military administration fought against this as late as the fall of 1917, when the crucial steps toward autonomy were to be taken. On October 20 the Lithuanian Taryba petitioned the Chancellor with a long list of grievances and proposals for improvement,[22] but virtually nothing happened. General Hoffmann, chief of staff at eastern headquarters, regarded the Lithuanians as completely incapable of self-government.[23] On November 4 the OHL met with Vice-Chancellor Helfferich and a number of department heads, to discuss the form in which the two provinces were to be integrated with Germany—it was to be as "autonomous" duchies, if possible with the king of Prussia as sovereign.

At this meeting Hoffmann insisted that the Lithuanians would opt for Germany if they were threatened with partititon. Even Ludendorff was willing to grant them certain favors to win them over as allies,[24] but what he really meant was that the country should live in perpetual enmity with Poland. This was to be done by extending it southward to the forest of Bialowiecz across territory that was partly or wholly Polish. The predominantly Polish Vilnyus was to become the capital, and the Lithuanian clergy was to be separated from the Polish episcopate. Since the disastrous failure of his Polish policy in 1916, Ludendorff had regarded the Poles as future enemies, even in the event of an "Austro-Polish solution," indeed, particularly in such an event. He wanted no efforts at conciliation and compromise among Germany's eastern neighbors, such as were proposed by the governor general in Warsaw, Beseler. Hindenburg added that the only principle to apply here was "divide and rule."[25]

These generals had not the least idea of conciliation and persuasion, but knew only orders, threats, and "territorial guarantees." Ludendorff, moreover, sought to realize here in the Baltic region some of his ideas with which we are already familiar—he wanted to make it a "breeding ground for men needed for further fighting in the east" (see Vol. III, p. 112), and also use it for creating "a human bulwark against Slavdom." True, he seems to have considered poverty-stricken Lithuania with its totally non-German population little suited to his colonization and Germanization plans;[26] but he pursued with all the greater energy the goal of making Courland German, and sweeping colonization plans were developed for that region. Figures and data of every kind were gathered and plans for obtaining land for settlement were established, using crown domains, clerical and secular institutions, and Baltic German latifundia, but also on the basis of whittling down the often quite large peasant estates of the Latvians. The Reich office of the interior and the foreign ministry were involved in these plans, all of which remained largely on paper, however. The whole design was in direct continuation and intensification of settlement plans and efforts already initiated by the Baltic aristocracy before the war. Considerable private means had been spent on increasing the German element, mainly by the settlement of German-speaking Russian peasants from Volhynia and the Volga region, with but modest success.

Now that these fine plans were to be realized and settlement societies and agrarian banks began to be interested, many unforeseen problems emerged. In the first place, a flood of Latvian refugees returning from Russia threatened to swamp Courland—only 270,000 of 675,000 Courlanders had stayed behind. By 1918 this stream was augmented by large numbers of ethnically German peasants and workers from Volhynia, Southern Russia, and the Volga region, most of whom were thoroughly Russianized, if not bolshevized. During the war they had been brutally deprived of their farms and jobs. It turned out, lastly, that only a fraction of these immigrants could actually be "settled," for almost everything to that end was lacking—houses, equipment, stock, roads, etc.

Efforts had to be made to dam the stream as quickly as possible. Germany, in the fourth year of the war, simply no longer had the strength and the resources to carry out such large and costly settlement projects—which in all likelihood would not even pay their own way. Reading the various memoranda and documents today, one can only marvel at the imaginative sweep of these plans, which contemplated turning swamps into meadows and roads, building houses, depots, bridges, canals—all the things that would have been indispensable for true economic reconstruction.[27]

The whole approach was utterly unrealistic, essentially a romantic dream. By late 1917 Courland and Lithuania were drained and impoverished to the point of acute emergency rather than suitable raw material for new states. Even Riga, once a flourishing industrial city, was in ruins when it fell into German hands. In the fall of 1915 the Russians had dismantled its entire plant and evacuated most of its workers, who were largely Latvian.[28] It was grotesque to say, as the generals did to Czernin, that in the fourth war year the Germans needed these regions for economic reasons.[29]

Economic considerations were almost certainly not behind Ludendorff's political stand, and by 1917 his settlement plans had at best taken second place. His true motive—and this applies to Hindenburg as well—was the traditional, not to say primitive drive of the soldier to render a beaten enemy harmless for all time by taking away as much of his land as possible. This policy was fervently approved by the Baltic Germans, who were one and all anti-Russian to the core.[30]

The main basis for Ludendorff's quarrel with the civil authority was that he not only expected his army and the German people to hold out until victory had been won on the battlefield but, beyond that, wished to create a favorable starting position, in both the east and the west, for the next war— his much-cited "Second Punic War." His mind was always on this goal.[31] Apparently he was never concerned—at least until August 1918—with the question of whether it might not exceed the military, economic, and moral resources of the German people. Since the Russians had sued for peace, he was even more convinced than before that the Germans would carry the day. By December a report from his headquarters spoke of plans he was considering for utterly smashing the enemy.[32]

The civilians in the foreign ministry talked themselves hoarse about the necessity for avoiding even the semblance of annexation, for reasons of domestic as well as foreign policy; but Ludendorff instructed his representatives in the peace delegation at Brest-Litovsk to demand the annexation of Lithuania and Courland with Riga and the islands, since "Germany needed more land for food." The national aspirations of the people of Lithuania and Courland could be considered only within the framework of annexation and even then only if the British did not occupy the Åland islands (Ahvenanmaa), Finland, Estonia, and Livonia. At the same time "self-determination" was to be recognized—but only when it was to Russia's disadvantage—the Russians were to evacuate Finland, Estonia, Livonia, Moldavia, East Galicia, and Armenia.[33]

The OHL had long wanted to capture Livonia and Estonia for Germany. In the Kreuznach agreement of August 9 a promise had been extracted from Michaelis to join the OHL in launching a pro-German propaganda campaign in those areas as well as in Finland and the Ukraine. The Ukrainians were to be persuaded to give tacit approval to friendly integration with Germany—this was long before the October Revolution, when the Ukrainian autonomy movement was only in its infancy.

In Finland and Estonia the ostensible motive for the German campaign was the "threat of British influence," manifested in land purchases.[34] Later on there was even occasional talk of the danger of British troop landings in the Baltic region.[35] In truth, however, the OHL's territorial greed far transcended Lithuania and Courland from the very outset. In October Lieutenant Colonel Buchfinck, chief of staff in Riga, wrote two memoranda in which he advocated advancing the German border to Lake Peipus;[36] and at the very beginning of the armistice negotiations Ludendorff instructed General Hoffmann, to the horror of the Austrians, to demand that the Russians get out of Livonia and Estonia. Only later did Hoffmann have a free hand to allow himself to be governed by circumstances and not let an armistice fail on account of such demands.[37] Yet when the German goals for Brest-Litovsk were discussed on December 18 between the OHL and the government, Hindenburg insisted that "for military reasons of eastern border security" Estonia and Livonia, including Riga and the islands in the gulf, must be closely joined to Germany, preferably by the Kaiser's cosovereignty *(Personalunion)*.

Precisely what military advantage was to arise from the addition of such a huge coastal strip, largely inhabited by people hostile to Germany, was not spelled out. So competent a military expert as General von Seeckt held that even the acquisition of Lithuania and Courland would worsen Germany's geographic situation.[38] Kühlmann, of course, ventured no military objections, contenting himself with the reservation that Russia could be completely cut off from the Baltic Sea only at the cost of perpetual mortal enmity. The Kaiser waved this aside with the frivolous remark that Russia should be encouraged to compensate itself for Riga and Tallin by grabbing territory on the Persian Gulf. It was ultimately agreed that the Estonians and Livonians should first be given a chance to voice their wishes.[39]

Ludendorff had actually already been on the receiving end of such expressions, though only on the part of the Baltic German nobility, who had been laying plans for a new pro-German Baltic state ever since the March Revolution and their subsequent ouster from political and social power by the Kerensky regime. Driven to desperation by the October Revolution and its consequences, they had redoubled their efforts to find support in Germany. On November 6, Ludendorff had received a Livonian delegation, which, according to Livonian sources, was given assurances of German protection all the way to the Narva, if the Baltic nobility, by means of extensive German-financed propaganda, won over the masses for some popular pro-German demonstrations that would satisfy the principle of self-determination, as demanded in parliamentary circles.

The result was a lively campaign, conducted at some risk and with the support of German military agencies. Petitions calling for German assistance were widely circulated. The Livonian and Estonian nobility went even further. Toward year's end the diet resolved the formal separation of the two regions from Russia; and on February 5, 1918, the Kaiser was directly petitioned, not only for protection, but for the entire Baltic region to become an integral part of the German Reich under the Hohenzollern crown.[40] The immediate consequence was that the Bolshevist government outlawed the entire Baltic nobility.

There can be little doubt, however, that wide sections of the population, not merely the nobility, were eager to get out from under the Russian Bolshevist reign of terror. Yet among the non-German elements, who constituted 90 per cent of the total, the catchword about "returning home to Germany" was received with a notable lack of enthusiasm; and it is virtually certain that the Germans would have ruined their chances at Brest-Litovsk, had they demanded at the outset that the Russians clear out of the whole Baltic region and leave it to Germany. Even inside Germany, to say nothing of Austria, such high-handed territorial demands would have had disastrous consequences. As for the Austrians, they were in a state of extreme exhaustion and war-weariness and had long looked on the German lust for conquest with distrust and resentment.[41]

Kühlmann could count himself fortunate that this demand, at least, was postponed on December 18. This, however, by no means settled the matter, which came up again and again in the ensuing months, with increasing urgency when the Baltic nobility addressed itself directly to the Kaiser, whose sense of chivalry was outraged at the thought of simply abandoning these royalists, for centuries the guardians and outposts of German culture in the northeast. He was supported in these sentiments by the unceasing activities of his intimate, the Baltic-German historian and publicist Theodor Schiemann of Berlin.[42] The Kaiser's lively dynastic ambitions were an added factor. During a parade on the entry of the troops into Riga, he had been jubilantly welcomed by the German populace, kindling visions of his playing a historic role as liberator and duke of the whole Baltic region.

All this must be borne in mind to appreciate the extremely awkward starting position of the German diplomats, Kühlmann and his associate Rosenberg, in the negotiations with the Soviet delegation during the Christmas season of 1917. Both the Kaiser and the OHL expected them to bring home a peace of conquest, albeit in somewhat disguised form, out of consideration for popular sentiment, as represented by the parties of the left. Kühlmann himself was far too much of a political realist and opportunist, wryly skeptical of all general principles, to look on self-determination as a sacred cow. He also appreciated its revolutionary potential. It is doubtful whether he had even a glimmer of the opportunity that existed for Germany to play a true liberator's role in the east. From his own words, he sought to use the self-determination catchword only to subvert the idea of peace without annexations, i.e., to camouflage an expansion of German power.[43] That could be accomplished only by the creation of buffer states, as Bethmann Hollweg called them, which would be conceded a measure of autonomy and expected to agree voluntarily to some form of integration with Germany.

On December 4 Kühlmann tried to set down for himself some general principles for the armistice and peace negotiations. "The fiction of self-determination must be kept alive as much as possible," he wrote. The primary condition to this end was at last to replace the military administration in Lithuania and Courland with civilian authority, whose immediate task it would be to effect a transition to indigenous hands.[44] The OHL, however, did not dream of surrendering its political power in the occupied territories. After offering stubborn opposition, it did agree on December 7 that Under Secretary von Falkenhausen should become a member of the administration in Lithuania and Courland, but only under the eastern commander-in-chief, and to serve in the main only as an information pipeline for the Chancellor. Yet his correspondence with the Chancellor and other agencies of the central government was to pass through channels, i.e., the eastern general staff and the OHL, affording an opportunity for military control. The minutes of this meeting speak of the necessity for maintaining a military administration "for years to come"; and as late as March 14, 1918, when the Chancellor was about to receive a Lithuanian delegation, Ludendorff insisted on it being told that both occupied countries would have to continue under military rule, even after they declared themselves independent, and that there would be no letup in the heavy economic burdens they would have to bear.[45]

In such circumstances, how could there be "voluntary" union between Lithuania and Germany? The Vilnyus Taryba was not intimidated when Prince Isenburg, the administrative chief, again threatened that the country would be divided up according to purely military contingencies, if the people remained obdurate.[46] Late in November it said that it was by no means prepared to place Lithuania as a satellite state under the rule of the Prussian crown and a Prussian viceroy, as desired by the OHL. On the contrary, it demanded as a first step the removal of the hated military regime and especially the dismissal of Prince Isenburg, a major administrative role for Lithuanian agencies, and the formal recognition of Lithuania as an independent democratically organized state within its proper ethnographic boundaries, including Vilnyus as the capital. A constituent assembly, democratically elected, was to be convened. If Germany were to recognize the independence of Lithuania and support its interest, the Taryba, representing the Lithuanian people, stood ready to join with Germany in a firm and perpetual alliance that would include economic and military conventions.[47]

The OHL was furious, the more so since a representative of the German foreign ministry had helped to draft this declaration. Hindenburg would not hear of independence, but insisted on the use of the kind of threats Isenburg had uttered, in order to force "voluntary" union with Germany, more specifically with the Prussian monarchy. He was unwilling to grant the Taryba any authority in foreign affairs, nor would he discuss any military convention. The Lithuanians were to be liable to service in the Prussian army and any administrative activities by Lithuanian agencies were to be under the control of the German military authorities. Apparently the generals never understood the obvious fact that this small peasant country would have had to come to terms with Germany even without military pressure, if it wished to achieve and maintain independence. Hindenburg was outraged that the Lithuanians had the audacity even to complain about the military administration, actually addressing the German government directly.

The foreign ministry responded to these objections with a very sharply worded memorandum, in which Kühlmann charged the OHL with improper intervention in political matters and emphasized that the German government no longer had a choice between granting Lithuania autonomy and annexing it, since its hands were tied as much by assurances that had been given the Lithuanians as by the general political situation. He charged that the OHL apparently still entertained the "old-fashioned" view that an occupied territory had to stand for anything that was done to it.

Tempers flared over this matter at meetings held in Berlin on December 6 and 7. The outcome was that in the wake of extremely difficult negotiations the Taryba was persuaded to issue another declaration on December 11, in which as "the only authentic representative of the Lithuanian people"—in other words, no longer requiring authority from a democratically elected constituent assembly—it proclaimed Lithuania independent of Russia. In its second part, this declaration asked for German aid and protection in creating a Lithuanian state. Without setting any terms in advance, the Taryba pledged a firm, perpetual alliance with Germany, embodied in military and transport conventions and a customs and currency union. The borders of the new state were not laid down in any way, though Vilnyus was named as the capital.[48]

In all ensuing negotiations the OHL and even the Chancellor kept invoking this "declaration," which left the door open for a purely authoritarian form of government and provided for unconditional integration with Germany. To the end of the war there was virtually no change in the military administration. True, Prince Isenburg was recalled soon afterward, but the OHL continued its stubborn opposition to the liberal policies of the foreign ministry and remained blind to the simple fact that the Lithuanians could not possibly be won over to the German cause, so long as their country was ruthlessly exploited as a prize of war. Controversy on this point continued throughout the winter and formal recognition of Lithuanian independence was postponed again and again.[49]

Part 2
The Negotiations at Brest-Litovsk

SELDOM HAVE peace negotiations begun with such lack of forthrightness on both sides as in Brest-Litovsk.[50] Both were utterly exhausted, both urgently needed peace. The Bolshevists, by their radical pacifist and revolutionary propaganda, had brought the Russian army to the point of complete unfitness for combat. It was, indeed, swiftly melting away; but the German high command too could be under no illusions that without the swift conclusion of peace in the east the cause of the Quadruple Alliance was lost, no military success of any consequence was in sight, and ultimate disaster could not be averted in the long run.

In awareness of these factors, the generals did swiftly conclude an armistice on very mild terms on December 15, without endangering the issue by demands for the evacuation of Livonia and Estonia, as originally planned; but then there ensued on each side an attempt to outmaneuver the other by means of the self-determination catchword. We already know how the Bolshevists interpreted that term—the international emancipation of the proletariat. Their only hope to avoid a harsh dictated peace was to foment trouble in the enemy camp by means of pacifist propaganda and to drag out negotiations until their own party rule in Russia was more firmly entrenched, while the enemy governments were subverted. We also know what the German side meant by self-determination—satellite status or outright annexation.

Caught squarely in the middle between the territorial greed of the OHL and the pressure from the majority parties for a swift peace without annexations, Kühlmann was in a quandary on how to satisfy the OHL without immediately undermining the credibility of the Hertling government, which had been formed largely on account of his intensive lobbying of the majority parties.[51] He was not a fighter by nature but rather a nimble opportunist.[52] All through the winter he managed with consummate skill to remain in the good graces of the parties of the left, eloquently reporting the negotiations with the Russians as successful. He glibly glossed over the increasingly sharp dispute that broke out between him and the OHL over these negotiations, for he had to remain on passable terms with Ludendorff and to think of effective ways in which he might fend off the impending attack from the right, supported by the OHL, against the allegedly "soft" line being taken at Brest-Litovsk.

Kühlmann himself was quite willing, in his own words, "to cut off as much as possible from the Russian body politic" with the help of self-determination, though without endangering the chances of peace and without violating liberal democratic principles too flagrantly. He knew how insecure were the foundations of the Bolshevist regime, and he opposed in principle a policy that completely forewent any gains at Russia's expense.[53]

But there was a consideration that troubled him even more than the Reichstag parties. Austria was horrified that peace might be unconscionably delayed solely on account of German gains in the Baltic area. Whenever the talks at Brest-Litovsk faltered, Czernin threatened that if worse came to worst he would conclude a separate peace with Russia. Kühlmann's outward reaction was as chilly as that of General Hoffmann, the General Staff representative, who remarked cynically that he would welcome such a thing, since it would free some twenty-five German divisions now required to stiffen the Austrian front; but both knew that Vienna could not even dream of casting adrift from Germany. In the face of so refractory an ally, the German negotiators nevertheless had a difficult time in trying to realize their power goals.[54]

Actually the Austrians were something less than sincere in pressing the Germans to accept the Russian peace formula. They could have scarcely been enthusiastic about self-determination, which, if rigidly applied, would have spelled the dissolution of the Austrian Empire. Formulating the Central Powers' first reply to the Soviet peace proposals jointly with Kühlmann on December 25, Czernin carefully added a clause that said: "The question of the national allegiance of nonsovereign entities cannot, in the view of the Quadruple Alliance, be settled by international negotiation but must be solved constitutionally by each state with its minorities."

Even this cautious formulation, which carried at least a hint of constitutional reform along nationalist lines, drew strong protest from the Czech and South Slav nationalist leaders. A statement issued by Czech deputies on January 6, 1918, demanded direct participation by their group in the peace negotiations.[55] This "Twelfth Night Declaration" was the first broadly visible sign of the tremendous ferment that now set in among the non-German elements within Austria, under the impact of Bolshevist propaganda. It spurred Czernin even more. He must not lose another week in bringing about peace along the lines of general conciliation.

But the attitude of Bulgaria stood in the way. Popov, the Bulgarian representative at Brest-Litovsk, would not hear of peace without annexations. The only reason why the Bulgarians had entered the war was to win back from the Serbs and Rumanians allegedly Bulgarian territory which they had lost in the Second Balkan War—and if possible a good deal more. Popov insisted on fulfillment of these goals, invoking the treaty assurances, and he was not put off by Kühlmann's and Czernin's arguments. Bulgaria's goals, he said, were directed not toward forcible acquisition but to the fulfillment of nationalist ideals, which were entirely compatible with self-determination. The Bulgarians might have been satisfied, if Kühlmann and Czernin had been prepared to incorporate their interpretation expressly into their reply to the Russians, but of course they refused. They merely promised to put forward the Bulgarian view at the negotiations, now as before. Czar Ferdinand's help had to be enlisted in overcoming Popov's opposition, even to make possible a joint note of reply by the four Central Powers.

Popov need scarcely have worried, for the reply of December 25 was a masterpiece of diplomatic dissimulation and shrewd adaptation to the Russian proposals. It was not meant seriously, as Popov was indeed advised. Its first part contained formulations that were intended to surprise Russia and the whole world by their seemingly unconditional acceptance of the principles proclaimed by the Soviets—a general peace of international reconciliation without forcible expansion of territory and war indemnities; but it expressly made such acceptance dependent on all the belligerents without exception obliging themselves, within an appropriate period of time, to observe faithfully a set of conditions that would be equally binding on all nations. Both authors of the note were convinced that the belligerents would do no such thing, if only because it had been made clear in recent speeches by cabinet members that the French would never forego Alsace-Lorraine nor the Italians South Tyrol.

The concord among the Central Powers thus had merely rhetorical value. It was to demonstrate dramatically to their war-weary people, especially in Austria, that they were ready to make peace and to shift the responsibility for any failure to the enemy. There was not even mention of self-determination in this first part;[56] and even in the second part it was recognized only with limitations, as a constitutionally guaranteed protection for minorities within existing states, and as a general principle only "insofar as it may be feasible."[57] Nor was there any mention of foregoing annexations in principle. It was merely stated that the Central Powers had no intention of "forcibly appropriating" the territories they held—which did not rule out their "integration" by treaty, especially since the time at which they would be relinquished was to be set only in the formal peace treaty, i.e., was left open for the time being.

In other words, the reply to the Soviets represented essentially though not in all points an effort at deception.[58] It is true beyond doubt that Kühlmann (like Czernin) could have wished he were able to bring about, on very moderate terms, not only a separate peace with Russia but a general peace;[59] but in this he stood alone among the German rulers. Neither the OHL nor even Chancellor Hertling[60] was looking for a peace with the Western powers just then, least of all one without any annexations at all. Ludendorff still desired to play what he thought his greatest military trump card, a battle of annihilation in France, using the concentrated power of the entire German army.

General Hoffmann felt ill at ease from the outset in this cunningly hypocritical diplomatic game. As a soldier he would have far preferred to lay his cards on the table, i.e., not to await Russian proposals, but simply to put forward the victor's minimum terms to which the Russians could then react. Prince Max of Baden later on severely criticized the tactics of the German peace delegation.[61] The Soviet delegation, he said, should never have been greeted with such exquisite courtesy, indeed almost flattery, which only served to make it difficult to come forward with subsequent moral indictments. They should have been received in a cool and businesslike way; and at the appropriate time their revolutionary propaganda should have been countered with a sensible and constructive German program for settling the situation in the east from the ground up. It should have been a program that would have truly liberated Russia's ethnic minorities, who were now threatened by the Red Terror, just as they had once been oppressed by czarist tyranny.

The criticism was certainly justified. The Germans not only left the initiative in peace propaganda to the Soviets, but countered the Russians' big words with duplicity and insincere declarations whose mendacity was soon bound to become apparent; but whom does the shoe pinch? Not necessarily Kühlmann, and even less so Czernin, who had his emperor's firm instruction in his pocket to leave nothing undone to bring home peace from Brest-Litovsk.62 Could these two diplomats have assumed the pose of the proud victor and simply swept the Russian peace slogans from the conference table? Among wide circles of the German people, especially on the left in the social democratic working class, this would have caused a furor, and in Austria it might even have precipitated revolution. This was shown on January 12 when General Hoffmann, in agreement with Kühlmann and Czernin, countered Russian arrogance with some plain speaking about the victorious position of the Quadruple Alliance and confronted their talk about "liberating the people" with the naked facts of the Soviet terror. The effect of this incident on public opinion in Germany and Austria was devastating. There was universal horror at the thought that brutal intransigence on the part of the German generals might yet wreck the chances of peace. Actually, Hoffmann had not, as was alleged, pounded the table. He was indeed at heart much more moderate and objective than his imperious overlord Ludendorff.63

The touchiness of public opinion merely reflected the basic fact that it was idle to speak of the Central Powers as though they were the unquestioned victors in the east. On December 25 Hindenburg, indignant at the German note of reply to the Soviet delegation with its seemingly unconditional renunciation of forcible annexations, had wired the Chancellor that "Russia needs peace rather than we." In the interest of the German fatherland he was hopeful that the Entente powers would be unwilling to conclude peace at this time and that the assurances given to the Russians thus would be null and void.64

This was a typically militarist misapprehension of the true situation. Germany too urgently needed peace and had long since, moreover, solemnly committed itself to peace. Kühlmann had no choice but to accept the Russian peace slogans in principle, nor had he any alternative to trying to make the world believe in Germany's willingness to negotiate, by demonstratively peaceful gestures toward the Russian delegation. To level moral indictments

of Bolshevist terror methods, to unmask the Russian pose of "national liberation," would have made sense only if Kühlmann himself had had a program
of true national liberation and self-determination to proclaim, together with
the authority to put it into effect. As we know, the immutable opposition of
the OHL and its Pan-German supporters forbade this, and they must shoulder
the blame for the politically unfortunate course of the negotiations at Brest-
Litovsk.

Any possibility of a peaceful settlement really went by the board within
twenty-four hours—when General Hoffmann made a confidential statement
to Joffe, leader of the Russian delegation, a statement that was at once
officially confirmed. It was to the effect that the Germans forewent forcible
territorial appropriation in principle only as it applied to occupied Russian
territory beyond the borders of Poland, Lithuania, Courland, Riga, and more
recently the occupied islands. These latter territories, it was claimed, had
already severed their ties with Russia on their own, and Germany was thus
free to deal directly with them concerning their future status.

Hoffmann felt compelled to make this statement, lest the Soviet delegation feel that that it had been deceived and not even return to Brest-Litovsk
after the ten-day adjournment that had been agreed on, during which it was
hoped that the Russians might entice the Western powers to the conference
table. In this purpose Hoffmann succeeded, for the Russian delegation did
return, though the enraged Allies left the Russian invitation unanswered. The
Russians, however, were now headed by a new negotiator, Foreign Minister
Trotzky, and their attitude was quite different, openly hostile. They bitterly
resented negotiating with a side that had the effrontery to talk about a
"peace without annexations," while at the same time severing some eighteen
provinces from Russia. Weeping tears of rage, the historian Pokrovsky, a
member of the delegation, had already made that clear on December 26.

Lenin's government was acutely embarrassed by this unexpected setback,
which it at first tried to keep from the Russian people. Within his own party
and even more among the social revolutionaries who formed the majority in
the Soviets there was much muttering over the predicament into which Russia
had slid, owing to unrestrained Bolshevist peace propaganda.[65] Trotzky had
little choice but to try to entangle the Germans in endless discussion, during
which he easily unmasked the German pretense of the allegedly voluntary
declarations by the Lithuanians, Courlanders, and Livonians in favor of integration with Germany. His efforts were also directed toward exposing the
covert annexationism of the OHL and its political omnipotence. Trotzky's
aim was to drag things out, to the point where the socialist masses in Germany and Austria might rise in impatience, war-weariness, hunger, and political indignation, forcing the diplomats to accept moderate peace terms.[66]

Had Kühlmann countered these tactics with table-pounding, threats, and ultimatums, he would have merely fed grist to the Russian mill. To avoid this, he was indefatigable in thinking up new arguments and compromise proposals to justify German policy in the occupied territories and to represent the declarations by the various "national councils" as legitimate expressions of the popular will. The debate went on for weeks on end, attended by the broadest publicity, for even in the armistice stage of negotiations the Russians had prevailed with a policy of putting the transactions of the conference on the wires immediately. Thus there were really no negotiations in the traditional sense. Each side was speaking "from the balcony," for propaganda purposes. This was a new style of diplomacy in which the two imperialist powers came off distinctly second-best. Kühlmann certainly failed in persuading the Soviets to recognize the "states" Germany had created—if such was his aim; but then, how could he have reached it, in the face of the OHL's determined efforts to allow his diplomacy no freedom of action whatever?

On December 27 Kühlmann sent Hertling a hasty personal report on the results of a discussion with the Russian delegates, limited to only a few persons. It shows the direction along which he wanted to proceed and what he thought he might obtain. This was before Trotzky appeared on the scene, and at this meeting it was shown that the Russians might agree to the separation of Poland, Lithuania, and Courland, and possibly even Livonia and Estonia, on condition that it accorded with the principles proclaimed by Lenin—that is, on the basis of a free and unequivocal expression of the people's will. They were not prepared to accept the resolutions of the specially convoked "national councils" (in Poland the "regency council") as such, though they displayed a reluctant willingness to acknowledge these declarations as "presumptive evidence."

What they asked for, in other words, was that the issue be settled by a constituent assembly or a popular referendum, but only after the Germans had completely evacuated these territories, for which they wanted a firm date in the not too distant future. The Russian delegates believed that only in this way could they render a peace treaty plausible to their people. Kühlmann counseled acceptance of these demands, especially since agreement had been swiftly reached on all other points, even in the economic sphere. He told Hertling that Czernin had threatened to conclude a separate Austrian peace, if the negotiations were to come to grief over this issue; but he foresaw that the OHL would fight to the bitter end in an effort to continue military occupation of the territories in question for years to come.[67]

These fears proved to be only too well-founded. To the very end of the negotiations at Brest-Litovsk, Kühlmann never succeeded in pinning down the OHL to a specific date for the withdrawal of troops from the occupied territories.[68] As early as December 29 the Chancellor received Hindenburg's first protest against the "morale-depressing" course of the negotiations. He criticized the second German offer of the preceding day—which was in accord with Kühlmann's proposals—because it spoke of a "broadly based popular vote" to confirm the declarations of the Baltic national councils. The military, he said, could tolerate no plebiscite whatever in the Polish border strip that had to be annexed at all costs, i.e., in the administrative districts of Suwalki-Augustowo and Bialystok-Grodno.[69]

Two days later the field marshal filed an even more sharply worded protest. Unless his demands prevailed, he would reject any responsibility for the peace. Poland must be limited to the size requested by the OHL; Polish border fortifications must be prohibited; Lithuania, to be extended southward to the forest of Bialowiecz must be integrated with Germany, as must be Courland, Riga, and the islands; any further right of self-determination in the territories occupied by Germany must be rejected; Russia must solemnly pledge to implement the right of self-determination in Livonia and Estonia and raise no objection to their integration with Germany; and lastly there must be recognition of the independence of Finland—which had actually declared its independence in May but which was threatened by a Communist revolt.

Hindenburg professed himself to be indignant over the manner in which the negotiations were being conducted at Brest-Litovsk. The whole affair was being widely considered a diplomatic defeat, with a bad effect on army morale. He insisted on a stronger voice and on the right of expressly approving all proposals and decisions that were made. He said he was instructing General Hoffmann to transmit all texts to headquarters beforehand, not merely by telephone but by telex. The message concluded with the histrionic assurance that Hindenburg would never authorize his representative to "sign a weak-kneed peace treaty out of character with the dignity of throne and fatherland."[70]

General Hoffmann actually was present at the negotiations only as a military adviser and observer; but it will be seen that the OHL held all the same that it shared responsibility for the peace treaty, indeed was the ultimate authority in steering the negotiations. If Kühlmann was to make any progress at all, he would have to try to bring about a decision in his favor on the part of the Kaiser, while at the same time fending off the attacks from the left and the right that rained down on him. The right was particularly angry on account of the German reply note of December 25. They insisted that the treaty should have been simply dictated to the Russians, instead of allowing them to present their own peace program. The Pan-German press ranted about a shameful "Jewish peace";[71] and with the aid of supreme headquarters a flood of protest telegrams was unleashed to the Kaiser, the Chancellor, and the OHL.[72]

One can only admire the courage and skill with which Kühlmann warded off these attacks on a trip to Berlin during the ten-day adjournment.[73] At a conference with representatives of all the parties he sought first of all to calm his opponents on the right by giving reasons why Germany was in no position to "force the Russians to their knees with bare knuckles," but had to try for a peaceful understanding. He explained that plebiscites in the event of territorial changes were nothing unprecedented—they had been held even in the days of Bismarck and Napoleon III.

The left naturally agreed but remained doubtful of acknowledging the resolutions of the national councils in Lithuania and Courland—and meanwhile those of the Riga chamber of commerce as well—as true expressions of the popular will. Scheidemann had visited the Baltic region and informed himself particularly well of the situation in Riga. Kühlmann nevertheless succeeded in overcoming his skepticism and convincing him of his own good intentions. In the joint caucus of the majority parties there were actually some voices that held that the kind of plebiscite the socialists wanted was impracticable and politically dangerous. Suspicion lingered, however—and with good reason—concerning the annexationist plans of the OHL.[74]

What now came home to roost was the failure on the part of the majority parties, when Hertling had been called to the chancellorship in October, to be sufficiently specific about the terms on which they were willing to pledge him their support. They had committed him to the reply note to the pope of September 18, 1917, but not to the peace resolution of July 19, which Hertling regarded as "obsolete" by mid-November.[75] Most importantly and counter to their original plan, they had not pinned him down to the most urgent element of a sound policy, breaking away from the OHL's apron strings.[76] Thus they could offer him scant support in his inevitable struggle with Ludendorff.

That struggle began the very next day, during a session of the foreign affairs committee of the federal council. Ludendorff was not content to give the briefing on the war situation for which he had been invited but moved on directly to put forward political demands. The Russian army was in such a hopeless state, he said, that Germany was under no necessity to make any concessions. "Should they refuse to yield, we shall have to revoke the armistice and beat them. . . . Our military situation is more favorable than it has been at any time during the three and a half years of war." The only problems were replacements in manpower, horses, feed, and rolling stock. The answer to that was to comb out the industrial workers even more rigorously and come to a swift end in the east. To pay any heed to Vienna was totally unnecessary—"We don't need Austria anymore in a military sense." Bulgarian military support was no longer of any consequence either, and Turkey was nothing but a military liability. As for the neutrals, Germany need not consider them. Sweden and the rest had forfeited any military importance as countries of transit. Germany, relying now wholly on its own resources, could at last pursue the great war aims of the OHL without any external considerations—secure borders, colonial domains, naval bases.

The program Ludendorff put forward shows that his main concern was not to forego annexations in the west. He called for a strong military rule in Alsace, which must on no account become "autonomous," i.e., federal territory. He wanted annexations in French Lorraine as well, the division of Belgium into a Flemish and a Walloon state with customs union with Germany, and above all sweeping annexations to create a wide German border strip against Poland, if that country were to fall to Austria. Even then he viewed Austria as a potential enemy, and in the event of an Austro-German conflict Silesia could not be held unless there were a major shift in the German border in the east.

Ludendorff had precious little to say about the issue actually on the floor, the negotiations at Brest-Litovsk, perhaps because he was short of the kind of objective arguments that alone would have impressed the members of the federal council. The supreme command, he said, had "hoped for firmer ties with Courland and Lithuania than now seem in sight. . . . We are afraid that the Brest agreements will not live up to the expectations we had entertained." This was a great worry and disappointment, but the most recent steps—Ludendorff probably meant the note of December 28—had somewhat raised army morale, and it was hoped that there would be no further damaging consequences.

Ludendorff's tone was much more subdued than the furious protest telegrams of the preceding week; and Kühlmann, in his reply, was careful not to add fuel to the flames. He tried rather to reassure the general. The question of the western borders was not acute, he said, for the Entente was certainly not willing to enter into peace negotiations; and when peace came the wartime coalition with Germany's three allies could not simply be dropped—Germany must try to "help them through the peace." No sweeping program of annexations in the east could be announced at this time, in the light of the temper of the Reichstag and public opinion, and in the wake of the commitments Germany had made in the note to the pope and the solemn declarations made by Hertling in his maiden speech as Chancellor in the Reichstag on November 29. It would be dangerous to provoke revolutionary ferment at home; and anyway, the controversial reply note to the Russians of December 25 included so many reservations and limitations that it did not really represent a commitment. Even so the German delegation had "reached 99½ per cent agreement" with its Russian counterpart, which had been ready to make sweeping concessions. It would be sheer madness to allow the chance for peace to be wrecked on the issue of plebiscites in the border states. Germany could not dictate peace—it must seek to convince the Russian delegates by means of searching discussion.

The conflict between militarist and diplomatic thinking was thus reduced to a straightforward formula: dictated or negotiated peace—that was the question to be settled. Hertling was dismayed by Ludendorff's attitude. "These generals," he said, "think only of what might happen in wartime; but it is necessary to think of peace as well." He admitted that he was rather apprehensive of bringing so many foreign elements into the Reich, even Livonia and Estonia, if Ludendorff had his way; but the federal council was simply not the kind of body to take major political decisions. Everyone wished that the conflict between war and politics might be peaceably settled. To cut off Russia from the sea entirely was considered questionable, yet German interest was to be fully safeguarded, especially in Poland, though elsewhere too, by improving the eastern borders. The most vociferous opposition was directed against placing the new Baltic states directly under the Prussian crown. This was regarded as being far too close to outright annexation; but dynastic jealousies were another factor. The representatives of Saxony and Mecklenburg registered doubts of such one-sided augmentation of Prussian power, all the more so since Ludendorff clearly wished to see Alsace-Lorraine placed under the Prussian crown as well. Saxony put forward claims to the ducal crowns of Lithuania and Courland; another candidate was the duke of Urach, a collateral relative of the king of Württemberg. Erzberger had inspired this campaign, but Premier Weizsäcker lent no support to it. In sum, there were signs that Kühlmann's basic policies were meeting with approval, even though the federal council was actually of little help to him. [77]

Everything now depended on the Kaiser's decision, and Kühlmann was in good spirits, because William II, in a private audience, had assured him of his agreement with his policies, indeed expressed warm appreciation for what had been achieved so far. Yet in the crown council session of January 2, on which everything depended, the conference at Brest-Litovsk seems to have been but briefly mentioned. Apparently Hindenburg and Ludendorff were content that the Baltic council declarations would have to be confirmed by a broadly based popular vote.[78] They vigorously urged that the negotiations be speeded up. The most important question, however, remained open—when the Germans would get out of the occupied territories. So long as the OHL was able to get away with refusing to set such a date, there was no hope of reaching an understanding with the Russians.

It was one of the Kaiser's quirks that he liked to gloss over irksome questions at such meetings, bringing up only such matters as were on his mind just then.[79] This happened to be the Polish problem. He was dismayed at Ludendorff's demand for the annexation of a border strip reaching all the way to Lodz, with several million Polish inhabitants, if Poland fell to Austria.

He had discussed this question with General Hoffmann in the morning and had been delighted to note that Hoffmann took a most reasonable stand. Like Kühlmann, Hoffmann was prepared to accept only minor, local border shifts, for the strategic or economic protection of certain vital points.

The Kaiser had had an appropriate map drawn, which he now presented to the generals as embodying his imperial decisions. Unfortunately, he cited General Hoffmann as his eastern expert, against Kühlmann's express advice and that of Hoffmann himself. Ludendorff was furious and could scarcely keep his temper. Feeling that the Kaiser had gone over his head, he offered the most vehement opposition. He was convinced that Hoffmann, his subordinate, had become Kühlmann's tool. The upshot was a most painful scene for all concerned, terminated by the Kaiser with a half-compromise—he said he wanted the OHL to report to him again in the matter. Ludendorff brusquely rejected the Kaiser's proposal that he go to Brest-Litovsk to convince himself that the negotiations were being properly conducted, and angrily slammed the door as he left.

It was the opening gun in a quarrel between the generals and the politicians, turning on nothing less than the final subjection of the Kaiser's will as "supreme warlord" to the omnipotent OHL. This time it was to be outright defiance rather than the persuasion used in the U-boat question the year before. On January 4 Ludendorff announced his impending resignation to the chief of the military cabinet and allowed—perhaps even caused—rumors to seep into the Pan-German press.[80] The result was as expected—there was an instant furor in nationalist circles and a flood of telegrams implored the Kaiser not to dismiss Ludendorff the hero.

The German crown prince asked his Bavarian counterpart by telephone to prevail on the king of Bavaria to intercede for Ludendorff's retention. Ludendorff's eastern policy was given as the sole reason for the clash with Kühlmann. The effort was said to enjoy Hindenburg's backing. The king of Bavaria did as requested, and appeals were also made to the kings of Württemberg and Saxony; but more detail was soon provided from Berlin by Count Lerchenfeld, who could scarcely conceal his indignation over Ludendorff's actions in mobilizing parliamentary and other circles on behalf of his views and inspiring attacks on the government in the press and the Reichstag.

Actually Crown Prince Rupprecht of Bavaria had been dismayed from the outset at the defiance of tradition manifested by the two generals in seeking to have their way by repeated threats of resignation, almost in the form of an ultimatum; but Rupprecht also shook his head over the Kaiser's attitude toward the OHL. "In the old days," he said, "it would have been impossible, as happened the other day in Cambrai, for the Kaiser, while visiting his troops, to convey greetings from the field marshal and express Hindenburg's praise for their performance." Rupprecht was convinced that taking non-

German elements into the Reich on a large scale was highly undesirable.

He was even more horrified at a secret memorandum by Colonel Bauer, sent to him by the German crown prince.[81] In a paraphrase of Ludendorff's political views, it asserted that Germany's military situation had never been better. Germany was winning, but failed to exploit its advantage. "The Russians are insolent while we are courteous. The Russians make demands and we yield." The result was a complete breakdown of German morale, "except among the red and golden international." The heart of the trouble was the Reichstag resolution of July 19, ruling out annexations of any kind. This would stand in the way of even a statesman who knew what he wanted, let alone Kühlmann, who was intent on staying in the good graces of the Reichstag majority.

It was a struggle between two opposed approaches. Either there was to be a strong peace that would safeguard Germany's future, which meant a strong and determined government; or Germany would pursue a policy of appeasement, leave the comity of nations both politically and militarily, and drift toward desuetude and Bolshevism.[82] Ranged on one side were Haase, Scheidemann, and Erzberger, favored by the Kaiser's entourage (this probably meant Valentini and Admiral Müller), and on the other side Hindenburg and Ludendorff. Once the Kaiser cast off his baleful advisers, Erzberger and Scheidemann would be finished. This would enormously boost nationalist morale, as had happened in August 1914, and Germany would press on to full victory.

Ludendorff did not actually write this memorandum, but it unmistakably specified the goal he was now pursuing. The Kaiser must separate himself from his "baleful" advisers. Kühlmann was to be the first victim. A direct petition to the Kaiser, signed by Hindenburg on January 7, enumerated all the shortcomings of the government. It still had not discarded the idea of autonomy for Alsace. It had displayed a lack of firmness in the Belgian question, in other words had done nothing toward securing Germany's western border. Matters were no better in the east. On January 2 Kühlmann had persuaded the Kaiser to cut down the Polish border strip, so that the hapless "Austro-Polish solution" had become completely untenable for the OHL. The declaration of December 25 had muddled the situation in Courland and Lithuania, where the prospect of plebiscites was bound to cause deep concern. The economic agreements reached at Brest-Litovsk were horrendous.[83] This stemmed directly from the lack of preparation for the peace treaty and the consistent German policy of compromise. Within the army this picture of weak-kneed diplomacy was causing profound alarm, and the rising tide of dissatisfaction was directed even against the OHL, which was held responsible for this failure. Questions were being asked whether the immense effort and sacrifices that would be exacted by the impending offensive in the west were actually worthwhile, or if the politicians would once again rob Germany of its well-earned gains, as was feared in the light of what was happening at Brest-Litovsk. The inevitable consequence would be deep frustration among the returning soldiers and the people, who would have to shoulder intolerable tax burdens.

This was, of course, a covert threat of revolution; nor was the threat of resignation lacking. Two reasons were given. The Kaiser had listened to the advice of General Hoffmann on a vital question, rather than to that of his superior officers; and the political differences between the general and Kühlmann were irreconcilable. The only end result of Kühlmann's policies would be to lead the monarchy "down from the heights to which Your Majesty and his illustrious forebears have brought Prussia and Germany." The Kaiser would have to choose. He could scarcely expect that the two generals would lend their names and authority to actions they held to be harmful.[84]

The poverty of these arguments was exceeded only by the arrogance with which they were put forward. Hindenburg's petition actually crossed a message from Hertling in which the Chancellor sought to reassure the field marshal, who was apparently not altogether happy with the line taken and who made some efforts to bring his quartermaster general to heel.[85] Yet when the Chancellor, at the Kaiser's behest and himself eager for conciliation, received the two generals on January 12, they bluntly demanded the dismissal of Kühlmann and Cabinet Chief Valentini. At one point, the edgy Ludendorff, for no reason whatever, reprimanded the aged Chancellor for inappropriate levity.[86]

Hertling declined to support the new OHL demands and gave vigorous backing to Kühlmann. He furthermore submitted to the generals for signature the draft of an "agreement" that was for the first time to delimit in writing the respective jurisdictions of the two sides. This document stated that constitutional responsibility for the peace negotiations fell completely and exclusively to the Chancellor, not only with respect to the ultimate goals, but to the tactics and results as well. The sole right and duty of the top military authorities was to take part in the negotiations in an advisory capacity, but this covered a very wide range, including tactics, army and navy morale, and even domestic policy, insofar as it affected the war. Their participation could only take the form of counsel, suggestions, reservations, or warnings. "The Chancellor," it was specified, "will see to it, in his decisions, that claims affecting the military conduct of the war will receive priority over all other claims." This implied, of course, that the military, if they were sufficiently ruthless, could completely paralyze the political decision-making process. In the event of inability to reach agreement, the issue was to be settled by the Kaiser.[87]

Hindenburg gave his signature only after a number of changes had been made in the draft, considerably enlarging his jurisdiction. Even so, he gruffly remarked that the declaration was really unnecessary, since the matter was already settled under the constitution. Besides, the German people completely trusted the OHL, which continued to feel that it shared responsibility for shaping the peace. From this responsibility no document could absolve it. Like Ludendorff, he would not dream of allowing anyone to limit his participation in political issues. To lend weight to this reservation, he insisted that the Chancellor promptly state his position on the petition of January 7, coincident with the "agreement." Nor was he slow in prescribing what that position should be. The Chancellor was to dissociate himself from the Reichstag resolution, since the premises on which it was adopted no longer applied. He was also to mention the OHL's serious objections to the first chapter in the Brest-Litovsk negotiations. This could only mean that he was also to disavow the controversial reply note of December 25 with its endorsement of a peace without annexations.[88]

Count Hertling met the generals only halfway. He ordered a lengthy memorandum entitled *Remarks on the Question of Responsibility,* to be based on an extensive report Kühlmann had submitted on January 10, at his request. Secretary of the Treasury Count Roedern and Under Secretary Radowitz of the chancellery had a hand in the final version,[89] which was submitted to the Kaiser on January 25 and subsequently transmitted to the OHL. It was the first and only time that the civil government sought to assert its authority over the military at such length and with constitutional arguments.

Within the German Reich, Hertling insisted, there was but one responsible minister, the Chancellor, while the power of ultimate decision, in military as in political questions, was the Kaiser's alone. Ludendorff regarded this as an act of provocation. He said in a marginal note that it was entirely up to the generals to decide how far their personal sense of responsibility should lead them. There were circumstances in which political considerations must give way to military ones: "Even a decision by His Majesty cannot relieve the generals from the dictates of their conscience." Hertling went on to warn the OHL against going too far in taking advantage of the confidence it enjoyed, by always insisting on its own way. In the long run this would be possible only if the two generals assumed political as well as military responsibility and leadership—and that would mean the total overturn of the Reich structure, which was bound to evoke serious domestic strife.

Hertling vainly protested that territorial expansion was not the only way or even the best way of safeguarding Germany's future. Security could also spring from good relations with neighboring countries, while forcible conquest bade fair to sow the seeds of future conflict, to say nothing of the unwelcome prospect of bringing non-German elements into the Reich, to which the Reichstag was unlikely to agree; but Ludendorff commented that only military border security would serve. What the government was really afraid of in the peace negotiations was to come to grips with opposing views. It made no proper effort to prevail. As for the undesired non-German influx, this "must be prevented by colonization." Austria was bound to wilt when Poland, under its aegis, grew strong enough to assert its own expansionist ambitions.

In the face of such obstinacy the Chancellor's efforts to set forth his policies and their motivations and to defend them against Ludendorff's charges were in vain. His caution in the questions of Alsace-Lorraine and Belgium went for nothing, as did his careful cultivation of good relations with allied Austria, his efforts to curb annexations in Poland, and his desire to relax political tensions in the east because of the great impending struggle in the west.

Hertling had gone to particular pains not only to justify the work of his foreign minister at Brest-Litovsk, but to underline its success. Yet this concluding part of his memorandum serves only to show how far removed his own policies were from the stand of the majority parties, and how little he understood Germany's plight. As he had already done in an earlier letter,[90] he carefully explained that the last word had not yet been spoken on the matter of the Polish border strip; and since the Western powers had absented themselves from the peace negotiations, Germany had a completely free hand for annexations in the west.

More than that, Hertling said that "the Reichstag resolution of July 19 was the product of a passing mood. . . . The situation has changed in the meantime and the government will now draw the political consequences that have become necessary in the new circumstances, without paying heed to the sentiments that are widely shared." It is true that in the discussions at Kreuznach on December 18 the Kaiser had already said that the decisions of the crown council of September 11 on Belgium were no longer valid, since the Entente had shown itself disinclined to enter into peace negotiations.[91] Hertling's words thus accorded with the Kaiser's attitude, but had this been made public, it would have unleashed a storm of indignation against him.

To his disavowal of the peace resolution he added the statement that he would never base his policies on popular and army sentiment—which was constantly cited from the side of the OHL—but solely on considerations of statesmanship. "The government must be strong enough to accept that responsibility, even if only later generations will have the wisdom to acknowledge that it took the right course." But did Hertling really possess the requisite strength and statesmanship? He was certainly not lacking in insight and goodwill, and in the determination not to be misled by patriotic sentiment. He was a man of moderation and compromise rather than a blind annexationist, but he was in no way equal to the brutal drive of a man like Ludendorff.

He was a Bavarian aristocrat and philosophy professor, without any proper experience in matters of grand policy. Old and physically worn, he was anything but a great political leader.

This was clearly shown in the settlement of the Ludendorff crisis. Outwardly it looked like a victory of the statesman over the generals, for Hertling did bring Hindenburg to the point of signing the declaration that neatly delimited military jurisdiction; but as we have already seen, it remained a victory on paper only, owing to the reservations the military had written into the document. Hertling even succeeded, in another discussion with the two generals ordered by the Kaiser on January 23, in persuading them to give way somewhat—they presented a new map that represented a compromise between the wishes voiced by the Kaiser on January 2 and their earlier sweeping demands;[92] but they did so only because they had in the meantime wrung another concession from the Kaiser, one that the monarch must have found quite humiliating. They felt that they could not push their luck just then.

Their military entourage seems to have talked them out of their intention to press once again for Kühlmann's ouster, a demand the Kaiser had rebuffed on January 12,[93, 94] but they insisted all the more stubbornly that Valentini must go. Actually the chief of the Kaiser's civil cabinet had nothing whatever to do with military matters and the peace negotiations in Brest-Litovsk; but at supreme headquarters he was accounted a baleful key figure at the imperial court. Colonel Bauer, especially, held this view, which was, in consequence, shared by the crown prince, who just then came in from the field. Ever since November the crown prince had made repeated efforts to secure Valentini's dismissal, an endeavor in which he enjoyed the eager support of the empress.[95] The charges against Valentini were always elusive and intangible. He was said to have erected a "Chinese wall" between the Kaiser and the people, to have misinformed him or informed him only inadequately. At heart his traducers accounted him the heir and representative of the spirit of Bethmann Hollweg, especially in matters of domestic policy; but this view utterly misconstrued the rigidly conservative cast of mind of Valentini, who was a Prussian aristocrat in the old tradition, besides wildly overestimating his political influence. We know today that after the war Ludendorff was completely engulfed in his own delusions, which ultimately turned him into a political simpleton and isolated him altogether. The sinister element is that such delusions were already a serious part of his thinking and that of his supporters during the last year of the war.

Ludendorff's ambition and power drive could not tolerate the possible failure of his attack on the "policy of weakness" he alleged was being pursued at Brest-Litovsk. When Hindenburg was summoned to attend a foreign policy conference on January 14,[96] Ludendorff persuaded him to advise the Kaiser subsequently, with the utmost firmness, the intention of the two generals to submit their resignations unless Valentini were dismissed at once and replaced by Provincial Governor von Berg, an inveterate conservative and confidant of the crown prince, and pretty much of a nonentity, as both a man and a politician.[97] A heated debate ensued, and what infuriated the Kaiser was that Hindenburg was quite unable to put forward any solid argument, limiting himself to generalities and political exhortations. In the end the Kaiser left the room, saying, "I don't need your paternal advice! " as he slammed the door.[98] General von Lyncker, at his behest, demanded that the field marshal give his reasons for the request in writing. Such a document arrived two days later, but it contained nothing more than rhetorical charges against the Bethmann Hollweg government, responsibility for whose faults Valentini was said to share. It was all in the typical style of Colonel Bauer, from whose pen it presumably came.[99]

There could be no doubt that Hindenburg was in dead earnest about his ultimatum; and after resisting the implorations of Colonel von Winterfeldt, the OHL representative assigned to the Chancellor and a shrewd and coolheaded intermediary, he and Ludendorff departed for Kreuznach in a cloud of imperial disfavor. Unfortunately this disfavor could not alter the course of events. Almost beside himself with rage and resentment, the Kaiser, on this as on previous occasions, did not dare let the two popular heroes leave his side. His state of mind bordered on desperation, and to spare him further agony Valentini, encouraged by Winterfeldt, decided to resign on his own. His request was granted, with every outward sign of imperial favor.

How bitterly the Kaiser resented this coercion and the loss of Valentini was shown by the words with which he greeted Valentini's successor, Berg: "I have been told in no uncertain terms that I must appoint you chief of my civil cabinet or else."[100] On January 24 he sent the two insubordinate generals Hertling's memorandum on the jurisdiction of the OHL, with an accompanying letter dripping with honeyed phrases—their "grateful king, well-disposed toward you, asks for your further cooperation." One can only marvel at the degree of self-control and dissimulation forced on the sovereign by his topmost generals. Not daring to consign them to their proper confines, he was content to voice the cautious hope that they would be able to devote themselves without diversion to the proper conduct of the war, now that the respective spheres had been delimited.

Valentini's dismissal may be regarded as a significant turning point in the history of the Prusso-German monarchy. Though his public responsibility was limited, he was a seasoned man of character on whom the Kaiser could rely absolutely; and for these very reasons his fall showed the Kaiser even more plainly than earlier incidents just how hollow his position as "supreme warlord" had grown.[101] He never seems to have got over this blow, and the result was not unlike the great shock of 1908. The Kaiser grew even more resigned and indolent in doing his work.

There is no need here to follow in detail the negotiations in Brest-Litovsk, which resumed on January 9, with Trotzky heading the Russian delegation, as already mentioned. In the light of the events we have described, they took the expected course. There were weeks of debate, mainly between Kühlmann and Trotzky, on the principles and realization of self-determination, in which neither was able to convince the other, while each tried to get the better of the other before the forum of world opinion. Neither side was in any particular hurry to reach a conclusion. By dragging out the issue, Trotsky hoped to kindle further unrest among the peoples of Austria and the socialist masses of Germany. Kühlmann, on his part, was primarily intent on a separate peace with the Ukrainian representatives, who had first appeared in Brest-Litovsk in mid-December and were now back in the role of peace negotiators. The expectations of both men were well-founded. Austria intermittently experienced menacing strikes, accompanied by huge demonstrations and open rebellion, the outgrowth of war-weariness, hunger, and distrust of German plans for military conquest, further fed by zealous radical socialist agitation, Soviet radio propaganda, and the activities of Slavic and anti-German nationalists. Late in January a great wave of strikes rolled over Germany. For the first time these strikes were politically as well as economically motivated—they were also directed against the reactionary Junker class and its sabotage of Prussian electoral reform. (We shall discuss these events at greater length in the next chapter.)

Once again it proved possible to bring urban rebellion under control in both countries. In Germany troops had to be called out, though moderate socialist leaders also succeeded in intervening. In Austria the acute food crisis was mitigated by prompt imports from Germany; but the foundations of law and order were beginning to crumble perceptibly. At times it seemed as though the great hope of the Bolshevist leaders might yet be realized— revolution in the original home of socialism while the war was still on.

Watching these events with a degree of concern bordering on despair was Count Czernin, who was already being reproached in the legislatures and political circles at home with being far too soft toward the Germans. Kühlmann too was in a considerable dilemma. Supreme headquarters was constantly pressing him to counter Trotzky's delaying tactics with far greater firmness and to use the weapon of the ultimatum to get on with the peace promptly. In a note at the bottom of a dispatch from Envoy Rosenberg in Brest-Litovsk, the Kaiser said: "We must make this scoundrel understand that we don't care in the least whether or not we sign with him. If he refuses to sign, out with him! We can afford to wait! There are others who will make peace."102

The OHL was completely out of sympathy with the diplomatic objective of at least trying for a negotiated peace, as demanded by the parties of the left and their followers. The generals also obstinately rejected any compromise on the issue of evacuation. The Kaiser stated his plans for conquest quite bluntly:

> (1) We have already conquered and occupied the Baltic region. (2) Russia will never get these regions back. (3) Since they contain many Germans, they will fall within Germany's sphere of influence. (4) Various parts of these regions will be granted libertarian institutions as soon as law and order have been restored, on the Russian borders as well. The Russian troops have already settled that the Baltic presents no obstacle to peace, when ceded to us. [What was meant was that the Russian troops had melted away.] Let us get a firm grip on things and do what we deem right, without allowing the maximalists to tell us what to do about plebiscites, etc., things they suppress and prevent at home.[103]

Such an attitude made it virtually impossible to carry out even a semblance of self-determination, as Kühlmann's policy contemplated.

With the appearance of a Ukrainian delegation at Brest-Litovsk, even Ludendorff was no longer interested in reaching agreement with the men who held the power in St. Petersburg. A peace treaty with them would merely get in the way of German power reaching out beyond Livonia and Estonia. As General von Bartenwerffer, head of Ludendorff's political section, had already set forth in a memorandum the preceding October, the Ukraine was, economically speaking, by far the most important Russian region.[104] If it were possible to detach the Ukraine from Greater Russia, using the principle of self-determination, and to conclude a treaty on favorable terms, this would not only cripple Soviet power but, hopefully, bring major, indeed decisive relief to the Central Powers in terms of food and raw materials.

No wonder the OHL pressed strongly for first seeking an understanding with the Ukrainian Rada, as a possible means for exerting pressure on the Soviets. Since both the OHL and the foreign ministry had been in touch with the Ukrainians ever since the preceding summer, they were well aware that these youthful intellectuals, who proved to be highly skilled, nimble, and tough negotiators, would put forward sweeping, if not presumptuous claims for their country.[105]

On December 27 Ludendorff had let the Chancellor know that the Ukrainians would lay claim to the districts of Kholm and East Galicia, the former belonging to Poland, the latter to Austria. He urged that these two countries be bluntly ignored and that territorial questions not be allowed to delay peace with the Ukrainians by a single day.[106] He gave appropriate directives to General Hoffmann as well.[107] We already know that Ludendorff was completely indifferent to the Austrians, whom he regarded as a millstone, and that he loathed the Poles. Taking away Kholm was probably intended to separate them from Greater Russia.

But in the event, it proved to be not quite so easy to come to an agreement with the Ukrainians, who saw through the critical situation of the Central Powers. At the slightest German attempt to play them off against Trotsky, they simply raised their demands until these ran deeply athwart Austrian interests. Were they to be accepted, Austria would have forfeited every vestige of Polish sympathy and indeed the loyalty of its Galician subjects—we shall hear more of this in Chapter 4.

Czernin, however, had no choice. Peace with the Ukraine was absolutely essential, for Austria's military strength was already crumbling from within, as shown by a serious naval mutiny in the port of Cattaro.[108] Austria's food economy, moreover, was facing total collapse, and the importation of at least one million tons of bread grain, held out to the Central Powers as part of a separate agreement, was virtually a matter of life and death. The economic clauses of such an agreement were being worked out with special care,[109] and they took additional time, for in these as in other matters the Ukrainians showed themselves to be as tough as they were inexperienced. Still another delaying factor was the civil war that was raging in the Ukraine. At times the Rada represented at Brest-Litovsk was virtually powerless in its own country, and just before the treaty was signed, on February 8, Kiev, the capital, fell to Soviet troops.[110]

All this did not deter Czernin and Kühlmann from their resolve to conclude a peace treaty with the Rada representatives. They counted on the changing fortunes of the civil war, in which the Germans had the option to intervene, and they hoped that the mere fact of a separate treaty would place Trotzky in a dilemma that would make him more inclined to compromise in the question of the Baltic border regions. By late January the Central Powers had formulated an ultimatum, which Ludendorff sought to word even more sharply when, as was customary, it was submitted to him. The Austrians, on their part, were reluctant to transmit it to the Russians until another effort for peaceful understanding was made, while Ludendorff was champing at the bit to break off negotiations and resume hostilities, this time with the goal of actually toppling the Soviet government itself.[111]

In long confidential talks with Trotzky, Czernin and the Austrian section head Gratz did manage to bring the divergent viewpoints a bit closer, but they never secured the kind of settlement that would have been acceptable to the OHL.[112] Kühlmann and Czernin were nevertheless eager to continue talking, hoping that they might persuade their Soviet counterparts to yield, if they threatened to break off negotiations within twenty-four hours; but the OHL no longer wanted any kind of peace with Trotzky. When the Russians, in a broadcast from St. Petersburg, openly called on German soldiers to disobey their officers, the OHL used the incident to extract a new ultimatum from the Kaiser. It took the form of a telegraphic military order to Hertling and Kühlmann on February 9:

Trotzky has until tomorrow tenth eight P.M. (at which time a report is to reach Homburg) to sign the treaty without further delay and accept our terms, immediate relinquishment of the Baltic area to the Narva-Pleskov-Dvinsk line inclusive without self-determination and acknowledging indemnity to all concerned in the Baltic.

If the Russian refused or tried delaying tactics the negotiations were to be broken off at eight o'clock and the armistice canceled, and the eastern command would begin advancing toward the prescribed line.[113]

It proved to be no more than one of those imperial gestures of which William II was so fond. Kühlmann had already protested to Hertling against a similar directive from the OHL to Hoffmann on February 8. He now offered serious objections and offered his resignation, insisting that he could not assume responsibility for such a step. He asked that the order be countermanded no later than 5:30 P.M. on February 10, and this was done promptly on time. The Kaiser now merely "recommended" that an agreement be reached under which Germany would assist the Livonians and Estonians in every way to create police formations that would enable them to carry out an orderly plebiscite to settle their future fate. Thus the minister's protest did succeed in averting failure from a nakedly martial posture that would have presumably disrupted the alliance with Austria and brought on grave domestic strife in Germany.[114]

But this dramatic confrontation was almost immediately superseded by an even more dramatic turn brought on by Trotzky. The leader of the Soviet delegation not only stubbornly resisted all further compromise proposals, but abruptly broke off the talks on his own. At the afternoon session on February 10 he delivered himself of a now famous declaration that took the whole world by surprise. The Soviet government, he said, refused to sign an "annexationist peace treaty," but at the same time regarded the war as terminated and was issuing orders for immediate demobilization to its troops on all fronts.

It was a daring gamble to exploit even the admission of Russia's complete military impotence for purposes of Russian propaganda. The utter peaceableness of the new "people's government" could scarcely have been contrasted more sharply and effectively with the naked imperialism of the German militarists and annexationists. Trotzky seriously counted on the Central Powers not daring to resume hostilities in the face of the pacifist mood of their masses. This was quite true of Austria, but not of Germany, as will be shown directly.[115]

Lenin had assessed the situation more realistically. It was only with extreme reluctance that he assented in the end, when Trotzky, late in January before the party central committee, broached the idea of breaking off the war without a formal peace. The whole problem of how to end the war led to extremely bitter clashes within the Bolshevist leadership, indeed to the gravest crisis that beset it in Lenin's lifetime.

In any event, all of the diplomats of the Quadruple Alliance assembled in Brest-Litovsk were initially prepared to follow Kühlmann's proposal and merely take note of the Russian declaration. They all wished to avoid acknowledging a formal end to the war, in order to keep open the door to its resumption, should that seem necessary or advisable for any reason at all. Kühlmann proposed that for the present the armistice be allowed to continue, since the Russians were obviously no longer able and willing to fight. All that had to be done was to fend off their political propaganda. Meanwhile there would be an opportunity to establish the new states of Lithuania and (urland in accordance with German policy and to squeeze something practical out of the peace treaty with the Ukraine.

Only General Hoffmann, acting on behalf of the OHL, favored immediate resumption of hostilities—Ludendorff had been waiting for this moment to carry out his planned advance to the outskirts of St. Petersburg. Thus the gap between political and military thinking immediately led to a new clash that at times threatened to precipitate a major crisis. The two sides waged a paper battle of wires and memoranda, settled only at a large meeting, set by the Kaiser for February 13 at Homburg castle.[116]

Hertling came and, for the first time, the parliamentary Vice-Chancellor, von Payer, whom illness had kept away from affairs. He was a moderate democrat from Swabia, the white hope of the majority parties and, at this juncture, of Kühlmann as well. As he had already done at Brest-Litovsk, the foreign minister based his opposition to Ludendorff's planned operation chiefly on the argument that it would prove virtually futile. "What would be the use of it? Will it bring peace, i.e., force Trotzky to sign? What would be the use of that? He will only fall."

As he had also explained at Brest-Litovsk, Kühlmann was convinced that such a campaign would take many months of what would probably be guerrilla fighting, tie down large masses of troops on the eastern front, exact enormous sacrifices, and fail in the end, even if the Germans chased the Bolshevists all the way to the Urals "with pen in one hand and sword in the other." Peace could not be brought about by force of military operations. The thought of stamping out a plague focus might seem tempting, but how to accomplish that? Even the capture of St. Petersburg would not bring the desired end. "All we will achieve by the use of force will be to fan the flames of Russian patriotism even more."

Kühlmann cited the historical precedent of the monarchist campaign in 1792 against the French Revolution as a warning. An attack on St. Petersburg would be inevitably interpreted as a crusade of imperialist reaction against the socialist revolution, rousing the indignant opposition of the war-weary masses. Austria especially would be a hotbed of such opposition;[117] but even in Germany morale would be endangered, and broad public support was essential to the great impending offensive in the west.[118] A resumed campaign in the east would undoubtedly encourage the German annexationists, and this would earn even greater distrust on the part of the socialist workers.

Kühlmann had his own suspicions. He had written Hertling from Brest-Litovsk of his fears that once Germany had occupied Livonia and Estonia the Baltic-German aristocracy would agitate for their permanent union with Germany. That would burden Germany with insoluble problems, besides drawing Russia's lasting enmity. He concluded that Germany should offer only indirect aid to the hard-pressed Balts, by establishing a militia to enforce law and order, providing supplies, etc. Nor was it Germany's business to free Russia from Bolshevist rule. The Russians would have to help themselves. He dismissed the idea of armed intervention in the Ukraine. Even military aid to the Ukrainian Rada could turn into a two-edged sword, for it might serve only to compromise the Rada in the eyes of the Ukrainian people.

Payer by and large supported these views. He pointed out in particular that a renewed advance into Russia would create an extremely painful impression in the Reichstag. Only a small minority of Germans were really interested in the Baltic issue. The predominant response would be horror that war was again being waged; and none knew how and when the German army would extricate itself from such an operation.

Unfortunately this argument, like Kühlmann's, was the weakest one with which to counter Ludendorff's plans. It grossly overestimated the Russians' ability and will to resist. Oddly enough, however, neither Hindenburg nor Ludendorff met the objections of the politicians by citing Russian military weakness. The reason may have been that they knew the weakness of their own field forces in the east even better than Russia's impotence. The best combat troops and virtually all heavy weapons had already been used to reinforce the western front. The forces in the east were a mere shadow of their former selves, wholly incapable of any large-scale aggressive action.[119]

To advance the eastern front all the way to Lake Peipus with only these Landwehr regiments—and this only a month before the scheduled date of the great western offensive—was a gamble.[120] The risk was further increased by the insistence of the two generals that auxiliary troops be sent to Finland and the Ukraine to put down Bolshevist rebellion.[121] They sought to counter this impression of irresponsibility by generalities and patriotic rhetoric, which pervade a paper Ludendorff had especially prepared for the session—actually it was the draft of a direct report to the Kaiser.

The situation had to be "clarified" in the east. Germany had to "act swiftly and decisively." The Bolshevist government had to be "overthrown" to "remove the threat to Germany's rear" in the impending gigantic struggle in the west, "the greatest military challenge any army ever faced." That struggle would be protracted and entail heavy fighting on more than one occasion. A successful campaign in the east was needed to provide the proper morale and arouse "new confidence in the military leadership."

Most importantly, the Bolshevists posed a serious threat to the Ukraine, Finland, and the Baltic regions, already "at the end of their strength." The Entente would take heart if Germany remained idle in the east instead of giving further proof of its power which, among other things, would also incline the Rumanians toward peace. On the home front too, resolute action could only have a favorable effect. If the German workers were convinced that everything that was being done was being done solely in the interest of peace, they would not engage in strikes.

Chancellor Hertling remained very reserved and it is unlikely that this inflated oratory made any impression on him. According to his son, he had decided, by the end of the morning session, to resign if hostilities were resumed in the east. According to Admiral Müller, Payer and Kühlmann had reached the same decision. The main impetus may have been the Kaiser's intervention in the debate, with a pathetically unrealistic speech. The Reichstag, he said, would have no voice at all in the matter. Should a military strike become necessary, it would not be listened to. Anything else would amount to the kind of republicanism that prevailed in France at the time of the Convention, and any such efforts would be suitably answered. The Bolshevists would have to be hunted down and killed like wild beasts. They were out to foment revolution in Germany and throw all the workers into one great pot. The money would come from the Entente, which wanted no peace with the Hohenzollerns. Strikes in Germany were being financed from abroad—there was a special committee for that in Paris. The Bolshevists were also being backed by Wilson with the help of world Jewry, the Grand Orient Lodge of the Freemasons. Germany had to establish law and order in Russia or else the British and Americans would show up there; and a Russia reorganized by the Anglo-Saxons would represent a great danger to Germany.

He could not accept responsibility for such developments, the Kaiser went on. It was not a matter of hostilities but of aid, chiefly to the hard-pressed Baltic Germans. A Baltic militia had to be created, to enforce law and order. Germany would advance to Narva and there negotiate with St. Petersburg. The Finns and Ukrainians would be included, to preserve appearances with the Russians. The Russian positions were, after all, unoccupied. There was nothing to stop the Germans and they must go forward, or the British would anticipate them. An advance was not merely a military necessity but also a political one.

What did the Kaiser really want? Was it to shoot down the Bolshevists or to negotiate with them from the vantage point of Narva, close to St. Petersburg? Or was the push to provoke another overturn in St. Petersburg? He probably did not know himself, any more than did Ludendorff, who was evidently as uncertain as the eastern command[122] whether his second-line troops would be able to do anything better than to gain some immediate tactical advantages–though in his paper he spoke of the possibility of giving the death blow to Bolshevism. At the meeting itself he seems to have reassured Hertling with a statement that only a short, sharp blow was planned immediately rather than any extended operations. In any event, Dvinsk would have to be taken, since that would "save Germany a division"; but he did reserve the right to advance farther. "Trotzky must be overthrown," he insisted. "A new government must sign the peace treaty."[123] The British, on their part, must be kept from coming to the aid of the "good" elements in Russia and the Baltic and from establishing a foothold on the north coast of Russia, which might happen if Germany abandoned Russia.

In sum, the generals, as always, pursued a highly aggressive policy, while their political aims were as fuzzy as ever. The afternoon session took place in the Kaiser's absence, and Hertling was swayed by the fact that the generals said they would limit their proposed advance to Dvinsk or Walk. They gave express assurances that an invasion of Livonia did not imply annexationist intentions. Its chief purpose would be to relieve the Ukrainians and help the hard-pressed Baltic Germans, which was to be accomplished solely by the establishment of a "police formation."[124]

The tenor of the discussion, however, was such as to lead Ludendorff to believe himself empowered to allow his troops to enter Finland and the Ukraine, if asked for assistance by non-Bolshevist governments in those countries. Hence Livonia's future remained open, and there too the "police troops" were to enter only if aid were implored by the local inhabitants. Payer was satisfied, while Kühlmann, whose suspicions lingered and who deplored Hertling's "compromise," nevertheless did not make good his intention to resign. Opportunist that he was, he justified this by arguing that the issue was purely one of political expediency.

Ludendorff had already received appeals for help from Livonia; hence the start of the advance into that region was immediately set for February 18, on expiration of the week's notice for revoking the armistice that had been agreed to at Brest-Litovsk–though the Germans did not propose to serve formal notice. Appeals from the Ukrainian Rada government also arrived, with surprising promptness, on February 16, as well as from Finland, on February 28. Thus the OHL was able to stage its whole far-flung action program by the end of the month.

The Livonian appeals were indubitably genuine.[125] Equally, there can be no doubt that they were not limited to the hard-pressed Baltic German upper crust. They accorded with the urgent desire of the Latvian people, especially the property-owning classes, for protection against banditry, "Red Terror," and violence of all kinds; and in Finland as well as the other Baltic regions the advancing German troops were jubilantly greeted as saviors.[126]

The real question is whether Germany, in the fourth year of the war and facing the last great decisive battle, was still capable of playing such a role so far from home and over such a broad expanse, without overstraining its resources. Actually, the cost in blood and military effort was much lower than the government had anticipated. Serious resistance in the Ukraine was mainly limited to a volunteer body of Czech prisoners and defectors. Even so, Kiev was occupied by March 1.

There was scarcely any fighting in Livonia. Usually there was little more to do than capture helpless staffs that had been abandoned by their troops and to collect large quantities of booty. The action there soon took on the curious form of a "railway campaign," in which the Germans moved on from station to station. Pskov and Lake Peipus were reached within the week, and the German parties of the left and their followers scarcely had time and occasion to protest the resumption of a war that had ceased to be a war in the proper sense. The Bolshevist terror regime, moreover, had evoked so much opposition that some kind of "police action" in Livonia seemed plausible.

The vicious aspects of a campaign waged against defenseless people were completely overshadowed; and Kühlmann himself was extremely skillful in concealing from public view the bitter quarrels that had arisen on these issues between him and the generals, and even more between the OHL and the Austrians. His cautious statement to the press and the party leaders on February 18 merely said that it had become necessary to "resume an active part on the Russian front," for the security of the Ukraine and the German-occupied Baltic regions.[127] On February 19, before the main committee of the Reichstag, he spoke somewhat more plainly of the need for creating a viable situation in Livonia and Estonia. In contrast to his stand at the Homburg crown council, however, he expressed the conviction that a mere show of force on Germany's part would suffice to bring the rulers in St. Petersburg to their senses quickly and to get them to acknowledge Germany's "just and reasonable position on the peace issue." As before, Germany stood ready to "grasp any hand extended in honesty and sincerity." On this point there was complete unity with Austria, and indeed at Brest-Litovsk there had never been even a shadow of disagreement with Germany's ally! [128]

All this sounded enormously reassuring, the more so since Kühlmann, when he presented the draft treaty with the Ukraine to the Reichstag on the following day, was able to announce that a telegram from St. Petersburg had been received the preceding day, in which the Soviet government stated its readiness to accept the peace terms proposed at Brest-Litovsk. To top the bill, Hertling was able to open the debate on the budget on February 25 with news of the acceptance of the new and stiffer terms that had been transmitted to the Soviets, who had already dispatched a delegation to Brest-Litovsk to sign the treaty.

The Chancellor emphasized that the resumed operations in the east had nothing to do with plans of conquest. Their sole purpose was to "secure the fruits of the treaty concluded with the Ukraine." They had been initiated by appeals for help from the Ukrainian government and "earnest representations by the Baltic peoples, asking protection against the atrocities and devastations of the Red Guards and other gangs." The Germans were acting purely from humanitarian motives and for no other reason. "We have no thought of settling down in Estonia and Livonia, but desire only to live in good neighborly relations with the new states that are rising there, once the war is over."129

In such circumstances and following this speech in the Reichstag, it would have been quite unnatural for the prevailing German mood to be marked by distrust of OHL annexationism and resentment of the resumption of hostilities, as had been feared in Homburg. True, socialist distrust continued, immediately finding a spokesman in Scheidemann; but in all the other parties simple joy predominated that after three and a half years of terrible war, the talk was at last of peace—a truly negotiated peace with the Ukraine and resistless capitulation on the part of the Soviet government. What critics and opponents of the OHL had but recently regarded as frivolous militarist action now took on a halo of historic achievement. "Perhaps never before in history," said Hertling, "have the words of Aristotle been so brilliantly confirmed: For the sake of peace we must be ready for war." The German sword had brought Germany peace.

No one, of course, had foreseen that the Soviet government would surrender so swiftly, an event that still seems puzzling today, in view of the furor, desperation, and resurgence of impassioned patriotism aroused in St. Petersburg by the German advance. Many of Lenin's closest followers condemned him as a traitor when he insisted on acceptance of the German peace terms as soon as they were known and had the news transmitted by radio on February 19. Despair and agitation among the leading Bolshevists rose to a peak when no reply had been received from the Germans by the morning of February 23, while at the same time they refused to grant another armistice before the signing of the peace treaty. The advance, in other words, would continue resistlessly, and everyone in Russia, including Lenin, thought that the goal was St. Petersburg. On February 16, when he first heard of the termination of the armistice, Lenin had said, "The beast is about to pounce—we must sign at once."130

Lenin's position as party leader—indeed, his very life—was never under such grave threat as during these anxious weeks. With ice-cold resolve and with a complete absence of any patriotic illusions about the disastrous Russian situation—for which he shared responsibility—he pursued but one goal: to maintain his revolutionary regime, even at the most frightful cost in territory and people. Under no circumstances could he allow the enemy to reach the capital, where his domestic enemies were already girding to welcome the Germans as saviors. He took preliminary steps for the evacuation of St. Petersburg and the transfer of the seat of government to Moscow—this was actually done on March 9—and he did not shrink from asking the representatives of the capitalist Entente powers whether there was any willingness to prevent the last extremity. The answer was disappointing, and Lenin's only hope was to halt the German advance and avoid the collapse of his revolution by swift and complete capitulation. To obtain the concurrence of the highest party organ was perhaps the most difficult and disturbing task of his life.

Trotzky resigned as commissar for foreign affairs; but Sokolnikov, who took his place as leader of the Russian peace delegation at Brest-Litovsk, saw to it that the widest publicity was given to the German policy of ruthlessness—the refusal to grant an armistice, the limitation of negotiations to three days, the subsequent stiffening of the ultimatum of February 21. Sokolnikov brusquely refused to discuss any of the details that had been negotiated at great length during the preceding months. On March 3 he signed, "gnashing my teeth," as he put it, and the treaty of Brest-Litovsk was thus indelibly stamped as a peace imposed by brute force.

Historians throughout the world have ever since regarded it as such, and it has time and again served the enemies of Germany as proof positive of the insatiable power drive and exploitation of the German imperialists and militarists. On March 22, the day after the great German offensive in the west began, the German Reichstag ratified the treaty by an overwhelming majority, drawing the same charge upon itself and allowing the peace resolution of July 19, 1917, to appear as the merest hypocrisy.

On the surface, the thing that frightened the world was the enormous territorial loss Russia had had to accept. Poland, Lithuania, Courland, and the western border regions of Livonia with Riga and the islands were simply cut away for good. Eastern Anatolia was to be returned to Turkey. Important regions in the Caucasus (Ardahan, Kars, Batum) were to be evacuated,[131] as were Livonia, Estonia, Finland, and Ahvenanmaa. Last but not least, the Soviets were to make peace with the social revolutionary anti-Bolshevist Rada government of the new Ukrainian "people's republic," in other words recognize that new state's peace treaty with the Central Powers and renounce its only vaguely defined territory.

The sum total of these losses to Russia was immense. It has been calculated that they comprised 34 per cent of the people, 32 per cent of the arable land, 85 per cent of the sugar beet crop, 54 per cent of all industrial enterprises, 89 per cent of all the coal mines, and virtually the entire cotton and oil production.[132] Actually, the Ukraine accounted for the most important part, and like Finland the Ukraine had already been effectively severed from Russia long before the Brest-Litovsk negotiations.

It is true that neither of these countries could have long maintained its independence without German military aid. Yet this aid was dispatched, not as an act of arbitrary military force, but in response to urgent entreaties by the local governments. In the case of the Ukraine, moreover, it was undeniably justified by the legitimate interest of the Central Powers in not allowing themselves to be deprived of the fruits of the peace treaties they had just signed with the Rada government.

Austria, in particular, was on the brink of famine, which it thought itself unable to avert without food imports from the Ukraine; and thus initial hesitations in Vienna to participate in the German occupation of that country were quickly overcome. The Austrians then proved to be even more ruthless than the Germans in exploiting the enforced collection of food and raw materials. These were all war measures, born of the exigencies of total economic exhaustion and the harsh Allied blockade. Indeed, the two treaties of Brest-Litovsk could never be anything more than provisional solutions of the eastern issues, for the war went on and its outcome was still uncertain. Few of even the Germans posted to the Ukraine could have thought that the country's separation from Great Russia would endure, in view of the close historical and economic ties between the two countries. Ultimately everything depended on how the Russian civil war would come out; and Lenin was not altogether wrong when he told his associates: "All the Germans are after in the Ukraine is wheat. Once they have got that, they will get out."[133]

The second great territorial loss was Poland. This too, however, had not really been left to the treaties of Brest-Litovsk. It had been in effect long before, indeed had been repeatedly acknowledged from the Russian side—one can almost say that it had become a historical necessity. Thus the actual bones of contention at Brest-Litovsk were the Baltic countries, and as our account has shown in detail, the constant intervention by the OHL and its obstinate refusal to set a date for evacuation made any diplomatic settlement all but impossible.

Even so, the German foreign ministry did succeed in embodying in the treaty text an explicit statement that the ultimate disposition of the countries west of the treaty line—i.e., Poland, Lithuania, Courland, and Riga—would be settled by the Central Powers "in concert with the local populations," which in essence excluded outright annexation.[134] All that was said about the future of Estonia and Livonia was that while the Russian troops and Red Guards were required to evacuate these regions, Germany would occupy them with police formations only until law and order were restored and local government institutions could offer a guarantee of security. There was no express demand that they be permanently severed from Russia. That was fixed only in a supplementary treaty of August 27, which carried certain exemptions, such as free commercial transit and free port areas for Russia.

Thus we cannot describe the peace as outright annexationist in character—or at least only in the sense that the Baltic articles were merely a cover for the intentions of the OHL and its political followers ultimately to establish one or more Baltic satellite states completely dependent on the Prussian crown. There can be no doubt that there were such intentions. Yet the final decision was deliberately avoided in the peace document and the struggle over this issue continued for a long time, though after March 3 there was even less mention of self-determination in Lithuania and Courland than before.

In the light of the legal situation created at Brest-Litovsk, Erzberger was well-entitled to make the statement that later drew so much criticism, namely that the treaty kept well within the frame of reference of the Reichstag resolution of July 19. Erzberger did add that the "police measures" in Livonia and Estonia were only "temporary" and hopefully would soon be terminated. Erzberger's suspicions concerning the OHL and the annexationists had by no means subsided. At a meeting of party leaders on March 12 he told Chancellor Hertling that if the right of self-determination were not swiftly, loyally, and honestly implemented for the Poles, Lithuanians, and Courlanders, the eastern peace treaty would not be worth the paper it was written on.

No one was more zealously opposed to the militarist policy of force in the Baltic countries than Erzberger, who did, however, try to defend the treaty of Brest-Litovsk against radical rejection by Haase and the extreme left.[135] A further element of congruence between that treaty and the Reichstag resolution was the fact that the former made no claims to war reparations and indemnities, and that while it exploited Germany's advantage in the economic clauses, these were by and large based on the principle of reciprocity; nor was Russia required to disarm permanently, merely to demobilize immediately, certainly a requirement that was indispensable while the war was on.[136]

All in all the treaty of Brest-Litovsk was rather better than its reputation, and despite its harshnesses it was not really a treaty of force.[137] All the same, there is one thing it was not: a treaty of reconciliation; and that was precisely the charge leveled by the German socialists. No sooner had the terms been announced in the Reichstag on February 26 when Scheidemann said: "What has happened to Russia is not in accordance with German social democratic intentions. We fought to defend our country, not to smash Russia." They were opposed to the creation of a spirit of revenge in Russia; they wished to foster a spirit of reconciliation and friendship. That was the reason why Scheidemann and his party, while they did not vote against the treaty, abstained. The social democrats were the only party of the majority of July 19 that remained completely true to its policy.

One may well ask whether a policy of reconciliation and future friendship with the Bolshevists was at all possible. The deep ideological split that has divided the world ever since they first appeared and that has not yet been healed even today, despite years of devoted comradeship-in-arms between East and West during the Second World War, was surely then an insurmountable obstacle to any true understanding in the questions of self-determination and the marginal areas. True, we have shown in detail how Kühlmann tried to reach a mutually acceptable compromise with the Russian delegation at Brest-Litovsk, only to be foiled time and again by the obstinacy, arrogant intervention, and shortsighted power strivings of the OHL; but that does not suggest that without such meddling Trotzky and Lenin would have agreed to allow the Lithuanians, Courlanders, Latvians, and Estonians to determine their own destiny in real freedom, independent of either side; nor that they would have agreed to an evacuation plan that would have been acceptable not only to the German occupying forces, but also to the non-Bolshevist elements—meaning the urban and rural propertied classes. What the Bolshevists wanted, after all—in the Baltic as in the Ukraine and Finland—was the Red Terror, the dictatorship of the proletariat and their party. It was this prospect rather than German intervention that drove both Finland and the Ukraine to defect from Great Russia and the Livonians and Estonians to appeal to a foreign power for help. The "smashing of Russia," rightly rejected by Scheidemann as a German war aim, sprang, not from the treaties of Brest-Litovsk, but from an internal process of disintegration.

German intervention in this process did expose the Germans to the charge of harboring ambitions for imperialist conquest—and to the degree that this charge was pointed at German military dictatorship, it was certainly not groundless; but most Germans at the time felt that in a moral sense it was inconceivable to stand by idly while such horrors were perpetrated in the Baltic region and to ignore the appeals of the substantial Baltic German elements, nor, even if only for the sake of suffering Austria, did it seem reasonable to forego the benefits that were anticipated from the peace treaty with the Ukrainians. Indeed, could a country fighting hard for its very survival be blamed for not foregoing the attempt to exploit for its own purposes the decay of so powerful an enemy as Russia?

The fault lay not in the attempt, it seems to us, but in the manner in which it was made. We thus return to our earlier assessment of Germany's situation (see pp. 81-83). In much greater measure than earlier wars, the First World War was a war of nations rather than cabinets; and the peace negotiations at Brest-Litovsk were attended by worldwide publicity of an intensity unparalleled in any comparable situation before. It was particularly important for Germany and Austria, once they had accepted the principles of self-determination and no annexations, to play their roles as "liberators of the oppressed" in such a fashion as to appear plausible rather than hypocritical.

And if it was impossible to bring the Russians around to a really service-able compromise—especially on the Baltic question—it should have been shown before all the world that the fault was theirs rather than the Germans'. The occupation regimes in the Baltic and Poland, moreover, and later on in the Ukraine as well, should have been conducted in such a way that the "police formations" did not appear to be in control. The occupation adminis-tration should have taken on the appearance of a real attempt at national construction rather than of a brutal dictatorship. The goal was, after all, to place a protective belt against the Red Menace around the Reich, as the Entente itself did later on, partly with the help of a vanquished Germany—or at least its soldiers. The real failure of the peace of Brest-Litovsk was that neither of the two eventualities occurred.

One immediate effect of the peace was to tell the world unequivocally who held the ultimate power of political decision in Germany—not the Reichstag, not the Kaiser, not the Chancellor, but Ludendorff. This elemental fact vitiated all the fine speeches of German statesmen who sought contact with the West and swore up and down that Germany was ready to negotiate peace. President Wilson said so very pointedly in a great fighting speech on April 6, in which he called on Americans to stake their full resources for victory.

The treaty of Brest-Litovsk also did much to engender a firm conviction in Russia that survives even today, namely that Germany was the intransigent aggressor, the world's public enemy. As shown by the rapprochement that took place under the Weimar Republic, that impression did not then become irrevocable—it was only Hitler who heightened Russian fears of German power politics to the level of a complex.

Quite apart from these psychological as well as political effects, the enor-mous extent of the German occupation zones laid down in the treaty brought on direct military consequences. Peace had returned in the east, but the German high command was still compelled to leave behind enormous masses of troops. On April 1, 1918, i.e., during the great western offensive, German troops remaining in the east (including Rumania and Turkey) numbered a million and a half, as against four million in the west. There were more than forty divisions, about half of them in the Ukraine and the South Russian occupation zone, which soon stretched to the Don region.[138]

True, these were garrison troops that had been combed out again and again, of limited combat effectiveness and with poor equipment. They would have been useless for the great western offensive; but their rolling stock at least might have served to close the gaping holes in the west and they would have been of great help in strengthening the rear echelons—if only the German military commitments in the east had been limited. It is, of course, not easy in retrospect to determine the extent to which that might have been possible. What is certain, however, is that the great overexpansion in the east seriously strained Germany's resources and that the practical results of the vast commitment in the Ukraine were a serious disappointment. Despite all the efforts of German military agencies and purchase commissions, that country, devastated by revolution and civil war and ravaged by political chaos, yielded but a small fraction of the food supplies that had been anticipated. It grew so difficult to deal with the impotent and refractory local authorities that the German generals in April abruptly staged a coup d'état and installed as dictator a former Russian guards officer, the Cossack hetman Scoropadsky. Intervention in the Russian civil war further entangled Germany in endless new problems, and Ludendorff did everything to make their solution even more difficult by plans for still greater expansion.

The greatest weakness of the peace of Brest-Litovsk was that it failed to create a true state of peace on the eastern front. Efforts to amputate further sections from the Russian empire continued. In Part 4 of Chapter 7 we shall trace the struggles between the OHL and the German foreign ministry, which sought to oppose this constant expansion of the theater of war.

3

Domestic Effects of the German Military Regime in the Fourth Winter of the War

Part 1
Unrest Among the Workers; The Electoral Issue in Prussia and the January Strike

DESPITE ALL the efforts on behalf of peace by the Reichstag majority, the pope, and the statesmen of both Central Powers, the war rounded into its universally dreaded fourth winter. The peace negotiations at Brest-Litovsk did not alter the fact that it continued in the west, where the last, greatest, and bloodiest confrontation lay still ahead. As had happened so many times before,[1] German youth—and not merely youth, but every German who could bear arms—was to be offered up to the slaughter of mechanized mass battle. The stranglehold of the British blockade had in the meantime pushed the food emergency for the civilian population to a new peak. Austria was close to famine.

The German government realized that in this plight it was more than ever dependent on the loyalty of the social democratic majority and its leaders, men like Scheidemann, Ebert, David, and Bauer. Only with their help could the growing unrest, impatience, and disaffection of the working class be held in check, open rebellion and political and hunger strikes be prevented, and the danger to army morale from radical pacifist propaganda be averted. The masses railed against the war-born economic hardships in their thousand and one irksome manifestations—profiteering, the black market, and countless other inequities—but political grievances were even more explosive. There were the activities of the fatherland party and of the annexationists, now universally reviled as "war prolongers"; the unabashed way in which the military countenanced this agitation; the biased and unfair handling of censorship; the endless delays in the negotiations at Brest-Litovsk; and not least the Prussian reactionaries who obstructed the reforms which the Kaiser had proclaimed in his famous Easter message of April 7.

What had now become of Bethmann Hollweg's high hopes that the comradeship of war would weld all classes together, that domestic reforms would create a new society? The rift that split right and left into hostile camps had only deepened. True, parliamentary leverage on the government had grown stronger with the formation of a firm, liberally and democratically oriented Reichstag majority and the appointment as Chancellor and Vice-Chancellor of such seasoned parliamentarians as Hertling and Payer; but with the fall of Bethmann Hollweg, the government had drifted into an even more abject dependence on the OHL; hence these changes had little practical significance.

The bitterest resentment was reserved to the party leaders in the joint caucus of the Reichstag. Even moderate democrats like Müller-Meiningen and Gothein spoke openly of an OHL military dictatorship that ignored the Reichstag majority; and the latter's desperate impotence was the strongest grievance of the social democrats. "Military policy is being conducted behind an impenetrable screen," as David put it.[2] There could be no democratization of any kind so long as no progress was made in the democratization of Prussian electoral law, which lay at the heart of the reform planned by Bethmann Hollweg.

A number of enemies of the general franchise within the Prussian cabinet had indeed been dismissed after Bethmann Hollweg's fall (see Vol. III, p. 478), to be replaced by men favorably disposed to reform. Bill Drews had succeeded Loebell as minister of the interior; and when the Bavarian Hertling took over as Prussian premier, the national-liberal Reichstag leader Friedberg became vice-premier. This cabinet did introduce in the diet the electoral reform bill that had been promised on July 11, and at its first reading on December 5 Hertling and Drews tried their best to emphasize its urgency. As expected, they immediately encountered strong opposition on the part of the conservatives, the national liberals, and even a considerable part of the center party; and this opposition was not overcome until October 15, 1918, just before Germany's collapse.

It mustered every parliamentary trick, all the complexities of the two-chamber system, every possible legal brake on constitutional change to drag out the issue and water down the government bill by counterproposals under which the propertied classes would have continued to command a majority. The second reading did not take place until May 2, when it was voted down, as happened again on the fifth reading on July 14. The bill was then buried in a committee of the upper house, from which it did not reemerge for serious discussion before the lower chamber until early October, when Count Roedern reported from supreme headquarters that in view of the new over-all military and political situation the OHL thought it time to give up opposition to the universal franchise. Until that happened, the Kaiser had never dared brave the resistance of the generals by doing the only thing he could have done to promote this urgent cause, threatening to prorogue the diet and hold new elections.

To avoid the domestic strife such a step would have been bound to elicit, the possibility had been discussed ever since the spring of 1917 of forcing through the universal franchise in all the federal states by Reich law. This was not, however, a practicable possibility, for it would have made a mockery of the federal structure of the Reich. Thus Prussia, together with Mecklenburg, remained until the end of the war an insurmountable obstacle on the road to democratic reform.[3]

Ludendorff and Hindenburg often vociferously declined to be drawn into partisan struggles—whenever the government tried to invoke their authority against the opposition of the parties of the right; but we have already seen, in the example of Bethmann Hollweg's fall and its background, how little that deterred the two generals from intervening in domestic policy. Writing to the then Prussian minister of the interior Drews on December 8, 1917, Ludendorff had explicitly stated that he welcomed Bethmann Hollweg's resignation mainly for domestic considerations—actually, of course, he had forced that resignation by giving the Kaiser an ultimatum. He charged Bethmann Hollweg with always having yielded to the left and strongly warned Drews against following such a line. "I regard a policy of surrender to the *Zeitgeist* as extremely dangerous," he wrote. "As history shows, it is bound to lead to perdition. . . . Our policy must be above party—it must lead the parties." For Ludendorff this kind of "leadership" meant fighting against the democratic *Zeitgeist*—the spirit of the times. Anything else was mere softness. "In my view the war has given us no·real reason for democratization and parliamentarization. Surely conditions in the democratically governed enemy countries offer us no inducement to emulate them." If the government were to force through the Reichstag electoral system in all the federal states (an emergency solution Drews did not wholly reject), this would be tantamount to an admission of bankruptcy, Ludendorff said. There was no reason for such a step, for there was no danger of a general strike or of widespread unrest. The preponderant part of the people were far too sensible and patriotic. Even the trade union leaders knew that failure to win the war would only impoverish the German workers; and if it did come to the test, there were forcible means for putting down rebellion.

Ludendorff wanted the minister of the interior to take these remarks merely as personal and confidential views rather than as official intervention into domestic affairs.[4] Yet could such a distinction be made? To be able to invoke the authority of the two popular heroes was of incalculable aid to the conservative opponents of the universal franchise in the diet, in justifying their own attitude. Drews did his utmost to convince both the Kaiser and the OHL that the failure to enact electoral reform would redound to the disadvantage of the policy of a "strong" peace, which they desired. In a long and rather verbose memorandum in mid-February, he tried to disprove or at least minimize the stubbornly held adverse judgment that the social democrats were in principle "enemies of the state." They had been well on the way, he said, toward developing into a moderate party of the working class, no longer irrevocably hostile to the middle class, and with a growing understanding of the needs of the whole nation, when the outbreak of the Russian March Revolution led to their radicalization and, soon, to their left wing splitting away. Since then the social democrats had experienced more and more trouble in maintaining leadership over the broad masses of the workers. Unfortunately the hapless action in the upper chamber in the spring of 1917[5] and the attitude of the parties of the right in the diet had made this task even more difficult, as did the activities of the fatherland party. The broad masses were increasingly distrustful of a reactionary regime, and combined with general dissatisfaction over the food situation and the snail's pace of the peace negotiations at Brest-Litovsk, this posed an ever-present threat of strikes. It was certain, nevertheless, that there was no lack of willingness even within the ranks of the majority parties to cast loose from the July resolution, or at least to accept a "strong" peace; but such a readiness for compromise was being stifled by the failure of the electoral reform bill to be carried in the diet and by nonfulfillment of the king's pledges of July 11. An even more alarming prospect was that the restive masses would now fall prey to extremist socialist agitation and slip from the grasp of the moderate leadership.[6]

The case had been put much more impressively, shrewdly, and concisely in a message which Hertling's adjutant, Under Secretary von Radowitz, had sent to supreme headquarters on January 17, with the Chancellor's vigorous support.[7] The Kaiser, the crown prince, and the OHL had all urged Hertling publicly to disavow the peace resolution of July 19, and Hertling was letting them know that he regarded it as obsolete, since the Western powers had never "taken notice" of it, proclaiming instead annexationist war aims of their own. Yet to make a public announcement would make it impossible for the majority social democrats to keep "face" before their followers. It would disrupt the existing Reichstag majority and create so broad an opposition that the government would not be able to carry on. The Chancellor would try to convince the Reichstag parties by and by that their peace resolution had been pointless, thus "freeing Germany of these self-imposed shackles."

On no account, however, must the social democrats be affronted, certainly not by the abandonment of electoral reform, as the conservatives wished, for then the trade unions would slip into the control of the independents altogether. Resentment over the failure to keep the reform pledge, combined with hunger, cold, and the effects of the Russian example, was bound to bring on chaos in short order. The OHL was mistaken in believing there was no danger of strikes. They could be avoided only so long as the goodwill of the social democrats was maintained. Machine guns would not achieve that. The future belonged to democratic monarchism, and if the crown, supported by a small group of powerful men, were to oppose the development of democratic ideas, the road would sooner or later lead into the abyss. Instead, an attempt should be made to transform the right wing of the social democratic party into a workers' party of nationalist orientation. Shortly before this Hertling had already advised the OHL that the treatment of the social democrats would require the utmost in political skill and caution. Any suppression of the *Vorwärts* should be considered with the greatest care. This was a question that lay entirely within the political sphere, and no one could relieve the Chancellor of responsibility for settling it, nor could he allow anyone else to do so.[8]

It is unlikely that this line of reasoning made any lasting impression on Ludendorff. His political concepts were limited to "leadership," "obedience," and "indoctrination." How little fear he had of working-class resistance was shown by the requests he made in September for modifications in the auxiliary service act—abolishing all provisions that favored the workers and extending liability for labor service down to the age of fifteen and for military service up to the age of sixty! The minister of war, Stein, rather than the Chancellor, had declared that these changes were out of the question for reasons of domestic morale.[9]

Ludendorff insisted that political unrest, grumbling, and rumormongering be combated by exhortation and propaganda. Censorship should be rigorously applied, and there should be centrally directed "briefings" for the press and for people in public life.[10] Since late July there had been an elaborate system of "patriotic indoctrination" for the troops, which aimed to counteract their disaffection stemming from defeatist sentiment on the home front.[11] The quartermaster general refused to acknowledge that there could be any limits to what could be achieved by his organizing genius, or that intellectual life was governed by rules of its own.[12] For such a man considerations of "popular sentiment" were inconceivable. Confidence in victory and willingness to fight were its only expressions he was willing to countenance in wartime. It was the business of the politicians to organize morale along such lines and to suppress any deviation. On the other hand, "army morale" was a factor he constantly cited in his debates with the government, and he insisted that it was of overriding importance.[13]

By late January, however, it developed that the manipulation of popular morale was not quite so simple a matter. For a few days after January 28 it looked as though the war industries might be seriously paralyzed by mass strikes. By the very testimony of the instigators, largely activist members of the independent social democratic group, they were being deliberately orga- nized as political protests rather than as mere hunger strikes, as had been the case before. On January 10, in a leaflet openly signed by its members, the independent social democrats called on the working people to demonstrate vigorously for a peace without annexations and indemnities, on the basis of self-determination, in order to impress the German delegation at Brest- Litovsk with the need for getting on with the job. A majority of the group had then rejected an open appeal for mass strikes as too dangerous for its authors.

But the extreme leftists, the so-called Spartacus group, nevertheless widely distributed leaflets and posters calling for mass strikes as a weapon of revolu- tionary rebellion, with the aim of preventing the great western offensive and creating a German people's republic on the Russian model.[14] Judging from the subsequent course of the strikes, the effectiveness of this propaganda should not be overestimated, even though since mid-January there had been alarming news from Austria, telling of great mass strikes in the industrial centers. Ebert and Scheidemann, the leaders of the social democratic majority party, used these reports before the main committee of the Reichstag to warn the government of growing unrest among the German workers as well; but their criticism was directed primarily against the OHL and the fatherland party rather than against the policies of the foreign ministry.[15] They were taken completely by surprise when a great mass strike broke out on January 28, organized by radical members of the "independents."

It was led mainly by Berlin metal workers in the arms industry and began with the formation of a "workers' council" at Berlin trade union headquar- ters, composed of 414 elected representatives from the various plants. This following of the Soviet example created a furor, as did the purely political strike program adopted by the meeting—lifting of censorship and the state of siege; unlimited rights of association, assembly, and bargaining; the universal franchise in Prussia; the immediate conclusion of peace on the basis of the Russian formula; and the participation of workers' representatives in the negotiations at Brest-Litovsk. Even more alarming was the swift spread of the strike, which at its peak is said to have embraced half a million workers in Berlin alone and which immediately affected other industrial centers like Hamburg, Altona, Kiel, Lübeck, Cologne, Bochum, Magdeburg, Nuremberg- Fürth, and ultimately even Wroclaw (Breslau). Despite all this, there was never any serious threat of revolution.

The strike of April 1917 had been called off when Groener proclaimed: "Anyone who strikes in wartime is a *Hundsfott* [roughly: son of a bitch]." In

October 1917, the German supreme court had described any strike in vital war industries as treason; and even among the radical independent social democrats fear of falling under this verdict and coming before a court-martial proved to be a strong deterrent; but scarcely less a factor was the sense of patriotic duty that continued to dominate large sections of the working class, despite their grievances and distrust and basic pacifism.

As for the trade union organizations, they held aloof from the strike movement from the beginning, aware of their special responsibility. They declared themselves neutral or, in the case of the Christian union movement, openly opposed. In the workers' council too the radicals found themselves unable to stampede the majority social democrats into a general strike. Indeed, the followers of the latter managed to have their leaders, Ebert, Scheidemann, and Braun, elected members of the strike committee, together with three "independent" deputies and nine of the striking workers. The majority men tried from the outset to exert a calming influence and to bring about an understanding with the government about the strike goals.

The manner in which this was attempted was thoroughly characteristic of the spirit of the German social democrats, who had long since lost their revolutionary fervor. It was only in Cologne and Bavaria that the authorities even agreed to meet with the strikers. The lord mayor of Cologne, Konrad Adenauer, and the Bavarian premier Dandl successfully appealed to the patriotism of the majority socialists. In Berlin the Reich minister of the interior, Wallraf, stubbornly refused to receive any representative of the strikers unless he had credentials for political negotiations, as either a Reichstag deputy or a trade union official.

When Scheidemann and Haase, both of them deputies (the latter representing the independent social democrats), presented themselves at the Reich office of the interior in the company of two strikers, Wallraf sent out a flunky to repeat his refusal. Instead of pushing the flunky aside and forcing their way in to see the minister, the members of the delegation subserviently waited outside and contented themselves with sending in word through another deputy that all they wanted was to tell him of the bad effect of the ban that had been promptly imposed on all meetings, including those of the workers' council and the strike committee.

Obviously the traditional authority of the state had not been breached in the least. The home military authorities proceeded with rigorous measures. The strike committee was declared dissolved and an emergency state of siege proclaimed, which meant the threat of courts martial. Seven plants in Berlin and a few elsewhere were "militarized"; i.e., the workers were drafted into military service and compelled to resume work under military supervision. A handful of ringleaders were arrested by the police.[16] As a result the strike faded in a matter of days. Apart from a few minor street riots, quickly controlled by the police without military aid, there were no attempts at revolutionary uprisings.

All the same, there were consequences of some significance. The social democratic workers were bitterly resentful of this demonstration of their complete impotence to influence grand policy in any way, whether in respect of the peace negotiations or of Prussian electoral reform. Not even their leading deputies had managed to secure a hearing for the representatives of the workers' council, which dealt a serious blow to the authority of these leaders. Above all, the strike had maneuvered the majority party into a precarious position. Its leaders had been called in at a time of crisis by their followers who were opposed to radicalism. Although they were initially reluctant, they could scarcely refuse this summons to the strike leadership without losing all control over the agitated masses. Moreover, they agreed with most of the people's demands and completely shared their distrust of the militarists and reactionaries.

At the strikers' meeting they had no choice but to use strong language, bordering on revolutionary agitation—this was true even of the eminently peaceful-minded Ebert, the party leader—but at the same time they had to assume a mediating role and seek to prevent the outbreak of real revolution. They could expect gratitude for their efforts from neither side. The bourgeois press waxed indignant over their joining the strike leadership, charging them with sharing responsibility for "a senseless crime against the fatherland"—and we may recall that this was brought up against Ebert even when he was president under the Weimar Republic. Stresemann and the national liberals refused to go on working with the social democrats in the joint caucus. The whole majority party coalition was close to disintegration, which, to cite the Austrian ambassador, would have had incalculable consequences for German foreign and domestic policy.[17] This extremity was ultimately avoided, but mutual confidence within the coalition was severely shaken. The majority social democrats had got themselves into a highly ambiguous position and even friendly observers doubted that they would still command a majority of the social democratic electorate. Here were the first intimations of the intensified domestic conflict that marked the final phase of the war.

The reaction of the OHL is shown with complete clarity in two letters which Ludendorff dispatched to the Chancellor and the war minister on February 17 and 18.[18] Colonel Bauer, already known to us for his political eccentricities, may be confidently assumed to be their intellectual author, for their content largely coincides with the draft of a direct report to the Kaiser which Bauer composed for Ludendorff in these days—it was immediately sent to the Kaiser's new cabinet chief, Berg, to serve as the basis for an oral presentation, and it was also sent to the crown prince.[19] Its basic ideas are precisely the same ones that Bauer had developed in the spring of 1917 in the memorandum that ushered in Ludendorff's campaign to topple Bethmann Hollweg (see Vol. III, pp. 455ff.).

The burden of the argument was that the social democrats—never mind their various factions—were the arch-enemies of the monarchist system and of Germany's military grandeur. When the war broke out, they had forfeited all political power, and if they had climbed back, it was owing solely to the weakness and everlasting appeasement of the government, which had failed to rally to its standard and give official support to those sections of the working class of nationalist persuasion—the Christian trade union movement, the Hirsch-Duncker organizations,[20] the Poles, and the unorganized—even though these "pro-free-enterprise elements" far outnumbered the "free" trade unions. The need of the day was to attack the social democrats and their trade unions rather than to treat them with kid gloves. Drews, whose February memorandum was the main target of this attack, was mistaken in his belief that such a frontal attack was not possible. The social democratic leaders shared moral responsibility for the January strike, which had amounted to outright treason. The government must exploit this fact in order to pillory them before the people.

Trade union leaders and deputies should be sharply confronted with the question of their attitude to strikes in wartime. If they condemned strikes, that would lead to a serious split in their ranks. If they did not do so outright, they would be unmasked as traitors and should be treated accordingly. It was necessary to isolate them, i.e., to separate them from the nationalist-minded majority of the workers—or at the very least a clean division should be brought about between nationalists and internationalists. Compromise would lead only to ever-higher demands. To govern meant to rule, and whoever wished to rule must base himself on loyalist strength rather than on those who sought to wrest power from his hands. There was no reason to be afraid of the social democrats. They would never dare refuse to vote for the war appropriations, and even if they did, a Reichstag majority could be put together without them. Even a general strike need not be feared, any more than other large-scale strikes that might impend. Like the January strikes, they would come to nothing, if only the government remained firm.

Least of all must concessions in the peace questions be made to the grumblers and the "Jewish and social democratic press." The peace resolution was long obsolete. At heart every German wanted a good peace that included territorial gains and war indemnities—even the social democrats, though they would not admit it, dogmatists that they were. As for Prussian electoral reform, well, the Kaiser had promised it and the attempt must therefore be made; but should difficulties arise in the Prussian diet, there was no hurry at all. Indeed, it was premature to allow only the noncombatants to decide the issue. The king had kept his promise, by allowing the bill to be written, but he had no particular obligation toward the social democrats, nor was there any reason to suppress the nationalist and monarchist elements among the people just to please the social democrats. The need was for economic and social rather than political reform—that was all the people and the army were interested in.

Such, then, were the notions on domestic policy which Ludendorff, through his creature, the new cabinet chief Berg, tried to carry to the Kaiser.[21] Toward the Chancellor he expressed himself in more cautious terms, not even touching on the electoral issue; but the basic thoughts were reiterated here too—no show of weakness, on no account democratization, and public exposure of the social democratic leaders. Ludendorff, in other words, was demanding precisely what had to be avoided at this juncture at all costs, the weakening or destruction of the authority over their followers of the moderate social democratic leaders. He lived in a world of illusions that could scarcely be surpassed.

The editors of the *Frankfurter Zeitung*, badly shaken by a talk with the OHL press chief, Lieutenant Colonel Nicolai, tried to puncture these illusions in a public memorandum addressed to Hindenburg. It warned insistently against the kind of propaganda along fatherland party lines that was only calculated to stifle whatever fighting morale still survived among the people and the army. The men at the front, it said, were certainly ready to make the supreme sacrifice in defense of the fatherland, but they were not willing to fight on for purposes of conquest. The impending great western offensive would be in danger from within, if it were susceptible to the interpretation that it constituted a campaign for conquest. Even now the OHL had forfeited the people's political confidence by virtue of its manifest opposition to the peace aims proclaimed by the government.[22]

This was one voice from the camp of the left. Possibly a stronger impression was registered on Ludendorff when his most loyal henchman, Stresemann, implored him in a letter not to intervene in the question of Prussian electoral reform, which was demanded by eighty-five per cent of the voters in Prussia and already taken for granted in South Germany. Stresemann especially warned Ludendorff against siding with the traditional Prussian reactionaries who opposed any dissolution of the Prussian diet in wartime. Such a step would dangerously reduce political confidence in the OHL.[23]

Ludendorff gave an evasive reply. At the time his military authority was still unshaken. Yet the great offensive on the western front, on which he had staked virtually everything, had already failed when he received Stresemann's letter. The war was virtually lost.

Part 2

The Problem of Alsace-Lorraine

THE DOMESTIC repercussions of the military regime were manifest throughout Germany, but nowhere more painfully than in the *Reichsland* Alsace-Lorraine, where its harsh pressures forfeited all the gains achieved in forty years of effort in "Germanizing" this population and implanting the seeds of a German national identity. The winter of 1917-1918 further showed that all attempts to assuage the rising resentment and alienation and to take the wind out of French propaganda by means of sweeping constitutional reform must falter hopelessly because of political and, even more importantly, military obstruction.

While they were part of Germany, Alsace and Lorraine always remained to a certain degree foreign bodies within the Reich. Bismarck's hopes in this respect were never fulfilled—he had anticipated that the Alsatians would automatically come to feel themselves to be Germans, once they were removed from rigid French government centralism and were given the opportunity to develop a vigorous Alsatian particularism. On the contrary, what particularism they developed was constantly nourished by their awareness of their historic, economic, and cultural allegiance to France, the pride their educated classes took in French culture, the family ties between large sections of the people and their many relatives who had emigrated to France, and ties with friends who worked in France. No fewer than some 300 generals and staff officers in the French army were natives of Alsace.

Still, by 1914—in the judgment of experts on the subject[24]—by far the greater proportion of the people, especially in the rural districts and among the younger generation, had come to take their allegiance to Germany for granted, and mobilization against France was effected without difficulty. There were even a few thousand volunteers from Alsace-Lorraine, despite the widespread resentment that had been aroused only recently by the Zabern incident and its bungled handling by the German authorities.[25] The most radical among the resisters, like the well-known publicist Abbé Wetterlé, left the country on the outbreak of the war, and some 3,000 young men evaded military service by flight; but by and large the loyal stand taken by the people and the press surprised the German authorities; nor was there any lack of generous patriotic demonstrations by leading political personages, publicists, and deputies.

It would, of course, have been surprising if contrary manifestations had been totally lacking. In Mulhouse, Altkirch, and Saarburg some of the local people joyously welcomed the invading French forces. There were traitors and spies in some areas near the front; and some of the military units were plagued with rebellious elements and defectors. Under wartime conditions public authority had passed almost entirely into the hands of the military, who often reacted to such incidents with excessive harshness. There were arrests without due process, largely on the basis of denunciations, and summary courts martial were likely to impose penalties that were grotesquely disproportionate to the alleged offenses.

Thus the inevitable hardships of war behind the front were greatly intensified, while the incarceration or expulsion of innocent persons aroused widespread resentment. Indeed, the temper of the people grew more rebellious in proportion to the severity of the military regime. Charges piled up before the military authorities, as did petitions of grievance before the civil authorities. The diet failed to serve as a safety valve for the general dissatisfaction, because the military authorities allowed it to meet only for brief business sessions, in which the sole discussion concerned budgetary questions and the like. Only in 1916 was the budget committee permitted to hear political complaints in secret session, and that was owing solely to the intervention of the central government. The only forum for voicing complaints that remained open to the Alsatian representatives was the Reichstag.

Deepening mutual dislike was the consequence. The military authorities thundered against the unreliability and insubordination of the people, while the old Alsatians chafed under what they called a Prussian military dictatorship. German distrust of Alsatian soldiers reached the point in 1916-1917 where such regiments were used almost exclusively on the eastern front. Alsatians were either removed or kept from military positions of trust, with the result that many loyal and valiant soldiers grew bitterly resentful, because they felt they were being mishandled and discriminated against as "inferior elements"—the Alsatian term was "third-class Germans." As disaffection grew, the question of the future of Alsace-Lorraine bulked more and more importantly in public discussion in the area.

Its urgency grew also from the fact that it had been discussed throughout Germany ever since the war began. There was universal agreement that the constitutional situation of semiautonomy created in 1911—a separate diet, but with an appointed governor and only limited voting rights in the federal council—had not stood up and must be changed; but opinion diverged sharply on the direction such a change should take. The people of Alsace and Lorraine naturally wanted full autonomy, i.e., equal status with the federal states of South Germany, with a head of state of their own; but would such autonomy really result in full integration with Germany? Might it not, on the contrary, further loosen the bonds and bring on defection, i.e., immediate pro-French demonstrations, which would seriously prejudice Germany's position in the peace negotiations to come?

There could be no unequivocal answer to these questions, if only because everything ultimately depended on how the war went and what the expectations were of the people of Alsace-Lorraine in that respect. They naturally expected that in the event of an Entente victory they would be enthusiastically welcomed as prodigal sons by the French, who would give them the democratic freedoms the Germans had withheld from them. They had no intimation of what would actually confront them: an orgy of French nationalism and conquerors' pride that would ruthlessly press the country into the way of life and administrative machinery of a rigorously centralized national state that had far less sympathy than Germany for peculiarities of language and culture and for regional autonomy, indeed, that regarded all these with suspicion, with the result that all immigrants from Germany and many old established Alsatians who were denounced as pro-German or unreliable were brutally expelled, while treason trials for Alsatian "autonomists" were promptly instituted.[26]

All this, of course, could not have been anticipated; but so long as a German victory was not certain, Alsatians necessarily took a risk in committing themselves publicly and irrevocably to the German cause. Conversely, the German government faced a risk, in such circumstances, in supplementing the constitutional changes of 1911 and granting Alsace-Lorraine full autonomy as a federal state in wartime. Even Bethmann Hollweg, who had pushed through the act of 1911 against much Prussian-conservative opposition, thought it was too early to take this risk in 1915, after the experience of the first war year.[27]

Two years later, in the spring of 1917, he had reached the point of regarding a division of the *Reichslande* between Prussia and Bavaria as urgently necessary, as an improvement on the provisional military dictatorship. He clung to this view firmly, against the entrenched opposition of Weizsäcker and the king of Württemberg.[28]

Most of the Germans who had gone to Alsace, especially the professors in Strasbourg—but also the Catholic Alsatian historian Ehrhard! —shared the view that autonomy was far too great a risk, in the light of war situation and the Alsatians' attitude. Most of the Strasbourg scholars believed that the important thing was to free the Alsatians from the shackles of their narrow provincial life and to bring them into closer contact with German life as a whole. Particularism, in other words, rather than being cultivated, should be overcome by integration with one of the larger federal states, either Prussia or Bavaria, or possibly by assigning Lorraine to Prussia and Alsace to Bavaria.

There were discussions on this subject within the Reichstag and the governments of the larger federal states, but dynastic ambitions and annexationism were complicating factors, especially in Bavaria, whose king, Louis III, had been dreaming of a greater Wittelsbach realm on the upper Rhine ever since the war's beginning. This mixture of dynastic and nationalist aspirations resulted in muddling the issue of Alsace-Lorraine more and more as well as in deepening rivalries among the larger federal states, who begrudged Bavaria and Prussia such a prize and demanded either a share of it or "compensation" in Poland or the Baltic region.

There was no other issue on which the Chancellor was so hemmed in in his freedom of action. Aside from the wishes of the people of Alsace-Lorraine, he had to take into account those of the OHL, the Reichstag, the Kaiser, the Prussian cabinet, and the various federal governments; for the *Reichsland* was the common property of all the federal states and could be reorganized or divided up only with their consent. In the event, there was a hopeless tangle of conflicting ambitions and opinions, even among the Reichstag parties. Some of these canceled each other out, and the result was endless negotiations that made no progress, since there was no solution that appealed to all. Only on one occasion, in midsummer and the fall of 1917, did there seem to be a turn that might have had immediate consequences of importance in the sphere of foreign policy.

This was associated with the solemn proclamation of *désannexion* of Alsace-Lorraine as a French war aim in the Paris chamber sessions of June 5 and 6; the Russian formula of peace without annexations and self-determination; and the peace resolution of the German Reichstag. In early July Helfferich proposed to the party leaders that the French annexationist claim be answered with a straightforward Reichstag declaration that Alsace was German in character;[29] but this would have scarcely been very effective, since the French could point to the fact that in forty-six years the Germans still had found no definitive solution to the problem of Alsace and dared not hold a plebiscite there, in implementation of self-determination, any more than they did in their Polish-speaking areas in the east.

There was wide agreement that the situation on Germany's western border must be stabilized. One solution would have been along OHL lines. German rule would be insured by a stronger show of force, French influence would be wholly eliminated, and the regions would be integrated with Prussia and Bavaria, thus abolishing their special status. This would have countered the French claims with a show of German resolve to hold this staging area toward France even more firmly than before, and it would have demonstrated a strong German faith in victory. On the other hand, Germany might muster the courage to satisfy the Alsatian desire for full autonomy, despite all the objections, in the expectation that this would persuade the people to come out officially and formally for Germany, which would take the wind out of French propaganda—likewise in anticipation of a German victory, without which Alsace-Lorraine would be lost in any event. If the Alsace diet did declare for Germany, this might make a deep impression abroad, especially in Britain, where there was still some hesitation in regarding the return of Alsace-Lorraine (in addition to the restoration of Belgium) as an indispensable war aim. Optimists entertained the hope that such a step might facilitate a negotiated peace.

The greatest such optimist was Matthias Erzberger, who was as firmly convinced of the infallible effect of such a policy as he was of the value of the Reichstag resolution. Yet he had but recently agreed with Lieutenant Colonel Bauer that an autonomous federal state of Alsace-Lorraine was tantamount to the loss of the whole area, and that it had therefore to be divided up, with the predominantly Catholic Alsace being joined to Bavaria.[30] Flexible as always, Erzberger changed his mind the moment the Reichstag mustered a majority for a negotiated peace. At the session on July 6 of the joint caucus of the Reichstag majority parties, the national liberal Strasbourg professor van Calker revised his earlier views and opted for combining the peace resolution with a declaration that Alsace-Lorraine was to become a federal state.

Erzberger picked up the idea with fervor. On the very day of the Reichstag resolution he urgently recommended, in a long letter to Michaelis that represented a kind of political guide for the new Chancellor, that an autonomous duchy of Alsace-Lorraine be created, assuring Michaelis that such a step would "trigger off an enormous international effect." The diet at Strasbourg, he predicted, would assent with great enthusiasm. The world would realize that this meant the realization of Alsatian ambitions, and that the war need not be continued for a single day on account of Alsace-Lorraine. The people would manifest their will in numerous demonstrations. The whole world would have to acknowledge that Alsace-Lorraine was no longer a prize for any country, including France. The French revanchists would find their most potent weapon struck from their hands. Peace-loving elements in France would find the degree of autonomy granted by Germany sufficient to concede that France had not fought in vain, since the two provinces would truly have achieved freedom. A main obstacle to peace would thus have been removed. The German government should introduce an appropriate bill at the next Reichstag session in September.[31]

Erzberger's naive enthusiasm completely misapprehended French war aims and manifestly overestimated Alsatian willingness to come out with declarations of loyalty. True, there had been such declarations in the Strasbourg diet more than once, sometimes couched in fervent terms, but they had not been adopted by the body as a whole, having been issued only by the presiding officers of the two chambers, whose evident aim it was to get the German military authorities to authorize diet sessions. Dr. Ricklin, president of the second chamber, had, moreover, used his concluding speech on June 12 to reject strongly Ribot's proclamation of *désannexion:*

> The people of Alsace-Lorraine [he had declared] emphatically reject
> the imputation that this terrible bloodshed is being continued on their
> account. Their sole aspiration is to continue their indissoluble allegiance
> to the German Reich, while maintaining, cultivating, and promoting
> their own legitimate character.

These wise and courageous words later on sealed the speaker's doom in the
Colmar autonomists' trial of 1928. Actually, a large number of deputies had
left the hall before they were spoken, and of those who remained behind only
a small number had applauded.[32]

Yet there can be no doubt that the promise of elevating Alsace-Lorraine to
the status of an autonomous federal state on the same level with the others in
the Reich would have still been greeted with great satisfaction in 1917, and
that the diet would have probably responded with a declaration that could
have been interpreted as an expression of allegiance to Germany, even though
it might have been couched in the most cautious terms, as a mere statement
of assent. Even newspaper reports that autonomy for Alsace-Lorraine would
be debated in the Reichstag elicited a most positive response, even though
this was coupled with understandable distrust that it might merely be pseudo
rather than real autonomy.[33] Was such distrust justified?

Two days after the Reichstag peace resolution, on July 21, a delegation
from the joint caucus called on Michaelis to present an agreement that had
been reached between the majority parties and the deputies from Alsace. The
diet of Alsace-Lorraine was to adopt a petition—it was assumed that this
would be unanimous[34]—for the granting of autonomy. The Alsatian delegation in the Reichstag would endorse this petition and submit it to the Reichstag and the government.

The proposal evidently made a strong impression on Michaelis, though the
Chancellor could not take a stand on it without first discussing it with the
OHL, the Kaiser, the federal governments, and the foreign ministry. He did,
however, say that he personally thought that domestic considerations had
made it impossible to divide up the *Reichslande.*[35] In Kühlmann's view,
considerations of foreign policy spoke even more compellingly against such a
solution. In a memorandum for the Chancellor, dated July 27, he said that in
the light of the principle of self-determination it was no longer possible to
carve up regions to satisfy dynastic ambitions, in the style of the Congress of
Vienna.

Kühlmann added that he had received the impression, during visits to Paris
prior to 1914, that politically influential Frenchmen, especially members of
the younger generation, were quite willing to let the question of Alsace-

Lorraine rest, as soon as the severed provinces had become fully reconciled to their new destiny and no longer sent out heartrending appeals to France.[36] Thus the German foreign ministry was in principle favorably disposed to raising Alsace-Lorraine to the level of a full-fledged federal state.

In the circumstances it seemed at first not unlikely that the government might yield to the pressure of the majority parties in the question of Alsace-Lorraine. On August 1, the Bavarian government did submit to the Chancellor a comprehensive memorandum in which it described a division of the *Reichslande* between Bavaria and Prussia as the only feasible solution; but it did not prevail. In any event, on August 20, during a visit to Berlin, the Bavarian premier, Count Hertling, gained the impression that the Reich government, for urgent reasons of foreign policy, would probably opt in favor of autonomy; and he seems to have decided not to oppose such a solution, if it resulted in a declaration of loyalty to the Reich on the part of Alsace-Lorraine. He won over the king of Bavaria to this stand; and the king gave his agreement when the leading Alsatian center party deputy, Charles Hauss, told him that the party wanted a member of the Wittelsbach dynasty appointed head of the federal state of Alsace-Lorraine.

Bavarian opposition, in other words, might have been overcome, if the central government had followed the desires of the majority parties and the deputies from Alsace-Lorraine and had brought in an autonomy bill or at least held out the definite prospect of one. Yet late in August, when the deputies were pressing for a decision, all that Michaelis could tell them was that while he himself would welcome autonomy in principle, he had not yet been able to secure a decision from the various agencies concerned.[37] Many obstacles had still to be overcome. The greatest of these, insurmountable for Michaelis, was the opposition of the OHL.

For Ludendorff, the only solution to the question of Alsace-Lorraine was forcible Germanization of the people, combined with rigorous military control. As he had declared early in April during a discussion with the governor of Alsace-Lorraine and a representative of the Reich office of the interior, "Alsace-Lorraine must become a German country, and it is necessary to train German soldiers there." Among the methods to be employed to this end were Germanization of the clergy and civil service; expropriation of the tremendous share of French real property and of all French commercial interests (supported in Upper Alsace almost exclusively by French capital); the settlement of Germans, mainly war veterans, in the French-speaking border regions, i.e., mainly in Lorraine; and the strengthening of military command authority.[38]

The OHL unswervingly stuck to this program, indeed, in later statements and memoranda the list of security measures to maintain the German character of Alsace-Lorraine was further expanded. In the Kreuznach program of

August 9, fixed during the first meeting with Michaelis, the OHL demanded the establishment of land acquisition societies for swift Germanization of real property; the purchase of forest land by Prussia; the separation from French influence of the clergy, and especially of school and hospital nurses; and the elimination of "inbreeding" in the Alsatian civil service. As earlier on in April, annexation by Prussia was declared to be the best solution by far, since Germany needed a broad and uniformly administered and occupied military border strip on its southwestern border. This would require three army corps, which only Prussia could muster—Bavaria could not even raise one.[39]

Michaelis did succeed in having the possibility of Alsace-Lorraine becoming a federal state, at the request of the Reichstag, at least considered. In such an eventuality, said the Kreuznach agreement, the security measures mentioned must be effected in such a manner that "Alsace-Lorraine would not lead a separate life." Its railway system would have to be joined to those of Prussia-Hesse, and the military sovereignty of the king of Prussia would have to remain intact.[40]

Ludendorff also made an effort to convince the Reichstag deputies and Reich agencies that the people of Alsace-Lorraine were "unreliable" in a nationalist sense, for the purpose of discouraging the granting of federal autonomy. He was vigorously supported by the Pan-Germans, who had the historian Dietrich Schäfer work out a memorandum on Alsace-Lorraine for the Chancellor—its date is August 27.[41]

The General Staff collected a pile of documents about political misdeeds in Alsace-Lorraine, which on August 1 were combined into a comprehensive indictment, duplicated in the Prussian war ministry for distribution to government agencies and Reichstag deputies.[42] Nor did Ludendorff, in private letters and memoranda to the Chancellor, neglect to warn the Chancellor against granting autonomy to Alsace-Lorraine, an act, he said, that was bound to bring on fateful consequences. "In my view an independent federal state of Alsace-Lorraine would be lost to Germany. It would become a breeding ground for unlimited French machinations."[43]

The OHL wheeled up its biggest guns late in the year, in a comprehensive memorandum that had been requested by Hertling. On this occasion, the list of indispensable security measures was once again expanded.[44] The main addition was a considerable prolongation of military control. In the event of annexation by Prussia—or Prussia and Bavaria—it was to last at least ten years; if the existing status were continued, twenty years; and if autonomy were granted, more than a generation.

The meaning was quite clear. Against such massive resistance, it is unlikely that autonomy could have been pushed through, even had it been demanded by an overwhelming Reichstag majority and the unanimous voices of the various government agencies concerned. No such thing happened. Once again the national liberals perceptibly departed from the line of the leftist parties. Despite the entreaties of the deputy van Calker, their central committee publicly and emphatically rejected "any unrolling of the so-called question of Alsace-Lorraine in wartime."[45]

The governor of Alsace-Lorraine, von Dallwitz, an old-style conservative Prussian civil servant to whom Michaelis appealed as his first adviser, seemed at first not inclined to radical rejection of autonomy; but like the OHL he made it dependent on a long series of security measures. They were formulated in more cautious terms than Ludendorff's. Among other things, Dallwitz called for financial support from the central government for financially weak Alsace-Lorraine and especially emphasized the need for training a cadre of civil servants and teachers, partly at German universities. This was almost certainly a well-founded demand, but such a measure would have been bound to weaken the effects of any autonomy act on the people of Alsace-Lorraine, especially since it was to be supplemented with military security measures.[46] Above all, these were minimum demands to which the Reich administration in Alsace-Lorraine might have become reconciled. They did not amount to anything like true autonomy.

Dallwitz subsequently prepared a memorandum for Hertling on the whole question,[47] from which it becomes plain that this doubtless competent and well-meaning bureaucrat had no better grasp than his colleagues of the true political meaning of the autonomy movement at this juncture. He rightly protested against the illusion that elevation of Alsace-Lorraine to the status of a federal state might put the French in a more conciliatory mood or even persuade them to make peace. The contemplated measure was as unlikely to conciliate the French as it was to result in the sudden conversion of the Alsatians into fervent German patriots.

What Erzberger and the representatives of the Reichstag majority wanted, of course, was primarily a declaration of allegiance to Germany by the Alsatian diet, which had been elected under the universal franchise. Such a declaration was expected to have an effect similar to that of the Reichstag resolution of July 19 and the public declaration foregoing German claims to Belgium, which the same parties had demanded. It was intended to counteract enemy propaganda and diminish enthusiasm for the war.

It was questionable whether the propaganda effect would have been commensurate with the risks that the step would have entailed, and the possible effects abroad must remain much in doubt. We do know today that the French argument that separation of Alsace-Lorraine from Germany would be merely an act of restoration (*désannexion*) rather than outright annexation of foreign territory did not by any means meet with immediate and undivided agreement in the Entente camp. By January 1918 the moral reservations entertained by Wilson and his advisers were still strong enough for the point to be passed over in silence in the first draft of the message to Congress of January 8, with its famous Fourteen Points. The second draft said that "if Alsace-Lorraine should again be apportioned to France, Germany should receive a similar advantage." The president cut this only at the last moment and found this formulation: "The wrong done to France by Prussia in 1871 in the matter of Alsace-Lorraine, which has unsettled the peace of the world for nearly fifty years, should [not must!] be righted. . . . " This language still left open whether and how this would be done, and whether a plebiscite would be part of such a plan.48

We know that in the winter of 1917-1918 the French government was deeply worried, lest the radical socialist demand for a plebiscite in Alsace-Lorraine prevail and deter British public opinion from unconditional support for *désannexion* and for a struggle to the end to achieve it. The attitude of the British leftist press and the Labour party did indeed lend weight to this French concern. Even Lloyd George was very cautious in his public utterances on Alsace-Lorraine. Only on January 18, in a discussion with trade union leaders, did he unequivocally concede the French the right to decide for themselves what would be a "fair" solution to the problem of Alsace-Lorraine. In the circumstances, a timely public declaration by the Strasbourg diet in favor of the creation of an autonomous German federal state might have seriously interfered with the designs of the Paris politicians, to whom the autonomy movement in Alsace-Lorraine had always been a thorn in the flesh.49

Surely here was a real political opportunity for Germany. It is characteristic of the mentality of the top bureaucracy in Germany that the existence of such a chance was scarcely appreciated. The foreign ministry had, after all, even under the leadership of so experienced a career diplomat as Kühlmann, failed to understand, or at least had underestimated the propaganda value of a public declaration on Belgium as well. What happened, in other words, was that the intensely political problem of Alsace-Lorraine fell into the hands of the bureaucrats. They may have been conscientious and knowledgeable men, but they were uniquely lacking in political audacity, and they failed to see that the favorable hour—if indeed there was such a time—passed as they engaged in their careful deliberations. In typical bureaucratic fashion, the question was being "closely studied," which meant that a decision was simply put off.50

In time the Alsatian Reichstag deputies grew impatient and tried to exert pressure on the government. On September 28, jointly with deputies of the majority parties, they introduced a motion before the main committee of the Reichstag in which they demanded an immediate bill for the creation of an autonomous state of Alsace-Lorraine and the simultaneous convocation of the Alsatian diet to settle the details.51 The democratic deputy Payer proposed that the diet first apply for the granting of autonomy, at the same time acknowledging the indissoluble allegiance of Alsace-Lorraine to Germany, and that the Reichstag only then give its assent. The Chancellor and Vice-Chancellor Helfferich strongly agreed. Both, however, tried hard to prevent immediate public discussion of this delicate question in the Reichstag, on the grounds that the government was not yet able to take a stand, having yet to discuss the matter with its allies. Michaelis promised to do so at once and to report back to the deputies within the week.

One wonders whether Chancellor and Vice-Chancellor were really aware of what was at stake in a political sense and whether they were prepared to back autonomy with the necessary energy. Helfferich thought autonomy extremely hazardous, much preferring annexation by Prussia; but he shrank from a conflict with the Reichstag and was not sure whether it might not be wise to grant autonomy in return for the psychological gain of a pro-German declaration by the Strasbourg diet—provided the guarantees asked by the governor could be included, to be supplemented by further military measures.[52]

Michaelis's own attitude appears to have been ambiguous. On September 29 he told the Württemberg chargé d'affaires that the reason why he had not rebuffed the party representatives was that the contemplated declaration might weaken the French position on *désannexion* and possibly hasten peace.[53] Two days later, on October 1, in the Prussian cabinet, he spoke in a rather different vein. The decision, he said, should be postponed until after the peace, if possible. It was a purely internal German matter and should not be discussed in sight of the enemy. He would do everything he could to keep the majority parties in the Reichstag from further action, speaking to the party leaders individually and also in the sevens committee and advising them of the serious objections to autonomy and the sweeping guarantees its grant would entail.

He also proposed that they should at the very least wait for the necessary initiative on the part of the Alsatian diet, anticipating that they would then be likely to desist from their undertaking. That, of course, was not certain. The Reichstag was evidently looking for a chance to demonstrate its power to the government, and it had picked the issue with considerable care, for the government could not risk an open conflict on it. That would have a devastating propaganda effect in Britain and France, where it would be cheerfully pointed out that the Germans simply did not know what to do about Alsace-Lorraine.

The cabinet responded as desired. There was a hail of objections from every side, not only to the granting of autonomy but to the power aspirations of the Reichstag, most pointedly from Drews, the Prussian minister of the interior. A stereotyped nationalist response was that Alsace-Lorraine, by its attitude, had simply not earned the boon of an autonomous constitution.

Drews said that to purchase peace at the cost of such a commitment would inevitably cause widespread resentment. The Alsatians would conclude that they owed their autonomy to France rather than to Germany. It was Count Roedern, one of the ministers, who gave the calmest, most lucid, and most objective judgment. He denied that the Reichstag demand was a bid for power and, as a former minister for Alsace, urgently warned against overestimating the defects in the existing constitution and the weight of the military indictment submitted by War Minister Stein.

Roedern described the guarantees demanded by the governor as excessive and in part politically dubious and urged that they be toned down. He favored the granting of autonomy, if, as Kühlmann thought, this would really shorten the war, even if it were by no more than two months; but even Roedern was opposed to precipitate action in so delicate a matter, unless there were compelling reasons of foreign policy, or unless the government could avert a conflict with the Reichstag in no other way.[54] Except for Roedern only Minister of Justice Spahn unequivocally supported the planned reform, though he too thought it had better be postponed until after the end of the war. Spahn did, however, wish to see a preliminary statement made, to the effect that constitutional changes were in prospect for Alsace-Lorraine.

Summarizing the discussion, Michaelis said that he still thought autonomy for Alsace-Lorraine should be considered, despite the numerous warnings against it he had received from various organizations, party groups, and political personages in Alsace. His tone sounded positive, but all that he probably meant was that he was unwilling to risk an open conflict with the Reichstag on the issue. What he wished to do immediately was to shelve it until war's end.

This was presumably the spirit in which he addressed the Kaiser in person on the following day at supreme headquarters—the cabinet meeting had actually been held in preparation for this audience. He told Admiral Müller that he was confident about the Reichstag. He hoped he had said enough in committee to avoid a statement on the floor.[55] It is not certain whether he took advantage of the opportunity to discuss the question of Alsace-Lorraine with Ludendorff.[56] Ludendorff did write him on October 6 that he had heard that the Chancellor was firmly resolved not to yield to the demands for the granting of autonomy to Alsace-Lorraine, a decision with which he strongly agreed. He added some advice on how South German annexationist desires might be circumvented without endangering border security. He naturally wanted all the areas that really mattered firmly integrated with Prussia, leaving Bavaria and Baden only a few rural districts devoid of strategic importance.[57]

When Michaelis received this letter he had already held the crucial discussion on the issue of Alsace with the representatives of the majority parties that had been agreed upon on September 29, departing once again for head-quarters immediately afterward, on the night of October 6-7.[58] Apparently he preserved silence before the deputies on the OHL stand, assuring them instead that he had in the meantime discussed the question of autonomy for Alsace-Lorraine with representatives of the three kingdoms [Bavaria, Saxony, and Württemberg] and Baden. He said that all the governments were opposed to the Reichstag dealing with the issue at the present time and to associating it with the question of peace. First to be settled were the terms for the creation of an autonomous federal state—in other words, the "guarantees." Negotiations on these matters were continuing with the governments con-cerned, and he hoped to have a bill ready by December.[59]

Was Michaelis in earnest about this promise, or was it merely an excuse to sweep the whole question of Alsace-Lorraine under the rug without precipi-tating a conflict with the Reichstag? From his statements in the cabinet, the latter conclusion is the more likely. It was surely a poor excuse to cite the alleged opposition of the major federated governments to the treatment of the autonomy issue, when Premier Weizsäcker had actually wired the tenta-tive agreement of the Württemberg government. True, Count Hertling had paid another visit to Berlin on September 30 to raise objections, but in the end he contented himself with warning against precipitate action and recom-mending that the whole thing be "properly staged." He had returned to Munich reassured, for Michaelis had strongly agreed and promised that he would first negotiate with Alsace-Lorraine on the "guarantees."[60]

There was actually no longer the slightest chance that autonomy for Alsace-Lorraine would come to pass. First and foremost, Ludendorff's abso-lute veto stood in the way. Its impact may be judged from the fact that during the "state of siege" the Strasbourg diet had not even been permitted to meet, let alone debate political matters, without the express authorization of the highest military authorities in Alsace-Lorraine. Then too, if Michaelis were really to make good his promise to negotiate further within the federal council on the prerequisites for the granting of autonomy, it was immediately predictable that more and more guarantees would be demanded. Even if, against all the odds, a bill were written by the end of the year, it would be so weighed down with reservations that the Alsatians would have no inducement to give Germany a loyalty declaration. Oddly enough neither Erzberger, the eternal optimist, nor his party friends and Reichstag associates foresaw this. They were content with the Chancellor's information and pledge.

They may have wavered in their attitude because of the unexpectedly reserved stand Kühlmann took in the conference between the parties and the Chancellor on September 29. Earlier on the minister had favored meeting Alsatian wishes and thus winning over the *Reichslande* to a clear and unequi-vocal profession of allegiance to the Reich.[61] Now he said that current discussion of the question of Alsace-Lorraine in the Reichstag would constitute a serious foreign policy handicap. At the moment a Reichstag resolution would be most undesirable. He had good reason to say this, on the basis of French intelligence received.62

What Kühlmann undoubtedly had in the back of his mind was the news from Brussels (see Chapter 1, Part 4) to the effect that Briand had agreed to secret talks with Envoy von der Lancken, on the subject of Alsace-Lorraine. Kühlmann had only just received a note from Lancken recommending that the prospect of elevating Alsace-Lorraine to the status of a full-fledged federal state be held out to the French as Germany's maximum concession, France being permitted to take the credit for this action.63 If the Reichstag were indeed to decide to grant Alsace-Lorraine autonomy immediately, the German negotiator would no longer hold a card he could play in his bid for peace.64

Actually, Kühlmann himself well knew that this kind of horse-trading for peace would be uncertain and uncongenial. He did admit that if the initiative came from Strasbourg and if the whole thing were properly staged he would have far fewer reservations. As we have already seen, this was Payer's proposal as well. It was indeed the only way that might have proved feasible – the kind of peace negotiations Kühlmann had in mind were the merest pipe dream. The Strasbourg diet, however, was unlikely to be persuaded to issue the desired declaration, unless it first had firm assurances of autonomy from the German government – and such assurances were precisely what Michaelis could not give.

A major share of the blame must, of course, be laid at the door of the OHL, with its unswerving opposition, though Michaelis avoided mention of this before the deputies and ministers; but it was not just the OHL. The risks of the measure in question were quite evidently considerable and success uncertain. An adverse opinion was voiced at the time even by the man whom Prince Max of Baden, in October 1918, was to dispatch as governor to Strasbourg, belatedly to create an autonomous regional government – much too late, as it turned out. This was Dr. Rudolf Schwander, mayor of Strasbourg, and from August to November 1917 Reich minister of economics. In a thoughtful memorandum he wrote for Hertling in December 1917, he strongly disagreed with the current German overestimate of French sympathies in Alsace-Lorraine; but he felt that years of military control had created such resentment that a sudden relinquishment of restrictions, such as autonomy was bound to bring, would have serious adverse effects. He was particularly apprehensive of the flood of emigrants who would return from France, filled with hatred of Germany and eager to agitate. In general, many serious problems would descend on the country after the war, and complete autonomy would make their solution more difficult, if not impossible. On the other hand, any measure of autonomy while a state of siege or emergency remained in effect could scarcely result in any substantial improvement in popular sentiment.[65]

In the face of such an accumulation of problems, any effort to meet the desires of the people of Alsace-Lorraine at a moment favorable to German foreign policy and thus to persuade them to profess their loyalty was foredoomed; and since this was so, there was little point in continuing even the discussion of autonomy versus partition, or annexation by Prussia or Bavaria. In the end it would be the outcome of the war itself that would settle the people's attitude, not the constitutional framework within which Alsace-Lorraine would be governed, nor whether it belonged to one German federal state or another. On October 9, after all, in an impassioned Reichstag speech, Kühlmann had declared that Germany would never relinquish Alsace-Lorraine (see Chapter 1, Part 4, above); and thus any pro-German declaration by the Strasbourg diet lacked credibility in advance. The enemy press would have derided it as a subservient echo to the master's voice rather than a free expression of the popular will.

We may now conclude our discussion of the question of Alsace-Lorraine. Despite countless reports, conferences, and exchanges of correspondence under Michaelis's successor, Count Hertling, not the slightest progress was made to the end of the war. Only two of the men Hertling asked for their opinion in December favored autonomy, Vice-Chancellor Payer without any strings, and Kühlmann with certain reservations. Payer gave the straightforward reason that autonomy was in keeping with the wishes of the Reichstag majority and constituted the only way of winning over the people to the cause of Germany. Kühlmann merely said that in the wake of the failure of Lancken's peace effort autonomy was the best solution in terms of foreign policy. It would be well-received throughout the world and possibly would even enable France to disengage itself from the goal of *désannexion.* He added that autonomy would forfeit value if it were hedged in by too many ifs and buts. One of the penalties to be paid would be that initially a wave of pro-French sympathy would seep through Alsace-Lorraine. Germany would have to stake its hopes on the chance that Alsace-Lorraine, consistently given its head, would find its way home to Germany.

The foreign minister did voice the fear that powerful military opposition would in the long run cripple such a policy, without which autonomy could not succeed. Germany would probably have to revert to the idea of partition or annexation by Prussia. The former would probably be bad for German foreign policy, the latter more favorable from a military point of view; but in view of the federal constituion it was unlikely that such annexation could be put over.[66]

Kühlmann's remarks struck a note of resignation, probably connected with the virulent quarrel between the military and the government that was raging around January 16; and Hertling could have scarcely wished to whip up the waves further by adding a debate over Alsace-Lorraine. As former premier of Bavaria he could not entirely dissociate himself from the annexationist ambitions of the king of Bavaria, which were well received by Ludendorff, out to ease the way for his plans for a Greater Balto-Prussia by concessions to the major federal states in the settlement of the question of Alsace-Lorraine.

In the wave of enthusiasm engendered by the early German successes in the great spring offensive, a vast territorial swap was worked out. Courland, Livonia, and Estonia would be joined to Prussia under direct Hohenzollern sovereignty. Lithuania would become a duchy under a Saxon prince, Poland a kingdom under a duke of Württemberg. In return, Lorraine would go to Prussia, Lower Alsace to Bavaria, and Upper Alsace to Baden. Actually, this project, agreed to between the Kaiser and Hertling on April 16 with Ludendorff's assent, was but the beginning of a whole series of plans for territorial exchange and compensation, involving more and more German federal princes and, among other things, discussion of an even more sweeping dismemberment of Alsace-Lorraine.

Against a backdrop of inexorably approaching military disaster, this free-for-all among the German dynasties for royal and ducal crowns and patches of territory here and there makes an almost spectral impression. Needless to say, it took place entirely behind closed doors. All through the winter the majority parties, especially the social democrats, worried about autonomy for Alsace-Lorraine and made further efforts on its behalf, though in time sentiment within the center party changed. By the spring of 1918 even Hertling seems to have slowly realized that no practical solution was possible until war's end, and that things would have to continue as they were until then. German interest in the question had sharply declined even before that time. Once again the people of Alsace-Lorraine were bitterly disappointed. By late January the Alsatian deputies Ricklin and Hauss had given up all hope that it would be possible to rally a majority in the Strasbourg diet for the hoped-for pro-German declaration.67

4

Growing Estrangement Between Germany and Austria: The Quarrel over Poland and the Rumanian Question in the Winter of 1917-1918

Part 1
The Quarrel Over Poland; How Far Did Obligations Go Under the Alliance?

THE GERMAN government was no more able to come to terms with the OHL on the future of Poland than it was on the question of Alsace-Lorraine. The destiny of these two marginal areas in the east and the west remained an unsolved problem to the end of the war. In the east, however, this gave rise to a diplomatic controversy with allied Austria that at times in the course of the winter of 1917-1918 came close to an open break and left a yawning chasm between the two allies.

We have already heard of the big Kreuznach conference of May 17 (Vol. III, p. 440f.), which Ludendorff had carefully staged to keep the Austrians from interfering with Prussian acquisition of Lithuania and Courland. The upshot had fallen short of a firm treaty, but the respective views and war aims were put down in writing. Austria conditionally renounced the idea of a Polish "condominium" to which it had steadfastly clung until then, the condition being that the greater part of Rumania would be left to Austria. Conceding this as a goal in the peace negotiations, the Germans on their part made the reservation that they were to be given the predominant share in the ownership and exploitation of Rumanian natural resources, on which there were to be further negotiations, and also that the deal was dependent on the acquisition of Lithuania and Courland and the integration of Poland with Germany being feasible.

Count Czernin had always entertained profound doubts about this highly involved agreement, and the summer had not yet passed when they proved amply justified. Rumania was certainly a tempting prize, but Czernin was in no position to renounce Poland for good without gravely compromising his own position. It was chiefly his doing that the Austrian Reichsrat was convoked in May, after being in recess for three years, once again providing a forum for venting the grievances of Austria's non-German elements. Oddly enough, the declarations of the Czech and South Slav deputies read at the opening of the parliament were much more moderate than that of the Poles. They did call for complete reorganization, transforming the Austro-Hungarian dual monarchy into a federation of free and equal national states; but quite unlike the various émigré groups abroad, they took for granted that these states would continue to be part of an Austrian empire, and on this as on earlier occasions, they did not neglect to reaffirm loyalty to the house of Hapsburg.

Among the Poles, however, the effect of the Russian propaganda campaign in favor of self-determination had had its effect, and their statement fell just short of outright disloyalty. Dominated by the leftist democrats among them, they called for the establishment of an autonomous Polish state comprising all of Galicia and Congress Poland (i.e., the border before the Congress of Vienna and partition), with direct access to the sea. Their continued loyalty to the empire would be entirely dependent on recognition for this maximum program.[1]

In the circumstances, the position of the newly formed Seidler government was extremely precarious. It was a purely bureaucratic government and had been unable to enlist any prominent nationalists. Czernin's own position was even more difficult, for there were rumors about that he was willing to leave Poland to the Germans, thus perpetuating the division of Galicia from Congress Poland. In early July Czernin began imploring the German government to preserve the strictest secrecy concerning Article 3 of the Kreuznach agreement, in which he had actually signed away Poland. More than that, he wanted the Germans to agree to his denying that any such agreement existed, if he were asked.

After some hesitation the Germans did so agree.[2] This, of course, poses the question of what practical political value can be taken to reside in an agreement which a signatory may disavow at any time, because he dare not acknowledge it. Count Wedel, the German ambassador, put the question in precisely such terms. He said that Germany's alliance policy urgently needed revision and he made a case for this position in a comprehensive report to Chancellor Michaelis on July 22, a document that played a crucial role in the further negotiations.[3]

In Wedel's view the Russian Revolution had completely destroyed the premises on which the Kreuznach agreement was based. If there were to be a Polish national state formed from Russian Poland and integrated with Germany, it was quite out of the question to exclude Galicia and keep that province as part of Austria. The Poles would not accept such a separation, even by force. The czarist downfall had lifted the Russian pressure from them and notably democratized them, to the point where they had almost completely lost interest in Austria. They preferred to seek their destiny as a nation within the framework of a democratized Russia rather than with Germany. Yet for Austria the loss of Galicia would be tantamount to losing the whole war against Russia—the great economic and military importance of Galicia had become fully evident only in the course of the war. Many Austrians would regard the relinquishment of Galicia as the beginning of the end and blame Austria's German ally, fanning the flames of anti-German and anti-Prussian sentiment, which had already taken on frightening dimensions. On the domestic scene too the Vienna government could scarcely put up with the permanent loss of its Polish-speaking Galician nationals, for it needed the Galician deputies as well as those from German-speaking Austria to maintain a parliamentary majority. Without them it could not push through the war appropriations.

Count Wedel saw but one chance to save Galicia for Austria and regain its allegiance for that country. That was the so-called "Austro-Polish solution." Polish national aspirations must be fulfilled within the framework of the Austrian Empire. He recommended this solution to the Chancellor in the German interest as well, pointing out that in return for foregoing a Polish satellite inhabited by people who hated Germany, a much harder bargain could be struck with Austria. The alliance could be enduringly strengthened by a military convention; a huge and highly integrated trading area, including the new Poland, could be created; and the agreement covering Rumania might be modified in Germany's favor. Wedel agreed that some adjustments in Germany's border with Poland were probably necessary but urgently recommended that they be held to a minimum. He regarded a "triolist" system as highly desirable in the reorganization of Austria. Under such a system, Poland would become the third partner, with Austria and Hungary. The Polish-speaking deputies would leave the Austrian parliament, which would then have a safe majority of German-speaking deputies.

We are by now quite familiar with such arguments and proposals. After all, they formed the substance of the endless, painful, and ultimately fruitless debates between German and Austrian governments that lasted from August 1914 to the spring of 1916 (see Vol. III, Chapter 4). We recall that Bethmann Hollweg at the time considered the Austro-Polish solution very seriously and concluded that it was the one "least unfavorable" to Germany; but he added the qualification that Germany's economic interests in Poland must be protected by a comprehensive Austro-German economic alliance. The Dual Alliance of 1879 would have to be greatly strengthened into a mutual assistance pact and Slavic predominance in Austria curbed by sweeping constitutional reform. All these objectives had then proved to be unattainable. Indeed, there had been virtually no common ground for an agreement on the problem of Poland.

Were the prospects now better? Constitutional change in Austria, especially an end to the obsolete "dualist" system, had become both more urgent and more perilous, for the whole country was threatened with disintegration. Since America's entry into the war, ultimate victory on the part of the Central Powers had become even more uncertain than before—at the very least it seemed further off than ever. After all, President Wilson—in his great peace speech of January 22, 1917—had outlined prospects for the Poles which the Central Powers could never match. Under his program, all areas inhabited by Poles were to be joined to form a new and independent Polish state. It is true that neither Britain nor France had immediately incorporated these maximum demands into their own war aims programs, though the émigré Poles led by the national democrat Dmovsky zealously beat the propaganda drum for them in all the capitals of Western Europe. The two powers were deterred by consideration for their Russian ally, prior to the October Revolution. Afterward Britain for some time still hesitated to opt for the "Balkanization" of Central Europe in the wake of Austrian disintegration. This, it felt, would destroy the last bulwarks against the spread of Bolshevism. For that reason London, even as late as December 1917 was far friendlier to the Austro-Polish solution than Count Wedel could have realized when he made his recommendations to Berlin. The kind of solution the British then favored would, of course, have ignored the integrity of German territory and driven a deep wedge between the two Central Powers. Either way, in the event of an Entente victory, glittering prospects would open up for the Poles, and this was formally confirmed when by the end of the year all the Western powers had recognized the Polish émigré national committee in Paris as a kind of government-in-exile.[4]

These developments did not at one stroke wreck the continuing efforts of the Central Powers to elaborate the new state they were creating, nor did they take the steam out of the controversy over whether Germany or Austria should be top dog in Poland. They did, however, greatly limit the immediate political significance of the quarrel; for in the end, much as in Alsace-Lorraine, the people's attitude and the success of the efforts at wooing them depended on the changing fortunes of war to a far greater extent than on what political steps the two Central Powers took and why they quarreled. Our own interest in the quarrel is limited to tracing the manner in which it once again expressed the conflict between political and military thinking.

Hindenburg almost immediately heard about Wedel's report in general terms through General Cramon, the German liaison officer at Austrian headquarters.5 Cramon, as a matter of fact, expressed agreement with the ambassador; and despite Wedel's warnings, he seems to have tried hard to get the OHL to agree as well. The OHL was simultaneously advised by Governor General Beseler that Michaelis had discussed Wedel's proposals with him, to Beseler's consternation. The result was what Wedel had feared from the beginning. Hindenburg voiced indignant objections to the Chancellor.6

We already know that Ludendorff had grown to loathe the Poles and that he was absolutely indifferent to Austrian needs and desires. He now let the Chancellor know, through Hindenburg, that a Poland in Austrian hands was quite unacceptable in a military sense. Austro-Polish influence would inevitably overflow into Lithuania and wreak havoc in the Polish-speaking parts of Prussia as well. Rather than leaving Poland to Austria, it would be in the German interest to hand the country back to Russia, exacting generous "border rectifications." Such a solution would pose fewer political and military dangers to Germany and would clarify the situation in a military sense. For the time being, the program of constructing a German-dominated Poland along Beseler's autonomy lines should continue. Here Ludendorff was striking a new note. Apparently he was beginning to anticipate that the Poles might openly defect to Austria.

Initially the new Chancellor displayed considerable uncertainty about the Polish question. He seemed to share the dislike of the new Poland entertained by Ludendorff and the Prussian conservatives and would have preferred to see it once again treated as occupied territory. Once a wide border strip had been ceded—as envisaged by the OHL—he was quite willing to leave the remainder to its own resources, i.e., to Russia. When he put this forward at a Vienna conference on August 1, it turned out that Count Wedel had not yet dropped even a hint to Czernin about his proposals. Czernin was at that time deeply involved in secret negotiations with France on a separate peace (see p. 34f., above), and he tried to persuade the new Chancellor to make concessions to the French in Alsace-Lorraine, as he had done with Bethmann Hollweg the preceding spring (see Vol. III, pp. 393, 396, and *passim*). He reiterated the offer he had made before. Austria would cede Galicia to the new German-oriented Polish state, if Germany were willing to relinquish at least part of Alsace-Lorraine in the cause of peace, and if Austria were compensated in Rumania.7 Although he was immediately rebuffed and opposed, he repeated the offer again at the large Berlin meeting on August 14, already discussed (see p. 35), and only then dropped it as hopeless.

At both these meetings he must have noticed, however, that his German allies had largely lost their zest for building up a German-oriented Polish national state.8 When Kühlmann visited Vienna on September 1, Czernin took advantage of the occasion to probe whether the Kreuznach agreement of May 18 might not be revised along the lines of Germany enjoying a stronger position of preference in Rumania, while the same would be true of Austria in Poland. The German minister did not reject the idea outright but predicted that the OHL would offer strenuous objections, which soon proved to be the case; yet Ludendorff, at this time, was indeed showing growing interest in German predominance in Rumania.[9]

Soon afterward Czernin voiced his desires even more plainly to Ambassador Wedel, who at once reported to Kühlmann, reminding him of his own proposals of July 27 and urgently commending Czernin's request. He grew even more insistent on September 29, following another talk with Czernin, who had bluntly told him that the Germano-Polish solution would make it impossible to preserve the alliance. Such a Poland would become an everlasting bone of contention, a second Schleswig-Holstein. Unless this issue were resolved, there would be no alternative. The two empires would have to "seek a different orientation."[10]

Here was no longer request or even demand but an unvarnished threat, marking an unexpectedly abrupt change of line. Wedel offered no counterarguments; on the contrary, he supported Czernin with political arguments of his own. Czernin, he said, was dependent on the Poles—nothing could be done with the Czechs. The Germans, who did not really need the Poles, might ignore them in formulating government policy, but in Vienna that was impossible. Wedel foresaw trouble for Czernin in the impending negotiations of the joint delegation of the Hungarian and Austrian parliaments. An Austro-Polish solution, he thought, would greatly ease the situation.

Even before this report reached Berlin there had been an abrupt change of view there. It emanated from the Kaiser himself, who had taken a fancy to fair and fertile Rumania during a front-line tour, while he had taken a corresponding dislike to the stark monotony of Poland. In September he took the Chancellor by surprise when he voiced a strong preference for exchanging Poland for Rumania. He thought this would please Austria and was dissuaded only with difficulty from passing on the good news to Emperor Charles on the way back, without consulting the foreign ministry or the OHL and without first settling the terms on which the exchange would be made. Nevertheless Michaelis and Kühlmann agreed with him in principle. Apparently Wedel's reports had convinced them. The sole remaining obstacle would be the OHL, whose opposition the Kaiser would personally seek to overcome.[11]

He met with only limited success, as was shown in a conference at Kreuznach on October 7 that lasted for many hours, with the Chancellor, the minister, and the generals participating. In favoring Polish integration with Austria, Kühlmann used essentially Wedel's arguments. Such an outcome could not be avoided in the long run and could now be granted in return for important advantages. Among these were a customs union, a military pact to strengthen the alliance, and economic predominance in Rumania.

Hindenburg and Ludendorff displayed deep distrust of Austria, indeed outright hostility, and viewed the relinquishment of Poland as highly dangerous. Hindenburg warned against any step that would strengthen Austria, which would only try to expand its dominion. He went so far as to say that if it came to war with Austria, the Hohenzollerns stood in danger of becoming Hapsburg vassals! Germany must make a show of strength to the Austrians instead of—as Ludendorff added—"always doing what the Austrians want us to do."

"Poland will bring war with Austria," Ludendorff went on, and this time Hindenburg added that the German element in Austria was really of no interest; but despite this obstructive bluster, the two generals allowed themselves to be drawn into a discussion of the terms that should be put to Austria if Poland were relinquished. In the wake of this discussion Ludendorff immediately submitted to Chancellor and foreign minister what were in effect the OHL's minimum terms, in the form of twenty-four points, the acceptance of which would have devalued the Austro-Polish solution completely, for both the Austrians and the Poles.

They included large cessions of Polish territory to Germany, sweeping economic guarantees for German industry, especially in terms of railway transport and natural resources, and certain general privileges for Germans in Poland.[12] In addition there were outright exactions from Austria, which was to cede the German parts of Austrian Silesia to Germany, i.e., the region of Teschen. Ludendorff's argument was that Germany needed direct passage to Hungary, but in a letter of October 11 to Michaelis he also mentioned considerations of popular sentiment. The acquisition of Teschen was likely to be the only quid pro quo the Germans might find acceptable in return for relinquishing Poland, gained at the cost of so much German blood.

Austria was also to cede a naval base on the Adriatic, Vlonë or Cattaro, renounce any intention of placing a Hapsburg on the Rumanian throne, leave Rumania politically, militarily, and economically entirely to Germany, facilitate German access to Rumania by way of the Danube, and above all pledge to continue in the war until German war aims too were achieved.[13] The Vienna government was further to agree not to intervene in any way in the settlement of questions affecting Germany's western border, including Belgium, while at the same time supporting Germany's claims to the return of its colonies and also to the acquisition of Lithuania and Courland. The questions of a customs union and a military convention were to remain open, and in a supplementary letter Ludendorff expressly reserved the right to put forward additional demands.

The whole matter had grown far beyond an exchange of territory into an attempt at blackmail. Austria's obvious dilemma in the Polish question was to be exploited for purposes of forcing the country into resistless acceptance of

German annexationist policies, while in return it was granted no more than a mutilated Poland completely dominated by Germany in an economic sense. This was a program oriented along lines altogether different from what Wedel and Kühlmann had envisaged. Naturally these two appreciated, as had Bethmann Hollweg in 1915-1916, that leaving Poland with its markedly Slavic character as a federal state to the feeble Vienna government held a certain danger for Germany—even though Kühlmann remarked that there were dangers in every solution to the Polish question, while there were no truly vital conflicts between the two allies.

The two statesmen did strongly press for strengthening the alliance over the long run, in both a military and a political sense, along the lines of the *Mitteleuropa* program of 1915-1916 (see Vol. III, Chapter 4). They further sought to establish the closest possible economic integration with Austria, in such a way that Austrian tariffs would not bar Germany's access to the Polish market, and through it to the Russian; but the two generals showed themselves utterly incapable of thinking about Austria in terms other than militant power politics.

Customs union and military convention, they said, could not be regarded as a satisfactory quid pro quo for the Austro-Polish solution. On the contrary, if that solution came about at all, Austria would virtually have to beg for so magnanimous a German gift. A customs union might bring Germany certain advantages, but only if a tariff wall against Austrian Poland were maintained.[14] As for a military convention, they concluded, the OHL was not in the least interested. The preceding discussion had already revealed the reason. When Michaelis had proposed that such a convention be "imposed" on Austria to suit Germany, Ludendorff had remarked that it would have to insure that Austria remained militarily weak. He viewed Austria as a potential enemy power, in other words, as one that must not on any account be strengthened.

Was this still a purely military approach? Hardly. Outright dislike manifestly played a part, together with the "popular sentiment" Ludendorff had already invoked. He could not bear to leave the great prize in the east to so vastly inferior an ally who had blundered so wretchedly—even though that prize might immediately appear to be a burden to Germany rather than a gain.[15]

Michaelis entertained similar fears. He anticipated that the relinquishment of Poland would expose his government to bitter attack and did not wish to commit himself finally until he had consulted the Reichstag parties.[16] Actually his government was already on the way out and his successor, Hertling, had long favored the Austro-Polish solution. The diplomats thus promptly went to work. Wedel prepared a long critical commentary on the OHL demands, many of which he found superfluous or at least not urgent. He did admit, however, that German public opinion would not regard German predominance in Rumania, which was relatively far away, as the full equivalent of Poland. He spoke vaguely of "expanding German power," but carefully avoided touching on the question of where this expansion was to take place.[17] He insistently warned against cutting a broad border strip away from Poland, preferring to seek border security in the east by means of a military convention that would bring the Austrian as well as the Polish military under German control. As for the cession of any part of Austrian Silesia, Wedel thought this quite unattainable and likely to bring a very bad reaction besides.

Only two days later Kühlmann agreed with Czernin on a common program, as yet only along very general lines.[18] Austria was to enter into a twenty-year mutual assistance pact with Germany, together with a military convention providing for uniform weapons systems and joint action on all necessary war measures. A conference of the leading statesmen of both countries was to work out guidelines for a union, in respect of financial policy, to lower tariff barriers as much as possible. In return, Germany agreed to adopt a position on the Belgian question that would insure that it would offer no obstacle to peace. There were to be neither territorial nor constitutional incursions, but instead a direct settlement with the king of Belgium. A reassuring statement to this effect was to be handed to Emperor Charles.

Germany further agreed to the kingdom of Poland coming under Hapsburg sovereignty, with appropriate guarantees—like Austria and Hungary, Poland would have to accept the German customs and army systems. Austria, in turn, with similar guarantees, pledged close integration of Rumania with Germany and an economic pact that would give special consideration to Rumanian goods in transit to Germany. Neither country would enforce these territorial clauses against the will of the people concerned, mutually agreeing to launch the propaganda necessary to that end. Czernin added a special clause: Courland and Lithuania would be granted autonomy and would become closely integrated with Germany—this was probably the "expansion" Wedel had had in mind.

This agreement of October 22 between the two foreign ministers represents the closest approximation to the idea of *Mitteleuropa* attained by Germany and Austria in the course of the war. Two days later the combined armies advanced at Flitsch and Tolmein on the Italian front, which promptly collapsed, once again bathing the two powers in the glory of a victorious comradeship-in-arms.

Kühlmann apparently now staked great hopes on the contemplated strengthening of the alliance that would bring enduring improvement in the power of both countries. Soon afterward, at a conference in Berlin, he cited Bismarck's policy of securing an alliance with Austria as soon as possible after the war of 1866. To make his proposals appear in a tempting light to the generals, he even spoke of a possible bloc of 230 million people in the heart of Europe—this was evidently meant to tie up with the *Mitteleuropa* movement of 1915.[19]

In the face of Austria's internal situation, all such hopes were bound to be uncertain and dubious, especially since the admission of some twenty million Poles to the Austrian Empire would water down its German character even further. This is probably the reason why the text of the agreement of October 22 spoke of only a loose connection between Poland and Austria, purely in terms of a Hapsburg sovereign. Evidently the "triolist" solution had already been abandoned as not feasible.

For the rest, the agreement did not pretend to be anything more than a preliminary guideline for further negotiations between the two allies. There were no formal signatures, and in the German copy the clause that came close to being the most important one for Czernin was afterward crossed out, probably because Kühlmann dropped it in the negotiations with the OHL that were soon to follow.[20]

This meeting took place in Berlin on November 3, a large and carefully prepared conference of all the departments concerned, to be supplemented by a Prussian cabinet meeting the following day, and concluded at an especially impressively staged crown council at Bellevue palace on November 5. Kühlmann, supported by Vice-Chancellor Helfferich and Count Roedern, made his case with his wonted diplomatic and oratorical skill, while the new Chancellor, Count Hertling, only just in office, virtually limited himself to the role of spectator.

During these discussions the Polish question was once again reviewed in all its aspects, its many and ultimately insoluble problems being aired at length. Once again Governor General Beseler served as the protagonist of the Germano-Polish solution. Yet the proponents of the Austro-Polish solution, countering the objections of the OHL which were put forward with undiminished sharpness, enjoyed the advantage of the argument that in one way or another the Austro-Polish solution was bound to prevail in the end, since so numerous a people as the Poles could scarcely be ruled against their will. If action were taken now, guarantees could be extracted from Austria.

A second argument proved perhaps even more effective in the Prussian cabinet—the Kaiser had already made up his mind; and indeed, at the crown council he fought vigorously for his latest pet notion, swapping Poland for Rumania, at times using very strong language. Of course the Austrians would never get their way with Poland without a quid pro quo. It was necessary to "pepper them with conditions until their eyes watered." Such language began to bring the resentful OHL round. Hindenburg at once announced that there would have to be large-scale strategic border improvements, from Upper

Silesia to East Prussia, reaching out particularly deeply east of Thorn, along the Warta and Vistula.[21]

The upshot was acceptance of the Austro-Polish solution; but also accepted as representing the preponderant view of the participants was the need for substantial "corrections" in Germany's eastern border, even if Poland were to fall to Germany.[22] The details of such a new line seem not to have been discussed; but at the crucial departmental meeting of November 3 Ludendorff pushed through virtually his entire list of twenty-four "conditions" that Austria must observe—even the demand that it must hold completely aloof from the Belgian question and agree to Germany's intended solution of the question of Courland and Lithuania, especially the integration with the latter of the districts of Vilnyus and Grodno.

Doubts did arise in connection with the cession of any part of Austrian Silesia. The Austrians would probably offer unswerving opposition. Consideration was given to the idea of resting content with a direct rail connection to Hungary, without Austrian control at any point. There was no agreement on the question of a military convention, which the OHL stubbornly rejected, arguing that Germany had no interest in further strengthening Austria. Kühlmann, on his part, thought it would forge a strong bond of unity and wished to see the convention expanded to include Poland.[23]

Immediately after the crown council the Austrian negotiators showed up in Berlin, and they were bound to be depressed when they heard what had happened. At the morning session on November 6, moreover, Ludendorff rather than Kühlmann played the major role, and this very fact made it abundantly clear where the ultimate power of decision lay on the German side. Ludendorff made no bones about his repugnance toward the Austro-Polish solution and the "tremendous increment in power" he thought it would bring Austria. He also voiced his distrust of Austria's ability to protect Germany against growing Polish ambitions directed toward Danzig (Gdansk) and the Polish-speaking provinces of Prussia. He demanded a further eastward shift, on the basis of German war gains and military necessity, as an indispensable guarantee against such dangers. To this end he produced a map prepared long before, which included the Polish coal and industrial region of Dombrova (Bendzin) in the south, allegedly indispensable to the military security of industrial Upper Silesia.

Ludendorff ignored Austrian objections that all this amounted to a fourth partition of Poland, in defiance of solemn promises given by the Central Powers on November 5, 1916, on the occasion of the founding of the Polish state. The Poles, he said, had completely failed to live up to the hopes the Germans then entertained. As for the idea that large-scale German annexations could serve only to fire the flames of Polish irredentism, that kind of thinking was utterly foreign to his soldier's mind. On the contrary, he pressed for effecting the annexations at once and paid no attention to the Austrian counterdemand that in that event the German rear-echelon area with Warsaw should be handed over to Austria at once. No understanding was reached, in other words.

At the afternoon session, during which the OHL was not represented, Ludendorff's twenty-four conditions for relinquishing Poland were presented to the Austrians, with the exception of the most delicate points, which Kühlmann apparently dared not mention—hands off Belgium, Austria to fight on for German war aims, the cession of parts of Austrian Silesia.[24] The disillusioned Austrians learned that all they would get in Poland was a kind of "condominium," with their German partners enjoying many economic and ethnic privileges.

Of course they demanded full parity—German predominance in Rumania, Austrian in Poland, everything clear and aboveboard. They declined to discuss any details of the long program with which they had been confronted, unless they first had a chance to consult the two premiers, in Vienna. There was no other course than to postpone the decisions. Both Vienna and Berlin were to work out a formal draft of the alliance between the two powers.[25] The question of a military convention was not even discussed. The German government was to provide an exposé on the economic issues, while an Austrian counterproposal for border rectifications was to be transmitted to Berlin and Kreuznach.

There was a clear desire to continue the talks, and they were, in fact, continued all through the winter; but Ludendorff's meddling, his mixing up all manner of military and economic conditions, infinitely complicated what had been originally planned as an approach to taking the strain off the wartime alliance. The severe challenges to both the Austrians and Poles could have but one predictable result. All the fine plans would bog down in talk and more talk.

The Russian October Revolution had in the meantime created a very different situation in the east. On the one hand military pressure on Poland ceased completely. On the other hand the conservative upper class and the Catholic clergy were much more afraid of the influence of the Bolshevist ideology. Czernin himself was deeply disappointed at the reaction of the Polish regency council to the result of the Berlin meetings—that is, German agreement in principle to the Austro-Polish solution—which had swiftly transpired because of a press leak. The Polish regents were much annoyed that the fate of their country had become the subject of decisions in which they were not even consulted—which indeed flew in the face of self-determination. Their spokesman, Ostrovsky, said that Poland insisted on complete independence and had no intention of accepting the sovereignty of any empire. Personally, he favored integration with Germany—this was probably because, as a Polish conservative, he was afraid of revolution, but perhaps he was also under the impression of the great German victory at Flitsch-Tolmein.[26] In any event, the views he expressed were certainly in keeping with Beseler's repeated predictions in Berlin, to the effect that the Poles were not in the least interested in an Austro-Polish solution. They did not wish to become an Austrian dependency.

Czernin was in a serious predicament. If he yielded to Ludendorff's demands for huge territorial cessions to Germany—he estimated that they ran to one-third of Congress Poland—he could never hope to regain Polish sympathies. He desperately searched for a way out. On November 18 he wrote to Ambassador Hohenlohe, asking whether General Arz, commander-in-chief of the Austrian army, might not come to a more moderate border strip agreement with the OHL directly, which could then be represented as merely an agreement between the generals, softening the shock effect a government pact would have on the Poles. And might the Germans not accept increased border security guaranteed by the right of military occupation in certain border areas rather than by outright annexation? In any event, the foreign ministry would secretly instruct Arz on precisely how far he could go.

It was all quite hopeless. German occupation rights in Polish border areas would lead to a kind of military condominium of the two powers on Polish soil that was bound to result in constant friction, quite apart from the fact that Ludendorff would never be satisfied. Czernin himself, furthermore, had insistently demanded that Emperor Charles must hold sole and unlimited military command power in Poland, which should be a full participant in any Austro-German military convention. The Poles should not be burdened with any manner of servitude, political or economic. All this flew directly in the face of some of the demands laid down in Ludendorff's twenty-four conditions.[27]

Late in November, in a "private letter," Czernin gave Kühlmann his "final word." Ludendorff's border demands were totally unacceptable, for Austria neither wished nor was in a position to force a dictated peace on the Poles. The minimum Czernin was willing to accept was Congress Poland, intact. If that were unattainable—which should be clear by Christmas—there was no point in further negotiations on *Mitteleuropa,* Rumania, economic union, or a closer alliance. The divided occupation of Poland would simply have to continue. In the face of the new situation on the Russian and Italian fronts, pacifist trends in Austria were growing, together with a distaste for a close and lasting association with Germany. There was a widespread desire for a free hand after the war.

Czernin was giving a kind of ultimatum, stiffened by his assertion that even the pro-German members of the Austrian interparliamentary delegation, including Count Tisza, shared his views. No one in his place, Czernin concluded, would be in a position to orient Austrian policy toward Germany unless Kreuznach yielded on the political issue; but all that Kühlmann could tell him in return was that he would do everything in his power to push through more moderate annexationist demands at the next crown council—he could hold out no hope that they would be dropped altogether. The answer was transmitted by Hohenlohe, who was not only angry over the OHL's political omnipotence but also resented its indiscretions—no confidential communication from Austria could be kept secret at German headquarters; all were instantly fed to the press for propaganda purposes.28

Czernin himself had in the meantime resorted to propaganda methods. On December 7, in a discussion among ministers of both Austria and Hungary, he had proposed that a formal press campaign be started to incite the German people against the OHL, which was to be represented as an obstacle to peace.29 Soon afterward he instructed the Austrian occupational authorities at Lublin to try to make it clear to the Poles that only an Austro-Polish solution would help them attain their goal of a national state. Since the Russian armistice, the Western powers were no longer able to do anything on behalf of Poland, while the Germans wanted an autonomous Poland on only the most modest scale. The border rectifications they were said to be planning reached close to the gates of Warsaw in the north and west. Austria would fight this and try to save as much territory as possible for Poland— indeed, try to gain further Russian territory for the Poles in the east!

Thus a propaganda campaign on behalf of the Austro-Polish solution, based on reason, had to be launched, using press reports and demonstrations. Let the Polish government plead for the retention of the military cordon against Bolshevist Russia, with the support of as many people and organizations as possible. The Polish regency council, ostensibly acting under a popular mandate, should offer the royal crown of Poland to Emperor Charles of Austria. The prospect of a coronation within six months' time could then be held out, and by that time Polish relations with Austria would have been settled.30

Was this an attempt to create a fait accompli in Poland, for the purpose of springing a surprise on Germany when the time came? There is probably no other interpretation. Yet in the event, things took an altogether different course.

For one thing, every effort to reach an understanding on border and territorial questions failed. At a Prussian cabinet meeting on December 8 Kühlmann sought support for his objections to Ludendorff's demand for the annexation of an area of 450 square miles with some two-and-a-half million Poles east of Thorn alone. He thought that improved protection for East Prussia could be obtained by advancing the border to near Ostrolenka on the Narev. Similarly, strategic cover for the industrial area of Upper Silesia might be gained by acquiring some of the high ground near Bendzin—certainly not by grabbing the Dombrova district, the most important Polish coal and industrial area by far. As for the great territorial acquisitions sought by Ludendorff east of the provinces of Poznan and West Prussia, Kühlmann thought them quite out of the question.

Kühlmann, in other words, was trying for a compromise, but enjoyed the support of only Interior Minister Drews, who warned against bringing so many Poles into the Reich. Most of the ministers dodged this precarious question; or they were so overawed by Ludendorff's authority that they were prepared to put national interest behind military concerns.[31] A similar compromise that included General Arz's counterproposals promised in Berlin fared no better. Arz was willing to rest content with better protection for East Prussia and the West Prussian-Poznan rail lines. He recommended that the southern border of East Prussia be advanced to the marshy Bobr-Narev line over a length of 125 miles. Only the northern part of the Suwalki district was to become German, in return for which the eastern border of Poland was to be advanced a bit.

Czernin still thought that these border changes were far too extensive— they would have involved some 3,600 square miles with about half a million inhabitants. Nevertheless he sent General Arz's map on to Kühlmann, as an earnest of his government's goodwill. He added that it represented a maximum offer rather than a basis for further negotiation and that he was not sure he could gain Polish assent.[32] Vain effort! Directly afterward, at the big Kreuznach meeting of December 18 over peace in the east (see p. 81) the Kaiser rejected Arz's counterproposal as unworthy of consideration. Hertling and Kühlmann vainly pointed out that there was much opposition within the Prussian cabinet to a large influx of Poles and that the Reichstag could also be expected to offer strong resistance.[33]

Before his military cronies and especially in Ludendorff's presence, the Kaiser was fond of playing the role of aggressive swashbuckler. We already know, however, that Ludendorff's sweeping annexationist plans left him ill at ease. He was greatly relieved when General Hoffmann on the morning of January 2 proposed to him on his own that the border corrections be limited to a few places of special importance (see p. 94f.). We have seen further, that when he did take a decision along these lines, he dared not uphold it against Ludendorff's furious opposition—with the effect that once again there was no hope for a meeting of the minds between Vienna and Berlin. A complicating factor was that in the meantime tension between the two allies over the peace negotiations at Brest-Litovsk had kept growing. Czernin found it intolerable that Germany should appropriate Courland and Lithuania, while Austria, having fought for three long years for Germany's war aims, should go empty-handed. He put the situation in these one-sided

terms to his emperor on December 24, proposing that two agreements covering an economic and a military association be worked out at once, to be
submitted to the Germans with a categorical declaration that they would
either have to turn over Poland to Austria on Austrian terms or face withdrawal of the Austrian propositions.[34]

If Czernin hoped that such a "proposition" might swerve the German OHL
from its inflexible attitude, he had completely misapprehended OHL sentiment. Nothing could have been less tempting to Ludendorff than the prospect of a closer alliance with Austria. Czernin's proposal, however, apparently
went back to an agreement he had reached at Brest-Litovsk with Kühlmann,
who was, after all, pulling in the same political direction. At the time, both
ministers were taking an active hand in discussions between German and
Austrian customs officials about coordinating the tariffs of the two countries.
Under way since July 1917, these talks had met heavy going and were in
danger of bogging down in a morass of detail.

The talks had been conducted in a purely routine fashion, in belated
continuation of similar efforts in 1916.[35] Now they suddenly took on great
political interest. On the German side no one was ready simply to offer to the
Austrians on a platter a Polish market that absorbed sixteen times as much in
German as in Austrian exports. Hence the feasibility of the Austro-German
solution depended in large part on the creation of an Austro-German customs
union, or at least on such a lowering of customs barriers as would prevent
German exporters from being placed at a serious disadvantage compared to
their Austrian counterparts when Poland entered the Austrian customs
sphere.

Kühlmann's intervention did bring some progress. On New Year's Day
1918 a Vienna conference agreed to reduce the remaining protective tariffs in
both number and volume and to review the entire customs system from time
to time. It did not go so far as to abolish customs duties between the two
partners altogether, mainly because the Austrians, on account of their backward industry, could not face up to such a prospect.

But the negotiations once again bogged down at this stage, for in the
course of January an Austro-Polish solution became less and less likely. The
first incident was a sharp clash between representatives of the two high commands, meeting on January 10 in Katowice to reach an agreement on the
German-Polish line to be drawn through Upper Silesia. To the horror of the
Austrians, Ludendorff's men now asked for four times as much Polish territory as Kühlmann had thought essential in his talks with Czernin at Brest-
Litovsk late in December. Not only that, they wanted a piece of Austrian
Galicia!

The reason given was merely that this was a strategically important line for the protection of the German coal pits in Upper Silesia rather than a matter of commercial gain. The Austrians found this grotesque, for the line ran straight through a highly industrialized region; and once the Poles lost the Dombrova coal region, they would be entirely dependent on imports of hard coal from Germany. There was no possibility of an understanding.[36] Vienna was well aware that a serious quarrel over the annexationist issue had in the meantime blown up between government and military in Germany (see p. 94f.). Vienna also feared that Ludendorff's iron will will prevail.

Even more lethal to Czernin's plans was the course of the negotiation at Brest-Litovsk—as we have seen, the Ukrainian delegation demanded that the Kholm region and East Galicia should go to the newly established Ukrainian state. The only concession Czernin was able to win was that while East Galicia would not be ceded outright, it would be combined with the Bukovina to form a new Ukrainian "crownland"; i.e., it would be severed from West Galicia. Predictably this surrender of Polish territory—or at least territory widely accounted to be Polish—would raise a furor in Poland. Reporting on these events before an Austrian crown council on January 22, Czernin aroused deep concern, especially on the part of the Hungarian premier, who feared that such outside interference and the formation of a crownland merely to satisfy nationalist aspirations might set a precedent that would bring on incalculable consequences.

Czernin vehemently disagreed. The Austrian foreign minister was in an unenviable predicament. It was dinned into his head day after day that Austria was close to starvation and under threat of domestic chaos—not a day must be lost in concluding a "bread peace" with the Ukraine. Hungary refused to supply enough food to Austria, or said it was unable to do so.[37] In the end Czernin did secure authorization, in view of the danger of famine, to continue talks with the Ukrainians, despite all the objections that had been voiced. In the face of Ludendorff's obstinacy—Czernin openly called Ludendorff Germany's dictator—it was decided to forego the Austro-Polish solution rather than accept a mutilated Poland that would continue to be economically oppressed and ruled by Germany. If necessary, an attempt would be made to find recompense in Rumania. In the event the Germans could not come to terms with Trotzky, the possibility of a separate Austrian peace with Russia was envisaged—it would probably take the form of Vienna simply declaring that the state of war between the two countries was terminated. So long as the Germans persisted in their annexationist demands, no further consideration was to be given to any talks with them on military and economic agreements.[38]

It was a bad end to the high hopes with which Czernin and Kühlmann, only three months before, had embarked on their alliance talks. An oppressive atmosphere hung over the crown council of January 22, meeting so soon after the bread riots and workers' rebellions, already mentioned, that broke out in the wake of the disastrous food situation. One of its consequences was increasing hostility between Austria and Hungary. Not without reason the Austrians reproached the Hungarians for failing to provide them sufficient bread grain, of which Hungary had more than enough. It is quite true that the new successor government to Count Tisza's, in a bid for popularity, had released the 1917 harvest to the people, to provide for themselves, with the result that the bulk of the supplies quickly disappeared into private hoards. Meanwhile the Rumanian emergency source had dried up, and Germany, implored time after time, was unable to continue shipments. When the crisis reached its peak, 50,000 troops had to be detailed to the task of ferreting out and forcibly seizing the flour and grain hoarded in Hungary.[39]

Sorely beset, Czernin had to stake everything on the chance of getting the German side to yield after all, thus giving him the sought-after political success of the Austro-Polish solution that would restore his authority. Directly after the crown council he instructed his ambassador in Berlin to go straight to German headquarters and make representations to Ludendorff.

Prince Hohenlohe preferred to speak to Kühlmann first and let the minister bargain with the general. Kühlmann was to tell Ludendorff that if excessive German demands were to sabotage the Austro-Polish solution, Austria would certainly seek to compensate itself in Rumania. If the Germans prevented that, there was no Austrian statesman who would be able to pursue the alliance policy as it now existed.

This was, of course, a carefully formulated threat to defect from the alliance. Surprisingly enough, it did not remain entirely without effect. At a discussion with Kühlmann and Hertling on January 23, of which we have already heard (see p. 100), Ludendorff said he would revise the border set for the coal district of Dombrova on January 10, if this became necessary for political reasons. He was only following orders from the Kaiser, who clung unconditionally to the Austro-Polish solution and had demanded to see a revised map.[40]

This was calculated to revive Czernin's flagging spirits, all the more so since the pro-Austrian propaganda his men had launched in Poland in December was just beginning to take effect. On January 28 and 29 Baron Ugron reported from Warsaw that the Polish council of ministers, in the presence of the regents, had decided to prepare for acceptance of the sovereignty of the Hapsburg emperor, keeping the preparations secret from the Germans. It seemed as though the Poles were now looking to Vienna for protection against Germany's annexationist plans, which was precisely what Czernin's propaganda had suggested.[41] It was soon to be shown, however, that this shift of sentiment in Warsaw had little practical significance. Even before then there was a serious clash with Ludendorff.

It came about during a frank exchange over concluding the talks at Brest-Litovsk, Czernin trying to get final clarification of the war aims to be pursued in common and of the limits to which the alliance obligated the partners. In Austria Czernin was being increasingly charged with allowing himself to be taken completely in tow by the OHL, which was forcing Austria to fight on for purely German goals of conquest. Even the German diplomats appreciated that Czernin was anxious to end this state of affairs.

On January 31 Count Wedel told Ambassador Mérey at the Austrian for-eign ministry that the German foreign ministry intended to hold talks with Ludendorff in the presence of Czernin and Wedel within the next few days. The purpose was to convince the general that in the long run it was impossible or at least extremely dangerous to have a German war for conquest run side by side with an Austrian war for purely defensive aims.[42] Wedel was afraid—and Hohenlohe confirmed this fear to the German foreign ministry—that the Vienna government, under pressure of public opinion, would not be able to hold out if Wilson someday offered it a separate peace that would not entail surrender of the German-speaking part of South Tyrol. All that Vienna wanted, according to Hohenlohe, was restoration of the status quo, at best with minor border rectifications and Mount Lovchen in Montenegro. In re-turn for an immediate peace, Vienna was willing to forego Poland, if only that country did not fall to Germany and the Poles were able to exercise self-determination. Unfortunately, distrust of Germany was responsible for rising tension, according to Hohenlohe, and Hertling's Reichstag speech of January 24, in which he had expressly declined to make a firm commitment about Belgium's future, had only served to deepen that distrust.[43]

In practical terms, the possibility of reaching an understanding with Aus-tria on the war aims question depended entirely on Ludendorff's attitude; out Ludendorff stuck to his guns tenaciously, despite his concessions in the mat-ter of the border strip at Dombrova, wrung from him by the Kaiser. Hertling apparently hoped that the Prussian cabinet would support him in his objec-tions to Prussia swallowing up large Polish territories and populations.

In any event, at a cabinet session on February 4—during the later stages of which Kühlmann and Ludendorff with his staff were summoned—Hertling had the minister of the interior recite the OHL demands. It turned out that the map produced by the OHL[44] still claimed an area of about 10,000 square miles, with a population of about two million. On January 22 and 23 there had already been consultations at the Reich office of the interior as to what could be done with the two million Poles and Jews, especially whether they might be resettled. Ludendorff envisaged a "Germanized" border strip that would separate the Poles in Prussia from their compatriots in the kingdom of Poland.

It had already become clear at the conference of November 3, with which we are familiar (see Note 22), that the forcible deportation of two million people was out of the question; but Ludendorff, stubborn as always, had insisted that the border strip must be resettled with German-speaking elements living inside Poland. On November 15 he had written: "We must have a dependable German population in the border strip that is to fall to Germany, from the Silesian to the East Prussian line."

At Ludendorff's request, his staff had worked out various plans for the mass expropriation of Polish smallholdings, on the pretext of creating military reservations and "protective strips" along the railway lines; for the Russian-owned estates that had been seized would have made room for a German influx of only 7.16 per cent, i.e., a tiny minority. Shipping off the Jews, more or less by force, preferably to America, had also been considered. Nothing had as yet been decided about these questions, but the idea of forcible expulsion and resettlement had met with serious objections on the part of the civil authorities, especially the foreign ministry. The Prussian cabinet was asked to react to these problems.45

If Hertling had indeed expected a vigorous protest against this possible increment of such a large number of foreign elements, he was to be bitterly disappointed. Ludendorff manifestly registered a strong impression with a presentation in which he developed clearly and concisely the great strategic advantages that would accrue from widening the eastern buffer zones beyond Silesia, Poznan, and West Prussia and flattening out the deep dent into the Prussian border culminating at Thorn, for purposes of future deployment against Russia.46 Not one of the ministers opposed Ludendorff's purely military argument with the crucial political consideration Hertling had put forward only days before, in his memorandum for the Kaiser and the OHL of January 23 (see p. 98f.), to the effect that borders might be secured by methods other than brute force exercised against a neighboring country and that the use of force would serve merely to deepen rather than mitigate resentment and hostility, thus enlarging the areas of political friction. It was left to Kühlmann to point out that once an autonomous Polish state had been established, Germany would no longer be able to grab its western provinces without consulting the Poles themselves—these provinces included the most highly industrialized areas and the most fertile land, densely covered with farms.

Ludendorff expressed surprise as well as indignation at the idea that the Poles should have anything to say in the matter. He had not the slightest inkling of the devastating political repercussions his plan would set off, in the face of a worldwide movement for self-determination. As for the Prussian ministers, they were bureaucrats lacking in political instinct and likewise ignorant of the implications. Their debate stuck almost entirely to technical questions. They wanted to know what economic and political demands would have to be put to Poland in the event of an Austro-Polish solution. Hertling was virtually alone in his effort to bring up the serious foreign and domestic problems he thought Ludendorff's plan would entail. The OHL's resettlement plans, presented by General Bartenwerffer, were scarcely discussed, though a desire was voiced repeatedly that the border strip east of Thorn should be narrower, which Ludendorff promised to consider.[47] No decisions were taken.

In the light of all this there was little prospect of success for the major conference with the Austrians, scheduled for the following day. True, there was swift agreement on the further course of the peace negotiations at Brest-Litovsk, but ˜greement on the question of the limits to obligations assumed under the alliance was purely formal, and there was no agreement on the Polish question at all. Czernin took the participants by surprise when he presented them with the secret agreement he had entered into with Bethmann Hollweg on March 27, 1917, in which the minimum program to be striven for jointly was stated to be restoration of the status quo of 1914 in east and west (see Vol. III, p. 395f.).[48] Czernin said that he envisaged broadening this agreement into a formal and solemn treaty, signed by the high commands of the two allies and possibly even by the two emperors, and binding them to limit participation in the war to the achievement of the status quo. The obligation to fight on would lapse the moment the Entente offered peace on such a basis.

This, in other words, was the precise opposite of what Ludendorff had demanded at Kreuznach on October 7 and pushed through at the departmental meeting on November 3 (see pp. 151, 155). Kühlmann, of course, had carefully kept this from the Austrian negotiators (see p. 155). He now declared himself to be in essential agreement with Czernin's proposal that Austria's obligation under the alliance was to be limited to purely defensive ends. He added, however, that it was sometimes hard to distinguish between such ends and territorial aims, and he proposed a typically diplomatic expedient. At Brest-Litovsk he and Czernin would seek to agree on a contingency formula that would envisage "positive" goals (i.e., territorial gains)—but only in the event of a great victory on the part of the Central Powers! [49] Czernin presented a preliminary draft to that end after the luncheon recess, and this was accepted as a basis for further consultations.[50]

Thus this delicate problem, which at times had threatened to precipitate a bitter conflict, was settled for the time being. Ludendorff had indeed protested vehemently against a status quo peace, which would be tantamount to a German defeat. Germany's industrial regions in both west and east lay so threateningly near to the borders that a "defensive" expansion was indispensable. Prince Hohenlohe emphatically rejected this view. Hertling, on his part, dared express himself only with some caution along Kühlmann's lines, for he wanted to keep the contemplated agreement a strict secret, so as not to commit himself before the Reichstag to a peace without annexations. During Ludendorff's outbursts he whispered reassuringly into Czernin's ear: "Let him be—the two of us will bring it off without Ludendorff."

Yet when the Polish question was brought up—an immediate and pressing problem, unlike the as yet purely theoretical limitations on the alliance— matters did come to a head with Ludendorff. Hertling, instead of asserting his political authority against Ludendorff, listened to the exchange in silence.[51] Initially it was the departmental experts on both sides who clashed. The Austrian section chief Gratz explained in detail that the twenty-four OHL demands, together with the requested border corrections, would subject Poland to such strain that it would be left as nothing more than an atrophied and mutilated state. Germany would be gagging the country in an economic sense, stopping up all of its sources of revenue. A resentful Poland maltreated in this way would be of no value to Austria.

These charges immediately brought in the German financial experts, Count Roedern and Helfferich. They were no longer able to offer expansion of Poland's eastern border by way of compensation, since the loss of the Kholm region had cut off Poland from the east; but they cited Germany's large investment in Poland and the strong German economic interest. This brought the discussion to an impasse, and Czernin stated bluntly that in the circumstances Austria would have to forego the integration of Congress Poland.

This would invalidate all the *Mitteleuropa* agreements, Czernin added, and since there could be no question of seeking compensation in Rumania, with which peace negotiations were impending, Austria would be compelled, willy-nilly, to go its own way after the war, a way that in the circumstances would diverge from Germany's. It would become impossible to get the Austrian people to accept a continuation of the alliance.

Further clashes were precipitated by Ludendorff's plans for peace negotiations with Rumania. Ludendorff wanted the victorious powers to impose the severest possible burdens on Rumania. The Austrian reaction was that such economic restrictions would be intolerable. They said it would amount to "squeezing the lemon dry." Prince Hohenlohe charged that the OHL was in veiled form trying to get Austria to forego Galicia, without seriously offering it any quid pro quo. The Germans did not seem to realize that their policies were leading into the abyss.

Czernin agreed. Austria, he said, would not allow itself to be pushed away from Poland and Galicia into the Balkans. He further complained that at the Katowice meeting the OHL representatives had conducted themselves with utter ruthlessness, a charge which Ludendorff sharply rejected. All avenues to an understanding between the allies seemed to be blocked, although appearances were preserved and there was no lack of assurances of loyalty on both sides, including even Ludendorff. Everyone was relieved when Czernin stated expressly that the over-all goal of his policy was to make continuance of the alliance possible, indeed to expand it along *Mitteleuropa* lines.

In fact, it had emerged beyond all doubt that the policies of the two countries in respect of Poland were irreconcilable and that without a satisfactory settlement of the Polish problem—i.e., unless Poland could somehow become part of the Austrian Empire—it would not be possible to put a *Mitteleuropa* policy into effect in the Hapsburg Empire. There was no alternative to putting off the hapless Polish question once again, unless the alliance were to be subjected to an even severer strain. This was what Hertling proposed to the Kaiser on the following day, and the Kaiser agreed.

Three days later conclusion of a "bread-and-butter peace" with the Ukraine became public, including separation of the Kholm region from Poland. News also soon transpired of the secret clauses holding out the prospect of the creation of a Ukrainian crownland, to include East Galicia. There was nationwide furor in Poland over "treacherous Austria" and "perfidious Prussia," with strikes and demonstrations in all the major cities, even in Galicia. In some towns the two emperors were publicly burned in effigy. In Vienna many members of the so-called "Polish club" in the imperial parliament voiced impassioned protests and went over to the opposition. Count Szepticky, a Pole, resigned as governor general in Lublin and the entire Polish government in Warsaw resigned in a body.

On February 14 the Polish regency council issued a proclamation to the Polish people, charging the occupying powers with breaking the law and violating the right of self-determination, planning a new partition of Poland, and going back on their pledge to establish a viable state—all on account of a province, the population of which was by no means purely Polish—without a word about Ludendorff's secret annexationist plans (rumors of which, however, had been widely circulating).

The bulk of the former Polish legion, on the Austrian front, tried to go over to the Russians on the night of February 15-16, or to join Polish troops that were assembling under the Russian banner. Only a small number succeeded, the rest being overwhelmed and led off into captivity by a Croat regiment. All possibility of an understanding among Poles, Germans, and Austrians seemed to have come to an end. For the moment, Czernin was the most hated man in Austria, and fears were expressed for his personal safety on his return trip from Brest-Litovsk to Vienna.

The Polish furor died away in time, however, and Czernin never stopped working quietly for an Austro-Polish solution, secretly warning the Poles of German annexationist intentions.[52] In a supplementary treaty with the Ukraine he managed to have the delimitation of the Kholm region carried out on ethnographic lines by a mixed commission, with the result that Polish opposition in the Vienna Reichsrat soon slackened. Mediation and harmonization efforts between Berlin and Warsaw also never ceased. General Beseler kept fighting Ludendorff's plan to deprive the Poles of their western territories and to encapsulate them completely against the east as well by a sweeping southward expansion of Lithuania, all the way to making contact with the Ukraine. By early April he had achieved a reorganization of the Polish government, with a very moderate program. Most importantly, the Reichstag majority parties zealously backed a policy of German-Polish reconciliation, in sharp and deliberate contrast to the OHL. In mid-March some notables and deputies came to an arrangement with leading German leftist politicians (Erzberger, Friedrich Naumann, David) which might have assumed great importance. A joint resolution was to be adopted in the Reichstag and the Polish state council, proclaiming a state of peace and friendship between Germans and Poles for all time and demanding a mutual nonaggression treaty that would guarantee the borders against irredentist challenge by the Poles as well as annexationist changes by the Germans. The Poles would be guaranteed the Congress borders as well as "sound eastward development" and a free port on the Baltic Sea. This, in other words, would be an attempt at reconciliation on a democratic basis.

It failed because of the opposition of the German government, which was suspicious of ultimate Polish aims[53] and reluctant to commit itself without an adequate quid pro quo. It invoked the alleged need for first negotiating with the Austrians, with whom there had already been the most serious problems, but at bottom it simply did not wish to see the Reichstag take a matter of foreign policy out of its hands. The real reason, as the indignant social democrats well realized, was the diametrically opposed policy of the OHL, which Hertling did not dare challenge—nor, for that matter, were the parties able to do so, for it was a point on which they could not be sure of the support of the majority of the German people. By openly challenging the government over Poland, as the social democrats wished, the majority parties feared they would provide grist for the extremist mill. Thus they contented themselves with a Reichstag resolution couched in very general terms—it was adopted on March 22—which merely demanded that the right of self-determination be honestly implemented for the marginal areas that had cast loose from Russia.[54]

This unsuccessful effort is of particular historical interest, because it represents the most sweeping effort on the German side to draw the sting out of the Polish problem. By complying with the most pressing Polish demands, it intended to persuade the Poles to forego any irredentist trends, especially any claims to Prussian territory. The significance of these parliamentary developments should not be overestimated, of course, for ultimately their success or failure depended on how the war came out. Should the Entente win, there would be no limits to what the Polish irredentists could get. What is significant for the situation in Germany at the stage of military predominance is that this effort at reconciliation did not even get off the ground. The guiding policy of the military was war, not reconciliation, not compromise.[55]

This is precisely what prevented any progress in the Austro-German talks on the Polish question. The Kaiser had already lost interest in the Austro-Polish solution by mid-March. This was due to continuing warnings by the OHL, which exploited his disappointment over the incipient peace negotiations to convince him that at bottom it was simply a matter of Hapsburg envy of the Hohenzollerns. Vienna showed no willingness to leave Rumania to the Germans, as the Kaiser had hoped; and Hindenburg thought that in the circumstances Austria should be denied a major success in Poland.[56]

Emperor Charles, on the other side, once the treaties of Brest-Litovsk had been made known, was bitterly resentful over the Polish stand and the treachery of the Polish auxiliary corps; and in consequence he seemed far less inclined to accept the Polish crown. During a talk between the two emperors at Homburg palace on February 22, the idea of a third solution cropped up, the so-called "candidate solution." The Poles were to choose as their king a German or Austrian prince who would be presented to them jointly. He would, of course, not get Galicia, and what would come into being would be no more than a "Little Poland," from which the two Central Powers would exempt in advance as many border districts as they deemed useful or necessary. The notion was well-received by the OHL, which henceforth adopted the candidate solution as its program.[57]

The discussion at Homburg had been entirely tentative, however. Within a few days, Emperor Charles reverted to the Austro-Polish solution, and beginning in early April he pursued it with great vigor.[58] Even the Kaiser did not immediately push the candidate solution hard. At a crown council on March 13 he seems to have achieved agreement with his ministers and generals on only one point: A new Polish state under a freely chosen king represented a danger for Germany and therefore must be firmly tied to that country. Still, no clear-cut decisions were taken;[59] and even the fall of 1918 did not see an end to the quarrel with Austria over the Polish question—indeed, after Czernin went on April 14 it only grew more embittered under his successor Burián.

Strangely, Czernin had also failed, by the time he disappeared from the stage, to secure the reformulation and limitation of alliance obligations which he had pursued so urgently.[60] Directly after the big Berlin conference of February 5 (see p. 165f.) he modified and passed on to Kühlmann at Brest-Litovsk the draft he had submitted on an interpretation of the alliance. Kühlmann took it with him to Berlin, to have it checked by the foreign ministry's legal division under Privy Councilor Kriege. Czernin prodded him on February 15, and the scrutiny was completed on the following day by Kriege, working jointly with Prince Hohenlohe. The upshot was a version formulated in more precise legal language, although it still closely followed the Austrian draft, even in the wording. There was virtually no change in the provisions contemplated.[61]

It came as a great surprise to Berlin when Czernin, on February 21, sharply rejected this revision, going so far as to threaten that Austria, if necessary, would advise the German government in a unilateral note that it stood ready to fight on only in defense of Germany's prewar territorial integrity and not for German conquest. Even Hohenlohe was at a loss to understand what might have set off this agitated protest, and the matter was left to further talks of Kühlmann and Kriege with Czernin, all three of whom were just then setting out for the Bucharest peace negotiations.

The documentary evidence does not unequivocally show why, though the men spent weeks together, no understanding was reached and the agreement was not finally signed. According to a review of the talks prepared for Czernin's successor late in April, there was really only one sticking point. The Germans insisted that an ally's obligation to fight on should cease only when the other ally's prewar territorial integrity had been secured "against all the enemy powers." This was to prevent Austria from concluding a separate peace until the German colonies had been regained from Britain and Alsace-Lorraine from France.

Czernin opposed this and proposed the following additional clause: "A partial peace with only one power may be concluded only by mutual agreement, but an ally whose . . . territorial integrity does not appear to be threatened by the power in question shall not withhold his agreement to such a peace." This might have enabled Austria to make peace, for example, with Italy (Wilson serving as the mediator) or with Rumania, while Germany could have made peace only with France or Britain, a most unlikely case. Kühlmann was unwilling to agree to this without first consulting his government and the Kaiser, and in the end Czernin proposed that the whole clause about ending the war prematurely be stricken out. Instead the first clause would be slightly expanded, to read that the alliance, in keeping with its purely defensive character, imposed on neither partner any obligations beyond the maintenance of its prewar territorial integrity against all enemy powers. Kühlmann did not reject this, though Kriege registered "some" reservations, which he did not specify. No conclusion was reached.

It would seem that what delayed agreement between the two ministers was a lingering suspicion on the German side concerning Austria's ultimate intentions. Czernin evidently found it difficult to commit Austria in writing to fight on for Alsace-Lorraine and the German colonies. Yet the remaining differences over the wording were not so great as to preclude the view that the two men might have bridged them but for Czernin's sudden fall; and the occasion for that fall, as we shall hear, involved a lapse of loyalty to the alliance on the part not of the minister but of his emperor, who was left in a very dubious light, deepening German suspicions even more.

Part 2

The OHL and the Peace with Rumania

THE FAILURE of the two Central Powers to agree on the Polish question had far-reaching effects on the course of the peace negotiations with Rumania, which immediately followed the talks at Brest-Litovsk. The Kaiser's readiness to leave Poland to the Austrians was dictated by his desire to acquire Rumania as a kind of German crown colony. Austria's claims to that country (which the Kreuznach agreement of May 18 had apportioned it as a "separate state") were to be indemnified, so to speak, by the Austro-Polish solution. This intention fell of its own weight, when excessive German demands prevented agreement on the Polish question; for when that happened, the Austrian claims of the preceding May were revived.

Actually, large-scale territorial gains had become quite out of the question for both powers since the October Revolution in Russia. This was particularly true of Austria, which even now could not manage the motley abundance of its non-German (and non-Hungarian) peoples. An additional crownland in Rumania would have completely disrupted the Austrian Empire which, as we know, was already at the end of its tether. Thus the dominant thought in Austrian policy in respect of Rumania was to make peace with this neighbor and former ally as soon as possible and achieve a stable modus vivendi. The German high command too was bound to want to see the Rumanian front dismantled as soon as possible. As for Rumania itself, the loss of its Russian ally had forced it into hopeless isolation. In the circumstances, it might have been thought that peace with Rumania would be concluded much more swiftly than had been the case with the Soviets. Actually, it took no less than five full months from armistice to peace, and the peace talks not only caused a serious crisis within the Quadruple Alliance but led to a furious clash among the German generals and statesmen.

Initially the Rumanian enemy had displayed unexpected military strength, which was scarcely impaired by the October Revolution in Russia. Pushed back into the Moldavian northwest corner of their country in the campaign of 1916, the Rumanians had done an excellent job of digging in there, exploiting every natural obstacle. The Rumanian army, moreover, had been thoroughly reorganized with the help of French instructors. Its morale withstood even the contagion of Bolshevist-pacifist propaganda and it remained firmly in the hands of its leaders.

A rash effort, inspired by Ludendorff, to take Moldavia in the wake of the counterblow against the Brusilov offensive in August 1917 failed with heavy losses,[62] and this defensive success greatly increased the confidence of King Ferdinand's government, foiling for the time being plans by conservative Rumanian politicians to depose his dynasty by a coup d'état in Bucharest and to make a separate peace with the Central Powers. Such plans had been carried to the German government ever since January. In August, during the Moldavian offensive, they were zealously taken up, on Ludendorff's instructions, at the headquarters of Mackensen's army group. The immediate aim was to reconcile the two leading Rumanian politicians, Carp and Marghiloman, and demoralize the Rumanian army by distributing leaflets with a peace offer. The German foreign ministry watched these activities with a great deal of skepticism, but a proposal by Field Marshal Mackensen was well received by the Kaiser. Mackensen wanted to support the creation, as soon as possible, of a new Rumanian government that would choose a German prince as king. Only in this way, he thought, could Germany anticipate the Austrians, who wished to tie the country to the Austrian Empire. The Kaiser eagerly assented and would have preferred to offer one of his own sons as a candidate for the Rumanian crown. He conferred with his wife, his generals, and Valentini on which one of them might be most suitable.

The immediate opposition he encountered stemmed not only from Chancellor Michaelis, but from Ludendorff as well. Both pointed out that under the agreement of May 18 Austria could well claim a position of political preference in Rumania, and they succeeded in obtaining a postponement of these plans for a coup d'état,[63] which became completely irrelevant when the Moldavian offensive failed. The Kaiser, nevertheless, continued to toy with the idea, and we shall not go far afield in conjecturing that it played a part in persuading him, after his Rumanian trip late in September, to voice a sudden desire to trade Poland for Rumania (see p. 150). By the end of the year this idea was revived by the same group of conservative Rumanian politicians who had put forward similar thoughts during the preceding summer, in the hope that a coup d'état and change of dynasty might gain their country a more favorable peace than was otherwise possible.

They were mainly out to safeguard the integrity of Rumania's prewar borders, not only against Bulgaria, which coveted the Dobrudja, but against Hungarian designs on the Carpathian mountain passes. The aged Carp was in the forefront of the movement to co-opt a German prince, such as the Kaiser's son Oscar, as King of Rumania. He thought that the Germans would scarcely expect such a sovereign to begin his reign with large-scale territorial cessions. Any Rumanian government would have, in fact, been unable to survive, if it discredited itself in advance as a mere tool of the victorious powers, by agreeing to such cessions. This was clearly perceived by Field Marshal Mackensen and such of his staff as Colonel Hentsch, administrative chief, and Legation Councilor Horstmann, chief of his political section, who tried to extract firm commitments to Rumania's territorial integrity at supreme headquarters.

Quite evidently they were intent on fulfilling the Kaiser's pet notion, but they also entertained other plans, which they necessarily kept secret from their Rumanian opposite numbers. According to a memorandum by Horstmann of January 1, 1918, Rumania was to serve as a bridgehead for a German position of dominance in the Middle East; and Colonel Hentsch, in another memorandum of January 6 for the OHL, explained that to that end Rumania would have to be reduced to the status of a mere German satellite. He did not use this precise expression, but spoke instead of a position similar to that of Egypt within the British Empire, while Horstmann used the comparison of the position of a British viceroy in India or governor general in Canada.

Hentsch proposed that the existing German military administration with its many special departments be taken over by the new Rumanian government lock, stock, and barrel, but at the same time that it be subordinated to a central German authority that might be given the harmless-sounding title of "consulate general" or "chief commissariat." This German diplomatic representation, however, would hold the sole civil power, just as the military power would lie in the hand of a German commander-in-chief.

Hentsch thought it would be simpler if the Kaiser himself rather than a German prince were to become the Rumanian sovereign. His orders, transmitted through a governor general, could then be put into effect directly by the consul general and the commander-in-chief. Rumanian pride at having Europe's most powerful ruler as the country's king, moreover, might comfort the people in their loss of autonomy. A German prince of lesser rank would have a far more difficult time–indeed, the people would probably tolerate continued German intervention in their domestic affairs for no more than a few years. In any event, the choice of a king must not antedate peace, as demanded by Carp, for the moral odium of such a peace must not be imputed to the new ruler.

Such were the fanciful dreams of German generals, who had come to think of themselves as absolute overlords in the occupied territory. This time, however, it was not Ludendorff who was the guiding spirit. On the contrary, Ludendorff seems to have taken the fantasies of his subordinate Hentsch as lightly as did the foreign ministry. He knew very well that Rumania was not to be had for the asking, unless Austria's ambition in Poland were satisfied.

On January 8 Ludendorff, through Hindenburg, transmitted to the Kaiser a direct report from Mackensen, dated January 31, in which the latter reviewed his difficulties in negotiating with Rumania. Ludendorff commented dryly that in view of the geographic distance to Rumania, Germany would find it difficult to exert political influence. Whether independent or integrated with Austria, moreover, Rumania would enjoy economic security. As for the Dobrudja, Bulgarian claims to it deserved greater consideration than those of Rumania, even though the right of unrestricted passage to the sea by way of the Danube was a matter of life and death for Rumania.

The Kaiser's marginal notes on Ludendorff's comments reveal not only his bitter disappointment, but also his helplessness in the face of Ludendorff's iron will. "More proof of an utter lack of political sense," he wrote. "This approach would completely foreclose a solution along the lines proposed by Mackensen, with which I fully concur. So far I have been unable to prevail over the chief of the General Staff . . . who in this way manages to paralyze every constructive political development in Rumania and the Balkans."

The Kaiser was amply justified in contrasting Ludendorff's opposition to the Austro-Polish solution and Ludendorff's border strip plans with the difficulties that existed in Rumania. The Austrians were watching the German-fostered plans for a Rumanian coup d'état with extreme suspicion.64 They were quite disinclined simply to leave Rumania to Germany, and they were busily engaged in counterpropaganda in the former country. The Kaiser once again blamed Ludendorff. Mackensen's report had, in fact, complained of Bulgarian and Austrian-Catholic propaganda, and the Kaiser commented bitterly that the reason lay in the failure to make any progress with the Austro-Polish solution, under which Austria would withdraw from Rumania. "The chief of staff simply won't accept the Polish borders I have proposed, else we should long since be in Rumania all by ourselves."

This was certainly an exaggeration. It was the Bulgarian rather than the Hungarian territorial demands that were the chief obstacle to an understanding. An added factor, soon to be shown, was that while the government of King Ferdinand was highly unpopular in German-occupied Walachia, it had gained a great deal of respect and loyalty, especially within the army, in Rumanian-controlled Moldavia; and the overthrow of the dynasty was inconceivable without the army.

Thus the talks with Carp and Marghiloman dragged on interminably and inconclusively. The two Rumanians never succeeded in drawing the Rumanian officer corps over to their side; nor was the impasse resolved by repeated declarations that on no account would there be negotiations with King Ferdinand and his prime minister, Bratianu, and that Rumania would almost certainly lose the Dobrudja, unless there were a change of dynasty.65

Meanwhile hostilities on the Russian front had died down, and continuation of the war had thus become futile for the Rumanians. The Rumanian army, however, together with Ukrainian and other non-Great-Russian troops, was still under the command of General Shcherbachev, a highly energetic soldier who, like the Ukrainian Rada, regarded himself as an enemy of the new powers in St. Petersburg and rejected the armistice concluded at Brest-Litovsk as not applying to his command. Mackensen's headquarters engaged in separate talks with him at Focshani, negotiating an armistice on December 9.[66]

But the ensuing peace negotiations made little progress, partly because of the continuing presence of Entente diplomats at Jassy. Shcherbachev was evidently intent on forming a new power focus on the South Russian front, based on the disciplined Rumanian troops and the remaining loyalist Ukrainian troops, amounting to about forty-eight divisions in all—the Bolshevist elements were being pushed off to the north. By comparison, the Germans and their allies still in Rumania by January were numerically much inferior, which precluded any strong military pressure on the Rumanian government.

That government remained steadfast. It is almost certain that its resistance and fighting spirit were only stiffened by news of the intrigues of certain Rumanian politicians, who were talking with the German command about deposing King Ferdinand and his prime minister Bratianu, the "war culprit" of 1916. In time, however, the political situation grew curiously warped. Germany was getting on with its peace with the Ukrainians, who were fighting the Bolshevists. The Rumanians were joining that struggle and in sometimes severe fighting repulsing the Soviet troops at their front. They thus became allies of the Germans, so to speak, or at least of Germany's Ukrainian partner. Military and political considerations were overlapping in strange ways.

In mid-January, when another four divisions were to be withdrawn for the western front, Field Marshal Mackensen, acting on behalf of the OHL, wished to put an ultimatum to the Rumanians: Unless they sued for peace within twenty-four hours, the armistice would be revoked. This, however, proved to be politically impossible. It would have endangered the peace negotiated with the Ukraine at Brest-Litovsk, and perhaps all the treaties negotiated there. Kühlmann, from Brest-Litovsk, urgently warned against it.[67]

Meanwhile conflicts over war aims had emerged prominently also among the powers of the Quadruple Alliance—so prominently that the alliance was at times in danger of being disrupted. The main bone of contention was Bulgaria's claim to the entire Dobrudja, the eastern part of Rumania between the Danube and the Black Sea. Under the treaty of alliance of 1915, Bulgaria did have a legal claim to the southern part, which it had lost only in the Second Balkan War in 1913; but Premier Radoslavov, using highly sophisticated if not downright fraudulent propaganda techniques, had convinced all Bulgaria by the fall of 1917 that it had a rightful claim to the entire province, including the Danube estuary, on the basis of an alleged promise by the Kaiser.

The Dobrudja was celebrated as "the cradle of Bulgaria," even though its northern part was inhabited predominantly by Rumanians and was indispensable to Rumania for transit from Walachia to the seaport of Constantza. An added factor was that the Turks, who had given highly effective military aid in the conquest of the Dobrudja, now asked for a quid pro quo in return for supporting the Bulgarian demands that went beyond what had been promised by treaty. What the Turks wanted was the return of a border area on the Maritsa, embracing in the main some of the suburbs of Adrianople (Edirne), ceded in 1915 to Bulgaria on Germany's urging, in order to persuade Bulgaria to enter the war.

Sofia, however, remained obdurate in the face of such claims, and these quarrels over relatively insignificant prizes threatened to make mortal enemies of Germany's Balkan allies. Both Radoslavov and the Turkish grand vizier, Talaat Pasha, declared that they could not stay in power unless they got what they wanted; and since their further participation in the war had long since become uncertain, there was now serious danger of their defection. The challenge to Kühlmann to act as a mediator was very urgent.

The foreign ministry in Berlin was convinced that the Rumanians would not in the long run stand for their country being cut off from the sea by the loss of the entire Dobrudja. Berlin also felt that it was not in the German interest to allow the only rail line from Bucharest to Constantza, and thus the only direct connection with Turkey, to fall into Bulgarian hands. Even Czernin was horrified over so crude a violation of the principle of peace without annexations and of self-determination.

Yet to reject the Bulgarian demand outright would have been far too dangerous, politically. It was vigorously supported by Ludendorff, moreover, who wished to assign a leading role to Bulgaria in the Balkans. In view of Austria's "unfriendly" attitude, which was bound to grow more hostile because of the Austro-Polish solution, Bulgaria's hand should be strengthened, Ludendorff thought, and the country should be placed under obligation to Germany by support for its claims. Ludendorff did, however, wish to acquire for Germany the Cernavoda-Constantza railway and the Black Sea port of Constantza itself, as a naval base. The Danube delta, on the other hand, he was willing to leave to the Rumanians.[68]

Of course Ludendorff's plans went even farther. Above all, he wanted to remove the king and the royal family from the country[69] and keep Walachia under military occupation for another five or six years after the conclusion of a general peace. This period was to be used for purposes of placing the country in a state of complete economic dependence on Germany. Its oil fields, railways, harbor works, and government estates were all to become the property of the German government or of German companies; a canal was to be built from the Danube to Constantza; and the Rumanian state finances were to be under permanent German control.[70]

All this meant a massive enlargement of Germany's share in the economic exploitation of Rumania. Actually, it had been agreed the preceding May that Germany should have a position of predominance. Czernin, in opposing it now, labored under the handicap that this agreement had been reached in May, despite the then contemplated Germano-Polish solution, at Ludendorff's insistence. Czernin himself, in keeping with the wishes of Emperor Charles, strongly favored a compromise peace with Rumania, conducive to long-time harmony; but in that endeavor he met with opposition even at home. Hungary, in particular, was not at all inclined to let off lightly a treacherous former ally who had stabbed the Central Powers in the back at a moment of grave military crisis and who had unceremoniously overrun Transylvania. Under Count Tisza's leadership, the Hungarians now called for vengeance and guarantees against future attack. They wanted a wide border strip taken away from Rumania and in general favored a strong rather than a weak peace, since only the former would impress the Western powers as a sign of strength.[71]

It was only in late January that all these differences took on practical importance and the German need to withdraw troops from Rumania to the west made it urgent to begin peace talks in earnest. Ludendorff at first planned to deny the Jassy government an extension of the armistice and to bring it to heel for peace talks by issuing a threatening ultimatum; but before these matters could even be discussed with the enemy, Emperor Charles had outmaneuvered Ludendorff's policy of bullying by pursuing a precisely opposite course—preservation rather than removal of the Rumanian dynasty, in the face of the threat of revolution to all monarchs; and understanding and friendship in place of vengeance and military force. On Czernin's advice, Emperor Charles, late in January, sent a secret message to King Ferdinand behind the backs of the Germans. It said that if the king now showed himself prepared to negotiate he could keep his dynasty intact and secure an honorable peace for his country. The delayed answer was couched in cautious terms, but on February 9 Bratianu was dismissed, to be replaced by General Averescu, thus removing the main obstacle to an understanding.

In the meantime the two Central Powers, on the occasion of the big Berlin conference on the eastern question of February 4-5 (see p. 163ff.), had tentatively agreed on a joint peace program, though they dared not immediately advise Rumania of its full scope.[72] Among other things, it contemplated cession of the entire Dobrudja, not to Bulgaria but to the four allies jointly; creation of a German free port (rather than a naval base) at Constantza; cession to Germany of the Cernavoda-Constantza railway; border fortifications in the Carpathians that would favor Austria; Rumanian territorial acquisitions in Bessarabia, in compensation for the Dobrudja; retention of the mobile Rumanian forces on the Ukrainian front (the Bolshevists having recently seized power in the Ukraine); continuing occupation of Rumania by the Central Powers under German command and administration—but only for the time being rather than a term of years—and lastly clauses covering rail transport, Danube shipping, economic questions, etc. Installation of a new government acceptable to the Central Powers was also demanded. Even this program showed that Ludendorff's far more sweeping plans were incapable of realization—not only on account of Austrian resistance but because, unlike the situation in Russia, the Germans lacked military power in Rumania, indeed at the moment needed the mobile Rumanian forces in South Russia as something in the nature of allies.

This was further shown as negotiations progressed. On February 13, when the Rumanians were having difficulty in forming their government, they requested that the armistice be extended for twenty days. Once again the OHL wanted to hasten the peace effort by military force, which was not only politically unwise but proved militarily impossible. Even Mackensen's staff concluded that Germany simply did not have the resources. By way of compromise, the peace negotiations were set to begin on February 22.

In the meantime, however, on February 17, as we have already learned, the Ukrainian Rada government had begun to send frantic appeals for help, and the OHL wished to use the Rumanians for giving aid against the Bolshevists. They not only were to occupy all of Bessarabia but were to advance all the way to Odessa. This became almost immediately unnecessary, for German troops invading the Ukraine reached Kiev with surprising speed, once again creating a new situation. It had now become possible to envelop the Rumanian army from behind, placing them in a hopeless trap. Averescu in consequence now said he was ready to talk and negotiations began—after still another delay—on February 24 at Focshani.

It developed immediately that the question of the Dobrudja precluded any agreement with Averescu, who said that the Rumanian army would fight to the last man before agreeing to cede the entirety of that region. In an effort to overcome this resistance, Czernin decided to seek out King Ferdinand personally for a face-to-face talk. This meeting took place on February 27 at a small railway station in Moldavia. Czernin told the king that nothing less than the survival of his dynasty, indeed of his whole country, was at stake and tried to soften cession of the Dobrudja by guaranteeing Rumania free access to Constantza and again offering part of Bessarabia by way of compensation. In the end he issued a forty-eight-hour ultimatum, demanding acceptance of the peace program of the Central Powers as a basis for negotiation.

The Germans and Austrians passed the forty-eight hours in a state of extreme tension. Peace with Rumania was an urgent necessity, so that German troops might be withdrawn and the Danube used without harassment as a waterway for the transport of Ukrainian grain. Several German divisions had just been pulled back from the front and one of them was already alerted for shipment to the west, against the event that King Ferdinand would yield.

If he did not, the question was whether Bulgarian ambitions were really worth a resumption of the bloodshed in Moldavia. General Hell, chief of staff of Mackensen's army group, anticipated a stubborn and bloody struggle, but the impatient Ludendorff pressed for swift action and revocation of the armistice, only to learn from the Chancellor that Emperor Charles, against the assurance given by his chief of staff, Arz, sternly rejected any participation by Austrian troops in a renewed Rumanian campaign; nor was Bulgarian and Turkish cooperation by any means assured—the Bulgarians were actually putting forward additional territorial demands as the price of theirs! Only five German divisions were available for the strike, and according to General Hell it would have been an act of futility to launch the attack with nothing more than that.

There was enormous relief when the morning of March 1 brought a dispatch from Jassy, expressing acceptance of the terms. Its language was held in general terms, however, and there was no indication that the Rumanians were prepared to sign a formal preliminary peace treaty. Hence the reply was rejected as unsatisfactory, though Czernin managed to secure another twenty-four-hour delay. Ludendorff protested, of course, and wanted the armistice canceled at once. He now managed to extract Charles's agreement to the Austrians participating in another passage at arms, if it were necessary—and Ludendorff was virtually certain that this would no longer be so.[73]

Averescu was advised on March 2 that military operations would commence on March 5 and that no further postponement would be granted, even for a matter of hours. This had its effect. Averescu's concurrence arrived on the afternoon of March 2 and on March 5 the draft of a preliminary peace treaty was signed at Bufta by a plenipotentiary of the Rumanian government.[74]

From that moment on the work of peace passed entirely into the hands of the diplomats, i.e., Kühlmann and Czernin, both of whom went to Bucharest, where they spent many weeks, in an effort to cope directly with a mountain of problems. The general framework fixed in Bufta had now to be filled in with numerous individual agreements. It was a difficult and time-consuming undertaking, in view of the continuing quarrels between Bulgars and Turks, conflicting Austrian and, Hungarian aims, differences arising among Vienna, Berlin, and the OHL, and not least the exceedingly technical economic aspects. More time was lost when the Averescu government resigned in mid-March, to be replaced by Marghiloman, a conservative opponent of Bratianu, rather pro-German, one of those who had stayed in Bucharest to engage for many months in talks with the occupying powers over peace possibilities. Czernin had been Austrian envoy in Bucharest from 1913 to 1916, and Marghiloman was an old acquaintance of his. Negotiations now took on a polite and almost friendly air, and in time the diplomats managed to turn the harsh dictate more and more into a peace of understanding.

In contrast to Ludendorff, Kühlmann tried hard not to push German economic predominance to the point desired in Germany and feared by Emperor Charles, i.e., to the point where Rumania would lose its political sovereignty, while Austrian influence would be completely submerged.[75] In common with Czernin, he pursued his *Mitteleuropa* plans, as before. Agreement between the Central Powers over Poland might have been foiled by the OHL, but on no account was Rumania now to become another bone of contention. Both countries were to share in the economic exploitation of Rumania's rich natural resources, by peaceful agreement, as Austria wanted it, rather than by brutal exploitation. Economic order was to be agreed on with the Rumanians, point by point. This took much time and careful detail work by the legal and economic experts of the German foreign ministry and economic office, as well as by Rumanian experts—much more time than the impatient Ludendorff was able to tolerate.

Ludendorff had the idea that the Rumanians must be kept under constant military pressure until the negotiations were concluded and the divisions intended for the west could be withdrawn. (We shall have occasion, further on, to discuss the effect this relentless pressure had on the diplomats.) On March 26, five days after the launching of the great western offensive, Ludendorff abruptly ordered General Hell to report by midnight of March 28-29 that the broad outlines of the treaty had been fixed, so that the divisions could begin rolling west. German successes in the west, he wired, forbade any further appeasement. By that time, however, the drafting of the most important clauses of the treaty had progressed to the point that they could be initialed that very day. There were some additions on March 29, and the divisions moved off, though detailed economic talks continued for a long time. They were not concluded until after Czernin had withdrawn, and the peace treaty was finally signed on May 7.

Unlike the peace of Brest-Litovsk, the peace of Bucharest was truly negotiated rather than dictated—apart from the cession of the Dobrudja, forced by the Bulgarians. Rumania's sovereignty had been largely preserved. There was no occupation of Moldavia, and the king was left a peacetime army of eight divisions, with four more at war strength in Bessarabia. There were no war indemnities. All the original demands of the Central Powers were substantially reduced. Hungarian border rectifications were essentially limited to a few uninhabited Carpathian passes, whose cession to Hungary could be justified on the grounds of improved Transylvanian border security. Czernin had enlisted the emperor's help to this end, against the Hungarian government. The future of the Dobrudja was in some measure left open in that for the time being its northern part, including the Cernavoda-Constantza rail line, was to fall to the Quadruple Alliance as a whole, while Bulgaria got back only the southern part it had lost in 1913. Rumania, moreover, was expressly guaranteed free access to the port of Constantza. How long the occupation was to continue was also left open, the precise term to be settled later; but occupation pressure was even now visibly lifted and the administrative transfer to the Rumanian authorities prepared.[76]

The settlements of the greatest importance to Germany were to be found in the numerous supplementary economic agreements, mainly those concerning oil and food production, which were absolutely vital to the Central Powers while the war was on. The Rumanian oil industry had in fact been largely developed by German capital, while the corrupt prewar Rumanian governments had been more of a hindrance than a help. Quite naturally, victorious Germany was now intent on securing the lion's share of the output. It had been originally planned that the royal monopoly and the oil-bearing land owned by the state should pass into the hands of a Central European oil company dominated by German capital. In the event, the company accepted long leases—up to ninety years—from the Rumanian state, which was to share in the profits. This form of control by German capital was supplemented by the creation of another German company that was to have a monopoly on marketing and utilizing the entire oil output. Austria managed to cut itself in on these enterprises. In addition both Central Powers concluded economic agreements with Rumania, which obligated itself to sell, or at least offer to sell to them, its entire agricultural and livestock surplus from 1918 to 1926, at strictly fixed prices. Some clauses dealt with rail freight and Danubian shipping, but did not seriously restrict Rumanian sovereignty.

All in all the peace treaty with its numerous economic supplements resulted in tying the Rumanian economy to that of the Central Powers, but not to the point of complete control. Some German economic interests were actually disappointed. They had anticipated far greater advantages and complained that their technical objections had been ignored because the negotiating diplomats placed such great stress on reaching a peaceful settlement with Marghiloman.

Czernin's ultimate aim, shared by his successor Burián, was to extend someday to Rumania the economic union with Germany that was being foreshadowed. This was to open up a major new market to Austrian industry, reducing the fear that German industry might gain a commanding position in Austria by virtue of lowered tariffs. Kühlmann and Hertling shared this approach, and Burián ultimately succeeded in overcoming the opposition of the

Hungarian government, which was afraid that a customs alliance with Rumania might threaten its agriculture. Thus on May 7, in a supplementary exchange of notes, Rumania stated that in the event of a customs union between Germany and Austria it was prepared to join in, under conditions to be negotiated. Months of painstaking effort had at last opened up the prospect of an expanded Central European economic community.

To the diplomats this represented a noteworthy success, but the generals regarded the whole work as flawed, since their aims and methods had not prevailed. Indeed, the Bucharest peace talks led to another serious clash between scepter and sword. On February 26 Kühlmann complained to the Chancellor about difficulties in persuading the Vienna government to joint action against balky Rumania, difficulties brought about by dismay and resentment over OHL tactics. "The major part of our troubles with Austria," he said, "stems from the fact that the OHL does not want an Austro-Polish solution and seeks to cross it up by means with which Your Excellency will be familiar."[77] The Austrians were afraid of being "fobbed off with a meager mess of pottage in Rumania, while getting little or nothing in return in Poland." Such political meddling by an authority without political responsibility had thoroughly soured Austro-German relations; and because it bore no such responsibility, it was unmindful of positive solutions, contenting itself with shooting down individual efforts that were essential in the over-all context.[78]

Nor did the pressure from supreme headquarters cease even when negotiations with Marghiloman had long since got on a smooth footing. On March 25 Kühlmann once again complained to the Chancellor. It was quite unreasonable, he said, still to threaten military intervention, imperiling the survival of the Marghiloman government, which had been formed only four days before, at a time when essential parts of the treaty were ready to be initialed in draft form the very next day. Kühlmann pleaded that the Kaiser be made to bring about a decision under which the armistice could be extended for ten rather than two days, giving the economic experts time to do their work. He added that Mackensen and his chief of staff, Hell, agreed with him and could not understand how Hindenburg concluded that the Rumanian government was being obstinate because it fully expected hostilities to be resumed. Delays in reaching agreement were solely due to technical reasons, indeed were the result of differences between the allies rather than of Rumanian stubbornness. Economic agreements obtained under duress offered no assurance of being observed once the occupation was lifted.

Kühlmann said that he had every hope of solving the problems posed in Bucharest, if only the OHL ceased to base its conclusions on uncontrollable and politically biased reports instead of keeping in constant touch with the Chancellor. It was, after all, being kept currently informed on the progress of the peace negotiations by its own representatives. Meaningful diplomatic work was possible only if it were governed by policies agreed on between himself and the Chancellor.

Ludendorff launched a counteroffensive the same day. In a long telegram he sharply criticized everything that had been done in Bucharest as well as Kühlmann's whole negotiating approach. On March 31 he insisted that all German authorities were agreed that Rumania must be integrated with Germany, which was not interested in weakening that country just to please its allies. In the Kreuznach agreement of May 18, 1917, even Austria had agreed to a "strongly preponderant" German participation in the Rumanian economy, despite the Germano-Polish solution that was then envisaged; but the German goals had not been attained, because of the failure to agree with the allies beforehand on a fixed program that would prevent the Rumanians from exploiting disunity on the other side. (He passed over in silence the Berlin program of February 5.) An added complaint concerned the slow pace of negotiations, which was harmful to German military contingencies. German diplomacy had been far too soft toward Germany's allies—in foregoing a naval base at Constantza, allowing Austro-Hungarian border corrections, abandoning certain financial demands that were to be put to Bulgaria. Germany was not getting its due, even though its forces had liberated Transylvania and held the strongest hand.

This wire was dispatched to the foreign ministry right during the great battle in the west. It contained many more comments on the initialed treaty text. Ludendorff did not let his responsibility for running the crucial western offensive deter him from dealing in minute detail with Balkan reorganization, in which he intervened again and again with long telegrams, concerning the settlement of Bulgarian war debts, safeguards for German mining, railway, and shipping interests in Bulgaria, questions of administration in the Dobrudja, etc. There were apparently no limits to his activist drive, his amazing ability to absorb information, and the versatility of his staff.

Ludendorff's staff stood ready at a moment's notice to find "material" when it came to mounting a campaign against some politician their chief did not like, as we have seen in Bethmann Hollweg's case (see Vol. III, p. 346). Even in Brest-Litovsk ambitious young officers had been "digging for dirt" in Kühlmann's private life, to report "topside." Hindenburg had told the Kaiser with a straight face that his foreign minister "was spending his time with an American game of chance called poker," but when he was half-jokingly challenged by the Kaiser, Kühlmann had been able to brush this off as an innocent pastime with Turkish and Bulgarian delegates.[79]

Even more harmful reports were now arriving from Bucharest, to be assiduously peddled to the Kaiser, and especially to the empress. During the crucial days in later March Kühlmann was said to have spent several days

duck hunting with Czernin. The Kaiser instantly wired Kühlmann a reprimand.[80] Apparently he now suspected that Hindenburg's complaints about
Kühlmann's inattention to affairs were justified. In any event, his cabinet
chief, Berg, told the Chancellor on March 29 that the Kaiser was furious over
Kühlmann's mode of life and had lost confidence that he was conducting the
negotiations with sufficient seriousness. The whole foreign ministry needed a
thorough overhaul. Berg apparently shared and even encouraged his master's
views, but Baron Grünau, foreign ministry representative to the Kaiser,
managed to defend his chief with some success. He was able to present a
message of protest in which Kühlmann showed that despite the technical
difficulties it had taken only a few days of negotiation with Marghiloman to
reach the stage when the treaty could be initialed and that his subsequent
invitation to Czernin to the brief excursion on the Danube had not delayed
matters by a single hour.

Chancellor Hertling clearly perceived the danger of these malicious attacks,
not only to Kühlmann personally but to government policy as a whole. He
took them very seriously and had Radowitz write a detailed reply. Addressed
to Berg, it was intended for the Kaiser, but it was apparently distributed also
to several other departments. Its significance goes far beyond the incident
that occasioned it, for it set forth Hertling's—and Kühlmann's—foreign policy
in broad outlines and with a clarity probably unequaled in any other document.[81]

It described Germany's relation with Austria as "the fulcrum of German
postwar policy." Any clouding of this relation would impair the value of
Germany's alliance with Bulgaria and render all the advantages secured in
Rumania illusory. Strengthening and firmly anchoring the Austro-German
alliance, on the other hand, would create a powerful Central European bloc
unprecedented in history. Germany must not allow itself to become isolated
after the war. The future of its relations with Russia was uncertain and would
depend on appropriate treatment of the marginal populations and on whether
Germany would succeed in finding a modus vivendi with the new rulers; and
if Germany won the war, the Western powers would be even more hostile
than before. A strong bloc in Central Europe to which even the Scandinavian
countries and Holland might give economic allegiance was an absolute
necessity.

Brest-Litovsk and Bucharest were dangerous shoals for the formation of
such a bloc, Hertling went on, and it was to Kühlmann's great credit that the
difficult negotiations had strengthened rather than weakened relations with
Austria. To wage a war of coalition was easy compared to the difficulty of
creating a peace that would satisfy all the members of the coalition. Kühlmann had managed a compromise among the demands of the four allies
without harming German interests, in full agreement with the two generals,

Mackensen and Hell, and even keeping on good terms with the pro-German Marghiloman government. It was unquestionably in Germany's interest to see to it that that government was encouraged and remained in power, and an alliance with it was a distinct possibility. The German occupation troops wanted by the OHL for the western front could have been withdrawn from Rumania without risk at any time after March 3. It was absolutely untrue to say that the foreign minister had dragged his feet or neglected his duties, and the malicious gossip being disseminated about him was as deplorable as was the general animosity against him that had been displayed by the OHL ever since the preceding fall. If Kühlmann's dismissal failed to bring about a change of the policy of alliance now being pursued, it would be superfluous and harmful. On the other hand, it might mean a turn away from the present policy in favor of one supported by the Pan-Germans and annexationists,"in which I [Hertling] would not be able to take part." The Kaiser should realize that the resignation of Kühlmann would mark the total collapse of an approach that had kept the majority of the German people and their representatives united and had succeeded in preventing strikes and unrest. There was hope at this time that the resolution of July 19, which had called for no annexations and indemnities, was fading into oblivion, but this would be true only so long as the government did not forfeit the people's confidence that it was prepared to make peace. Kühlmann's fall would shake that confidence. It was quite true that his policy was one of skillful negotiation rather than of striking the proud pose of the victor; but Kühlmann would certainly not hesitate for a moment, in peace negotiations to come, to insist on terms commensurate with the sacrifices Germany had made. A program that went too far, however, like the continued or partial annexation of Belgium, would represent an intolerable strain on Germany's future domestic situation.

None of this made any impression on Hindenburg. In a direct report to the Kaiser on April 2 he stuck to Ludendorff's charges. Kühlmann had not properly safeguarded German interests at Bucharest.[82] It was to be anticipated that this would be repeated when it came to negotiations with the Western powers, for the German diplomats had amply demonstrated that they were in the habit of tackling their job without adequate preparation. They simply refused to keep their eyes on German power, as revealed in the great successes in the field, already a matter of record in Rumania and now again heralded in the west. Kühlmann had failed to take charge of the negotiations at the outset, nor did he keep the reins firmly in his hand. He should never have allowed Czernin to tell the king of Rumania that Emperor Charles was holding out the hand of peace. He totally lacked any firm program for the negotiations, nor had there been any general directives for the various economic subcommittees, which were staffed with unsuitable men, while Kühlmann himself was unfamiliar with the technicalities. This had opened the door to

Rumania's delaying tactics, and the foreign ministry with its bureaucratic pedantry had simply not been up to the job. As for Czernin, who was praised for cultivating the alliance so carefully, he had entered into separate agreements with the Rumanians behind the backs of the Germans.[83] On Kühlmann's demeanor outside office hours there was a report by Major von Kessler. It showed that the German diplomats diverted themselves in ways incompatible with the standards of German officers and civil servants. Mackensen might disagree, but he, Hindenburg, thought German prestige suffered from this kind of conduct.

Kühlmann had little difficulty, in a report of April 9, demonstrating in detail that all these charges were completely baseless. In this report he praised the exemplary and self-sacrificing work of his associates, singling out especially his seasoned economic adviser von Koerner.[84] He complained in turn of the underhanded way in which the OHL had secured biased and unverified reports from Bucharest behind his back. Hertling forwarded this protest to the Kaiser with a covering letter of his own in which he endorsed Kühlmann's complaints.[85] As had happened before in January, everything possible was being done to keep the foreign minister in his post. Yet it was foreseeable even now that the OHL would leave no stone unturned until it someday brought about his ouster.

Beyond any disagreements on details, it was at bottom a radical conflict in basic political attitudes that made the presence of a man like Kühlmann intolerable to Ludendorff. This contrast emerged even more clearly during the negotiations at Bucharest than it had in Brest-Litovsk. It was indeed a straightforward clash between the sword and the scepter. As Hertling correctly perceived, the peace negotiations at Bucharest were a masterly achievement in diplomacy, giving full scope to the special abilities of Kühlmann, the skillful tactician. As shown in his memoirs, Kühlmann himself evidently regarded these weeks and months in Rumania as the high point of his career. A highly sophisticated connoisseur of life, he thoroughly enjoyed his long sojourn in this southeastern corner of Europe with its colorful exotic life. He studied its art treasures and historic monuments under expert guidance, devoted every leisure hour to lively company and conversation with cultured Rumanians, and applied himself vigorously to the pleasures of the table in a land that was not yet going hungry. He was delighted to find in Field Marshal Mackensen and his shrewd chief of staff Hell sympathetic partners, advisers, and collaborators rather than adversaries. It was thus easy for his ill-wishers to send in reports about his "undignified hobnobbing with the enemy" and "easygoing mode of life." Servile subalterns, down to bribed chauffeurs, were all too willing to provide such intelligence. There were even slanderous charges of immorality that got into the Pan-German press and forced Kühlmann to sue for libel.[86] Every stop was pulled out to bring the Rumanian peace and its author into disrepute, and but for the concentration of public interest on the great battle in France, these attacks would have presented an even graver threat to Kühlmann.

The ultimate motive behind all these personal attacks was Ludendorff's deep resentment that the diplomat had outmaneuvered him in his efforts to end the war with Rumania with another peace dictated in the "proud pose of the victor," as Hertling put it. Ludendorff had no sympathy whatever with Kühlmann's successful endeavor to heal the deep rift with Vienna as much as possible by close collaboration in the Rumanian question.

5

European Diplomacy
and War Propaganda on the Eve
of the Decisive Battle

Part 1
The Struggle for World Opinion;
Peace by Victory or Compromise?

EVEN AFTER Russia made its final exit from the theater of war, there was no change in the decision of the Entente powers of October 6, 1917. There were to be no diplomatic negotiations with Germany unless there were a certainty in advance that the most important war aims of the Entente had been attained, and that no single power would engage in separate negotiations with the enemy (see Chapter 1, Part 4, p. 65f.). Lloyd George had always regarded a negotiated peace as a half measure, and this was rejected out of hand in favor of full and complete victory, i.e., the crushing of Prussian-German military power. Until then there was to be no peace.

But to reach an understanding on such a program at government level was altogether different from convincing the Allied peoples of its iron necessity. The difficulty of this task increased as the hardships of war affected the Entente countries more and more. The U-boat campaign did not exactly bring on a food crisis in Britain, but imports were very perceptibly curtailed. Late in February 1918 food rationing was introduced. In the end, the scarcity of bottoms, even for military purposes, was overcome only by forcible measures against neutral Holland, which in March 1918 was forced under brutal threat to surrender most of its ships.

Of far greater importance was the necessity for calling to the colors hundreds of thousands of civilians hitherto spared war service, to replace the tremendous losses of the preceding summer and stiffen the defensive front in France. This measure especially disturbed the British trade unions and served to strengthen pacifist sentiment. How much longer was the war to last? The German western front was being greatly strengthened in the wake of peace in the east. The American forces were being built up and transported overseas with maddening slowness and they were far from ready for combat. In the face of these difficulties the Allied General Staffs could not even think of mounting another spring offensive. The war might yet last for months, if not years.

To keep the nations prepared for hardships and struggle over such a long period was no easy task. It was rendered all the more difficult by the constant barrage of radio proclamations in which Bolshevist Russia called on the workers of the world to rise against their capitalist governments and force them to make peace on reasonable terms. Never was the need for political mass propaganda more urgent than during these anxious final months before the great decisive battle. This led to a long series of war speeches by the leading men, especially in Britain and America, with frequent replies from the side of the Central Powers, setting off a kind of continuing debate across the fighting fronts.

To compensate for the defection of Russia, the Western powers also made many efforts to split off Austria from Germany, by way of open propaganda as well as secret diplomacy, and in the end also by inciting the Slavic minorities in Austria to rise in rebellion. As for the German politicians, they tried to develop new and more effective methods of counterpropaganda, aimed at breaking morale, especially in Britain, so that the task of the impending great German offensive might be eased, if indeed it might not be avoided altogether. A few German politicians even undertook the hopeless effort of trying to establish contact with liberal British opposition groups and with their help find a basis for peaceful understanding at the last moment.

The strongest impetus was given by the surprising emergence of Lord Lansdowne, conservative leader in the House of Lords and former foreign secretary, who issued an urgent exhortation for the revision of British war policy. We have already heard of his vain efforts in the fall of 1916 to persuade the British cabinet to conclude peace by negotiation rather than victory (see Vol. III, p. 260ff.). Lansdowne now appealed to Foreign Secretary Balfour in a confidential memorandum and simultaneously, on November 9, 1917, to the British people in a letter to the editor of the *Daily Telegraph.*

He reminded the former, as he had the cabinet the preceding year, of future dangers and the uncertain prospects of victory. Eschewing this line in his open letter, he appealed to his fellow countrymen's sense of chivalry. Germany must be beaten, he said, not for revenge but because the recurrence of so dreadful a disaster as occurred in 1914 must be prevented for all time. The world was virtually unanimous on how that was to be accomplished.

Wilson, the German Chancellor, the pope, the Austrian government, and Balfour had all said so—and Lansdowne quoted them liberally. An enduring international organization must be created for the peaceful settlement of disputes.

There would have to be international sanctions to prevent war, of a military as well as an economic character, and on these points it should be possible to reach agreement. It was hard to find solutions right now to the concrete problems at issue, but even Asquith had admitted that the territorial goals proclaimed by the Allies in January 1917 did not constitute an inflexible program immune to revision. That, of course, was not true of all the points then put forward. Belgium, for example, must be liberated and indemnified; but discussion was possible on many points, especially on Balkan questions.

To reach an understanding with the Central Powers, their people must be stirred to force their governments to adopt a reasonable attitude. That meant freeing them of the fear of enemy vengeance and intolerably harsh peace terms. Ministers should publicly declare that Britain (1) did not desire to destroy Germany as a great power; (2) would not force on Germany a form of government it did not want; (3) apart from war measures, did not begrudge Germany its place among the world's great economic communities; (4) stood ready after the war to reexamine with other powers the problems subsumed under the catchword of "freedom of the seas"; and (5) stood ready to enter into a world pact that would serve to settle international disputes by peaceful means.

Lansdowne's letter unleashed a movement that spread farther and farther into the summer of 1918, with demonstrations of various kinds, involving prominent political personages like the former secretary of war, Haldane. It was indeed a classic expression of all the forces in the ancient cradle of liberalism that were opposed to the fanatical militancy and irreconcilable power and victory drive of the new era of total war. They represented the old Anglo-Saxon faith that all the world's political problems could be resolved peacefully around a table by the application of common sense. They were also liberally infused with the revulsion the ancient British peerage felt against the unrestrained warmongering of the great demagogue Lloyd George with his appeal to the proletarian masses, as shown by many letters to Lansdowne and other correspondents.[1]

But was there still a serious chance of steering British policy into calmer waters, away from its course of impassioned militancy and the blind pursuit of victory? Could the bonds that tied Britain to its continental allies be loosened and the dynamics of total war brought to a halt? Surely this was possible only—and even then not with certainty—if there were a change on the German side too, away from the obdurate pugnacity of the military regime now in power. Even so, the fruitless efforts of British and German liberals to follow Lansdowne's lead, achieve a rapprochement, and even establish actual contact, represent a fascinating spectacle that deserves to be followed.

The statesmen in charge of British policy were greatly embarrassed by Lansdowne's performance. Asquith, the liberal leader in the House of Commons, could scarcely allow the conservatives to outdo him in declarations of readiness for peace in principle. He tried to trivialize Lansdowne's letter, as though it were merely an effort to avoid any misapprehension of British war efforts. No one in Britain, he insisted, wanted to humiliate the German people or cause them misfortune. The sole goal was to destroy Prussian militarism and make the Germans understand that a policy of brute force without regard to international law did not pay.[2]

Lloyd George wheeled up heavier guns. On December 14 he declared that there was no middle way between victory and defeat. It was absurd to conclude treaties to secure world peace with a notorious treaty breaker. It was as though a judge let a murderer, arsonist, bandit, burglar, swindler, and pirate go scot-free—and all these descriptions fitted Germany. Indeed, it was like giving such a felon a policeman's badge, merely because the court was bored or fatigued with the trial. A nation whose professors had always taught that crime was within the law if it led to the country's aggrandizement and enrichment would always be a threat to world peace. It was Britain's divine mission to see to justice and thus to establish enduring peace for Englishmen and the children of Englishmen. True, to fight on even a single day when there was no hope would be criminal; but the fact was that despite all the disappointments, ultimate victory was certain. It might take a long time, but Britain had better build a firm bridge to a new and better world rather than one that shook and swayed.[3]

It was a fighting speech that arrogantly enlarged the traditional Whig claim to Britain's mission as the guardian of freedom and law. Hertling almost immediately gave a press interview in which he countered this crude invective hurled against the German people in a thoroughly dignified form. He said he would abstain from conducting a political debate by rude insults "in the style of Homeric heroes." He added that since the speech no one in Germany believed any longer that it was possible to reach agreement with a government headed by Lloyd George.[4] This was quite true. Those in Germany who still hoped for a negotiated peace counted on Lloyd George being brought down by his political enemies.

Lloyd George himself was by no means as confident of victory as he tried to make the public believe. This is shown by the zeal with which he was endeavoring at this very time to bring about a separate peace with Austria, efforts of which we shall hear further on. It is shown equally plainly in a letter he is supposed to have addressed to Clémenceau in mid-December, according to an intelligence report that reached German hands,[5] in which he voiced concern that American aid might not bring tangible military results.

In such an atmosphere of uncertainty there were, as notably Balfour emphasized in the cabinet,[6] certain political risks in any public commitment to a definite war aims program. If the program were kept modest, it might discourage the Allies. If its demands went too far, it would arouse liberal and socialist opposition at home. Strong opposition along such lines was indeed voiced in the House of Commons on December 19, when there was a debate on the secret Allied war aims treaties, which the Bolshevists had been making public one by one since late November. Balfour had a difficult time in justifying them to the opposition as essential.[7]

And then, on December 25, came the Russian invitation to take part in the peace conference at Brest-Litovsk, where general peace was to be made without annexations and indemnities! It was scarcely possible to reject such an invitation without public proof, in the form of a British peace program, that the war had to go on for good reasons and a just cause. Lloyd George absolved himself of this difficult task with consummate rhetorical skill, in his famous speech to British trade union delegates on January 5, 1918.[8] This speech had been carefully prepared to the last detail—it had been discussed within the cabinet, with Asquith and Grey of the liberal opposition, with labor leaders, and with representatives of the chief dominions. It became a basic document for British policy down to the days of Versailles. Three days later President Wilson, acting from similar considerations, followed suit with his even more famous Fourteen Points. The whole Western world was to be convinced that its governments were intent on moderate, reasonable, and highly moral war aims rather than on peace by force alone.

In order to register an impression of this kind. Lloyd George's first task had to be to paint Germany as the aggressor and public enemy who trampled international law underfoot and defied the dictates of humanity, and whose power for evil must on all accounts be broken. There were, of course, the customary assurances that no one dreamed of destroying the German people and their state, nor of forcing a different form of government on them. The only goal was to lead them back to their true mission as a great cultural force—and the speaker had a few well-chosen words of praise for German culture. What Britain desired was that the Germans themselves grow aware of the anachronistic character of their "autocracy" and earn the confidence of the world by a thoroughgoing process of democratization. All the German peace offers that had become known so far, including the latest statement of December 25, had been vague and inadequate, indeed almost devoid of real content.[9] Any future peace treaty must be built on the popular will, freely expressed, i.e., on the right of self-determination, which applied to all nations, large and small, rather than being based on the whims and power rivalries of governments, as had been true in Vienna in 1814-1815.

This assertion of nationalism and self-determination as the basis for a new order in Europe was the heart of the British prime minister's speech. Wielding this weapon with consummate skill, he was able to gild Entente power politics with a halo of morality and idealism. His task was made easier than it had been in January 1917, for he could speak freely, without fear of meddling by Britain's allies.

The return of Belgium, he said, was not enough. The high reparations Germany would have to pay were amply justified in atonement for the wrong that had been done. As Asquith had done before him (see p. 49), Lloyd George now described the German seizure of Alsace-Lorraine in 1871, without reference to the desires of the people, as an outright crime—this, of course, completely ignored the knotty problem of what really was the nationality of the Alsatians. Reconsideration of this wrong, which had poisoned the peace of Europe for half a century, was as much a moral obligation as it was an indispensable means toward securing that peace.

The union into an independent state of all Poles who wished to be so joined was justified by similar arguments; but Lloyd George was rather more cautious about Italian, Rumanian, and South Slav ambitions. He did not want to affront Austria openly, which would have nipped in the bud any new or continuing hopes in Vienna for a tolerable separate peace. He did say that all peoples of common descent and language had the right to be joined into separate states, but his language was vague, and Italy's sweeping war aims along the Adriatic were not even mentioned. Instead there was still another assurance that Britain desired no dismemberment of the Austrian Empire, any more than did America.

As for Turkey, the "liberation" of the Arabs, Armenians, Mesopotamians, Syrians, and Palestinians from the Turkish yoke did amount to total dismemberment of the Ottoman Empire; but the Turks were to remain unmolested in their homelands of Asia Minor, with Istanbul. The notorious London treaties of 1915, which were just then becoming known to the world, were brushed aside with a reassuring statement that all such agreements were subject to revision, according to the war situation.

Lastly, the right of self-determination was applied also to the blacks in the German colonies, though in rather labored phraseology and not without a certain embarrassment. The irksome fact that the askaris in German East Africa had fought on the German side with a degree of bravery that aroused admiration throughout the world was disposed of by describing them as a "privileged minority," thus picturing them as a kind of feudal caste.

Amends for wrongs that had been done, assertion of the principle of self-determination for all nations, and—as the keystone—disarmament and the creation of international organizations along Wilson's lines, to secure enduring peace–this was indeed a war aims program bound to make a great impact. In his closing words Lloyd George rose to heights of passion, cursing war as a relic of barbarism that must be promptly rooted out. What he was actually proclaiming and justifying in this speech, however, was continuation of the war with undiminished and merciless severity.

Clémenceau understandably lost no time in congratulating the British prime minister on an oratorical triumph that absolved France from the necessity of giving any detailed reasons why, against the will of the socialists, it should stay away from the peace negotiations at Brest-Litovsk.[10] There was little that German propaganda could do to make up for the moral advantage the great British demagogue had gained with his speech and to discredit him in the eyes of his fellow countrymen. The Germans might have countered the charge of reckless conquest, if, at Brest-Litovsk, they had appeared in the role of liberators and if they had really set about the realization of their Christmas peace program; but as we already know, this fine-sounding program, holding out the hope of negotiated peace, was replaced only three days later with another much more concrete program that made the proclamation of December 25 seem the merest hypocrisy.

Thus Wilson, in his great propaganda speech of January 8, was able to begin with the question of who was really in charge on the German side. Was it the liberal German and Austrian statesmen who stood behind the peace declaration of December 25, or was it the military leaders, incapable of any thought other than to hold on to what they had? For whom did the negotiators of the Central Powers speak, their parliamentary majorities or the military and other domestic minorities that had hitherto dictated their policy? The fateful dichotomy of German policy, the craven dependence of German statesmen on the generals, could have scarcely been characterized more bluntly.[11]

Actually, the note which Wilson sounded was on this occasion notably conciliatory, unlike his reply of August 27 to the papal peace note (see p. 26). He carefully avoided invective and blanket charges. America felt no envy of the achievements and distinctions in science and peaceful pursuits that had established such a brilliant and enviable reputation for Germany. There was no desire to injure Germany in any way or to block its rightful influence and power. There was indeed no desire to fight Germany, either with arms or by means of economic sanctions, if only Germany were willing to join with America and the other peace-loving nations of the world in an order based on law, justice, and fair play. To this end Germany needed only to accept equal status with other nations in the world as it existed today, instead of seeking to dominate them. Neither was there any desire to meddle with Germany's constitutional institutions. What was necessary was to know who were Germany's true spokesmen.

Such was the tenor of the Fourteen Points speech; and later on, when its military power had collapsed, Germany desperately clung to these words as its last hope. By 1919, when this hope was so bitterly disappointed, they were decried as hypocritical. How can they be explained?

Wilson was deeply impressed with the vigor with which Bolshevist Russia pressed for peace, without annexations and the right of self-determination. Lansdowne's open letter had impressed him equally. Like his intimate, House, Wilson thought that the time had come to put forward a peace program that would plainly show the world that America was not prepared to fight for the selfish aims of European powers—"with the possible exception of Alsace-Lorraine," as he cautiously added in a wire to House.12 America was fighting solely for a just and enduring peace, in the sense of the American ideology he had proclaimed so often before.

Ever since the arguments over the papal note, Wilson had been afraid that there would be disagreement between America and the European Allies over the details of his program, when it came to putting general principles into concrete proposals, especially in the settlement of territorial questions. In preparation for these issues, so foreign to American political experience, Wilson had asked House in September to form a special "commission of inquiry" of scholars and publicists that would write position papers on ethnographic, economic, and territorial matters affecting Europe. It became the precursor of his subsequent advisory staff at the Versailles peace conference and, in a sense, of the whole latter-day American approach to foreign relations. First activated for the drafting of the Fourteen Points speech, it did not cover itself with glory on that occasion.

Wilson felt a special sense of urgency, on account of Trotzky's appeal to the world of December 29, which he thought would have a profound effect on the Western peoples. Then too there was House's disappointing experience at an Allied conference in Paris early in December, when the American had vainly tried to extract a positive reply to the Soviet peace proclamation. Well, if the Allies fumbled, the president himself would leap into the breach! Without calling in his shrewd secretary of state Lansing, whose skeptical attitude toward the revolutionary doctrine of self-determination he knew and feared, Wilson locked himself in his study, as usual, with only House. The final draft was actually ready on January 5, and Wilson learned only then that Lloyd George—worried on his part about unwelcome statements by the American prophet of peace—had anticipated him on that day.

Wilson's speech, such as it was, was not intended to serve as a program for a negotiated peace, to which none of the Allies would have agreed. Its purpose was to encourage some revision of Allied war aims and to help assuage the concern if not the fury of liberals and socialists throughout the world, which was aroused by the secret Allied treaties that had been recently publicized. To this end the president was compelled, in his Fourteen Points, to come to grips for the first time with concrete controversial questions, especially those of a territorial nature. He did not find it at all easy. Beyond this, however, his aim was also agitational. The Russians were to be deterred from a separate peace with the Central Powers and encouraged to stick with the Allies. The German social democrats were to be incited against the military regime of the OHL and against the Pan-Germans, the Austrians heartened to make peace separately.

In pursuit of the first of these aims, Wilson had fulsome words of praise for the Russian people, their unswerving love of liberty, the grandeur of their concepts, the nobility of their sentiments, their steadfast and selfless adherence to ideals. Coupled with this were solemn but vague assurances of assistance, but this was less a pledge than a challenge to all "sister nations" to put their goodwill to the test. In Paris and London the Russians were long since regarded as traitors and the Bolshevist regime was openly opposed, but Wilson had not a word of criticism for the new rule of force. His diplomats and agents kept him very poorly informed about conditions in Russia, indeed misled him outright.[13] Wilson seems at the time to have had no clearer picture of the true nature of Bolshevism than did his successor Franklin D. Roosevelt in the Second World War. He was totally unrealistic in trying to encourage Russia to engage in new military exploits on the Allied side. Long since helpless and defenseless, the Russian nation was in a state of chaos.

His attempt to exhort the Germans seemed more promising. Once the leaders of the Reichstag majority were put in charge of foreign policy, it would be seen that they need not anticipate an intolerable peace, dictated by force. The treaty would be freely and openly negotiated. It would provide for freedom of the seas, removal of economic restrictions, general disarmament, and a strictly impartial settlement of colonial claims, taking the wishes of the colonial peoples into account. Of course the return and restoration of Belgium and occupied France would be demanded.

As the president well knew, the most delicate question was that of Alsace-Lorraine. We have already heard (p. 137) that he was hesitant even to mention it and that he was searching for a compromise formula; but on the point of demanding the restoration of an independent Polish national state he was quite uncompromising. Following the wishes of the émigré Polish national committee, he insisted that the new Poland comprise the Polish ethnographic borders and have free access to the sea. He did add the qualification that only areas of "incontestably Polish population" should be included.

Wilson was very eager to learn the effect of this program on the German parties of the left and issued instructions that the German socialist press be carefully scrutinized. Immediately, his two territorial demands proved an obstacle to the success for which he had hoped, especially the cession of

Alsace-Lorraine, even though this was formulated only indirectly. Yet the speech did make a certain impression on the Germans, and in the fall of 1918, after the military disaster, it invested its author with a certain charisma.

In Austria—which was rather ostentatiously treated with kid gloves—the immediate effect was stronger. Wilson was firmly opposed to dissolving the Austrian Empire—indeed, his inquiry commission had urgently recommended that it be preserved as a large and uniform economic area. The peoples within the empire, however, were to have the freest opportunity for autonomous development. The borders of Italy were to be revised, but solely along clearly recognizable national lines. This meant that the Italian-speaking part of South Tyrol was to be ceded to Italy, but not the German-speaking part, a position Wilson is known to have taken at Versailles initially—he was, in fact, highly critical of the extravagant Italian annexationist demands.

The American president, like his inquiry commission, had only the vaguest notions about the complexities of the Balkan problem and expanded on it only in cautious general terms. As for Turkey, he developed a program not unlike that of Lloyd George. All in all, nothing that was completely unacceptable was put to Austria; we shall examine the effect of this at greater length further on.

There was in Germany a group of convinced liberals who, ever since publication of Lansdowne's letter, thought they perceived a split in British public opinion that might trip up Lloyd George and his "knockout" policy, if only Germany lent a vigorous hand. The leading spirit seems to have been a young publicist and later pedagogue, Kurt Hahn, political adviser to Prince Max of Baden and his liberal coterie. Hahn at the time held down the British desk in the German foreign ministry's military department, which was headed by Colonel Haeften and served as a liaison agency between the ministry and the OHL. One of its tasks was to supply the OHL with intelligence about the foreign press.

We have already met Haeften in the role of Ludendorff's confidant in the winter of 1914-1915 (Vol. III, p. 48ff.). At the time now in point, he had been strongly influenced by his new environment. He had begun to understand that political problems did not necessarily yield to military solutions, and in the last year of the war he did his best to influence his chief along such lines. This led to repeated mediation efforts with the diplomats, but Haeften was never able to escape from his acceptance of strict military discipline, and in his subordinate role he was unable to pursue a coherent policy.

Through Hahn Haeften was put in touch with Prince Max of Baden, brother and heir presumptive to the reigning grand duke of Baden. Prince Max was a high aristocrat of indubitably liberal and humane convictions, though he was lacking in political stature and instinct. Urged on by his friends, the prince, in the winter of 1917-1918, repeatedly tried to influence public opinion at home and abroad along moderately liberal but still patriotic lines. Even though he was not always pursuing concrete goals, his speeches and interviews earned him much sympathy on the part of liberals.

The prince was always guided by his friend Wilhelm Solf, the colonial minister, an unswerving enemy of the Pan-Germans whom Hertling regularly consulted in matters of foreign policy.[14] Greatest admirer of the prince was the democratic deputy Haussmann, who kept in constant touch with him and had recommended him as a candidate for the chancellorship after the fall of Bethmann Hollweg and again when Michaelis left that post.

Hahn was disappointed when Kühlmann and the foreign ministry failed to come to Lansdowne's support with a public declaration on the relinquishment of Belgium. In his memoirs Prince Max reproduced a memorandum of December 11, intended to persuade Ludendorff to come out in favor of Germany relinquishing Belgium. Almost certainly written by Hahn, it tends to show that Hahn, despite his close official connections with the OHL, was only imperfectly aware of Ludendorff's political stand.[15] Ludendorff's views on the Belgian question never wavered. On the contrary, in the winter of 1917-1918 he repeatedly tried to dissuade the OHL as well as Hertling from the limitations placed on German claims to Belgium at the crown council of September 11 (see p. 51f.).[16]

Oddly enough, neither Hahn nor Haeften was deterred by these efforts. On January 14 they themselves tried to gain OHL approval for an unequivocal public declaration on Belgium. The ostensible occasion was the new situation created by the speeches of Lloyd George and Wilson which, in their view, required a German response. To that end they projected a program in a memorandum intended for Ludendorff and conceived in terms of his purely military thinking.

A new German peace offer, they said, was decidedly counterindicated. In Britain such an offer would be interpreted merely as a sign of weakness. It would serve to mobilize only the extreme pacifists, whose activities were of no conceivable interest to Germany, while it would weaken if not discredit the position of Lansdowne and his followers. An attempt to ingratiate oneself with Lloyd George in the style of Erzberger, following the crude invective the British prime minister had hurled against Germany in his speech of December 14, was the last thing to be done. Even Kühlmann's secret peace feeler of the preceding September had been wide of the mark, the crucial flaw being that it was based on a belief that Lloyd George's government might be ready to negotiate.

No, what now needed to be done was to move openly to the attack against Lloyd George the warmonger. It would have to be made clear beyond doubt to the British that the only factor responsible for the continuation of the war was Lloyd George's "knockout" policy. Germany had to provide Lansdowne with the weapons he needed to topple the present British government. If the intelligence and the many hints from Britain were to be trusted, this could be done only by the issuance of a declaration on Belgium that would avoid the equivocation of the past, such as the demand for "dependable guarantees," etc.

Such a declaration should become the core of an intensive propaganda campaign, which was urgently needed by way of political preparation for the great spring offensive contemplated. By the time German military operations commenced, the British home front must have become so demoralized that German military successes would register the greatest possible effect. "Today words have become battles. The right words are battles won, the wrong words are battles lost." The authors were clearly trying to make up for the sins of omission of the early fall, now that the great decisive battle impended. They still wished to enlist world opinion on Germany's side, and by couching their demands in strongly militant terms they hoped to gain the approval of the all-powerful OHL.

They were badly deceived. On the very day that this memorandum was written, Ludendorff sent word to the Chancellor, demanding that he disavow the Reichstag peace resolution, "since the conditions that gave it birth no longer apply."[17] Ludendorff liked the idea of mounting a political propaganda campaign that might topple Lloyd George, especially since Haeften's memorandum seriously criticized the passive attitude of German diplomacy. He may also have been impressed with the detailed knowledge of internal British difficulties shown in the memorandum, which he transmitted to the government as an OHL program—but with every reference to Belgium deleted, which, of course, rendered the whole exercise pointless.[18]

The German diplomats scarcely could be expected to score any bull's-eyes with mere charges aimed at Lloyd George, no matter how massive. Haeften did make one further feeble attempt to convert Ludendorff. On February 4 Ludendorff voiced great enthusiasm over the peace treaty with the Ukraine and developed grandiose plans for the future. Haeften remarked that Germany would do well to take the fullest advantage of its successes in the east, so that an offensive in the west might become superfluous. Germany could well afford to let Belgium go and thus secure a negotiated peace.

Ludendorff, supported by his section chief Wetzell, naturally would not hear of such a thing. Belgium must remain in German hands at all costs, he said. "I found this plausible," Haeften wrote in his 1918 notes, "and I remained silent."[19] Kurt Hahn was instructed to stop working for a declaration on Belgium. He protested in vain.[20]

Hertling passed on the memorandum of January 14 to Kühlmann, but the foreign minister, as we already know (see p. 95f.), was just then embroiled in his own serious conflict with Ludendorff, and he apparently left the memorandum unanswered.[21] Shortly before this the Chancellor had asked his advice on what he should say in response to the speeches of Lloyd George and Wilson. His reply of January 10 shows that he too thought an aggressive reply to Lloyd George indicated. His main recommendation was that the vast power drive and territorial ambitions hiding behind the fine words about minority rights and enduring peace be laid bare. Here Alsace-Lorraine was to be annexed, Italian and Rumanian greed supported, Turkey dismembered, and the German colonies reapportioned, ostensibly taking into account the wishes of their people—a policy which Britain completely ignored in Ireland, India, and Egypt.[22]

This might indeed have weakened the impact of Lloyd George's speech in Britain, but it would not have accomplished much more than that. At the time it would have been not merely dangerous but completely futile for Kühlmann to propose a declaration foregoing Belgium. Hertling would not have acceded to such a plan.[23] Hence the foreign minister did not wish to see the Belgian question even discussed. He did propose a declaration to the effect that Germany and its allies were not in the least interested in anything Lloyd George might have to say on the question of peace, unless there were full recognition of the territorial integrity of the entire Quadruple Alliance, not merely Germany.

That would have represented a very sharp rebuff, and one is tempted to conclude that at the time Kühlmann had given up all hope of an understanding with Britain—or at any rate with any government under Lloyd George.[24] Hertling, however, did not follow him in this attitude. In his reply to Lloyd George and Wilson, given before the main committee of the Reichstag on January 24, he resisted the temptation to score what would almost certainly have been a most effective point—indeed, might have seriously embarrassed Wilson[25] —namely, to ask which was the true Allied policy, Wilson's Fourteen Points or the secret treaties that had just been made public. Recognizing that both his adversaries had struck a somewhat milder tone than before, he sought to defend Germany against their charges. He argued Germany's historic right to Alsace-Lorraine and endeavored to show that most of the president's Fourteen Points were acceptable to the Central Powers—at least as a basis for serious peace talks. Hertling did criticize Lloyd George's continuing hostility, but his speech was not conceived as a gage of battle for the British prime minister, but rather as an effort to demonstrate to the British, and especially to the Americans, that Germany was basically in a conciliatory mood and was willing to reach a peaceful compromise. They were to be made to realize that it was unnecessary to fight on to the bitter end and to be challenged to revise their war aims. Hertling, of course, did not fail to mention Germany's tremendous military strength, now that the war on the eastern front was at an end.

It was a speech that accorded well with the desires of German liberals—except for the decisive point of the treatment of Belgium, in which the Chancellor showed himself more dependent on the good graces of the OHL than on the will of the majority parties. Hertling merely referred to the repeated declarations of his predecessors in office, who had stated that Germany's peace program did not include the forcible integration of Belgium. Actually, the details of this question would have to be settled in "war and peace negotiations." They certainly could not be taken for granted so long as the enemy refused to acknowledge the territorial integrity of the Central Powers as a self-evident basis for peace. Thus everything was once again left open and the political effect of the speech was blurred.26

Still dissatisfied, a group of liberal politicians and intellectuals on February 11 tried once again to win over the OHL for an open declaration on Belgium. Their comprehensive memorandum, written by the sociologist Alfred Weber with Kurt Hahn, also bore the signatures of Friedrich Naumann, the publicist Jäckh, Dr. Robert Bosch, and the trade union officials Legien and Stegerwald.27 It argued that a prompt end to the war had become a matter of urgency for the Central Powers, not least because Germany's allies were wasting away. The impending great offensive would exact huge bloodshed, which the German people would accept uncomplainingly only if they were convinced that the enemy had forced it on them. On the other side, the morale of the British workers was also bound to suffer if Germany succeeded in spreading the same conviction there. This was possible only with the aid of a broadly conceived propaganda offensive, and this in turn could succeed only on the basis of completely unequivocal statements about Belgium, demonstrating to the world that the war was being continued solely to enable the French to annex Alsace-Lorraine. Even if it should prove impossible to topple the Lloyd George government, the war on the British side would deteriorate from a people's war into a government war, dooming it to failure.

Prince Max of Baden gave vigorous support to this approach, though seemingly only after hesitating for some time. He was not sure that his position as a member of a ruling dynasty permitted him to emerge in so strongly political a role, virtually as leader of an opposition group.28 In the end, detailed information from Hahn on the situation in Britain apparently convinced him that a mood of political depression and crisis prevailing there simply had to be exploited. Haussmann had repeatedly met with politically motivated—or charged—British emissaries in Switzerland since December, gaining the impression that peaceful tendencies were gathering force in Britain29 and also bringing back a report by the well-known Swiss military writer Hermann Stegemann that deeply impressed the circle around Haeften. It held that the German spring offensive was bound to bring considerable political gains, but it certainly would not bring about a decision. Hence it was an urgent matter to capitalize immediately on Allied fears of the offensive along the lines of the Weber-Hahn memorandum.

Prince Max, according to his own report, met with outright rejection on the part of the Chancellor. Hertling said that a declaration on Belgium would be of no use to Germany at this time. It would be taken no more seriously in the enemy camp than all the preceding statements. British public opinion could be decisively influenced only by great military successes, in which Hertling had boundless faith. Kühlmann, on his part, remained skeptical. He did not believe that the offensive would have any miraculous effects or that another Belgian declaration would meet with any success, apart from the fact that the generals would not have it.[30]

The prince now decided to visit Ludendorff at headquarters, which he did on February 19. He was strongly impressed with the serious and responsible cast of Ludendorff's mind. The general listened to him with courteous interest, but the prince was quite unable to get him to modify his Belgian program.[31] Three days later Ludendorff sent his reply to the authors of the memorandum of February 11. It dealt exclusively with the military necessity for the great offensive and swept aside the political proposals in the memorandum with a single sentence: "So long as we seek an economically strong and secure fatherland, we do not have the alternative of peace or war."[32]

To try to change Ludendorff's mind by means of written arguments was probably a priori a hopeless undertaking. Kühlmann, moreover, was probably justified in his skepticism—it was already too late for declarations about Belgium. On February 4 the Supreme Allied War Council at Versailles—though with the United States represented only by an observer—had put out a brusquely worded statement. It said that the latest speeches by Hertling and Czernin—who had spoken in even more conciliatory tones than the Chancellor—showed no real accommodation to the "moderate war aims" of the Allies. The course of the negotiations at Brest-Litovsk only served to deepen this impression. At odds with the idealistic principles initially proclaimed there, the Central Powers were now openly out for conquest and aggrandizement. In the event, the Allies could only resolve to stand shoulder to shoulder, mustering all their resources toward carrying on the war. In the face of unrepentant aggressive militarism, the Allies could only hope that their joint efforts would persuade the enemy to make peace on the basis of freedom, justice, and respect for international law.[33]

This meant formal rejection of the continuing public peace dialogue among the political leaders as futile. Paris had evidently taken alarm over the effect on the Central Powers statesmen of Wilson's Fourteen Points, anticipating that Allied morale might be weakened by conciliatory speeches by German and Austrian ministers. The American State Department, however, immediately protested that it should not be held responsible for the Versailles declaration.[34] Indeed, on February 11 Wilson delivered an even more conciliatory speech before the Congress—it was certainly more conciliatory in respect of Austria, to which it was primarily addressed, as we shall hear further on.

Toward Hertling the president explicitly displayed distrust and ill will. He refrained from reproaching the Chancellor for his vague statements about Belgium, but did describe Hertling's speech as highly confusing. He grossly misinterpreted and even distorted some of Hertling's statements, which, he complained, were lacking in the spirit of the peace resolution of July 19. Wilson's speech culminated in four additional points, moral principles as a general basis for peace, which amounted in essence to recognition of the right of self-determination in all territorial changes.[35]

Lloyd George and Balfour, on February 12 and 13, at once tried to weaken the impression made by this speech with statements of their own in which Czernin's and especially Hertling's replies to Wilson's Fourteen Points were scored as displaying the same old militarism. The British prime minister emphasized the absence of any satisfactory statements on Belgium and Alsace-Lorraine in Hertling's speech. Balfour defended the Versailles proclamation against vehement opposition attacks in the House of Commons; and on February 15 a semiofficial commentary in a Reuters dispatch opposed any further pressure for a revision of Allied war aims. The statements by Lloyd George and Wilson already constituted a minimum program, it said, and it was illusory to believe that the Central Powers could be converted to more moderate war aims—the German people did not desire an enduring democratic peace.[36]

Considerable pressure was now built up on Hertling to discredit this point of view. He tried to do so in another Reichstag speech on February 25. He told Prince Hohenlohe that he had little hope of practical effects, but felt the need for easing his conscience by meeting the other side as much as was to his mind compatible with the dignity of the German Reich.[37] In this endeavor he would seem to have been strongly influenced by suggestions that had been made to Haussmann by the Englishmen with whom he had had discussions in Switzerland.[38] The most important passage in Hertling's new speech, however, which dealt with Belgium, was held in the same vague terms as before and certainly was not calculated to make any impression abroad. Thus the fact that Hertling accepted Wilson's additional four points virtually without reservations as a basis for negotiations availed him little.[39]

In his reply, Balfour had an even easier time in disposing of this agreement as practically immaterial, since in those very days the Germans had resumed their advance on St. Petersburg. The dictated peace of Brest-Litovsk gave him a welcome opportunity to charge the Germans once again with intolerable militarism, which he represented as something more than merely the policy of a few ambitious generals. It represented the views of important sections of the German intelligentsia which, he said, firmly aspired to world dominion and wished to see the rest of the civilized world crawling at its feet.[40]

Thus the dialogue among the statesmen of the world ended in bitter vituperations. In a second open letter on March 5, Lord Lansdowne vainly implored his fellow countrymen not to persist in an unyieldingly militant stance, but to continue discussions among a small circle, as proposed by Hertling. He also vainly implored the German Chancellor to elucidate the meaning of his statement on Belgium without equivocation. Was it intended in the spirit of the papal note, which had demanded not only the complete evacuation of Belgium, but also guarantees that Belgium would enjoy full political, military, and economic independence from all the powers? Or did it carry the qualifications imputed by Balfour?

The circle around Prince Max of Baden spent much vain effort to persuade Hertling to give a public reply to these questions,[41] which would have provided Lansdowne with the strongest possible weapon for his peace initiative and his fight against the Entente's annexationist demands. The Chancellor possessed neither the power nor the courage for such an act. As the Austrian ambassador Hohenlohe told the prince to his face on February 17, there was no possibility of political propaganda in Germany, except by leave of the OHL. He also told Kühlmann that the time for playing hide-and-seek and engaging in diplomatic shadowboxing in the Belgian question was past. Germany could well afford to come out in the open at last and say in so many words what it proposed to do with Belgium. "I am firmly convinced," he added, "that unless we succeed in terminating the world war by negotiation with Britain before the western offensive begins, we shall with absolute certainty drift into universal disaster, no matter how the offensive may come out." The ambassador felt that Count Hertling was too old and irresolute to stand up manfully for his convictions, regardless of the views and ideas of the OHL.[42]

No doubt he was right. It is more than uncertain that in the wake of events at Brest-Litovsk even the kind of declaration on Belgium he desired would have persuaded Britain to pursue a more conciliatory policy and make an effort to reach a peaceful understanding. Yet the impact on world opinion, including America, would have been a powerful one, especially since such a statement would have come at a time when German military strength was at its peak. We can scarcely disagree with Bethmann Hollweg, who took the clear-cut position—which he vainly tried to get his successor Hertling to adopt—that Germany, whatever it expected of its offensive, must embark on such a venture only after having stated its stand on Belgium in unequivocal terms.[43] The unfortunate fact was that no one anywhere seriously trusted Germany's military rulers with adopting a policy of moderation.

There were two ways in which Ludendorff's military triumph at Brest-Litovsk exerted an unfavorable effect on all the attempts to reach an understanding. Within Germany it aroused patriotic pride and a new confidence in victory that reached all the way into the ranks of the majority parties, making many Germans believe that the Reichstag resolution of July 19 was an obsolete and indeed irksome commitment. On the other side, especially in America, it was felt to be a triumph of German imperialism and as such a threat to the world, stifling any inclination toward compromise. This was brought home to Prince Max's liberal group when certain peace discussions that seemed likely early in March via the American legation at The Hague failed to eventuate. Private talks which Haeften and Hahn conducted there with a German-American intermediary showed that there would not be the slightest chance of any further American peace initiative, unless there were a revision of the peace treaty of Brest-Litovsk.[44]

Part 2
Attempts to Wean Away Austria from the German War Alliance

THE LONG SERIES of war speeches by German, American, and British statesmen during the final winter of the war represented in the end nothing more than a struggle for world opinion. Both sides tried to persuade their people that continuation of the war to the bitter end was inevitable and the best guarantee for a just and enduring peace to come. It is true that on the German side there were repeated statements in favor of a compromise peace, but they were given without conviction and without willingness to forego any part of pre-1914 German territory; and then there was the matter of Germany's powerful expansionist drive in the east, either embodied in the treaties of Brest-Litovsk or predictable from them.

Unlike the numberless soundings taken by German diplomats ever since 1915 in Scandinavia, Switzerland, Belgium, and Holland,[45] there was not a single peace feeler from the Allied side that might have been taken as laying the groundwork for a negotiated peace with Germany. The sole attempt, emanating from Belgium and planned by Briand in 1917, was instantly squelched and did not even get off the ground (see p. 60f.). Allied efforts to get Germany's failing allies, especially Austria, to defect were, however, pursued with all the greater frequency and vigor.[46] The war speeches by Allied statesmen which we have just examined were essentially part of the effort. They were intended to deepen Austrian war-weariness by representing Prussian militarism and its insatiable appetite for conquest as the true and sole reason why the war was still going on.

We have already heard of the first and very serious French peace feeler launched by War Minister Painlevé in August 1917 (see p. 35ff.). It failed because of Czernin's unshakable loyalty to the German alliance. About the same time there seemed also to be a prospect of peace talks with the British envoy in Holland, Sir Walter Tawnley, initiated by the Dutch foreign minister Loudon and another unidentified person. Preliminary discussions among the intermediaries dragged on until November. Late in October, during the great Austro-German offensive on the Italian front, London called off these talks, which were soon afterward resumed, however, only to be broken off in the end by the Austrian side, which was unwilling to allow the British to tempt them into a peace offer laid down in writing.

Nevertheless these talks were not entirely negative, in that the Austrians learned on October 20 that while the British government had expressed its solidarity with France in respect of Alsace-Lorraine, it would very much like to see France ease up on its intransigent point of view. Conversely, Czernin sent word to Britain via the Dutch intermediaries that Austria had enough influence to get Germany to relinquish Belgium and that Belgium would represent no obstacle to peace. On the question of Alsace-Lorraine, however, Austria was entirely on Germany's side. If Britain were to insist on the return to France of these provinces, that would mean indefinite prolongation of the war.[47]

On this occasion too, in other words, Austria's attitude was impeccably loyal to the alliance. In his comprehensive situation report of July 22[48] (see p. 146f.) Count Wedel had mentioned that hatred and resentment of "the Prussians" prevailed in Austria, and that if a plebiscite were held, most Austrians—though not the Hungarians—would vote for lining up on the Allied side against Germany. The German-speaking Bohemians formed an exception. Their entire aristocracy—the Fürstenbergs, Clams, Czernins, and Nostizes—as well as their merchant class were pillars of the German alliance.

Czernin was indeed a member of this group. We recall his sharp clash with the Berlin politicians as recently as August 1917, when he demanded that German war aims be limited and applied this demand to Alsace-Lorraine as well (see p. 35f.). He had now convinced himself that the Germans would never voluntarily forego those provinces, any more than the Austrians would forego South Tyrol, and he calmly cast up the balance. "If anyone asks whether we are fighting for Alsace-Lorraine," he told a group of Hungarian deputies in Budapest on December 6, "the answer is yes—we are fighting for Alsace-Lorraine, just as Germany is fighting for us, and has fought for Lvov and Trieste. I see no difference between Strasbourg and Trieste."

Czernin did say in the same address that following Kühlmann's Reichstag declaration it was now clear beyond any doubt that the sole remaining obstacle to peace was Alsace-Lorraine, with Belgium no longer figuring in the picture. Germany's allies need not, therefore, fear that they would have to fight for non-German prizes.[49] This prompted Hindenburg to lodge a strong protest with the Chancellor. Since the discussions at the crown council of September 11 no longer applied, the agreements of April 23 with respect to Belgium were back in force, he insisted.[50] It was an ungrateful reaction to the Austrian minister's loyalty declaration.

Czernin naturally had to see to it, on the other hand, that he was not in any way identified with the spirit of "Prussian militarism," or he would have earned a reputation of being a mere puppet. He did this in a famous and controversial peace speech in Budapest on October 2. To universal surprise, he declared his fervent allegiance to a program of general disarmament and settlement of all postwar conflicts among nations by international courts of arbitration.[51] This speech may well have helped strengthen his reputation in Britain and America as a moderate statesman who was in favor of peace. At any rate, when Wilson, in a most curious speech on December 4, asked the American Congress to declare war against Austria-Hungary, he avoided criticizing Czernin in any way. He heaped obloquy on the German statesmen, proclaiming that the extermination of their "autocracy" was an urgent war aim; but he allowed Austria, Bulgaria, and Turkey to appear as mere tools and helpless victims of these "sinister masters" and their ambitious intrigues. According to Wilson, the war against the Austrian Empire (actually declared at the behest of the Allies, especially Italy) was virtually a war of liberation of these German "satellites." Austria was expressly assured that America would not dream of weakening it or meddling with its internal affairs, or of depriving it of free access to the sea, to which it was as much entitled as the Serbs and Poles.[52] In another Budapest speech of December 6 Czernin immediately expressed gratification over these assurances, adding, however, his own assurances with which we are already familiar, namely that Austria would remain true to its ally.

This was of particular significance, since at about this time a new chance of entering into peace talks with Britain was opening up, an opportunity that had to be taken very seriously. The first hint came through the British envoy in Switzerland early in November. This was followed a month later by a second approach in which it was stated that the British suggested a discussion between two notable political personages who would serve as delegates from the two countries. This discussion was to take place on the neutral soil of Switzerland, directly accessible from Austria.[53] The man behind this plan was none less than Lloyd George, who early in December in the Allied war council had vigorously and in the end successfully pressed for agreement on a British effort to drive a wedge between Germany and Austria and possibly disrupt the alliance, providing some compensation for Russia's defection, so to speak.[54] These peace talks did take place, and they remain virtually unique in the history of the First World War, on account of both the high political rank of the two participants and the high intellectual level of the exchanges.

The British representative at the meeting on December 18 and 19 in Geneva was the former Boer general Smuts, then a member of the British war cabinet. Smuts was accompanied by Lloyd George's private secretary, Philip Kerr. On the Austrian side was Count Mensdorff, former ambassador in London, where he was well thought of. Mensdorff immediately rejected any idea of a separate peace with Austria with such finality that there was no further talk on this subject. What Smuts tried to do instead was to paint such a tempting picture of Austria's possible future as to make it appear most attractive to abandon Germany. Internally liberalized and at peace by virtue of having been transformed into a "league of free nationalities," freed of domination by Prussia-Germany, and enlarged by the inclusion of Poland, the Austrian Empire would take Russia's place as a counterpoise to the powerful German Reich, which was forever threatening the peace of Europe. At the same time Austria would enjoy the full sympathy and support of the Western powers.

It was all couched in rather vague terms, and Mensdorff's assurances that Austria would certainly be amenable to new goals after the war were small comfort. For the time being he merely promised that Austria would seek to exert a moderating influence on German war aims. He was not very forthcoming in respect of the British emissary's efforts to get Vienna to make concessions to Italy, Serbia, and Rumania. Indeed, nothing whatever of a concrete nature arose from these discussions. What made them memorable nevertheless was the absolute clarity with which two reasonable statesmen from the hostile power blocs, sitting down to talk together calmly, established the fact that it was impossible to negotiate peace with Germany—a country which Smuts personally professed to admire! Even if Germany were now to join a league of nations, he said, it would form a continuing threat to the world, simply on account of its frightening military superiority. The fear and danger looming over Europe that led to the present war would go on, leading to ever-greater armaments. Everything depended on breaking Germany's military dictatorship and erecting a protective wall of alliances against the aggressor.

In moving words Mensdorff vainly implored Smuts to consider that the war, indefinitely continued, could result only in the hopeless destruction of Europe's power and culture, while America would become the financial and economic center of the world. What would such a victory avail Britain, he asked? In vain he sought to convince Smuts that the German government stood ready indeed to moderate its war aims. The recent rise of liberal democratic forces was unmistakable, men from the working class had become thoroughly capable of conducting the business of government, and the German socialist party was the largest in Europe. The power of the OHL would instantly collapse, once peace talks were started in earnest.

Smuts pointed out, however, that fear and distrust of the all-powerful Prussian military caste were so deeply rooted in British public opinion that there could be no question of direct Anglo-German peace talks. He insisted sorrowfully that Britain would have to carry on the war, indefinitely if necessary, but in any event until victory was achieved or the dark forces of revolution had done their work, as in Russia. The threat to Britain was no smaller than the threat that had once been posed by Napoleon, and the British people were determined to meet it with even greater resolution.[55]

Lloyd George's splitting maneuver, in other words, failed out of hand. Yet General Smuts did gain certain lasting impressions—of Mensdorff's high caliber, of his statements that Vienna stood ready to exert strong pressure on its German partner for more moderate war aims, of Austrian satisfaction that no one in London dreamed of carving up the Austrian Empire, of Emperor Charles's determination to grant his peoples scope for autonomous development within the framework of the empire. On January 2 Balfour forwarded this intelligence to Colonel House for President Wilson's benefit;[56] and indeed, Wilson's Fourteen Points included no demands that were unacceptable to Austria. There was mention only of "autonomous development" for its peoples, and correction of the Italian border along "clearly recognizable national lines."

Wilson's speech made a great impression on Czernin. He thought he read from it a possibility of American peace mediation, and immediately seized on this prospect with his wonted vigor. In the ensuing weeks, he made one effort after another to establish contact with Washington. The Slavic populations within the Austrian Empire were threatening to defect—the Czechs, for example, issued their famous Epiphany Declaration in January 1918—and at this point of crisis Czernin had to cling to every straw of hope for peace. Soon after Wilson's speech, he allowed word to transpire to Washington via The Hague and Stockholm that he regarded Wilson's Fourteen Points on the whole as reasonable.[57]

To pave the way for contact with Wilson, Czernin, in his response of January 24, treated Wilson's speech with even greater respect than did Hertling on the same day. Czernin called it a "peace offer," more or less agreed to the Fourteen Points—or, in the delicate questions of Belgium and Alsace-Lorraine, gave them a wide berth—expressed himself in highly conciliatory terms on Poland, and formally invited the president to an exchange of ideas with Austria, whose interests conflicted with those of America least among all the belligerents. He called on Wilson to use his great influence on the Allies for the purpose of initiating general peace talks.[58]

Intelligence that reached America via Switzerland indicated that the basic attitude expressed in Czernin's speech was set by Emperor Charles, who had requested that its text be dispatched to the president beforehand via Holland or Denmark.[59] Not content with that, the emperor immediately sent to Switzerland with secret orders—probably without Czernin's knowledge[60]—one of his confidants, the Vienna professor of international law Lammasch, a member of the Austrian upper chamber. Lammasch, with the deputy Professor Joseph Redlich and the well-known Munich pacifist Professor Friedrich Wilhelm Foerster, was a member of Charles's intimate circle of advisers who constantly kept alive the Austrian emperor's opposition to German war policy and urged him to make peace promptly and, if necessary, separately.[61]

By his own testimony, Lammasch was repeatedly asked by the emperor to form a new cabinet, but as a cloistered scholar he did not feel equal to the task, though he did regard himself as a suitable successor to Czernin—actually, in late October, when the Austrian monarchy collapsed, Lammasch did become prime minister and foreign minister for a few brief days. What he expected of Wilson emerges from the detailed reports (partly in shorthand) the American legation in Berne sent Lansing early in February about Lammasch's top-secret talks with all manner of intermediaries, chief among whom was the American theologian Professor Herron. Herron was an American expatriate who entertained highly unconventional political ideas. A complete amateur who busied himself in Switzerland without any official diplomatic credentials, he nevertheless proved invaluable to the American legation, which he kept informed about the activities of the swarms of agents and peace apostles from all over the world who infested Switzerland. Herron looked on himself as a prophet of Wilsonian democracy and worshiped the American president as a kind of world redeemer—though later on he turned against Wilson. Oddly enough, he was taken quite seriously by many politicians, including the Swiss, as an alleged confidant of Wilson, whom, in fact, he had never met. Lammasch had been put in touch with him through Foerster and was naive enough to put Austria's fate in Herron's hands, so to speak, even though the outlandish character of Herron's political ideas should have been abundantly clear from his conversations.[62]

The burden of what Lammasch told Herron on February 3, 1918, was that Emperor Charles urgently wanted to be rid of Prussian dominance. If Wilson made a conciliatory reply to Czernin's speech of January 24, Austria would almost certainly ask Germany to modify Hertling's speech of the same date, in the direction of unreserved acceptance of the Fourteen Points. If Germany refused, there would be an open break, and Austria would conclude a separate peace with the Allies, by American mediation. As Lammasch envisaged it, Charles would write and make public a long letter to the pope in which he would make known to the world plans for a reorganization of the Austrian Empire along federal lines, which he had long discussed with his Catholic and pacifist advisers. They ran to the creation of a federal union of states which were to be newly established, each comprising a single nationality. Wilson's ideas on disarmament, a league of nations, and self-determination would be accepted—but they must apply also to Ireland and the disputed Italian areas.

In his speech Czernin had politely but firmly ruled out any form of foreign intervention in Austria's internal affairs. Lammasch took a different line. Charles implored the president, he said, to issue a peace ultimatum that would pave the way for internal Austrian reorganization, abolition of intolerable Hungarian dominance, and removal of the Prussian yoke. Germany dare not reject an American peace offer on such a basis, since otherwise Bavaria and Württemberg, indeed all of South Germany, would defect from Prussia. If Berlin did remain obdurate, Austria would make peace separately.

The American chargé d'affaires shook his head as he reported all this to Washington word for word. He thought it represented an almost incredible and utterly hopeless adventure by the youthful Austrian emperor. Wilson, however, took the news very seriously. It seemed to him to confirm what he had heard on February 8 from Balfour via House, namely that Austria was close to a break with Germany and that Czernin—dismayed just then by the delay at Brest-Litovsk occasioned by the demands of the OHL—was only looking for a pretext. Balfour thought a favorable juncture had been reached for American mediation between the Entente and Austria—even though he was afraid of a highly unfavorable reaction in Italy.[63]

Wilson took the hint. He sent for House at once and the two drafted the text for Wilson's next speech of February 11.[64] It was completely oriented in the direction of Vienna and praised Czernin's goodwill and clear insight into the problems of peace. It even excused his silence on certain delicate problems by his dependence on the rulers of Germany. The four new principles with which the speech concluded (see p. 203f.) were expressly calculated to pave the way for immediate peace talks with Czernin. Wilson called them a test of whether such talks had any prospect of success. Hertling's reply, on the other hand, was criticized with unmerited sharpness; and at the end, in a calculated phrase suggested by Colonel House, Wilson spoke of the military and annexationist party in Germany, which did not shrink from sending milllions of men to their deaths, to forestall the justice on which all the world was now agreed.[65]

This sharp distinction between the attitudes of Czernin and Hertling was manifestly and deliberately at odds with the brusque declaration of the Versailles war council of February 4, which had treated both statesmen as equally obdurate adversaries (see p. 203). Czernin was gratified. He had been afraid that Wilson would hold him partly responsible for the course of the negotiations at Brest-Litovsk, and he now thought that the shrewd Wilson fully appreciated Austria's predicament.66 He gathered new heart and decided to try direct American-Austrian peace mediation in the form of a personal letter he persuaded Emperor Charles to address to the American head of state on February 18, via the king of Spain.67

Unlike the proposals only recently submitted to the president by Lammasch via Herron, there was now no mention of a separate peace with Austria, only of secret and preliminary Austro-American discussions that might lead to general peace. Charles's political uncertainty and insincerity toward his minister is characterized by the fact that on the very day on which he wrote to Wilson, Lammasch was able to tell Herron that the emperor was in complete agreement with what the two emissaries had discussed and that he would soon act accordingly.68

Wilson, in other words, received two separate offers from the Austrian monarch at one and the same time, each quite different in approach, indeed contradictory. Czernin's foray was a skillful diplomatic effort to ensnare the professorial theoretician Wilson in his own solemnly proclaimed principles. He let the emperor declare his agreement, one by one, with the four points set forth in Wilson's speech of February 11. At the same time, however, Czernin wanted to see a serious beginning made with the principle of peace without annexations or conquest. The territorial questions, said the emperor's letter, could be very simply solved, if only all the belligerents, including America's allies, accepted and carried out this principle. If the president prevailed with such an endeavor, the emperor would try the same with his allies. Certain border changes, made by agreement among those concerned, would evidently not conflict with Wilson's principles, nor would a final and satisfactory settlement of the Balkan borders, which had not yet been attained, for example in respect of the portions of Macedonia inhabited by Bulgars. Surely the president wanted to see nationalist claims met only to the degree that this would not create new unrest and conflict.

The Austrian government was in a position to establish conclusively that some of these claims were actually not in keeping with either the wishes of the people concerned or the interests of the countries. This was especially true of the Italian claims to South Tyrol, whose inhabitants had time and again unequivocally professed their allegiance to Austria. The principle of the status quo would, of course, require the complete relinquishment of Belgium, and there should be little difficulty in reaching agreement on Serbia's desire for economic security and access to the sea. As for the questions of securing the peace, achieving general disarmament, and guaranteeing freedom of the seas, there were no differences of opinion whatever on these matters.

This letter from Emperor Charles is of great historical interest, since it marks the limits to which Central Powers policy—or at least the policy of

Austria—was willing to go in making concessions to the enemy on the eve of the last decisive battle. There was no mention of eastern questions, and there could not be, for at this very moment the Germans were again advancing on St. Petersburg and the issue was still open. For the rest, there were actually but two points on which any effort at negotiations was bound to founder, Alsace-Lorraine (which was not even mentioned) and South Tyrol. This became even plainer in the further course of this initiative.

It is rather strange that Wilson, declared enemy of all "secret diplomacy," nevertheless consented to give a secret reply in this instance. He had first directed an inquiry to Balfour through House, as to what he might be expected to do. This led to a very remarkable response from the British foreign secretary. Balfour thought it futile to negotiate on the proposals in the emperor's letter at all. He thought that the demanded restoration of the status quo would represent a great success for the Central Powers and was incompatible with the declarations Wilson had made so far. Even the offer transmitted through Lammasch carried considerable risk. It simply bypassed Italy's territorial claims and promised the Slavic peoples inside Austria no more than what they had been often promised before, home rule within the empire, without necessarily abolishing German and Hungarian dominance. The Slavs regarded this as merely the old slavery under a new name. If they now learned that the American president was secretly negotiating peace with the Austrian emperor, they, like the Italians, would feel bitterly disillusioned, indeed betrayed, and would make their peace with the Central Powers. In order to end the war successfully, the Allies needed the enthusiasm of the Italians and the anti-German zeal of the Slavic populations.[69]

The favorable moment for Austria had clearly passed. As recently as early January, Lloyd George had outdone Wilson in public assurances that the Entente did not dream of dissolving the Austrian Empire. That was done with for now—for reasons we shall still have to consider. In London the desires of the Slavic peoples had suddenly become more important than the preservation of the Hapsburg state as a whole. As for the status quo, i.e., the question of Alsace-Lorraine and South Tyrol, there was no inclination at all to make this the subject of negotiation.

Wilson did not immediately follow this radical turn in British policy. He first wanted to try to establish, as he asked House to tell London, whether there might not be a true desire for peace, with moderate war aims, behind the emperor's letter, which he, like Balfour, seems to have regarded as a peace feeler concerted with Berlin. If his findings were negative, German militarism would once again be laid bare to the world.

One wonders whether Wilson still really believed that a general negotiated peace might be attainable with Austria's help—despite Lansing's earnest warnings against a policy of grasping at straws, which would merely create an effect of weakness and arouse Allied distrust, especially in Italy. House too voiced objections, and Wilson sought further support by discussing the matter with the French ambassador Jusserand. Very probably his democratic and pacifist principles made him hesitate to ignore a letter from the enemy camp that seemed to bespeak so much goodwill—and a letter from an emperor, to boot!

He did reply, on March 5, in very courteous terms—but he rejected as superfluous the emperor's crucial request for direct talks with an American delegate. Instead, he asked for concrete details on the peace settlement proposed by the emperor, touching only on questions that concerned Austria exclusively, which suggests that he was thinking of a separate rather than a general peace.[70]

Owing to the snail's pace of Spanish diplomacy, this letter apparently took weeks to reach Vienna. Czernin replied to it (through Emperor Charles) only on March 23, after the great offensive on the western front had already begun. Once again he tried to demonstrate that Austria's war aims coincided completely with the president's principles. Neither in the Balkans nor along the Adriatic coast would there be likely obstacles to an understanding. Only Italy's annexationist demands were beyond fulfillment—but then, they were completely at odds with the president's principles as well. If these were taken at face value, no cession to Italy could be regarded as justified—and surely this included cession of the Trentino. At the end of the message, the remaining point at issue was precisely formulated: "There is but one obstacle to peace that is nonnegotiable: the French and Italian greed for territorial aggrandizement."[71]

On that note the correspondence ended. Actually, Spain did not pass on this second letter from the emperor at all, and it reached Washington only through unofficial channels, through the British secret service, which intercepted and decoded it as it had the first one. After all, with the beginning of the great offensive, the time for such negotiations was over.

Throughout the winter, Czernin had staked his greatest hopes on the success of this offensive. "I never believed in the success of the U-boat campaign," he wrote in his memoirs, "but I did believe there would be a breakthrough on the western front, and throughout the winter of 1917-1918 I subsisted on the hope that this would break the obstinate destructive will of our enemies"; and to a friend he wrote on November 17, 1917, "So far Hindenburg has kept all of his predictions—you must leave him that." In other words, he laid the false prophecies in the U-boat question at the door of the German navy rather than at that of the field marshal.[72] This alone would explain his resistance to every temptation for a separate peace that came to him in the course of the winter.

"The Austrian ship of state," he had written Tisza as long ago as the early summer of 1917, "is constantly veering away from the alliance course." It was necessary to counter this trend. "After all, one can change course and steer that followed by the Entente, if one believes oneself capable of carrying it off. But then one should have the courage to go the whole way. This flirting with treason without ever getting to the point is simply stupid. We stand to lose all credit in Berlin, without gaining anything in London or Paris."[73]

This was aimed at the policy of Emperor Charles and his Bourbon kin and pacifist advisers, with which Czernin found himself more and more at odds. At bottom Czernin thought that to win a tolerable peace for Austria without and against Germany was impossible; nor was his only reason his anticipation that the Germans would meet such an undertaking by marching into Austria.[74] Czernin was indeed willing to reach an understanding, but there were certain limits beyond which he was quite unwilling to make concessions. His most impassioned objections were reserved for the cession of the German-speaking part of South Tyrol. This was a sacrifice that could not be made while a spark of life was left, he held, no more than a man in a runaway sleigh would throw his own child to the pursuing wolves to save himself.[75]

Yet he fought tooth and nail against the cession of Alsace-Lorraine. This became plain in his arguments with Count Revertera, Charles's confidant who in August 1917 had negotiated with the French major, Count Armand (see p. 35), and who seems to have clung tenaciously to his hopes for a separate peace with France. In September, on Czernin's instructions, the talks had been discontinued (see p. 39); but the emperor was forever concerned with not letting the tenuous connection with Paris break off and urged Revertera by October to resume the talks with Armand. In his view, it was solely owing to the obstinacy of the OHL that Berlin refused to forego Alsace-Lorraine in return for the compensation that had been offered in the east (see p. 35). Revertera shared his further view that Austria must cast loose from German leadership.[76]

There was a serious quarrel between Revertera and Czernin, who went so far as to suggest that Revertera should succeed him as foreign minister, so that he could change Austrian policy; but in the end, in a joint audience with the emperor on October 10, Czernin had his way, and Revertera did not immediately return to Switzerland. At the emperor's request, however, he did inquire of Paris through his Swiss middleman in early November whether there were a possibility of resuming the talks with Armand. This was almost certainly done without the knowledge of Czernin, who would scarcely have approved such importunities from the Austrian side, unless there had been a further French initiative.

The French General Staff was not averse to a resumption of the talks, but first consulted Clémenceau, who had just become premier. It got a laconic reply: "Listen! Say nothing!"[77] In consequence, Armand did encourage

Revertera, but for the time being Revertera delayed his departure for Switzerland. On January 14, however, Revertera reported to Czernin that to his great astonishment he had received an invitation to a new meeting from Armand, through Armand's Swiss middleman. Should he accept? On January 17 Czernin agreed to the meeting, but added a condition that clearly shows his distaste for such secret and unofficial talks, which were almost impossible to control. Revertera was to tell Armand that there would be no further secret talks. If the French were in earnest about making peace, let them send their foreign minister or an official representative. These secret gropings no longer made any sense.[78]

This did not deter the Austrian diplomat from having long talks with Count Armand on February 2 and 3–the very time when Lammasch was negotiating with Herron! Armand did not by any means stick to Clémenceau's instructions to listen and say nothing. On the contrary, he was extremely voluble. We cannot be sure of everything the two discussed. If the Frenchman's report is to be trusted, Revertera left no doubts whatever concerning Charles's and Czernin's loathing of Ludendorff and his policies; and the Austrian strongly recommended a separate peace between Austria and France. He also voiced considerable skepticism about the impending great German offensive.

According to Revertera's own report to Czernin, he evaded the question of a separate peace and indignantly rebuffed the Frenchman, when Armand tried to discuss so "unjust a demand" as the cession to France of Alsace-Lorraine, part of the ancient German empire–or rather, when Armand suggested that the issue be reconsidered in Berlin. The two reports agree only on one point, namely that the question of Alsace-Lorraine appeared to be the crucial obstacle to an understanding. Revertera did all he could to encourage his minister to continue the talks, emphasizing that the French, including Clémenceau, were indeed prepared to negotiate and were waiting only for counterproposals to the peace program they had transmitted in August. Revertera insisted that on this occasion Armand expressed himself far less definitively than five months earlier.[79]

He stayed on in Switzerland himself to be available for further talks, which in fact took place on February 23 and 25, but which ended without result since Czernin had in the meantime wired his legation councilor: "As soon as France foregoes its territorial ambitions, the talks will stand a chance of success. Without that concession I regard matters as hopeless."[80] Revertera was now under the necessity of making a statement to that effect, which he had to do in writing, at Armand's request. It was formulated with exquisite care, however, and sounded almost like an Austrian plea not to allow negotiations to fail because of the question of the status quo, since otherwise there was much hope for success.[81] The answer Clémenceau gave on March 2 was, of course, negative. France could not commit itself to forego any annexation. Thus the whole enterprise came to nothing.

The same fate was met by another British peace feeler, the origins of which appear to be rather mysterious. The British cabinet minutes show that Lloyd George was very much concerned with seeing that General Smuts meet Czernin as soon as possible or, if necessary, that he meet Mensdorff once more, in Switzerland, as had been agreed in the December talks, though only as a vague possibility. Evidently the British prime minister hoped that he might move very much nearer a separate peace in such a second encounter. He pressed for such a meeting beginning on January 2, 1918, and even went so far as to gain Clémenceau's approval.

Smuts himself hesitated and warned against overeagerness. Czernin's response to the war speeches of Lloyd George and Wilson should first be awaited. Into these deliberations there suddenly burst a dispatch from the British envoy Rumbold in Berne, on January 12. It said that Count Skrzynski, an Austrian legation councilor in Montreux, assigned to the Berne legation, had let Rumbold know through intermediaries that Czernin stood ready to meet the British prime minister in Switzerland to discuss some points in his speech of January 5 and Wilson's of January 8, on which an understanding might well be possible. This created understandable excitement in London.

In his memoirs Lloyd George insists that he took this invitation seriously and was strongly inclined to accept it, in the hope of thus achieving a separate peace with Austria and destroying the morale of the Austrian forces. But apparently his memory deserted him. The British war cabinet deliberated the matter on January 18, instantly concluded that a world sensation like a meeting between the British prime minister and the Austrian foreign minister was much too hazardous, and was willing to go only as far as another Swiss meeting with General Smuts.

The British also read the Berne report to mean that the Austrian government was now out for bigger game than a separate peace. Lloyd George leaped to the conclusion that Kühlmann might have a hand in the affair—he might have irrevocably broken with the OHL and joined Czernin in pursuing a more moderate peace program. Let Smuts try to drive a wedge between the OHL and the statesmen of the Central Powers. They might well be eager to reach an accommodation with the Allies before the OHL launched its costly offensive in the west. Of course it would be a mistake to enter into peace negotiations before British war aims had been attained; but at some point there would have to be talks to learn whether the enemy was prepared to accept the British terms. History would severely condemn any government that failed to take note of such significant overtures. Smuts should therefore try to inform himself from Czernin's lips as to the general attitude of the

Central Powers on the peace question. A wire was dispatched to Berne saying that Czernin could indeed meet with a British statesman, but only with Smuts rather than Lloyd George.

Clearly, what Kühlmann's peace feeler of the preceding September had not been able to gain, namely British readiness for confidential exchanges among responsible statesmen, now seemed within reach after all, in the face of the impending German offensive. Surely this represented a surprising success for the Austrian invitation!

The point at issue was whether the invitation was genuine. The British Foreign Office immediately voiced serious doubts that the news transmitted from Skrzynski was reliable, pointing to a number of far-fetched assertions in the Berne telegram of January 12.[82] Skrzynski himself was a dubious figure. He had indiscreetly passed on to his Polish compatriots a report on the secret talks between Mensdorff and Smuts, in an effort to ingratiate himself with them as well as with the British. Apparently he hoped to play a major role in the free Poland to come.[83]

When one compares the London files with those in Vienna, it becomes abundantly clear that Skrzynski had no official authorization for his swashbuckling initiative to bring Czernin and a British cabinet member together. It was entirely his own idea, and to this end he fed intelligence to the British legation in Berne through such obscure intermediaries as the Anglo-Egyptian professor Parodi and the Egyptian prince Tusun, who told the British that Czernin did want a separate peace but hoped that President Wilson would mediate between Austria and the Entente. Czernin was alleged to have fallen out completely with the Germans, who regarded him as a defeatist of the worst kind, though he enjoyed the favor of Emperor Charles, who was most eager for peace. Charles, however, might lose his throne any day, and if there were to be any understanding with him, it would have to be soon. To seek peace with the Germans was hopeless, for since they had conquered large parts of Russia, they were plentifully supplied with food and raw materials.

All this was reported in the form of vague hints rather than as precise information, in thoroughly conspiratorial style; and it seems strange that Rumbold, the British envoy, passed on this gossip credulously rather than remaining severely suspicious of it. The Foreign Office, however, clung to its skepticism, which was confirmed by Czernin's public speeches directed to America rather than Britain. These did not at all gibe with Skrzynski's information, any more than with the content of the letter which Emperor Charles had sent Wilson via Spain. In the end the war cabinet decided on March 5 to send Philip Kerr to Switzerland, rather than Smuts. Kerr was to talk personally with Skrzynski in an effort to determine how much truth there was to Skrzynski's overture. Was Kühlmann possibly behind it, as well as Czernin? Did Vienna really wish to conclude a separate peace? [84]

In the meantime Skrzynski had told the Austrian legation on February 27 that he had learned through Prince Tusun that the British government was ready for another meeting along the lines of the one between Mensdorff and Smuts, but this was to deal only with questions concerning Austria itself, i.e., Italy, Albania, Serbia, Poland, and Rumania—which was what Skrzynski himself had proposed to Rumbold! Count Mensdorff advised Czernin to delay a reply until the negotiations in Brest-Litovsk and Bucharest had been concluded. Czernin immediately went further, however, and on March 4 wired Skrzynski, forbidding him for the time being to have any further contact with representatives of enemy countries. He was to rebuff any approaches. "They are apparently trying to play us false," he said, causing acute embarrassment to Skrzynski, whose standing with the British as an alleged insider and political intermediary for Czernin was badly compromised.

On March 7 and 9 Skrzynski told Vienna that his middlemen and the British envoy Rumbold were very much put out by the sudden distrust shown them. Parodi had invaded his room unannounced as he lay ill abed, to give him the important news that Mr. Philip Kerr was coming to Switzerland for the special purpose of visiting him in Montreux—a visit that then actually took place. Czernin thereupon gave permission for a noncommittal exchange in Montreux on March 14.

In Berne Kerr had initially gained the optimistic impression from Anglo-Austrian intermediaries that Austria was well on the way to casting loose from Germany and preparing for a separate peace.[85] But he met an unexpectedly chilly reserve from Skrzynski, who told him, in keeping with Czernin's instructions, that there was doubt in Vienna of a serious British interest in peace. All Britain was trying to do was to alienate Austria from Germany.

The Briton was naturally at pains to dispel these suspicions. Britain was anxious to concretize the attractive principles proclaimed by Czernin in his speech, and to prepare for an enduring general peace that would satisfy all the nations and be fair even to Germany. This, of course, would not necessarily rule out certain concessions to Italy, in accordance with the nationality principle. The German militarists, Germany's real overlords, constituted the only remaining obstacle to peace—and that was the reason why Britain could not negotiate with the Germans. Skrzynski, following his instructions, declined to discuss these matters. Kerr departed for London on the following day, leaving word that any reply should be sent to him through Parodi.

Count Mensdorff now advised Czernin to insist that Austria act as mediator between the Entente and Germany. Czernin rebuffed him brusquely and instructed Skrzynski to tell Parodi that Kerr's "generalities" could not possibly be taken seriously, the true reason for the prolongation of the war, the annexationist ambitions of France and Italy, having simply been ignored. The moment Italy and France declared that they were willing to forego Austrian and German territory, there would obviously be no further obstacle to peace. For the rest, the Central Powers would not permit any intervention in their internal affairs, especially since they themselves had not the least intention of intervening in the internal affairs of the Entente.

This was Czernin's final word, and to make certain that his diplomats did not weaken or falsify it, he set it down in a brief memorandum he managed to get into British hands, whence it also reached Colonel House in America.[86] Philip Kerr was mistaken in his belief that Czernin had changed his mind once again at the last moment, believing that American mediation was more to be relied on than British and merely wishing to drag out the negotiations. Czernin's attitude in the matters of a separate peace, Alsace-Lorraine, and South Tyrol remained unchanged throughout the winter. He allowed no doubt of his country's loyalty to the alliance.[87]

Czernin had staked everything on the success of the great breakthrough offensive, which he was unwilling to compromise by political double-dealing. Yet tragically enough, his loyalty to the alliance not only did not delay but actually accelerated his country's internal disintegration and disastrous fate. As we have already heard, until the end of 1917 nationalist uprisings among the non-German minorities in the Austrian Empire aimed only at achieving home rule; and even the notorious Epiphany Declaration of the Czech deputies on January 6, 1918 (see p. 210), represented a compromise among royal and radical elements—at any rate, it avoided an unequivocal call to dissolve the empire, and by January 1918 the Entente governments too were still anxious to avoid such a public commitment, to the despair of Czech and South Slav émigré groups, which were trying to push them in that direction. These groups enjoyed only limited support in the Entente countries. The South Slavs, in particular, had little contact with the Allied governments and were financially strapped until the spring of 1918. The reason for this reticence was that the Entente statesmen clung tenaciously to their hopes for a separate peace with Vienna and were unwilling to do anything to destroy those hopes. No one was more afraid that such a separate peace might be concluded than Masaryk, Beneš, and the other leaders of the Slav emigration.[88]

This situation changed when it became clear that it would not be possible to pry Austria away from Germany by the time the great spring offensive began. The historian Seton-Watson and the London *Times* correspondent Wickham Steed, pro-Slav propagandists and friends of Masaryk who had long inveighed in Britain against the Hapsburg Empire, now greatly gained in influence. In mid-February Steed wrote a comprehensive memorandum in which he tried to convince Balfour that the time had come to mobilize the thirty-one million anti-German elements within the Hapsburg Empire against the twenty-one million pro-German elements. A policy of separate peace was hopeless, he contended. Influence along the same lines was brought to bear on House.[89]

Balfour did not at once admit that there was any alternative. He thought that one could lend encouragement to the non-German peoples of Austria, while at the same time pursuing the idea of a separate peace. Actually, everything was done henceforth to intensify the autonomy movement among the Slavic peoples to the level of separatism. Italy was the main base for these propaganda activities. Steed had established contact with the propaganda service of the Italian General Staff. In early April Rome was the scene of a great meeting of Slav émigré activists, and a major manifesto supporting separatism for the "suppressed nations" was issued.

This conference did not yet manage to bridge the often serious internal divisions among Serbs and Croats, South Slavs and Italians; nor did it succeed in having the dissolution of the Austrian Empire formally declared a new Entente war aim. It did, however, make important progress in that direction, mainly by the creation of a united front of South Slavs to overturn the Hapsburg monarchy. The émigré groups also obtained official recognition from the military authorities for their subversive activities.

The chief danger to Austria from all this was that the propaganda was carried right into the ranks of its military forces; and since the beginning of the war it had been the army with its iron discipline that had primarily held together this multinational state, beyond any expectation and despite internal tensions and conflict. Austria's military deficiencies and failures, so often mentioned in these pages, should not blind us to this political achievement, bordering on the miraculous; nor should we deprecate the heroism of many Austrian units, especially those from German-speaking, Croat, Slovene, and Hungarian areas. Unfortunately, even this strongest buttress of imperial authority began to crumble in the spring of 1918. The worsening supply situation certainly played a part in this deterioration, but enemy propaganda was even more damaging. Hundreds of thousands of prisoners returning from Russia brought back the message of Bolshevism, while in the south Italian and Yugoslav deserters began to form partisan bands behind the front.

Foreign Minister Czernin was not a man possessed of the iron nerve that would have been necessary to meet these symptoms of decay effectively. He sensed that the ground was giving way more and more under his policy of sticking it out by the side of the German ally and that Emperor Charles's confidence in him was waning. The annexationist obsessions of the German OHL had long interfered seriously with his efforts to convince his people that Austria wanted a compromise peace, that they were not being asked to support foreign conquest. The treaties of Brest-Litovsk had succeeded in bringing a measure of reassurance on these points, while the negotiations at Bucharest seemed to hold out the hope of creating a more enduring Central European community.

It was at this juncture that the nationalist opposition of the non-German peoples in Austria, especially the Czechs, began to grow more radical, deepening into outright separatism. At the same time, the imperial court saw a considerable growth in the influence of those advisers who wanted peace with the enemy at any price, and of others who despised Czernin as a defeatist.

To defend himself against these charges Czernin, on April 2, 1918, delivered his last major speech, before the Vienna borough council, especially summoned to serve as a sounding board. It was the speech that was to break him.

Czernin tried to shake off the invidious charge that he was a "war prolonger," first of all by giving publicity to his most recent secret peace exchanges with Wilson, going into greater detail about Rumania, Serbia, and other Balkan issues. His next tactic was to hurl the charge back at his detractors. "As God is my witness," he said, "we have tried everything possible to avoid the new offensive; but the Entente would not have it." With great lack of caution and discretion, he revealed, by way of evidence, the secret Paris peace feeler of February 2 and its failure, owing solely to the question of Alsace-Lorraine.[90]

At the same time he charged the Czech nationalist leaders—whom he did not identify by name—not only with prolonging the war, but with treason. Under the protection of parliamentary immunity, their speeches were virtually calling on the enemy to destroy the monarchy. They were working hand in glove with "that wretched Masaryk." All efforts on behalf of a negotiated peace had failed because of the "sudden change in the wind" in the Western capitals, occasioned by the disastrous decline inside Austria, which persuaded the enemy statesmen to wait, against the possibility that the Hapsburg Empire might be further subverted from within.

There was considerable substance to these charges, which were flung out with great pathos and patriotic resentment.[91] Czernin took pains, moreover, to make a distinction between the Czech people and their parliamentary representatives; yet by thunderously calling on Germans and Hungarians to "fight the traitors," he gave the impression that he was lumping all the Slav peoples together in that category, which deeply wounded the small but persistently loyal Czech parliamentary delegation. The result was a unanimously adopted reply by the Czech Union, imposing on the Czechs a kind of obligation to stand for the creation of an autonomous Czech-Slovak state.

The consequences of Czernin's challenge to the French premier were even worse. The story has often been told. In the ensuing press coverage, Clémenceau, the seasoned journalist and parliamentarian, swiftly enlisted world opinion on his side. In this endeavor he did not always fight fairly, but resorted to distortion in trying to turn the tables on Czernin, whom he described as having taken the initiative in the talks between Armand and Revertera. Indeed, he went so far as to say that Austria kept virtually begging for peace.

Clémenceau was in possession of an absolutely lethal weapon, which he wielded with consummate mastery. This was the secret letter which Emperor Charles had addressed to Prince Sixtus of Parma on March 24, 1917, professing warm friendship for France and promising to do all in his power to support France's "just claim for the return of Alsace-Lorraine." This revelation was all the more damaging since Czernin, in his speech, had praised to the skies Charles's allegedly unshakable loyalty to the alliance—probably for the very reason that he knew the emperor to be vacillating and wished to pin him down in public.

The worst aspect of the affair was that the monarch who had been thus highly lauded disavowed the letter, on his "word of honor"—first it was said not to have been sent at all, and then to have been falsified en route to Paris. He thus stood revealed as a miserable liar, even toward his own minister, and as a weakling totally lacking in character, forfeiting every shred of credibility before his people. The German-speaking Austrians even more than the Hungarians lost faith in the emperor, and the foundations of the dual monarchy were even further undermined.

Czernin, who had innocently set off this scandal, wound up as its victim. The only dignified course the emperor could have adopted would have been to withdraw at least temporarily from the business of government. In a political sense, however, this held risks of its own. Charles himself was initially not unwilling; but Empress Zita proved to have the stronger will. She would not hear of such a withdrawal—and if it had to be, she herself wished to assume the regency. Hence the minister had no alternative to accepting the role of whipping boy, by himself resigning, on April 14. It was a bitter end to his career, but the Vienna politicians of the day were to agree that no Austrian statesman ever was so popular as Czernin after this political debacle.92

In the sphere of foreign affairs the "Sixtus scandal" proved extremely harmful to Austria, most of all to the efforts on behalf of a separate peace which Emperor Charles had pursued. Until that time President Wilson had always shown sympathy for these efforts and sharply recoiled from "Balkanizing" the Danubian area. True, he had also displayed sympathy for the Polish cause, but this did not extend to Masaryk, the Czech leader, and the South Slav émigrés. As soon as Clémenceau brought the Sixtus letter to world attention, the statesmen in Washington realized that it had become impossible to conclude a separate peace with Charles and his circle, let alone behind the back of the Austrian government, for his own people now regarded him as a traitor.

It was fully expected that the Germans would henceforth keep their ally on a very short military and political leash. When Emperor Charles went to

Spa in mid-May to meet the Kaiser, the American press concluded that he had been summoned to do penance, like the German emperor Henry IV at Canossa. Austria was described as having declined to the status of a mere satellite, an instrument of Prussian militarism. As will be seen further on, in Chapter 7, Part 1, this was a gross exaggeration, if not a complete misreading of the real situation; but American public opinion would not have countenanced any Austrian flirtations on the part of the president, and the men in the State Department, Lansing in the lead, insisted on a complete turnabout in America's Austrian policy.

Not without considerable qualms, on May 29 Wilson approved a declaration by Lansing in which the government of the United States openly voiced its sympathy for the liberation of "Czechoslovaks" and "Yugoslavs"—then newly coined names—along the lines massively proclaimed to the world by the "Congress of Oppressed Austrian Peoples" that had met in Rome the preceding month. Charles, Lansing told Wilson in a memorandum, had forfeited all earlier sympathies when he "signed away his birthright" at German headquarters. It was now settled American policy that Austria-Hungary should be expunged as a political entity.

Thus the final act in the tragedy of the Austrian Empire opened with a call to its non-German peoples to rise in rebellion. Wilson himself, in a speech on May 18, declared that no peace feeler would henceforth swerve America from its grim determination to win victory on the battlefield.[93]

TWO

The Leaders Ask for
More than Germany's Dwindling
Resources Can Provide;
Revolution and Collapse

6

Excessive Strain and
Failure of the Military Forces
in the Summer of 1918

I F THE GREAT "Michael offensive" of March 21, 1918, seemed to the Germans a political as well as a military necessity, an act of salvation, to be welcomed with the warmest hopes, the increasingly visible internal decay of the Austrian dual monarchy and the vacillations of its ruler, bordering on treachery, were but two of the reasons. Year by year, the merciless pressure of the British blockade had borne down with increasing effect on the peoples of Central Europe. Austria was not the only country in which hunger, physical exhaustion, unending hardship, and war casualties had engendered a deep war-weariness. Those who did not already secretly count the war as lost staked all their hopes on a last great decisive battle, to be launched before it was too late, i.e., before the Americans appeared on European soil in force. The German army, of course, longed for an end to everlasting trench warfare, hoping that someday it would be possible, as it had been in the summer of 1915 in Russia, to break through the enemy front and overwhelm the enemy in the open field.

The present author was then a front-line officer at the crucial breakthrough point near St. Quentin in the sector of the eighteenth army and well remembers the mood of his comrades and of the men of his infantry battalion. He remembers equally well the anxious doubts that befell him and others, in the face of the wretchedly equipped supply units, the makeshift vehicles, the dejected nags with their bones sticking out, the largely overage, poorly trained, and thoroughly weary men. Was such an army really capable of advancing swiftly across the cratered battlefield of the Somme with its elaborate trench system, to reach the sea and totally destroy the Anglo-French armies?

We know all too well today that such doubts were well-founded. Technical preparations—especially in the artillery—for the tremendous attack of March 21 had been executed in masterly fashion.[1] New artillery barrage effects, carried out with complete surprise, proved absolutely devastating. The initial breakthrough was many times more successful than anything Germany's enemies had been able to achieve since their offensives in 1916, even marshaling their greatest resources. Still, there can be no shadow of a doubt that the German chances of success were only slight from the very outset, on account of German supply deficiencies and enemy superiority in manpower and matériel. There never really was any prospect of "total victory." What might have been achieved at best—and nearly was achieved, because of surprisingly serious strategic errors on the other side—was to drive a deep wedge between the British and French armies.

Ludendorff and his staff were, of course, fully aware of the weaknesses of the German army in the fourth year of the war. He himself seems never to have shared the belief of the army and the people that he could really end the war at one fell stroke. In his Homburg memorandum of February 13 (see p. 107f.), he spoke of "a tremendous struggle, beginning in one place and continued in another, and taking a long time," all in all "the greatest military challenge ever thrown down to any army."[2]

Elsewhere too Ludendorff made statements suggesting that he did not think the contemplated offensive would result in immediate and total success.[3] He seems to have counted on a continuing series of "battles of attrition," which were indeed launched one after another throughout the summer, following the strategic failure of the great initial attack. It is virtually certain that the idea of a swift succession of attacks at different sectors of the front interfered with the consistent execution of the Michael offensive on its north wing, and it has also been established that there was no fixed OHL plan for the operational exploitation of any breakthrough that might be achieved. Before the beginning of the offensive there was some talk about rolling up the entire British front from the south, but once the battle was joined the orders were to fan out against the British and the French at the same time.

In the opinion of General Kuhl and other military experts this resulted in excessive strain on the German forces. Ludendorff was indeed averse on principle to operational planning so long as the tactical success of a breakthrough was uncertain. Until that point was reached, he was unwilling to listen to "operational considerations." Early in April he told the chief of Crown Prince Rupprecht's army group: "We shall simply tear open a hole, and the rest will follow. That is the way we did it in Russia."[4] This approach, tactical rather than strategic, carried dangers. It stemmed from a restless drive for constant activity, intent on one impressive partial success after another, without due consideration to the campaign plan as a whole and the limits of German resources.[5]

In retrospect Ludendorff's planning courts the criticism that even the great breakthrough attempt of March 21 was unrealistic and motivated by political considerations rather than by a sober military estimate of the situation. Ludendorff was obsessed by the idea of "final victory."[6] The immense bloodshed incurred in the initial offensive—total casualties were 230,000, rising to 424,000 by late April—was futile and could have been avoided, if defense rather than attack had been considered from the outset, and if the defenses had been made virtually impregnable by the timely elaboration of a system in depth of trenches, machine gun emplacements, artillery positions, and bunkers, reaching back to the Meuse and the Vosges.

The necessary labor force for this purpose, about a million men, would have been available, indeed considerably more than that number, had Germany's goals in the east been limited. In such an event, the immobility of so many German divisions, stemming from the lack of vehicles, would have been not nearly so disastrous as it proved to be in the offensive phase. Shortening the front would have made it possible to enlarge the reserves. Exhausted units could have been given essential rest periods, rear-echelon training would have stood a better chance, and defenses, notably against the new weapon of the tank, could have been improved. The burden of attacking across shattered areas would have fallen to the enemy. The experiences of 1916 and 1917 had left the Allies with such a profound revulsion against this course that the supreme war council, in December 1917, contemplated another offensive only at a time when the American forces would have been fully deployed, i.e., not earlier than 1919.

Even by the fall of 1918, with the German army completely exhausted, the Allies did not succeed in tearing open the German defensive front at any point. This certainly justifies the conclusion that a defensive strategy based on a mobile front, with local sorties, would have proved invincible, at least in 1918. For the first time in the war almost four-fifths of the total German forces were assigned to the western front. As a result of the Hindenburg program and quite unlike the Battle of the Somme in 1916, they were abundantly supplied with artillery and ordnance. Had the Germans adopted such a defensive strategy, it might even have been possible to leave stronger forces at the most vulnerable locations on the eastern front—Macedonia and Turkey— than could be spared with the complete concentration of offensive power on the western front. The consequences, during the final months of the war, were disastrous.[7]

Was it then an unequivocal blunder even to attempt a breakthrough offensive in the west, powered by a complete concentration of force? Those who reach such a conclusion may, in our view, be right in a purely military sense; but they do Ludendorff an injustice when they ignore that there was more behind the decision to launch the great offensive than the vaunted offensive spirit of the German General Staff. There were the hopes and longings of the German people that now at last, peace having been achieved in the east and the two-front war ended, it would prove possible to deal the western enemies so hard a blow that they too would become amenable to peace, and that this should be done swiftly, before the American forces could intervene. No doubts had yet arisen concerning the strategic genius of the two great field captains, Hindenburg and Ludendorff, and it seemed that now, for the first time since taking over the OHL, they had been given the effective means for really winning "final victory."

One may go so far as to say that the very charisma which the two generals radiated made it impossible for them to forego the great "decisive battle" and to use their swollen forces on the western front to build a stronger system of entrenchments. All soldiers take the will to victory for granted, and the German people had not yet by any means buried their hopes for victory. On the contrary, the peace treaties that had been concluded in the east served as a promising augury of ultimate success in the war. In such a situation to forego the great breakthrough effort in the west would have been politically impossible.

This situation changed radically in late April, once it had become clear that the Michael offensive was mired beyond hope and even its extension into Flanders had led to only half a success. For the front-line soldiers this was a crushing disappointment. Once again war's end had receded into the distant future, once again hecatombs had done no more than haplessly lengthen the front; and how could what had not been achieved in the first great blow, struck with every resource, full surprise, and tremendous artillery barrages, now be won with far weaker forces, consisting largely of decimated and exhausted divisions?

Even the ordinary soldier in the ranks had to ask himself this question. Colonel von Thaer, a shrewd General Staff officer stationed on the Flemish front, has described in his diary the discouragement that spread as early as April. He was dismayed about how remote from the front the OHL was. The men at the top showed not the least sympathy for his worries and warnings. Hindenburg brushed them off with complacent optimism, while Ludendorff bitterly and quite unfairly scored the alleged "failure" of the front-line officers.[8]

There can be no question that the reason for the slow decline of morale within the German army over the final months of the war was the feeling of the soldiers that they were being ground to pieces in one useless, pointless, and hopeless offensive action after another. Radical and subversive propaganda, mainly from soldiers who had been shipped to the dreaded western front from the east or from Russian prisoner-of-war camps, was by comparison of only subsidiary importance. Ludendorff always inclined to ascribe every failure, every cave-in of the front, to the "failure" of subalterns. His hasty interventions reached more and more deeply into local tactical situations, often by means of endless telephone conversations. By ruthlessly recalling and transferring General Staff officers who dared to contradict him or were otherwise irksome to him, he stifled all initiative on the part of his subordinates.

It was, in truth, the OHL rather than the troops in the field that was responsible for the unhappy course of the campaign. Its policy of wearing down the enemy by strike after local strike was basically unsound. It grossly overestimated German resources and at the same time underestimated even more grossly the enemy's single-minded tenacity and the abundance of his matériel. Rather than the enemy being worn down, it was the fighting power of the German army that was being squandered with dismaying swiftness. When Ludendorff's major strategic assistant, Major Wetzell, kept insisting in numerous memoranda to his chief that everything depended on "wresting the initiative" from and "forcing our will" on the enemy, this was nothing more than military dogmatism. What good was initiative that could never lead to definitive success and thus became an end in itself, so to speak? It achieved but one result. The German people, and the government too, by being continually fed with reports of offensive "victories," were completely deceived about the gravity of the situation. Hopes were thus kept alive that the next blow must at last compel the enemy to yield.

The shrewd and calculating General Hoffmann had long since inwardly turned against Ludendorff. He agreed that there had been no alternative to attempting a breakthrough in the west, since the Germans could not possibly sit by and twiddle their thumbs in the face of impending landings by American forces and continuing threats in the east that cast doubt on the adequacy of the food supply. "The day the OHL realized, however, that it could not take Amiens," he writes, "in other words, that the breakthrough had not succeeded, it should also have realized that decisive victory on the western front was no longer within reach. . . . The day the OHL ordered the offensive against Amiens halted, it was its bounden duty to tell the government that the time had come to begin peace negotiations and that there was no prospect of ending the war on the western front with a decisive victory."[9]

The German army and the German people drifted into disaster because Ludendorff was simply incapable of making such an admission in time. There was no lack of exhortatory voices among the front-line leaders, urgently advising him to move from the offensive to the defensive. Particularly illuminating and memorable is a report about a talk which General Fritz von Lossberg, chief of staff of the fourth army, held with Ludendorff on July 18, after the setback at Villers-Cotterêts. Lossberg insistently counseled Ludendorff to adopt a systematic policy of defense at the expense of yielding ground.

Ludendorff was impressed with Lossberg's arguments and replied after a long pause: "I think your proposals are pertinent, but I cannot follow them, for political reasons." What political reasons?" Lossberg asked. "I must think of the impression on the enemy, on our own army, and on the home front." Lossberg countered sharply that the surrender of military necessity to political expediency always led to trouble. Ludendorff's response is not undisputed, but according to Lossberg he was struck with consternation and said in a tone of despair that he would resign.[10]

Ludendorff did not resign, and neither did he follow Lossberg's advice. Again and again he clung to the unrealistic hope that the next strike must bend the enemy to his will.[11] His iron and obsessive will in the end blinded his military reason. This blindness and remoteness from reality at supreme headquarters is highlighted in a memorandum Major Wetzell wrote as late as June, in which he anticipated that a major attack on Paris might be launched by mid-September. As another sidelight, the OHL forbade General von Below's troops to dig in in rough territory after an enemy advance, to preserve the semblance that they would soon move to the attack—all this despite devastating enemy artillery and air attacks![12]

These incidents foreshadow Hitler's frantic strategy in the final stages of the Second World War. Ludendorff tried to justify himself to Colonel von Thaer by arguing that he certainly could not be expected to make "peace at any price" and that the enemy had made no serious peace offers.[13] This was quite true, but in the face of rising Entente prospects it was futile to keep on waiting for such offers. All Germany's hopes for victory had been staked on the single card of the great breakthrough battle. When this turned out to be something less than a trump card, the game was lost beyond retrieval, and it was absurd to dream of "victory." The proper consequences should have been drawn in time, i.e., a German peace offer at a military juncture that was not yet completely hopeless, but still afforded scope for protracted and tenacious resistance, if the enemy offered terms that were too severe.

If there were any means at all to keep the Allies from making such terms, it would have been this: The world must be convinced that the Central Powers were ready to make peace on extremely moderate terms of their own and if necessary even to agree to certain border corrections—if such action would lift the panic fear of German militarism. This could probably have been achieved only at the cost of a change in the German military command, and probably of the government as well, although it must remain uncertain whether even such changes would have brought the desired effect. It would have at least lifted from the German troops the nagging sense of being ground to pieces in futile attacks. It might even have returned to them the confidence that they were indeed only defending their native soil and Germany's legitimate interests from brutal violation. Had such a policy been followed, coupled with a timely shift to a system of operational defense zones in depth, as proposed to the OHL by General von Lossberg,[14] the increased incidence of open mutiny on troop trains, of desertion and unresisting surrender in the field after May of 1918, might have been prevented. The politicians might have gained time to negotiate, and on the Allied side the prospect of continuing costly offensive operations might have strengthened peace sentiment.

All this is the merest conjecture. Manifestly there never was the slightest possibility of such major shifts in policy and strategy. Despite the grave setbacks on the western front, the German people's confidence in those two infallible military heroes, Hindenburg and Ludendorff, was still unbroken by midsummer. Where could the German statesman be found who possessed the insight, the valor, and above all the authority to force through such basic changes? From June onward Count Hertling was almost continually at headquarters in Spa, for political as well as health reasons; and while he was there, he grew more and more dependent on the OHL rather than being in a position to influence it. He was an old man, tired and worn-out,[15] in a sense the physical symbol of Germany's political impotence during the final stages of imperial rule.

But it was not only the feebleness of the hands that held the reins that lay behind the impotence. The German people, misled by un unending sequence of victory reports, unshaken—at least so far as the middle class was concerned—in their national pride and confidence, stubbornly refused to entertain the idea that a war waged at such sacrifice, with such heroism, and with so many battlefield triumphs could end in defeat. To hold off that defeat would have been the military challenge, to soften its impact the political. Both would have called for a high measure of self-abnegation, for keen insight into the true situation of Germany and its allies in the fourth year of the war. It was not the OHL alone that was lacking in these qualities. Down to the fall of 1918, in the face of the continuing mood of victory, it was extremely difficult to launch a policy of timely conciliation—and day by day the chances for such a policy to succeed grew dimmer. None dared enlighten the people about the true situation; and when Kühlmann, in a Reichstag speech late in June, dropped cautious hints in that direction, the OHL at once secured his dismissal.

The degree of utter blindness on the German side is shown most plainly by the vast plans for German expansion in the east that were dreamed up and actually worked out at supreme headquarters all through the summer and right down to the moment of total collapse. The juxtaposition of these outlandish eastern plans and the unceasing and increasing military failure in the west is among the most typical features of Ludendorffian militarism.

7

Exaggerated Political Goals during the Final Phase of the War

Part 1
Arguments with Austria;
The Polish Question

THERE WERE ecstatic hopes of victory in the camp of the Central Powers in the wake of the auspicious start of the great March offensive. German prestige rose to a new high among Germany's allies and with the Poles and Rumanians as well. It was into this exalted mood that the revelations about the Sixtus letter of 1917 burst, as we have seen in Part 2 of Chapter 5. In the event, the damage to Emperor Charles's prestige, both at home and in Germany, was even greater, by virtue of his wretched efforts to extricate himself with transparently mendacious disavowals.

Naturally much thought was given at German headquarters to the question of how to react to these unfortunate revelations. The Kaiser was irate, and there was agreement that Germany must protect itself against a recurrence of such escapades on the part of the Austrian court. Austria, in other words, had to be tied more firmly to the German alliance. Yet the interests of monarchism required an avoidance of public reproaches and of any appearance of formal penance. Reminding the Kaiser of Austria's critical domestic situation, Hertling insisted that it must not be aggravated by any public signs of disunity among the two allies.[1]

General von Cramon, the German liaison officer with the Austrian high command, played an important role as mediator. He proposed that the Kaiser invite Charles to pay him a visit, and that Charles beg his pardon and, on this occasion, in the presence of the newly appointed foreign minister Burián, pledge in writing henceforth not to establish contact with any foreign power, let alone make any offers without the prior knowledge of the Kaiser.[2] No written assurance of this kind is known to exist. Apparently the oral promise Charles gave during his long-delayed visit to the Kaiser at Spa on May 12 was considered satisfactory.[3]

The occasion was, however, to be used for securing stronger political, economic, and possibly even military ties between Austria and Germany. A written draft was prepared by both sides, apparently not without contact between their diplomatic representatives. In a political sense, the Dual Alliance of 1879 was to be renewed, specifying in general terms the conditions in which it would come into force—which were not limited to an attack by Russia—and extending it over a longer period of time, something like twenty years.

The documents in the Vienna archives show concern on the part of the Austrian diplomats, based on domestic as well as foreign considerations, lest Austria come into the odor of being more and more dependent on its German ally, and these fears were to prove to be only too well-justified. For these reasons Count Burián wanted the treaty not only to be kept strictly secret but to come into effect only after the conclusion of general peace, i.e., not earlier than January 1, 1920, a goal with which he failed to prevail. He also looked for formulations that would keep Austria from being drawn into international and colonial controversies.[4]

The Austrians realized that closer ties with Germany had become inevitable, but they wanted to get off as cheaply as possible, and in this they succeeded to a surprising degree. What the two emperors were given to sign as a result of their discussions—and what was countersigned by Hertling and Burián—was a kind of agreement to agree rather than a formal treaty of state. Both monarchs bound themselves to instruct their governments to work out and conclude with every dispatch certain agreements on the following three points: (1) a close long-term political alliance that would serve the defense and security of both empires; (2) the creation of a military alliance; and (3) the conclusion of a customs and economic union in which tariffs would be gradually reduced, with the ultimate goal of paving the way for the complete abolition of customs duties between the two powers. This customs and economic union was to be devoid of any aggressive aims directed against other countries.

In other words, everything was left rather unsettled. Only a seven-point supplementary military agreement drafted by General Cramon and signed by Hindenburg and Colonel General Arz contained somewhat more clearly defined terms. It provided for full utilization of defense resources in both countries, coordinated organization and use of troops, standardized arms, exchange of officers, joint war planning, and extension of the rail network, profiting from the experiences of the war.

As recently as October 1917, Ludendorff had sharply rejected a military convention with Austria (see p. 151). Now he agreed to it in a preliminary meeting, remarking that Germany had failed in the past to press strongly enough for improvements in the Austrian army. The tactical and strategic training of Austrian and Hungarian officers had to be standardized.[5] He was, however, concerned about military security in the Austrian army, which he described as being riddled with traitors. The impending separation of the Hungarian army from the over-all Austro-Hungarian army system also rightly worried him. It was indeed already too late for a military convention between the two Central Powers. As we already know, it was precisely at this time that the whole structure of the Austrian Empire began to come apart, while nationalist propaganda had begun to undermine the cohesion of the Austrian army. Soon afterward this process was sharply accelerated with the swift failure of the Austrian offensive on the Piave in June and its tremendous casualties.

Thus Cramon's military alliance remained a mere scrap of paper, and there never were any further discussions about putting it into effect.[6] The pledge of an economic alliance did have some consequences. It led to a revival of the customs negotiations that had got stuck early in the year (see p. 160f.). Beginning July 8, these talks were resumed in Salzburg by the experts on both sides; but the Austrians still clung to their anxious reservations about abolishing protective tariffs. The Germans, on their part, were far more reasonable, and in the end there was a compromise that held out the prospect of removing these barriers at a later date.[7] Actually, these negotiations were concluded only on October 11, a time when the Austrian Empire was about to break up for good.

As in the winter before, the creation of a joint customs area was to help solve the Polish question, which continued to form the main obstacle to an understanding between the two powers. Indeed, during the ensuing months, it played a much more important part than the strengthening of the alliance, a subject in which the German side soon manifestly lost interest as the internal decay of the Hapsburg Empire gathered speed. Even during the preparations for the meeting of the two emperors in Spa it became clear that the OHL, and Hertling as well, were mainly concerned with exploiting Austria's political difficulties for purposes of getting away from the Austro-Polish solution. The Chancellor thought, however, that it would be going too far to confront Emperor Charles immediately with a formal demand to surrender his Polish claims in return for a German rapprochement.[8] He was content to include the following clause in the draft alliance: "The high contracting parties agree that a final solution to the questions dealt with in this treaty will require an understanding on the Polish question."

Had this clause been taken seriously, the alliance negotiations might well have foundered on it, for as we shall see, there was no understanding on the

Polish question. Count Burián, however, was intent all the same to push through the contemplated reforms in the Dual Alliance of 1879 and complained about lagging German interest in implementing the agreement of May 12.[9] It became clear that he was actually concerned with loosening rather than strengthening the alliance. The draft he presented in Berlin on June 11 did provide for extending the alliance until 1940, but at the same time it sought to water down the mutual aid requirements as against the original treaty concluded by Bismarck.[10]

The Germans presented a counterproposal, drafted by Kühlmann, but even after this had been significantly diluted, Burián accepted it only as a basis for further negotiations.[11] Subsequently there were objections, mainly to the fact that in the German draft the supplementary agreement on the military expenditures and obligations of the two allies—in other words, the military pact—was not only mentioned but described as an essential part of the treaty. To this Burián did not want to commit himself.[12] Foreign Minister Hintze, who carried on the talks after Kühlmann's fall, met Burián's reservations on this point, but was unwilling to accept further changes demanded by Burián with pedantic tenacity. The final draft, revised by the foreign ministry in Berlin, was transmitted to Vienna by Hintze on September 5, 1918,[13] but at that time much more urgent questions were to the fore in that city—when and how hostilities might be broken off and the enemy persuaded to negotiate; whether this should be attempted by an appeal to all the belligerents, as Burián wished, or by neutral mediation, as proposed by the German side; whether it must be done at once or if there was still time. The Dual Alliance of 1879, in other words, was already breaking up for good. To proclaim its solemn renewal would have been a mere act of histrionics. Hintze gave such little importance to it that he did not even mention the treaty project during the talks.[14]

Even before this he had rejected an attempt by Burián to combine renewal of the Dual Alliance with an agreement to limit mutual alliance obligations, as sought by Czernin during the preceding spring (see Chapter 4, Part 1, especially pp. 165f. and 169f.). The occasion was the OHL's request, voiced on June 18, that the Austrian high command make six divisions available for strengthening the western front. This desperate cry for aid caused embarrassment at Austrian headquarters for many reasons and was ultimately met only very imperfectly, with two divisions.[15] The fact that Burián, even at this juncture, thought it necessary to stand on his treaty rights, which forbade the use of Austrian troops for German territorial goals, was considered irrelevant in Berlin, indeed in curious conflict with the efforts to tighten the alliance that were going on at the same time. Hintze was very blunt about it and refused to be put off by counterarguments.[16]

All in all one can scarcely avoid the conclusion that the meeting at Spa failed to live up to German expectations. Not only was the alliance not strengthened but on the contrary, with Burián again in charge, there were the same old frictions, the same tug-of-war over minor advantages, just as there were during the time before Czernin (see Vol. III, Chapters 3, 4, and 7). It was the quarrel over Poland, above all, that now became quite hopeless. It scarcely seems worthwhile to trace in detail the endless exchanges and meetings that took place between Vienna and Berlin from mid-June on.[17] They turned on the same old issues, with which we are by now thoroughly familiar, and in the end nothing was accomplished, for Poland's fate no longer depended entirely on the two Central Powers. The actual question was when Allied victory would usher in an independent Poland with access to the sea, on which the Entente powers had long since been agreed.

Burián stuck to his old demand, the Austro-Polish solution, even though his backing at home was growing progressively shakier. The German-speaking Austrians were now beginning to be disaffected, as far as the Hapsburg dynasty was concerned; and as for Emperor Charles, he continued to be obsessed by the single thought of ending the war as soon as possible and was afraid that peace would be more difficult if he assumed the rule over Poland. Even at the meeting between the two sovereigns on May 12 he had plainly hinted that he was averse to the Austro-Polish solution—which was most useful to German diplomacy in its arguments with Burián.

On the German side there was a firm determination not to allow Poland to fall into Austrian hands in any circumstances. The Austro-Polish solution was now unequivocally rejected even by Count Wedel, who had backed it so vigorously in 1917 on the grounds that it was indispensable to cure the trouble both inside Austria and with the Central European alliance (see p. 146f.). In his view Austria was already in an advanced state of disintegration and was no longer capable of digesting Poland.[18] It was Ludendorff rather than Wedel, however, who decided German policy. Ludendorff set forth his views on the Polish problem in a comprehensive OHL report of July 5. It is one of the most remarkable expressions of his militant philosophy.[19]

He rejected as totally unrealistic any attempt to turn the Poles into good neighbors of Germany by a policy of compromise and conciliation and to settle Poland's borders by treaty. There was only one way of protecting Germany's eastern border against Polish greed and hostility, the creation of a German-dominated border strip. Retreating somewhat from earlier and still more sweeping demands, Ludendorff still wanted this strip to comprise some 8,000 square miles, of which something more than 3,000 were to be cleared of Poles by expropriation and resettled by Germans. This was to be accomplished by the use of military requisition methods on which his staff had been working during the preceding winter (see p. 163f.).

In Ludendorff's view only a protective wall of loyal Germans, separating the new kingdom of Poland from the Poles in Prussia's eastern provinces, could preclude the danger of Polish irredentism. He airily waved aside humanitarian considerations against the expropriation of Polish private property and the expulsion of the inhabitants. "Modern concepts of law in respect of property and personal freedom have changed," he said. "Sweeping public intervention into private life and property rights that would have seemed inconceivable only a few years ago is today countenanced as expressing the natural rights of sovereignty."

These are remarkable statements indeed, foreshadowing the militaristic totalitarian state that was to arrive a generation later. Ludendorff claimed that eastern experts had described his resettlement plan as necessary and feasible and he appended to his memorandum a compilation of "voices from the border regions" that applauded him; but rather different opinions were expressed by the Reich and Prussian agencies concerned, whose leaders met on August 9 at the invitation of Vice-Chancellor Payer. They not only objected to the large size of the contemplated border strip but unanimously declared that the expropriation and resettlement schemes envisaged were totally impracticable, for reasons of finance as well as international law.[20]

Ludendorff was right, of course, in holding that it was impossible at this late date to halt, let alone overcome Polish irredentism by a policy of conciliation. If there had ever been such a possibility, the time was now long past. Yet his alternative, his "protective wall of Germans," to replace the Poles expelled from the border belt, was even more unrealistic and quite properly discarded. At the big war aims conference held on July 2 under the Kaiser's chairmanship. Ludendorff did prevail, however, in having the Austro-Polish replaced by the so-called "candidate" solution, i.e., leaving it to the Poles themselves whom they wanted as their ruler. The kingdom thus created would embrace only Congress Poland, i.e., the former Polish regions of Russia, and even these would be substantially reduced in size by a wide border strip to be annexed by Germany, including the coal districts of Dombrova and Bendzin. This Poland was to be economically dominated by Germany, which would control its railways and exact war contributions.[21] That the Polish army would be under German command had already been settled in 1916-1917. The new country, in other words, would become a satellite rather than an ally, a far from enticing prospect to the Poles.

During August, however, the general situation at the western front changed so unequivocally that even Ludendorff's confidence in victory lessened perceptibly, and so did his political authority. The Polish notables close to the regency council were now in the agreeable position of being able to exploit for their own purposes the differences between the two Central Powers. In a certain measure they were even wooed by both. They were told in Berlin that if they chose a king acceptable to Germany and entered into close ties with the Reich, large-scale border corrections would not be necessary and the Kholm region would even be restored to them. If, on the other hand, they preferred the Austro-Polish solution, Germany would have to annex a wide border strip to protect itself.[22] In Vienna, by contrast, union with Galicia was held out to them in that event, which meant an increment of twenty million Slavs, 80 per cent of them Polish.

Late in August Foreign Minister Hintze asked Ludendorff whether the Poles could not after all be promised certain acquisitions to the north of their country, mainly the city of Vilnyus and the region around it, as an inducement for choosing a German candidate to their throne. Hintze recommended such a course. To his surprise, Ludendorff was amenable to it. He still very much wanted to bring the Polish question to a swift conclusion in the face of the threatening collapse of the western front, and he had been progressively disillusioned by the political sentiments of the Lithuanians, to whom Vilnyus had been firmly promised as their capital in 1917. He did insist on the closest ties between Germany and the new Poland. The borders of East Prussia were to be secured by "bridgeheads" on the Narev; and oddly enough he demanded the famous primeval forest of Bialowice as a Prussian state domain.[23]

At the Vienna discussion of September 5, already mentioned, Burián was equally worried. He too wanted to secure the Polish prize before the Entente could intervene and general peace came. He implored Hintze not to create a dangerous focus of permanent unrest and conspiracy in the east by mutilating Poland, and he swore up and down that German fears of an Austro-Polish solution were groundless. Germany's political and military needs could well be met even in such an event.[24] Hintze was not swayed in the least. He said that the creation of a large and independent Poland without a militarily secure border strip was far too dangerous for Germany and ran counter to its national interests.

In order to avoid an open break, there was agreement in the end to submit the issue for further clarification to a mixed commission. Thus we have the grotesque spectacle of a commission of German and Austrian experts meeting—of course without reaching agreement—for five days, September 24-28, in Berlin, to discuss the Polish question in full depth and length, up to the very moment when Ludendorff finally gave up the war as lost and demanded an immediate armistice.[25] In a spectacle no less grotesque, an Austrian crown council on September 27, held for the purpose of discussing the desperate situation created by Bulgaria's open defection from the alliance, decided on Burián's motion to ask Germany not only to make peace at once but to confirm its assent to the Austro-Polish solution.[26] The quarrel over the Polish question between the two Central Powers lasted right down to October 18,[27] the very moment at which Emperor Charles's proclamation to the peoples under his rule of federal reorganization ushered in the complete disintegration of the Austrian Empire.

Part 2
Struggles Over the Future of Lithuania and the Baltic

EVER SINCE his plans for military recruitment in Poland had failed (see Vol. III, Chapter 7), Ludendorff had viewed that new country as nothing more than a dangerous neighbor, to be guarded against by the annexation of the largest possible border areas. His basic attitude in this respect did not change with the concessions he was prepared to make to the Poles in the summer of 1918 to facilitate the candidacy of a German prince in Warsaw. He clung with equal tenacity to the hope and desire of placing Lithuania and the Baltic coastal countries into a position of complete dependence on Germany—more precisely, on the Prussian crown—short of outright annexation.

As we have already seen (Chapter 2, Part 1), one of the obstacles was the desire of the German government to come to an agreement with the Soviets on a peace without annexations. At the same time, neither Kühlmann nor Hertling were inclined to stick to the principle of self-determination as an article of faith. Both were predisposed to compromises under which German power in the east might be expanded or at least secured by more or less "voluntary" adherence of the Lithuanians and Balts, so that the semblance of even camouflaged annexation might be avoided.

Angliederung, roughly translated as integration, was a newly devised catchword to that end. Its ambiguity, under both constitutional and international law, was to become apparent as soon as serious attempts were made to apply it, as we shall see. OHL and government were agreed on the desirability of integration, but there were considerable differences between them concerning the method and scope of this policy. In Hertling's and Kühlmann's view, while Livonia and Estonia were to receive support against the Red Terror, as had been decided at the Homburg crown council of February 13 (see p. 106ff.), they were in peacetime to remain outside the German power sphere. The OHL, on the other hand, wanted to see these two provinces combined with Courland into a Greater Baltic State under the Kaiser's direct sovereignty, in other words as a kind of Prussian crown colony.

If politicians and generals were agreed that Courland and Lithuania should be "integrated," the question still remained of how this was to be accomplished. To the military administrations both regions represented primarily prizes of war, to be exploited and used for purposes of military security, their non-German inhabitants expected to obey unprotestingly. The Chancellor and the foreign ministry, on the other hand, tried zealously and in the end vainly to secure local cooperation with Germany, by granting as much freedom and autonomy as possible, so that self-determination would not become a mere mockery. The Chancellor was virtually forced to try for this again and again, because the majority parties in the Reichstag reacted to the weakness of his policy vis-à-vis the OHL with increasing distrust and fought Ludendorff's annexationist policies, which they held responsible for prolonging the war; but the deputies of the joint party caucus never succeeded in gaining any lasting influence over the course of policy. Yet it is plain that except for their continual pressure for implementing the right of self-determination, the aged Chancellor would have displayed even greater weakness toward the OHL.[28]

That weakness was shown particularly in the case of Lithuania. We have already seen how difficult it was to assemble a Lithuanian council or Taryba that might have been represented as the legitimate representative of the popular will. With considerable effort, this assembly, on December 11, 1917, was persuaded to adopt a resolution in which German aid in the creation of a Lithuanian state was solicited and a "firm and everlasting alliance" with the Reich envisaged (see Chapter 2, Part 2). Ludendorff, however, was quite unwilling to mitigate the harshness of the existing military administration on the basis of this declaration, as shown by his indignant complaint to Kühlmann and Hertling about Privy Councilor Nadolny, eastern expert of the foreign ministry, who had discussed the future of Lithuania with representatives of the Taryba late in January without the consent of the military commander. Nadolny had given them certain rather vague pledges that Germany would recognize Lithuanian independence. Ludendorff's wire charged that the intervention of civil agencies like that of Nadolny undermined the authority of the military and served merely to enhance the effrontery of the Lithuanian opposition. He requested that the foreign ministry dispatch no further representatives to Lithuania.[29]

This was in itself a rather sweeping challenge; but Ludendorff's sensitivity in this matter was not wholly unprovoked. The Lithuanians did of course stiffen their stand as they noticed more and more that there were sharp differences between the OHL and the foreign ministry on how they should be treated, while at the same time the Reichstag majority was favorably disposed toward their cause. Deputy Erzberger never tired of assuring them of that, with the result that eastern headquarters, in the bluff military words of General Max Hoffmann, characterized Erzberger's activities as *Schweinerei* (outrageous mischief).[30]

For the rest, the military were not entirely consistent in their attitude. In mid-February two high Lithuanian clergymen presented themselves at supreme headquarters as spokesmen of an anti-Polish group that was prepared to cooperate closely with the Germans. Ludendorff initially displayed alacrity in assenting to the recognition of a Lithuanian state, in order to prevent the Polonization and Bolshevization of the country, against which the clergymen warned. Hertling was delighted and pressed for formal and public acknowl-edgment of the Taryba resolution of December 11 by the Kaiser and for allowing the Lithuanian council at last to participate in local administration.

But here he met with objections on the part of both the military and the civil administrative chiefs, Waldersee and Falkenhausen.[31] Both feared that Lithuania would swiftly slip from the German grasp if it were proclaimed to be autonomous. These objections received strong support from a Taryba resolution of February 16 which, contrary to the declaration of December 11, demanded the creation of an independent Lithuania on a democratic basis with the aid of a constituent assembly that was to be convened promptly. There was no mention this time of invoking German "protection."

The Chancellor was quite willing to ignore this new declaration and pro-posed to the Kaiser that Lithuanian autonomy be recognized on the basis of the December resolution of the Taryba, anticipating a possible similar declara-tion on the part of the French.[32] The Kaiser agreed, but Falkenhausen and the OHL, in the person of Bartenwerffer, thought this impossible unless the Lithuanians "atoned for their disloyalty" of February 16 by issuing still another declaration. It was decided on February 20 to wait and see, mean-while negotiating with the representatives of Courland.

These were the days of the German advance to Lake Peipus. Ludendorff was so incensed over the Lithuanians that he demanded the recall of Bonin, the German diplomatic representative in Vilnyus, who had accepted the Taryba declaration of February 16 and passed it on to the foreign ministry without going through military channels. The military actually considered arresting the originators of the declaration and dissolving the Taryba; but in the end they rested content with prohibiting publication of the declaration and issuing a sharp reprimand to the Taryba.[33] All this did not swerve Hert-ling. Directly following the final conclusion of the peace of Brest-Litovsk he asked eastern headquarters to see to it that a properly authorized delegation from the Lithuanian council be dispatched to Berlin to request German recog-nition under the terms of December 11.[34]

The OHL immediately fought back. Ludendorff, who only on February 10 had said that immediate recognition of Lithuania was necessary to prevent the country from becoming Polonized and Bolshevized, now, on March 6, insisted that autonomy would merely serve to enhance these dangers, bringing on domestic strife that would alienate Lithuania from Germany.[35] He wanted to see recognition indefinitely postponed, first seeking to de-Polonize the Lithuanian clergy, particularly the archiepiscopal see at Vilnyus, bring the agrarian bank at Vilnyus and the Polish latifundian estates under German control, and at the same time effect major border changes in the south that would turn Lithuania into a bastion protecting Germany from Poland. Indeed, he wished to establish a common frontier between Lithuania and the Ukraine, shutting off Poland to the east. This, however, would have meant adding large Polish-speaking regions like Bialystok-Grodno to Lithuania, thus promoting rather than discouraging "Polonization."

What Ludendorff was really after was to set Lithuania and Poland at each other's throats. He wanted Germany to continue ruling the country and had no real intention of granting autonomy. He demanded to be shown the Chancellor's reply before it was handed to the Lithuanian delegation and even submitted a draft of his own, a very model of the military mind. The Lithuanians were to be told no more than that the military administration—not the German government!—would examine the conditions necessary for the creation of a Lithuanian national state, in cooperation with individual representatives of the Lithuanian people. The delegation was to be left in no doubts about the demands Germany would put forward in the various areas. The Chancellor was to advise them—and a delegation from Courland as well, which was expected on March 14—that both countries would continue under military rule and have to bear their full share of the economic burdens imposed by the war. There would be no change in the exploitation of the two countries for German war purposes. Ludendorff added that the borders to be assigned at a future date would depend on the behavior of the Lithuanians. He was willing to accept reforms in the military administration only on a very minor scale. No Lithuanian was to be permitted to occupy any leading position, but eastern headquarters would reexamine the question of whether individual Lithuanians might serve in inferior positions with the military agencies, after the Russian manner.[36]

Like the foreign ministry diplomats, Count Keyserlingk, Reich commissioner for the Baltic regions, strongly protested these demands. They held that any further effort to delay Lithuanian recognition would have a bad effect, at home and abroad. Hertling, as a matter of fact, did not submit his reply to the Lithuanian delegation in advance to the generals of the OHL.[37] Ludendorff was furious. He told Legation Councilor Lersner on March 19 that the Chancellor ignored military interests and had simply gone over his head, as usual.[38] But had Hertling given way to the general's demands, he would certainly have drawn fire from the majority parties and might even have risked having the war appropriations bills voted down, possibly jeopardizing the work of Brest-Litovsk. This emerges quite clearly from the difficult negotiations which the Chancellor had to conduct with the majority party leaders during those very days. Erzberger, particularly, insisted that self-determination for the Poles, Lithuanians, and Courlanders be swiftly, loyally, and honestly implemented.[39]

Hertling got out of his dilemma by means of a compromise. To the Lithuanian delegation on March 23 he said nothing about any continuation of military rule, but neither did he promise that it would be abolished. He did, however, make the unwelcome announcement that Lithuania would have to share Germany's war burdens, which, after all, also served the liberation of Lithuania.[40] Lastly he solemnly proclaimed, in the name and at the behest of the Kaiser, that Lithuania now formed a "free and independent" state, with German assistance. In practical terms, there were no changes in the situation of the Lithuanians and their Taryba.

Similar recognition had already been granted the state of Courland on March 15. Its council, which had a German-Baltic majority, had offered the Kaiser its ducal crown on March 8, directly after the conclusion of the peace of Brest-Litovsk, together with close military and economic ties with Germany. The desire had also been expressed to join with Livonia and Estonia, which had just been occupied by German troops, to form an all-Baltic state, an idea that immediately met with serious objections in the German Reichstag.[41]

This would indeed have been in sharp contravention of the terms of the treaty of Brest-Litovsk and of the pledges Hertling had given on the floor of the Reichstag on February 25, when explaining the German advance into Livonia and Estonia. He had stated categorically that Germany was not out for conquest. The goal was to establish law and order, in the interest of the peace-loving inhabitants. Germany did not dream of gaining a foothold in Estonia and Livonia. [42]

The OHL, however, had shown its displeasure over these words by early March. Word came from supreme headquarters that the army was still meeting much trouble from armed gangs and was resentful of the government's lack of interest in holding onto these areas. It was important that their future still be left open. The Kaiser responded by stating that army sentiment could not be ignored, and despite the representations that were made to him, he insisted that these countries must not be left to their fate. The best solution would be to turn them into crown colonies in the British style. [43]

At a conference on March 10 Ludendorff said that the time had not yet come to discuss a union of all the Baltic countries, but he did agree to promote the union of Livonia and Estonia into a single state, developing sweeping plans for delimiting such a state against Soviet Russia, establishing reconstruction commissions, concluding mutual aid treaties, convening a diet, forming an economic and transport union, and even entering into a secret military pact. The new state was to forego any separate diplomatic representation—in other words, it was to become a German satellite. [44]

This was once again sharply at odds with the views of the foreign ministry, which had long warned against "integrating" these distant lands with the aid of a thin upper crust of German-Baltic landed proprietors and wealthy merchants, in the face of opposition from the bulk of Estonians and Latvians. Kühlmann himself was always extremely reluctant to court everlasting Russian hostility by taking away the Baltic ports for good.[45] This opposition, however, was short-lived in view of the Kaiser's explicit wishes and reports about pro-German demonstrations in the Baltic regions.

On March 21 the Riga municipal council voted unanimously for the establishment of a hereditary monarchy composed of Estonia, Livonia, and Riga, directly under the German imperial crown. The Estonian and Livonian councils followed suit on April 9 and 10, and so, on April 12, did an assembly that had been convened as the joint diet of these three regions, plus the island of Sarema (Oesel).[46]

Hertling seems to have been deeply impressed. By April 16 he had reached agreement with the Kaiser in a conference at Spa, at which Ludendorff was not present, though he gladly agreed with its results. All three Baltic countries were to be joined directly to the Prussian crown. The ambitions of the other German federal states were to be met by allotting Lithuania to an "elected" Saxon prince. Lorraine would fall to Prussia, but Lower Alsatia would go to Bavaria, Upper Alsatia to Baden. Poland would choose a Württemberg prince as its king. [47]

All this was no more than a tentative solution, to be kept strictly secret—one is almost tempted to say that it amounted to no more than wishful thinking. Hertling realized that not a word must be allowed to transpire—indeed, he was seriously concerned that his own government might be in danger if the Kaiser now gave binding assurances to the united Balts. He saw to it that the Kaiser, on April 18, sent them a warmly worded but evasive reply. Actually drafted by Kühlmann, it merely promised to "examine" the Baltic diet's request for integration with Germany.[48] On April 24 the Chancellor himself received a delegation from that diet, now embracing Courland as well. He employed similar words of restrained goodwill, expressing the hope that final integration might soon be effected.

Both Hertling and the foreign ministry, however, seem to have soon become reconciled to the prospect that union of all three Baltic countries could not be prevented in the long run, if only for moral reasons.[49] They did succeed in keeping Livonia and Estonia from being torn from Russia by force. The separation was actually effected by diplomatic agreement, in the form of a supplement to the treaty of Brest-Litovsk, on August 27, of which we shall hear more. There was no mention of integration with Germany in this document; but Ludendorff's view of the future of the Baltic countries was plainly revealed in the big war aims conference that took place in Spa on July 2 under the Kaiser's chairmanship. He looked on the whole Baltic area as little more than a deployment area for the German army and navy against Soviet

Russia, and he put forward corresponding demands, jointly with the naval representatives. The east shore of Lake Peipus was to become Russia's western border, but even Dvinsk was to be "held" as the terminal of the railway from Riga—though this violated the treaty of Brest-Litovsk and had to be fought for by diplomatic negotiations with the Bolshevist government.[50] Ludendorff rejected demilitarization of the Ahvenanmaa (Aland) islands, wanted by both Sweden and Russia, and wished to reserve the right to fortify Tallin, which the Russians regarded as a massive threat to St. Petersburg. Lepaya was to become a major naval base, and the navy even wanted the right to establish a submarine base in Tallin. None of these demands made any sense unless the Baltic region were to remain in German hands for good.

How was all this to be made to happen? Directly following the occupation of Livonia and Estonia Ludendorff had evidently planned to proceed there much as he had before in Lithuania and Courland. There would be a military administration that would keep out civil agencies and create a fait accompli. On March 19 Ludendorff bitterly complained to Hertling, who had appointed Count Keyserlingk as Reich commissioner for the occupied eastern territories, with the mission of establishing uniform policies for Lithuania and the other Baltic regions, under the guidance of the Chancellor. The general insisted that to place a civil agency beside the military to share administrative responsibility would merely create confusion. He was particularly incensed over the fact that at Hertling's behest Keyserlingk was to visit Livonia and Estonia to conduct political talks with representative inhabitants. "In my view," he wired the Chancellor, "authority for such talks, to be conducted according to directives issued by Your Excellency through the OHL, rests exclusively with the local military command." He cited the "tragic experience" of Lithuania, mentioning Nadolny's disturbing appearance in Vilnyus, which must not be repeated.

Ludendorff was, in effect, claiming a political monopoly from the government. The Chancellor responded with considerable tartness. Through his chancellery chief Radowitz he advised Ludendorff that an added reason for rejecting this claim was the fact that as yet there was no military administration in Livonia and Estonia, only troops detailed for police duties. The political aspects of these territories were under the Chancellor's jurisdiction; hence he was entitled to send his representatives there. Presumably he himself would not be barred from these regions, if he decided to visit them! It was intended that Keyserlingk inform himself at firsthand of sentiment in Livonia, maintaining liaison with the military, of course, to insure uniform procedures. "Policy will be determined by the Chancellor, who will first coordinate with the military agencies. The Chancellor agrees substantively with the OHL in seeking a friendly relationship between Germany and Livonia and Estonia. Since we wish to maintain peaceful relations with Russia as well, this must not lead to cutting off Russia's economic access to the sea."

Ludendorff's reply, dictated during the first flush of success of the western offensive, shows him at the height of his political arrogance. There was no objection to Keyserlingk seeking information, "but I cannot permit any political activities. They are the concern of the military authorities, proceeding by OHL directives." These directives were, of course, claimed to accord with agreements reached with the Chancellor. There must not be two separate agencies working side by side. Undivided military authority was particularly important in Livonia and Estonia.

Ludendorff insisted that he too was intent on good relations with Russia; but Russia was still far from strong, and would not be strong for at least another generation. Settlement of Livonian and Estonian matters could not wait that long. Ludendorff added two new complaints about Keyserlingk. In Riga the count had tried to get the local representatives to postpone issuing their declaration in favor of integration with Germany, claiming that Ludendorff agreed to this. On OHL orders the local eighth army command had already intervened, and the Chancellor was asked to do likewise. Evidently intimidated, Hertling did so at once.

The Chancellor did, however, criticize the fact that the military were propagandizing the Lithuanians without regard to the demands of over-all policy. This only led to still another complaint by Ludendorff. He had only belatedly learned that the Lithuanian delegation had been received on March 23. He was now informed that it had been promised recognition even though there had been no satisfactory Lithuanian declarations. He requested that he be told the reason for this action, together with instructions on how the military administration was to protect German interests henceforth, in the face of probable Lithuanian resistance.

Hertling replied in an explanatory if not apologetic vein. He expressed the hope that the eastern high command's rear-echelon military administration might be promptly dissolved and all administration placed on a peacetime basis, with Lithuanians participating under German leadership. Ludendorff at once refused this outright. He even complained that Lithuanians were permitted to travel to Berlin, which merely served the purpose of strengthening Erzberger's hand. The Lithuanians should be told that unofficial talks prior to the official negotiations could only have a harmful effect; and protests by pro-Lithuanian Germans in Berlin should be given no weight.

In the light of all these factors, Count Keyserlingk understandably voiced considerable concern about the eastern policies of the OHL and its organs, on the basis of the impressions he had received during his visit. He said that the eighth army military administration was run by a former assistant judge and in consequence was amateurish in the extreme. Inveterate OHL distrust of central government agencies led to the military doing pretty much as it pleased in the east, which in turn led to constant friction. Any integration in keeping with German interests was impossible, unless the Chancellor gained administrative control of the eastern territories.[51]

Hertling fully intended to reserve to himself the ultimate political disposition of the Baltic states and their relations with Germany; but military arrogance time and again foiled this purpose. It does seem, however, that the OHL did not meddle with the detailed consultations that were held in the Reich office of the interior from May onward to set down in treaty form the integration with Germany of the new states, mainly Courland and Lithuania, and to prepare their constitutions.[52] Virtually all the top government agencies participated in these talks, in addition to the war ministry and still other Prussian agencies, and initially also representatives of the military administration staff of eastern headquarters.

It soon became apparent that the task was fraught with internal contradictions, if, indeed, it was at all soluble. "Integration" was not to be tantamount to annexation; but neither was it to be a mere alliance under international law. At bottom what was expected was something like the union in 1870 of the South German states with the North German League. Yet Lithuania and Courland were not to become part of the German Reich proper, for that would have been annexation, which never would have got by the German chambers. The new states were to have no vote in the federal council, the Reichstag, or the Prussian diet; yet they were to be governed by German law, especially in respect of the economic and tax systems, even though they could have no part in making such law, but simply would have to accept it.

In terms of international law Lithuania and Courland were not to be juridical entities, since they were to be represented by Germany, with no foreign services of their own. Their armed forces were to become part of the German army, i.e., to be under German command. Foreign Minister Hintze, Kühlmann's successor, strongly objected to these terms. He insisted that the "integrated" states should be granted a limited freedom of action in foreign affairs and a seat and a voice in the federal council, at least when Baltic questions were on the agenda. A military alliance and mutual aid pact should be concluded with them instead of their forces being incorporated into the German army. He also wanted their share of war burdens to be determined by their capacity to pay rather than their population.[53] There was opposition to all this, and it was ruled out of order by Reich Commissioner Falkenhausen, who was presiding.

There was unanimity, however, on the establishment of a uniform economic area, with a common currency, state bank, post and telegraph, railways, and customs—this was all intended to help tie the new states to Germany; and the various Reich agencies now competed with one another in seeking to expand their authority by "integration." This bureaucratic overlap resulted in a host of special claims and considerations that for months kept any progress from being made. The talks never went beyond the interests of the various Reich and Prussian agencies. At bottom the whole effort was pointless and wasted. Such conclusions as were reached could never have received the assent of the peoples of Lithuania and Courland, nor of their councils—to the extent that these could be taken seriously in a political sense—let alone of the Reichstag. If integration were ever to mean anything more than poorly camouflaged annexation, the peoples concerned would have had to be granted a modicum of true autonomy and liberty. This would have been possible only if Germany had been able to count on their future friendship. Yet in view of the dreadful events of the war years, which were still continuing, how could a relationship of true confidence have arisen between Germany and the Lithuanians?

It was precisely this mutual distrust that was to make the question of writing constitutions for the new states so difficult. The only reason for granting the Lithuanians the universal franchise would have been for the purpose of holding the Polish estate owners and upper middle-class in check. Yet that would have meant giving the Lithuanians a right the Prussians did not yet possess; and talks with the Taryba in the winter of 1917-1918 had shown that only a thin conservative-clerical upper crust was seriously prepared for integration with Germany, as in Poland more from fear of Bolshevist revolution than from friendship for Germany. No one could foresee the lines along which a democratically based Lithuanian state would develop as an "integrated" neighbor of Germany. Conversely, the only way to preserve German-Baltic political dominance in Courland, Livonia, and Estonia would have been to avoid radical democratization and grant political privileges to landowners, whether by means of a graduated class franchise or the creation of corporate institutions, highly artificial methods either way, with small chance of surviving. In practice the deliberations on these difficult questions never reached a conclusion even within the Reich office of the interior.

The only point of agreement was that Lithuania and Courland must not become republics but constitutional monarchies on the model of the German federal states. That at once raised new difficulties. Who was to occupy the thrones of the new "duchy" of Courland and the "grand duchy" of Lithuania? If they were given to candidates from the ranks of the federated German dynasties—Lithuania, for example, to a prince of Saxony or Württemberg—international representation of the integrated states through the Kaiser as the supreme Reich organ would become even more complex. Most importantly, there would be the same danger that loomed in the case of the so-called "candidate solution" to the question of the Polish succession. By the second generation at the latest, the imported new dynasty might become alienated from its German origins and interests. Indeed, this was bound to happen, if the rulers wanted to maintain themselves.

It was such consideration that commended the solution proposed by the Baltic councils: to vest sovereignty over the new states—at least in the case of Courland—directly in the German Kaiser. Put more precisely, he would exercise this sovereignty in his capacity as king of Prussia, since the Hohenzollerns were a royal Prussian dynasty rather than an imperial German one; but this in turn raised complex constitutional issues: Was the German Reichstag or the Prussian diet the authority for legitimizing such an act of state? Even more difficult was the prospect that such an augmentation of the power of the Prussian crown would instantly arouse the jealousy of other dynasties in North and South Germany, whose assent was essential for acts of the federal council. We are already familiar with these rivalries in the case of the question of Alsace-Lorraine (see Chapter 3, Part 2), and we shall not here take the time to trace the ramifications that resulted from the government's continuing efforts to find a compromise. Lithuania and the Baltic states, like Alsace-Lorraine and Poland, became mere bargaining counters in competing dynastic ambitions.[54]

The man who presided over the preliminary work within the Reich office of the interior, Reich Commissioner Falkenhausen, long clung to the hope that it should be possible to secure *Personalunion* of the Prussian crown with ducal sovereignty over the entire Baltic region, including Livonia and Estonia, in which case the Lithuanians too might be prevailed on to choose the king of Prussia as their ruler.[55] In this purpose he was not swerved even by the highly arbitrary action of the Lithuanian Taryba, which on June 4, tired of waiting endlessly and fruitlessly for the situation within the country to improve and for the constitutional reforms that had been promised, elected as king of Lithuania Duke William of Urach, a collateral member of the Württemberg dynasty. He was to rule as Mindaugas II and create a purely Lithuanian court in Vilnyus, a plan to which he assented. This royal election, which took the military government completely by surprise, was in the main the work of Matthias Erzberger, who had long espoused the cause of the peasant people of Lithuania and wanted to see to it that they got a Catholic ruler.[56] The German government brusquely rejected it as premature, and thus the act did not take effect. In formulating this rejection, Hertling followed Ludendorff's proposals quite closely.[57]

In a political sense—and not only from the German point of view—this royal election was certainly a dubious venture, a typical *Schwabenstreich* (Swabian prank). The throne of Mindaugas II would have undoubtedly soon vanished into the abyss. Yet the purely negative and passive spirit in which the Chancellor met the wishes of the Lithuanians once again served only to demonstrate the helplessness of his eastern policy. It is true that the military administration of Lithuania was taken away from the eastern command, that restrictions on travel were lifted, and that other concessions were made; but this did not alter the fact that the Taryba was growing more and more rebellious. It demanded a final settlement of the Lithuanian question. Among the majority parties in the Reichstag too dissatisfaction was growing over what the social democrat David called the "outrageous" situation in the eastern regions. Yet as late as September 14 Hertling was still rejecting all the Taryba demands, holding out for the treaties that were to come, but that actually had never eventuated by the time of his fall.

Hertling's successor, Prince Max of Baden, did try to appease the Lithuanians by a sweeping compliance with their wishes; but in the meantime the German occupation troops, long since weary of war service, had succumbed to revolutionary ferment and were no longer able to protect the new democratic state against the banditry that was rampant in the country. The reconstruction of Lithuania was now taken on by the Taryba directly. On November 3 the Kaiser abolished the military administration in Lithuania and Courland, and five days later Prince Max abolished the Reich commissariat as well. The following day, November 9, revolution broke out in Berlin, and another two days later, just when the Lithuanian Professor Woldemaras was forming a national government, the armistice was signed at Compiègne, revoking the treaty of Brest-Litovsk with all its clauses concerning Lithuania and Courland.

Thus ended all the grandiose plans of German annexationists for a greater Baltic state integrated with Germany. It is astonishing in retrospect how long and tenaciously Germans and German Balts clung to these hopes. As late as August 15, when the military defeat in the west was already clearly foreshadowed, a report from the Prussian cabinet demanded the *Personalunion* of Courland, Livonia, Estonia, and Lithuania with Prussia or Germany.[58] The supplement to the treaty of Brest-Litovsk, already mentioned, was framed so as to facilitate the execution of such plans. The reopening of the University of Riga as a purely German-speaking academy was brilliantly celebrated on September 14, marking the high point of German Baltic hopes. All this was now mere outward show. In a report for the Chancellor on September 18, Foreign Minister Hintze manfully opposed all integration plans—and Hertling was fond of crediting Hintze with speaking up bluntly and openly to the military rather than avoiding open conflict by remaining silent at critical moments, like his predecessor Kühlmann.[59]

Hintze insisted that *Personalunion* would fly in the face of all the protestations by the German government that it desired no annexations, stamping it as hypocritical before all the world. It would compel the Kaiser to be represented in the Baltic countries by viceroys, which would inevitably favor the rise of republican and even Bolshevist trends. Most importantly, it would not be possible to adopt the same policies in the east as in the Reich, and this too would bring on dangerous political complications. Prussian sovereignty, moreover, would cause serious resentment in Dresden and at the South German courts; and lastly, the Reichstag would never agree to integration.[60]

These representations did not fail of their purpose. Reich Commissioner Falkenhausen, always strongly influenced by the military approach,[61] did stand up for the spirit of Ludendorff. He said that in the end all depended on the strength of the government, which must not shrink from the charge of annexationism—not to be avoided in any event—but should pursue Baltic integration at all costs; and at another meeting with the Chancellor on September 20 it was stated that to forego *Personalunion* would make a mockery of Germany's entire eastern policy and resettlement plans. But simple continuation of these policies was nevertheless considered far too risky, and it was decided to postpone a decision, even on the contemplated pacts with the Baltic states. Falkenhausen submitted treaty drafts on October 7, but there was little point to the effort. In view of the disastrous German military situation, no consultations on them were ever held.

This was a tremendous disappointment to the Baltic Germans. They tried vainly in October and even early November to secure the union of Courland, Livonia, and Estonia into a single Baltic state on a broad popular basis, by resolutions of their joint diet. Hopes of Baltic integration with Germany and of preserving the traditional dominance of the Baltic Germans were swept away in the maelstrom of the November Revolution and the great military disaster.

Part 3
Germany and the Russian Civil War

THE ONLY REASON why the Germans were able to pursue the policy of Baltic integration for such a long time was that by the summer of 1918 the Bolshevist regime had lapsed into a severe internal crisis that at times seemed to herald its end.[62, 63] Its moral authority had been shaken for many reasons— its signing of the imposed peace of Brest-Litovsk, which was generally considered a shameful act of surrender and which was exploited for increasingly strident attacks by the great rival party of the people, the social revolutionaries; the inability of the Communist apparatchiks to cope with concrete economic problems of transport and administration, which steadily worsened the chaotic situation at home; the bloody terror by which it sought to support its minority rule; and above all the growing danger from abroad, which the Bolshevists, since the disintegration of the old army, could meet only with the highly inadequate Red Guards and a few reasonably reliable Latvian regiments.

This danger arose at just about the time when the peace treaty of Brest-Litovsk was signed, removing the last hopes of the Allies that their Russian ally might still be brought into action once more against the Central Powers. Greatly overestimating German strength, the Allies were henceforth haunted by the fear that Germany might in time control the vast eastern spaces all the way to the Urals and beyond, which would have lastingly destroyed the balance of Europe. By May 1918 the British General Staff entertained the grotesque idea that if the war continued for a long time, the Germans might recruit some two million workers and soldiers in the east, throwing about half of them into the western front. To prevent this and save from the German grasp the extensive war material stored in the ports of Murmansk and Vladivostok, where they had been delivered by the Allies, and possibly to hinder the withdrawal of German occupation troops for the western front, Britain tried hard, from April onward, to organize military intervention in Russia, involving Japan as well as the United States.

It is well-established today that at least until the fall of 1918 this intervention was directed not so much against the Bolshevist regime as against Germany. Somehow a new eastern front was to be brought into being; and following the initial success of the German western offensive this was felt to be so urgent a need that utterly absurd plans were considered, such as an advance by Japanese and American troops from the Yellow Sea to the Urals and beyond.

The actual resources committed to this intervention were relatively slight; but the situation grew dangerous for the Bolshevists when, after a trifling incident, the Czech legion, which was to be sent to the western front in France via Vladivostok, on May 14 rose in open rebellion against the Soviet government. This legion, composed of some 50,000 Czech defectors and prisoners-of-war, had been formed in the summer of 1917. Armed at the time by the provisional revolutionary government, it had been committed on the southeastern front and now represented the only intact force in the Russian chaos.

Following this rebellion, the Czech legion served as a tool of Western interventionist policy. Britain hoped that the troops it and America had landed on the shores of the White Sea might link up with the Czechs fighting in the Urals and Siberia. Even more dangerous to Lenin's government was the possibility that its internal enemies, the liberals and monarchists, and the Volga and Don Cossacks, might establish contact with the Czech legion and form a rival government with its help. Wherever the Czechs ruled the countryside, they formed regional and local governments of various party colorations.

By midsummer the situation looked desperate for the Bolshevists. There were numerous putsches and hunger revolts in the cities, agrarian unrest in the open country, and political uprisings of every kind. From the north the Entente troops, reinforced since June, advanced by way of Murmansk and Archangel, from the south the Cossack generals Alexeyev and Krasnov, in the Caucasus the Turks, in the east the Czechs from Siberia and the Urals. At times Lenin considered abandoning Moscow, to avoid complete disaster.

What should German policy have been in the face of this Russian chaos? It was certainly tempting to exploit the extraordinary and still increasing weakness of the Soviet government by joining with its internal enemies, who were all more or less eager for such a combination. Swift military intervention in Moscow and St. Petersburg—which, in the opinion of military experts, would have been possible with relatively small forces—might then have put an end to the Bolshevist mischief. A moderate government might have been helped into power and "law and order" in the conventional political sense restored.

We know from our account of the Homburg crown council of February 13 (see Chapter 2, Part 2) that Ludendorff intended to take such steps to "clarify the situation." He clung to this goal throughout the summer. It is noteworthy, moreover, that his views were shared beyond military headquarters. Nearly all the German diplomats in Moscow were inclined to favor German intervention in the Russian civil war and a German alliance with the anti-Bolshevists. The first German envoy in Moscow, Count Mirbach, initially very critical of the anti-Bolshevist groups that were wooing German support, because he distrusted both their intentions and their capacities, soon gained such a gloomy impression of the situation of the Bolshevist leaders that he foresaw an impending *Götterdämmerung* and advised Berlin to prepare in time for a possible change in power. His successor Helfferich was an even stronger advocate of an anti-Bolshevist policy, encouraged by his Moscow associates, all of whom without exception, military or civilian, regarded the Bolshevist government as close to death and beyond hope of recovery—apart from their doubts that it was sincere in its desire to cooperate with Germany.

Amazingly enough the German foreign ministry never wavered in its total rejection of intervention in the Russian civil war, a fact that was to have historic consequences. The ministry stood firm against the judgment of its own diplomatic experts, let alone the interventionist desires of the OHL, consistently objecting to any effort to go beyond the provisions of the treaty of Brest-Litovsk and wrest further territory by military force from the still-weak Soviet government. Kühlmann, like his successor Hintze, who followed exactly the same course, presented impressive arguments in favor of such a policy.

Late in April Ludendorff recommended that the foreign ministry establish secret contacts with monarchist opponents of the Soviet government. Kühl-

mann objected in a telegram sent from Bucharest on May 3.[64] The crumbling
of the Russian empire and the resultant bursting of the enemy ring around
Germany, he said, constituted Germany's greatest political success in the war.
So long as the war lasted, Germany had to do all it could to prevent Russia
from regaining its strength rather than promoting such a development. The
territorial losses Russia had suffered by virtue of the peace of Brest-Litovsk—
especially its being cut off from the Baltic and Black Seas by the ensuing
expeditions of the German armies—would force any future Russian regime
that consolidated its position to pursue an imperialist policy to regain the lost
territories. This would be particularly true if the regime were monarchist. The
German parties of the left, furthermore, would take it badly if Germany were
to fight for the restoration of czarism. Lastly, there were no discernible
economic advantages a restored Greater Russia might offer Germany in time
for the needs of the current war.

Kühlmann voiced similar sentiments time and again. He was a confirmed
opponent of any further expansion of the German occupation, not only
because he was afraid of committing still greater German forces in the east,
but mainly for political considerations. German policy would forfeit credibility if it ignored the treaty provisions of Brest-Litovsk. Kühlmann thought it
was decidedly in the German interest to keep the Bolshevist regime in power
as long as possible since it was the only one prepared to accept the treaty of
Brest-Litovsk as an established fact, despite all the patriotic protests within
the Bolshevist party. Its chaotic regime of violence, moreover, kept the country in a state of perpetual ferment, preventing the formation of another
eastern front, especially since Lenin rejected any further military adventure
on principle.

Support of the Bolshevist regime by conservative-monarchist Germany may
certainly be considered to have been paradoxical if not Machiavellian;[65] but
Germany, caught up in a struggle for survival, had little choice. In the preceding year the Germans themselves had brought Lenin to St. Petersburg,
thus launching the Bolshevist ferment in Russia; and it was only logical to
allow that ferment to run its course. An added factor was that not one of the
anti-Bolshevist groups suing for German support had any reasonable chance
of success. Some consisted of officers without men, others of men without
leaders. Many sought support from the Germans and the Entente in turn and
none was capable of competent organization and leadership.

Kühlmann believed that it would be utterly irresponsible for Germany to
intervene in this ferment of savagely contending forces. He found corrobora-
tion in the judgment of a former Russian diplomat with expert knowledge,
who confidently predicted that if the Bolshevist regime were to fall, the lion's
share of political and economic reconstruction would fall to the Germans,
who would swiftly draw the hatred of the Russians as their oppressors and

disciplinarians.[66] A foreign ministry report of early May urgently warned against listening to the pleas of Russian reactionaries.[67] Germany, it said, would be elected to do the dirty job of driving out the Bolshevists, only to make room for the reactionaries, who would pursue the same old policies toward Germany used by the czarist government during the preceding decades.

Kühlmann was at pains to deepen the conflict between Bolshevist-governed Russia and its marginal areas, especially the Ukraine, at least "for the time being," i.e., while the war was on, and to suppress federalist tendencies in the territories occupied by Germany. This was the reason why he welcomed the establishment of a civil government under Hetman Scoropadsky in the Ukraine. This did not mean he thought Russia could or should be permanently split up into smaller states. Like other German experts on eastern questions—including even Ludendorff—he thought that a Ukrainian national state could be only a temporary solution and that the Ukraine would not be able to survive separated from Greater Russia.

Indeed, Kühlmann felt that the whole peace of Brest-Litovsk was only a temporary expedient. That was why he was concerned lest Russia become permanently estranged from Germany by virtue of being cut off from the Baltic and Black Seas. Yet he too entertained doubts that Lenin's rule would endure, as indeed did everyone else, including even Lenin himself. He firmly rejected the idea occasionally put forward by his eastern expert Nadolny, that German military forces should be committed for the purpose of maintaining the Bolshevists in power. He was nevertheless prepared to give them some diplomatic relief at critical moments,[68] just so long as their regime seemed to him useful to Germany.

Germany's remaining strength at the end of the war would never have sufficed to root out Bolshevism and revolutionary socialism in general by force of arms. The experience in the Ukraine had demonstrated that. There occupation forces running to 600,000 had been unable to cope with the rural social-revolutionary movement and establish a bourgeois regime that could prove reasonably durable. It may have seemed easy at times to take St. Petersburg or Moscow and thus topple the Red regime, but the incalculable chaos unloosed in 1917 could never have been contained with bayonets. This was a fact never understood by Kühlmann's adversaries at supreme headquarters—nor was it grasped by even so shrewd a politician as Helfferich, who severely criticized the foreign ministry's stand from his conservative-monarchist point of view; but Helfferich was never able to outline an alternative policy that might have offered a better chance.

Even sharper, of course, was the clash of views between Kühlmann and the OHL, which drew its political intelligence from a kind of parallel military foreign service that bypassed the foreign ministry. The leading military voice on eastern questions seems always to have been that of Colonel Barten-werffer, head of the General Staff's political section. Since the German army archives have been destroyed, we cannot tell precisely to what extent Barten-werffer influenced Ludendorff's views, which often seem startlingly primitive.

In a wire to the Chancellor on June 9, for example, Ludendorff admitted that the German divisions stationed in the east would not be strong enough if the situation there worsened. Hence they must be reinforced by a Finnish army and a German-organized Georgian army—and if possible also by the Cossack tribes this side of the Caucasus, if Germany were in a position to arm them. The Soviet government would have to continue to be regarded with the deepest suspicion. It represented a permanent danger, which could be lessened only if it went on acknowledging Germany as its absolute overlord and proved itself compliant, from fear of Germany and concern for its own survival. To sharpen these fears, Germany should establish contact with monarchist-inclined, rightist, anti-Bolshevist circles. They were the only ones on whom reliance could be placed, for unlike the other groups, they were not beholden to the Entente. The goal of German efforts must be to have the monarchist movement march entirely to the German tune, once it had achieved authority.

Typically militarist in spirit, this was surely a highly amateurish approach. Two weeks later it was raised to grotesque proportions, when the OHL learned of certain proposals by the German ambassador in Moscow, Mirbach, which Kühlmann had instantly rejected. Mirbach had suggested that Germany anticipate certain Entente efforts to win over the Russian counterrevolutionaries by making offers of its own. Hindenburg thereupon addressed both the Kaiser and the Chancellor on June 23, stating it as his opinion that the situation in Russia had grown extremely tense, requiring Germany to take a clear-cut decision. "From the military point of view I must demand . . . that Greater Russia be opened up to us for purposes of military intervention aimed at capturing the major rail lines and transport centers so that we may establish a government willing and able to proceed with us against the Entente"![69]

This happened just before Kühlmann's fall, but Legation Councilor Grünau, Kühlmann's representative with the Kaiser, was able to win him over to Kühlmann's view, by presenting the foreign minister's arguments before Hindenburg's. After Kühlmann left, it was Colonel Haeften who tried hard to end the unceasing tension between the OHL and the foreign ministry, in an effort to strengthen German policy abroad as well as at home. To this end he developed a war aims program which, in his view, stood a chance of gaining the approval of both the generals and the politicians. Haeften, among other things, wrote a report entitled *Aims of German Policy,* which he claimed was based on discussions he had held with Ludendorff on June 26-28 and which he had Ludendorff expressly confirm. Allegedly representing Ludendorff's views, its style and argumentation raise doubts of the degree to which this was true; for Haeften's activities as a mediator were marked by his peculiar ability both to adapt himself to the views of his chief and to read his own thoughts into his chief's statements.[70] The report nevertheless affords interesting insight into the world of Ludendorff's political ideas, even though he may not have actually formulated them in this case. The practical effects were nil, and in the foreign ministry, where the report wound up, it was simply filed away.

Germany, the report said, must see to it that Russia become "a reliable friend and ally who not only poses no danger to Germany's political future but forms a source of military strength while being kept in the greatest possible political, military, and economic dependence on Germany"–Russia, in other words, was to be at once friend, satellite, and object of exploitation! Only in this way could Germany secure dominion over Europe and pave the way for a European-Asian bloc. Only in this way could Germany maintain its world position against the two other world states that were in the process of formation, the Pan-American bloc and the British bloc with its dominions.[71]

But how could this friendship and dependence of Russia be secured? Entente policies, consciously directed toward overthrowing the Bolshevist regime in combination with the Russian "cadets," "octobrists," and monarchist groups, compelled Germany to become active in the same direction even now. Under no circumstances must the Russia of the future be allowed to owe its liberation from Bolshevism to the Entente. Germany would have to take the lead, i.e., seek contact with all the pro-German groups in Russia and propagandize them for the German cause. They would have to accept the treaty of Brest-Litovsk, however, as well as the separation from the Russian empire of Finland, the Baltic regions, Lithuania, Poland, and Georgia. Let the remainder join in a federal scheme, provided there were firm economic integration with Germany for the purpose of opening up Russian economic resources and protecting both countries against raw material blockades. The immediate goal was a clear-cut decision in favor of the pro-German groups among the counterrevolutionaries, and a single propaganda front extending from Helsinki to Tiflis.[72] Such a relationship with Russia, settled for decades to come, would greatly facilitate the tasks of German diplomacy when a general peace was concluded.

German-Bolshevist relations reached a critical climax when the German envoy, Count Mirbach, was assassinated on July 6 by two fanatics from left social revolutionary circles. Their intention was to rekindle the war with Germany. The Bolshevist government showed itself incapable of controlling the political chaos even in Moscow, and all the anti-Bolshevists now hoped that Germany would break with Lenin. Understandably enough, Mirbach's associates, Legation Councilor Riezler in the lead, also wanted diplomatic relations broken off; but the foreign ministry, under the new minister, Rear Admiral Hintze, clung unswervingly to Kühlmann's policy and viewed the assassination as a mere incident for which the Bolshevists were not to be held responsible. It rejected a diplomatic break.

Nor did this change when early in August, directly after the arrival of Helfferich as Mirbach's successor in Moscow, revolutionary unrest in that city reached such heights that the German diplomatic mission was under grave new assassination threats. The Soviet government enjoined Helfferich from visiting the Kremlin, since it was unable to guarantee his safety en route. Foreign Commissar Chicherin actually called at the German legation in person to pick up the new envoy's credentials.

Lenin was so desperate at this time that on August 1 he demeaned himself by virtually asking the Germans for military aid against the British, advancing from the north.[73] Small wonder that Helfferich described it as useless to enter into any further treaties with such a government. Any such policy was bound to break down promptly and infamously. Contact with the anti-Bolshevists had to be sought at once. Helfferich proposed that a show be made of complying with the Bolshevist government's plea for help, but that the troops actually march to overthrow the Bolshevists. To win over the counterrevolutionaries to the German cause, Helfferich was prepared to revise the treaty of Brest-Litovsk, even to return the Ukraine to Russia.

Hintze manfully resisted any such policy, nor was he swerved by doubts voiced from among his associates in Berlin.[74] He recalled Helfferich to Berlin for consultation, which resulted in the virtual dissolution of the German diplomatic mission in Soviet Russia.[75] Even before the envoy arrived, Hintze had prepared the ground for the major review of eastern policy that was now bound to ensue. In a personally drafted letter to Ludendorff of August 6 he presented his stand with great clarity and in a way shrewdly calculated to appeal to the headquarters mentality.[76]

The only language understood there was one that uncompromisingly placed the exigencies of war and German power interest ahead of all other considerations. Ludendorff had offered the minister six to seven divisions in the north and a few more in the south, for purposes of intervention in the civil war, along the lines proposed by Helfferich. Ostensibly they were to support Lenin's government against its enemies, especially the British invasion on the north coast. The covert purpose would be to overthrow the Bolshevists with its aid. As Ludendorff put it in a wire on August 6, such forces could buttress a new Russian government that would have popular support.

Hintze immediately replied that a government enjoying popular support would not need the Germans, since it would rise to power with the help of the people. As for the troops offered for use against the Entente in the north, the Czechs in the east, and the Cossack general Alexeyev in the south, they could be committed regardless of the kind of government that was in power or might come into power. It so happened that it was the Bolshevist government that had asked German aid. Any other government would immediately or at any rate very soon become a friend and ally of the Entente. Germany had no friends worth mentioning in Russia. Anyone who told Ludendorff anything else was deceived. The Bolshevists had certainly fallen on hard times, but they were by no means threatened as yet by a popular uprising. Germany had no occasion to wish for or hasten their demise. They were certainly nasty people, undeserving of sympathy; but that had not kept Germany from forcing the peace of Brest-Litovsk on them and from depriving them of people and land even beyond that. Germany had got what it could out of them and the exigencies of war dictated that it go on doing so as long as the Bolshevists were in power. Whether this was done with enthusiasm or not was quite beside the point. History had shown it to be an expensive luxury to introduce emotions into politics. Such indulgence in Germany's present situation would be unpardonable. Collaboration with the Bolshevists could not be abandoned because they were disliked or even loathed. To the present day and for many years to come, politics would always be a matter of practical realities.

There were indeed signs that the Bolshevist regime was nearing its end, Hintze went on. But such an event should be calmly awaited rather than hastened. The anti-Bolshevists, whom Hintze described in some detail, were so divided that only a Russian genius could unify them. Such a genius was not in sight. One thing the anti-Bolshevists did have in common was their hostility to Germany. Germany's goal in the east was the military paralysis of Russia. The Bolshevists were taking care of that better than any other Russian party could, without Germany risking a penny or a single man. Germany certainly could not expect love from the Russians. Let it then be content with their impotence and cultivate their differences with the Entente. Helfferich was speaking of modifying the peace of Brest-Litovsk, even of returning the Ukraine, in order to win over the antirevolutionary parties. Others spoke of restoring Russia within its old borders. Why all this? Was Germany to forfeit the fruits of its victories for the sole reason of escaping the odium of collaborating with the Bolshevists? Germany was not really working with them—it was exploiting them. Such, after all, was the very essence of politics. Was the OHL really ready to relinquish the Baltic, Lithuania, the Ukraine—to say nothing of the Crimea, Tabriz, the Donetz basin, the return of all of which would be certainly demanded?

Hintze's arguments were so unanswerable, especially in their concluding rhetorical questions, that even Ludendorff was left with nothing to say—he received the document on the eve of the great military disaster of August 8.

He now said that it had never been his intention to secure a sudden change in German Bolshevist policy and that he concurred in general with Hintze's line.[77] It was the first foreign ministry victory over the all-powerful OHL on a major policy issue. It is true that at this time, in early August, Ludendorff, as shown in the obscure and sometimes ambiguous wording of his wires, was no longer quite certain that his eastern divisions were strong enough to carry out a great anti-Bolshevist coup; nor did he entirely give up hope of such a thing, even after Hintze's memorandum, as shown by his continuing preparations for an advance on St. Petersburg; but by his resolute demeanor, the foreign minister did gain political control of eastern policy until the end of the war.

How is Hintze's program to be taken? Did he really aim at a policy of unending brutal oppression of Russia, of unrestrained expansionism and continued annexations?[78] Or did the foreign minister intend merely to underline Germany's grave war exigencies, in an attempt to frighten the imperialist Ludendorff with the prospect that the anti-Bolshevist alliance he was pursuing could be purchased only at great territorial cost? The answer is seen clearly from Hintze's unequivocal rejection of all efforts to integrate Livonia and Estonia with Prussia through *Personalunion,* a stand that has already been discussed (see p. 255f.). He expressed himself even more plainly in a discussion with the parliamentary leaders of the major parties in the Reichstag on August 21:

> The Russian people possess great powers of resistance, and they will become an important factor in the life of nations. From our point of view those may be right who wish to see our policy approached from the aspect of closer economic ties in the future; but the exigencies of war require that we do not allow Russia to rise again while the war is on. Where are the people with whom we could overthrow the present government and then reach a settlement?

There were no promising opponents of the Bolshevists in Russia, he went on, and for the time being not even the Entente could do anything decisive against them. Should that change, Germany would have to intervene. The proper policy was to wait calmly, so long as it was possible to postpone that time. Germany did have the sincere intention of establishing good neighborly relations with Russia.[79] Even more persuasive than these words is the tenacious struggle which Hintze waged, in continuation of Kühlmann's policies, for the supplement to the treaty of Brest-Litovsk, to put an end to the unending tension between Germany and Russia and "keep the generals on a short leash," as it was covertly put inside the foreign ministry.

There had been negotiations over the supplement ever since June. It was intended to settle a number of questions still left open at Brest-Litovsk. Berlin hoped it would defuse the political atmosphere, which had been poisoned by the excesses of the German occupation power, far transcending the limits set at Brest-Litovsk. The separation of Livonia and Estonia from the Russian body politic had long been a settled matter at headquarters, and among other things the foreign ministry wished to bring this about by peaceful negotiations rather than force.

Lastly, an attempt was to be made to revive economic relations with Russia, which had been interrupted by the war. German industry, especially heavy industry and the big banks, was deeply interested in this effort. It importuned the Reich agencies with its demands, which were tantamount to the greatest possible financial penetration of Russia. Germany was to exploit its military dominance and the terms of the treaty of Brest-Litovsk to place the Russian economy in a state of far-reaching dependence on the German economy. The Russian market was to be opened up to German goods, Russian natural resources were to be exploited for German industry, and the Russian rail network was to be dominated by German capital, if that were possible.

The program put forward by German heavy industry unhesitatingly went far beyond the limits of economic and political demands. Permanent military occupation of the European access routes to North Russia, i.e., the Baltic islands, especially Sarema and Ahvenanmaa, Finland, and the coast of Murmansk, was declared to be necessary. The required capital, initially some two million marks, was to be provided by government-guaranteed public loans. On June 4 a conference of representatives of heavy industry and the big banks with men from the OHL and government agencies was held at the Reich economic office. It was decided to establish a syndicate for the purpose of German economic expansion in the east, initially only with privately subscribed capital amounting to 100 million marks.[80] Furthermore, an "economic staff" of Eastern experts was established at the German embassy in Moscow.

This syndicate, however, never gained any practical importance, for the grandiose plans of the German industrialists soon proved to have been built on air rather than on the solid soil of economic and political realities. The foreign ministry had from the outset entertained doubts that German industry would still be able to engage in large-scale expansion in the fourth year of the war. At a departmental conference on May 15, convened by Under Secretary von dem Bussche, it developed that German capital could participate in the reconstruction of the Russian rail system to only a very limited degree; and in a report from Moscow, Legation Councilor Riezler warned against any illusions that capitalist methods could prevail in a country whose economic policies were in open conflict with capitalism.

"Sweeping financial penetration" of Russia was indeed precluded by the fact that the Soviet government had decreed a state monopoly of foreign trade in April. The result was that German businessmen got into unending difficulties with the Soviet authorities. This virtually paralyzed all trade, and the general chaos in business and government did not help. All prospects of "penetration" by German capital were finally buried when the nationalization of all major Russian industrial undertakings was decreed on June 28—as a matter of fact, as a deliberate step to foil the expansionist plans of German heavy industry.

This, however, kept neither Lenin nor his ambassador Joffe in Berlin from repeatedly holding out to the Germans the bait of economic concessions that were to usher in a flourishing Russo-German trade. Their intent was to mobilize German economic interests against the territorial ambitions of the "war party," i.e., the OHL. These Soviet offers, hedged in as they were with all kinds of reservations, were used by the foreign ministry to persuade the OHL that ministry policy was correct. The ministry insisted that negotiation might exact considerable advantages from the Bolshevists, provided the continuing advances of German troops in the east were halted, and with them the breakaway of more and more regions from the Russian body politic.

The OHL response of May 28 showed that supreme headquarters entertained ideas very similar to those of heavy industry, though they were couched in much harsher militarist terms. It was important to German industry in both war and peace, said the OHL, for Germany to attract Russian exports and gain a foothold in Russian economic life. This would be facilitated if Germany controlled Russia's export ports, "with the exception of Archangel and the Siberian railway." These goals would never be attained by military or political compromise. Russia would never be Germany's friend and must be weakened and tied to Germany by force. The weaker marginal states, on the other hand, must be strengthened as well as made economically dependent on Germany. On no account must the Russians be allowed to enter into any substantial economic relations with the Entente. Similarly, Germany must retain the right to intervene in Russia's relations with rich marginal states, like the oil regions in the Caucasus, even though the Soviet government had expressly demanded that Germany refrain from such intervention.

In the circumstances, the foreign ministry was exposed to constant friction and clashes with the OHL in its negotiations with the Soviet government, whose policies were considered to be insincere if not malicious, not only at supreme headquarters but by the Kaiser personally. Further delays and complications were caused by the continuing German advances in South Russia and the Caucasus (to be discussed in Part 4), as well as by Ludendorff's efforts at political contact with the rebellious Don Cossacks. This in turn made German policies appear insincere and malicious to the government in Moscow.

It was thus rather surprising that the supplementary treaties should have been concluded at all. Initialed on August 10, they were finally signed on August 27. During this period, however, there was a perceptible slackening of OHL interest in eastern questions, as a result of the disastrous situation on the western front. In Moscow too the treaty was no longer taken very seriously, since a German defeat was more and more clearly foreshadowed. A final obstacle was the opposition offered from the ranks of the majority parties in the Reichstag, notably by Erzberger and Ebert. Hintze, however, by a skillful and frank presentation on August 21 of his war aims for the east, managed to win over a majority of the parliamentary leaders. The sticking point for the deputies was the severe additional exactions from Russia imposed by the supplementary treaty—final separation of Estonia and Livonia, though the Russians were granted free port areas at Tallin, Riga, and Ventspils, together with preferential trade and customs terms. The Russians agreed to Germany recognizing Georgia as an independent state, in return for a German promise to evacuate the Black Sea regions after the war, as well as White Russia east of the Beresina, dependent on whether the payments agreed to in the financial section were actually remitted. A payment of considerable size, six billion marks, was indeed set, though not in the form of an outright contribution, but rather as a blanket indemnification for all civil damage and costs inflicted up to July 1 by such Russian measures as repudiation of the government debt and expropriations, as well as for German expenditures for prisoners-of-war.

As against these exactions, the supplementary treaty also brought the Soviets considerable advantages. Germany pledged nonintervention in relations between Great Russia and its various territories and agreed not to promote the formation of any further independent states on Russian soil. Russia promised to drive out the Entente troops from Murmansk and Baku, to which end it was assured of the help of German troops. Germany agreed to prevent any third power (this meant Turkey) from advancing into the Baku oil region. In return it was to receive a share of the Baku oil output, while Russia was to share in Donetz coal as long as the German occupation continued. Russia's title to the warships seized from it was recognized, as was the Russian claim for compensation at a later date for supplies seized elsewhere than in the Ukraine and Finland.

All in all the treaty did quite clearly aim at settling controversial points and harmonizing conflicting interests, though it did not remove the inequities of the treaty of Brest-Litovsk or undo what happened subsequently. It was soon shown, moreover, that Germany, at the end of its strength, was no longer able to fulfill all the promises made in the supplementary treaty.

It may nevertheless be asserted that the foreign ministry did here succeed essentially in prevailing over the OHL with policies directed toward compromise rather than force. This will become plainer as we now proceed to follow Germany's military expeditions in the wake of the treaty of Brest-Litovsk, together with the associated political plans of the OHL.

Part 4
Military Expeditions in the East and the OHL's Plans for the Future

EVEN BEFORE the treaty of Brest-Litovsk was signed, the OHL began to transcend the territorial limits laid down in it. As early as February 21, when an emissary of the moderate government of Finland was in Kreuznach, it promised to dispatch an auxiliary corps to help drive out the Red Guards who had been fighting the Finnish White Guards under General Mannerheim since late January.[81] The foreign ministry was not even advised of the text and scope of these assurances. On March 5, at the Kaiser's order, German troops landed on the Åland islands (Ahvenanmaa), which were to serve as a base for an invasion of Finland. This was two days after the signing of the treaty of Brest-Litovsk!

Ice conditions and mined seaways, however, prevented passage to Finland for the time being, and the Baltic division of some 10,000 men under General Rüdiger von der Goltz, which had been reserved for this purpose, had to be held in Danzig until early April. This gave the politicians the opportunity to make their objections to the whole undertaking known to the Kaiser, who flew into a rage. He felt himself morally bound to the project and described Hertling's telegram of objection as outrageous meddling with purely military matters.[82]

The political objections to the Finland expedition were obvious. It had indeed been agreed on February 13 at Homburg that Germany would dispatch "police troops" in response to pleas for help from the Baltic area, and Finland and the Ukraine actually had been mentioned in this connection (see p.109). Article 6 of the treaty of Brest-Litovsk, moreover, obligated the Soviet Russians to immediate withdrawal of the Red Guards from Finland and Ahvenanmaa, as well as of the Russian fleet and naval forces from Finnish ports. Yet politically and from the viewpoint of international law it seemed highly dubious to mobilize a sizable force against the Red Guards before the treaty was even ratified, and without giving the Soviet government time to carry out its obligations. It was an act of force that immediately downgraded the treaty, possibly jeopardizing its ratification by the Russians, and it also necessarily appeared in the light of intervention into the internal affairs of a foreign state.

Would the Reichstag majority be prepared to authorize the necessary appropriations? Was Germany to play the role of world policeman, spending substantial means to that end at this particular time? Unpopular new military operations might well endanger passage of the war credits that were about to come up in the Reichstag. An invasion of the Ukraine possibly might have been justified on the basis of the critical food situation of the Central Powers, which stood in urgent need of grain shipments from this allegedly opulent "breadbasket"; but what business had Germany in Finland? Holtzendorff, who strongly supported the Finnish enterprise, spoke of securing the Baltic Sea against Anglo-American attempts at intervention, which raised the suspicion that the German navy was out to acquire naval bases.

But what was the ultimate aim of the OHL? This was described as the heart of the matter at a ministerial conference called by the Chancellor on March 11 and attended by Roedern, Wallraf, Krause, Solf, Bussche, Payer, Winterfeldt, and Radowitz, at which these objections were to be aired. The minister of justice sought to disarm the reservations put forward on grounds of constitutional and international law, doing so with considerable pettifoggery.[83] Yet there remained much concern that the OHL might involve Germany in another adventure with incalculable consequences.[84] Hence Hertling decided to ask the Kaiser to delay the expedition, in such a way as to give the Russians a definite time limit for evacuating Finland. On its expiration combat with regular Russian forces might then be justified under international law. The Russians were also to be told that there was no intention of intervening in the internal affairs of Finland; and the OHL and navy were to pledge themselves not to go after permanent occupation and naval bases in Finland.[85]

I have been unable to verify that this compromise was actually presented to the Kaiser for approval, but if so it apparently made no impression on him; for at a crown council on March 12 he seemed to follow completely the arguments of Ludendorff, who left nothing undone to counter the government position. He sensed that its reservations actually betokened an intention to halt the Finnish expedition altogether and proceeded to paint a gruesome picture of the dangers that threatened Germany from the northeast.

The whole trend of the Bolshevist chaos, he insisted, was directed against Germany—and never mind the treaty terms. There was no assurance of where the internal situation in Russia would wind up; hence it was essential to have a show of strength on the northern border of Russia. Hindenburg sent a wire saying that with proper military support Finland, on account of its geographic situation with respect to St. Petersburg, might exert salutary pressure on Great Russia. Like the Ukraine, Finland would be Germany's natural ally in peacetime. German vacillation was bound to shake Finnish confidence in Germany. The expedition would secure the Baltic Sea, threatened by Britain and America since the landings at Murmansk, and thus would secure the peace as well. If Germany did not help the Finns, they would appeal to Britain. If they succumbed to the Reds, it would mean opening another floodgate to the Russians. Germany might even have to mount another campaign against Great Russia, which would certainly cost a great deal more than a Finnish expedition. A firm alliance with Finland and the Ukraine would secure Germany's rear against the Western powers. Then too, Germany's economic situation might be relieved by deliveries of such Finnish raw materials as lumber. Lastly, Germany had given its word and must keep it.[86]

The decision was to be taken at the crown council of March 12, which was held at Bellevue palace, with considerable circumstance. The Chancellor's objections were supported by Under Secretary Bussche,[87] who pointed out that many Finns, including especially General Mannerheim, desired no German armed aid, that a German invasion of Finland would cause a strong reaction in Denmark and Norway, and that in any event Germany would have to wait until Russia ratified the treaty of Brest-Litovsk on March 17.

The Kaiser, however, seemed completely convinced that such an expedition was necessary. A bulwark against the Russian flood had to be erected; the Bolshevists had to be exterminated; Finland could give Germany security against renewed attacks from the Red army; the Norwegians were *Schweinehunde* (pig-dogs—a German term of abuse); and Finnish covetousness of Norwegian territory should be encouraged. The expedition was no more than a police action, much like the one that had been mounted in China to halt the Boxer rebellion—if it were peacetime, all the nations would participate. As for the question of postponement, this would take care of itself, in view of Holtzendorff's statement that the expedition could not get under way until April, for technical reasons.[88]

Kühlmann was still detained in Bucharest and the Chancellor had written him for his opinion. He replied on March 12 in a skeptical and resigned vein. The OHL had not told him whether it planned a large-scale expedition or merely the dispatch of a few battalions, nor did he know what Hindenburg had promised the Finns. The British bogey, which kept popping up in the OHL argumentation, could scarcely be taken seriously; and to move against the Russian Revolution was not Germany's business. He said he was unaware of any economic advantages such an expedition might secure or whether there were any understandings on this subject. It was true, however, that in view of Russia's weakness the possibility of Russian resentment was not an important consideration. Russo-German relations were already as bad as they could be, because the retention of German troops on the borders of Estonia and Livonia was in the long run intolerable to North Russia and St. Petersburg.

In his own view, Kühlmann went on, it would be better merely to supply the Finns with arms, and to commit no more than some minor units, which could be represented as volunteers. In the light of the Homburg talks of February 13 and the occupation of Ahvenanmaa, however, it was unlikely that the OHL could be persuaded to abandon the expedition. In that event it would at least be highly desirable for the Germans to get out again as soon as possible, without constituting a power factor in Finland. A skilled military negotiator should also be sent to Finland, with the mission of minimizing friction and of trying to get the country to share in the costs of the expedition. The whole matter was not important enough to risk a vote of confidence.

Kühlmann was dodging a clear-cut stand, and thus the OHL's militant drive for action prevailed without much difficulty. The expedition itself was crowned with brilliant success—it took no more than a month to clear the Finnish countryside of Red Guards, and German casualties were light. At the request of the Finnish government, some of the German forces under Goltz stayed until the end of the war, to help in organizing and training a Finnish national army. From the viewpoint of the Western, anti-Communist world, the liberation of civilized Finland from the "Red Peril" was an act of great historic importance that could have scarcely succeeded without German participation.[89] The Germans here truly played the role of liberators and were welcomed as such by the Finnish politicians.

This role nevertheless amounted to sweeping intervention into the affairs of a country whose dominant party, the social democrats, was largely on the Bolshevist side in the civil war that had broken out in January.[90] And the position of power so swiftly won in Finland kept tempting the OHL to exploit it for purposes of carrying out a crusade to overthrow Lenin's government.

The government of the pro-German premier and later regent Svinhufvud was a moderate minority government that could not have maintained itself in democratic Finland but for the fact that the social democrats were virtually excluded from the diet by the arrest of most of their deputies. The government tried to strengthen its position by introducing a monarchial constitution, and it wanted Prince Oscar of Hohenzollern, one of the Kaiser's sons, as its candidate for the throne. This, it was hoped, would commit Germany to permanent support of Finland and its sweeping expansionist ambitions, especially in eastern Karelia. The OHL strongly supported this plan, and there were direct negotiations between Goltz and Svinhufvud. It was the political section of the General Staff under Bartenwerffer—in direct touch with the Kaiser through Berg, head of the civilian cabinet—rather than the foreign ministry which issued the directives, and the German envoy in Helsinki was simply bypassed. In the weeks following Kühlmann's fall this was a rather perilous state of affairs, ended only in late July by the vigorous intervention of the new minister, Hintze.[91]

Finnish intermediaries advised the generals to have some military figure issue a semiofficial declaration that German support for Finland's ambitions for Karelian expansion could be expected only if the country became a monarchy. On July 6 Ludendorff proposed to the Chancellor that the formation of a Finnish monarchy under a prince who was German to the core was in the interest of Germany and of its federal dynasties, to counter the growing democratic and republican trends of the time. A republican Finland, on the other hand, was bound to slip swiftly into Entente hands. A semiofficial statement by Goltz along the lines proposed would win the wavering Finnish politicians, especially those of the smallholders' agrarian party, to the monarchist cause. Leading Finns actually hoped for a certain pressure in this direction.

From July 1 on Chancellor Hertling was at headquarters in Spa virtually all the time, and after discussions with the Kaiser, he offered no objections to a semiofficial statement in favor of the monarchist form of government.[92] The Kaiser himself, however, would not hear of his own son or indeed any Prussian prince exposing himself to the vicissitudes of a Finnish throne candidacy and constitutional democratic monarchy. This the Chancellor and the foreign ministry also firmly rejected—the dignity of the imperial house would be imperiled if the prince were unable to maintain himself. Germany would share responsibility for Finnish policy, and its relations with Sweden and Russia would be prejudiced. If Russia were to grow strong again and be in a position to demand concessions from Finland, this would become much more difficult with a Prussian prince on the throne of Finland. It would also be a complicating factor when a general peace was concluded. Lastly, a Prussian throne candidacy would meet opposition from the majority parties and the federal dynasties.[93]

German policy, in other words, shrank from excessively close ties with the recently established state in the far north, to the great disgust of the OHL. Hindenburg wrote that a swift transition to a monarchy in Finland was desirable "in the military interest," and that political considerations should not delay let alone imperil such a development. German policy lacked the kind of firm direction that would turn Finland into an unwaveringly loyal ally of Germany, of which Germany stood in great need, against Russia, and also against Britain in the Baltic Sea and northern waters.[94]

So intense a reaction, however, was scarcely necessary, for neither the Kaiser nor Hertling had any objections to some other prince, and the first candidate to be proposed was Prince Adolph Frederic of Mecklenburg. Largely because the emissary of this prince conducted his propaganda with great crudity, this candidacy met objections from the Finnish government, and still other princes were considered, the last one being Prince Frederic Carl of Hesse, a brother-in-law of the Kaiser, who was actually elected king by the

Finnish diet on October 8, shortly before the German collapse. This election, however, was informal, and virtually nothing happened in consequence.

Svinhufvud had great difficulty in finding an adequate majority for his constitution and tenaciously clung to Prince Oscar for a long time. He also negotiated with General Goltz concerning a secret German-Finnish military pact, combined with assurances of German support in the question of eastern Karelia. Though he later disputed it to the German envoy, he allegedly pleaded for authorization to advise his diet that only the installation of a German monarch would persuade Germany that Finland really intended to conclude an alliance with Germany, which alone would provide the basis for a military pact.[95] In this endeavor he enjoyed the support of the OHL, which kept pressing him to promote the establishment of a monarchy in Finland by every possible means.[96]

The German foreign ministry, however, displayed considerable reserve. Hintze entertained at best the idea of a military convention rather than of a military pact. Such a convention would provide for German help in organizing and training a regular Finnish army. Hintze protested vigorously against purely military agencies entering into negotiations on matters of high policy and insisted that the OHL instruct Goltz not to exceed his authority, since otherwise a clear-cut policy line for Finland would be made very much more difficult if not impossible. As a result of this uncommon bluntness, the OHL saw itself obliged to defend the general's actions to the Chancellor and to admit that any commitments he might have made were not binding, likewise an unwonted spectacle.[97]

Hintze's reservations were well-founded, as seen from sobering reports by the German envoy, Freiherr von Brück. They showed that the parliamentary position of the Svinhufvud government was weak and that there was virtually no broadly based monarchist movement in Finland. Monarchist agitation was entirely a government affair and had only limited success. The constitutional reform bill brought in by Svinhufvud was voted down on August 9, despite sustained and skillful propaganda; but on the following day the government was nevertheless charged with preparing for a royal election. This was done only by a rather labored interpretation of the existing constitution, supposedly a continuation of the constitution of 1772. In view of the general mood of the workers and peasants, this was nevertheless regarded as an act of force. Many voices were raised against excessively close ties with Germany, especially in the field of trade and big business. A German monarch in Finland, Baron Brück wrote, would face formidable difficulties, particularly since reentry of the social democrats into political life might bring on a radical shift in power.[98]

Since the Finnish royal election dragged on until October, the intimate ties of which the foreign ministry was apprehensive were in the end avoided. The headlong nationalist power drive of the Finns, however, caused no little trouble for German policy. This began as early as May, when the Finns asked for German armed aid in the siege of the Russian fort Ino, which was located near Kronstadt and formed a kind of key to access to St. Petersburg. The OHL stood ready, but the Chancellor firmly opposed the action. He wired Hindenburg that Germany must not drive Russia to desperation on behalf of some interest quite foreign to Germany. On the contrary, Germany should mediate peace between Finland and Russia as soon as possible. In the meantime the Russian commander blew up the fort, which thus fell into Finnish hands after all, though only in a state of destruction. The Finns obstinately refused to relinquish Ino and thus the Russo-Finnish negotiations favored by the OHL as well came to nothing.

Ludendorff had wanted to sponsor a compromise between the two countries on the basis of an exchange of territory. In return for Ino the Finns were to get a piece of the Murmansk coast. There had also been repeated talk of an exchange of Finnish territory near St. Petersburg against eastern Karelia.[99] The Soviets accepted both proposals as a basis for negotiations, but these failed because of the sweeping territorial demands of the Finns. What the OHL wanted was to expel the British from the Murmansk coast, thus banishing the risk of a new eastern front, which it greatly overestimated. To this end a whole series of strategic plans was developed in the course of the summer, predicting now Russo-Finnish, now German-Finnish or Russo-German cooperation.

We have already heard (p. 263) that by early August Lenin felt so beset that he virtually pleaded with the Germans to help him against the British, who were bombarding Archangel and had occupied extensive sections of the Murmansk railway with Allied troops. We have also heard that there was strong inclination on the German side to take political advantage of this crisis by initially occupying St. Petersburg, which might well have led to the overthrow of the Bolshevist government. In a military sense, this approach might have been justified on the ground that such a campaign could be executed only with the use of the Murmansk railway (which terminated in St. Petersburg), since the supply routes through eastern Karelia were wholly inadequate.

The Soviet government, however, not only was seriously worried that passage of German troops through St. Petersburg might lead to a political disaster, in view of the mood of the people, but also was distrustful of ultimate OHL intentions. We know today that this distrust was amply justified. Eastern headquarters and the naval command had worked out a plan to gain control of Kronstadt and thus of the port of St. Petersburg with the help of the German fleet, and at the same time to advance against the city by rail four divisions from Pleskov and Narva, as well as the Baltic division of

General Goltz from Finland.[100] As a precautionary measure, the area near Ino had been mined in mid-August on Lenin's orders. There were, in addition, weeks of negotiation with the Germans on whether and how the German expedition might bypass St. Petersburg, which entailed detailed reconnaissance by German officers of road conditions between Lakes Ladoga and Onega. The commencement of the expedition thus kept being put off, and in September it was finally called off altogether. This was the moment when Ludendorff conclusively gave up the war as lost.

The foreign ministry had meanwhile found a way of assuaging Russian distrust, in the supplementary treaty of August 27. This treaty obligated Russia to "employ promptly every possible resource to preserve its neutrality by removing the Entente forces from its northern territories." A secret exchange between Hintze and the Russian ambassador Joffe added the provision that if Russian action did not "promptly" lead to the desired goal, Germany would find itself compelled to carry it out itself, possibly with the help of Finnish troops. The Russian areas around St. Petersburg, however, would not be entered without the consent of the Russian government.

In Finland the Germans may have been able to maintain their pose as liberators; but in the Ukraine, contrary to their original intention, they swiftly turned into ruthless exploiters. On March 6, only five days after the capture of Kiev, Ludendorff was still sending the Chancellor reassuring reports about OHL intentions.[101] In Lithuania, Courland, Estonia, and Livonia, he said, the Germans in a certain sense had to continue as overlords, but in the case of Finland and the Ukraine the last thing Germany wanted was to remain permanently. Germany would have to proceed with the greatest care to gain trust and disarm any suspicions of its intentions. He had issued instructions along these lines, in keeping with the Chancellor's latest telegrams to the president of the Rada.

A few weeks later, on April 23, General Groener, chief of staff of the Eichhorn army group at Kiev, received a private letter from the same Ludendorff, encouraging him to proceed ruthlessly: "Your situation is not easy; but I think the thing can be done, with strong pressure on the Rada, or even its removal. The Russian still wants to feel the knout. So go to it—you may be sure of my support."[102] Five days later a military coup d'état dissolved the Rada and the government fell. German soldiers invaded a Rada session, shouting, "Hands up!" and arrested several ministers. The former Russian guards officer and Cossack hetman Scoropadsky was installed and formed a government that became a willing and skillful tool of the German occupation power. The sovereign state of the Ukraine, with which Germany had concluded a treaty of peace and amity on February 9, was turned into a ruthlessly exploited occupation area, a kind of government general.

Kühlmann and Hertling made every effort to oppose these developments, seeking to maintain the legal basis of the treaties of Brest-Litovsk, and urging the generals to negotiate with the Rada government in good faith instead of helping themselves to the country's supplies. Hertling was furious over the clumsy and brutal tactics employed in toppling the Rada government, and he succeeded in having the responsible town commandant in Kiev removed from his post. Also recalled was the "military plenipotentiary" whom the OHL had dispatched to Kiev to settle all political matters, though there was already a diplomatic representative of the foreign ministry in Kiev, Freiherr von Mumm zu Schwarzenstein. Actually the government was able to exert only a limited influence on the course of events in the Ukraine. The ultimate power of decision lay with the military regime, which was firmly under the thumb of General Groener, chief of staff of the Eichhorn army group. As Groener on one occasion wrote his wife: "We do what we think right and useful and don't concern ourselves with what the Wilhelmstrasse in Berlin or Erzberger and company may say."103

Actually, Groener was by no means a blind follower and admirer of Ludendorff, but rather a man with a mind and critical faculties of his own. We have seen him in this light when he was head of the *Kriegsamt* (see Vol. III, p. 353f.). He can scarcely be described as a militarist. He was a cool-headed pragmatist with the natural inclination of the strong-willed to simplify mounting problems instead of allowing himself to be overwhelmed. His position was exceedingly difficult. His mission was to extract as much food and raw material from the Ukraine as possible, without violating that country's sovereignty. The diplomat Mumm himself described this as tantamount to trying to square the circle.

Groener soon concluded that virtually nothing could be accomplished with the Rada government and "its ministerial jokers and greenhorns," and that it was pointless to kowtow to them. They were opinionated young men without a popular following, without experience, with neither an army nor a civil service, and all they were able to achieve was chaos. In keeping with their social revolutionary ideology, they had simply delivered the big estates to the mercy of the peasants, without creating any new agrarian constitution. As a result agricultural enterprise soon languished, and the unresolved property relations paralyzed peasant working morale. An order by the military on April 6, requiring the tilling of the fields, brought no improvement.

Revolution and civil war had destroyed or dispersed much of the food supply, and what was left was usually concealed from the Germans with great care, often buried in the ground. Naturally the new overlords were regarded with the greatest distrust and hostility, since the people feared that they would restore the status quo and revoke the "achievements of the revolution." Many of the peasants had secured arms from soldiers of the derelict Russian army and were wont to defend their property by force, which led to bloody guerrilla warfare. The Rada resisted every German effort to obtain the hoped-for goods on the free market, i.e., through purchasing agents; but on the other hand it was quite unable even to come near to fulfilling the deliveries prescribed in the treaty of Brest-Litovsk and its supplements of mid-April.

Unless the Ukraine expedition was simply to fail, what alternative was there to the use of force in the circumstances? Groener shrank from the collection methods of the Austrians, who simply requisitioned food supplies, without engaging in long negotiations with governments; but he saw no method that promised success, short of creating a compliant government that would, for one thing, also restore the property rights of the estate owners. "The people in Berlin," he complained in his diary, taking aim at the foreign ministry, "view the Ukraine as a butter barrel, into which one merely has to stick one's fingers and then lick them off. They look on me as some kind of magician who can create grain and hogs from nothing, or who at least can send them home by rail." What motivated Groener to disperse the Rada government was certainly not militarism, nor the desire to exercise power arbitrarily, but the serious predicament in which he found himself. The diplomat Mumm shared this view and in the end even the foreign ministry was reconciled to it—though the brutal manner in which the coup was staged continued to be condemned.

Field Marshal Eichhorn, a man of considerable intellectual stature, sent word to the Chancellor through the OHL that no one familiar with the situation in the Ukraine could be in any doubt that in so extraordinary a situation only extraordinary methods would serve. No doubt this was true, but unfortunately not even extraordinary methods were able, in this case, to achieve results in keeping with the enormous investment in funds and manpower, to say nothing of the loss of moral authority. Despite every effort, food and raw material deliveries from the Ukraine yielded only a fraction of what the Rada had agreed to by treaty. Most of what was found was used up in maintaining the troops in the country.[104] The Kaiser, and at times Groener too, had hoped that the moderate Scoropadsky government, composed of experienced men, might create something like an enduring focus of law and order amid the Russian chaos, counteracting the forces of Bolshevism, but this too failed.

Ukrainian nationalism turned out to be limited to small groups of intellectuals, without any real attraction for the masses, whose allegiance still lay with Great Russia. Hence the Ukrainian state remained nothing more than a synthetic product, unable to survive the departure of the German troops. In mid-May Ludendorff was still under considerable illusions in this respect.[105] He wanted to withdraw part of the occupation force to the west, their role to be taken over by a Ukrainian administration. It soon developed that in fact the troops would have to be greatly augmented, if military requisitions were to produce the required food deliveries by force. Two Ukrainian divisions had been organized from prisoners-of-war in March and equipped with picturesque uniforms, but they soon had to be dissolved, since the men promptly defected to the Bolshevists. Ludendorff had still other plans. The Ukrainians were to supply him with workers' battalions, and their industry was to supplement the German war effort, though in fact it had long since gone to rack and ruin. Ukrainian grain deliveries were to be increased to the point where Germany might supply neighboring neutrals like Holland and Denmark, so that these might then be forbidden to deliver up their merchant ships to Britain under threat. "A tremendous goal," he wrote, "and well worth the effort."

In reality revolutionary ferment continued undiminished in the unhappy country. Not unexpectedly, there were brutal atrocities on the part of military units in connection with the enforced rounding up of food supplies and livestock, and this led to bitter resistance. The Austrian envoy, Count Forgách, gave a horrifying account of conditions in a report of July 3. Murder, rapine, bloody uprisings, guerrilla skirmishes, arson, bomb outrages, and drumhead courts-martial were the order of the day, he said.[106] Field Marshal Eichhorn was assassinated by a social revolutionary on July 30, showing in a flash the deep hatred in which the German regime was held.

By the time of this terrible blow, Groener had long since realized that a durable Ukrainian state was still far off. On June 3 he had written Ludendorff that the creation of such a state would require the sternest exercise of power, many years of occupation, and huge capital investment.[107] Could such prospects be seriously entertained by Germany in the fourth year of the war? Yet astonishingly enough, the German military administration, working closely with the various government departments in Berlin, as well as with heavy industry and the big banks, put forward the most Herculean efforts to start up industry in the Ukraine and occupied South Russia, to exploit the economy in the German interest, and to improve the rail system—all this not just for the duration of the war but far beyond.[108] Its economic office in Kiev became the center for German-Ukrainian trade. The efforts of the Scoropadsky government at agrarian reform with the aim of creating an affluent peasantry were strongly supported by the Germans and seem to have met with some success, yet ultimately the whole endeavor was in vain. This was not only because the political situation remained unresolved in view of the steadily worsening situation on the western front, but even more because the price in men, industrial production, and capital was far beyond Germany's means.[109]

German resources would have been under even severer strain, had the Germans yielded to the temptation of forming an alliance with the anti-

Bolshevist groups that infested Kiev and made such offers almost daily. By and by representatives of nearly all the underground groups, from the historian Milyukov, leader of the "cadets," to the Volga and Don Cossacks, frequented Groener's office in the hope of winning Germany to their cause. Groener's own attitude toward them seems to have been rather ambiguous. His conservative antecedents made him reluctant to abandon hope that it was possible to destroy the Bolshevist regime from within by supporting its foes, in view of the many serious threats from without and within.

Like all General Staff officers he was critical of the foreign ministry, that "bunch of pussyfooters," as he called them. He inveighed against its policies, which in his view were shoring up the Bolshevist government in Moscow. He thought they were "playing up" to the Russians and working on a new treaty with them that would not be worth the paper it was written on. On the other hand Groener was quite well aware that for the time being at least the monarchist movement inside Russia was far too weak to stage a successful uprising. The mass of the Russian peasants were totally uninterested, and even so a returning monarchy would have faced insoluble problems. He also knew that many of the anti-Bolshevists were trying to establish contact with the Entente, while Lenin's government fought back stubbornly against such intervention. Lastly, he realized that the treaty of Brest-Litovsk, and with it the independence of the Ukraine and the division of Russia, could not be maintained permanently, even if Germany were in league with the Russian monarchists and other patriots. For the time being, he remarked, Germany would have to play for time with the Bolshevist rulers, until the monarchist movement, which was largely pro-German, had regained enough strength to form a government.[110]

In practice, however, this sober assessment[111] did not keep Groener from seeking contact with the anti-Bolshevists, in the spirit of the OHL and at its behest, mainly for the purpose of foiling foreign ministry policy, his main target being General Krasnov, the Don Cossack hetman. Kühlmann was outraged that the German invasion army under Groener, advancing by rail, moved directly on into the Donetz basin and the Crimea, halting in May only at Rostov on the Sea of Azov, and doing even this only on urgent pressure from the government. This meant heedlessly ignoring the eastern border of the Ukraine, as expressly laid down in the treaties of Brest-Litovsk, and cutting off Great Russia from the Black Sea, putting it in an intolerable situation.

The situation became completely impossible when Ludendorff's great dream was fulfilled and a southeastern Russian state, extending all the way to the Caucasus, was created. Wholly under German influence, purged of Bolshevists, and based on bourgeois principles, it arose out of Scoropadsky's connections with Krasnov, who, in letters to the Kaiser, had pleaded for a

German advance to the Volga to cover his flank against the Czech legion and also asked for German arms and funds. The OHL, through the Kiev command, readily supplied arms depots and no less than fifteen million rubles!

In late June the eastern high command inquired whether the Eichhorn army group could take Kursk and Bryansk en route to Moscow.[112] The Chancellor had to intercede with Hindenburg in the sharpest terms, indirectly threatening his resignation, and the wires were kept humming before support for the Cossack general—which clearly contravened the Brest-Litovsk agreements—was withdrawn, at least for the time being, until the supplementary treaty with Moscow had been signed.[113] Actually, the conclusion of this treaty was imperiled as late as August, when Krasnov made further efforts to secure an alliance with Germany. In the meantime, however, not only top government circles but Groener and the OHL had come to entertain doubts concerning the utility of the whole Ukrainian operation and the permanence of the Ukrainian state. A major factor was that the German forces, scattered far and wide over the countryside, gave themselves up to a blend of idleness and bloody police action which undermined their morale and cohesion and made them easy prey for revolutionary propaganda.

The Ukrainian project failed, but it was planned on a broad scale and motivated by Germany's critical situation, with the idea of utilizing Russia's richest areas for German war purposes. By comparison, the military expeditions which Ludendorff launched on the Black Sea and in the Caucasus, seem like the merest adventurism.

This applies primarily to the occupation of the Crimea. A Tartar government had established itself there in the summer of 1917, only to be overthrown by the Bolshevists. In the spring of 1918, however, it swept back into power, asking aid from the German troops advancing into the Ukraine. This was granted, against the wishes of the foreign ministry, on the ground that Germany needed to gain control of the port of Sevastopol and the Russian Black Sea fleet stationed there, in order to insure safe sea passage on the Black Sea, which was indeed essential for the export of Ukrainian products. The desirability of generally utilizing Crimean resources and ports was also cited.

The fuzziness of Ludendorff's political ideas, however, was promptly demonstrated by his proposal, quite properly rejected in Berlin, to appease the Turks for their losses in Mesopotamia and Palestine by offering them the Crimea by way of compensation. There was also talk at headquarters of cleansing the Crimea of Bolshevist elements after the fashion of Livonia; and General Hoffmann, chief of staff of eastern headquarters, glibly prated of a "German Riviera."

The German government found itself confronted with military faits accomplis, as dramatically illustrated in a conference held at headquarters on

May 13 with the Chancellor and Kühlmann. Hertling carefully sounded out the ground, merely asking what goals the OHL was pursuing in the Crimea and, when Ludendorff answered evasively, suggesting that Germany engage itself there as little as possible. Ludendorff said that when the time came the OHL would, "as always" [sic] consult the foreign ministry on what the German policy in the Crimea should be.

When the Chancellor insisted that in all such projects purely German interest must supersede any general interest in establishing law and order, Ludendorff then argued that the Black Sea must be made safe for shipping; and when the Chancellor referred this question to Kühlmann, the foreign minister was obliging enough to confirm that enemy vessels in the Black Sea should indeed be neutralized. Kühlmann added, however, that it was in Germany's interest to avoid seeing a Bolshevist government replaced by an even more radical government. It would be a very good thing if it could be stated one day that German operations in Russia were definitely at an end. Ludendorff then said that this point had now been reached, a statement of considerable significance.[114]

But Ludendorff's dreams of power did not end with the limited goal of making Black Sea shipping secure. The problem that increasingly worried him during the heavy fighting on the western front was his rapidly dwindling manpower. He developed a fantastic plan for creating a pool of German-speaking Russians in the Crimea and South Russia. They were to be conscripted and would augment the military reserves which he then still expected from Finland and Georgia, where German training officers were to organize national armies.

The former colonial minister Lindequist, together with a certain Reverend Winkler, acting as spokesman for the Black Sea Germans, provided Ludendorff with the idea of establishing a German colony in the Crimea, by resettling all the German colonists in South Russia, from Bessarabia, the Chersonese, Volhynia, the Volga region, and the Caucasus. When this met with strong opposition from the Ukrainian government, he shifted to the creation of a Crimean-Tabriz state that was to federate with the Ukraine, much as Bavaria was joined to Prussia. Such a federation, possibly joined by Georgia, would be under strong German influence, guaranteed by the concentration of German-speaking settlers, which would bring Germany major economic advantages. Holtzendorff proposed that Sevastopol should become a base for the naval forces allied with Germany, under German command, of course. It was not actually to be a German naval base, since the German navy was unlikely to have any mission in the Black Sea, once peace had returned.

Early in July Ludendorff submitted these plans to the Chancellor. Even before this time Lindequist and Winkler had launched a propaganda campaign, advocating the establishment of a German crown colony among the

German-speaking Russians and creating a considerable stir. Ludendorff expected that the result would be a powerful remigration movement, which was to be organized under government auspices. At a crown council at Spa on July 2 he brought up the desire of German colonists in the Ukraine to acquire German citizenship and protection. He wanted to use as many of them as possible to settle the Polish border strip.

"But if we grant them citizenship," he said, "they will have to serve under our flag. The army needs men. If we give them the assurance [that they can become German citizens], they will be willing to do what we ask."[115] In his mind's eye he already saw a flood of returning Germans from other countries as well, especially overseas. The various groups should be allotted land in the newly acquired territories–French Lorraine, the Polish border strip, Lithuania, the other Baltic regions. Since there would not be enough to go around, additional land inside Germany would have to be found, and this should be mainly land acquired by war profiteers.

Ludendorff was convinced that these returnees would constitute a rich recruiting ground, but again he would allow them to acquire citizenship only if they were prepared to do military service. The German Mennonites in Russia, for example, numbering some 50,000, should be admitted only if they were willing to serve.[116] The government departments were, of course, horrified at these rantings, and even Groener strongly disapproved. He angrily remarked to Mumm that there would probably never be peace at the top in Germany until Ludendorff became both chief of staff and Chancellor.

The foreign ministry urgently warned against massing German colonists in the Crimea and Tabriz, which was bound to alienate the Ukrainians and drive them back into the arms of Great Russia. Kühlmann thought that the interests of the German colonists would be adequately protected by treaty guarantees from Russia and the successor states.[117] In the supplementary treaty of August 27 Germany, against the wishes of the OHL, agreed to evacuate all German territory beyond the Ukraine on the conclusion of a general peace. Ludendorff's request for recognition of the Crimean Tartar government formed in June under German "protection" was not met.

Ludendorff's ambitions were not limited to the land forces and coastal regions. He also wished to bring under German control the Russian fleet stationed at Sevastopol, which included, among others, two large armored vessels. There was more difficulty with the foreign ministry over this, and even with the naval command.

As a pretext for the seizure of the Russian Black Sea fleet, Ludendorff wanted to use the fact that certain marine detachments had taken part in the fighting for Nicolayev, the Chersonese, and Simferopol. Some separated naval units had also fought minor engagements with German-allied naval forces along the coast of Tabriz. Ludendorff viewed this as a violation of Article 5 of the treaty of Brest-Litovsk, which required Russian warships to be neutralized or disarmed, and wanted to claim the entire Russian fleet as a "prize of war." He further cited the fact that the Russian naval crews, most of them belonging to the social revolutionary party, sometimes defied the orders of the Bolshevist government. He regarded their activities as a kind of Red Guard piracy that must be sternly dealt with.

Neither the foreign ministry nor the naval high command could agree with Ludendorff's "war prize" theory. Kriege, the Wilhelmstrasse's legal expert, wrote a memorandum in which he maintained that even if all the vessels had engaged in hostilities, their seizure would constitute a breach of international law and of the treaty of Brest-Litovsk. The German admiralty and even the naval command in the Crimea felt that seizure of the ships after the signing of the peace was an unchivalrous act of force, and they denied that any German naval interest required such a policy. The admiralty representative in Berlin, Captain Vanselow, proposed instead a kind of testamentary apportionment, by distributing the vessels among the marginal states establishing themselves on Russian soil—the Ukraine, Tabriz, the Caucasus, etc.[118] Apparently the admiralty was also resentful of the autocratic way in which Ludendorff had treated the naval commander at Sevastopol as an OHL subordinate ever since the German troops had arrived, and of his arrogation of the right to dispose of the Russian fleet. Ludendorff wanted to assign the major Russian vessels to Turkey and had promised this to Enver Pasha without consulting the government. Representatives of the foreign ministry, the OHL, and the admiralty met in Berlin on May 13 and in the end reached a compromise agreement. The states of the succession bordering on the Black Sea were to be told that they would get most if not all of the Russian ships, provided they lend some of them in return to Germany for the duration of the war.

Ludendorff rejected this compromise and bitterly resented that Admiralty Chief Holtzendorff allowed his representative to support the foreign ministry view. He sent word to the admiral that he regarded this as a flagrant act of disloyalty and that henceforth there would be an unbridgeable gulf between them. Holtzendorff vainly tried to appease the general by subsequent alterations in the minutes and by laboriously putting a different face on his stand. Ludendorff brought all his resources into play and did not rest until Holtzendorff, repeatedly subjected to deliberate provocations, resigned in August, thus following men like Bethmann Hollweg, Caprivi, and Kühlmann into the outer darkness.

To avoid bombardment from the shore and seizure, the Russian Black Sea fleet had meanwhile weighed anchor on the night of April 30 and left Sevastopol for Novorossiysk, the last usable Black Sea port still at the disposal of the Soviets. Since this could be interpreted as contravening the treaty of Brest-Litovsk, the German envoy, Count Mirbach, requested the Russian government to order the fleet to return to Sevastopol immediately and to have it disarmed. This would not forfeit Russia's title to the ships, but if the request was refused, a German advance on Novorossiysk was threatened.

The discrepancy between German political and military thinking was unmistakably revealed in the negotiations over this request, which was certainly humiliating to the Russians. The government in Moscow, of course, tried to take advantage of the German interest in its Black Sea fleet. It said it would order the fleet back, if Germany would cease to advance in South Russia and Finland and fix the borders of the occupation area in final form, excluding Sevastopol. It further insisted that Russian ownership of the naval vessels must be in no way prejudiced.

The German foreign ministry was well aware of Lenin's difficulties vis-à-vis his own radicals and urged that the "salami technique" with respect to Russia be called off, as Ludendorff had promised Kühlmann on May 13. It wanted to see the Soviet demand accepted. On May 19 the Kaiser was indeed prevailed on to call off the advance on Novorossiysk. Ludendorff, on his part, complained of the foreign ministry taking up a question of strategy directly with the Kaiser without his knowledge. He would agree to demarcation lines only if the Russian fleet was back in Sevastopol within six days. This led to new talks on questions of timing, which we need not cover in detail here.

An unexpected incident complicated the situation. A band of some 10,000 Bolshevist troops, operating entirely on their own, made a landing at Taganrog and was immediately destroyed. Ludendorff wanted to use this as a pretext for carrying out the advance on Novorossiysk after all, but the foreign ministry wanted the matter amicably settled and insisted to the OHL that two big warships did not warrant a major clash. Kühlmann strongly warned against depriving Soviet Russia of its last food resources by occupying the Don region and the near coast of the Caucasus. Into these talks burst the news that on orders from the Moscow government the Russian fleet had been scuttled on the morning of May 18. One of the two men-o'-war had failed to follow orders and had set sail for Sevastopol with sixteen torpedo boat destroyers. This squadron arrived in Sevastopol in due time.

The prize at issue had dwindled, in other words. Kühlmann had promised the Soviet ambassador in May that if the vessels returned to Sevastopol, Germany would not make use of them in any way. Ludendorff, however, now insisted that their employment was a "military necessity," by which he meant their use for protecting Istanbul and the straits, threatened by a British attack in the OHL's view. At the big Spa conference on July 2—presided over by the Kaiser though completely dominated by Ludendorff, with Kühlmann and Holtzendorff absent—the general largely had his way. The ships were to be available for German use for the duration of the war, without any prejudice to their Russian ownership.[119] Foreign Minister Hintze ultimately saw to it that this "availability" was written into the supplementary treaty with Russia of August 27 rather than being exacted by force. A secret clause in that treaty specified that Germany might use the ships during the war for such peaceful purposes as mine clearance and police duty—but also for combat, if necessitated by the exigencies of war. Full indemnification was pledged for any damage.

On October 1, as a result of this treaty, the big warship *Volya* and a few others were manned with German crews. Effected without attracting attention and with the help of a Russian commissar, this action was virtually wasted, since Turkey collapsed immediately afterward. Ludendorff's "military necessity," never acknowledged by the German navy, turned out to be not so urgent after all.

As in the Crimea and the Black Sea, it was Turkey that provided the original impetus for additional German ventures and expeditions in the Caucasus. The discrepancy between the scope and political goals of these escapades and the modest military forces available for them was grotesque.

We have already learned (Chapter 2, Note 131) that in the end stages of peace negotiations with Russia early in March Turkey had suddenly come out with a demand that the Caucasian areas of Kars, Ardahan, and Batum, which had belonged to Turkey until 1878, should be returned to it. The OHL had supported these demands, because it was concerned with diverting the Turks from the demands they put to Bulgaria in the matter of the Maritsa (see p. 176), thus facilitating peace with Rumania. The Turks, it held furthermore, deserved compensation for their heavy losses in Mesopotamia and Palestine.

By contrast, the foreign ministry was afraid that these new demands would hamper the peace negotiations and precipitate a Russo-Turkish conflict later on, since the regions in point were very rich in natural resources and also quite indispensable to the Russians for purposes of transit. The Black Sea port of Batum was especially important, as the terminal of the railway that led through Armenia to Persian Tabriz. In the end a compromise was found. The areas in point were not to be ceded, but they were to be evacuated by Russian troops. As soon as the treaty was signed, however, Turkey did occupy them, in pursuit of the same ambitions for power in the Black Sea regions that had made it reach for the Crimea.[120]

After the October Revolution, in the wake of the general disintegration in Russia, a Trans-Caucasian republic had formed in the Caucasus, comprising Georgia, Armenia, and Azerbaijan, together with the great Baku oilfields. Turkey got into a quarrel with this new state and declared war on it on April 14. Batum fell the very next day and Trans-Caucasia had to sue for an armistice. Peace negotiations commenced in Batum, and Germany tried to intervene in them.

Germany did indeed have a political interest in these regions, at least until the treaty of Brest-Litovsk was signed. Ever since the war started, there had been efforts to incite the Caucasian montagnards against the czarist empire. These efforts were led by a revolutionary committee of Georgian émigrés, and millions in cash and arms had been pumped into the movement. After Brest-Litovsk, Germany's interest was limited to the economic sphere, but that interest was considerable. The most urgent immediate needs were for Trans-Caucasian oil and manganese ore, to aid the German war effort. Beyond that there were the trade routes from Batum to North Persia and the cotton-growing regions of Turkistan, which needed to be kept open and expanded.

A foreign ministry Eastern expert, Trautmann, had set forth the views of his department on April 1. He urgently cautioned against the Pan-Turanian plans of Enver Pasha, the Turkish commander-in-chief. These plans were directed toward the conquest of all Trans-Caucasia and would probably lead to terrible atrocities among the Armenians, for which Germany would have to share responsibility in the public eye. The annexation of the Mohammedan areas of Kars and Ardahan might at worst be accepted; but the flourishing port of Batum with a predominantly Christian population was the only one to serve the Caucasian hinterland and should be allowed to remain in the hands of friendly Georgia. The Turks did not need it, since they did not even know what to do with Trebizond; but for the Germans it was important as a terminal for the trade routes to Middle Asia and Persia. Even before the war, Germany had expended considerable effort to open up the Trans-Caucasian route to Persia, against Russian resistance; and during the war it had spent millions to create a pro-German Caucasian state to serve as a bridge to Central Asia. All this would have been in vain if the Turks were allowed to annex Batum and Trans-Caucasia, which would put Germany at their mercy in both the political and the economic spheres. If Germany could not prevent such an annexation, it should at least seek assurances of certain trade, transport, and oil privileges. Sweeping privileges of this kind were outlined in detail.[121]

The German foreign ministry stuck to this position. It mentioned as a further argument that the contemplated Turkish action would constitute a grave violation of international law. Germany's signature to the treaty of Brest-Litovsk implied that it would help implement that treaty. Turkey, moreover, did not have the resources to organize such a large region, which would weaken rather than strengthen it. There was indeed the possibility that Turkey would have to implore German armed aid. Hostilities between Christians and Muslims were to be expected.[122]

In the light of all these considerations, the Turkish action was a great embarrassment to Germany, which wished neither to alienate Turkey nor to imperil the treaty of Brest-Litovsk. By the same token, it did not wish simply to throw overboard the needs of German war industry. It is, of course, quite understandable that General Seeckt, then chief of staff of the Turkish army, should have felt some obligation and tried to strike the best bargain for Turkey in the controversy over Georgia. In this he was in agreement with the OHL, which once again took a benevolent attitude toward Turkish expansionism.123 Kühlmann counseled caution and reserve until the Turko-Bulgarian quarrel about the Maritsa line were resolved. On April 22 an interdepartmental meeting took place under Helfferich in his capacity as minister in charge of peace preparations. It was decided to seek both Soviet and Ukrainian recognition for the new Trans-Caucasian republic. A representative was to be sent to the Batum negotiations to ask the Turks to restrict their claims to the three areas designated at Brest-Litovsk, leaving Batum and the Trans-Caucasian railway lines to the German sphere. To make this easier for them, Germany would forego concluding a political alliance with Trans-Caucasia, limiting itself to purely economic agreement—denationalization of the railways and the port of Batum in favor of a Turko-German private corporation and exploitation of natural resources by a monopoly shared between Germany and Trans-Caucasia. By agreement between the *Kriegsamt* and the Reich economic office, a group of representatives from the German mining industry had already been dispatched to Batum and Poti to scout the possibilities of getting manganese ore out of the Caucasus. German war industry stood in urgent need of this raw material.

The conclusion of a compromise peace between Turkey and Trans-Caucasia was a task of great delicacy that required considerable diplomatic skill. Unfortunately—though to Seeckt's satisfaction—a general rather than a career diplomat was sent to Batum as the German representative; this was the military attaché at Pera, General Lossow, who later played such an important role in Hitler's putsch of 1923. Instead of trying to reach an understanding with the Turkish representatives, he immediately began quarreling with them; and in his rage he demanded that German troops be sent into Caucasia, which was precisely what Seeckt wanted. The Turks paid no attention and broke off the talks after a single meeting, immediately commencing an advance into the interior of Armenia, nearly all of which they claimed as their own. Thereupon the Trans-Caucasian republic disintegrated into its three component parts, Georgia, Armenia, and Azerbaijan. Since the Azerbaijanis were Muslims who sympathized with the Turks, the Georgian leaders were now entirely dependent on Germany. The Georgian leader Tshchenkeli established contact with Lossow and declared that Georgia might well apply for integration with Germany, either as a federal state with a German sovereign or like a British dominion with a German viceroy.

Lossow took this outlandish prospect quite seriously and in his reports raved about this great and rich country that was going begging, an opportunity that might not recur for centuries. He concluded a series of provisional agreements with Tshchenkeli, which made the port of Poti and the Georgian railways, among other things, available to Germany, provided they were occupied by German troops. The OHL was convinced that a Caucasian expedition would be a profitable undertaking, and on its insistence the dispatch of German troops was decided in Berlin and Spa.

On May 10 Ludendorff submitted daring plans to the foreign ministry, calling for joint action with the Turks against Persia. "If we lay claim to world leadership, we need a viable Turkey," he said. "Even during the present war, we must think of using Turkey to gain a foothold on the Caspian Sea, laying the basis for military cooperation with Afghanistan against Britain in Persia and India."[124] Bussche wrote "nonsense!" in the margin. The foreign ministry was giving no thought to campaigns in Inner Asia while the desperate life-and-death struggle raged on the western front. Kühlmann felt uncomfortable at the prospect of dispatching even a single battalion to Caucasia as railway guards.[125] He sensed that any German appearance on that stage would bring dangerous new responsibilities and might readily lead to open conflict with Turkey. He thought that Ludendorff was indulging in fantasies, as he put it in a marginal note, if he thought that the Turks, supported by Germany, might advance from Caucasia into Persia and Mesopotamia, barring any further advances by Britain in the area to the Caspian Sea; and he characterized the Turkish actions in Caucasia as sheer madness.

In a meeting with the Chancellor on May 11, Ludendorff nevertheless succeeded in having "a few" battalions dispatched to the Caucasus. Hertling objected that additional military involvements would merely serve to prolong the war, but Hindenburg asserted the precise opposite. "We are not fighting a new enemy, but an old one. . . . The precise spot where our troops do our fighting does not matter."[126] Certainly a most curious conclusion!

At Ludendorff's suggestion, however, it was also decided to dispatch another military man, Colonel—later General—Kress von Kressenstein, to Tiflis to scout out the situation, this time with the consent of Kühlmann, who was intent on reaching an understanding with the Soviets over Caucasia rather than allowing that area to become a bone of contention. This became quite clear in talks that were held in Berlin after Lossow's return. The military attaché gave a glowing report of the enormous economic advantages that were waiting in the Caucasus, but Kühlmann declined to enter into long-term commitments to the Caucasians. There was to be only a wartime treaty with the Georgians, who had the relatively best-organized state. Germany would have to try to navigate between the Scylla of a break with Russia and the Charybdis of one with Turkey. The Soviets would never forego Baku and its oil, though an attempt should be made to get them to agree to the separate existence of Georgia, possibly with a share of the Baku oil. At the same time, a compromise ought to be sought with Turkey. Kühlmann rejected as highly dubious the dispatch of German troops to the Caucasus, as well as Lossow's organization of former German prisoners-of-war as railway guards.

In sharp contrast to these cautious political arguments, Ludendorff, in mid-June, on the occasion of Colonel Kress's departure, formulated some wildly fantastic plans, which he dispatched to the Kiev army group in mid-June.[127] Both the Kaiser and he had been deeply impressed by Lossow's presentation. His hopes were not limited to the seizure for the German war effort of large quantities of important raw materials that were allegedly available. He wanted to utilize Georgian manpower by establishing an army with the help of a small German cadre. This force might conceivably fight on Germany's side against Russia.[128] Germany was to recognize Georgia's independence and see to it that a peace treaty was concluded as soon as possible between the new state and the Quadruple Alliance. Georgian pleas for integration with Germany were to be complied with.

Ludendorff's plans actually went much further. Lossow had brought back from Batum a Georgian delegation under Tshchenkeli, as well as a representative of the Kalmucks, Prince Tundutov, hetman of the Volga Cossacks and former adjutant to the czar, whom the foreign ministry rejected as a mere adventurer. Tundutov had already offered Germany a protectorate over his homeland and proposed the occupation by German troops of Tsaritsyn, the later Stalingrad. Groener had met him on his return to Astrakhan and was equally critical of him, but confidentially advised the foreign ministry, via Mumm, of Ludendorff's ideas.

Despite foreign ministry warnings, however, Tundutov was received at supreme headquarters, where he inspired Ludendorff's fanciful plans. The Kalmuck prince briefed Ludendorff on his old plan of creating an anti-Bolshevist federation in Southeast Russia, in which the North Caucasian montagnards would join with the Volga, Don, Kuban, and Terek Cossacks. The general and his political section under Bartenwerffer were deeply impressed, as they were by Lossow's reports about the desires of the Armenians and North Caucasian montagnards for integration with Germany. Ludendorff evidently thought that such a federation was a practical possibility, if Germany gained a firm foothold in Georgia and showed, by establishing a small force of German effectives there, that it was prepared to maintain its interest in the Caucasus. Other Caucasian states would fall into line, and thus a bloc allied with Germany might arise, which would be of the greatest importance to Germany, not only by supplying raw materials while the war was still on but by establishing an effective military counterpoise to Russia after the war as well as a barrier to British economic penetration of the Caucasus.

The difference between the dreams of the power-hungry militarists and the sober political reflections of the diplomat Kühlmann with his policy of careful maneuvering between Scylla and Charybdis could scarcely be more sharply expressed than in this Ludendorff memorandum, almost certainly drafted by Bartenwerffer. Ludendorff admitted that the current political situation precluded the pursuit of sweeping programs in Moscow at the present time, but he demanded that a "first step" be taken in Georgia. He had advised Tundutov that the Cossacks should declare their own independence and establish liaison with the Ukrainian government. The OHL would see to it that the necessary arms and munitions would reach the Cossacks from Kiev, on the pretext that in order to safeguard the lives of German prisoners-of-war in the Cossack regions, the Cossacks must be armed against the Bolshevists. Later on the Cossacks and North Caucasian montagnards were to get arms and munitions from Tiflis as well. Tiflis would thus become the center of a "Caucasian bloc," composed of non-Russian Christians, Muslim Tartars, and Buddhist Kalmucks, in other words largely non-Slavs. This would favor Germany against the great Slav bloc that was bound to arise when the inevitable reunion of the Ukraine with Great Russia came to pass.

As was to be expected, Lossow's presentation made a profound impression on the Kaiser as well. William II immediately drafted a grandiose plan of his own, in which Russia was subdivided into four "czardoms," the Ukraine still being separated from Great Russia. He spoke of striking a bridge to Central Asia to threaten the British position in India and assented to Lossow's proposals, though only in vague terms. Ludendorff exploited this in forwarding his own ideas to the foreign ministry, allegedly as an imperial directive. He also dispatched this to Count Bernstorff, the former German ambassador in Washington, now in Istanbul, and to Colonel Kress. Bernstorff was not misled, saying that he could follow only directives from the foreign ministry itself. Because he was stationed in Turkey, he could see even more clearly than Berlin the danger of the break with Turkey that would necessarily follow if Germany did indeed establish a foothold in the Caucasus; and thus, among all the German diplomats, Bernstorff was probably the most outspoken in rejecting the OHL policy in the Caucasus. He thought that it was much more important to retain the integrity of the Quadruple Alliance and the painstakingly negotiated peace with Russia than to play around with the unreliable Caucasians, who might themselves become easy prey to revolution. To lose the tested Turkish ally—whose defection in a separate peace with Britain he also considered a possibility—in favor of the Caucasians meant sitting down between two chairs. Lossow's policy in Batum had been a policy of power—except that there was no power. The pursuit of German interests in the Caucasus would be easier in concert with Turkey and Russia rather than against them. Recognition of Georgian independence would avail the Georgians little, unless Germany were prepared to resort to arms on behalf of their independence. In a political sense, Germany had no business whatever in the Caucasus. To seek a foothold there meant, in Bismarck's words, to "court jeopardy beyond the political sphere assigned to Germany by God." 129 Bernstorff's advice that it was far better to mediate between Turks and Russians, keeping Germany's own economic interests to the fore, was entirely in accordance with Kühlmann's views.130

Kühlmann resisted the repeated OHL importunities for official recognition of Georgian independence, stating that for the time being this state could certainly not be integrated with Germany, either as a protectorate or in any other loose form. Nor could he see any political profit in the organization of a Georgian army. He proposed a conference on the Georgian question, to be held in Istanbul, i.e., far outside the OHL's immediate sphere of influence, with the formal participation of a Soviet representative. This conference was repeatedly postponed and never did eventuate.

As the diplomats had feared, tension with Turkey meanwhile rose more and more, mainly owing to the actions of the OHL. Lossow's reports about the refractory attitude of the Turkish high command and its excessive territorial claims had certainly modified Ludendorff's pro-Turkish attitude; another factor was that all his efforts to divert the Turkish advance into Persia and Mesopotamia had remained fruitless. The Turks proved themselves hard-headed rivals of Germany in the Caucasus; and Ludendorff let the Turkish minister of war know in threatening terms that he could not recognize Turkish treaties with the Caucasian states concluded without the knowledge of Turkey's allies. This position, by the way, was shared by Kühlmann.131

Immediately afterward, on June 9, Hindenburg demanded that Enver Pasha evacuate all Caucasian regions occupied beyond the provisions of the treaty of Brest-Litovsk. He had no political authority whatever for so sweeping a diplomatic step. Enver responded by threatening to resign. At this same time there were actual military clashes between German and Turkish troops in the Caucasus. The alliance seemed virtually doomed, and Bernstorff reiterated that Germany's policy in the Caucasus was dangerously unrealistic.

Enver Pasha was an old friend of Germany, and his threat to resign dismayed Ludendorff, who now took a conciliatory line and asked Seeckt to pave the way for diplomatic mediation, a mission in which that skilled officer succeeded in the course of June and July, though he himself was infected with fanciful notions of the need for a "land bridge" to Turkistan.132 Ludendorff now advised the foreign ministry that he was willing to concentrate on purely military matters in the Caucasus, leaving all political decisions to the foreign ministry.133

What contributed to this decision was undoubtedly the fact that Caucasian military and political affairs were growing more and more tangled. Colonel Kress's reports from Georgia had a sobering effect. In the face of the wretched realities there, Ludendorff's orders to Kress now seemed almost grotesque–to organize an army from the irregulars and investigate the possibility of establishing a link to India, where Britain (once France had been defeated) could be struck in its most sensitive spot. The Georgian government turned out to be exceedingly feeble and without the military resources to prevail over the Red Guards. Hence the urgent pleas for German troops, grain from the Ukraine, and fuel from Rumania and the Ukraine for the railways and public utilities. Did all this warrant a major political and military commitment?

No. Georgia was a thoroughgoing disappointment to German industrial interests, and the fact that the Georgian government tried very hard to get financial help by granting rights for the exploitation of natural resources did not change this in any way. In July some preliminary contracts were signed in Berlin with German mining companies, looking toward the establishment of companies to mine manganese ore and run railways and ports.[134] But they never came into force, since they were to be effective only when Germany recognized the Georgian republic; and the foreign ministry was quite unwilling to grant such recognition without first reaching agreement with Russia, since otherwise the treaty of Brest-Litovsk would have been contravened.[135] In the end, in Article 13 of the supplementary treaty of August 27, Hintze did secure Russian consent to German recognition of Georgian independence.

In July, at the request of Colonel Kress, the OHL ordered two further battalions and three field batteries transferred from the Crimea to Caucasia, via Poti, with virtually no effect. Germany was quite unable to dispatch sufficient troops for effective intervention. Indeed, the OHL was reduced to asking the Austrian high command to make a few battalions available to protect the Armenians.[136] The Baku oilfields, so essential to the German war economy, remained beyond reach, though late in the summer and in the fall a dramatic struggle for possession of the wells broke out, subjecting Germany to the dual danger of alienating both the Russians and the Turks.

The rich Baku oil flow was as important to Russia as it was to the German war economy, for Russian rail and river shipping was largely fueled with oil. The Soviets never left any doubts of their determination to hold on to Baku. They would sooner have blown up the entire oilfield than let it fall into the hands of a foreign power. If Germany really wanted a share of the oil, it therefore had to negotiate with the Russians, the more so since it lacked tankers and tank cars for direct oil exports via Batum. Even the OHL ultimately came around to the need for an oil agreement with Russia.[137] It took a great deal of effort and time, but in the end the supplementary treaty of August 27 did pledge that Germany should receive one-fourth of the Baku oil output—though this was at a time when Russia was no longer in full control of Baku, which by early July was threatened by the Turkish advance toward the Caspian Sea. The Germans found it necessary to restrain their own ally, an effort in which the OHL vigorously participated. They achieved virtually nothing, for the Turkish front-line generals paid no attention to Enver's directives.

The situation changed instantly on July 31 when the Bolshevist government in Baku was overthrown and had to flee. The government that succeeded it, composed of social revolutionaries, Mensheviks, and other groups, was friendly to the Entente, and invited a British force stationed in Persia to occupy the city, which was accomplished by August 17, initially with light forces. The OHL thereupon proposed that German and Turkish troops cooperate in regaining the town for Russia, naturally in return for economic concessions. The foreign ministry thought the undertaking sufficiently important to ask the OHL to make several German divisions available, though there was doubt that the Soviets would countenance Turkish participation. Foreign Minister Hintze, worried about getting the supplementary treaty signed, was prepared to risk Turkish displeasure and agreed with the Soviet ambassador Joffe that German troops would advance on Baku, keep the Russian civil administration in power, and evacuate the town, once the British had been driven out. Under Article 14 of the supplementary treaty, the Turks were to be confined behind a certain demarcation line to the west and south of Baku.138

Hintze, however, had gone too far. There was profound resentment at the Sublime Porte and Grand Vizier Talaat Pasha at once departed for talks in Berlin. Kress, moreover—though Ludendorff had in the meantime given him further troops—said that in view of the resolute stand of the Osmanli front-line generals he would not be able to halt a Turkish advance on Baku. The Turks did actually enter Baku on September 14.

This makes it seem almost grotesque that as late as September 13 the OHL was still ordering General Kress to prepare an attack on Baku. Even during the latter part of September the OHL was counting on gaining control of the Caspian Sea with the help of the navy, after the capture of Baku, set for mid-October. To this end a U-boat and several fast motorboats were to be disassembled and shipped by rail from Batum to Baku, where they were to be reassembled. On October 3 a detachment of the Mediterranean division was to leave for Baku for naval defense, according to an order issued on September 23.139

The machinery of military command ground on, without regard to the general situation. Even German diplomats were far from idle; on September 23 Hintze was able to conclude a secret agreement with the grand vizier which conceded to Germany control of the Baku oilfields, the Tiflis-Baku railway, and the Baku-Batum pipeline. Agreement with the indignant Russians no longer seemed possible. A few days later, however, Bulgaria's military collapse compelled Turkey to drop its Caucasian campaign. On October 3 a

Russo-Turkish agreement, guaranteed by Germany, ordained the evacuation of all of the Caucasus beyond the lines laid down in the treaty of Brest-Litovsk.

Thus the Caucasian chimera ended a month before final disaster overtook Germany. It remains remarkable that the ghostly game was continued as long as it was.

8

Vain Peace Feelers in the West; Kühlmann's Fall

T HE GREAT German breakthrough offensive in the spring of 1918 had failed in its goal. From May onward it was clear that only partial strikes with limited aim were still possible and that a complete defeat of the Western powers to the extinction of their fighting power was out of the question. This, however, kept the OHL neither from continuing its military expansion in the east nor from clinging to its plans for Belgium, of which we shall hear more and which could not possibly be realized unless Britain were first subjugated. Even Count Hertling still had illusions, though ever since his major Reichstag speech of February 25 (see p. 204) he had endeavored to convince the enemy statesmen of the sincerity of his protestations that Germany was ready to conclude a moderate peace on the basis of the Four Points in Wilson's speech of February 11. His main target was the American president himself who, in his speech, had charged the German chancellor with insincerity, in contrast to Czernin. Hertling's task was rendered all the more urgent by the fact that the Germans had, in the meantime, advanced to Lake Peipus and (on March 3) imposed the peace of Brest-Litovsk, two actions that seemed to lend the most convincing confirmation to Wilson's charges and that set off a new worldwide wave of moral indignation over the German militarists and imperialists.

Yet unlike the German liberals who kept pressing for public declarations concerning the relinquishment of Belgium, Hertling and Kühlmann thought it futile to continue the exchange of high-level policy speeches that had been so numerous during the winter of 1917-1918 (see Chapter 5, Part 1). Instead, Hertling looked for ways of reaching Wilson through secret channels. Such opportunities beckoned when almost simultaneously in early March the German foreign ministry was on the receiving end of offers from two American intermediaries.

One originated with a German naval officer, Senior Lieutenant Mensing, who had been charged ever since 1917 with cultivating clandestine connections with America through his father-in-law, a certain Vice Consul McNally in Zurich,[1] for which purpose he had been provided with a special passport. Mensing expected to meet his father-in-law in Zurich on March 26 and offered to get a message to Wilson through McNally, concerning Germany's political intentions. Hertling received him in person and gave him instructions—Kühlmann being away in Bucharest at the time. Only on March 9, through the German legation in Berne, did Mensing receive the foreign ministry text of what was meant to figure as a personal statement by Hertling, constituting his message to Wilson.[2]

Unfortunately the French police detained McNally as a suspected spy, and the Americans managed to get him released only with difficulty. In consequence McNally did not arrive at the home of his daughter in Zurich until early May, while his son-in-law, in order to disarm the suspicions of the Swiss police, had returned to Germany in mid-April. McNally was a somewhat dubious and ambiguous figure whom many Americans in France thought to be a "paid German agent," though he had served his government well with useful information on German military matters. The Germans, on the other hand, thought they could trust him, especially since his son-in-law insisted that he was sincerely eager to help bring about a negotiated peace.

He seems to have been rather hesitant to accept the role Mensing wished him to play, and he first obtained the permission of the American State Department to discuss political questions with his son-in-law. He got this authority, couched in rather vague terms, on May 17, apparently describing it to the Germans in rather more positive terms than may have been warranted.[3] Oddly enough nothing happened for quite a while, possibly because the German foreign ministry had in the meantime received reports from Zurich that made it doubt whether McNally could be considered a serious intermediary.[4]

It was only on July 8 that the German legation in Berne learned that McNally had received a surprising wire from his "top chief" (Wilson?): "Contact son-in-law immediately, cable German peace terms, and guarantee complete sincerity."[5] There was consternation in Berlin. Under Secretary von dem Bussche, deputizing for Kühlmann, who had just been ousted, thought that the message might reasonably suggest a certain eagerness on Wilson's part to secure peace. He instantly dispatched the agreeable news to headquarters and sent Mensing off to Zurich.

The Kaiser's response was that "the shoe was on the other foot" and that it was up to Wilson to set forth his peace terms;[6] but McNally sent word through Mensing that the notes he had received about earlier German negotiating proposals were insufficient and that Germany would have to expressly accept the latest Four Points Wilson had proclaimed in his speech at the grave of George Washington. Hertling then persuaded the Kaiser to consent; which he did, however, only with a reservation proposed by the foreign ministry, namely that the first of the Four Points—providing for the destruction or neutralization of any "arbitrary" force that threatened world peace—was not directed against Germany.

On July 29 the American State Department received a wire from McNally, reporting that the German government had accepted the Four Points—with the reservation stated—as a basis for peace negotiations.[7] The form of the message shows quite clearly that McNally had no official authorization whatever to forward such communications. The alleged directive from his "top chief" in Washington, which he had transmitted to the German authorities on July 8, was purely fictitious, dreamed up solely to elicit further communications from the Germans, which McNally might use to inflate his importance in Washington. A notation on his original telegram shows that it was seen by Wilson; but it was by now late July, and the Allied counteroffensive could look back on its first great successes. Thus the message remained without any effect whatever.[8]

This first effort to establish clandestine contact with the president, therefore, turned out to be a blind alley. A second route seemed at first to hold out better prospects. The man who offered himself was Harold F. McCormick, a major industrialist of international stature, who lived in Zurich.[9] A member of a prominent Chicago family, McCormick was a son-in-law of John D. Rockefeller. He had already seen to it in 1917 that an article he had written, *Via Pacis,* got into the hands of the German foreign ministry, and he now offered to go to America at a suitable time to try to influence President Wilson in favor of a negotiated peace. The offer was made—or rather renewed—through his friend, the German Professor Nathan, head of a well-known Zurich chemical institute. McCormick sent word early in March that President Wilson, a friend of his since college days, was poorly informed about conditions in Europe, a state of affairs he was prepared to improve in private talks, provided he were given the requisite information. Hertling was sufficiently impressed to accept von dem Bussche's proposal to dispatch the envoy Baron Haniel von Haimhausen to Zurich, where talks actually took place between McCormick and Haniel from March 17 to 19, resulting in a series of notes in English which Haniel dictated to the American.[10] McCormick divided this text into a "message" from Hertling to Wilson, and a set of personal explanations and additions from Haniel. Both were to serve as the basis for an exchange with Wilson.

Essentially, though incompletely, this document coincided with what McNally had been told, so that these two contacts may be considered under a single heading. One main endeavor was to justify German eastern policy and the peace of Brest-Litovsk. German policy was represented as having been dictated by the need to create order in an area close to Germany, just as America had had to do in Mexico. Hertling insisted that Germany was not bent on conquest but merely wished to stem the tide of anarchism. Russia's marginal regions had separated from the mother country of their own free will. Germany could neither deny them the protection they sought nor could it in its own interest withdraw the occupation forces while the war was on.

As far as Belgium was concerned, Germany had no expectation of keeping it or infringing its sovereignty. It sincerely assented to the Four Points proclaimed by President Wilson on February 11, as well as to his proposals for securing the peace to come—league of nations, freedom of the seas, international court of arbitration. It was further prepared to discuss all questions at issue, with the sole exception of the integrity of Germany's borders.

There could be no more scope for negotiating over Alsace-Lorraine than Britain would accept with respect to Ireland or America to Texas and New Mexico. Germany was certainly ready to discuss any economic issues that might come up, but it would not stand for a trade boycott or commercial discrimination after the war. Assertions abroad that the German government was tyrannized by a military caste were completely incorrect. The German army was a people's army rather than a professional force, and only a few of its officers were professionals. Thus there could be no question of a military caste. Of course the General Staff carried crucial weight in purely military questions and also had a voice when military and political problems overlapped; but it had nothing whatever to say in purely political matters. When the German government decided to support the principle of self-determination, for example, the military authorities were not even consulted.

Haniel himself added that the existing situation in the east must be considered only provisional and did not yet accord with Wilson's Four Points. Germany was anticipating broadly based plebiscites that would settle the future of the marginal states. Germany had undergone progressive democratization during the preceding year, to the point where no step of any political significance could be taken without prior consultation with the Reichstag and its committees. The Reichstag's power of the purse was a reliable guarantee against autocracy. A considerable number of officials of cabinet rank were former parliamentarians. There was no chance of revolution. A majority in the Reichstag were solidly behind planned constitutional democratization.

In the matter of Belgium, Germany's current Flemish policy had no bearing on the question of ultimate Belgian sovereignty. This was rather a matter that fell under the heading of self-determination. To continue the war indefinitely would be a dangerous policy, for German resentment would rise to a level preventing any moderate peace policy. The best way to peace would be confidential talks among representatives of both sides. Germany was convinced that where there was a will all differences could be ironed out. Public speeches by the statesmen led nowhere.[11]

There certainly was no argument about this last statement; but would Wilson, known to be opposed to all secret diplomacy, agree to top secret preliminary talks with the Germans, merely on the say-so of a private person? We have already seen that he rejected a similar bid that came to him in Emperor Charles's letter from Vienna about the same time (see Chapter 5, Part 2, p. 212f.). That the governments of both Central Powers should have approached him with such offers is a sign of the extraordinary authority he commanded among their statesmen since his speech of January 8.

It is rather odd, however, that Germany, instead of appealing to a neutral country, chose as an intermediary an American with no official standing. The expectation was almost certainly that McCormick would do a good deal more than simply send Wilson a transcript of his meetings. It was hoped that he would speak to the president in person and do everything in his power to persuade him that the Germans were sincerely striving for peace.

Afraid of the attentions of the French political police, McCormick applied to the American legation in Berne for a diplomatic passport, but was rebuffed, whereupon he sent word to the president that he was in receipt of a message he must deliver in person and asked for an appointment.[12] The reply was a request to transmit the message through the legation in Berne. McCormick consulted Haniel who advised him to say that the message could only be delivered in person.

On May 11 Lansing suggested by cable that McCormick's message to the president be included in a diplomatic pouch to be carried by courier. These were anxious days, when Germany was scoring major military successes in France, and America was growing uncertain how the war would end. McCormick in consequence settled for a compromise. He would let his message (which was dated May 20) go by courier to Washington through diplomatic channels but at the same time would go to Washington himself. Haniel agreed with some reluctance.

McCormick did depart for America and was received by Wilson on June 13. It seems to have been only a brief meeting,[13] and it apparently got nowhere at all. Wilson did not even open McCormick's letter of May 20 with its extensive documentation, which had traveled sealed in the diplomatic pouch, and it was filed unread.[14] By mid-June, in other words, the president was no longer interested in such an approach, and it is true that this one would scarcely have told him anything new.[15] American troops were soon to be committed to combat in force, and the president may have been reluctant to risk further delay. He did not wish to give even a semblance of betraying his allies or of disavowing his own war policy, by engaging in any further mediation efforts.

Wilson had publicly proclaimed his firm opposition to secret peace talks on May 18. In a propaganda speech to the Red Cross he had said that hypocritical peace feelers would not swerve America from its grim determination to win the war. He added that he had examined these confidential communications and could state with a clear conscience that they were lacking in sincerity. He viewed them for what they were—attempts to gain a free hand in the east in order to realize designs for conquest and expansion. Every proposal for an understanding in the west was coupled with reservations concerning the east. This sounded like a direct retort to McCormick's message. He may have got wind of its content before it reached him, though on the other hand he may have been referring only to the appeal from Emperor Charles, with which we are already familiar.[16]

All that the German foreign ministry knew was that McCormick had arrived in America, but it exploited this news for purposes of opposing a new lunatic plan hatched by the OHL and the naval command. They wanted to declare the American coastal regions a war zone to be patrolled by three German super U-boats, so-called U-boat cruisers. Von dem Bussche told the Kaiser that this would be a direct affront to the president at the very time when he was being approached with a bid to enter into confidential peace talks.[17] Actually the foreign ministry did not know by mid-August how this bid had fared. It could not even be sure that McCormick's message had reached Wilson.[18] As for the intermediary himself, apparently nothing further was heard from him.

Switzerland was the launching platform for German efforts to come into contact with the Americans, but it was from neutral Holland that the Central Powers tried to communicate with the British. Kühlmann had established a "British desk" at the legation in The Hague, and this soon became the foreign office's main source of information about conditions in Britain. By the early summer of 1918, in the wake of the first great German successes in France, it seemed for a while as though the Lansdowne group (see Chapter 4, Part 1) was gaining in public influence and British statesmen were increasingly worried lest they become too greatly beholden to America at the peace table. These vagaries were closely followed in The Hague, not only by the German envoy, Friedrich Rosen, but the Dutch government as well. The Dutch foreign minister Loudon left no stone unturned in his efforts to bring about a negotiated peace between the two great neighbor states, Germany and Britain, if only to gain relief for his own sorely oppressed country.

On May 12 Rosen reported at length to the Chancellor on impressions brought back from a trip to Britain by a Dutch oil magnate whom he knew well, the former general and war minister Colijn. In the matter of war aims and peace terms Colijn had encountered quite moderate views when he met General Smuts and Sir William Tyrrell, Sir Edward Grey's former chief secretary and now chief of intelligence at the Foreign Office. No doubt this had something to do with the initial German successes on the western front. Tyrrell did inquire whether the Germans might not be minded to cede at least some part of Lorraine, possibly the French-speaking regions. If they were, Britain would undoubtedly stand ready to make sweeping concessions in eastern Europe—though the treaty of Brest-Litovsk would have to be revised, of course! [19]

Kühlmann thought of Sir William Tyrrell as a close friend of long standing and set great store by Sir William's political views. Particular credence was lent to the news transmitted by Colijn because at this very time, on May 17, General Smuts held a speech in Glasgow in which he said that the war would never come to an end unless there were first confidential and unofficial talks to pave the way for peace. He added that one should not cast stones at every peace feeler from the other side nor suspect every such effort of being insincere. On the contrary, one should try to learn at the proper time what concessions the enemy was prepared to make.[20]

But to Rosen's chagrin, Kühlmann did not immediately rise to Colijn's offer to continue playing the intermediary. In the course of June Kühlmann did, however, let the Dutch know that Anglo-German peace talks were possible only if three conditions were fulfilled: The integrity of the entire territory of Germany, including Alsace-Lorraine, would have to be guaranteed. An appropriate German colonial empire in Africa would have to be established— not necessarily by a return of Germany's prewar colonies. There would have to be absolute assurances against any trade war after the end of hostilities.

These were, of course, precisely the same demands we know from Kühlmann's peace feeler of September 1917 (see Chapter 1, Part 4). Colijn aired them in a long letter of June 26 addressed to Tyrrell and offered to come to London again for personal talks. Tyrrell replied only in mid-July, negatively. There was no point in engaging in such talks, he said, so long as there was such a wide gap between the views of the dominant military party in Germany and those of President Wilson.[21]

In the meantime another approach to peace talks with British politicians had opened up. It involved the talks on an exchange of prisoners, which were to be resumed at The Hague. Rosen reported on June 5 that the British government would, on this occasion, send a cabinet member, Home Secretary Sir George Cave. The Dutch diplomats with whom this piece of news originated surmised that Britain expected the Germans to send a statesman of equal rank. If this expectation were disappointed, it might be interpreted as an expression of lack of interest in any political contact.[22]

The British cabinet papers do not bear this out—it may have been no more than a wishful dream of the Dutch. The Home Secretary was actually dispatched to The Hague only to appease British public opinion—there was the greatest interest in Britain in these prisoner-of-war talks.[23] Sir George Cave had no political mission, any more than did the second British delegate, Lord Newton, assistant under secretary for propaganda and prisoner-of-war questions in the Foreign Office. Lord Newton had participated in earlier negotiations on the prisoner-of-war issue.[24]

Kühlmann evidently had a better understanding of the situation and did not share the expectations of the Dutch foreign minister Loudon.[25] He asked the minister of the interior, Delbrück, whether he would care to take part in the negotiations. When Delbrück declined, Kühlmann considered sending the colonial minister, Solf; but although Loudon kept pressing for action, Kühlmann was reluctant to insist on the attendance of Solf, who was recuperating from a serious illness in Switzerland. He merely held Solf in reserve, so to speak. For the time being he was content to stick to Prince Hermann Hatzfeldt, who was to represent the foreign ministry as the appropriately responsible member of the Red Cross organization.[26] Kühlmann has words of praise in his memoirs for his friend Hatzfeldt, son of a former German ambassador in London. He thought the prince very urbane and well-qualified for confidential soundings because of his many contacts in Britain. Rosen at The Hague did not share this view, which is certainly not confirmed in the least by such reports from Hatzfeldt as are available.[27]

Like Sir George Cave and Lord Newton, however, Prince Hatzfeldt was given no political instructions. In his memoirs Kühlmann insists that he summoned Hatzfeldt to Berlin for precisely this purpose and provided him with a top secret code for his reports, so restricted that it was not known even to the German legation at The Hague. This is demonstrably false.[28] That Hatzfeldt probably had no directives from the German foreign ministry is seen from his rather startled letter to Kühlmann after a political discussion with Lord Newton that took him completely by surprise. Hatzfeldt wrote that he could have wished the talk had taken place at a latter date, "once I am aware of your intentions."

It is not even certain that Kühlmann told Hatzfeldt to propose to the British that there be a secret conference of properly empowered persons at which peace questions could be discussed noncommittally in a preliminary way. In an effort to emphasize the ominous character of his fall from office early in July, Kühlmann, in his memoirs, makes a great thing of his alleged plan for meeting his "old political friend" Sir William Tyrrell for such secret talks at the Dutch castle of Middachten, claiming that he had had an exchange of views with Tyrrell through the intermediary of a neutral personage— evidently a reference to Colijn. Tyrrell had sent word that he was in agreement with the three demands put forward by Kühlmann, but this is difficult to reconcile with Tyrrell's letter to Colijn, already cited. Apparently Kühlmann decided only late in June to go to Holland himself for any secret talks, possibly because he had meanwhile realized that Hatzfeldt was not equal to such a task. Actually Hatzfeldt was at such a loss, even at his very first talk with Lord Newton, that on June 13 he appealed to Kühlmann for help immediately.[29]

The extended political discussions between the two men from June 12 on thus took place on the initiative of neither Hatzfeldt nor Kühlmann. Nor was it the British side that gave the original impetus but rather the Dutch. Yet as early as June 5 Sir Walter Tawnley, the British envoy at The Hague, did call the attention of his government to the possibility of such peace talks. The Germans, he said, had concluded from the appointment of the Home Secretary as the chief delegate that the British were interested in opening up confidential talks on the peace question. That was why they, on their part, had appointed Prince Hatzfeldt as their delegate. Three weeks earlier, Tawnley went on, the Dutch envoy Baron Vredenborch, arriving from Stockholm to take the role of middleman, had proposed to him that the occasion of the prisoner-of-war conference might be exploited for the purpose of setting up peace talks between Tawnley and Rosen, both of whom might be appointed delegates to the conference to that end. Tawnley said that he had responded with considerable reserve and skepticism. Vredenborch, however, kept insisting that the Germans were now extremely eager to make peace on acceptable terms, and he cited both Rosen and von dem Bussche to that effect. Tawnley's reply was that the peace treaties of Brest-Litovsk and Bucharest made the wide gap abundantly clear between German and British ideas of what constituted a "reasonable" peace. He did tell London of other evidence that the Germans were now intent on making peace on much more favorable terms than might be assumed from their recent public statements. If Britain did agree to peace talks with them, they were likely to show themselves conciliatory on the prisoner-of-war issue as well.[30]

Tawnley's wire immediately resulted in an interesting debate within the war cabinet. Balfour reminded his colleagues that he had but recently said in public that Britain stood ready to listen to what the enemy might have to say on the chances for peace; and Lloyd George expressed sharp opposition to Clémenceau's refusal to enter into any kind of peace discussions, a stand that had met with much resentment, especially among the French workers, as Lloyd George had learned on his last trip to France. A directive was dispatched to Cave, instructing him to listen to anything he might be told on the peace question, but to take no stand, merely to report.[31]

Cave was at no particular pains to implement this directive by seeking political talks with the Germans. From accounts by Rosen and the German delegates as well as from Lord Newton's memoirs, he was ill-suited to international negotiation, brusque and arrogant in his demands and occasionally tactless in his speech. Lord Newton tried all the more eagerly to engage Prince

Hatzfeldt in talks. On June 12, directly following the first session of the commission, he sent word through Vredenborch that he would like to meet Hatzfeldt secretly. The German delegate was taken completely by surprise and in his confusion could put forward nothing better than vague generalities and a desire to arrange a talk "among gentlemen" on the peace question.

Hatzfeldt thought Newton naive and "typically British"—i.e., arrogant—in being willing to carry German peace proposals back to London without first discussing them here and now. In other words, he completely misread the character of his opposite number, who was undoubtedly a man of good will. Subsequently he had qualms about having gone too far in his utterances and sent word to Newton through Vredenborch that any unilateral transmission of German proposals to Britain was out of the question. At a second two-hour discussion on June 16 he tackled the peace question in the clumsiest possible way. In view of its great military triumphs, he said, Germany could under no circumstances enter into peace with its position as a world power diminished.

As was to be expected, Newton's response was on the vehement side. Britain's greatest fear, he said, lay in the opposite direction—that in the wake of Russia's total collapse Germany might exercise something like unlimited dominion over Europe. In the early stages of the war it was a great Russian victory that had been feared, and thought was given to the possibility of Anglo-German cooperation against an all-powerful Russian empire; but today the situation had changed. It was precisely in the East that German power had waxed excessively, and British security and interest in the Middle East dictated opposition to such a major shift in power.

Instead of taking advantage of the occasion to tell Britain what the Red Peril meant to western Europe; what the role of the newly created marginal states as a *cordon sanitaire* was; how German troops were urgently needed to police these regions, and above all that the whole system created at Brest-Litovsk was purely provisional, Hatzfeldt was content to mouth trite reassurances. British interests in the East, including Turkey, he said, could surely be satisfied by appropriate treaties, as had been the case at the time of the controversy over the Baghdad railway. The Belgian issue was scarcely mentioned, Hatzfeldt only remarking that by way of indemnifying Belgium Germany might purchase the Congo from it. To Newton's disappointment he said that there was no point at all in discussing Alsace-Lorraine. The Germans, Newton pointed out, had not always been so obdurately opposed to compromise. He did not reject outright Hatzfeldt's demand for the return of Germany's colonies, possibly in somewhat altered form, but mentioned the strong views the British dominions held on this subject. He emphasized that America fully shared British apprehensions of excessive German power.

There was more talk at this meeting, but that was all—not the slightest opening for a policy of mutual understanding. What was clear was that the Germans insisted on the status quo and were bitterly opposed to any form of postwar economic reprisal. Lord Newton complained at the end that he had been given nothing concrete to report to London. The British government could scarcely be expected to seek further exchanges, in the light of talks that had brought nothing new. Rather than interpreting this as a challenge to say something more positive, Hatzfeldt concluded that his task was completed. He told Kühlmann that he wished to depart and warned him against doing anything further in the matter. Germany would have to wait and see what the British would do and must not "run after them." Lord Newton was quite unsuitable as a negotiator and had no authority whatever. He, Hatzfeldt, had been at pains to mention Tyrrell's name more than once during the talks.

Kühlmann took quite a different view. Evidently surprised at Newton's conciliatory attitude, he wished to see the discussions continued and recommended that Tawnley be included, if possible.[32] In the meantime Loudon, the Dutch foreign minister, had got busy as well, communicating with Cave in an effort to win him over to the idea of a Dutch mediation initiative, a project Hatzfeldt thought distinctly "inopportune." What worried Hatzfeldt most in that connection was the prospect of being challenged to make an unequivocal statement about Belgium. Loudon quoted Cave as saying that the British government would agree to peace talks with Germany only if Germany were ready to relinquish Belgium without any reservations.

Hatzfeldt remarked that this would have repercussions at home and abroad and on that account it was quite out of the question unless Germany were compelled to do so. On June 21 he begged Kühlmann to provide him with a cleverly evasive formulation on Germany's Belgian policy which he might use with Loudon—he thought it too risky to devise one of his own. Almost immediately he regretted having embarrassed Kühlmann, since any statement on Belgium was likely to have serious consequences. He kept Loudon on a string, insisting that he must ask Berlin what was planned for Belgium's future and that a reply might be long in coming. At the same time he considered whether he might say that he did not think it appropriate to ask Berlin at all at the behest of a third party, since the foreign minister, like himself, was bound to regard unconditional German assent to the British viewpoint on Belgium as out of the question.[33]

Hatzfeldt, in other words, was a political innocent who had no real idea of the importance of his mission. In his uncertainty he kept inveighing against the British negotiators, whom he described as quite unsuitable for peace talks and without political instructions. General Friedrich, the military member of the commission for prisoner-of-war exchange, served only to reinforce Hatzfeldt's antipathy. Friedrich refused to accept a statement from Cave, because of its supposed arrogance. Besides, the OHL and the German admiralty kept flooding him with directives, all insisting that the British must yield, since they would be vanquished by winter anyhow.

Hatzfeldt asked himself whether Ludendorff would even consider an understanding with Britain. Evidently he too was strongly influenced by OHL views. On more than one occasion the prisoner-of-war commission seemed about to founder, usually on account of subsidiary issues that were blown up out of all proportion by the OHL. It was only owing to the telegraphic intervention of Kühlmann and von dem Bussche that the meeting was continued at all—to gain time for the political talks. Newton left Hatzfeldt in no doubt that if the commission blew it, it would mark the end of any hope for peace talks.

Although Lord Newton continued the secret discussions with amazing pertinacity, Hatzfeldt simply had no conception of how to take advantage of his opportunities. On June 23, in another meeting that lasted more than two hours, Newton said he was willing to apprise Balfour and possibly even Lloyd George.[34] In the end the Dutch diplomats appealed directly to the German foreign ministry and to Rosen, the German envoy, whom Hatzfeldt had kept in the dark about his talks with Lord Newton.

On June 25 Vredenborch wrote von dem Bussche privately that he had talked with Cave, who was the leader of the British delegation and the only one with authority.[35] Cave had told him in deepest confidence that he was ready to talk peace with the Germans, but not with Hatzfeldt—it had to be someone of higher political rank. Vredenborch had proposed Solf and Cave had agreed—"certainly a very good man." Asked specifically during a second talk whether he was prepared to enter into confidential talks with Solf, Cave had replied in the affirmative.

In consequence the Dutchman urgently advised that Solf be promptly dispatched to The Hague. He gave the same counsel to Rosen, who at once told the German foreign ministry about it by wire. Rosen did voice some reservations—he was not certain whether Cave's alleged willingness to hold talks was spontaneous or merely inspired by Vrendenborch. Some thought also had to be given to the impression a trip by Solf to Holland would make. Rosen added that he had discussed all this with Hatzfeldt, who would come to Berlin on June 26 for further instructions.

These reservations apparently prevailed with Kühlmann and Hertling,[36] who decided for domestic reasons that Solf should not be sent to The Hague for the time being. All that Kühlmann would concede was that he might revert to the matter after talking with Hatzfeldt. This interim solution stemmed from the fact that by June 26 Kühlmann's position was already in grave danger. Among the conservatives and at headquarters his Reichstag speech of June 24, still to be discussed, had created a furor, and Ludendorff had already decided to force his resignation. The Chancellor was trying to keep him for at least a while longer—at such a juncture a new political affront could not be risked. Hatzfeldt himself, moreover, did everything in his power to convince Kühlmann that virtually nothing could be accomplished through Newton and Cave.

Was he right? The British documents show quite clearly that no one in London had had any thought of entrusting the two delegates with secret peace negotiations or even with paving the way for such talks. The British were interested only in learning how the Germans envisaged their peace terms, now that their great western offensive had suffered its first setbacks. When Cave was instructed to listen to them and report what they might have to say, this was immediately communicated to the Allied governments—Balfour was ever concerned lest the alliance be shaken by fears and suspicions of a separate British peace.

Many years later, in 1931, when Rosen asked General Smuts whether the British government in the summer of 1918 was still seriously considering a negotiated peace, Smuts replied with a vehement yes;[37] but not too much credence should be given to this belated recollection, for Smuts's own attitude at the time was equivocal. On the one hand, on the basis of his own bitter experiences as the loser in the Boer War, he shrank from fighting until the enemy should be "crushed." Then too, like Field Marshal Haig he overestimated German powers of resistance during the final war months. Hence Smuts rejected—even in public—the idea of going on to march on Berlin; and as we have already seen, he warned against rejecting every German peace feeler in advance. On the other hand, Smuts was afraid that moderate German peace offers might compel the Allies to enter into negotiations before Germany's military defeat was sealed and its military prestige broken for all time.[38]

In the light of all these considerations the historical significance of the peace talks at The Hague should not be overestimated. Still, it is frustrating to see how Kühlmann's negotiator did everything in his power to discourage and foil the peace initiative of those very Dutchmen whose queen, only a few weeks later, when the last hopes of "victory" had gone aglimmering, was implored by the Germans to serve as an intermediary. It would seem that Kühlmann never really abandoned the idea of paving the way to a negotiated peace through confidential talks with the British. As we shall see, even his speech of June 24, which tripped him up, served this purpose.

It is not easy to perceive, however, just what Kühlmann expected of these talks, seeing that he provided his man with no concrete directives—not even in the Belgian question. He could scarcely have expected, now that the great German offensive had failed and more and more American troops were arriving in Europe, to persuade the British government to negotiate, without offering some attractive inducement; and this is precisely what he lacked, owing to the inflexible attitude of the OHL and his own refusal even to discuss the question of Alsace-Lorraine. In our view the bankruptcy of Kühlmann's peace policy had long since been apparent by late June 1918, and all his continuing efforts to salvage it were mere acts of desperation.

This includes his notion of offering himself to the British as a negotiator in place of Solf, a proposal originating with Hatzfeldt, as we have seen, only to be suddenly taken up by Kühlmann himself, now that it was too late. Hatzfeldt had sounded out Lord Newton on June 23, getting a positive reaction. A few days later Berlin learned that Cave had said approving words about Kühlmann's Reichstag speech—which von dem Bussche promptly wired on to headquarters.[39] Unfortunately Cave was recalled to Britain on June 30, for purely domestic reasons, and Kühlmann himself was dismissed on July 8.

Only shortly before, Hatzfeldt, probably acting on Kühlmann's instructions, was still energetically trying to arrange confidential talks between his principal and Tyrrell "this side of the border" for a later time; and he found Newton quite willing to cooperate. Newton was, of course, severely disappointed at Kühlmann's sudden fall; but Hatzfeldt entertained the opinion that this was no reason for the line to be broken—indeed, that Kühlmann might still serve as negotiator. Anticipating such a meeting, he described Loudon's mediation initiative as premature, to Loudon's bitter disappointment.[40] Oddly enough Kühlmann himself continued to keep himself available for such a mission—provided only that any directives he would receive were so formulated as not to preclude the success of the talks in advance; and Hertling sent Hatzfeldt word to continue negotiations along the same lines, without regard to Kühlmann's ouster.[41]

Hertling also asked Solf to be ready to go to The Hague, and the Kaiser remarked that in the event it did not matter particularly who was sent.[42] What a complete misconception this was! Lord Newton, nevertheless, agreed to the dispatch of the fallen minister provided he were properly empowered; and Hatzfeldt was naive enough to conclude that the British government—it was by now July 16! – seemed to be a bit more receptive to the idea of a negotiated peace, perhaps from fear of American dominance and the rise of socialism.[43] An end was put to all these illusions by a letter from Vredenborch in Stockholm on August 8, which was a black day for the German army. Vredenborch included the text of a wire from London, politely stating that the idea of confidential peace talks was now outdated.[44]

In his memoirs Kühlmann has described the haste with which he had to prepare his well-known Reichstag speech of June 24 and the physical exhaustion, due to overwork, from which he suffered when he delivered it. No doubt this was true,[45] yet the speech was by no means an improvisation. It was most carefully prepared,[46] a highly characteristic expression of Kühlmann's political character. It began with a broad overview of Germany's foreign policy situation, its relations with its allies, and its eastern policy–all painted in the rosiest colors, without revealing any trace of the serious difference between government and OHL, especially in eastern questions. To deny or at least conceal these differences was inviolable government policy, shared even by the democratic Vice Chancellor von Payer.

The speech closed on a note of boundless confidence in victory, based on Germany's battlefield position, its immense reserves of matériel, its firm domestic situation. Kühlmann insisted that all these factors would soon persuade the enemy to see that the notion of an Entente victory was a snare and a delusion. This, of course, was merely meant to disarm the OHL and the super-patriots. The real purpose of the speech was to appeal to the British with whom Prince Hatzfeld was just then holding talks at the Hague. Kühlmann earnestly pleaded with the British to lend no credence to the idea that Germany had initiated the war to achieve world dominion, or that it still strove for such dominion, as Balfour had reiterated only a few days ago, on June 20. In the German view it was Russia rather than Britain that was guilty of having started the war in 1914. Germany's own war aims were solely the maintenance of its historic boundaries together with a proper share of colonies and world trade. These alone were the preconditions for peace talks, all else was subject to negotiation, including Belgium. On that subject Germany was scarcely in a position to make a public statement, since that might be interpreted as an advance commitment without in any way binding its enemies; for it was certainly a foregone conclusion that Allied terms would not be limited to the relinquishment of Belgium.

Public declarations from the rostrum, Kühlmann said, would bring peace no nearer. Germany shared the view Asquith had put forward in the House of Commons on May 16–the door would never be closed if the enemy were to make proposals resting on a firm foundation.[47] Some day, after all, an exchange between the contesting parties would be necessary, and it would come about only when each side conceded the other a measure of decency and chivalry instead of denouncing every hint of peaceful intentions as a trap or malicious plot to sow dissension among allies. Without such exchange military decisions alone, unaccompanied by diplomatic efforts, could scarcely be expected to bring this vast war of coalition to a definitive end, in view of the number of powers involved, including those overseas.

It was this final passage that spelled Kühlmann's doom. What it said sounded as though it were self-evident, and most of the deputies and even the Chancellor originally viewed it in that light and gave it little notice. It was the conservative party leader Count Westarp who (supposedly after a telephone call from Ludendorff) blew it up into a full-fledged scandal on the floor of the Reichstag, vigorously supported by Stresemann. The OHL, perceiving a welcome opportunity to get rid of the hated Kühlmann, instantly and brusquely made its protest public[48] and insisted that the Kaiser dismiss Kühlmann.

Obviously Kühlmann's final passage applied only if a dictated peace, to be simply foisted on the enemy after final victory, without any diplomatic negotiation, were ruled out. But not even at Brest-Litovsk had things gone that way—at least not from the beginning, only after the second subjugation of Russia early in March; yet neither Ludendorff nor Westarp could have imagined that the spectacle of Brest-Litovsk would be repeated with Britain, France, Italy, and America.[49] To pillory Kühlmann as a defeatist and become exercised over the supposedly "devastating" effect of the speech on the army and the people was thus a malicious distortion of his words.

It was not Kühlmann's speech that brought unfavorable consequences but the reaction from the right and the OHL that it set off. Kühlmann wished to tell the world that Germany was ready to negotiate and that diplomatic peace feelers could be discussed as openly in the Reichstag as Smuts and Asquith were able to do in Britain. This intent was thoroughly frustrated. Kühlmann's policy would be openly disavowed and the continuing dominance of the military demonstrated to all the world, if the OHL succeeded in having Kühlmann instantly dismissed by the Kaiser.

Viewed in this light, Kühlmann was a martyr to a good cause. The pity of it is that the cause was already lost before he made his speech and that his appeal to the British was as illusory as the secret talks he had staged at The Hague. By the time the speech triggered a Reichstag controversy over a negotiated peace, the Germans no longer had any chance of a negotiated peace. Kühlmann's adversaries were right when they gave out the slogan "No peace without victory." They were even worse deluded, however, when they believed that "final victory" in the sense of a complete unilateral triumph could still fall to the Germans.

Kühlmann assures us in his memoirs that it was the intention of his speech to bring the German people to their senses. Such a process of disillusion was overdue. Had it taken place in time, i.e., had the German political and military leaders appreciated (and convinced the people) that the only possible course of compelling the enemy to offer moderate peace terms was by waging so tenacious a defensive struggle as to delay his triumph indefinitely or make it as costly as possible—had this been done, at least the terrible shock of the disaster in the fall of 1918 might have been softened, and with it possibly the revolution and the sudden loss of confidence in the political and military authority of the Reich avoided.

This, however, would have required a good deal more than a single carefully formulated passage in Kühlmann's speech, which avoided any mention of his differences with the OHL and concluded on a note of pretended confidence in victory, thus losing much of its effect. Had Kühlmann really wanted to shake up the German people, he would have had to attack the official system of mendacity head on—the insistence on concealing the truth and giving out false victory slogans. In so doing, Kühlmann would also have been risking his political survival, but he would have been assured of a memorable exit.

"Negotiated peace" was no longer an appealing catchword. Twentieth-century total war, whipping up the passions of the people, admits less and less scope for "negotiation" the longer it lasts—at least of the kind of old-style diplomatic settlement, the tradition of which dominated Kühlmann's thinking. To shake off at last political dominance by the military became a goal that grew more and more attractive as the myth of the "unconquerable" captains ebbed away on the battlefields of France.

On this occasion protest against the military regime emerged with far greater force on the floor of the Reichstag, especially in the speeches of the social democrats, than had been the case a year earlier, when Bethmann Hollweg fell. David delivered a major speech, brilliantly prepared and based on an intimate knowledge of the facts. It served to vent the dammed-up resentment of the majority parties over the eastern policies of the OHL, which they had vainly opposed time and again. It was also an impassioned indictment of military misrule in the occupied eastern territories. Noske and Scheidemann supplemented these charges with vigorous protests against the official policy of braggadocio and the trumpeting of victory which had long since lost all credence. Accusing the government of pusillanimity, they demanded a "truth offensive." The government, they said, did not have the courage to tell the generals what all others had long since realized. Germany could not force its will on the whole world. Military illusions had to be abandoned.

The parties of the right, represented by such as Westarp and Stresemann, were not slow in responding, and a hidebound Pan-German spokesman persisted in long-winded tirades. The extreme left sought to outdo David's indictment with atrocity tales from Lithuania and the Baltic. Thus the last Reichstag session under the Hertling government turned into a searching debate on the goals and methods of German war policy, revealing to the world the deep rift that had split Germany into two hostile parts at the end of the first year of full Ludendorffian militarism and frantic activity on the part of the fatherland party. Scheidemann was so incensed at the wishy-washy attitude of the Hertling government that he gave formal notice of his party's defection. It took protracted and difficult negotiations in the joint party caucus to have this step softened and limited[50]—in fact, the caucus came close to breaking up over the matter.

Kühlmann's attitude in these Reichstag debates severely disappointed his followers on the left. Hertling had tried to help him by affording him a chance on June 25 to supplement and explain his speech. His political instinct should have told him what the occasion called for—a brief and incisive statement in which he objected to Westarp's malicious distortion of his words—as though he had said the war could be ended only by negotiation rather than force of arms. This should have been coupled with an equally sharp protest against the OHL's unceasing intervention in political matters, which had now reached the point where the OHL tried to exercise military censorship over the speeches of cabinet members.

But instead of defending himself by attacking, Kühlmann made long-winded excuses, in which he tried to refute Westarp's charges letter by letter, insisting that he had mentioned the diplomatic exploitation of military victory "only theoretically," i.e., presumably without any intention to draw political consequences from it. What this meant was that he was virtually surrendering his whole position, his policy of seeking a negotiated peace. In consequence he immediately lost face and stature as a leading statesman. Noske and Scheidemann did stand up for him on the floor of the Reichstag, but not without passing severe judgment on him themselves.

Payer wrote the Chancellor a long letter, warning him against dismissing Kühlmann, which might have disastrous results at home and abroad; but even the majority parties, like Hertling himself, now began to entertain doubts that Kühlmann had the caliber of a statesman. Discussing the case at headquarters with the OHL, the Chancellor tried to have the ouster postponed for at least two weeks, until the appropriations bill had been passed. He did win over the Kaiser; but von Berg, the Kaiser's arch-conservative cabinet chief, long since intent on tripping up Kühlmann (and if possible Hertling as well), had a series of stormy sessions with the monarch in which he prevailed with his demand for immediate dismissal, an accomplishment on which he subsequently prided himself.[51] That dismissal was already a settled matter when Kühlmann appeared in Spa on July 8, and his representations, particularly with reference to the secret negotiations at The Hague, made no impression.[52]

Thus Kühlmann suffered the same fate as Bethmann Hollweg had a year before. At the moment of supreme crisis none was ready to offer effective opposition to the omnipotent OHL and the slavering rightist press. Kühlmann's fall, however, was to be their last political triumph, and even it was less than complete; for against the expectations of both the liberals and the Pan-Germans, the man whom the Kaiser summoned to replace Kühlmann, his favorite, Envoy Hintze[53] turned out to be neither an expansionist nor a pliable tool of the OHL, though he did manage to restore tolerably good relations between the OHL and the foreign ministry. As we saw in Chapter 7, he unswervingly stuck to his predecessor's course, the difference being that he displayed greater vigor and clarity of purpose.

In his policies toward the Western powers, and indeed on the peace question in general, Hintze was clear-headed and realistic. It is true, however, that he was under greater pressure to seek an accommodation with the OHL in these areas than in the East, unless he wanted to risk suffering Kühlmann's fate. As we shall see, these contingencies repeatedly imposed serious handicaps on his freedom of action. By the time Hintze took office it was probably already far too late to bring the war to an end "by diplomatic means," as Kühlmann had imagined possible. If there had been any intention to salvage what could still be saved by political methods, the first and foremost step would have been to send Ludendorff packing—and this none dared consider.

9

The Disaster

Part 1

Incipient Collapse of the German Front and Final Diplomatic Salvage Efforts (August-September, 1918)

FROM MAY 1918 onward, Ludendorff, the man of iron will, had an occasional inkling that his star was about to set and that the *Endsieg* (final victory) was moving farther and farther into the dim distance. He always managed to suppress such glimmerings. It was after the failure of the second offensive in Flanders that his adviser, Colonel Haeften, thought he first noticed a touch of uncertainty in Ludendorff, who told him that victory could be in prospect only if he were promptly given 200,000 serviceable field replacements, a goal neither the Chancellor nor the war minister knew any way of reaching.

It then became clear to Haeften that peace could not be secured by force of arms alone, and he worked out a long memorandum that demanded a "peace offensive," a propaganda campaign to break down the enemy's will to fight on. What he envisaged was a rallying of prominent Germans from every walk of life who could be considered absolutely reliable in a nationalist sense—princes, aristocrats, retired statesmen and diplomats, parliamentarians of the "national party" (i.e., social democrats would not qualify), leaders of business, finance and industry, the cream of the universities. These were to join in a propaganda campaign in defense of German policy, especially in the east. The charge that Germany was responsible for the war was to be refuted and Entente policy attacked. There were to be public demonstrations on behalf of world-wide social objectives—freedom of the seas, social legislation on the German model, etc. This was to give the impression abroad that there was a strong nationalist peace party in Germany.

The whole campaign was to be officially organized, and every public statement was to be carefully scrutinized in advance; but this centralized control was to be most carefully concealed behind a show of spontaneity. At the same time the world was to be misled into believing that another German peace offer impended. Even the question of Belgium could be touched on, though only within the limitations of public statements on this matter made by the Chancellor and his predecessor.

In order to win Ludendorff to his plan, Haeften expressly rejected any effort at a new German peace offer, though a single passage did contradict this. "It is a well-established Prussian tradition to practice the greatest moderation in putting forward political demands, even when one has gained the most brilliant military successes. If there be a sincere desire for an understanding on the part of Germany's enemies, we should stand ready to conclude a peace that would be compatible with their honor and their interest, as well as ours."

The other side would, of course, have promptly seen through the purpose of such a peace offensive—to create confusion in the Allied camp; nor would the Western powers have failed to perceive the official, centralized direction. Haeften nevertheless set great store by the idea of such a campaign. Unleashed during an interval between two major offensives, it would, he thought, mobilize all those forces in Britain that sought a swift peace and opposed the government of Lloyd George. Then, if a new great military blow burst quite unexpectedly into this political turmoil, the whole hatred of the deceived and disappointed people would be vented on the warmongers, and a great wave of resentment would topple the present government. Once the British home front collapsed, it stood to reason that morale would crumble in France and Italy as well.

It is not surprising that Ludendorff found such rosy prospects reassuring, gave his approval to the memorandum, and warmly recommended to the Chancellor that Haeften's plan be put into effect. What is difficult to understand is that Haeften was so completely deceived about the situation in Britain, on which he should have been particularly well-informed through Hahn and the Hague legation. Even more surprising is the fact that, according to Haeften's own statement, experienced career diplomats and men with an intimate knowledge of foreign affairs like Wolff-Metternich, Romberg, Stumm, and Colonial Minister Solf collaborated with him on his memorandum—or at least did not advise him against it.[1] Once again Haeften was entangled in a web of illusions in his quixotic endeavors to mediate between the war policy of Ludendorff and the conciliatory course of the foreign ministry.

When Haeften's plan was discussed at the Chancellor's office on June 19 in the presence of its authors, Payer, Kühlmann, and Radowitz, it was greeted with general skepticism.[2] Hertling held that there was no prospect of the plan being put into effect so long as the OHL and the government were at odds on the Belgian question. Haeften hastened to report that at his most recent discussion with Ludendorff he had found the general holding rather moderate views. He felt sure that agreement on this central issue could be reached, if the government manfully stood its ground. The group was surprised and impressed. On Kühlmann's proposal, the Colonel was entrusted with implementing his own plan, a seasoned senior diplomat being assigned to him as adviser. Kühlmann was emboldened to deliver his fateful speech by the passage in Haeften's memorandum that said that military success alone would not bring peace. He actually thought he had authority from the OHL for his peace initiative.

This, of course, was a colossal misunderstanding, a fact that, oddly enough, has not been noticed by historians. Haeften's proposed "peace offensive" was, in the words of its own author, "not intended to bring about peace, but to support the war," by methodically destroying the enemy's home front while strengthening Germany's. It was, in other words, the precise opposite of what Kühlmann pursued. It expressly rejected all "peace feelers," on the ground that they would serve only to slacken the German war fervor. The moment he realized how Kühlmann had misinterpreted Haeften's peace offensive, Ludendorff forbade Haeften to have any part in it.[3]

Had Ludendorff really changed his mind on the Belgian question, as Haeften insisted? If the Colonel's memoirs, written at a later date, are to be trusted,[4] Ludendorff told him on May 7 when pressed by Haeften that he was willing to forego annexations in Belgium but that Germany must insure its further influence by fostering the Flemish nationalist movement. Haeften goes on to say in this highly colored report that he gained the impression that Ludendorff had already inwardly given up Belgium but feared that any such declaration from him would be interpreted as "a sign of weakness" and thus have a bad effect. Haeften thought that the government would have to proceed on its own, without letting it become known that the OHL agreed. What this meant was that Ludendorff was to be permitted to "pass the buck" to the government, so that he could keep on playing the role of the strong man and keep in the good graces of the Pan-Germans. This was certainly a very odd way of playing politics. We must keep in mind, however, that we are here dealing with nothing more substantial than highly subjective impressions on the part of Colonel Haeften, who was ever eager to play the mediator. If Ludendorff had really more or less foresworn Belgium by May 7, Haeften would have had no need of including such a meaningless formulation about Belgium in his memorandum.

A week after the meeting in the Chancellor's office, Haeften was discussing with Ludendorff what should be done to wipe out the impression of weak-

ness created by Kühlmann's speech. The upshot was another report by Haeften on *Aims of German Policy,* formulating extravagant plans for the east
with which we are already familiar (see p. 261f.). This document, however,
included remarks on the Belgian question, evidently in further elaboration of
Haeften's talk with Ludendorff on May 7. British sensibilities might be
spared, it said, by nominally preserving Belgian sovereignty and territorial
integrity while using the Flemish nationalist movement as a political, military,
and economic fulcrum for Germany's interests, to make certain that Belgium
would never become a military staging area for Britain. This ultimate aim of
German policy in Flanders was not to be publicized at all, but to be pushed
only at the peace table, where, Haeften insisted in a rather remarkable statement, Germany was bound to hold the stronger position, because of the
divergent interests of the Entente powers! An official declaration that Germany stood ready to restore Belgium's sovereignty and integrity, however,
should be issued only when the warmongering government in London had
fallen, to support the peace-loving forces in Britain.

We see once again an effort by Haeften to reconcile Ludendorff's imperialism with the conciliatory policy of the German foreign ministry. This
was scarcely Ludendorff's own thinking. That clearly emerged in the major
war aims conference which took place in Spa shortly afterward, in the absence of Kühlmann, who was already counted out. The Kaiser himself presided at these talks at which in the main questions of eastern policy were
discussed.[5] As for the west, it was agreed that Belgium should be formally
divided into two separate states under a single sovereign and with close economic ties. Both were also to be firmly tied to Germany by means of a
customs union, common rail system, complete disarmament (at least for the
time being), protracted occupation, etc. Last to be evacuated would be the
coast of Flanders and the city of Liège, and even these only if Belgium came
into the closest ties with Germany and the Flemish coast were protected
beyond any question.[6]

Such, then, were Ludendorff's real ideas concerning Belgium! Haeften
may have believed them to be "moderate," because there was no longer talk
of outright and direct annexation, but obviously this was a totally unacceptable basis for peace talks, as far as Britain was concerned. By early July the
OHL had still not grasped the seriousness of Germany's plight, even though it
was sending vocal appeals to Berlin for more reserves and replacements, proposing that they be procured by forcible means, even by conscription in the
Ukraine and the Crimea, as we have already seen.[7] With these appeals the
OHL slipped more and more into conflict with the frontline generals and how
they saw the situation (see Chapter 6). As early as June 1 Crown Prince
Rupprecht of Bavaria had written Hertling a most reasonable letter in which
he pulled no punches in explaining the gravity of the military situation and

urgently advised the immediate initiation of peace negotiations, while Germany still held a few military trump cards. He was aghast at Ludendorff's faith in some miracle by means of which the morale of one of the western enemies would suddenly crumble.[8]

Unfortunately the Chancellor was deaf to this entreaty. Hertling clung to the ideas propagated by Haeften in his memorandum asking for a peace offensive, ideas that were long since obsolete. He thought that some day the pacifist movement in Britain might come into its own, under the impact of continuing German military hammer blows and in disappointment over American aid. He simply put off the political decision demanded by the Bavarian crown prince, saying that he would talk to him in July. On July 1 he put the question directly to Ludendorff: "Can we destroy Britain?" Ludendorff replied: "We cannot destroy it, but we can seriously weaken it." Hertling persisted: "If Britain, in order to avoid falling completely under American influence, should some day be ready to talk, should we listen?"

This was certainly a curious question for a statesman to put to a general. Ludendorff replied: "The OHL is always willing to listen, but any step we take must carry a dignity and strength commensurate with our achievements."[9] Hertling agreed. Both Hertling and Ludendorff, in other words, thought they could afford to wait until Britain made some peace offer;[10] and presumably the Chancellor's directive to Prince Hatzfeldt (which followed soon afterward), to the effect of keeping the same negotiating line in The Hague (see p. 310), was dictated by this expectation.

On the Belgian question Hertling made a statement before the main committee of the Reichstag on July 11. It was intended to reassure the deputies that there would be no change in German foreign policy but actually stuck closely to the policy outlined at Spa on July 3 and mentioned closer economic integration with Belgium and future political guarantees. Only under pressure from the majority parties did Hertling on the following day modify the statement to include a promise of full relinquishment at a later date and represent close economic integration as being in Belgium's interest.

Both of these statements were made in executive session and classified as "strictly confidential," for the Chancellor did not wish the OHL to know their text. When leaks from certain indiscreet deputies nevertheless forced publication of the second statement, the conservatives insisted that the first statement also be published, in the *Norddeutsche Allgemeine Zeitung,* with the result that the two statements virtually cancelled each other out.[11] The Chancellor did emphatically express his government's continuing readiness to enter into peace talks if the enemy dispatched negotiators with plenipotentiary authority rather than mere agents.

A few days later the German army command unmistakably lost the strategic initiative on the western front. The complete failure of the Rheims offensive and the successful breakthrough achieved by a French tank attack southwest of Soissons prevented the Germans from launching any more major strikes and forced them on the defensive. The so-called Marne salient to the west of Rheims—i.e., almost the entire ground gained in the great offensive push of late May—had to be relinquished and the front withdrawn to behind the Vesle.

Ludendorff's closest associates and a number of high-ranking combat officers all testify to the fact that Ludendorff took this withdrawal with its shift to the defensive very badly. He was desperately afraid that the German people—and even more so Germany's allies—would lose confidence in the German military leadership. For hours on end he lapsed into a deep depression and nervous restlessness that paralyzed his usual self-assured command.[12]

Until early August, however, Ludendorff kept telling himself that most of the withdrawals were taking place in good order, that the enemy had failed to score a really decisive breakthrough, and that the German forces at no time gave the impression of being a beaten and routed army.[13] As late as August 2 an order to the army group commands spoke of resuming the offensive in the near future; and time and again Ludendorff resisted surrendering field positions that had become untenable.[14] It was only after the grave setback of August 8, when the German lines on the Somme were overrun by massed armor and some of the German troops actually turned tail, that Ludendorff, by his own testimony, realized that the war had turned into an irresponsible gamble and could not be won by an *Endsieg*. "The destiny of the German people," he says in his memoirs, "was too high a stake to gamble with. The war had to be ended."

But what did Ludendorff now do to turn this conclusion into practice? After that black August 8, why did almost another two months elapse before a plea for an armistice went out to Germany's enemies? For when it did go out Germany's situation, on account of the collapse of its allies, had become completely hopeless. Germany was unable even to protest the most humiliating armistice terms—terms that did violence to military honor. Who bore the responsibility? Was it the military command? Or was it the government, as Ludendorff maintained in a memorandum as early as October 31, directly after his dismissal? [15]

When the quartermaster general, together with Hindenburg, officially apprised the Kaiser of the grave defeat at the Somme, he seems to have wasted not a single word on the need for concluding peace as quickly as possible. Instead, he complained of poor morale, of abject failure on the part of the troops. Some men returning from the front had called members of an attacking division strike-breakers and war-prolongers, Ludendorff said.

It was the Kaiser who thereupon insisted that much too much had long since been expected of the men, and he cited the crown prince in support. When Ludendorff protested, the Kaiser said: "I perceive that we shall have to cast up the balance. We have reached the limits of our capacity. The war must be ended."[16]

The Kaiser summoned the two generals to Spa to discuss the question; but the talks that took place there on August 13 and 14 (the Kaiser presiding on the second day) brought no clear-cut result and only skirted the heart of the matter—what might be done to bring the war to a swift end. Before the talks started Ludendorff had privately admitted to Foreign Minister Hintze that he was no longer as firmly confident as in mid-May. He was not certain he could break the enemy's will and compel him to make peace. Hintze, profoundly shaken, asked how Ludendorff now envisaged his further strategy. Ludendorff replied that the German forces would gradually paralyze the enemy's will by strategic defense action. They would not necessarily forego occasional offensive blows.

At the crown council on August 14 Hindenburg actually expressed the hope that the German forces would manage to stand fast while still on French soil and ultimately force their will on the enemy—in editing the notes, Ludendorff turned this hope into certainty! When the two generals had discussed the matter beforehand, however, Ludendorff (according to Haeften) had emphasized that the government must be informed without pulling any punches.[17] Yet at the sessions proper he seemed intent mainly on protecting himself and the OHL against criticism of their strategy by inveighing against the defeatism and indiscipline on the home front which had now begun to infect the combat troops, and by complaining bitterly of how Hertling's government and its agencies had failed him.[18] In doing so he neglected the most urgent order of the day, to tell the leading men how serious the military situation was with such conviction that they would feel constrained to take immediate diplomatic steps. Thus it was left mainly to Hintze to bring up the subject in the first place. He did try and went to particular lengths in picturing the danger of sudden collapse or defection on the part of Germany's allies—which Ludendorff characterized as "crepe-hanging."

As it turned out, the talks were devoted mainly to the domestic front. The Kaiser insisted that the government take rigorous measures to implement its authority and suppress defeatist tendencies. A propaganda commission was to be established to mount a great campaign along the lines of Haeften's "peace offensive," with which we are already familiar (see p. 317ff.). for the purpose of "weakening the enemies' confidence in victory while raising that of the German people."

At the very moment of military collapse, in other words, there was to be official manipulation of opinion, an undertaking doomed even before it began. The miscalculation was all the greater since the only way to build up "confidence" was to misrepresent Germany's critical situation, when what would have been necessary was to enlighten the people rather than to fill them with war propaganda. They had to be brought, step by step, to the point of accepting the fact that the war would end unfavorably—and they had to accept this without giving way to despair and losing their self-respect.

Deutelmoser, the foreign ministry's publicity head, had no doubts whatever that war propaganda at this juncture stood not the slightest chance of success. "Out with the truth," he demanded, "right up to the limit of where we would be playing into the enemy's hands!" But how was it to be done? During the ensuing weeks he and Haeften worked out "directives for informational activities" that still amounted to no more than glossing over the situation. Deutelmoser insisted that the OHL had pledged itself to maintain the front in the west—and surely this was an unrealistic if not misleading claim. It is virtually certain that the big propaganda campaign of the final war months did more mischief than good.[19]

As regards foreign affairs, the Spa crown council of August 14 did not go beyond a demand by the Kaiser that a suitable time must be chosen to reach an understanding with the enemy, preferably through the king of Spain as a mediator, or better yet, the queen of Holland. Hertling said that a "suitable time" would be "after the next German success in the west"—but there was no such further success. Hintze failed to protest this indefinite postponement, even though he was much more pessimistic than the generals with respect to the overall political and military situation. It is fair to say that it should have been his job, at the crucial session of August 14, to push with the greatest vigor for an immediate peace initiative.

If his own report is to be believed, he did remonstrate with Hertling, even before the meeting, actually threatening to resign if the crown council decided adversely;[20] but neither the Kaiser nor Hertling let matters reach this pass. After all, there would be action, "after the next military success"! Hintze's position was undoubtedly difficult. In office for only a few weeks, he was himself a professional naval officer, filled with deep respect for the military achievements of Hindenburg and Ludendorff, whom he described as the greatest captains the war had produced. He was deeply affected by Germany's hopeless situation,[21] and neither personally nor in his official capacity could he bring himself to give up the war as lost beyond redemption. He clung to the view that Germany's two popular heroes still had a right to be heard, and he was not yet ready to try to seize the helm from the Chancellor's senile hands—that happened only a few weeks later—and force the stern decision to sue for an armistice at once.

In later years he always emphasized that he had taken a much gloomier view than the generals, the Kaiser, and the Chancellor; but his attitude shows that he was no more ready for immediate surrender than the others. Presumably he anticipated that the German front would still hold up for some weeks or months to come, giving the politicians time to prepare for armistice or peace.

But were there any possibilities left to stage talks in preparation for a tolerable peace? Why should the enemy governments still enter into such talks, now that their armies were advancing triumphantly? Late in August Romberg, the German envoy in Berne, reported that his sources in Paris and London were speaking of a heightened mood of victory in those cities and there were similar stories out of Washington. Romberg had questioned the Swiss envoy in Washington, Sulzer, home on a visit, and Sulzer told him that, in his view, talks with any prominent American were out of the question.

After some hesitation Sulzer did, however, offer to see that upon his return to Washington Wilson was apprised of Germany's moderate peace aims, in the form of a purely private communication.[22] It was made quite clear that one of these aims must be complete relinquishment and restoration of Belgium. Even so, since March the brother-in-law of the king of Belgium, Count Törring-Jettenbach (already known to us from his secret talks in the winter of 1915-1916, see Vol. III, p. 240ff.), had been discussing questions of peace with the Belgian envoy in Switzerland, de Peltzer.[23] For Hintze the Belgian issue was certainly very much to the fore.

In his subsequent controversy with Ludendorff, Hintze maintained that he had been ready from the beginning to accept the complete relinquishment of Belgium and its restoration to pre-1914 neutral status but had been obstructed by Ludendorff's obstinate resistance. On August 13 Ludendorff was still insisting on the sweeping Belgium program of July 3 (see p. 321).[24] Ludendorff, however, denied as early as August 21 that he had discussed the Belgian issue with Hintze at all.[25] At best, therefore, there can have been only the briefest exchange on the subject.[26] Certain passages in letters Hintze wrote in late September cast some doubt on whether he realized the full urgency of the Belgian issue. Did he share the desire of most of the generals— especially naval officers—to salvage as much as possible of the Belgian booty for Germany? [27] The files of the German foreign ministry fail to provide a clear picture.

Private talks between Törring and de Peltzer conducted in the Dutch legation in Berne show that King Albert's government was willing, within limits, to listen to any German peace offers that went beyond Hertling's declaration of February 25.[28] As before, in 1916, the Belgians were almost certainly afraid (as Lancken soon afterward reported from Brussels) that Allied "liberation," coupled with German "withdrawal," would complete the transformation of their country into a heap of rubble.[29]

The Belgians, in other words, wanted to get out of the war as soon as possible and hoped that a favorable German statement on Belgium might lead to a prompt general peace. In his talk with de Peltzer on June 30, Count Törring had inquired as to what France and Britain were likely to say, if there were a German-Belgian understanding. He asked for another meeting on July 15 to receive a reply. Hymans, the Belgian foreign minister, did ask the Allies, keeping America to the last, and for this purpose postponed another meeting. In his own opinion no serious peace offer should be rejected without serious examination. The British government thoroughly agreed.[30] Thus early in August contact with the enemy, so long sought in vain, did at last begin to materialize.

At the foreign ministry in Berlin the importance of Törring's effort seems not to have been immediately appreciated. The first response, at any rate, was to send the count a newspaper clipping with Hertling's statement of July 12, when he requested instructions. This document, of course, proved almost useless. Törring then went directly to Hintze, urging the minister not to demand Belgian integration with Germany (as had been done in 1916), but to accept its return to full neutral status. Hintze agreed to this proposal only with reservations.[31]

When the Bavarian count returned to Berne on August 10, de Peltzer would not see him. Törring was given a communication from the Belgian government, however, to the effect that Hertling's statement in the Reichstag on July 10 and 12 made it impossible to continue with the contemplated talks. The Chancellor's speech had been unanimously rejected by both Allies and neutrals—indeed, it had met with criticism on the part of sections of even the German public. To speak of hostages and guarantees was in obvious contradiction to the reply Belgium had given to the papal note in 1917. So long as this approach was maintained, any further discussion was fruitless.

If the Germans had really wanted to continue the talks, there would have been only one possibility. All reservations and limitations in respect of the relinquishment of Belgium would have had to go by the board, and Germany would have had to promise also to give whole-hearted assistance in restoring that country. This Hintze did not dare offer. He and Törring met in Spa on August 13 and 14[32]—coincidentally with the fateful crown council—and Hintze tried to reassure Törring about the use of the term *Faustpfand* (hostage or bargaining counter). It was directed not against Belgium but against the Entente and America. It was up to Belgium to persuade its allies to relinquish the colonies, etc., which Germany wished to redeem with its "bargaining counters."

A Dutch intermediary had reported that the Belgians were afraid the Germans might do what they had done in Russia, i.e., subsequently keep adding to their demands without limit. On this too Hintze sought to reassure Törring. He said that the Flemish question was open to discussion, as was true of Belgian desires for guarantees of full independence and economic autonomy.

Indeed, all the Belgian aims were open to discussion, save only the matter of indemnity. On that point Hintze proposed that Törring consult Count Roedern, the minister of finance.

But apparently the situation demanded much more than mere German willingness to discuss what the Belgians wanted. The same inadequacy applies to the wire which the minister sent the foreign ministry on August 15 as a directive to Romberg for "instructing a certain party." There would be neither annexation nor satellite status or any similar state of dependence. Instead, there would be close economic relations and guarantees against Belgium becoming a staging area for Germany's enemies.[33]

Under Secretary Stumm immediately registered objections by wire. Mention of "guarantees" would immediately vitiate the effect of any German statement. He proposed a different phrasing for Törring, who was about to depart for Switzerland for new talks and urgently requested better instructions:[34] Return to the status quo, i.e., neither annexation nor satellite status nor any similar state of dependence, close economic relations, guarantees of political and military independence, from Germany as well as Germany's enemies.

The controversy now revolved around the meaning of the term status quo. Hintze gave instructions by wire on August 17 that it should be struck out of the new version. Von dem Bussche thought that impossible and wished to make this clear to the minister in person. Apparently he succeeded after Hintze returned to Berlin, for Hintze now tried to change Ludendorff's mind.

The occasion[35] was a speech Colonial Minister Solf was to deliver on August 20 as part of the new "propaganda offensive"–he was working on it with Haeften. The speech was simply to mention the "restoration" of Belgium. Hintze was afraid that even so, Ludendorff would object, but tried to secure the general's assent by pointing out that Ludendorff himself, according to Haeften, had tacitly agreed to the "restitution" of Belgium late in June. Ludendorff at once denounced this as a misinterpretation of his earlier statement. He said that Belgium must remain Germany's *Faustpfand* as long as it remained under occupation. To prevail with the necessary guarantees for the future was strictly up to the politicians. He maintained that he had never spoken of the restitution of Belgium in the sense of restoring the status quo.[36]

It is hard for us to understand today why the German foreign ministry took such account of a general who had already been beaten in the field, allowing him to impede its decisions; but such was the case. Romberg reported from Berne on August 20 that restoration of the status quo in Belgium was an indispensable precondition for the resumption of talks. Any equivocation on this point would render them impossible. He pleaded to be given immediate authority to talk to Sulzer along these lines, since Sulzer was bound to raise the status quo question, and any evasion would merely serve to deepen the unfortunate impression left by Hertling's *Faustpfand* formula, possibly disrupting the connection altogether.

Romberg also pleaded for omitting any mention of "guarantees." That term had long since acquired an unpleasant connotation; but Romberg never got the instructions he sought, and in his talk with the Swiss envoy he had to evade the questions of both Belgium and Alsace-Lorraine, while he could drop only vague hints about a possible revision of the peace treaties of Brest-Litovsk.[37]

Törring meanwhile had continued his talks with de Peltzer, apparently with considerable diplomatic skill and some success. The one point on which no altogether satisfactory answer could be given was the delicate question of how the independence promised Belgium could be reconciled with the assurance Germany had given the Flemish nationalists. Questioned on August 25, the foreign ministry immediately replied that German support for the Flemish nationalist movement was purely a wartime measure, continued for reasons of expediency. In any event, after the war the Belgian government would have to come to terms with the Flemish nationalist movement, and an amnesty for its leaders would be a matter of self-interest. Törring should have no hesitation in proposing such an amnesty.

At the conclusion of the second of two discussions, held on August 24 and 26, the count handed the Belgian envoy an extended statement in letter form, dated August 23. It went far beyond any earlier statement by a German statesman on Belgium in its willingness to give back to that unhappy land its political and economic independence as well as restoring its status quo as a neutral country. It is noteworthy that there was no mention of indemnities and reparations.[38]

Hintze was greatly irked that Count Törring had exceeded his instructions on his own by delivering a written statement in which he expressly cited his talks with the Chancellor and the minister, thus giving rise to the impression that the proposals had official standing. He insisted that the count had been empowered only to voice a private opinion of the Belgian problem. In the preliminary talks at Berlin there had never been any mention of Germany foregoing the Belgian colonial territories, as Törring had pledged. Hintze was very much afraid that this "offer" might be made public and reserved the right to disavow it.[39]

The obvious question is of what use a purely "private opinion" of the Bavarian count would have been. A possible explanation for Hintze's ire is that he feared a new dispute with Ludendorff, with whom he had only just painfully patched up a compromise on the Belgian question. On August 25 Vice Chancellor Payer had made a special trip to headquarters at Avesnes for this purpose, presenting for approval a formula on the Belgian question which he and Hertling had prepared in Spa. What it amounted to was that with the coming of peace Germany would surrender Belgium without reservation and residual claim, but in such a form that no other country should enjoy political or economic privileges with respect to Belgium in excess of those accruing to Germany. The details were to be settled between Germany and Belgium directly.

The OHL did not reject this formulation outright but on August 26 requested an addition that deprived the whole thing of its political value. The formula was to be preceded by a bitter indictment of Britain: it was only ostensibly fighting for Belgian independence, its real goals being the conquest of Germany's colonies, the acquisition of territory in Turkey, and Germany's political and economic destruction. In pursuing these goals, Britain was apparently unaware that it would be destroying itself. It was also intent on gaining a foothold in Belgium and France, thus strengthening its world dominance. This Germany could not tolerate. There was to be another addition, to the effect that Germany and Belgium would have to agree on the Flemish question as well. A final phrase was to read: "In return, we demand our colonies and the renunciation of British claims to Calais."

The government did at least succeed in having this provocative last phrase as well as the no less provocative remark about Britain's unconscious self-destruction struck from the draft.[40] Hintze further insisted that the consent of the admiralty be sought, and this was obtained on August 31. Yet it is difficult to envisage just what it was hoped to achieve. True, there was now agreement among the leading statesmen and military men, but the document could certainly not have been made public, except at the cost of creating a furor at home and abroad. It was decided to keep this hapless compromise in reserve, as the basis for a public statement "at a suitable time." Payer did just that when he delivered a patriotic speech in Stuttgart on September 12—but he was careful to suppress the provocative phraseology. Instead, he accused Belgium of having participated in the pre-1914 "encirclement" of Germany. Without wasting a word on the question of restitution, he said that Germany would generously forego the war indemnities to which it was really entitled. In consequence the effect of this speech abroad was entirely negative.[41]

Initially Törring's letter to de Peltzer seemed to meet with greater success. On August 27 Törring reported that the Belgian diplomat had expressed himself most approvingly about the concessions offered by Germany, which in the main coincided with Belgium's known terms. Törring said that de Peltzer's report was being eagerly awaited in Le Havre. The envoy had been asked to send extracts in the night of August 24-25, immediately following the first talk. These were now being promptly submitted to the Entente governments for reaction. Replies could be expected in only about two weeks. Törring said he had immediately inquired when detailed negotiations might commence—which Hintze thought somewhat premature.

But de Peltzer was to be severely disappointed in his hopes. They may have been initially shared to a certain degree by the Belgian foreign minister Hymans; but Hymans was reluctant to respond without first consulting the governments of America, Britain, France, Italy, and Japan. By the time he communicated the content of Törring's letter to the envoys of the United States and the Entente powers on September 9, Hymans had already grown very doubtful. He admitted that the statement of his intermediary deserved attention and represented a step forward toward a just solution of the Belgian question; but he then contrived all kinds of arguments to put the German statement in an insincere light.[42]

Hymans, in other words, anticipated an unfavorable response on the part of the Allies and was getting set for it. That rejection was not long in coming. Lansing wired on September 11, without giving any reasons, that Törring's letter deserved no favorable reception; and Balfour, falling in with Hymans's views, advised that Törring's letter be left unanswered, at least for the time being. Obviously the German offer had come too late. Virtually the only effect was that Entente propaganda tried to represent Törring's letter as a malicious German attempt to split Belgium away from the Allies by means of a separate peace, thus forestalling an Allied advance through Belgium. The Belgian government did meet this calumny by issuing a statement to the effect that there had been no negotiations on a separate German-Belgian peace;[43] but in an official press statement of September 19 it reiterated all of Hymans's critical arguments and advised Törring that de Peltzer was not authorized to engage in any further talks.[44]

Hintze's attempt to reach Wilson with peace proposals via Switzerland had no better luck. Apparently he authorized Romberg to talk with Sulzer about the restoration of the status quo in Belgium only after he had actually secured OHL and admiralty agreement to Payer's Belgian formula.[45] At any rate, he provided Romberg with a detailed directive, including the controversial concession, only on August 31. This document also mentioned Brest-Litovsk and Wilson's Fourteen Points. The latter were to be described as open to discussion, provided Wilson meant them as suggestions rather than firm demands. This was also true of the question of Alsace-Lorraine—though Romberg was advised to try to evade this question in his talks with Sulzer, if appropriate, saying only that peace would not be allowed to fail on account of the question of satisfying French self-respect. On Brest-Litovsk Romberg was to say that Germany regarded the treaties negotiated there as compatible with the right of self-determination, but stood ready to discuss this issue with Wilson in an effort to provide sound arguments for its position.[46]

It scarcely needs saying that no progress could be expected in Washington from such half-measures. The Swiss federal president, Calonder, originally agreeing to Sulzer's private peace mission, soon grew apprehensive. He held that any diplomatic step on the part of Germany was hopeless, unless it were accompanied by a clear statement of German peace terms; and thus he withdrew his authorization to Sulzer. Romberg reported on September 23 that Sulzer's departure would be delayed until October 6. Even at an earlier date, however, his mission would have been fruitless.

Thus week followed week, and peace negotiations came not a step nearer. Actually, Ludendorff's reluctance to accept radical concessions in the Belgian question, while delaying the progress of German policy, did not cripple it crucially. The really decisive element was the notion on the part of the leading men that they had to wait for the "right psychological moment," i.e., until the German withdrawals were completed—though actually no firm front was ever reestablished. Hertling said on September 3 at a Prussian cabinet meeting that no new German peace offer must be made. Germany's enemies would merely regard it as a sign of weakness and brusquely reject it. Contact with the enemy should be established, however, preferably through neutral or other suitable personages. The enemy should be told in so many words: You see now that you cannot vanquish us, but we are always prepared to conclude an honorable peace. Unfortunately, morale on the home front was poor, though the military situation was not as bad as all that. Morale must be improved by every possible means and that was the purpose of the great propaganda organization that had been created.[47] Obviously the aged Hertling had no idea of how dreadfully serious the situation really was, nor did he understand the necessity of enlightening at least the ministers and deputies and preparing them for the inevitable.

Hintze was far removed from such primitive optimism, though he too lived in a world of illusion. "I shall keep my eyes and ears open," he had told the Austrian ambassador, Prince Hohenlohe, on July 27, "to be able to react instantly to the slightest whispers of peace on the part of our enemies." Outwardly, however, he added, he acknowledged but three words: "We shall win," and he hoped to hypnotize the public with them, so to speak.[48]

Hohenlohe had promptly told him that he regarded this policy as basically misguided. Hintze, nevertheless, kept outwardly within the propaganda framework decided on at Spa. He saw his task as one of concealing Germany's military weakness and displaying an infectious confidence in victory.[49] On August 21, in a major talk to the party leaders on matters of eastern policy (see p. 265ff.), he boldly asserted that in the view of the OHL "there was no reason to doubt ultimate victory. We shall be vanquished only when we doubt that we will win. We . . . are entitled to anticipate that we shall achieve a military position from which we shall be able to gain a satisfactory peace."[50]

Two days later Hintze admitted to Count Westarp that he had somewhat exaggerated, in order to stem the sense of depression that prevailed in Berlin;

but even now he clung to the view that no vacillation must be shown and that the people must be supported in standing firm, following the example from above. For these reasons he recommended that the Pan-Germans and conservatives continue to maintain their sweeping demands in the Belgian question.[51]

But this policy of standing pat and waiting it out brought Hintze into conflict with Germany's Austrian ally. On the afternoon of August 14 Emperor Charles had appeared in Spa, accompanied by his chief of staff, Baron Arz, and his foreign minister, Count Burián. The latter there revealed his plan of long standing to issue a universal call for peace on the Soviet model as soon as possible. It was to be an appeal for the prompt convocation at some neutral venue of peace talks to be attended by delegates of all the belligerents. These talks were to be initially confidential and noncommittal.

On August 23, following consultations with the ambassadors of Bulgaria and Turkey, a draft for such an appeal was presented in Berlin.[52] It was a rather long-winded document that cited the alleged rapprochement of the views of the two sides, increasing ever since 1916, but carefully avoided any mention of peace terms by the Central Powers. The impression of a unilateral peace offer, let alone a surrender, was to be be carefully avoided, in other words. Yet considering Austria's wretched plight at the time, this broadcast appeal was nevertheless bound to create the impression of a drowning man shouting for help.

Austria's time had indeed run out. The Austrian state was already far along the way to complete disintegration. A final major offensive in June in Venetia, completely misplanned, failed, and with that failure the offensive power of the Austrian forces came to an end. Not only that, the army proceeded to crumble at an alarming rate. Within three months after July 1 defectors and deserters reduced the effective strength of the southwestern front by almost half. Confidence in the leadership had waned throughout the country. A particularly glaring expression of this decline was the dismissal of Conrad von Hötzendorf who, as commander-in-chief on the South Tyrol front, bore a major share of the responsibility for the disaster.[53]

Mutinies, especially among the non-German-speaking replacement troops, became more and more common. Large bands of deserters rendered the countryside unsafe—by fall there were estimated to be at least a quarter-million. The army, like the people, suffered dreadfully from a want of almost everything. Food, clothing, and equipment were lacking. The Honved Division, dispatched to the German western front in mid-June as a relief unit, arrived there for the most part unshod.[54]

Perhaps the main feature was the helpless political decline of the multination state. From July-August onward, "national councils" began forming, at first among the Slavic peoples. Early in October German-speaking Austria was also affected. There the social democrats pursued a radical pacifist course, abandoned all confidence in the Hapsburg dynasty and proclaimed a separate German-Austrian state on October 3. Soon afterward Hungary cast loose from the monarchy in a sequence of revolutionary acts which Emperor Charles and his advisers vainly sought to stem at the last moment by reorganizing the Austrian empire as a federation.

In the light of this overall situation, the impatience with which Burián and his emperor greeted German hesitation to end the war before it was too late becomes understandable. Tempers flared in the ensuing debate, though both allies at bottom wanted the same thing, a secret conference with plenipotentiaries of the Entente rather than a straightforward downing of arms. Burián was prepared to wait no longer than another ten days before asking for such a conference, and he wished to go directly to the enemy rather than by way of a neutral mediator, like the Germans. In Burián's view such a detour not only meant unnecessary delay but was virtually hopeless. Neutrals would think twice before agreeing to accept the onus of engaging in "unfriendly activities" from the Entente side. Even if this hurdle were surmounted, why should a small neutral state like Holland expect to gain a hearing in the camp of the big enemy powers, having nothing to offer but a statement on the part of the Central Powers that they were generally ready to talk peace—but without putting forward any concrete terms?

Hintze, of course, was able to counter that an Austrian broadcast appeal had even less chance to be taken seriously by the Entente. Its unconventional diplomatic form would make it appear an act of desperation, eliciting only mingled sentiments of scorn and triumph on the other side. The effect would be very different if, say, the queen of Holland were to appeal on her own to the major powers, urging them to put an end to the frightful slaughter and to this end to allow a preliminary conference to meet promptly at her residence, The Hague, for the purpose of seeking a common basis for peace. Particularly as a woman, as well as the head of a trading nation known to be peacefully inclined and lacking in any great power ambitions of its own, she would lend plausibility to the purely humanitarian character of such an appeal. Germany, moreover, was perfectly willing to communicate to the mediating power its peace terms, as a basis for the mediation—provided the other side did the same. At this time, late August, however, it was still too early for such a step. So long as Germany's enemies were still riding high, their confidence in victory at its peak, they were unlikely to respond to a peace appeal. The military situation, however, was bound to change in Germany's favor and the enemy offensive would be brought to a halt. If worse came to worst, the enemy could always still be approached directly.

Hintze was unwilling to admit to himself and the others that worse had already come to worst. This emerges with particular clarity from a talk he held on August 29 with the Dutch envoy, Baron von Gevers. According to Hintze's notes made the same day, Gevers approached him on the matter of the recent severe setbacks on the western front. "I took advantage of the opportunity," writes the minister, "to describe these setbacks as strategically insignificant and to give detailed reasons for our confidence that the enemy would exhaust himself. At the end of my argument Gevers said that the queen and Loudon were eagerly anticipating the moment when they might do something to bring about peace.

Here was the mediator Hintze sought offering his services voluntarily! Hintze took the hint all the more seriously, for during the discussion he learned that the Dutch government was fully prepared to meet with resistance on the part of the Entente and still did not flinch from the task; but instead of starting up the contemplated action at once, his response was to display diplomatic reserve.

> I explained that we had on several occasions expressed ourselves on the matter of our willingness to conclude peace, always meeting the response that we had to be destroyed. The German people stood united to prevent that. I said that what I envisaged was not a peace offer but an exchange of views, direct and noncommittal, by representatives of the belligerents meeting in a neutral place. Speeches by statesmen had served only to exacerbate the situation, and this was true of demonstrations as well. Gevers agreed.

Hintze then apparently diverted the discussion to other matters.

He was, however, now able to tell Burián that the Austrian need not worry about enlisting a mediator. To reassure Burián and win him to his own plans, Hintze went to Vienna on September 2. Such a visit had become urgent, for the Malinov government in Bulgaria, in office only since June, was more or less ready to negotiate with the Entente and urged that the four central allies approve the Austrian peace appeal.[55]

Vienna then became the scene of the great meeting on questions of eastern policy on September 5 of which we have already heard (see pp. 240 and 242f.), a long and ultimately fruitless discussion on the peace initiative. Burián disagreed strongly with Hintze's view that peace terms might be made mutually known through a neutral mediator. He said that if the Central Powers put forward moderate terms, this would be precisely the kind of surrender that was not wanted. If, on the other hand, the terms were obviously inspired by confidence, they would be brusquely rejected. In any event, soundings would have to be taken in America and among the Entente, to establish that neutral mediation would be acceptable, and that would take far too long. Holland had too little power and authority to earn anything but rejection.

Hintze disputed this and suggested that the peace terms should be made known first in the confidential talks for which Holland would issue the invitation, but he lacked persuasive arguments as to why Dutch mediation would have better prospects of success than the peace appeal proposed by Vienna. At bottom Hintze's proposal was as unrealistic as the Austrian's, and Burián was quite right when he insisted that the fiction of a purely neutral, purely Dutch, and purely humanitarian peace initiative could not be maintained for more than a day.

Yet an open plea for peace negotiations, issuing spontaneously from the Central Powers, was utterly at odds with the propaganda campaign still being pursued in Germany, and Hintze was obviously afraid of the consternation such a step would occasion. The Austrian peace appeal, he said, would have the effect of an admission of weakness. The German people would feel that Austria was betraying them; and in Austria the peace movement would go wholly out of control.

Burián observed dryly that Austria was already facing the abyss. There was no more time to lose. The Austrian people demanded immediate action on peace. There was grave danger if the impression got abroad in Austria that Germany was restraining the Austrian government. And after all, the Germans too were at the end of their strength.[56]

Austrian policy, in other words, was directly at odds with German. In Austria there was no longer any fear that the people would react badly to sudden enlightenment about the true situation. Despair had already begun to spread in that country. Hintze and his under secretary, Stumm, traveled back to Berlin in a state of deep depression. They were particularly irate that Charles and his government wanted to play the role of peace agents at any cost, for the sole purpose of shoring up their declining popularity.[57] Hintze thought this the main reason why Burián so obstinately rejected his proposal for at least trying for Dutch mediation. He was left with no alternative to beating the Austrians to the punch with his own plan, instead of waiting another three weeks, as he had proposed in Vienna.[58] He promptly departed for headquarters in order to secure the consent of the Kaiser and the OHL.

When he arrived, he found the OHL in considerable turmoil. Numerous staff officers and chiefs of staff of the major armies and army groups all testified that the setbacks of recent weeks had severely shaken Ludendorff's iron nerve and self-assurance.[59] He apparently felt he had lost his old authority as a strategic genius and his principle of not surrendering an inch of ground without tenacious resistance had obviously failed. In consequence he gave way to outbursts of extreme irritation in which he inveighed beyond all reason against the alleged failure of his subordinate officers.

Ludendorff was especially depressed by a deep penetration of the positions of the 17th German army on September 2, which forced large elements of the front to be withdrawn to the one-time Siegfried line. The day before he had admitted to Colonel Mertz von Quirnheim that he had no idea how he could manage to continue the battle at the present level of intensity for even another two weeks. When Mertz asked whether Hintze should not be advised of the gravity of the situation, Ludendorff replied that that was quite out of the question. The foreign ministry was always scared of its own shadow and if it were to learn the truth of the situation there would be hell to pay.

But when General Oldershausen, chief of the railways service, told Ludendorff on September 2 that the leading men in Berlin were still far too optimistic, he rang up Colonel Winterfeldt, his liaison officer at the Chancellor's office, and instructed him to tell Hintze at once the unvarnished truth about the disaster that had befallen the 17th army. The minister, he added, would have to draw his own conclusions. Yet when a request for information about the situation at the front arrived from the Chancellor's office subsequently, an optimistic reply was dispatched once again.[60]

Hintze arrived at supreme headquarters on September 9 and had little difficulty in securing Hindenburg's consent for the immediate initiation of a peace effort by the queen of Holland. The field marshal, at the same time, strenuously objected to the idea of the Austrian peace appeal. On September 11 Hintze had identical dispatches sent to Vienna, Sofia and Istanbul, saying that "His Majesty and the supreme army command agree to the immediate initiation of a démarche with a neutral power." All three allies were invited to join in this measure or at least to consent to it.[61]

Hintze was a bit proud of this success. He told Ambassador Hohenlohe that Vienna was quite mistaken in looking on him as a mere puppet of the OHL—actually he had wrested many concessions from it; but Hintze was himself mistaken in believing that he had outmaneuvered Burián. It is true that on September 7 Emperor Charles had agreed to delay his peace appeal briefly,[62] but he was by no means deterred from his project by news of the German démarche in Holland or by the various diplomatic representations. Indeed, Burián gave notice on September 12 that the world appeal would be issued two days later—and he was as good as his word.

Thus Hintze's own project was foiled at the last moment, to the Kaiser's fury. William II thought the action of his fellow sovereign "insolent" and said as much in a wire in which he minced no words.[63] There was resentment in Sofia and Istanbul as well, and most of all in the foreign ministry in Berlin. The Vienna action had made it quite impossible to represent any peace initiative on the part of the queen of Holland as "independent" and "neutral."

When Hintze met with the leaders of the majority parties on September 14, he made no bones about his anger and said that he would make a public statement dissociating himself from the Austrian appeal; but here, to his surprise, he met strong and unanimous opposition, which hardened substantially the next day at a meeting in which the Chancellor participated. The deputies admitted in unison that the independent Austrian step was a grave blunder; but since the German government had not been able to prevent it—a serious diplomatic failure, by the way! —it would be an even graver blunder to disavow it now. Such a passive stand would merely confirm the widespread suspicion that there was a serious rift in the alliance. Any ensuing peace negotiations must on no account be left solely to the Austrians. Germany would have to grasp the leadership and at once state its eagerness to participate.

The opposition to Hintze was led by Erzberger, who continued to maintain close ties with Austrian diplomatic and court circles. Another reason behind it was that virtually all the deputies of the left were apprehensive lest the weak-kneed Hertling government lead them down the path of perdition. The speeches of the social democrats, especially, revealed wide-spread distrust of the synthetic optimism expressed in the army dispatches.[64] None really knew the full gravity of the military situation, but Scheidemann voiced the general sentiment when he said that there was no point in waiting with Hertling for the "psychological moment." There was unlikely to be any military turn in Germany's favor, he added, and confidence in the government had vanished completely. David spoke even more plainly. The last hope of victory was gone, he said, and Germany must accept the fact that there was no possibility of winning by the sword.

These developments plainly heralded a government crisis, and Hertling did his utmost to delay or prevent another meeting of the main committee of the Reichstag, as demanded by the deputies. Hintze on his part found it necessary to give a much more positive note to his statement on the Austrian peace appeal. Above all, he was under the greatest pressure to stage a prompt peace initiative of his own.

We already know of his vain and inadequate efforts to send German peace proposals to Washington via Switzerland (see p. 325f.). On September 18 he asked Germany's allies to agree to an effort to "superimpose" a Dutch mediation initiative on the Austrian démarche, the very kind of effort he himself, with Hertling, had only recently thought out of the question.[65] Hintze wished to ask the queen to offer her official residence as the scene of the contemplated conference, as well as hospitality to the delegates. If necessary, she could be asked to preside.

Agreement from Germany's allies was promptly forthcoming,[66] and on September 19 Hintze presented his idea to the Dutch envoy, Baron Gevers, as representing the common desire of all the members of the Quadruple Alliance. He met a sympathetic reception, but the Dutch very much doubted whether the other side were yet ready to engage in preliminary negotiations.[67]

The German envoy at The Hague, Rosen, was nevertheless instructed to talk to the Dutch foreign minister—van Karnebeek had held the office only since September 9—and here too the reception, as reported on September 21, was sympathetic. The minister was willing to consult with his colleagues and the queen. In his view Holland's neutrality was not to be taken to be a purely passive affair.

Rosen was obliged to add before the day was over that van Karnebeek thought it impossible to disavow the German initiative or even to keep it quiet. He urged that it be represented as stemming from Austria—in other words, The Hague should be offered as the seat for the talks proposed by Burián. It was not advisable to reveal that the Germans were actually behind the effort.

This was a great letdown for Hintze, who now found his own political initiative entirely overshadowed by the Austrian. He had Rosen tell the Dutch that the idea came from all the powers in the Quadruple Alliance rather than from Germany alone, adding that German participation would have to be made known. Actually, he had no choice but to communicate the Dutch proposal to Burián, who was of course delighted, particularly since his peace note had, in the meantime, met with universal rejection in the Entente camp.

On September 24 Burián promptly told the Austrian chargé d'affaires at The Hague to take appropriate action, and the Dutch government reacted with equal promptness. By September 26 all the Dutch missions in the Entente countries had received instructions to advise the governments to which they were accredited that the queen of Holland would be happy to make her official residence available for any talks the belligerent powers might care to hold there. The Dutch diplomats were to mention only an inquiry from Austria as the impetus, but Rosen had been told confidentially that the queen was ready to engage in far more sweeping mediation. The trouble was that a leading Dutch party politician had received a hint that Britain would regard this as a distinctly unfriendly act.[68]

The Dutch bid was little more than an empty formality. No one in the Entente camp had the least inclination to enter into peace talks of any kind with the Central Powers. On September 12 American troops had scored their first major offensive success. They had broken deep into the southern front of the German army group C, forcing a precipitate withdrawal from the projecting St. Mihiel salient, between Verdun and Metz, attended by heavy German losses.

News of the Bulgarian request for an armistice broke in the middle of the German negotiations with Holland. Bulgaria's fighting power had abruptly collapsed. Any hope for a negotiated peace had thus gone by the board. Actually, Lloyd George had already announced in a Manchester speech on September 12 that there was no possibility of a compromise between freedom and force. Only victory could bring a secure peace, and the German people would have to learn at last that wrong was bound to be punished.

On September 16 Foreign Secretary Balfour rejected Burián's peace bid on the ground that it was quite unrealistic, citing German Vice Chancellor Payer's Stuttgart speech of September 12 as a crude effort at deception, intemperate in its demands—even though the proposals in that self-same speech were regarded as extremely moderate throughout Germany. The mailed fist always showed through, Balfour said, no matter how hard the Germans tried to disguise it.

The French reply to Burián was a deliberate insult. The Vienna government was brusquely referred to the newspaper version of a speech Clémenceau delivered in the French senate on September 17. It was a speech brimming with confidence in victory, a savage outburst of nationalist hatred and scorn, of an intemperance without example in the history of Europe.

A speech by Wilson on September 27 put finis to all these exchanges. Germany kept on hinting of terms it was prepared to accept, he said, only to discover on each occasion that the world was in no mood for peace terms of any kind. It wanted the definitive triumph of justice and fair play.[69]

Part 2
Initiation of Armistice Negotiations with Wilson

IN THE MEANTIME the OHL's stubbornly maintained belief that it could "force its will upon the enemy" by sustained military resistance had collapsed. The suddenness with which this change came has always been a matter of surprise. The previously unshakable German determination to win lapsed abruptly into total despair. An end was now frantically sought. On September 20 Ludendorff, speaking to Lersner, was still refusing to set forth the full gravity of the military situation to the foreign ministry. "Do not push me too hard," he said. "I'm the one who made Hindenburg's reputation, and officially he still doesn't know what's going on."

A few days later he was telling Groener that he could still hold out for several months, "but there must be peace by Christmas."[70] On September 25 the army groups received an order denying that there was any plan to retire to "operational positions in the rear"—in other words, a voluntary withdrawal. Any such talk was calculated to weaken the will to carry out the decisive struggle in the present positions.[71] The policy of defending every foot of ground was to be continued.

That same day Colonel Heye pleaded with his chief that there was no alternative to his going to Berlin immediately to see the Kaiser and Hintze and press for the prompt initiation of peace measures; but Ludendorff still shrank from an open admission of defeat and insisted that Hintze was already fully informed and doing everything he could to bring about peace. That same night Ludendorff tried to reassure his staff with the news that pneumonic plague had broken out in the French army, a fact he said he had immediately reported to Berlin. When Surgeon General Schjerning denied the truth of this rumor, insisting that there were only a few cases of typhus and grippe, the general was profoundly shaken. "I clung to that news like a drowning man to a straw," he said.

These words revealed as though in a flash the deep uncertainty, indeed, despair, behind the rigidly maintained mask of iron calm and assurance; and the incident led to a most unusual step, a kind of palace revolution of the departmental chiefs. On September 26 Colonel Mertz von Quirnheim made this note in his diary: "His Excellency is still desperate enough to continue the fight but lacks the courage to put an end to it. He will never jump that hurdle unless he is forced to do so." He consulted with General Bartenwerffer, head of the political section, Colonel Heye, and later on Legation Councilor Lersner as well, how this might be accomplished. Lersner was told of what Ludendorff had said and was persuaded to summon Hintze to headquarters urgently by telephone. In other words, the generals, at the end of their tether, were calling in the politicians.

The bad news that Bulgaria wanted a separate peace had reached Spa in the night of September 25-26. German and Austrian divisions were instantly dispatched to Bulgaria, but this action was too late and did not keep the Bulgarians from concluding an armistice on September 30. The suddenness of this unexpected disaster had an important bearing on Ludendorff's decisions. There was the prospect of an exposed flank in the southeast, of the Danube being blocked, of Rumania re-entering the war, of the loss of the Rumanian oil fields, of the swift collapse of Turkey. On September 30 Ludendorff told General Kuhl: "We can't stand up against that; we can't fight the whole world." When Lersner told him that Hintze would arrive on September 29 for an extremely grave confrontation with the OHL, Ludendorff showed no reaction. Indeed, on the eve of that meeting he reluctantly agreed with Hindenburg that a peace and armistice offer would have to be made at once.

In his war memoirs Ludendorff gives a dramatic account of the climatic discussion with Hindenburg, who apparently gave his consent without the slightest hesitation. Ludendorff insists that he was thinking only of an armistice that would allow orderly evacuation of the territories occupied by Germany, with the possibility of resuming hostilities at the borders of Germany, if necessary. No doubt this is true. Ludendorff almost certainly did not simply wish to run up the white flag and surrender, as the Bulgarian command was already doing and the Austrian command was to do only a month later.

What he apparently envisaged was, first of all, to gain a breathing pause for his totally exhausted troops, and then to resume the struggle at the German border, if he had to, in order to gain better peace terms. He hoped that his armies would retain enough power to prevent a "shameful" peace. In a technical sense, he looked for an armistice commission, to be composed of top-ranking generals with the diplomatic participation of Lersner, while the German foreign ministry would issue a peace offer to all the enemy powers, proposing immediate peace negotiations at The Hague and simultaneous armistice negotiations at the front.[72]

Ludendorff was obviously suffering from a profound misapprehension. A plea for an armistice, disguised as an "offer," was quite unlikely to persuade the Allies to halt their victorious advance and give the Germans a chance to catch their breath. Their immediate aim was to make it impossible for Germany to resume hostilities at its pleasure. Either Germany's position was really hopeless, in which case it would have no choice but to surrender, in order to prevent futile bloodshed; or it was not quite so desperate and there were still ultimate possibilities of resistance, if the peace and armistice terms were intolerably harsh.

The latter alternative might have been open, had the OHL taken the advice of most of the army group commanders for a timely, methodical, and well-prepared withdrawal to a defensible position on a substantially shortened front, with sufficient reserves spared. But this was precisely what Ludendorff had forestalled with his policy of clinging to every foot of ground. Now he had to anticipate a major breakthrough—with much of the thin German line held virtually only by officers manning machine guns. The outcome could only be a wild and chaotic rout, with the surrender or capture of masses of troops no longer capable of defending themselves.

Strangely enough, no such breakthrough eventuated after all, owing to uncertainty and waning élan on the Allied side and the valor of small groups of German soldiers who remained ready to stake their lives for their country down to the last moment. Yet the possibility of such a disaster haunted Ludendorff into mid-October. It led to the curious paradox of his spurring on the politicians and insisting that the "offer" could not wait another day, while at the same time refusing to consider capitulation. He may have believed from the beginning that if worse came to worst the Germans might be made to fight on in one final spasmodic effort, a *furor teutonicus,* even if it ended in annihilation.[73] The idea may have been high-minded; but it was certainly misguided, and in the course of October and November it did a great deal of mischief, actually fostering the outbreak of the revolution.

Hintze says that while he was willing to grant that some individuals might be willing to fight to the death for the sake of "honor," he never for a moment believed that could be true of a nation of seventy millions. Germany as a nation was bound to survive, and it was pure self-deception to believe—as did certain literary figures and men of the stripe of Walther Rathenau—that the half-starved country, plagued by a severe grippe epidemic, fine-tooth-combed by the army over and over again, its patriotism long since strained to the breaking point, could be once more kindled into a *furor teutonicus* and formed into a *levée en masse*.

Yet in the absence of formal surrender what could the government do to achieve a half-way tolerable armistice and peace? Actually, Hintze displayed amazing initiative from the moment when the pleas of the section chiefs at headquarters reached him. He seems to have realized at the outset that Hertling's government had no chance whatever of having any "peace offer" taken seriously abroad—just as there was no chance for Ludendorff to get anything out of a military armistice commission except an outright surrender.

On September 28 Hintze had his foreign ministry work out a most extraordinary document, an entirely new domestic and foreign policy program for Germany. It demanded the immediate formation of a new government on a broad national basis, by the voluntary action of the Kaiser. "To this end it would be desirable if by tomorrow night a message were received, accepting the proffered resignation of Count Hertling and charging Vice Chancellor Payer with immediately making proposals to the Kaiser concerning a new chancellor and the composition of a new government." Such proposals were to be worked out in closest cooperation with the elected representatives of the people, and they were to encompass the full resources of the nation on the broadest possible basis.

Hintze himself dubbed this proposal a "revolution from above." The term does not quite fit, for it did not yet contemplate a truly democratic government, nor even one that would be formed from delegates of the majority parties, but only "joint action" with the Reichstag, strong emphasis being placed on the imperial initiative. Yet undoubtedly the "broadest possible national basis" meant that social democrats were to enter the government, and this was bound to send a shudder through all the conservative elements in traditionally imperial Germany, including Hertling himself who—as Hintze well knew from talks he had had with him during the preceding weeks—was opposed to any increased parliamentarianism in his government and particularly the inclusion of administratively untrained social democrats.[74]

But Hintze was convinced that what he was proposing was absolutely essential. On the domestic scene, democratization was the only way of softening the impact of Germany's impending defeat on the masses, in other words, of forestalling a "revolution from below." As for the field of foreign affairs, Hintze was equally convinced that a more united nation with stronger confidence in its government was an essential element in the armistice negotiations to come. Lastly, Hintze had been repeatedly told by his foreign service that Hertling's government—including, alas, himself—was accounted abroad a mere tool in the hands of the militarists, which would virtually preclude the kind of confidential talks with Wilson which Hintze contemplated.[75] He drew the appropriate consequences himself, immediately asking to be relieved and getting his resignation accepted by October 4, against the vigorous opposition of the Kaiser and even representations on the part of Ludendorff, who then still regarded him as an essential diplomatic savior.

During the last weeks in September, moreover, the majority parties had lost faith more and more in Hertling's leadership. This led to the drafting—in the first instance by the social democrats—of a comprehensive program for a new government, the main feature of which was to be far greater independence from the OHL.[76] By the time Hintze had his own program worked out in the foreign ministry on September 28, he could thus be sure that he would find powerful political backing in the Reichstag. Still, it was a most extraordinary thing for a minister to sponsor a document predicating the resignation of his chief without even informing him.[77]

Hintze's program proposed that the new German government should, "at the proper time," approach Wilson with the request that he take charge of restoring peace and to that end ask all the belligerent powers to send plenipotentiary delegates to Washington. "In accordance with whatever wishes may be voiced by the military, the president may be asked to invite the belligerents at the same time to conclude an immediate armistice." He was further to be advised that the Quadruple Alliance was disposed, under certain conditions, to accept his well-known Fourteen Points as a basis for peace negotiations.

It will be seen that even then the German foreign ministry was not yet contemplating asking for an immediate armistice. What Hintze envisaged was to continue and intensify his efforts, long since underway, to reach President Wilson through a Swiss or American intermediary and to enlist the president himself as an intermediary in the achievement of a moderate peace.[78] The memorandum of September 28 said at the end that wires would be immediately dispatched to the various German missions in neutral countries, asking for opinions on which American envoy might be most suitable for the transmission of a confidential message to Wilson.[79]

In his reply from Switzerland Romberg said that the American envoy in Berne was totally unsuitable for such a mission. He also rejected an expedient proposed by Hintze, namely that the American envoy at The Hague, John W. Garrett, be recruited—he happened to be in Berne and was known both as an eminently reasonable man and a personal friend of the president. This approach would be merely interpreted as another German trick, and the Americans would not fall for it. Romberg thought that Sulzer might be more suitable, or McNally, whom he described as "absolutely reliable" [sic]. Romberg also made reference to Wilson's speech of September 27 (see p. 339), which made it seem quite hopeless to discuss with the American president any peace program other than his own. Wilson expected that program to be accepted without reservations.[80]

Burián in Vienna voiced strong objections against using an American intermediary in Hintze's peace plan, to which he agreed in principle. A secret diplomatic approach merely risked outright rejection or an unacceptable response that would amount to intervention in the internal affairs of the Central Powers.[81] Berlin was apparently impressed with this argument, especially since it had been the intention there from the outset to leave it to Wilson whether he wished to conduct the talks in private or in public. A more important consideration was that secret preliminary talks would have taken time, and time was precisely what was lacking, as Hintze discovered in the discussions he held at Spa on September 29, first with the OHL and then with the Kaiser.

The skill and vigor with which the minister managed to advance his own program of the preceding day are truly remarkable. Both Ludendorff and the Kaiser were too badly shaken to dare protest even the "revolution from above"—the formation of a parliamentary government to include the social democrats.[82] Hintze shrewdly explained to them that there was a definite danger of revolution in the wake of the immense shock that would convulse the nation with the news of the armistice request and the realization that the war was lost beyond recall. There were only two ways of meeting this threat: either a new popular government, or a military dictatorship. It was clear that the latter alternative was scarcely feasible at the moment of complete defeat.

Hertling arrived at Spa in the afternoon—Hintze had deliberately anticipated him—and almost persuaded the Kaiser to revoke his assent to a change in the government and to the so-called "peace offer"; but Hintze intervened once again with the greatest vigor, citing the urgent OHL demand for an armistice. He virtually snatched the signed decree he had prepared from under the Kaiser's hands. He promptly made the decision to appeal to Wilson for an armistice and for peace irrevocable by having the proposal wired to Vienna and Istanbul that same evening.

But Hintze also successfully stood up to the OHL, which demanded that the Armistice appeal be issued at once, even before the reorganization of the government. He did pledge, however, that the new government would be formed by October 1, i.e., within two days! To this end he immediately returned to Berlin where, on October 1, he dropped the idea of confidential preliminary talks with Wilson. He wired Vienna that the peace note would be transmitted to the president through normal diplomatic channels, i.e., through Switzerland, which was acting as the protective power.

Hintze's firm and clear-cut program made him, for the moment, the central figure on the German political scene following Hertling's fall, which he had staged. Indeed, from this time on, OHL dominance within the German government began to dwindle. In its relations with the new parliamentary government, the OHL gradually declined to the level of a mere advisory agency rather than being the one that made all the important decisions; but this development took a good deal of time and in retrospect we can only marvel at the caution, indeed, the outright timidity with which the new men treated the military views and public authority of the famed Ludendorff, down to the end of October, when making their political decisions.

This brought serious consequences during the very first days, while the new government was being formed. It was put together with incredible haste and casual legality, for by October 1, Ludendorff was wiring every few hours, demanding that the peace offer be made instantly, without waiting for a new government. The front was still holding, but there was no way of foretelling what the morrow would bring: "If by seven or eight o'clock tonight there is assurance that Prince Max of Baden will form a government, I agree to a delay until tomorrow morning. If there is any doubt about the formation of a government, the declaration to the foreign governments should, in my view, be issued tonight."

The formation of a parliamentary coalition government is probably one of the most time-consuming political endeavors. Vice Chancellor Payer had been entrusted with the formation of the new government, on Hintze's proposal, but Payer refused to take on the chancellorship himself, insisting that the change in the political system must be made as outwardly visible as possible. Instead, he got the majority parties to agree to the appointment of Prince Max of Baden, whose appearance on the political stage is surely one of the strangest phenomena in the history of the Wilhelminian Germany.

The summoning of Prince Max was the work of his liberal democratic friends, above all of the democratic deputy Haussmann, who had been promoting his candidature ever since 1917. Another man behind it was Colonel Haeften, Ludendorff's confidant and go-between, but also enjoying the trust of Prince Max. Haeften was henceforth to play an amazingly important political role.[83] His feat of gaining Ludendorff's assent to the appointment of Prince Max, while certainly not saddling the OHL with responsibility for it, may have ultimately carried the day with the Kaiser, who was originally reluctant to summon the prince.

What the OHL was responsible for was the haste with which the deliberations of the majority parties on the formation of the new government took place on October 1. The politicians were told that their democratization plans were in danger, unless they promptly agreed on a cabinet. One gains the impression that even so, the politicians were very much at a loss.[84] All manner of lists were got up, covering the distribution of cabinet posts among the parties, but no proposals were forthcoming at all for the most important post, that of Chancellor, when Payer declined. There was a general air of resignation when Prince Max suddenly appeared in Berlin, summoned on the very morning of October 1 by Colonel Haeften, by agreement with the Kaiser's cabinet chief, Berg.

The prince was a man of character and considerable appeal who soon managed to win over even a Scheidemann, but beyond any doubt his appointment was a blunder, based on misconceptions. It was Payer's intention to emphasize to the world that the political system had changed in Germany, but the appointment to the Chancellorship of a leading aristocrat was calculated to accomplish the precise opposite, particularly since the prince had not even been nominated by the Reichstag. It was soon clear, moreover, that owing to his delicate health and lack of political experience he could not have conducted his high office at all without the close support of his deputy, Payer. In practice it was Payer who presided over by far the greater number of meetings of the new war cabinet.

The prince himself, like his friends and followers, greatly overestimated his prestige at home and abroad as a liberal statesman, as well as his influence on the Kaiser by virtue of his status as a federal sovereign. Haussmann, moreover, was quite mistaken in regarding the prince's own political program as "democratic" in any proper sense; and this error is not easy to explain, even taking into account the fuzzy idealism that marked many of the prince's earlier political pronouncements.[85]

We are already familiar with his plans and hopes in the field of foreign affairs, and those of his youthful adviser Kurt Hahn, whom he kept near him as a kind of amanuensis when he became Chancellor. The prince always remained dedicated to a negotiated peace, never realizing that the time for such a peace had long passed. He was horrified when he learned, on the afternoon of October 1, that his first act as Chancellor was to be to sign a peace and armistice offer to Germany's enemies. What he had envisaged as his first act was to deliver a major speech before the Reichstag, convincing the world of Germany's just cause and the new government's moderate peace aims, and making the German people understand why a new peace offer must now be made. The prince, however, also wished to proclaim Germany's absolute determination to "fight to the death, if it were confronted with dishonorable terms." This, in his view, would paralyze the enemy's aggressive power.[86]

These were high-minded notions of an upright patriot; but would such a speech have made the slightest impression abroad? Would it not have been taken as a sign that German "militarism" was continuing unchanged, even under the new government, especially since Ludendorff was remaining at his post? The Entente would scarcely have read any reason for moderating its war aims into such a speech. On the domestic scene it would have certainly reassured many German patriots; and indeed, Payer had justified the prince's appointment as Chancellor on the grounds that as a leading aristocrat he stood above party and would succeed in reconciling even rightist circles to the government's new course. It needs saying, however, that any appeal to "fight to the death" would have only alienated the terrified and over-propagandized masses of the left, whose confidence had to be maintained above all. Prince Max's own vision of his mission—to reconcile extreme left and extreme right—was based on pure delusion.

On the other side, the nervous haste with which Ludendorff kept pressing for an immediate armistice offer had fateful political consequences, especially after Ludendorff's emissary, Major von dem Bussche, drew an unvarnished picture of the situation at the front for the Berlin deputies—for the conservative leaders on September 30, for the other party leaders on the morning of October 2.[87] So abrupt a reversal from supreme confidence to utter defeatism, coming without any warning, was bound to all but destroy faith in the political as well as the military leadership, with incalculable and possibly revolutionary implications. It was quite in keeping with Ludendorff's brand of militarism to ignore these implications and concentrate exclusively on the disastrous threat to the fighting front—which was actually exaggerated. The OHL had no clear picture of what the step it so urgently requested meant in political terms. By October 5 the OHL was not yet even familiar with the text of Wilson's Fourteen Points.[88]

We thus have the contradictory pictures of a government that wished to "stick it out," and of a military command that wished to give up at once. It looked for a while as though Prince Max would refuse to accept the office of Chancellor. He said he would withdraw unless Ludendorff granted him a brief grace period to deliver his speech and gauge its effect—initially he spoke of two weeks, then of two or three days. When none of this availed and he found himself completely isolated among the leading political personalities, he accepted on the evening of October 3 and at once signed the note to Wilson which Hintze submitted to him. In addition to asking for the convocation of a peace conference, it accepted without reservation all the peace programs the president had put forward from January 8 to September 27, as a basis for peace negotiations. It further requested the immediate conclusion of an armistice.

This note was dispatched to Berne during the night of October 3-4. Once again Ludendorff's will proved to be the stronger, and in yielding, the prince gave away his political authority at the very moment of his appointment. All the same, his political stand was objectively untenable. Delaying the note by a matter of days or weeks would not have altered its political effect or its admission of defeat. The semblance of a voluntary act, on which the prince was so intent, could not have been attained in any event. No one anywhere would have believed that the new government was suing for an armistice from pure love of peace, without the harshest kind of military pressure.

It was proper, even though rather unusual, for the armistice plea to be included in the Chancellor's peace note, in accordance with Hintze's proposal, rather than being left to the generals. This seemed the only way of playing off the American president as an intermediary from the outset—and the Germans staked their last hopes in Wilson, whose sense of justice they thought they could trust, even though his statements on Alsace-Lorraine and the Polish-speaking provinces of Germany in his Fourteen Points speech had always given them serious pause for thought.

By not letting the OHL—i.e., Hindenburg and Ludendorff—make the pilgrimage to the enemy camp, white flag in hand, the civil government did, however, invite grave moral odium. Ignorant of the true situation or unwilling to admit it, the extreme nationalists ever after charged it with treason to the German cause. Prince Max on his part, for reasons of policy as well as decency, never made public the fact that the armistice plea originated with the military and that they were the ones who pressed it so anxiously. The leaders of the majority parties, by the way, were equally hesitant, though they were well aware that a myth of a "stab in the back" might be in the making.[89]

For lack of space alone we must forego giving the depressing details of the new war cabinet's October deliberations on the course of the negotiations with Wilson.[90] The meetings were often turbulent, initially revealing more than once the new Chancellor's reluctance to leave Germany's destiny to the American president without let or hindrance. The ministers who had been brought into the cabinet from the majority parties—mainly Erzberger and Scheidemann, but also the new foreign minister, Solf—on their part wished by all means to avoid impeding Wilson in his possible role of peace mediator.

In his first Reichstag speech, scheduled for October 5, Prince Max wished to discuss Wilson's Fourteen Points at length in their application to German interests. He wanted to show the enemy that "we still have our breath," thereby "expunging the humiliation" implicit in the German peace note; but he encountered so much resistance that it almost came to another government crisis.[91] The prince was forced to yield, to the deep disappointment of his adjutant Hahn who had already drafted the speech, together with Privy Councilor Simons of the foreign ministry.

A more serious crisis arose after October 9, when a Swiss newspaper published a highly indiscreet letter which the prince had sent on January 12 to his cousin, Prince Alexander of Hohenlohe-Schillingsfürst, who lived in Switzerland and was a radical pacifist. The letter had bitterly attacked the Reichstag's peace resolution and sharply criticized parliamentarianization of the government. For the moment it seemed as though the "new era" Prince Max had just proclaimed in the Reichstag had forfeited all claim to credibility, and that he would have to resign. It casts a glaring light on the predicament of the majority parties that in the end the deputies accepted Haussmann's reassurances and the shrewd and dignified defense the prince himself put forward.

In America, however, the letter was grist for the mill of anti-German propaganda, and Wilson himself lost any confidence he may have had in the new German government.[92] The new Chancellor's authority with his associates and with the majority parties was, of course, seriously impaired. Henceforth the policy of caution, resignation, and indulgence in respect of Wilson's demands gained the upper hand even more completely within the German cabinet.

That cabinet, however, was at a serious disadvantage, since it was reduced largely to guesswork, where the American president was concerned. Its members were more or less in the dark about the ultimate purposes he pursued. Much intelligence on this subject kept coming in from neutral countries; but it was full of contradictions and largely recognizable as mere conjecture and rumormongering. The German foreign ministry did treat Romberg's reports from Switzerland with considerable respect; but Romberg's source, McNally, about whom we heard in Chapter 8, got his intelligence almost exclusively at second hand, from discussions with American diplomats and politicians in Switzerland.[93] His assignment from Washington was purely military rather than political.

Wilson's first note of reply, on October 8, was couched in such moderate and courteous terms as to create a false sense of reassurance. The Germans had long anticipated that they would have to accept the Fourteen Points without reservations, together with evacuation of the occupied territories in the west, before an armistice would be granted; and they were confident of being able to give a plausible answer to the question asked at the conclusion of the note: Did the Chancellor speak in the name of the German people, or did he still represent the powers that had been in control of the war so far? The reply would be that the new government sprang from negotiations with the Reichstag, hence represented the popular will.

After consulting McNally, Romberg, however, urged that a clear picture be given of the domestic political changes that had been instituted, in order to redress the American people's ignorance of the situation in Germany. In consequence the German foreign ministry, on October 13, sent Romberg a report giving a brief account of the constitutional changes that had either been effected or impended and picturing them as the beginning of a sharp turn of course. Romberg was to try to have the Swiss envoy inform the president in person of these circumstances, but this proved to be impracticable.[94]

Unfortunately, at this very moment, on October 12, a young U-boat commander sank the British passenger ship *Leinster,* not with one but with two torpedoes, a disaster in which some 600 people died, including a great many women and children.[95] This incident completely precluded any personal contact with Wilson, such as had been contemplated. It hit Wilson at his most sensitive spot, reviving his ire over "barbaric German militarism" and immediately introducing a much sharper note into the exchange of messages.

In the preparation of the first German reply note of October 12 the OHL was consulted, but there were no serious difficulties about its text. Ludendorff could have wished that it were expressly specified that the armistice should begin even before the evacuation of the occupied territories, and that several weeks would be allowed to effect that evacuation; but he was reconciled to these clauses being cut, evidently in the expectation that this matter could be settled in the "mixed commission" proposed by the Germans for that purpose. Nor did he pick up the demand then being put to the government by the conservative leaders and Walther Rathenau: Refuse to evacuate and break off negotiations with Wilson! When the Chancellor asked him very precisely formulated questions about the military situation, he answered cautiously and evasively rather than confidently, though the panic of the early October days had clearly ebbed.

There was general agreement that Germany would not accept armistice terms making it impossible to resume hostilities and doing violence to German honor. Ludendorff did say expressly that it were better to withdraw to the German borders, there to resume the struggle if it became necessary, rather than to risk a breakthrough of the present untenable positions. He put no faith in the kind of *levée en masse* propagated by Rathenau. What is highly significant is that one phrase was taken into the reply note at the request of the OHL: Germany expected that the powers allied with America would also base themselves on Wilson's Fourteen Points. This was very welcome to Wilson and facilitated his peace policy.

The exchange with the president thus seemed initially to develop with good prospects of success—when suddenly a second note on October 14 destroyed all hope and brought on a serious German political crisis; but before we discuss this at length it will be useful to consider Wilson's own political situation, his ultimate purposes, and the attitude of his allies.

Part 3

Wilson's Ambiguous Attitude;
The Allies Intent upon Victory

THE UNCERTAINTY about Wilson's ultimate goals that haunted the German statesmen was not purely a matter of inadequate intelligence. In America too none really knew precisely what he wanted. The American president's policies at this late stage of the war were not only wavering but downright contradictory.

On the one hand he clung steadfastly to his ideal of a "just and enduring peace" that would satisfy all the nations of the world, and to the democratic right of self-determination. On the other hand, he had proclaimed that the war was being fought to "make the world safe for democracy," and he understood this to mean the destruction of the system of "willful autocracy" which he saw embodied in Germany. This, of course, implied the most active intervention in the traditional German body politic, without any regard to "self-determination."

Wilson told the British diplomat Wiseman on October 16 that he was dismayed at his fellow countrymen's war fervor, and he rejected utterly any "peace of vengeance."[96] This, however, did not keep him from telling another foreign visitor that the German leaders would have to be tried in a court of justice after their defeat.[97]

The ambivalence of Wilson's stand was very apparent in his speech of September 27, already cited. It proclaimed once again with warmth and ardor the American ideals of "impartial justice" and durable international peace, summarized in five points; but in it Wilson also said that it was impossible to make agreements with the governments of the Central Powers, for they were without honor and did not keep their word.[98] In rejecting the bargaining process on principle, he was, of course, opening the door to a dictated peace, the very thing he condemned time and again. He probably never viewed this as a contradiction himself, for his ideal war aims included the liberation of the Germans from their "autocratic and militaristic overlords." Once they were gone, it should be possible to reach an understanding with the democratically governed German people, who were surely as peaceable as any other.

In these circumstances the German government probably followed the best possible counsel in asking Wilson to convoke a peace conference on the basis of his Fourteen Points, which it accepted in advance without any reservations; for this was indeed Wilson's great dream. As head of the American superpower, he wanted to bring the world a peace fashioned after his own idealistic program, with a fair balance of justice, freedom of the seas, and a league of nations. Now the Germans seemed at last ready for such a thing, indeed, were beseeching him to get the great enterprise underway as swiftly as possible—and he could not simply refuse without going back on his own word. Nor could he simply delay his reply, as Colonel House proposed, for in that case the Germans were likely to lose faith in him. They might then address their peace proposals directly to London and Paris, which would deprive Wilson of his great role as mediator and arbitrator.

Actually, Wilson stood quite alone with his pacifist ideals among his people and even his advisers. The American people had gone quite war-mad, as House put it, since American arms had won such visibly great successes on European soil, and the Germans, vaunted as the world's soldiers, seemed to be succumbing to them. No one wanted peace or armistice until full military triumph had been tasted, possibly a march right through the gates of Berlin. "Unconditional surrender" was the watchword of the day, not peace and armistice talks.

Even the usually moderate Colonel House thought that Generalissimo Foch should be encouraged to drive more and more wedges into the German front, until it were completely disrupted, Wilson meanwhile wearing down the Germans by diplomatic attrition.[99] No peace with the Hohenzollerns, cried the *New York Times,* America's most important political opinion-maker, on October 6, when the German peace request was received. If Germany wanted peace, let it depose its irresponsible braggart of a Kaiser and let a people's government speak.

On the same day a Republican Senator introduced a resolution that rejected any thought of armistice until the Germans had dissolved their army, delivered to the victorious powers their arms, munitions, and warships, agreed to pay to the last cent for all the war damage they had caused, repaid the French war indemnity of 1871, and punished all "war criminals," whether they had committed their crimes on land or at sea. Senator Henry Cabot Lodge, a leading Republican member of the Senate Foreign Affairs Committee, wrote to Theodore Roosevelt that if America granted an armistice or bargained for a negotiated peace, it would have lost the war. American soldiers would bitterly resent being kept from marching into Germany. The German peace request was widely regarded as a mere trap, to tempt Wilson into a negotiated peace and obtain a breathing space for the exhausted German army.

Thus the president was subjected to a great many pressures of public opinion in making his decisions. What lent these pressures even greater force was the fact that Congressional elections impended on November 5. Their outcome would determine whether Wilson's party, the Democrats, kept their narrow majority. His main adversary, former president Theodore Roosevelt, and the Republican party were doing their best to fan the flames of war enthusiasm in an effort to undermine Wilson's position. His Fourteen Points were extremely unpopular, and his first reply note to the government of Prince Max of Baden aroused much criticism because of its mild tone. The Allies too were disappointed by it.

This conciliatory tone, however, was by no means a sign of peace sentiments, but rather nothing more than a tactical calculation. The Germans were to be encouraged to continue negotiating with the president for the time being, until the Fourteen Points program had been formally fixed—they were really Wilson's foremost concern. He was not nearly so much interested in the chief concern of the Germans—the swift conclusion of an armistice—especially when all America was screaming for "unconditional surrender."

It is true that Wilson did not want a "peace of vengeance," nor a dictated peace, as the Republicans demanded. He was concerned lest the chance for peace be missed because his European allies scaled the price too high, and he certainly did not wish to slam the door in the Germans' face. Yet when the Allies, in a series of telegrams on October 9, insisted that only their generals in the field were in a position to judge when and how the din of battle was to be silenced, Wilson yielded to their demands. Let the war council in Versailles decide whether the time had come for an armistice, and settle its terms as well. They would probably be too harsh for the vanquished, perhaps altogether unacceptable—but in that case the governments could still intervene.

When Wilson, on October 14, dispatched Colonel House to Paris as his deputy on the supreme war council, he gave the colonel no instructions whatever concerning the armistice question. He did, however, agree with the colonel on this formulation: Once the Germans were beaten, they would accept any terms. If they were not yet beaten, America did not wish them to accept any terms—in other words, the Germans were not to be allowed to make it more difficult, by their conciliatory attitude, for America to continue the war.

Presenting this approach to the British diplomat, Sir William Wiseman, Wilson justified his distrust of Prince Max's government by reference to the prince's hapless letter to his cousin Hohenlohe, which had become known to Wilson on October 6.[100] The "experts," consulted by the American State Department, could not agree on what the constitutional reforms contemplated by the Germans meant.[101] Some warned against excessive intervention in the domestic affairs of Germany. President Lowell of Harvard University wrote that when institutions expected to enjoy popular support appeared to be forced on the people, they were almost certain to lose their popularity swiftly. Another called for the Kaiser's abdication, while still another thought that unimportant.

Most of the advisers did agree, however, that the reforms effected by Prince Max of Baden were inadequate. Even William C. Bullitt, an expert on Germany, a friend of Kurt Hahn, and later on American ambassador in Russia, initially doubted that the new Chancellor was able and willing to form a government responsible to the legislature and thus deriving its power from the people. On October 4 he told Wilson that in his view the reins of power still lay in the hands of the Kaiser and the military leaders.

The crucial element for Wilson and his foreign secretary Lansing was the pressure of public opinion rather than the judgment of the "experts."[102] The president, in countless speeches and solemn pronouncements, had charged German "autocracy" with kindling the war and continually threatening the peace of the world. He had proclaimed the destruction of that autocracy to be the proper goal of the war. Now he had become the prisoner of his own war propaganda, so to speak. The American man in the street was not in the least interested in whatever reforms the Germans might effect in their complex constitution. For him the Kaiser was the epitome of the sinister despot, while Ludendorff was the archetype of the German militarist. Both would have to go before anyone could believe that Germany was liberated and converted to democracy. Not just newspaper editorials but petitions by mass organizations implored the president to tell the Germans unmistakably that they must push the man who had initiated this barbarous war off the throne. The sinking of the *Leinster* came at just the right moment to raise American war passions to white heat.

Wilson had no choice but to strike an altogether different note in his second message to the German government, if he wished to maintain his position of leadership. It was dispatched on October 14 and demanded not only evacuation of all occupied territory but fully satisfactory guarantees for the continuance of Allied military superiority. It further leveled serious charges against the continuing inhuman methods of naval warfare practiced by the German U-boats, as well as against the allegedly unprovoked and barbarous destruction of French and Belgian localities by the receding German troops. Above all, it grew extremely discursive and deliberately ambiguous in speaking of the necessity for putting an end to the arbitrary military power that had hitherto governed the destiny of the German people and that represented a threat to the whole world. Germany had it within its power to change this; and it would never have peace unless this change were effected in a clear-cut and satisfactory way.

It was not exactly an open appeal to the German people to rise in revolution; but it was a subtle and carefully calculated effort to create domestic confusion within Germany and thus to cripple German fighting morale beyond redemption. This was indeed the goal Wilson had been pursuing in his war speeches for years. Did he really want the German monarchy to fall by revolution? Was he deliberately aiming at a German republic, in the expectation that it would be a better guarantor of peace in the world?

We shall yet have to consider the devastating effect on the German people of Wilson's second note, and the frantic efforts of the German government to discover by diplomatic hook or crook whether the president really wanted the Hohenzollern dynasty deposed, or whether he would be content if it were transformed into a merely ceremonial institution on the British model.

Even today, with much source material from inside Wilson's immediate environment available, the question cannot be unequivocally answered. It may not even have interested Wilson particularly. Presumably he was not as much concerned with the form of the German government as such as with making it clear to the world that autocracy and militarism had no future in Germany, i.e., that the Hohenzollern dynasty no longer held any power. He needed a visible blow of that kind, for its propaganda effect, to safeguard his own position, and not least, to influence the Congressional elections. He had to show himself as the strong man who was willing and able to tackle the awesome and centuries-old House of Hohenzollern and bring it down.

Yet as an ally of the British Empire, Wilson could not openly throw down the gage to the monarchial system as such; and even in his most radical formulations he barely skirted doing so. He told Wiseman on October 16 that if the Allies really cornered and humiliated the German people, they would destroy all governmental authority and Bolshevism would rush into the resulting vacuum. Germany must not be ground into the dust, or there would be nothing left to build on.

Wilson was considerably embarrassed by the shrewdly formulated reply of the German government to his second note. Drafted after the bitterest arguments, it pointed to the sweeping changes in the German constitution, along liberal democratic lines, already effected with the greatest dispatch. It was certainly not feasible to deny outright that any such reforms had taken place. Yet the Republicans professed fury over the latest German "trick"; and Senator Lodge proposed in the Senate that the president be enjoined from any further negotiation with Germany.

Wilson engaged in long deliberations with his cabinet on what was to be done, but opinion was sharply divided and there was much uncertainty. In the end he voiced his fears that in the event of an upheaval in Germany Bolshevism might spread in Europe. The Kaiser would probably have to be kept, he said, to control the Bolshevist menace and maintain some form of order. On the following day, October 23, he convened his smaller war cabinet, where he initially displayed the same uncertainty.

Ultimately, however, he drew from his pocket the finished draft of a third note, which outdid all its predecessors in its massive attacks on Germany's "military rulers and monarchist autocrats." The German people, he said, still lacked the means of ordering the military authorities to submit to the popular will; and as for the power of the kings of Prussia to control the policies of the German Reich, it seemed virtually indestructible. The United States would have to decline to negotiate with these entrenched powers, which were undeserving of trust. If they remained at the helm, Germany would be in no position to talk about peace terms. It would have to surrender.

It is clear that while the president was apprehensive of the danger of revolution, he did not, in the event, shrink from actually unleashing it by an act of crude intervention in the internal political life of Germany; and contemplating the incalculable historical consequences of that intervention, it is depressing to note how closely it was meshed with electioneering in the American style and with considerations of strengthening the president's position at home.

It is no less depressing to note, however, that there was no real substance to Wilson's claim that Allied terms for an armistice and peace depended on the overthrow of the "old powers." The British and the French, who presently had a much closer hold on Germany's destiny than the American peace prophet, never dreamed of making their peace and armistice terms dependent on any degree of German "democratization."[103] It is true that Lloyd George had also proclaimed time and again that the war must not end until the power of German militarism were broken. Like Wilson, he distrusted the government of Prince Max of Baden, who had been designated by the *Kriegsrat* (war council) rather than a democratic body. As for the democratization of Germany, Lloyd George regarded that as a dummy façade, a mere ruse to deceive the Allies.

Yet Lloyd George did not dream of making an armistice dependent on Germany actually carrying out its program of democratization. All he wanted was to see the Germans militarily subjugated to the will of their vanquishers. They would have to be beaten in the field beyond any doubt, for any other issue of the war would represent a tremendous triumph for them.[104] The British field marshal, Wilson, was profoundly irked that the president was unwilling to treat with the Hohenzollerns. That was merely paving the way for Bolshevism.

When the British war cabinet debated Wilson's second peace note and the German reply, there was much dissatisfaction over the fact that the president was so deeply preoccupied with problems of German domestic politics instead of discussing the military aspects of an armistice with his allies. Washington was always talking about not permitting a "peace of vengeance," Austen Chamberlain complained; but did not the demand for the elimination of "arbitrary power" in Germany amount to precisely such a peace? Such an American policy was strongly reminiscent of the notorious slogan, "No Peace with Huerta!" (the former president of Mexico). Other cabinet members asked what was the use of the German constitutional reforms so eagerly pursued by Wilson. Even if Germany had the same kind of liberal constitution as Great Britain and the United States, surely that was no guarantee against further military surprises.[105]

Paris was no less irate over Wilson's peace notes. Initially Clémenceau disdained even to take notice of the German-American negotiations, since they had been initiated and conducted without consultation with the Allies. Immediately after the dispatch of the first German peace note, he had Marshal Foch work out armistice terms in draft form, and this was done by

October 8. The terms were tantamount to an unconditional surrender by Germany. Belgium, France, Alsace-Lorraine, and Luxembourg were to be evacuated within two weeks and their inhabitants repatriated. Any remaining troops—for example, the wounded—would become prisoners-of-war.

To enable the Allies to resume hostilities, if necessary, two or three bridgeheads on the far side of the Rhine were to be occupied within two weeks—at Rastatt, Strasbourg, and Neu-Breisach, each the center of a twenty-mile semicircle. Within thirty days German troops were to clear out of the whole left bank of the Rhine, which would be occupied and administered by the Allies, in order to insure the payment of reparations to be fixed at a later date.

All war material and supplies that could not be easily moved were to be left behind intact, likewise all rail equipment and military and industrial installations. In return, hostilities were to cease twenty-four hours after the Germans signed these terms. They were approved by Clémenceau, intensively discussed with the British in the ensuing weeks and expanded and made more stringent but without essential alterations.

Equally zealous efforts were underway in Britain to crystallize peace terms without respect to American ideas. Sir Henry Wilson, the British chief of staff, thought it a piece of effrontery that the Germans had approached the American president at all. He felt there should be no treating with the *boches* until they were disarmed and pushed back beyond the Rhine. Most active of all were the British admirals, who had begun their discussions about the armistice even before the first German peace note had arrived in Washington. They wanted the entire German high seas fleet surrendered, including all U-boats. There were protracted debates on these matters, and Lloyd George's government did not reach agreement with the generals and admirals as swiftly as Clémenceau did with Foch—nor for that matter did the British generals and admirals among themselves.

Nevertheless, all the Entente powers were intent on preventing Wilson from hammering out the armistice terms with Germany alone. As early as October 6, they jointly approved the general outlines of an armistice with the Quadruple Alliance—complete evacuation of France, Belgium, Luxembourg, and Italy; a withdrawal not merely to the old German borders but beyond the Rhine; evacuation of Alsace-Lorraine without occupation by Allied forces; the same procedure in the South Tyrol and Istria; evacuation of Serbia, Montenegro, and the Caucasus; preparations for the immediate withdrawal from all former Russian and Rumanian territory; immediate cessation of U-boat warfare with continuation of the Allied blockade. On October 8 these terms were hardened. Prisoners-of-war held by the Germans were to be returned at once, while German prisoners were to be retained to help in the reconstruction of ruined areas. The fortresses of Metz, Thionville, Strasbourg, and Neu-Breisach, and the fortifications of Lille and the island of Heligoland were to be surrendered to the Allies at once. The justification for all this was that no credence could be given to any promise given by the Germans, who could not be relied upon to abide by the ordinary code of honor.

Talks on this program went on until November 4, and we need not trace them in detail. German hopes that Wilson would succeed in moderating the terms proved vain. He did wire House on October 28 pleading for such moderation. He agreed that the terms should be such as to preclude the Germans resuming hostilities, but beyond that goal they should be as moderate and reasonable as possible, for going too far in the matter of guarantees would make it difficult if not impossible to conclude a real peace. The somewhat more moderate-sounding proposals put forward by Haig, Milner, and Pétain, as relayed to Wilson by Pershing, seemed to the president safer than those of Foch. Foresight was wiser than immediate advantage.[106]

On October 26 the president issued a concrete directive to Pershing through his secretary of war, Newton Diehl Baker. He was to raise the question of whether Allied or American occupation of Alsace-Lorraine after the German evacuation were really necessary. The president also doubted whether any occupation of German territory on the right bank of the Rhine were advisable. Armistice or no, such a thing would virtually amount to an invasion of Germany. In sum, Wilson thought the armistice terms must be sufficiently severe to prevent a resumption of hostilities by the Germans, but not humiliating beyond that point, since otherwise they would merely serve to strengthen the hand of the military party in Germany.[107]

Wilson was clearly in earnest about his program for a moderate and therefore durable peace. On occasion he did manage to impress his European allies with his moral fervor. Late in October, at a session of the British war cabinet, Lloyd George said in his nonchalant way that now at last the Allies were free to put the lash on the Germans' backs, and he asked whether this should not be continued for a while, even though the Germans were now giving up. After all, France's industry had been devastated, while Germany's had got off virtually unscathed! Many people in Britain were calling for retribution.

When he was done, Foreign Secretary Balfour read a report from Wiseman, to whom Wilson had said shortly before that he would be ashamed to call himself an American if American troops were to destroy even a single German town. That put an immediate end to the discussion, and there was no further call for continuing the war, if a favorable armistice could be secured now. Actually, this had been the predominant view right along.[108]

Thus Wilson did exert a certain influence over the European allies in exhorting and warning them against unrestrained vengeance. Yet he was too remote from the focus of military decision to be effective in that area, nor did he have the necessary insight into the military and technical contingencies which the Allied high command had to consider. Indeed, American generals had only a small share in these discussions. The armistice platforms of October 6 and 8 were deliberately formulated in their absence, in order to show that the Allies did not wish to be masterminded by Wilson.

General Tasker H. Bliss, American representative on the Allied war council, was shown these plans only subsequently. He did not dare subscribe to them at once, without instructions from Washington, although personally he agreed with them. What worried him was that the Allied generals were even now transcending the military sphere and fixing terms that anticipated the peace to come.[109] His concern was amply justified.

Late in October General Bliss proposed that in place of an armistice Germany's land and naval forces be completely disarmed and demobilized. It was a highly impractical proposal, and it was not taken seriously in the war council. As it happened, General John J. Pershing, commander-in-chief of the American forces, was the only general among the Allies who strongly opposed an armistice and wished to continue the war, along the lines advocated by the pro-war press in the United States. (Pershing seems to have been close to the Republican party.)

There was thus no American advocate of milder peace terms in the Allied war council. The lone dissenter was Field Marshal Haig, who had a very high opinion of German discipline and fighting power and was loath to drive the Germans to desperation. It was Foch who saw clearly that German fighting power was at an end.

It was only on October 26 that Colonel House at last appeared in Paris as Wilson's representative, but he too raised no particular objections to the armistice terms the generals had agreed on. House's main concern, pursued with the greatest tenacity, was to put over Wilson's Fourteen Points as the basis for armistice and peace. He fought for this goal with considerable vigor, not even shrinking from political threats, especially against the British, who wanted no part of "freedom of the seas," which would mean foregoing their naval hegemony and blockade rights.

This constituted a serious conflict of interests between the new world power and the old, and no real settlement was reached, only a compromise formula which postponed the settlement to a later date. House thought himself highly successful in securing this compromise and fending off further objections to the Fourteen Points by Clémenceau. Thus the German tactics did result in formal assurances that the peace would be concluded on the basis of the American program. Unfortunately Wilson stood absolutely alone among his own people with his Fourteen Points, and his program was so vaguely formulated and permitted so many interpretations that its practical success was severely circumscribed.

In the end the Germans could only thank their lucky stars that they were granted an armistice at all, instead of it being denied them, as the American people would have preferred. When Colonel House asked Field Marshal Foch whether it would not be better to fight on, the Frenchman gave a very characteristic reply:

> I don't wage war just for its own sake. If an armistice fulfills the conditions we wish to impose on Germany, I shall be content. Once the goal has been attained, none has the right to shed even one further drop of blood.[110]

It was a typical soldier's reply; and it is quite true that the French marshal was guided by purely military considerations in formulating his armistice terms, harsh as they were for the Germans. France was to be protected at all costs against another Schlieffen Plan, by the occupation if not annexation of the left bank of the Rhine, together with the "bridgeheads." Like the Versailles treaty later on, this was really a sign that the victorious French felt by no means certain of their military superiority.

Foch left it to the politicians to consider the political consequences of this occupation policy for Franco-German relations. Every representative of the Entente powers who had any part in concerting these armistice terms was apparently quite clear about the fact that they were exceedingly harsh. Balfour said on October 29 that in their final form they were surely unacceptable and harsher than the peace terms that had been imposed on France in 1871.[111] Clémenceau and Foch on their part could not understand why the British were so insistent that the German battle fleet be surrendered, since it had proved to be practically without value during the war.

Balfour took the danger of Bolshevist revolution in a beaten and humbled Germany very seriously, while Clémenceau thought it was mere German propaganda talk. Both Lloyd George and Colonel House were very uneasy about French occupation troops being advanced beyond the Rhine. Clémenceau reassured them by pledging his word that the French troops would withdraw after the fulfillment of the peace terms—which had then not even been discussed! The French premier's promise was not exactly rendered more credible by his additional remark that the French chamber would surely oust him, if the treaty did not provide for occupation of the Rhineland.[112]

All these differences of opinion were of little political use to the Germans. By late October the OHL was still cruelly deceiving itself into believing that it could count on a certain measure of goodwill on the part of the Americans and it instructed its armistice commission to exploit to the fullest any differences between the Americans and the Anglo-French.[113]

Neither in Versailles nor in Paris nor in London did anyone waste a single word on the abdication of William II and the question of whether the Hohenzollern dynasty should stay or go.

Part 4

The Exchange of Notes with Wilson Continues (Latter Part of October); Ludendorff Dismissed

GERMAN hopes of avoiding unconditional surrender by negotiating with Wilson received a disastrous setback with his second note. Against the background of the cruel political realities as they are now known to us, the German war cabinet deliberations on how to answer this note take on an almost spectral quality. The Germans were groping in the dark, wavering between conflicting delusions. There were those who still staked their hopes on the president's good will and thought that further compromise might encourage him; and there was the angry group that had set its face darkly against any further concessions and demanded that negotiations be broken off at once.

The first to take the latter course was the Kaiser himself. "Wilson's note," he wrote his cousin, Prince Max of Baden, "is a piece of unmitigated frivolous nonsense. You must use it to rouse the entire people to rally round their emperor in defense of their sacred heritage, just as the government must stand shoulder to shoulder behind him. This impudent intervention in our political affairs must be properly exposed to all."[114]

As a first reaction this was perfectly understandable; but Germany had no means at all to "expose" the enemy; and the day was long past when the people could be rallied round their emperor in defense of their heritage, sacred or not. Indeed, the question of the Kaiser's abdication had been openly mooted for a number of weeks; and Wilson's note kindled anti-Hohenzollern sentiments that had long been smoldering.

Prince Max, on the same day, noted down a kind of program for the next steps to be taken by the government, and in it he refused to call immediately for a final struggle of desperation. "No doubt some are toying with the idea of perishing with honor," he wrote; "but a responsible statesman must conclude that the broad masses have a right to demand quite baldly that they be allowed to live rather than to die in beauty." The Chancellor nevertheless was willing to make another effort to maneuver Wilson into the role of mediator.[115]

The prince's attitude, in other words, had changed radically since his first week in office. This at once put him at odds with Ludendorff, and the differences were needlessly exacerbated by the excessive zeal of Colonel Haeften as representative of the OHL;[116] for since the receipt of Wilson's note the political temper at headquarters had abruptly shifted for the second time,

the mood of deep resignation this time giving way to one of renewed determination to fight on. On no account were Hindenburg and Ludendorff
minded to put up with humiliating armistice terms and a "peace of dis-
honor."

They demanded that the government unleash a patriotic *levée en masse* as
a last ditch defense. Hindenburg sent word to the Chancellor on October 24
that the home front information service, as now organized, was woefully
inadequate. He proposed that the publicity head of the Reich Chancellery be
given an advisory council composed of businessmen, rural proprietors, journalists, writers, poets, trade union leaders, and others. Since it would be many
weeks before any armistice could come into effect, it was important for army
morale that morale on the home front remain strong, and this must be encouraged by every possible means. Regional advisory councils must be created
in the federal states.[117]

As was to be expected, identical demands were raised in the press and by
the leaders of the rightist parties, and the Chancellor was inundated with
countless petitions and demonstrations. The radicals of the left, on the other
hand, thought that their hour had struck, since the foundations of the monarchy were evidently about to cave in. Most importantly, the long frustrated
yearning of the masses for peace was swelling more and more into a revolutionary movement. It was almost intolerable even so that the armistice negotiations had been dragging on for weeks on end; but what was really beginning to infuriate the masses was that according to Wilson's note still further
delay threatened, because the old imperial power continued in the saddle.
The last remnants of national unity crumbled over this issue; and week by
week the leaders of the socialist majority parties—Ebert, Scheidemann,
Noske, David, and their publicity men—had a harder time assuaging the impatient masses.

Traditional patriotism and respect for military expertise, however, were
still so deeply ingrained even on the left that it was decided once again to
discuss the "military situation" with the generals. This time the talks were
not limited to Ludendorff and (with the Kaiser's gracious permission!) other
top troop leaders were consulted—resulting in an immediate threat of resignation from Ludendorff. He appeared in person in Berlin on October 17, where
he was confronted with a long list of questions intended to clarify whether
there was any possibility of improving Germany's situation by doggedly fighting on.

Ludendorff's answers sounded reasonably confident, but they were far too
vague to serve as the basis for so important a political decision as breaking off
negotiations with Wilson. On closer scrutiny, War Minister Scheüch's promise
of another 600,000 reserves proved to be futile in practice. This contingent
was to consist in part of militarily unfit, indeed rebellious elements, in part of

raw eighteen-year-olds who could not possibly reach the front for months to come.

Prince Max has stated that it was at this long cabinet session that he lost confidence in Ludendorff as a man. Instead of giving factual information, Ludendorff delivered propaganda speeches. Yet the draft note which the prince presented to his cabinet was couched in rather prouder terms than its predecessors. All who were present agreed that Germany could not simply play doormat; and the draft stated that precipitate changes in the form of government held out little promise of enduring. It would be folly "if Germany, to please other countries, allowed itself to be pushed with indecent haste into constitutional changes that did not accord with its character and traditions."

These were brave words, but the cabinet felt they were too provocative and they were struck out. All that was left was the assurance that the recent reforms had brought about a fundamental change in German political life. The hope was expressed that in settling the armistice questions the president "would not approve demands that would be incompatible with the honor of the German nation and with creating the proper spirit for a peace of justice." Lastly, Wilson's charges of allegedly inhuman acts by the German army and navy were rejected with dignity and objectivity.

A serious clash between the Chancellor on one hand and the OHL and admiralty on the other nevertheless ensued. Both military agencies insisted that the U-boat campaign be continued, and in this they had the Kaiser's approval.[118] Oddly enough, a cabinet majority led by Payer and Erzberger was also initially against dropping U-boat warfare altogether; but when some of the German ambassadors were consulted at another meeting, the group grew convinced that the U-boat campaign had become an act of futility that simply could not be reconciled with the continuation of negotiations with Wilson.[119] In the end Prince Max succeeded in wresting from the Kaiser a passage in the reply note that expressly renounced the torpedoing of passenger vessels (which virtually meant the end of U-boat warfare). To gain this concession, however, the prince had to threaten his resignation.

This decision by the Kaiser had one consequence that is noteworthy within the context of our main theme. The ministers insisted that Ludendorff be forced to give his express assent to the note, which the general obstinately refused to do, though War Minister Scheüch and Haeften made long representations to him by telephone, to the effect that failure of the armistice deal could not be risked on account of the U-boat campaign, which had already become highly unpopular and virtually useless. As always when it came to differences with the OHL, the ministers were afraid they would be publicly accused of stabbing the army in the back, if it became known that Ludendorff had disapproved of the note.

Over all this concern, they failed to note that they were indirectly conceding the general a voice in what was ultimately a purely political decision; nor were they appeased by Ludendorff's oral assurances that the Kaiser's decision settled the matter for him. He reaffirmed that the OHL had no political functions and promised not to publicize his disagreement. The suspicions of the politicians were not allayed. In the end Haeften and Hahn together resorted to the expedient of persuading the gentlemen that they could give no better proof of their newfound power than to show that they had overruled the military on this issue.

Haeften also persuaded Ludendorff to sign a written declaration which Haeften had drafted, to the effect that the OHL did not look on itself as a political power factor and hence bore no political responsibility either. In the current controversy, it would not swerve from its loyalty to the government and would avoid airing any disagreements. Despite its military dissent in the question of U-boat warfare, the OHL acknowledged that it lacked both jurisdiction and expert knowledge for judging the political necessity of the note that had just been agreed on.[120]

It sounded like a definitive retreat from politics. But a few days later, on the arrival of Wilson's third note with its massive attack against Germany's "military rulers and monarchist autocrats," it grew amply clear that Ludendorff contemplated no such withdrawal. Of course the note could not fail to infuriate the men at supreme headquarters. Colonel Haeften communicated the gist of it to the OHL by telephone on the morning of October 24, and he did everything in his power to translate military indignation into instant political action. He implored his chief to come to Berlin immediately, with Hindenburg—against the Chancellor's express wish! – in order to discuss the new situation with Prince Max. He said he distrusted the influence of the war cabinet on the Chancellor, especially that of the new foreign minister, Solf.

Haeften, in other words, was inciting the OHL against the policy of the government, and he also wanted the generals to persuade the Kaiser to take up the active defense of his throne himself, break off negotiations with Wilson at once, and rally the people for a fervent last-ditch fight against dishonorable peace terms.[121] Ludendorff eagerly agreed at once; but before departing for Berlin he took a step that was to be his undoing. For this too Colonel Haeften bears part of the responsibility.

At a meeting of high government publicity heads at the foreign ministry on October 24, Haeften reported that the OHL was demanding immediate discontinuance of negotiations with Wilson and continuation of the war. "Soldiers' honor can ask no less." Further talks would inevitably lead to the fall of the monarchy, with the German nation rendered defenseless. Privy Councilor Stumm made some additional ambiguous statements, and these, together with Haeften's, were taken by one of the attending representatives of the war press office to mean that the government shared the views expressed, in other words that Haeften had been speaking more or less semiofficially.

This version was at once transmitted by telephone to supreme headquarters, where the deputy chief of intelligence, Major Kroeger, instantly drafted an order to be distributed to all troops down to company level. The "surrender" demanded by Wilson, it said, was unacceptable and proof

> that our enemies merely pay lip service to the idea of a just peace in order to deceive us and break our resistance. For us soldiers Wilson's reply can therefore only constitute a challenge to continue resisting to the limit of our strength. Once the enemy realizes that the German front cannot be pierced by all the power in the world, he will be ready to conclude a peace that will safeguard Germany's future, especially for the broad masses of the people.

The political implications of this statement were inescapable. The very fact that it was issued before there had been any official statement by the government, though it flew in the face of the course the government had been following, was bound to make government policy appear abjectly dependent on the military. Hindenburg nevertheless immediately signed the order. Ludendorff, according to his own report, was initially startled, but accepted Major Kroeger's assurance that from the statements made at the press conference there could be no doubt that the order represented the government view. Without checking with the foreign ministry or the government, or at least reporting the action to them, he too signed.

More thoughtful General Staff officers like Colonel Thaer at once anticipated that there would be a "big stink."[122] The proclamation to the troops, nevertheless, went out that very night, being distributed down to battalion level and also, "confidentially," at a briefing session of the war press office. Only when the army group Gallwitz on October 25 voiced serious objections was Colonel Heye, Ludendorff's deputy—the general himself had meanwhile departed for Berlin—persuaded to countermand the order.[123]

It was only by way of the press conference that the Chancellor learned of this latest escapade of Ludendorff. The news was virtually the straw that broke the camel's back. Prince Max was exhausted and ill, and at this moment he was terrified of further quarrels with Ludendorff on the armistice question. He was being urgently warned from all sides against OHL demands and military pledges. On October 18 Crown Prince Rupprecht of Bavaria had reported to him on the truly desperate plight of the army. "Ludendorff doesn't accept the seriousness of the situation," he said. "We must at all costs secure peace before the enemy forces his way into Germany."[124]

From headquarters itself Lersner reported that the military situation was still at least as hopeless as it had been three weeks before. Upon inquiry he added that the greater part of the army would now welcome Ludendorff's dismissal.[125] The cabinet members were already much put out over Ludendorff; and on October 20 Solf had assured the foreign affairs committee of the federal council that the government would not be intimidated by any further resignation threats from the OHL. He quoted the war minister as giving positive assurances that he had replacements for both Hindenburg and Ludendorff.[126]

Wilson's note had, of course, specifically attacked Germany's "military rulers," and on October 24 there were discussions within the war cabinet of how Ludendorff might be got rid of without a fuss.[127] Quite independently and without consulting his ministers, Prince Max was drafting a direct appeal to the Kaiser to put an end to "dual government" and dismiss Ludendorff, but to persuade Hindenburg to remain, if possible. The prince threatened to resign if this were not done. This communication was delivered to the Kaiser on the evening of October 25, after the Chancellor had heard of the new army order.

Both generals had meanwhile arrived in Berlin on the afternoon of October 25. That morning the Chancellor, through Kurt Hahn, had requested Haeften to persuade the two to keep out of the matter of the reply to Wilson's note. Haeften not only declined this request but implored the generals to submit their resignations to the Kaiser if the government refused to break off negotiations with Wilson at once. Once again, as so often before, they were to impose their will on the Kaiser by means of an ultimatum.[128]

Ludendorff at once agreed. At the audience in Bellevue palace that ensued immediately, he implored the Kaiser to see to it that the government unequivocally broke off negotiations with Wilson and at last rallied the country to put forth its utmost efforts. He insisted that little could be expected of the new government and was in no way swayed by the counterarguments put forward by Delbrück (who, at the Chancellor's request, had succeeded Berg as the Kaiser's cabinet chief.)[129]

The Kaiser balked and referred the generals to the Chancellor, who declined to receive them and referred them in turn to his deputy Payer. Late that night Payer's home was the scene of a dramatic three-hour meeting which, according to the reports of those who took part in it, may be characterized as the final classic confrontation between the German political leadership and Ludendorffian militarism.[130]

Payer, hardheaded Swabian that he was, was not influenced by Ludendorff's grandiloquence about "soldiers' honor," "shameful challenges," "inspiring the nation's morale," and "rallying all the country's resources." He observed calmly that a nation of seventy million must not be driven into a last hopeless adventure on mere hope and against all the discernible facts.

Payer is supposed to have said that he could not acknowledge "soldiers' honor" as a political motive. "I am a plain ordinary citizen and civilian. All I can see is people who are starving." Ludendorff's voice rose: "In that case, Your Excellency, I fling the whole shame of the fatherland in your face and in the faces of your colleagues. . . . We two do not understand each other and we shall never understand each other. We live in two different worlds." That was indeed true.

Ludendorff was drafting his resignation on the following morning, when Haeften suddenly came storming in to bring him news he had just got hold of in a roundabout way in the lobby of the Reich chancellery. At the request of the Chancellor, the Kaiser proposed to fire Ludendorff. Haeften wished to prepare Ludendorff for the painful scene that was likely to take place in Bellevue palace, but he did his chief a poor service, for Hindenburg had just persuaded Ludendorff to hold back his resignation until he, Hindenburg, made another effort to change the Chancellor's mind.

It is alleged that the Kaiser, too, was at the last moment persuaded by his adjutant, Major Niemann, to accept a compromise. The political section of the General Staff was to be disestablished, Ludendorff was to pledge to keep out of politics altogether, and in return the Chancellor was to forego his request for Ludendorff's dismissal.[131] None of this held out much hope of success.

Ludendorff was virtually beside himself. His hands shook to such an extent that he could barely manage to button his uniform. It was a poor augury for the ensuing audience, which took a very stormy course—certainly much stormier than Ludendorff later described it in his memoirs. The Kaiser complained about the army order of October 24 and the repeated abrupt changes in the OHL stand. Ludendorff seems to have responded with vehement accusations against the government for not siding with the General Staff when it was unfairly attacked. From his own report to Colonel Thaer, he reminded the Kaiser of what the monarch owed his General Staff and demanded in extremely brusque tones to be relieved.

According to a report by Hindenburg, the tone grew so sharp that the Kaiser at one time said: "You seem to forget that you are addressing your king." It is not quite clear to what extent Ludendorff, in demanding to be relieved, was influenced by the fact that the Kaiser had told him of his intention to ask two other seasoned field generals to give him an assessment of the situation. This must have played some part in getting Ludendorff's back up.

It will be recalled the Ludendorff's predecessor Falkenhayn, on being relieved of office, agreed to accept a major appointment as commander of an army group; and Conrad von Hötzendorf acted similarly; but when the Kaiser made him such an offer, Ludendorff brusquely rejected it, though the Kaiser, flying into a rage, told the general that it was solely up to him as "supreme war lord" to decide when and even whether Ludendorff was to go.[132] Ludendorff's response was to repeat his request to be relieved, and this time it was granted, albeit ungraciously.

The crowning disappointment for Ludendorff concerned Hindenburg. Instead of supporting his quartermaster general, the field marshal had kept his counsel, though at the end he did ask to be relieved himself. When the Kaiser brusquely replied: "You will stay," Hindenburg merely bowed from the waist. Ludendorff departed as soon as his resignation had been accepted, but Hindenburg seems to have stayed behind for a brief talk with the monarch, to whose desire that he remain in office he yielded without any great show of reluctance.[133]

Words were exchanged between the two generals outside the palace. Ludendorff accused the field marshal of "treachery." The two men drove back to the General Staff separately; and Ludendorff never forgave his former chief and longtime comrade-in-arms this "betrayal." It will be recalled that some years later, without notable success, he did what he could, in vicious polemics, to destroy the myth of Hindenburg the great general.

What did Ludendorff mean by treachery and betrayal? Was he merely giving vent to bitter human frustration at being sent out into the wilderness alone, which rendered his ouster far less sensational than it might otherwise have been? Was he enraged over broken comradeship? Or did it mean the failure of a last political effort such as Haeften had recommended to the two generals—an attempt to change course abruptly once again by offering their resignations at the same time and thus forcing the negotiations with Wilson to be discontinued?

If the latter interpretation is the correct one, the resignation Ludendorff was drafting early that day did not signify that he had abandoned all hope, as suggested in his memoirs, but that he was engaged in one final power ploy that went wrong. There can be no certainty on this matter. During the final audience, however, Ludendorff showed no sign of having given up hope. He confronted his "supreme war lord" with obstinacy and arrogance, not to say insolence, and thus inevitably, even in Hindenburg's view, brought on his own dismissal himself. In the circumstances, the field marshal's support would have meant very little.

Prince Max's war cabinet took the outcome of the affair with great relief, indeed rejoiced over it. It would now no longer be necessary to wage a serious struggle over the reply to Wilson's third note—though there was to be some bickering over the wording, which the prince wished to make as steadfast and dignified as possible. It was abundantly plain by now that negotiations could no longer be broken off and that Germany would have to ask for the enemy's terms.

An aggravating factor was that Austria's total collapse, long expected, now actually took place. On October 27 Emperor Charles advised his German ally that he was compelled to conclude a separate peace with the Entente. That same day saw the dispatch of the fourth and last German note to Wilson. It could say no more than what the situation required, but managed to avoid the terms "conditions" and "request." It simply said that Germany "looked forward to proposals for an armistice that would usher in a peace of justice as outlined by the president in his proclamations."

Nine days elapsed before a reply was received—terrible days of incipient general disintegration. Turkey surrendered on October 31, Austria on November 2 without waiting for the mediation requested of Wilson. On November 3 it became clear that despite Emperor Charles's pledges the Austrian armistice agreement did not rule out the transit of enemy troops through Austria to South Germany, indeed, specifically authorized it, holding out the prospect that Hungarian, Czech, and Yugoslav troops might participate. Hence Germany was now under threat on its southern flank as well; and news was already being received, suggesting that Bavaria was wavering in its loyalty toward the Reich. Immediately afterward, revolution broke out in Germany, sweeping away the last remnants of military resistance and creating political chaos.

Part 5
Revolution and Imposed Armistice

THE REVOLUTION in Germany began as a widespread mutiny, not unlike that in Russia in 1917. It was a reaction to the intolerable pressure of the state on the physical and moral resources of the nation, continued over many years. Naturally revolutionary sentiment was also nurtured by the incessant propaganda activities of the socialists and their "independent" offshoot, with their constant opposition to all military and government authority. A major contribution came from the small group of revolutionary activists under the leadership of Karl Liebknecht and Rosa Luxemburg, who called themselves "Spartacists," used Soviet propaganda material smuggled into Berlin by the Russian ambassador Joffe, and followed directives from Moscow; but because of the amazing loyalty and patriotism of the broad German working masses under the leadership of the majority socialists, these groups would not have succeeded, except for the general exhaustion and malnutrition, the serious grippe epidemic, the complete lack of the necessities of life, the shock of the sudden and unexpected military collapse, the intolerably protracted negotiations with Wilson, and above all the American president's repeated and insistent appeal to shake off traditional authority.

There was no republican party of any consequence in Germany. The left socialists did have a republican program, but their followers were in a hopeless minority. In a Reichstag by-election in October, the majority socialist candidate garnered three times as many votes as the independent, while the candidate of the progressive people's party obtained an absolute majority over both socialist groups.[134] There was no anti-Kaiser movement in either the army or the navy, but the average German soldier did not exactly "love" or "venerate" his sovereign—he did not really know him. As for the snappy and cliché ridden speeches the Kaiser occasionally delivered at parades, they elicited irritation and headshaking rather than enthusiasm. The soldier in the ranks was fighting, not for Prussia or Bavaria or Württemberg, but simply for Germany—certainly not for the Kaiser, to whom he felt as indifferent as he did to all matters of higher politics.[135]

But neither did the soldier hate the Kaiser. In the modern mass army a relationship of personal loyalty between the "supreme war lord" and his following of soldiers, bound to him by the oath to the flag, survived only in theory. At the top of the military pyramid, especially among the generals, the old feudal relation of liege and vassal did live on. Nevertheless, a great many factors had to coincide to turn the brave and steady German frontline soldiers, seasoned in a thousand and one emergencies and tight spots, into the kind of mutinous and undisciplined rabble, wearing red scarves as a kind of badge, that could be seen idling about on the streets of virtually every German city in November-December 1918.

William II had not been really popular since the "affair" of 1908, and during the war years his image had faded almost beyond recognition. It was Hindenburg who had become a legend. Huge wooden statues of him had been erected in the squares of many German cities, and the populace was given the privilege of driving a nail into the wood, in return for a contribution to the war chest. The field marshal had long put the Kaiser in the shade. As we have seen, the OHL had often forced the Kaiser to do its bidding in major issues, but the new government of Prince Max of Baden scarcely troubled to cut him in on its deliberations about the exchanges with Wilson (which were rather confused even so!) or even to submit the completed texts to him for approval. Yet no one in Germany gave any serious thought to demanding the Kaiser's abdication until the armistice request was made by Wilson. We can trace rather closely how this theme grew into prominence in the course of the exchanges with Wilson, swelling step by step into a mass movement as Wilson's demands became more and more massive.

The first voices from the majority socialist camp to demand the Kaiser's abdication in the interest of concluding a more favorable peace came from

Bavaria, in an article that appeared on October 10–i.e., directly after Wilson's first note of October 8–in the Nuremberg paper *Fränkische Tagespost*. It created a considerable stir. When Wilson's second note of October 14 with its much sharper tone became known, doubts that the Kaiser could be retained against the will of the Entente began to be voiced in moderate circles as well.[136] Even the conservatives were affected.

It was only after Wilson's third note, however, that public reticence on the issue was abandoned. Until that time the official mouthpieces of the major parties, including the social democrats, had been circumspect, in contrast to the provincial press. It had been quite impossible to keep the Wilson note secret even temporarily, as Haeften had asked the Chancellor to do; nor did the foreign ministry have any luck with its request to the press not to open a discussion on the abdication issue. Even censorship was unable to restrain an impassioned debate on Wilson's demand for the abolition of "monarchist autocracy."[137]

All this put Prince Max's government in a serious predicament. None of the political parties in it had republican wings pressing for abolition of the monarchy. Scheidemann, undoubtedly the most radical among the newly appointed ministers from the Reichstag, said after the second Wilson note that it was shameful to have to make all the progressive consititutional changes under enemy pressure; but even he was unwilling to believe that Wilson wanted anything more than to see the Kaiser's arbitrary power curbed, along the lines of parliamentary government. (These statements were made on October 16 and 18.)

On October 24 Scheidemann expressed keen regret that Wilson's third note expressed opposition to the OHL and the Kaiser rather outspokenly. On that same occasion he did admit, however, that according to his information, the people would vote for abdication if the issue came before them, adding that the danger of Bolshevism was growing more and more.[138] In the end this was the factor that decided him. If the left socialists could make the monarchist label stick on the social democrats, his party was likely to lose a large number of its followers to them.

Scheidemann was appalled when he saw Liebknecht, the Spartacist leader whose pardon he had secured, triumphantly borne away from the penitentiary gate on the shoulders of soldiers wearing the ribbon of the Iron Cross. Like other members of the government, he was even more dismayed by the scenes in the Reichstag on October 22-24, when the independent socialists openly called for the abolition of the whole monarchist system, proclaiming that "the Hohenzollerns mean war, no Hohenzollerns mean no war!" These were also the days when the Poles, Danes and Alsatians in Germany openly avowed their separatist stand.

By late October, Scheidemann was the cabinet member who was agitating most actively for the Kaiser's abdication—but not for forcible deposition, for Scheidemann wanted the Kaiser to depart with dignity rather than being thrust off his throne by a popular rebellion. He had the support of many moderates of stature, of civil servants, and even of officers up to the rank of colonel, many of whom he had consulted.

The most determined opponent of abdication was Scheidemann's cabinet colleague Erzberger. It was not that Erzberger had any illusions that the Kaiser had sufficient personal attributes to keep him for any length of time on his throne after a lost war. He simply thought it stupid and undignified to press for abdication before arms were downed. Such a thing would merely split army and people. It would be more seemly to await the enemy's armistice terms. The Kaiser would then have the option of rejecting them, thus creating the proper occasion for his abdication, as Czar Ferdinand of Bulgaria and King Constantine of Greece had done before him.

To be oversensitive to opinion abroad seemed particularly demeaning to Erzberger, and he thought it downright criminal to ask the opinion of prominent foreigners. On October 31 Erzberger still thought that public opinion was sharply divided—he may have been thinking of the surprising loyalty demonstrations being staged on behalf of the Kaiser by the Catholic trade unions and associations just then. He reported to the cabinet that a Swiss acquaintance had told him:

> If Germany now drives the Kaiser off the throne, people abroad will say that the Germans, when victorious, are brutal, and when vanquished, contemptible; and they will be right, if you try to use the Kaiser as a pawn. You may think you can get better terms by his abdication, but I am convinced the terms have long since been fixed; and then you will have gone to all that trouble in vain.[139]

Matthias Erzberger, so often the naive optimist, on this occasion called the shots with surgical precision; but he was alone with his views, and the heavy fog in which the discussions in the war cabinet took place was steadily thickened by the constant influx of intelligence and rumor from abroad. As a federal prince himself, Prince Max was particularly reluctant to exert the slightest pressure on his imperial cousin; and he tried all he could to get authoritative information on Wilson's ultimate intentions through people abroad whom he trusted.

In mid-October, following Wilson's second note, the Chancellor dispatched his adjutant Hahn to The Hague, where Hahn managed to have a two-hour talk with Alexander C. Kirk, first secretary and former chargé d'affaires of the American legation. Hahn tried to convince the American that Prince Max was in dead earnest with his reform endeavors; but he also insisted that constitutional reform could endure only if it were based on evolution rather than revolution.[140]

According to Hahn's own report, transmitted through the German legation, there was a direct exchange on the question of the Kaiser. Hahn told the American quite bluntly that for America to raise that question at all was an act of coercion. Kirk assured him that Wilson certainly did not expect the Kaiser to abdicate. He did hope that the monarch's position might take on a more ceremonial character, as in Britain, adding that a clear-cut rejection of the present system was essential. The Emperor's command power needed to be abolished, the Chancellor's responsibility clearly defined, the Reichstag given the authority to declare war, and such reforms needed to be firmly anchored in law. Otherwise there would always be a lingering suspicion that the old autocracy might some day return. All this sounded reassuring enough, though Hahn gained the impression that the president no longer had complete freedom of action and was bound particularly by the prevailing anti-German mood in Britain.[141]

It was rather unfortunate that the Chancellor immediately passed on this encouraging news to the OHL, which promptly issued a round robin communication to the various army commands, the contents of which became known to an American "agent" in Switzerland, presumably McNally. Whoever it was reported to the State Department that Prince Max had postponed any further pressure on the Kaiser to abdicate, since he had learned at The Hague through Kirk that Wilson did not insist on such a thing. Lansing promptly queried The Hague. Kirk denied everything. Not a word had been said in his talk with Hahn on the question of the Kaiser or on the attitude of the government of the United States. The American secretary of state gave instructions that Hahn was to be informed that his report about the president's stand was without any foundation.[142]

Kirk may have expressed himself ambiguously, but whatever the misunderstanding, it was worsened by a statement from another confidential American source at The Hague, reported by the German envoy, Rosen, on October 27.[143] It said that the dismissal of Ludendorff had a highly beneficial effect, while at this juncture the Kaiser's abdication and the crown prince's renunciation of the throne were likely to make an unfavorable impression and at best to bring only inconsequential improvement in the armistice terms. It would be far better if the Kaiser issued a manifesto supporting democratic reforms, which should then be explained in clear-cut fashion by the Chancellor. It might be well too if there were no further crown council meetings.

Apparently these were no more than the personal views of an American who was well-disposed toward the Germans but lacked any official standing whatever.[144] The German foreign ministry, however, had long been aware— not least on account of many exhortations issuing from Switzerland—that much depended on convincing Wilson of a genuine political change in Germany and of the importance of the constitutional changes that were being deliberated in the federal council and in the Reichstag with almost breathless haste. Germany had to appear in a "democratic" guise.

On October 27 the foreign ministry drafted a report that concisely summarized what had been done. "Personal rule," it said, had become impossible for all time to come. An English translation was immediately wired to the German legation in Berne in plain language and cabled to Washington on October 28 by the Swiss government as an official communication to the president.[145] On November 1, Prince Max discussed the report at length with a Dutch journalist, whom he sought to convince that a true "revolution from above" had taken place in Germany. The Dutchman at once passed on these remarks to the American chargé d'affaires at The Hague, Robert W. Bliss, who had them promptly cabled to Lansing. As a direct result, Bliss, on November 4, asked for the full text of all the new measures which the federal council and the Reichstag had passed.[146]

Prince Max still felt that the intelligence reaching him from Holland was inadequate and continued his quest for more information. On October 25 he had the German legation in Copenhagen ask the Danish foreign minister, Scavenius, to inquire of Wilson or Colonel House as to the meaning of the latter part of Wilson's third note. The minister politely declined this as a hopeless undertaking,[147] whereupon Prince Max sent his adjutant Hahn to Copenhagen to seek contact with Secretary Lithgow Osborne of the American legation, with whom he had long been friendly. This mission was successful, and Hahn had a long talk with Osborne and another unnamed American diplomat.[148]

He was told that Wilson himself thought the Kaiser's abdication of secondary importance, but was no longer able to prevail with this view, being at odds with the British and French governments on the armistice issue. He would probably have to yield, unless he received further support. The best support he could get would be the Kaiser's abdication, for it was widely believed that Germany was likely to relapse into a monarchial system, unless the Kaiser went. Wilson did not want to see a Bolshevist-type revolution in Germany; and if the Kaiser did abdicate, there was a chance that he might refuse to go along with excessively severe armistice terms, since the Entente might then get into a precarious situation; but there would have to be swift action.

As summarized by Count Brockdorff-Rantzau, these Copenhagen talks made a profound impression on Prince Max, and rightly so, for they came very close to the truth. The impression was reinforced by a flood of intelligence and rumor that had been pouring in from Belgium and Switzerland since late September. Much of this originated with a source already known to us, the busybody McNally and his son-in-law Mensing, both of whom seemed to enjoy the particular confidence of the German legation and the members of a prisoners-of-war exchange delegation working in Switzerland.[149]

The gist of all these reports was that Germany needed to hurry in initiating democratization in earnest, in getting rid of such notorious militarists as Ludendorff, Bartenwerffer, Bauer, and Nicolai, and above all, in getting the Kaiser to abdicate and the crown prince to renounce the succession.[150] Members of the Swiss federal council gave similar well-meant advice. Much of this "foreign intelligence" has been shown today to have been mere rumor-mongering; and McNally is now known to have been an unreliable informant.[151]

McNally was skating on very thin ice when he told the State Department that Germany was willing to submit to the president's will, particularly in the matter of the Kaiser. He cited his talks with the German envoy Romberg and the members of the prisoner-of-war exchange commission.[152] As for Prince Max, he seems to have been rather suspicious of the reliability of this American source,[153] but the overall impression of the news coming from Switzerland was persuasive.

He was perhaps most deeply affected by a long letter sent to him by his cousin, Prince Ernst zu Hohenlohe-Langenburg, chairman of the German prisoners-of-war commission. Written on October 25, it reached the Chancellor two days later via Mensing and another officer. It painted a grim picture of the hopelessness of any call for a "struggle to the death" and combined this with an "authoritative" interpretation that Wilson's third note was aimed at none other than the Kaiser, the crown prince, and Ludendorff. Unless they vanished from the scene, there would be no further bargaining about the armistice and the peace—his view was undoubtedly derived from McNally.

News was at the same time flowing out of Bavaria, indicating that the deeply ingrained hatred of all things Prussian that marked that state was now more and more turning on the Hohenzollern dynasty. Indeed, in the Bavarian diet there had been an actual suggestion that Bavaria conclude a separate peace.[154] There seemed no other way out. Official sanction had to be given to the suggestion that the Kaiser abdicate voluntarily.[155]

Prince Max long shrank from such a step. At first he simply limited himself to "informing" the Kaiser about the growing threat to his throne. He then tried to get Augustus William, one of the Kaiser's sons, to persuade his father; and he also tried vainly to enlist a fellow sovereign, Prince Frederic Charles of Hesse. He polled all the federal princes, most of whose representatives in the federal council strongly backed abdication. Lastly he dispatched the Prussian minister of the interior, Drews, to Spa with a detailed situation report, in the hope that this would change the Kaiser's mind.

On October 19 Count Lerchenfeld had had a discussion with the Kaiser in which he called the monarch's attention to the growing threat of revolutionary action. William II had declared sternly and resolutely: "A successor of Frederic the Great does not abdicate."[156] He stuck to this decision with iron resolve until November 9, pledging his six sons on their honor not to make themselves available for the succession or regency. To escape the pervasive influences of the politicians, the Kaiser left Berlin on October 29 in such haste as to resemble almost a flight,[157] returning to headquarters and its purely military environment where he was safe from importunities to abdicate.

It was an unfortunate step that made close contact between the Kaiser and his government impossible during the fateful days of November. Grotesquely, the fate of the monarchy and the Reich became the subject of continual and endless bargaining by telephone. The situation made it abundantly clear that the Kaiser lived in a world of political illusions. The king of Prussia, he said, was not a "deserter" who would yield to the urgings of "weak-kneed civilians." He would never voluntarily surrender his role as "supreme war lord," merely from fear of the "rebellious rabble." He would be obliged and certainly able to put down any revolt at the head of his troops. He was emperor by the grace of God, and his office was not his to give up.

It is impossible to do justice to the Kaiser's stand, indeed, even to comprehend it, unless one enters into this frame of reference, extraordinary as it may seem to the modern mind.[158] To his own mind it was a sense of duty rather than obstinacy that caused him to cling to his royal office to the last moment, and in this stand he knew himself to be at one with his military entourage, including even Groener, whom Hindenburg had summoned to Spa as Ludendorff's successor, and whom we already know as a politically astute man, sensitive to public opinion.

On Hindenburg's orders Groener told Prince Max's cabinet on November 5 that the field marshal would consider himself a blackguard if he now abandoned the Kaiser—"and this view, gentlemen, is shared by all soldiers with a sense of honor."[159] This stand came as a bitter disappointment to the social democratic leaders, among whom Groener, as the former head of the *Kriegsamt,* enjoyed much confidence. In a confrontation on November 6, they implored him to persuade the Kaiser to abdicate—paradoxically, in order to preserve the monarchy, which was then a hope shared by countless Germans; but Groener's rejection of this approach was consistent with the spirit of traditional Prussian monarchism, based on military authority and obedience. The Kaiser's authority, in his view, was rooted in history—it was not by the grace of the people. It was quite beyond the German generals to imagine that such an authority could be simply dropped. Such a thing was bound to destroy the cohesion of army, people, and Reich, to invite open chaos, in other words. This was more than the generals could envisage. The imperial power was more than an institution—it was a political and historical symbol.

Actually, resistance to any interference with this symbol and the belief that it could be preserved intact were not nearly so unrealistic as it may appear to the historian in the light of the events of November 9. By late October and early November there was still no anti-Kaiser movement in the German army and navy, despite the fact that war weariness, incipient insubordination, and rebelliousness were rife among many units. The Kaiser himself, moreover, had repeatedly and solemnly expressed his approval of the constitutional reforms that had just been initiated, including even the lifting of his unlimited command power.[160] He certainly offered no opposition to its revocation and he was understandably upset—one reason for his flight from Berlin—that the new government deliberately omitted to give any publicity to his willingness to accept reforms from fear that this might stir up debate over the Kaiser even further.

At home as well as abroad, some voices were heard to express doubts that the Kaiser was able to adapt himself to the new era. The social democrat Landsberg told the joint Reichstag caucus on November 5: "This man, on the threshold of his sixties, cannot be expected to learn a new set of rules. . . . We must depose him."[161] William II, he added, would never become a "people's Kaiser," he would always stick with the generals. This was probably a correct assessment. In any event, it clearly threw down the challenge of an era that no longer wished to have any part of the generals and Prussian militarism. What it meant, in other words, was revolution rather than careful preservation of the monarchy by way of the Kaiser's allegedly voluntary abdication, as contemplated by Prince Max's government and the leaders of the majority social democrats as well, notably Ebert, who told the Chancellor: "Unless the Kaiser abdicates, social revolution is inevitable. I do not want such a revolution, I hate it like sin."[162]

Could the monarchy have been saved if William II had abdicated in time? The liberals of the time gave an affirmative answer to this question, and it has long been customary to endorse this view. Prince Max is charged with the grave failure of not having "forced" the Kaiser to abdicate;[163] but the prince could have done so only by forcibly pushing the Kaiser off the throne, thus himself giving the impetus for revolution. Surely this was too much to expect of him.

But assuming for the moment that William could have been persuaded if Prince Max had convincingly threatened to resign—and this is precisely what he is known to have tried in vain as late as November 8—was there any assurance that a monarchy worthy of the name could have been preserved? When positions of power founded on traditional authority are destroyed, they can be replaced only by new powers based on trust; but Wilson's propaganda and the way the war was ending had destroyed the faith of the masses in the monarchial leadership beyond redemption. The Kaiser might have gained some moral credit if, by foregoing the throne, he had secured some improvement in the armistice terms, and if such an achievement had been made known and rendered plausible to the public; but as we have seen, there was no such possibility.[164]

Thus, had the Kaiser abdicated before the armistice, this would have been interpreted merely as an admission of his own failure and war guilt, without the prospect of any discernible gain in the peace question; and where was the Hohenzollern prince who could have taken the Kaiser's place and drawn the trust of the public, in the light of the lost war and the domestic chaos that was opening up in November 1918? The government of Prince Max actually conducted a frantic search for some suitable personage who might have been put forward with some hope of success as a temporary regent for the eldest of the Kaiser's grandsons, then twelve years old, or as a "deputy" for the Kaiser himself.[165] For one thing, there were almost insoluble constitutional difficulties in the way of a regency, arising from the federal structure of the Reich and the special position of Prussia within it.

We conclude that the republic of 1918 stemmed from a situation that had become hopeless for the monarchy rather than from any "failures" or coincidences. It was the achievements of their army, acknowledged to be the best in Europe, that had raised the Hohenzollerns to the status of a great power. Once that instrumentality of power was smashed, synthetic constitutional expedients were of little avail.

What was totally unexpected and truly extraordinary, however, was that the collapse should take place so abruptly and completely, rendering all organs of the state utterly helpless. This was a direct result of the great naval mutiny which from November 4 on spread like wildfire throughout Germany. This phenomenon is hard to explain. In a word, it stemmed from the extreme accentuation of Prusso-German militarism, which "blew its top," so to speak, and thus brought about its own downfall.

Since the summer of 1918 the German navy had been under the supreme command of Admiral Scheer, the great German naval hero of the Battle of Jutland. We know him as an extremely aggressive proponent of ruthless tactics from the controversy over U-boat warfare in 1916 (see Vol. III, Chapter 5, Part 3, and Chapter 8, Part 3). Late in August 1918, he had created a separate *Seekriegsleitung* (naval war command) which was intended to secure for the German navy the kind of power and autonomy with respect to the Kaiser which the OHL had long enjoyed. Scheer's chief of staff was Rear Admiral Levetzow, who was as hard-hitting as Scheer himself; and he was further assisted by Admiral Trotha, chief of staff of the high seas fleet and an impassioned admirer and follower of Tirpitz. These are the three men chiefly responsible for the disaster of November 1918.

The initial plan of the *Seekriegsleitung* was to increase U-boat construction to the limit. The so-called "Scheer program"—named on the model of the "Hindenburg program" of 1916—contemplated no fewer than thirty-six new units per month. Its aim was to enable the German navy at last to score major successes, late as it was in the war. This plan quickly failed, because Ludendorff was unable to release from the army—despite Colonel Bauer's promises—the 15,000-20,000 skilled workers needed by the shipyards.

Failure also met Scheer's and Levetzow's efforts, supported by the OHL, to continue with unrestricted U-boat warfare during the armistice negotiations, in defiance of Wilson's second note. In the wake of this failure, the navy at once sought to score in still another way. Prevented from using its U-boats, it would at last commit its men-o'-war and strike a last heavy blow against Britain. Trotha's sense of urgency in this matter was fed by reports that Ludendorff, talking to a naval officer, had hinted that a British request for surrender of the German fleet would probably have to be complied with, and that, by and large, it was probably the German navy that would have to "pay the piper." Such a statement would have been entirely in keeping with the traditional aversion within the General Staff to the huge but "useless" armored fleet.[166]

Well, if the fleet were to be surrendered some day, it must have one last fling, to demonstrate its power and usefulness to the world, and especially to Britain; and this must be done promptly, before an armistice supervened. On October 6 Trotha had put down on paper *Reflections at an Hour of Crisis,* to be transmitted to the *Seekriegsleitung.* They contained the nucleus of a great battle plan. Once U-boat warfare were abandoned, Trotha said, the fleet would be freed for missions other than submarine cover, and a strike by the combined high seas forces should be undertaken, accepting the risk of full commitment, since otherwise all that the navy had to look forward to was a shameful end.

Such a climactic battle must be envisaged, Trotha wrote, unless the war were to end without an opportunity for the navy to demonstrate the full striking power inherent in the German nation. Such honorable naval combat, even if it were to prove to be a death struggle, was bound to give birth to the German fleet of the future, unless Germany utterly failed the test of nationhood. There would be no future for a fleet shackled by a humiliating peace. In a covering letter of October 8 to Levetzow, Trotha wrote:

It goes without saying that we are filled with shame and apprehension at the thought of the fleet being given over to destruction from within, without ever having had an opportunity to strike. A commitment to perish with honor would certainly still be worthwhile, for we would be bound to inflict serious injury on Britain.[167]

These were fine words in terms of national honor and military ambition, but they were quite lacking in any technical military rationale. From that point of view, it would have been utter madness, at a time—it would have then been late October—when the Flemish ports had long been evacuated and the U-boats had been withdrawn from their stations there,[168] to risk tens of thousands of lives in a naval battle that could not possibly help the receding German front in the slightest. Another totally unrealistic plan was put forward by Captain Michaelis of the Reich naval office, who admitted that committing the entire fleet would be an outright gamble but held that a prompt and substantial naval success might affect morale on the home front in such a way as to save Germany from general disaster. In any event, he added, the risk of losing the fleet was comparatively small, since by comparison with the army it represented no major power potential.

The *Seekriegsleitung* immediately adopted Trotha's plan, as recorded on October 16. "It is unthinkable," says the note in point, "that the fleet should remain idle during the final struggle preceding an armistice, whether it come now or later. The navy must be committed. Even though it cannot be expected that this will decisively influence the course of events, it is a question of honor and morale if not survival for the navy to do its utmost in the final struggle."

Trotha's *Reflections at an Hour of Crisis* still provided for the ultimate decision in so crucial a matter to be made by "the highest authority." Scheer, however, always looked on the Kaiser's supreme command of the German navy as purely "nominal." On the occasion of reporting to the Kaiser on October 18, he merely said that "the abandonment of U-boat warfare without an armistice would cancel the present restraints on the high seas fleet, which would become available for other missions." The Kaiser naturally received this statement with satisfaction.[169]

Scheer employed similarly unrevealing phraseology with Prince Max two days later: "Abandonment of U-boat warfare has now released the high seas fleet from checks on its operational freedom of action." Advocates of the naval point of view have argued that this constituted an adequate briefing. Admiral Levetzow agreed that Prince Max may not have understood what was meant by "operational freedom," but then, that was scarcely surprising, since the Chancellor was not really qualified for his office. Besides, it was none of his business. On October 30, 1918, Levetzow told the deputy chief of the Kaiser's naval cabinet that the reason His Majesty had so far not been informed about the contemplated strike was that it was a project not requiring the Kaiser's authorization.

The naval high command, in other words, deliberately concealed its fateful plan from the government, on the premise that the government would never give its consent.[170] Ludendorff alone was made a party to the secret, with the request of keeping it as such. The general was in full agreement; and on October 22 Admiral Hipper, head of the high seas fleet, received orders to be prepared to commit his forces for a strike against the British fleet.[171] This was two days before Ludendorff's notorious order proclaiming arbitrarily that negotiations with Wilson were being broken off—the order that led to his dismissal.

The date of the strike by the combined German high seas forces into the Strait of Dover behind a U-boat screen was set for October 30; but on the evening of October 29, when the unit commanders met on Hipper's flagship in the outer harbor of Wilhelmshaven to receive their orders, news was received that there had been serious trouble with the crews in the third squadron. The men were refusing to carry out orders. Much additional news of the same kind soon began to flood in, and Hipper was obliged to call off the planned undertaking.

Despite every effort at secrecy, a rumor that the officers had decided to take the fleet on a death strike against the will of the government and solely to satisfy the "honor" of the navy began to spread among the crews on October 22, leading to an open mutiny. This soon reached a stage compelling Scheer and Levetzow to seek the aid of the democratic government of Prince Max, which they despised. A proclamation written in the editorial offices of the social democratic newspaper *Vorwärts* and signed by the Chancellor, Scheidemann, and Ritter von Mann, head of the Reich naval office, was now widely distributed among the men as a flyer. It denied that there had been any differences between the government and the naval officer corps and characterized the story about a "death strike" as a silly rumor. It was all in vain. The mutiny spread farther and farther and got entirely out of control.

We need not here trace in detail the reasons for the mutiny nor its actual course,[172] since these matters have been thoroughly covered elsewhere. Much attention has been devoted to the fact that seamen, in the difficult, confined, and monotonous life in the bowels of great warships were particularly susceptible to the demoralizing influence of leftist propaganda. It was the kind of life in which conflict between officers and men was inevitable; but the situation in the fall of 1918 was further aggravated by the political attitude of the officers toward the new democratic regime.

Still, all this does not fully explain the phenomenon. Most of the German naval officers seem to have responded to the general uprising of their men with almost complete passivity and helplessness.[173] It was evidently quite beyond their comprehension that the patriotic dedication of their men should have ended so abruptly and completely. Military discipline soon went out the window altogether. There was something highly contagious, especially to already disaffected elements, in the experience that one could refuse to carry out orders, strip officers of their insignia, indeed threaten their lives, and actually shoot them down, without instantly being summoned before a court martial and shot oneself.

But there were moderates among the rebels as well. A delegation of some twenty seamen was sent to Berlin, to explain the attitude of the mutineers to the government and put forward their claims, only a few of which had any political tinge. In essence, the men wanted assurances that there would be no reprisals—or at least no excessive reprisals—against the rebels; that there be an end to excessive spit and polish; that the right of assembly be granted and the men be permitted to read whatever newspapers they wished; and that working conditions for seamen be improved.

Clearly this was at heart no political revolution but rather an elementary mass reaction to military coercion that had become almost unbearable because of the excessive strain to which patriotic sentiment had been subjected. Then there was the last straw, the nightmarish attempt to compel the men to display a last-ditch heroism by glibly ordering them about. It is true, of course, that from the very beginning Bolshevist propaganda played its part. One outward sign was the immediate formation of workers' and soldiers' councils on the Soviet model, which sought to concentrate all power in their hands. It was probably owing to this leftist propaganda as well that a demand for the abdication of the Hohenzollern dynasty soon emerged. It is not at all clear how many of the mutineers really supported this demand.[174]

Attempts were made to isolate the Kiel garrison, which was the focus of the mutiny, but they failed completely, as did efforts to keep the roving sailors out of the big cities. The events of Kiel were soon re-enacted in different form in many other places. Workers' and soldiers' councils were formed everywhere, while public authority vanished almost resistlessly. Perhaps the most grotesque instance took place on November 7 in Munich, where a leftist writer who scarcely deserved to be taken seriously managed, with the support of a few hundred men, to proclaim a republic and drive the king of Bavaria off his throne.[175]

Everywhere the driving force behind the movement was the desire for immediate peace, together with the notion, nurtured by Wilson's note, that the old powers, with the Kaiser and the crown prince in the lead, stood in the way of peace. Everywhere the troops in the garrison towns went over to the mutineers. None was willing to risk his life to put down the rebellion, none to be sent to the western front. Not the least element to contribute to the distrust and agitation among the workers was the fact that conscription levies were still operating by late October and early November.[176]

As chaos spread, the last German hopes of being able to avert a "shameful," intolerably harsh, imposed armistice by threatening at least temporary resumption of hostilities vanished. Groener later concluded that but for the great mutiny there should have been little difficulty in effecting an orderly retreat behind the Rhine, where a new line of resistance might have been built up.[177] Whether he was right is a moot point, but in any event such a course would have caused the devastation of the countryside and cities on the left bank of the Rhine. It was, however, precisely what Lloyd George and Field Marshal Haig feared. The Germans, finding the armistice terms too harsh, might dig in behind the Rhine and force the Allies to fight on for another winter on roads that had been rendered impassable. Lloyd George thought that in such an event it was more than doubtful whether the British and French would go along merely for the purpose of wresting the eastern conquests from Germany's hands.[178]

But all such fears, consideratons, and prospects were now proved at one stroke to be groundless. Nothing is more impressive than the sudden change in Groener's attitude when he personally came up against the full scope of the impending chaos during a visit to Berlin. On November 5 he had still furnished the cabinet with a grave but not entirely hopeless situation report that counted on an orderly withdrawal of the army within the old borders of the Reich. He said it would take eight to ten days to dig in at the new line, at which time Germany would be ready to receive armistice terms—terms Groener did not yet commit himself to accept.

But on the following day, under the impress of the news from Kiel, Bavaria, and the big cities of West Germany,[179] he bluntly told the Chancellor that there was no more time to wait for Wilson's reply. As the Kaiser had already proposed on the day before, Germany would have to walk into the enemy camp, white flag in hand. "Surely we have another week!" exclaimed the horrified prince. "We do not have that much time," said Groener. "Can we wait until Monday [November 11]?" the Chancellor asked. "Even that is too long," Groener replied. "Saturday [November 9] is the last possible day."

The cabinet agreed and an armistice commission was organized. It was to depart that same afternoon, with instructions to cross the enemy lines. It was not until shortly before midnight, long after all this had been settled, that Wilson's fourth and last note was received, announcing that Marshal Foch had been authorized by the American and Allied governments to receive properly empowered representatives of the German government who would be advised of the armistice terms.[180]

The clear implication was that the armistice terms would be imposed by the Allies, and it was immediately explained that their purpose would be the full protection of the interests of the nations united against Germany. Germany was to be compelled to carry out the details of Wilson's Fourteen Points, which it had already accepted as a basis for peace. It was solemnly stated that the Allied powers too had committed themselves to the Fourteen Points, with the exception of "freedom of the seas," and with an almost unlimited expansion of the concepts of "restoration" and "restitution."

The wording of the note, like the entire preceding exchange, showed that this was to be no purely military surrender but a blend of armistice and preliminary peace negotiations. It was thus entirely in keeping that the negotiations with Foch were not to be left to the military alone, but that the German armistice commission was composed of both civilians and military men. It included Erzberger as the representative of the newly democratized Germany.

Erzberger did not volunteer for this daunting mission; on the contrary, he was originally reluctant to serve. He probably did not fathom the full burden of obloquy he was shouldering—as we know, it subsequently cost him his life. It was only on the following day that he was nominated as chairman of the commission, on the motion of Lersner at headquarters. Together with the highly skilled diplomat, Count Oberndorff, he achieved as much as was humanly possible with Germany's supremely self-assured enemies, during the painful sessions of November 8-11 in the forest of Compiègne, in what could scarcely be called "negotiations" between the two armistice commissions. Groener had realized at the outset that it would be impossible to have the armistice terms softened in any substantial way.[181]

During these talks, which were announced to the German people on November 6, the great mutiny continued on its resistless course. It now threatened even Berlin, which the military tried in vain to bar to the rebels. The Chancellor's telephone calls to Spa grew more and more urgent. He was trying to persuade the Kaiser to abdicate "voluntarily" at once. The majority socialists were afraid of losing their hold over the masses of left socialists and Bolshevists, unless they could serve up the sop of the Kaiser's abdication.

At a cabinet meeting on November 6, Erzberger and Gröber, another centrist deputy who had been drafted into the cabinet, still held out, with the Chancellor's support, for the question of the Kaiser to be postponed until after an armistice had been concluded; but this solution no longer seemed tenable, for any moment might bring on open revolution in Berlin under the Spartacist banner; and all the troops that were standing ready or had been summoned were proving to be unreliable.

And thus, on November 9, Spa witnessed the pathetic tragedy of the German empire that has been described so often. Resolved to the last not to lay down his crown, William II affirmed his determination to defend it and if necessary to put down the revolution by force of arms. His highest advisers, including Groener and Hindenburg, were convinced by the evening of November 8 that any such attempt would be utterly futile.

On the morning of November 9, the crown prince appeared, accompanied by his chief of staff, Count Schulenburg, and the Kaiser resorted to the half-measure of agreeing to abdicate as emperor of Germany but remaining with his forces as king of Prussia.[182] In the end he faced the bitter necessity of fleeing to Holland in his special train, since his safety could not be guaran- even at headquarters.[183]

The end of the ancient and renowned Hohenzollern dynasty was anything but heroic. It dodged and faded without putting up a fight, just as other dynasties have ended without a struggle. After all, neither of the two Napoleons, the elder of whom is accounted a military hero, sought death on the battlefield when their cause was lost.

Should William II have given a synthetic heroic cast to the end of his rule, as many officers of his General Staff, including Groener and Colonel Heye, seem to have wished? Should he have marched out into the trenches or staged a miniature action in which all OHL officers would have taken part and sacrificed their lives? [184]

In a military sense any such histrionics would have been pointless, and the whole thing would have smacked of "collective suicide" rather than patriotic heroism. Its effect on German morale must be considered doubtful, even if it had been carried out without a technical flaw, something that cannot be regarded as certain, in view of the disruption at the front at this time and, even so, the vast "emptiness" of modern battlefields.

No, such an act would have been an admission of guilt rather than an act of heroism, the confession of a man who certainly cannot be held responsible for everything that happened. If he drew any hatred on the part of the people, it was because the people had believed in the myth of imperial omnipotence which he himself had created.

Perhaps the Kaiser's own dream would have constituted the most dignified end—to fall, sword in hand, in defense of his throne and the restoration of order. Yet it would have been virtually impossible to carry out such a design—trying to put down a mutiny with a handful of officers and men, his back to the western front. Least of all was it possible under his leadership at the end of a lost war. Some tried to form volunteer units of officers in Berlin, but it was already too late.

The facts were immutable. The ancient glamour of the Hohenzollern crown had dimmed for good, and with it the glory of Frederic the Great, the soldier king. They could no longer be rekindled by tricks and artifices. A new era was dawning, in which the relation of the sword and the scepter, of politics and war, was to undergo a profound change. It was a terrible fact that on November 10, when Erzberger asked for plenipotentiary authority to sign the armistice agreement at Compiègne, there existed in Berlin no government that could regard itself as empowered to grant such authority, so that the OHL had to leap into the breach.[185] From the first moment of their power, the social democratic men of the people, who were struggling in Berlin to create something akin to a new state authority that might reduce chaos to order, were dependent on the support of the army.

Abbreviations

and Abbreviated Book Titles Used in the Notes

AA	Political archive of the foreign ministry *(Auswärtiges Amt)*, Bonn.
AF	Documentary Studies *(Archivalische Forschungen):* History of the German Labor Movement *(Geschichte der Deutschen Arbeiterbewegung)*, 4/II and 4/III. Repercussions of the Great Socialist October Revolution in Germany *(Die Auswirkungen der grossen Sozialistischen Oktoberrevolution auf Deutschland)*, ed. by L. Stern, G. Schrade, and H. Weber, Berlin (1959).
AHR	*American Historical Review.*
AU	Official Documents *(Amtliche Urkunden)* on the Background of the 1918 Armistice, published by the foreign ministry *et al.*, 2nd ed., Berlin (1924).
BA	Federal archive *(Bundesarchiv)*, Koblenz.
BMH	*Berliner Monatshefte.*
EL	Alsace-Lorraine *(Das Reichsland Elsass-Lothringen)*, published for the Research Institute of Alsatians in Germany at the University of Frankfurt, ed. by G. Wolfram, 4 vols. (1931-1937).
FO	British Foreign Office.
FR	*Papers Relating to the Foreign Relations of the United States,* Washington.
GHQ	Supreme headquarters.
GSTA	Secret state archive *(Geheimes Staatsarchiv)*, Munich.
GWU	*Geschichte in Wissenschaft und Unterricht.*
HHSTA	Dynastic, court, and state archives *(Haus-, Hof- und Staatsarchiv)*, Vienna.
HSTA	Court and state archives *(Hof- und Staatsarchiv)*, Stuttgart.
ÖU	Austria-Hungary's Last War *(Österreich-Ungarns Letzter Krieg 1914-1918)*, published by the Austrian Federal Ministry of Defense and the War Archive, Vols. 6 and 7, with supplements (1936, 1938).
PD	The Parliamentary Debates (Official Report), V, Vol. 96 (1917, Vol. 7).
PRO	Public Record Office, London.
RAW	Official war history *(Reichsarchivwerk)*, *Der Weltkrieg 1914-1918*, ed. by Reich Archive, Berlin, Vols. 5ff. (1929ff.).
RK	Reich Chancellery *(Reichskanzlei)*.
Sch&Gr	A. Scherer and J. Grunewald (eds.), *L'Allemagne et les problèmes de*

	la paix pendant la première guerre mondiale. Documents extraits des Archives de l'Office Allemand des Affaires Etrangères, Paris, Vol. 1 (1962); Vol. 2 (1964).
UA	Investigating committee *(Untersuchungsausschuss)* of the national assembly and Reichstag following the First World War, 4th series, *The Causes of the German Collapse,* ed. by Albrecht Philipp et al., Vols. 1-12, Berlin (1925ff.).
UABL	*Ibidem,* 2nd Subcommittee, No. 31: *The Armistice and Peace Negotiations at Brest-Litovsk* (on microfilm).
WC	British war cabinet.
WG	*Die Welt als Geschichte.*
WK	First World War *(Weltkrieg).*
ZA	Central archive *(Zentralarchiv),* Potsdam.
ZGO	*Zeitschrift für Geschichte des Oberrheines.*

Ahlswede (1)	Dieter Ahlswede, *Friedensbemühungen zwischen dem deutschen Reich und Grossbritannien 1914-1918,* dissertation, Bonn (1959).
Ahlswede (2)	Dieter Ahlswede, *Deutsch-britische Friedensgespräche im Haag 1918,* WG, Vol. 20 (1960).
Arz	Artur Arz, *Zur Geschichte des Grossen Krieges* (1924).
Baker	Ray Stannard Baker, *Woodrow Wilson. Life and Letters,* Vol. 8, *The Armistice,* London (1938).
Barth	E. Barth, *Aus der Werkstatt der deutschen Revolution* (1920).
Basler	Werner Basler, *Deutsche Annexionspolitik in Polen und im Baltikum 1914-1918,* Berlin (1962).
Baumgart (1)	Winfried Baumgart, "Ludendorff und das Auswärtige Amt zur Besetzung der Krim 1918," *Jahrbuch für Geschichte Osteuropas,* Vol. 14 (1966).
Baumgart (2)	Winfried Baumgart, "Dokumentation: Die militärpolitischen Berichte des Freiherrn von Keyserlingk aus Petersburg, Januar-Februar 1918." *Vierteljahreshefte für Zeitgeschichte,* Vol. 15 (1967), pp. 87ff.
Baumgart (3)	Winfried Baumgart, *Deutsche Ostpolitik 1918. Von Brest-Litowsk bis zum Ende des 1. Weltkriegs,* Munich (1966).
Baumont	Maurice Baumont, *L'Abdication de Guillaume II,* Paris (1930).
Benedikt	Heinrich Benedikt, *Die Friedensaktion der Meinl-Gruppe 1917-1918,* No. 48, publications of the commission for recent Austrian history, Graz and Cologne (1962).
Bertie	Lord Bertie of Thame, *The Diary,* ed by Lady Algernon G. Lennox, Vol. 2 (1924).
Beyer	Hans Beyer, "Die Mittelmächte und die Ukraine 1918," *Jahrbuch für Geschichte Osteuropas,* Supplement 2 (1956).
Bonhard	O. Bonhard, *Geschichte des alldeutschen Verbands* (1920).
Bonnefous	Georges Bonnefous, *Histoire politique de la Troisième République,* Vol. 2, *La grande Guerre 1914-1918* (1956).
Brecht	Arnold Brecht, *Aus nächster Nähe. Lebenserinnerungen* (1966).
Breucker	Wilhelm Breucker, *Die Tragik Ludendorffs* (1953).
Briggs	Mitchell Pirie Briggs, *George D. Herron and the European Settlement,* Stanford (1932).
Bülow	Prince Bernhard von Bülow, *Denkwürdigkeiten,* 4 vols., Berlin (1930-1932).
Bunyan-Fisher	J. Bunyan and H. H. Fisher, *The Bolshevik Revolution 1917-1918,* 2nd ed. (1961).
Charles-Roux	François Charles-Roux, *La Paix des Empires Continentaux* (1947).
Conze	Werner Conze, *Polnische Nation und deutsche Politik im Ersten Weltkrieg,* Cologne and Graz (1958).

Cramon	August von Cramon, *Unser österreichisch-ungarischer Bundesgenosse im Weltkriege,* Berlin (1920).
Czernin	Graf Ottokar Czernin, *Im Weltkriege,* Berlin and Vienna (1919).
Deist (1)	Wilhelm Deist, "Die Politik der Seekriegsleitung und die Rebellion der Flotte Ende Oktober 1918," *Vierteljahreshefte für Zeitgeschichte,* Vol. 14 (1966), pp. 341ff.
Deist (2)	Wilhelm Deist, "Die militärischen Bestimmungen der Pariser Vorortverträge," in *Ideologie und Machtpolitik,* ed. by H. Rössler (1966).
Demblin	A. Demblin, *Czernin und die Sixtus-Affaire* (1920).
Deuerlein (1)	Ernst Deuerlein, *Der Bundesratsausschuss für die Auswärtigen Angelegenheiten 1870 bis 1918,* Regensburg (1955).
Deuerlein (2)	Ernst Deuerlein, "Zur Friedensaktion Benedikts XV," *Stimmen der Zeit,* Vol. 155 (1955).
Dorpalen	Andreas Dorpalen, "Empress Auguste Victoria and the Fall of the German Monarchy," AHR (1952).
Drahn-Leonhard	Drahn and Leonhard, *Unterirdische Literatur im revolutionären Deutschland während des Weltkriegs,* Berlin (1920).
Dugdale	Blanche E. C. Dugdale, *Arthur James Balfour II,* London (1936).
Eisenhart-Rothe	E. von Eisenhart-Rothe, *Im Banne der Persönlichkeit,* Berlin (1931).
Engel-Janosi (1)	Fr. Engel-Janosi, "Die Friedensbemühungen Kaiser Karls mit Besonderer Berücksichtigung der Besprechungen des Grafen Revertera mit Comte Armand," *Proceedings of the Twelfth International Congress of the Historical Sciences,* Vol. 4, Vienna (1965).
Engel-Janosi (2)	Fr. Engel-Janosi, "Die Friedensgespräche Graf Reverteras mit Comte A. Armand 1917-1918," *Anzeiger der österreichischen Akademie,* Vol. 102 (1965).
Engel-Janosi (3)	Fr. Engel-Janosi, *Österreich und der Vatikan,* Vol. 2, *Die Pontifikate Pius X. und Benedikt XV., 1903-1918,* Graz (1960).
Epstein	Klaus Epstein, *Matthias Erzberger und das Dilemma der deutschen Demokratie,* Berlin (1962).
Erzberger	Matthias Erzberger, *Erlebnisse im Weltkrieg,* Stuttgart (1920).
Feldman	Gerald D. Feldman, *Army, Industry and Labour in Germany 1914-1918,* Princeton (1966).
Fester (1)	Richard Fester, *Die politischen Kämpfe um den Frieden (1916-1918) und das Deutschtum,* Munich (1938).
Fester (2)	Richard Fester, *Die Politik Kaiser Karls* (1923).
Fischer	Fritz Fischer, *Griff nach der Weltmacht. Die Kriegszielpolitik des Kaiserlichen Deutschlands 1914-1918,* 3rd amended ed., Düsseldorf (1964).
Foch	Ferdinand Foch, *Mémoires pour servir à l'histoire de la guerre de 1914-1918,* Vol. 2, Paris (1931).
Foerster (1)	Wolfgang Foerster, *Graf Schlieffen und der Weltkrieg,* 2nd ed. (1925).
Foerster (2)	Wolfgang Foerster, *Der Feldherr Ludendorff im Unglück,* Wiesbaden (1952).
Gatzke	Hans W. Gatzke, "Dokumentation zu den deutsch-russischen Beziehungen im Sommer 1918," *Vierteljahreshefte für Zeitgeschichte,* Vol. 3 (1955), pp. 84ff.
Geiss	Imanuel Geiss, *Der polnische Grenzstreifen 1914-1918,* Historische Studien, No. 378, Lübeck (1960).
Glaise-Horstenau	Edmund von Glaise-Horstenau, *Die Katastrophe. Die Zertrümmerung Österreich-Ungarns und das Werden der Nachfolgestaaten* (1929).
Goltz	Count Rüdiger von der Goltz, *Meine Sendung in Finnland und im Baltikum* (1920).
Gratz-Schüller	G. Gratz and R. Schüller, *Die äussere Wirtschaftspolitik Österreich-*

	Ungarns während des Krieges (1925). English version published in 1928 as part of the Carnegie Foundation's *Economic and Social History of the World War*.
Groener (1)	Wilhelm Groener, *Lebenserinnerungen. Jugend, Generalstab, Weltkrieg,* ed. by Friedrich Freiherr Hiller von Gaertringen, Göttingen (1957).
Groener (2)	Wilhelm Groener, "Politik und Kriegführung. Ein Rückblick auf den Weltkrieg," *Deutsche Revue* (1920).
Haegy	*Das Elsass von 1870-1932,* ed. by Abbé J. Rossé *et al.* in memory of Abbé Haegy, 4 vols., Colmar (1936-1938).
Hamilton	Mary Agnes Hamilton, *Arthur Henderson. A Biography,* London and Toronto (1938).
Hancock	W. H. Hancock, *Smuts. The Sanguine Years 1870-1919,* Cambridge (1962).
Hardinge	Charles Lord Hardinge, *Old Diplomacy; the Reminiscences of Lord Hardinge of Penshurst,* London (1947).
Haussmann	Conrad Haussmann, *Schlaglichter. Reichstagsbriefe und Aufzeichnungen,* ed. by U. Zeller, Frankfurt (1924).
Helfferich	Karl Helfferich, *Der Weltkrieg,* 3 vols. Berlin (1919).
Hendrick	Burton J. Hendrick, *The Life and Letters of Walter Hines Page,* 3 vols., New York (1923).
Herre	Paul Herre, *Kronprinz Wilhelm. Seine Rolle in der deutschen Politik* (1956).
Hertling	Count Karl von Hertling, *Ein Jahr in der Reichskanzlei. Erinnerungen an die Kanzlerschaft meines Vaters,* Freiburg/Breisgau (1919).
Hersfeld	Hans Hersfeld, *Die deutsche Sozialdemokratie und die Auflösung der nationalen Einheitsfront,* Leipzig (1928).
Hoffmann	Max Hoffmann, *Die Aufzeichnungen des Generalmajors Max Hoffmann,* ed. by K. F. Nowak, 2 vols., Berlin (1929).
Hölzle	Erwin Hölzle, "Das Experiment des Friedens im Ersten Weltkrieg 1914-1917," GWU: Vol. 13 (1962).
House	Edward Mandell House, *The Intimate Papers of Colonel House,* arranged as a narrative by Charles Seymour, 4 vols., London (1928).
Hubatsch	W. Hubatsch, "Finnland in der deutschen Ostseepolitik 1917-1918," *Ostdeutsche Wissenschaft,* Vol. 2 (1955).
Hutten-Czapski	Count Bogdan von Hutten-Czapski, *Sechzig Jahre Gesellschaft und Politik,* Vol. 2, Berlin (1936).
Janssen	Karl Heinz Janssen, *Macht und Verblendung. Kriegszielpolitik der deutschen Bundesstaaten 1914-1918,* Göttingen (1963).
John	Volkwart John, "Brest-Litowsk. Verhandlungen und Friedensverträge im Osten 1917-1918," dissertation, Bonn (1937), in *Beiträge zur Geschichte der nachbismarckschen Zeit und des Weltkrieges,* No. 35.
Johnson	Humphrey Johnson, *Vatican Diplomacy in the World War,* Oxford (1933).
Jutikkala-Pirinen	Eino Jutikkala and Kauka Pirinen, *Geschichte Finnlands,* German trans., Stuttgart (1964).
Kaehler (1)	Siegfried A. Kaehler, "Vier quellenkritische Untersuchungen zum Kriegsende 1918," *Nachrichten der Akademie der Wissenschaften,* No. 8, Göttingen (1960), reprinted in *Studien zur Geschichte des 19. und 20. Jahrhunderts,* ed. by W. Bussmann (1961).
Kaehler (2)	Siegfried A. Kaehler, "Zur Beurteilung Ludendorffs in Sommer 1918," *Nachrichten der Akademie der Wissenschaften,* No. 1, Göttingen (1953).
Kann	Robert A. Kann, "J. M. Baernreither und Graf Czernins fragmen-

	tarische Darstellung der Sixtusaffäre," *Mitteilungen des österreichischen Staatsarchivs,* Vol. 16 (1963).
Keit	E. Keit, *Der Waffenstillstand und die Rheinfrage 1918-1919,* dissertation, Heidelberg (1919).
Kennan	George F. Kennan, *Soviet-American Relations 1917-1920. Russia Leaves the War,* Princeton (1956), German trans., *Amerika und die Sowjetmacht,* Vol. 1, *Der Sieg der Revolution,* Stuttgart (1959?).
Klimas	P. Klimas, *Der Werdegang des litauischen Staates bis zur Bildung der provisorischen Regierung im November 1918,* Berlin (1919).
Knesebeck	L. G. von der Knesebeck, *Die Wahrheit über den Propagandafeldzug und Deutschlands Zusammenbruch. Der Kampf der Publizistik im Weltkriege,* Munich (1927).
Kruck	Alfred Kruck, *Geschichte des Alldeutschen Verbandes 1890-1939,* Wiesbaden (1954).
Kühlmann	Richard von Kühlmann, *Erinnerungen,* Heidelberg (1948).
Lama	F. Ritter von Lama, *Die Friedensvermittlung Papst Benedikts XV. und ihre Vereitelung durch den deutschen Reichskanzler Michaelis,* Munich (1932).
Lammasch-Sperl	Heinrich Lammasch, *Seine Aufzeichnungen, sein Wirken und seine Politik,* ed by Lammasch and H. Sperl, Vienna and Leipzig (1922).
Landwehr	Ottokar Landwehr, *Hunger. Die Erschöpfungsjahre der Mittelmächte 1917-1918,* Vienna (1931).
Lansdowne	The Marquess of Lansdowne, "The 'Peace Letters' of 1917," *The Nineteenth Century and After* (March 1934).
Lewerenz	Lilli Lewerenz, *Die deutsche Politik im Baltikum 1914-1918,* dissertation, Hamburg (1958).
L'Hôpital	René Michel M. L'Hôpital, *Foch, L'Armistice et la Paix* (1938).
Linde	Gerd Linde, *Die deutsche Politik in Litauen im Ersten Weltkrieg,* Wiesbaden (1965).
Lloyd George	David Lloyd George, *War Memoirs,* 6 vols., London and Boston (1933-1937).
Lossberg	Fritz von Lossberg, *Meine Tätigkeit im Weltkrieg 1914-1918,* Berlin (1939).
Ludendorff (1)	Erich von Ludendorff, *Urkunden der Obersten Heeresleitung über ihre Tätigkeit 1916-1918,* Berlin (1920).
Ludendorff (2)	Erich von Ludendorff, *Meine Kriegserinnerungen 1914-1918,* Berlin (1919).
Lutz	R. H. Lutz, *The Fall of the German Empire,* 2 vols., Stanford (1932).
Mamatey	Victor S. Mamatey, *The United States and East Central Europe 1914-1918. A Study in Wilsonian Diplomacy and Propaganda,* Princeton (1957).
Mann	Bernhard Mann, *Die baltischen Länder in der deutschen Kriegspublizistik 1914-1918,* Tübingen (1965) *(Studien zur Geschichte und Politik).*
Martens-Triepel	G. F. de Martens and H. Triepel, *Nouveau recueil général de traités et autres actes relatifs aux rapports de droit international. Continuation du grand recueil de G. F. de Martens,* 3rd series, Vol. 10 (1921).
Martini (1)	A. Martini, "La preparazione dell'appello di Benedetto XV ai governi belligeranti," *La Civiltà Cattolica* Vol. 4 (1962), pp. 120 ff.
Martini (2)	A. Martini, "La Nota di Benedetto XV ai Capi della nazioni belligeranti (1. Agosto 1917)," *La Civiltà Cattolica,* Vol. 4 (1962), pp. 417-429.
Matthias-Morsey (1)	Erich Matthias and R. Morsey, eds., *Der Interfraktionelle Ausschuss 1917-1918,* 1st series, Vol. 1, I and II, *Quellen zur Geschichte des*

Parlamentarismus und der politischen Parteien, ed. by W. Conze, Düsseldorf (1959).

Matthias-Morsey (2) Erich Matthias and R. Morsey, eds., *Die Regierung des Prinzen Max von Baden,* 1st series, Vol. 2, *Quellen zur Geschichte des Parlamentarismus und der politischen Parteien,* ed. by W. Conze, Düsseldorf (1962).

Max   Prince Max von Baden, *Erinnerungen und Dokumente* (1927).

Meier-Welcker (1)   Hans Meier-Welcker, "Die deutsche Führung an der Westfront im Frühsommer 1918. Zum Problem der militärischen Lagebeurteilung," WG, No. 3 (1961).

Meier-Welcker (2)   Hans Meier-Welcker, *Die militärischen Planungen und ihre Ergebnisse 1917-1918. Weltwende 1917,* Ranke Society, Göttingen (1965).

Meinecke (1)   Friedrich Meinecke, *Erlebtes 1862-1919,* Stuttgart (1964).

Meinecke (2)   Friedrich Meinecke, "Kühlmann und die päpstliche Friedensaktion von 1917," *Proceedings of the Academy of Sciences,* Berlin (1928).

Mermeix   Mermeix (G. Terrail), *Les négociations secrètes et les quatre armistices,* Paris (1919).

Metternich-Solf   Wolff Metternich and Wilhelm Solf, *Gegen die Unvernunft. Der Briefwechsel zwischen Graf Wolff Metternich und Wilhelm Solf 1915-1918,* ed. by E. von Vietsch, Bremen (1964).

Michaelis (1)   Georg Michaelis, *Für Staat und Volk* (1922).

Michaelis (2)   Wilhelm Michaelis, "Der Reichskanzler Michaelis und die päpstliche Friedensaktion von 1917," GWU (1956).

Michaelis (3)   Wilhelm Michaelis, "Der Reichskanzler Michaelis und die päpstliche Friedensaktion 1917. Neue Dokumente," GWU (1961).

Michaelis (4)   Wilhelm Michaelis, "Zum Problem des Königstodes am Ende der Hohenzollernmonarchie," GWU (1962).

Mitchell   Allan Mitchell, *Revolution in Bavaria 1918-1919. The Eisner Regime and the Soviet Republic,* Princeton (1965).

Mordacq   Général Mordacq, *Le ministère Clémenceau. Journal d'un tèmoin,* Vol. 2, Paris (1930).

Müller   Georg Alexander von Müller, *Regierte der Kaiser? Kriegstagebücher, Aufzeichnungen und Briefe . . . 1917-1918,* ed. by W. Görlitz, Göttingen (1959).

Murphy   Robert Murphy, *Diplomat Among Warriors,* New York (1965).

Nabokoff   C. Nabokoff, *The Ordeal of a Diplomat,* London (1921).

Naumann   Viktor Naumann, *Dokumente und Argumente,* Berlin (1928).

Neu   H. Neu, *Die revolutionäre Bewegung auf der deutschen Flotte 1917-1918* (1930).

Newton (1)   Lord Thomas Newton, *Lord Lansdowne,* London (1928).

Newton (2)   Lord Thomas Newton, *Retrospection,* London (1941).

Niemann (1)   Alfred Niemann, *Kaiser und Revolution. Die entscheidenden Ereignisse im Grossen Hauptquartier,* new ed. (1928).

Niemann (2)   Alfred Niemann, *Revolution von oben. Umsturz von unten. Entwicklung und Verlauf der Staatsumwälzungen in Deutschland 1914-1918,* Berlin (1927).

Noske   Gustav Noske, *Von Kiel bis Kapp,* Berlin (1920).

Nowak   K. F. Nowak, *Sturz der Mittelmächte,* Munich (1921).

Painlevé   P. Painlevé, *Comment j'ai nommé Foch et Pétain. La politique de guerre de 1917. Le Commandement unique interallié* (1924).

Patemann   R. Patemann, *Der Kampf um die preussische Wahlreform im Ersten Weltkrieg,* Düsseldorf (1964).

Payer   Friedrich Freiherr von Payer, *Von Bethmann Hollweg bis Ebert. Erinnerungen und Bilder,* Frankfurt (1923).

Pipes   Richard Pipes, *The Formation of the Soviet Union. Communism and Nationalism,* Princeton (1957).

Poincaré	Raymond Poincaré, *Au Service de la France. Neuf années de souvenirs,* Vols. 9 and 10, Paris (1932).
Poll	H. Poll, "Die Reichsleitung, die Oberste Heeresleitung und der Abschluss des Waffenstillstands November 1918," *Annual Report and Minutes of the Görres Society* (1954).
Renouvin	P. Renouvin, "Les buts de guerre du Gouvernement Français 1914-1918," *Revue Historique,* Vol. 235 (January 1966).
Reshetar	John S. Reshetar, *The Ukrainian Revolution 1917-1920,* Princeton (1952).
Revertera	Count Nikolaus von Revertera, "Kaiser Karls Bündnistreue," *Historisch-Politische Blätter für das katholische Deutschland,* Vol. 169 (1922).
Ribot (1)	Alexandre Ribot, *Journal d'Alexandre Ribot,* Paris (1936).
Ribot (2)	Alexandre Ribot, *Lettres à un Ami. Souvenirs de ma Vie Politique,* Paris (1934).
Riddell	Lord Riddell, *Lord Riddell's War Diary 1914-1918,* London (1933).
Rosen	Friedrich Rosen, *Aus einem diplomatischen Wanderleben,* Vols. 3 and 4, Wiesbaden (1959).
Rudin	H. Rudin, *Armistice 1918,* New Haven (1944).
Rupprecht	Crown Prince Rupprecht, *Mein Kriegstagebuch,* ed. by E. Frauenholz, Vols. 2 and 3, Munich (1929).
Scheidemann (1)	Philipp Scheidemann, *Der Zusammenbruch,* Berlin (1921).
Scheidemann (2)	Philipp Scheidemann, *Memoiren eines Sozialdemokraten,* 2 vols., Dresden (1928).
Schiffer	Eugen Schiffer, *Ein Leben für den Liberalismus* (1951).
Schmidt	Charles Schmidt, *Die geheimen Pläne der deutschen Politik in Elsass-Lothringen (1915-1918),* Paris (1923).
Schulthess	*Schulthess' Europäischer Geschichtskalender,* ed. by E. Jäckh and K. Höhn, new series, Vols. 32ff., Munich (1921).
Schwabe	Klaus Schwabe, *Die deutschen Professoren und die politischen Grundfragen des Ersten Weltkrieges,* unpublished dissertation, Freiburg (1958).
Schweinitz	Wilhelm von Schweinitz, "Abriss meiner Haager Berichterstattung. Ein Beitrag zur Geschichte des letzten Kriegsjahrs," *Grenzboten,* Vol. 80 (1921).
Scott	James Brown Scott, *Official Statements of War Aims and Peace Proposals, December 1916 to November 1918,* Carnegie Endowment, Washington (1920).
Seeckt	Hans von Seeckt, *Aus meinem Leben 1866-1917,* ed. by Freiherr von Rabenau, Leipzig (1938).
Seymour	Charles Seymour, *American Diplomacy During the World War,* Baltimore (1934).
Sharp	*The War Memoirs of William G. Sharp, American Ambassador to France 1914-1919,* London (1931).
Sixtus	Prince Sixtus of Bourbon-Parma, *L'Offre de paix separée de l'Autriche,* Paris (1920).
Snell (1)	John L. Snell, "Germany and the Fourteen Points," *Journal of Modern History,* Vol. 26 (1954).
Snell (2)	John L. Snell, "Die Republik aus Versäumnissen," WG, Vol. 15 (1955).
Solf	See Metternich-Solf.
Steglich (1)	Wolfgang Steglich, "Bündnissicherung oder Verständigungsfrieden. Untersuchungen zu dem Friedensangebot der Mittelmächte vom 12. Dezember 1916," *Göttinger Bausteine zur Geschichtswissenschaft,* Vol. 28, Göttingen (1958).
Steglich (2)	Wolfgang Steglich, *Die Friedenspolitik der Mittelmächte 1917-1918,* Vol. 1, Wiesbaden (1964).

Stupperich   Robert Stupperich, "Siedlungspläne im Gebiet des Oberbefehls-
                      habers Ost, Militärverwaltung Litauen und Kurland, während des
                      Weltkrieges," *Jomsburg*, 5 (1941).
Stutzenberger   Admiral Stutzenberger "Die Abdankung Kaiser Wilhelms II. Die
                      Entstehung und Entwicklung der Kaiserfrage und die Haltung der
                      Presse," *Historische Studien*, Berlin, No. 312 (1937).
Suarez   Georges Suarez, *Briand, Sa Vie.—Son oeuvre, avec son journal et de
                      nombreux documents inédits*, Vol. 4, Paris (1940).
Tardieu   André Tardieu, *La Paix* (1922).
Thaer   Albrecht von Thaer, *Generalstabsdienst an der Front und in der
                      OHL. Briefe und Tagebuchaufzeichnungen 1915-1919*, ed. by S.
                      Kaehler, Göttingen (1958).
Thimme   Annelise Thimme, *Hans Delbrück als Kritiker der wilhelminischen
                      Epoche*, Düsseldorf (1955).
Tobien   Alexander von Tobien, *Die livländische Ritterschaft in ihrem
                      Verhältnis zum Zarentum und russischen Nationalismus* (1930).
Trotzky   Leon Trotzky, *Mein Leben. Versuch einer Autobiographie*, Berlin
                      (1930).
Ullmann   Richard H. Ullmann, *Intervention and the War. Anglo-Soviet
                      Relations 1917-1920*, Princeton (1961).
Valentini   Rudolf V. von Valentini, *Kaiser und Kabinettschef. Nach eigenen
                      Aufzeichnungen und dem Briefwechsel des Wirklichen Geheimen
                      Rats R. V. von Valentini*, ed. by B. Schwertfeger, Oldenburg (1931).
Vogel   W. Vogel, "Die Organisation der amtlichen Presse- und Propaganda-
                      politik des deutschen Reiches bis zum Beginn des Jahres 1918,"
                      Zeitungswissenschaft, Vol. 16, No. 8/9, Berlin (1941).
Volkmann   Erich O. Volkmann, *Der Marxismus und das deutsche Heer im
                      Weltkrieg*, Berlin (1925).
Volkmann   Erich O. Volkmann, *Annexionsfragen:* See UA IV, vol. 12.
Wehler   H. U. Wehler, "Elsass-Lothringen von 1870-1918," ZGO (1961).
Westarp   Count Kuno von Westarp, *Das Ende der Monarchie am 9. November
                      1918*, with an epilogue by W. Conze (1952).
Wheeler-Bennett   John W. Wheeler-Bennett, *Brest-Litovsk. The Forgotten Peace,
                      March 1918*, 3rd ed. (1956).
William   Crown Prince William, *Erinnerungen*, ed by K. Rosner, Berlin and
                      Stuttgart (1922).
Wippermann-Purlitz Deutscher Geschichtskalender. *Der europäische Krieg in aktenmäs-
                      siger Darstellung*, Vol. 7 (1917).
Wortmann   Karl Wortmann, *Geschichte der Vaterlandspartei* (1926).
Wrisberg   Ernst von Wrisberg, *Erinnerungen an die Kriegsjahre im Königlich
                      Preussischen Kriegsministerium*, 3 vols., Berlin (1921-1922).
Zeisler   K. Zeisler, "Die revolutionäre Matrosenbewegung in Deutschland im
                      Oktober/November 1918," in *Revolutionäre Ereignisse und Prob-
                      leme in Deutschland während der Periode der Grossen Sozialisti-
                      schen Oktoberrevolution 1917-1918*, Berlin (1957).
Zeman (1)   Zbyněk A. B. Zeman (ed.), *Germany and the Revolution in Russia
                      1915-1918, Documents from the Archives of the German Foreign
                      Ministry*, Oxford (1958).
Zeman (2)   Zbyněk A. B. Zeman, *The Break-up of the Hapsburg Empire
                      1914-1918. A Study in National and Social Revolution*, London
                      (1961) (German trans., 1963).
Zeman-Scharlau   Zbyněk A. B. Zeman and W. B. Scharlau, *Parvus Helphand.
                      Freibeuter der Revolution*, Cologne (1965).

Notes

Notes to Chapter 1

1. Painlevé, pp. 135ff.; British cabinet session, PRO, Cab. 23/16, WC, 159a.
2. See Riddell, pp. 267f.
3. See esp. Hardinge, pp. 220ff.
4. Lloyd George, Vol. 4, p. 2040.
5. Bertie, pp. 183 and 193, about his discussions with General Messimy (former war minister) and Colonel Aubrey, who had been dispatched to Albania (September 15 and October 2). Aubrey thought France should be satisfied with recovering only part of Alsace-Lorraine.
6. Hendrick, Vol. 3, pp. 381ff., 391; Sharp, Vol. 3, pp. 184, 196ff.
7. Sharp, p. 199, message to Wilson, August 24, 1917.
8. Hendrick, Vol. 2, pp. 267f., 275, 289; Vol. 3, pp. 381ff.; Lloyd George, *The Truth About the Peace Treaties,* Vol. 1 (1938), pp. 66f.
9. Hendrick, Vol. 2, pp. 217ff., 267ff., 275, 289ff. Page's letters, esp. those to his son of March 25 and July 8, 1917, show a marked literary flair, expressive of the fact that the writer was a journalist and publisher.
10. Ribot (2), pp. 252f., also 241ff.; see also Poincaré, Vol. 9, p. 184. Poincaré was much concerned about socialist "double-dealing." The socialists wanted a referendum in Alsace-Lorraine.
11. Details in Ribot (2), pp. 243f., 261; Bonnefous, pp. 241ff.; Suarez, pp. 215ff.
12. Millerand, on June 27, urgently warned against any attempt at a separate peace: *Ce sera un acheminement vers la paix générale* (Poincaré, Vol. 9, p. 177).
13. The situation was different in Britain. I seriously doubt, however, whether anyone in the Western camp still had any question by the summer of 1917 that Germany would allow the chance of peace to be wrecked over the Belgian issue. That Bethmann Hollweg was prepared to relinquish Belgium had probably transpired through the Vatican and through Belgian and American sources, especially the confidential disclosure of German war aims to Wilson on January 31 (Sch&Gr, Vol. 1, No. 476; see my Vol. III, pp. 303, 334). The preface to Johnson by Count Salis, British envoy to the Vatican, hints that Salis knew about Bethmann Hollweg's talk with the papal nuncio Pacelli on June 26 (my Vol. III, p. 461).
14. The talks at St. Jean-de-Maurienne on April 19, 1917, offer a classic example. They are dramatically described in Ribot (2), pp. 272ff.; see also my Vol. III, p. 384. For Sonnino's and Boselli's speeches in the chamber, see Schulthess, Vol. 2, 1917, pp. 504ff.

15. There were negotiations with Wilson in February 1917, see my Vol. III, p. 338, and peace feelers through Count Mensdorff in Scandinavia, *ibidem,* p. 385; further, there were peace feelers with Turkey in April 1917, *ibidem,* p. 374. At a Paris conference in July Lloyd George vainly suggested separate peace negotiations with Austria and Turkey. He complained that the Allies were completely lacking in imagination and pigheaded in sticking to their war aims (Riddell, p. 258, July 30, 1917). In December he authorized Smuts to talk with Mensdorff (Steglich [2], pp. 257ff.).
16. At any rate, that is how Page described the situation in a letter to Wilson on February 22 (Hendrick, Vol. 3, pp. 370ff.).
17. Ribot (2), pp. 258f. The date is not given, but from the context it must have been May.
18. Riddell, p. 247, April 1, 1917.
19. Riddell, p. 272, September 9, 1917.
20. Hendrick, Vol. 2, p. 246; Lloyd George, *The Truth About the Peace Treaties,* pp. 60ff.
21. Hamilton, p. 138, August 1, 1917.
22. Hamilton, pp. 138ff., gives a detailed account, which corrects the account by Lloyd George. Nabokoff also throws light on Lloyd George's intrigue staged with alleged telegrams from St. Petersburg and Stockholm, obtained from the Russian embassy. It is worth noting that a trip to St. Petersburg which MacDonald planned to undertake in June was forestalled by a seamen's strike especially staged for the purpose.
23. Helfferich did so, among others (Vol. 3, p. 140); see also Michaelis (1), p. 330.
24. MacDonald complained about this in the House of Commons on July 26. Actually, a specially printed comprehensive *Memorandum on German War Aims,* prepared by the Foreign Office Intelligence Bureau (and signed E. R. B., J. W. H.), was submitted to the members of the cabinet on July 15 and 27. It presented a surprisingly accurate picture of German war aims policy and the significance of the Reichstag resolution (PRO, Cab. 24/23, pp. 498ff.). I have no information on how the Reichstag resolution was received in the French press, which presumably also ignored it.
25. The following is taken from PD, pp. 1479ff.
26. There was an Allied conference in Paris, but neither Lloyd George nor Balfour attended.
27. German and Dutch liberals immediately and hopefully spoke of "a bold effort on behalf of peace," because Asquith (reacting to an interjection by Snowden) put his question in such formal terms (see Max, p. 132; Rosen, pp. 108f.). Kühlmann's reaction was similar (see Part 3 of this chapter). The differences between statements by Asquith and Bonar Law were especially emphasized in these circles.
28. Riezler before the UA, December 20, 1921, according to Steglich (2), p. 457, Note 78. See also my Vol. III, p. 482.
29. Speech in Glasgow, June 29, 1917 (see Scott, pp. 109, 112).
30. Riddell, p. 309, January 27, 1918.
31. According to Michaelis (1), p. 329, it was simply an "act of insincerity," since its authors continued to entertain claims to substantial annexations and indemnities, which they subsequently put forward with the help of various tricky interpretations. No doubt this is quite true, but at the time the resolution was adopted Bethmann Hollweg and the Reichstag majority were certainly and sincerely ready for a negotiated peace that would have foregone annexations.
32. According to Friedrich Naumann, before the joint party caucus on August 28 (see Matthias-Morsey [1], p. 121). Michaelis initially hoped to have the Reichstag resolution withdrawn altogether and to exact official approval of his speech by all the political parties instead; but as he reported to Prince Hohenlohe, he was unable to prevail with this plan (Hohenlohe to Czernin, July 17, 18, and 19,

HHSTA, Prussia, Vol. 3, p. 173). Michaelis could have entertained this hope only because he was unfamiliar with the background of the resolution (see my Vol. III, pp. 467ff.).

33. Michaelis (1), pp. 329ff. and esp. 335f. On July 26 Michaelis wrote the crown prince that his interpretation (i.e., the clause he had added) had blunted the menace of the "notorious" resolution. He added that almost any kind of peace might be concluded on its basis (Here, p. 107; Scheidemann [2] Vol. 2, pp. 52f. The most charitable interpretation of this notorious letter is that it shows its author's extreme political insecurity.

34. See Michaelis (1), p. 332, and plausible confirmation by Michaelis's son, Dr. Wilhelm Michaelis, a high municipal official, in GWU, 1956, pp. 17f.; 1961, p. 428; 1962, p. 699, in addition to personal communications from the son to the author, always accompanied by documentary evidence. When Prince Hohenlohe had his first talk with the new Chancellor on July 17, he also got the impression that Michaelis was unwilling to allow himself to be "raped" by either the conservatives or the Pan-Germans and was sincerely aspiring to conclude a prompt negotiated peace. The American Feldman (pp. 408f.) rightly emphasizes that the Michaelis-inspired cabinet appointments were far from reactionary, as was Michaelis's institution of the "Sevens Committee."

35. Matthias-Morsey (1), I, pp. 138ff.

36. On Kapp, see my Vol. III, p. 530f, Note 3. For the rest, see Schwabe, Chapter 8, Wortmann, and Kruck. Feldman (p. 430) regards the fatherland party as a direct instrumentality of the OHL, arranged through the OHL's propaganda chief Nicolai. Feldman cites a memorandum by Major General Magirus of Württemberg in 1916, which already fully outlined the basic idea behind the fatherland party. Personally, I do not believe that the evidence fully supports this theory.

37. From the first day onward, Pan-German circles, notably the industrialist Röchling, besieged Michaelis to be "tough" in the face of the Reichstag's "soft" peace policy. They urged him to bear in mind what had happened to Bethmann Hollweg. (They were, of course, supported by the OHL! See Röchling, July 15, ZA, RK [Reich chancellery], Vol. 9, p. 14.) On September 1 Dietrich Schäfer sent Lieutenant Colonel Bauer at the OHL a formal political "directive" intended for the new Chancellor. Michaelis, Schäfter said, was still lacking in experience and required support (see the Bauer papers, BA).

38. Johnson, pp. 14ff. For the following, see also Martini (2), pp. 119-132, 417-429; Engel-Janosi (3), pp. 296ff.; Steglich (1), pp. 168f.; Steglich (2), pp. 117ff. In view of Steglich's meticulous source studies, there is no need for me to review the evidence in detail.

39. Sch&Gr, Vol. 2, p. 109; Naumann, pp. 235ff. More details in Steglich (2), p. 449, Note 8, p. 453, Note 32; Engel-Janosi (3), pp. 302ff.

40. Czernin encouraged Erzberger, among others, to act as an intermediary along these lines. See my Vol. III, p. 579, Note 67; also Steglich (2), p. 453, Note 32. On Erzberger's activities with Pacelli, see *ibidem*, p. 451, Note 12.

41. Report from Grünau to Bethmann Hollweg, July 3, 1917 (Sch&Gr, Vol. 2, No. 157); draft of the Kaiser's reply to the pope, July 14 (*ibidem*, No. 165).

42. Bethmann Hollweg, in a letter to Professor Hans Delbrück, August 5, 1918, in which he also said that in his Reichstag speech of December 19, 1915, he had purposely refrained from describing Belgium as a "hostage" (cited in Steglich [2], p. 452, Note 19).

43. Steglich (2), pp. 132ff., presents a searching study on Zimmermann's "changed attitude" late in July and the probable reasons for it. The real question is whether Zimmermann, about to leave office, could have done anything else but register objections and mention guarantees for Germany, in the changed situation after July 13. Zimmermann's counterdraft to the draft of the note transmitted by Pacelli on July 24, dated July 28, is found in AA (WK 25, papal peace appeal, Vol. 1). It was approved by Michaelis and Kühlmann and also submitted to the

OHL, which offered no objections, but it was passed on to Pacelli only on August 12, i.e., at the time the papal peace note went out. Thus it was virtually without effect. Details in Steglich (2), pp. 137f. and 462, Note 132; also Sch&Gr, Vol. 2, Nos. 175, 183 (peace note of August 2).

44. FR, 1917, Supplement 2, Vol. 1, pp. 172, 175; Johnson, p. 34.

45. FR, 1917, Supplement 2, Vol. 1, p. 167 (Jay to Lansing, August 21); Sonnino's speech in the chamber on October 25, Johnson, pp. 33, 37f.

46. FR,, *loc. cit.,* pp. 166 (Lansing to Wilson), 175 (Sharp to Lansing, August 24), 180 (Francis to Lansing, August 24); House, Vol. 3, p. 162 (August 19); Ribot (1), p. 180; Lloyd George, Vol. 4, p. 2059.

47. Poincaré, Vol. 9, p. 251 (the date given, August 17, is probably wrong and should be August 16); Ribot (1), pp. 177ff., 183.

48. FR, 1917, Supplement 2, Vol. 1, pp. 170f. (Sharp to Lansing, August 21), also for the following.

49. House, Vol. 3, pp. 164f. On August 24 de Margerie displayed (or pretended to display) indignation to Sharp that the pope made no moral distinction between the aggressors and their victims and evidently wished to see Germany preserved as a great power (FR, *loc. cit.,* pp. 175ff.). Note also Poincaré's anger about papal neutrality (Vol. 9, p. 250).

50. A very shrewd observation! In the end it proved to be unfortunate that Wilson, instead, still imagined he could revive flagging Russian spirits by warnings of the specter of German militarism (which did, however, meet with the approval of Tereschenko). On Wilson's Russian policy in general, see Hölzle, pp. 486ff.

51. House, Vol. 3, pp. 157f., 160f. (House to Wilson, August 15 and 17).

52. These illusions seem less important when one reads, in House's letter to Wilson of July 19 (*loc. cit.,* pp. 162f.), how the colonel warned.the Russian ambassador against any public demonstrations directed against the Kaiser or Germany's "military caste." The Germans, with their monarchist and militarist indoctrination, would never understand such a thing. They should, however, be tempted with the idea of "representative government," which could then fob off responsibility for the war on the "autocrats."

53. Wiseman, at Balfour's behest, to House, August 11; Balfour to House, August 22 (House, Vol. 3, pp. 156, 160). Sharp to Lansing, August 21 (FR, 1917, Supplement 2, Vol. 1, p. 171).

54. "If these terms included the evacuation of Belgium, it would show a marked advance on the part of the Central Powers towards a settlement" (PRO, Cab. 23/3, WC 220 [1], August 20, 1918). Preliminary meetings took place on August 8 (*ibidem,* WC 20, 10) and August 15 (*ibidem,* WC 215 [4]). On August 21 Balfour submitted the draft of his directive to Count Salis (*ibidem,* WC 221, 8).

55. This is the way in which Salis himself subsequently interpreted Balfour's intentions— he was intent that no "doubts of Britain's good faith" should be aroused. See Salis's preface to Johnson; Ribot (1), p. 184; Lloyd George, Vol. 4, p. 2060.

56. The text of the directive, as given in the British White Book of 1919 (*The Peace Proposals Made by the Pope . . . on January 8, 1917, and Correspondence Relative Thereto,* Misc. No. 7), differs materially from the version wired to Washington and Paris (FR, 1917, Supplement 2, Vol. 1, pp. 167f.; Ribot [1], p. 185). Strangely enough, the originals of the documents published in the White Book could be found neither in the Foreign Office files nor among the papers of Balfour and Cecil.

57. As late as September 17 he was still waiting for a German reply to the papal note. He told the war cabinet that a few trial balloons in the German press left the impression that a German peace program would follow after all (PRO, Cab. 23/3, WC 234 [2]).

58. Steglich (2), p. 177, where the belief is expressed that this brief telegraphic communication from Cecil was indubitably and quite deliberately intended to turn the diversion contemplated by Ribot into its direct opposite. I do not think

this probable and doubt that it can be demonstrated. Any effort to sabotage Ribot's plans in Rome would have made sense only if Cecil had been willing to risk a break with Paris, and that is quite unthinkable. Apparently Cecil oversimplified or misunderstood Ribot's views, which were communicated to him in the first instance through the French chargé d'affaires de Fleuriau and only subsequently by letter, as shown by Cecil's wire to Lord Bertie on August 22 (Scott, No. 3).

59. Steglich (2), p. 179, Note 352, notes correctly that the French translation (given in Michaelis [1], pp. 343f.) departs from the English text (Scott, No. 2), not merely in stylistic respects (which might have been a matter of coding), but by omitting the dubious opening sentence: "H. M. Government . . . cannot say whether it would serve any useful purpose to offer a reply thereto [i.e., to the papal note of August 1] or if so, what form any such reply should take."

60. Ribot (1), p. 188 (Ribot to de Fleuriau, August 25). Commission executed on August 27 (Scott, No. 8). French memorandum of August 26, Cecil to Salis, same date (Scott, No. 7). From the fact that Salis did not wish to intervene in ongoing German-Vatican negotiations but preferred to allow things to run their course, Steglich (1), p. 179, seeks to gain further support for his above-mentioned theory that the British government was then really engaged in a serious peace feeler. But what could Salis have done to interrupt Gasparri's negotiations with Kühlmann, particularly since he had only just stated that a moderate German declaration on Belgium was desirable? And why should he oppose the continuation of such negotiations? If Germany forewent Belgium unconditionally, that was highly desirable, without in any way obliging Britain to forego the Allied war aims. If Germany refused, that would offer excellent new opportunities to accuse German militarism before all the world. The interpretation of a casual and irrelevant statement by Count Salis on September 1, as given in Steglich (2), p. 182, second paragraph, seems to me contrived.

61. Hendrick, Vol. 2, p. 321 (to House, September 1917); Vol. 3, pp. 406ff. (to Wilson, September 25).

62. Riddell, p. 277 (September 26); Lloyd George, Vol. 4, p. 2069.

63. Ribot (1), p. 190.

64. Hölzle, p. 489.

65. Directive by Balfour to Bertie in Paris, also communicated to Rome, St. Petersburg, Le Havre, Tokyo, and Washington on September 1. The British government rejected the communiqué proposed by France, looked for the time being for a German response to the papal peace note, and did not wish to issue a new Allied peace aims declaration, preferring to concentrate on Wilson's declaration, though only up to the point of not regarding any further response to the pope as necessary after Wilson's note. "There are phrases in the president's note about economic policy and the impossibility of treating with the present German government, etc., which make it difficult to go further than this." A rather remarkable reservation! (See the Balfour papers, British Museum, Manuscript Division, London, No. 49699.)

66. In January 1917 the German journalist Heinrich May, stationed in Amsterdam, heard from Camille Huysmans, secretary general of the Second International, that King Albert of Belgium had stated he would welcome a negotiated peace without annexations or indemnities, provided Belgium were unconditionally restored. To relieve Franco-German tension in the predominantly French-speaking parts of Lorraine, he also recommended a referendum. May reported this to Scheidemann, only to be sharply upbraided: "Young man, I can't take anyone seriously in a political sense who acknowledges that there is such a thing as an issue over Alsace-Lorraine." On July 26, 1962, Dr. Wilhelm Michaelis, the Chancellor's son, made May's report public in a West German broadcast. On the Stockholm talks of Scheidemann and Ebert see my Vol. III, p. 459.

67. See the account of the Reichstag session of October 6, 1917 (Kühlmann, p. 496).

68. Kühlmann, p. 472.
69. Memorandum for Michaelis and the Kaiser, September 3, 1917 (Michaelis [3], pp. 429ff., from the Chancellor's papers; also in AA, WK 15, secret, Vol. 4, copy, and WK 20, a, secret; also now in Sch&Gr, Vol. 2, No. 235). Further notes by Kühlmann of September 8 (Michaelis [3], pp. 432ff.). A memorandum of July 27 (Meinecke [2], pp. 191f. [20f.]).
70. Kühlmann, p. 473.
71. The following materials are available on the Kreuznach talks of August 9: (a) A formulation of the "conclusions," undertaken by Ludendorff and wired on August 14 to Michaelis, who authenticated it by his signature. Points 10-18 are reproduced in UA, Vol. 12, pp. 204ff., and the complete text is in AA, WK 15, secret, Vol. 4, reprinted in Sch&Gr, Vol. 2, No. 207. See Steglich (2), p. 463, Note 138. (b) A copy of Points 12-14, 15 (in greatly abbreviated form), and 18, wired ahead of time by Ludendorff (through Lersner) to Michaelis, for use in the talks with Czernin (AA, WK 15, secret, Vol. 4. I owe my copy to Steglich's courtesy). (c) A slightly different version from the Reich chancellery, with marginal notes comparing it with Ludendorff's version, authenticated by Lersner (ZA, RK II, Kr. 1, Adh. 5, Ed. 1). I have a photostat of this document.

On August 9 Ludendorff sent Michaelis detailed proposals for central press coordination, drafted by Colonel Nicolai (ZA, RK II, Kr. 10, Vol. 13). The next day Hindenburg dispatched a similar "directive" to Michaelis. It went into great detail on the necessary close collaboration between government and OHL, previously lacking through Bethmann Hollweg's fault, with the result "that I [Hindenburg] felt obliged to oppose Herr von Bethmann Hollweg before His Majesty.... The view that statesmanship and strategy can be separated has always been wrong. It is particularly wrong in a war that intimately involves the entire nation." The two top authorities, Hindenburg went on, must work closely together, presumably equipped with equal power, and they must trust each other completely (UA, Vol. 2, pp. 39ff.). Judging by its characteristic tone as well as its content, this memorandum is clearly traceable to Colonel Bauer. On August 15 a third "directive" followed, containing information about the threat posed by the impending new international socialist conference, which "would sit in judgment on Germany" and call for a general strike for peace, which would certainly have harmful repercussions on army morale. "I leave it to Your Excellency to draw the appropriate conclusions" (ZA, RK IX, 15). This time, however, Michaelis objected and on August 27 he tried to explain to the OHL why the attendance of German social democrats at the Stockholm conference was desirable, while to keep them away would be dangerous *(ibidem)*. Colonel Bauer was not only Ludendorff's political adviser but at the same time the confidant of the annexationists and Pan-Germans at the OHL, as shown by the numerous letters addressed to him by the historian, Dietrich Schäfer, the industrialist Röchling, *et al.,* found among his papers. On September 1 Schäfer admonished him that the new Chancellor needed support, if not written directives from the OHL, for both his domestic and foreign policy, since he was not yet equal to his post and would first have to settle in. Schäfer generously appended a handwritten draft for such a directive! Subsequently, on October 17, Bauer drafted a message to Michaelis, providing counsel on domestic policy, especially the treatment of the press and social problems, all given in rather schoolmasterly fashion (BA, Bauer papers, Portfolio 11, Sheet 64; Portfolio 2, Sheets 179ff.).
72. ZA, RK II, 1, III, GHQ 21, App., Vol. 1 (the so-called Bingen conference).
73. See my Vol. III, p. 440.
74. The claim for Liège is found included only in the OHL formulation given in UA and not in the Reich chancellery version or in the wire to Michaelis dispatched on August 13 (see Note 71). Perhaps it was subsequently cut, which might explain what Colonel Haeften, under the influence of an emissary from Prince Max of Baden, claims he achieved in a presentation to Ludendorff directly after the

discussion with the Chancellor (for Haeften's statement before the investigating committee on March 2, 1922, see Max, p. 135, and Steglich [2] p. 468, Note 181). Also cut in the chancellery version is this sentence: "For the time being we are not interested in Austria renouncing Galicia."

75. It is true that the OHL offered no objection on August 9 to the "countermemorandum" to Pacelli's *Pro Memoria* of July 24 (see Note 43). This countermemorandum, however, produced by the German foreign ministry while it was under Zimmermann's direction, was so carefully worded that the OHL could read its wishes into it without trouble.

76. See Steglich (2), pp. 147f., for the evidence. The Kaiser was strongly impressed by the need for reaching peace soon (Sch&Gr, Vol. 2, No. 177, Czernin to Hohenlohe, July 24, Hohenlohe's report of the following. day). Ludendorff advised the minister to proclaim a sweeping annexationist program and thus win the support of public opinion! Czernin was horrified and replied that his last speech, based on the Reichstag resolution of July 19, had met with the warmest approval on the part of all Austria's political parties, without exception. The only reason why his uncompromising allegiance to the alliance was accepted at home, even by Czechs and Poles, was that he kept emphasizing the purely defensive character of the war. Ludendorff, in his reply, said that one had to hold out big goals and strike a pose of strength to the outside world. The only alternative was to surrender. There was no middle way. A modest demeanor merely served to encourage enemy greed. It was a typically militarist response. (HHSTA, 47/3-20 and 13, secret, Czernin to Ludendorff via Cramon, wire by telephone, July 30; Ludendorff to Czernin, July 31.)

77. See the highly interesting letters of British officer prisoners-of-war about the high level of British morale, as shown by the outstanding success of the voluntary bread-rationing program, the dying-down of the U-boat scare, etc., in Rupprecht, Vol. 2, pp. 244ff. (August 13, 1917).

78. ZA, RK II, 2, III, GHQ 21, App., Vol. 1. The note taker was presumably Legation Secretary von Prittwitz. The formulation of the key words is rather awkward, in part almost incomprehensible, as is always true in minutes taken by Prittwitz. For minutes of the preceding meeting in Vienna, see Sch&Gr, Vol. 2, No. 181.

79. Discussion with Ludendorff, see Note 76. The tears were reported by Legation Councilor Krafft to Hertling on September 1, 1917, in the course of an account of a visit by the Chancellor to Crown Prince Rupprecht's headquarters in Munich on August 31 (GSTA, Pol. A, VII, 39).

80. Details on the Armand-Revertera talks are in Steglich (2), pp. 146, 148, 150, 158, 160, 162f., 169. See also Fester (2), pp. 166-188; Fester (1), pp. 108-119. Fester, with a Pan-German bias, seeks to present Czernin and Revertera as traitors. French sources (as yet few) are cited. See more recently Engel-Janosi (1), pp. 287ff. This author had access to the family archive of Count Revertera-Salandra. See also Engel-Janosi (2), p. 24; Charles-Roux. The explanations which Count Armand, according to Engel-Janosi (1), p. 289, is supposed to have given on the stand of the Paris government seem so peculiar that one is inclined to question that Revertera could have been serious in writing the notes which Engel-Janosi used. The German legation in Berne under Romberg was continually informed about the French peace feelers through Frau Zuckerkandl, the wife of an Austrian court councilor and a resident of Switzerland, who received a steady stream of political reports (and a number of visits) from her sister, a sister-in-law of Clémenceau and a friend of Painlevé. These reports suggested that Painlevé was certainly ready to make peace before the war went on to the bitter end, but felt isolated among his fellow cabinet members. Painlevé apparently would have been satisfied personally with the cession of Alsace and was prepared to repay such a concession generously with colonies and commercial privileges (see Sch&Gr, Vol. 2, Nos. 198f., 204, 214, 224, 246, 270, 279, 281, and esp. 292).

81. Ribot (1), pp. 174, 176.

82. Report by Legation Councilor Krafft von Dellmensingen to Hertling, September 4, 1917, on discussions between Michaelis and Crown Prince Rupprecht on August 31, 1917 (GSTA, Pol. A, VII, 39).
83. Müller, p. 315, August 24.
84. UA, Vol. 12, pp. 206ff.; Sch&Gr, Vol. 2, No. 211.
85. Evidence in Steglich (2), pp. 158ff.; see also Sch&Gr, Vol. 2, Nos. 231, 233.
86. According to Steglich, *loc. cit.,* pp. 151f., the Vienna government balked at the wishes of the Holy See.
87. It is noteworthy that Czernin (pp. 224ff.) speaks only of an Entente demand for the cession of all of Tyrol to the Brenner—which was certainly no longer true of the program Armand presented on August 22. Czernin apparently believed that the Entente would never be able to get away from the pledges made in the London pact.
88. RAW, Vol. 13, pp. 214ff. Fester (2) rather tends to overdramatize the military events.
89. Czernin, p. 223. On Kühlmann's stand, see Steglich (2), p. 477, Note 292, where the evidence is presented.
90. Minutes of August 15, ZA, RK II, 2, III, GHQ 21, Supplement, Vol. 1. Evidence is cited in Steglich (2), p. 467, Note 169. See also Sch&Gr, Vol. 2, No. 190.
91. AA, WK 25, papal peace appeal, Vol. 2, August 24. See also Sch&Gr, Vol. 2, No. 222.
92. Berlin's explanations are given in Steglich (2), pp. 150f.
93. Michaelis wired the Kaiser on August 21. After receiving the Kaiser's consent, he wired Wedel the next day that Czernin, out of consideration for the pope, would send a friendly but noncommittal reply. Czernin would actually drag his feet in the matter and wait and see what the enemy might say. Czernin's sole interest was to see to it that the enemy would be blamed for any failure (AA, WK 25, papal peace appeal, Vol. 2; Sch&Gr, Vol. 2, No. 216).
94. In the final version of the reply note, the passages on disarmament and arbitration were worded with exquisite care (Ludendorff [1], pp. 435ff.; Schulthess, 1917, Vol. 1, pp. 801f.). These formulations were influenced by a report from Kriege of the foreign ministry's legal department, which stated that the papal proposals on these subjects were neither feasible nor acceptable. (Two earlier reports are cited.) Even Kriege, however, recommended avoidance of total and direct rejection (AA, WK 24, papal peace appeal, Vol. 2).
95. See Note 43. Kühlmann's assertion rested on a message from Pacelli to Bergen on August 15 (Sch&Gr, Vol. 2, No. 205) and another to Erzberger on August 24 (Matthias-Morsey [1], I, p. 127, Note 9). On August 18 Pacelli again urged Bergen to see to it that papal mediation was promptly accepted (Sch&Gr, Vol. 2, Nos. 187, 191, 195, 212, 213, August 6-18, 1917).
96. On the arguments about this question between Berlin and Vienna, see Steglich (2), pp. 157, 170f., 192ff. There was such difficulty with the reply note in Sofia and Istanbul that the only version of the text Kühlmann dared transmit there was one that did not contain the reference to the peace resolution of July 19 subsequently added at the behest of the Reichstag!
97. For drafts dated August 25 and 27, the second written after consultation with Erzberger by the Bavarian legation councilor von Stockhammern, who was detailed to the foreign ministry, see AA, WK 25, papal peace appeal, Vol. 2. This same volume contains the following messages by Erzberger: To Bergen, August 18 (translation of the papal peace note); to Michaelis and Kühlmann, August 18 and 21; to Bergen, August 20 (reports from Switzerland on the excellent impression registered in Entente circles by the papal note, described as a masterpiece of papal diplomacy); to Michaelis and Kühlmann, August 21; draft of a reply note, by Erzberger, August 25; to Kühlmann, August 27 (reports from Rotterdam on opinions in England and France).
98. Letter to Haussmann, Matthias-Morsey (1), I, No. 27. What follows is from the

material on the proceedings of the joint party caucus and the so-called Sevens Committee, collected in *loc. cit.* The footnotes in this work provide all the necessary references to secondary sources, hence these need not be reviewed here.

99. Michaelis to Ambassador Count Wedel for Czernin, August 19. Michaelis asked for permission, if need be, to let the party leaders know confidentially about the earlier foreign ministry reply (counterdraft) of July 28, still drafted by Zimmermann, in response to the draft note submitted by Pacelli on July 24 (see Note 43). Czernin gave his consent (wire from Wedel, August 20), but asked for a clause to be added to the claim for guarantees of Belgian neutrality, namely that this "in no way involved a change in Belgium's borders." Actually, the contemplated briefing of the party leaders never took place, as recorded in a marginal note, probably by Kühlmann (AA, WK 25, papal peace appeal, Vol. 2).

100. On the meeting with the party leaders on the morning of August 21, when Michaelis, without having to go into the details of the note, gave assurances in keeping with the wishes of the joint party caucus, see Matthias-Morsey (1), I, pp. 126f. It is characteristic of Erzberger's cast of mind that he grandiloquently told Pacelli he had been charged jointly with Bergen with drafting the reply note (*loc. cit.*, p. 127, Note 9). Erzberger, in other words, unhesitatingly equated himself with the proposed committee of deputies.

101. Matthias-Morsey (1), I, p. 181, Note 3; Erzberger, pp. 276f.; *ibidem,* p. 207, on communications of the Belgian envoy in Berne; *ibidem,* p. 278, on Czernin's personal insistence in Berlin on September 6. Pacelli's repeated intercession with Erzberger and Bergen, urging acceptance of the papal proposals, was also probably not without effect. On the liberals and Rosen, see Max, pp. 132ff.; Rosen, pp. 108ff. Reports by Rosen to Michaelis and the foreign ministry of August 7, 24, and 25, all in the sense described, are found in AA, WK 15, secret, Vol. 4, also reproduced in Sch&Gr, Vol. 2, Nos. 189, 218f. They go back to reports from pacifist circles in Britain and Holland and also to statements by the Dutch prime minister Heemskerk and the foreign minister Loudon. Not mentioned by Rosen in his memoirs is the fact that by August 28 he was singing a different tune: a "reliable German" had learned from British journalists that British morale was supremely confident of victory and far removed from any inclination toward peace. The papal note had met with universal rejection. Hopes were centered on victory with American aid. Rosen concluded that a declaration on Belgium at this time would be harmful after all. "Unless we receive credible assurance from Britain, I do not think we should make such a statement now" (AA, WK 25, papal peace appeal, Vol. 2). Kühlmann, on September 10 (see further on), used Rosen's report before the Sevens Committee as an encouraging sign of a British conciliatory mood, though on September 9 he had told the envoy that the foreign ministry was giving unceasing attention to the Belgian issue. There was no desire to discourage peace efforts, but at this time any public declaration on Belgium would be "completely inopportune." At a more propitious juncture Germany would see to it that its intentions were properly brought home to the belligerents (this was probably an allusion to the Villalobar effort). The policy, in other words, was to spin out the peace threads but not to allow Germany to become committed by a public declaration (AA, WK 15, secret, Vol. 4, and WK 20, a, secret; Sch&Gr, Vol. 2, No. 239). At this very time there was meaningful contact in the Hague between the Austrian envoy Szögény and the British envoy Sir Walter Tawnley, arranged through an unidentified intermediary and promoted by the Dutch foreign minister Loudon. This too involved a general peace feeler rather than a separate peace, and these feelers were continued until about the end of the year. I have this correspondence from HHSTA, Kr. 25/27. It has also been used by Steglich (2), pp. 222ff.

102. To Count Wedel for Czernin, August 27 (AA, WK 25, papal peace appeal, Vol. 2).

103. Varnbüler to Weizsäcker, September 1 (HSTA, E 49-51, Vz. 12, Kr. IV-2, not

included in Matthias-Morsey [1]). Lerchenfeld's report on a session of the foreign policy (8th) committee of the federal council of August 20 (which met on the papal note) clearly shows that anything but unity prevailed among the members of the federal council. Only Weizsäcker and Hertling inclined toward a decidedly positive response (Deuerlein [2], pp. 247ff.).

104. See p. 31.
105. Details in Steglich (2), pp. 172f. The note was transmitted and made public on September 20, shortly after rather than before the German note.
106. Michaelis (3), pp. 432f.
107. Steglich (2), p. 482, Note 354; Sch&Gr, Vol. 2, No. 230.
108. Steglich (2), pp. 167f.
109. This seems to me to be established by Pacelli's subsequent testimony (letter to Michaelis, May 8, 1930, Michaelis [3], p. 424) and by that of Erzberger himself (Lama, p. 157, Note 19), as well as by Erzberger's further attitude. His willingness to trust Kühlmann would be quite incomprehensible if he had known the text of the letter.
110. Report by Lerchenfeld in Steglich (2), p. 174 (not included in Matthias-Morsey [1]).
111. Matthias-Morsey (1), I, p. 187.
112. Scheidemann (1), pp. 110ff.
113. According to the report of Württemberg's Berlin chargé d'affaires, Fabre du Faure, on the committee meeting of September 10, Kühlmann then said "he knew that it would certainly not be unwelcome to the Vatican if the reply note said nothing on the Belgian issue. The cardinal secretary of state had sent word to the Chancellor, asking to be told confidentially about his stand on Belgium" (HSTA, E 73, Vz. 61, Fz. 12, 1, II, not used in Matthias-Morsey [1], II).
114. Report by Fabre du Faure, see preceding Note.
115. Details in Steglich (2), pp. 196ff. See also Sch&Gr, Vol. 2, Nos. 237, 243, 256, 260, 262, 263.
116. The statement by Kühlmann before the Reichstag investigating committee on June 8, 1922, cited in Steglich (2), p. 485, Note 394, shows how strongly Kühlmann responded to the pressure of agitated public opinion on his policies.
117. Pacelli to Bergen, August 18 (AA, WK 25, papal peace appeal, Vol. 2).
118. Scott, pp. 141ff.
119. Michaelis to Hertling, September 12, after Fischer, p. 550.
120. Rupprecht, Vol. 2, pp. 252ff. Michaelis replied to these objections that Ludendorff had told him he was glad that he would have nothing more to do with politics henceforth. Apparently Ludendorff regarded the new Chancellor as a pliable tool, to whom politics could be confidently left. (Report by Legation Councilor Krafft to Hertling on Michaelis's visit, September 4, GSTA, Pol. A, VII). In a long letter to Hertling of July 19, 1917, which showed deep concern, Rupprecht favored an immediate peace with Russia, in which Germany would forego all annexations and indemnities, including even Courland. He further advised that peace negotiations be initiated with the Western powers after the conclusion of the British breakthrough offensive, through the mediation of Spain or Sweden, on the basis of the status quo and with Germany renouncing its colonies (Herzfeld, pp. 391ff.).
121. A certain youthful nonchalance, superimposed on his political immaturity, seems to have made the crown prince easy prey to the influence of his immediate entourage. The author clearly remembers some details about Michaelis's courtesy visit to the crown prince at Charleville, about which the former Chancellor, then a high municipal official in Stettin, told him in the late fall of 1918 and which had clearly flabbergasted Michaelis. Earlier, on July 18, the crown prince had written him requesting him to remove Valentini, Lyncker, and Müller from the court, because they were disruptive pessimists who were undermining morale. Unfortunately, Michaelis's reply, written in the first few days after he took office, shows that he was then still very far from seeing through the prince's political dilettantism (Scheidemann [2], Vol. 2, pp. 51ff.).

122. Details on the crown prince's policies as well as sources and references are found in Herre, pp. 83ff., 103ff., 114. See also Naumann, pp. 264ff., 463ff.
123. Helfferich, Vol. 3, p. 172.
124. Michaelis to Hindenburg, September 2, 1917. In his reply of September 3, Hindenburg welcomed the proposed talks, but hoped they would bring "positive results" in the matter of border expansions in the east, which were urgently needed (ZA, II, Kr. 1, Adh. 5, Vol. 1).
125. Fischer, pp. 550f. One wonders whether this session may not have been the same one discussed by Kühlmann in his memoirs, p. 479, and also before the investigating committee on December 6, 1921, when the date was given as September 10, 1917 (see also Steglich [2], p. 484, Note 389). According to Kühlmann's memoirs, the essential point at issue was to establish before the ministers that U-boat warfare no longer offered any prospect of victory and peace overtures would therefore have to be made. Michaelis made similar representations about Belgium at a Prussian cabinet meeting on September 4 (Sch&Gr, Vol. 2, No. 236). His remarks show, among other things, how foreign the idea of parliamentary government was from his thinking. On the one hand he declared that it was inadvisable to dissolve the Reichstag, since this would be a "gamble for the parties of the right." On the other hand he threatened that "if the Reichstag, having been advised of the official government stand through its leading men [i.e., the Sevens Committee], still refused to see reason and proceeded in pursuit of its own power goals, prorogation would have to be considered." The ministers present were notably objective in their estimate of the situation and their war aims, especially Roedern, who regarded the acquisition of Longwy-Briey as superfluous—he said it was not worth even five days of what it cost to prosecute the war—and who projected a very gloomy picture of Reich finances, which rather shook the participants.
126. Michaelis (3), pp. 433f.
127. Reports by Roedern (notes in his papers) and Kühlmann, p. 482. There seems also to have been talk of returning the German colonies and refusing all reparation payments (Michaelis to Hindenburg, September 12, Michaelis [3] p. 353).
128. See pp. 45f. and 51; Michaelis to Hindenburg, August 12, Michaelis (3), pp. 352f.
129. Roedern took part in the crown council as a financial expert, and in a note (found among his papers) he states expressly that the Kaiser "passed over the OHL demand to retain Liège but did not take a decision not to keep it." I have used this note, in addition to the sources enumerated in Steglich (2), p. 454, Notes 388-390, and carefully evaluated there, pp. 558ff. This renders obsolete the study by Meinecke (2), pp. 179ff., on the crown council of September 11. I think the most reliable source remains the note that Michaelis dictated on the very day of the crown council and had signed by the Kaiser. The "notice" which Michaelis released to the press on July 26, 1919 (Steglich [2], p. 559), is in my view an excerpt that is supposed to represent the crown council decision. The objections which Kühlmann raised against the Chancellor's letter to Hindenburg of September 12 (Kühlmann, p. 483) are probably explained by the fact that the issue of economic integration was only briefly touched on and not discussed in any detail; but of course Michaelis knew the OHL view, which he tried to satisfy by projecting OHL wishes, so to speak, into the proceedings, including the OHL stand on Liège, and subsequently accepting them as a "program for negotiation." The only thing he was interested in at the time was preventing subsequent opposition by the OHL, but in this he did not succeed; for Ludendorff's long memorandum of September 14 immediately reestablished an unconscionable annexationist program (UA, Vol. 2, pp. 102ff.; also in Ludendorff [1], pp. 428ff.). Hindenburg gave Ludendorff his support, see his reply to Michaelis of September 15 (UA, Vol. 8, p. 140f.; also in UA, Vol. 2, p. 240). Holtzendorff indignantly protested against dropping the German claim to the Flemish coast (letter to Michaelis, September 14, UA, Vol. 2, p. 141).
130. Steglich (2), p. 561, after unpublished documents of the investigating committee. A

few documents on the Villalobar project have now been published in Sch&Gr, Vol. 2, Nos. 241ff., 257.

131. Michaelis to Hindenburg and Holtzendorff, September 12 (Michaelis [3], pp. 352ff.; Ludendorff [1], pp. 434f.; Sch&Gr, Vol. 2, Nos. 247, 251). For the replies see also UA, Vol. 2, pp. 102ff., 140f. The almost incredible anonymous memorandum on the papal peace note which Ludendorff forwarded to the Kaiser, Hindenburg, and Michaelis late in August (Sch&Gr, Vol. 2, No. 245) could very well have been written by Bauer, judging from the style and content.

132. Tirpitz to Michaelis, September 15 (ZA, II, Kr. 1, Adh. 5, Vol. 1).

133. Kühlmann before the investigating committee, December 17, 1926 (UA, Vol. 7, II, p. 143).

134. Declaration by Kühlmann (UA, Vol. 7, II, pp. 139f.). See also Michaelis's statement of July 26, 1919 (Ludendorff [1], p. 429).

135. This is due to the researches of Steglich, who made the crucial documents available to Michaelis's son (Dr. Wilhelm Michaelis) even before Steglich's book was published—see Michaelis (3) as well as Michaelis (2), also Epstein, pp. 243ff. Meinecke (2) recognized the true meaning of Michaelis's letter as early as 1928. According to Engel-Janosi (3), Erzberger at around this time told a South German of some standing that he attributed the greatest importance to the German reply to the pope. He said he was "proud to have worked on it with Herr von Bergen. It will move the conclusion of peace significantly closer" (documents in HHSTA). What is not clear is whether he meant the reply of September 18 or the secret one of September 24.

136. This obscurity has not been completely illuminated even by the admirably comprehensive and critical researches reported in Steglich (2), pp. 207-221, which draw on all the published sources.

137. Reported by Kühlmann. I cannot accept the hypothesis of political objections given in Steglich (2), pp. 208f.

138. Nowhere is there even a word about any peace effort on the part of Marquis Villalobar in the British documents I have scanned—the files of the war cabinet and Foreign Office, and Balfour's private correspondence (among his papers at the PRO, FO 800/201, and in the manuscript division of the British Museum, Vol. 49699). The Foreign Office index of key words includes no reference under *Villalobar, Tawnley,* or *peace proposals.* In the files discussion of this question always begins with Hardinge's dispatch of September 18. Before the Reichstag investigating committee both Kühlmann and Lancken stated as a fact that Villalobar went to The Hague directly after September 11, where he drew the British envoy Tawnley into his confidence, though without revealing the substance of his mission. Even if this is true, there were certainly no practical consequences. Lloyd George, Vol. 4, pp. 2084ff., gives deciphered versions of the correspondence between Villalobar and Lema, but I have been unable to establish just when that correspondence fell into British hands. According to Lloyd George's statement, at any rate, it was not yet known in London by September 20 (p. 2092). It contained nothing, by the way, about Kühlmann's conditions for the relinquishment of Belgium. Nowhere in the cabinet proceedings is there any mention of this correspondence.

139. Lloyd George, Vol. 4, pp. 2093ff. Draft with corrections in Balfour's hand in Balfour's papers (British Museum, Manuscript Division, No. 49699, 32-42).

140. Lloyd George, Vol. 4, pp. 2098ff., also for the following.

141. The statements by Lancken and his Belgian partners are carefully compared in Steglich (2), pp. 495f., Note 552. Lancken's correspondence with the foreign ministry has now been published in Sch&Gr, Vol. 2, Nos. 97, 116, 139, 146, 151, 154, 160, 164, 166, 188, 192, 194, 227f., 255, 259, 265, 273, 282. Item No. 265 (report by Lancken, September 23) clearly shows that he was willing to grant the French no more than the elevation of Alsace-Lorraine to the status of a full-fledged federal state. He regarded as "totally unacceptable" sweeping

concessions by Briand–immediate neutralization of the provinces with a subsequent plebiscite and large indemnities to be paid to Germany. Lancken himself counted on the failure of the negotiations but thought that subsequently a separate understanding on Belgium (by way of Broqueville and King Albert) might not be wholly impossible.

142. Suarez, p. 273.
143. Report by Cambon on his talk with Balfour, Ribot (1), pp. 212f., Suarez, pp. 280f. What is not at all clear is how Cambon came to report alleged concessions by Lancken that were far more sweeping–the restoration of Serbia, territorial cessions to Italy, and colonial cessions to Britain. This is what Balfour told the war cabinet on September 24. Lloyd George's report (Vol. 4, p. 2099) is based on the handwritten minutes of this secret session, taken down at great length by Cabinet Secretary Hankey. Exceptionally, and like the minutes of September 27, it gives not merely the cabinet decisions but the statements of all who took part in the discussion (PRO, Cab. 23/16, WC 238a [September 24], and WC 239a [September 27]). Surely Cambon did not make up these concessions from the whole cloth!
144. On September 28 Gasparri sent copies of the German and Austrian replies to Lloyd George and tried to represent them as constituting assent to the peace effort, for the continuation of which he sought Allied assent. The Holy See, he said, had good reason for believing that the German reference to the Reichstag resolution virtually meant acceptance of Points 3 and 4 of the peace appeal, i.e., evacuation of France and Belgium. Lloyd George seems to have taken this seriously, for he agreed on October 6 when Lord Riddell described this communication as "the first step towards the peace" and predicted that there would be further "telephone calls" of this nature. Public statements must not be permitted to interfere with this process. For the evidence, see Steglich (2), pp. 203f., also Riddell, p. 281. Steglich attempts to make a case for the British initially having been inclined to reply to the papal communication of September 28 in a positive sense–actually, it was brusquely rejected by merely being acknowledged verbally–but he fails to convince me, any more than does his conjecture that the British response might have been different, had the German reply to the pope included a satisfactory statement on Belgium.
145. Ribot thought so, as shown in his statement to Poincaré on September 23 (Poincaré, Vol. 9, p. 298). In October the matter led to a parliamentary quarrel between Ribot and Briand, in which the two rivals sought to compromise each other. Briand ultimately won out, Ribot being compelled to surrender his office on account of a socialist vote of nonconfidence. For details, and the minutes of the secret chamber session of October 16, see Bonnefous, pp. 318ff.
146. A piece of evidence is a diary note made by Briand on February 1, 1918, in which he quotes Lloyd George as saying, when told by Briand of the Lancken project, that it was a serious blunder to have sabotaged the effort, and as expressing vehement regret that he was not properly briefed on the situation at the time (Suarez, p. 316).
147. Lloyd George, Vol. 4, p. 2101, *ibidem,* his report to the war cabinet. For the following, see Painlevé, pp. 249f.
148. For that reason he criticized as "unwise" Asquith's speech of September 26, in which Asquith had pledged that Britain would fight on not merely for Alsace-Lorraine but for the liberation of occupied Russian territories.
149. Pierre Cambon, on September 24, also reported to Painlevé that this concern inclined him toward peace (Ribot [1], p. 216, Note 1).
150. Lloyd George, Vol. 4, p. 2104. Lloyd George wrongly gives October 8 as the date of the conference, and this error is perpetuated in other British biographies (FR, 1917, Supplement 2, Vol. 1, pp. 226ff., report by Page to Lansing, October 8). Page's interesting report of October 8, published there, on discussions with officers of the British intelligence service, shows London believing that

Kühlmann's inquiry could not have been made without OHL approval and that the Germans were evidently now prepared to relinquish Belgium and Alsace-Lorraine–the General Staff because it had no more hope of victory left, and Kühlmann because he hoped thus to buy German access to world trade–but the Allies would not consider such an agreement!

151. Steglich (2), pp. 218ff., was the first to show that Villalobar received his information and orders from Madrid. I find myself unable, however, to accept his conjecture that the marquis avoided passing it on to Berlin to nip any Spanish mediation initiative in the bud. According to Sch&Gr, Vol. 2, No. 290 (wire from Villalobar, October 13), the Spaniard hesitated to pass on the disappointingly curt response from London only because he hoped or wished to be able to pass on a more "complete" reply. As Villalobar should have foreseen, the consequences of this act of omission to German diplomacy were incalculable. Since Berlin did not respond at all to the British declaration, the other side was able to interpret this silence as meaning that the feeler was not intended seriously in the first place. As General Smuts wrote Count Mensdorff on December 19 (BMH, Vol. 15, 1937, p. 412), an especially unfavorable effect was exerted by an article in *Vorwärts* which maintained that it had been decided at a crown council to seek contact with Britain, but that subsequently the military had once again gained the upper hand.

152. Kühlmann, p. 495. This account clearly overdramatizes the events. Kühlmann did not immediately take the floor on the issue of Alsace-Lorraine but initially spoke on Peru's threatened declaration of war and on the papal note, in the normal course of a debate on a foreign affairs report to the main committee, rendered by Fehrenbach.

153. See the sessions of August 6 and October 9, 1917 (*Proceedings* of the Reichstag, 13th legislative period, 2nd session, Vol. 310, pp. 3714ff.). On October 6 the majority socialist Landsberg put a question on political agitation within the army, amply documenting existing abuses. Michaelis tried to assuage Landsberg in the main committee on October 8, but without success. The following day, on the floor of the Reichstag itself, there ensued the notorious clash with Dittmann and the "independents," which rendered Michaelis's position untenable. Michaelis made defamatory statements about the revolutionary propaganda allegedly engaged in by Dittmann and the independents, which caused a particular stir on the left, since there had been an express understanding between the Chancellor and the party leaders that nothing should be said about Dittmann's alleged connection with the mutinous seamen, unless the German attorney general were able to proceed against certain deputies for treason. Thus when Michaelis broke this agreement, it was anticipated that he had new incriminating material to present. Actually, most of the deputies agreed with the Chancellor in morally condemning the agitation. For details, see Wrisberg, Vol. 1, *Der Weg zur Revolution* (1921), p. 80. There is no substance whatever to the statement in Fischer, p. 570, that Michaelis fell mainly because of his reactionary stand toward implementing Prussian electoral reform. This issue played no part in the event, and on October 12, Michaelis actually assured the social democrat Südekum that he was in the best imaginable position to effect electoral reforms, precisely because he was a conservative and enjoyed the confidence of Prussia's county councilors. It was for that very reason that he initially tried to stay on as premier of Prussia–see Matthias-Morsey (1), I, pp. 225, 370, and *passim.*

154. Schulthess, 1917, Vol. 2, p. 336.

155. Schulthess, 1917, Vol. 1, pp. 803, 823ff. In the session of September 28, Erzberger zealously defended government policy and said that even the German reply of September 19 to the papal note was eminently satisfactory: "There is no need for a second, public declaration. . . . Those who do not understand the reply note are political ignoramuses." One may well wonder whether it was he who wrote the Munich article.

156. Steglich (2), p. 498, Note 576. In his memoirs Kühlmann says that what motivated his clarification were Ribot's hints about German willingness to make concessions in Alsace, offered in a secret chamber session; but this is a case of faulty memory, for Ribot's "revelations" in the chamber about Briand's readiness to negotiate, as well as Briand's counterblow which led to Ribot's fall, took place only on October 12. Kühlmann may have confused these incidents in the French chamber with certain rumors emanating from St. Petersburg, about an alleged separate Franco-German understanding, on which Lancken had just reported (dispatch of October 4, Sch&Gr, Vol. 2, No. 273). He was merely following Lancken's advice in meeting exaggerated French hopes about German willingness to offer concessions with a brusque "never! " His action, however, may also have been associated with the efforts of the majority parties and the Alsatian Reichstag deputies to elevate the Reichland to the status of an autonomous federal state, which will be discussed in Part 2 of Chapter 3. Kühlmann favored this goal, but probably sought to prevent government approval of it from being interpreted as a sign of German weakness.
157. This declaration is certain to have been made easier for him by Asquith's speech, referred to in Note 118. The speech reassured him that on this point no liberal opposition was to be anticipated.

Notes to Chapter 2

1. See the impressive and colorful account in the German version of Kennan, pp. 28ff.
2. Only Kühlmann's OHL-engineered ouster, which Hertling was unable to forestall, provided the occasion for Scheidemann to terminate his support of Hertling—see Payer, p. 57.
3. On the debates of the joint party caucus, see Matthias-Morsey (1), I, pp. 614ff., II, pp. 7-335. On the attempts in Stockholm to seek contact with the Bolshevists, see Scheidemann (2), pp. 122ff. Initially, the professional conspirator Parvus-Helphand, already known to us from Vol. III, p. 400f., played a role as mediator, but Lenin rejected him. See Zeman-Scharlau (an excellent biography, based in part on Bonn diplomatic files), pp. 284ff. Erzberger tried to put the joint party caucus into direct contact with the Bolshevists—*ibidem,* p. 291; Matthias-Morsey (1), I, p. 611. It is characteristic of Scheidemann's over-all attitude that he immediately yielded to the desires of the foreign ministry not to endanger official negotiations with the Russian government by party-to-party negotiations.
4. Schulthess, 1917, Vol. 2, p. 758.
5. My account is based on the relevant writings of Lenin and Stalin (Lenin, *Ausgewählte Werke,* 2 vols., Moscow [1946]; Stalin, "Marxismus und nationale Frage," in the anthology, *Der Marxismus und die nationale und koloniale Frage,* Berlin [1952]) and above all on Pipes. See also the interesting articles by Fritz Kopp on the relationship between communism and the nations and national consciousness, in *Ostbriefe, Monatsschrift der Ostdeutschen Akademie,* Nos. 71/72, 73, 74 (1961).
6. Bunyan-Fisher, p. 395. There is an almost cynical note to Stalin's reply to a question by the Menshevik Martov, who wanted to know why the demand for a referendum in Poland, Courland, and Lithuania was being put forward so insistently at Brest-Litovsk, while only manual workers were granted the franchise in the Ukraine, the Caucasus, Finland, etc. Stalin said that in the Ukraine the stage of bourgeois parliamentarianism was already over, while in Poland, Courland, and Lithuania, the "yoke of autocracy" had not yet been shaken off.
7. Linde, p. 38, after a Lithuanian source (Klimas). Communications from Minister Roedern to deputies of the majority parties on January 18, 1918. Communications from Kühlmann to party representatives on January 23—Matthias-Morsey (1), II, pp. 118, 146.

8. Erzberger, pp. 242f.; Matthias-Morsey (1), II, pp. 59, 117, 121f.
9. See. Vol. III, p. 69f. On June 14, 1915, Jagow too, speaking on behalf of the foreign ministry, had expressed serious reservations concerning a visit by the Baltic "council of trust" (Colonel von Veh) formed during the war. He said he doubted that the Baltic peoples really wanted to join the German Reich–even among German-speaking Balts this was by no means the rule (Lewerenz, p. 167, after the papers of Johannes Haller).
10. See Vol. III, p. 508, Note 66.
11. One of these was Hans Delbrück (Thimme, pp. 129ff.). A good overview of the growth of the pro-Baltic movement is found in Lewerenz, an excellent dissertation, pp. 50ff. See *ibidem*, p. 117, for the mass petition to Bethmann Hollweg drafted by Johannes Haller and signed, among others, by Friedrich Meinecke. Fischer, p. 608, ignores the extreme caution with which Bethmann Hollweg responded to this petition. He said he favored separation of Courland from Russia, and only of Courland, and he opposed full integration. See also Fischer and Schwabe (Chapter 3) for the moderate stand of Otto Hoetzsch, in sharp contrast to that of Theodor Schiemann.
12. See his arguments before the federal council foreign affairs committee on May 8, 1917, in Vol. III, p. 427.
13. UA, Vol. 12, p. 200.
14. For the minutes see Basler App. 11, pp. 400ff. The Bingen program was based on proposals offered on July 10 by Gossler, administrative head in Courland (see the Gossler papers, BA). Professor Gerhardt Giese of Berlin, who knew Gossler well, has described him to me as a responsible and humane man in the finest Prussian tradition.
15. Details in Lewerenz, pp. 173ff. It is probably going too far to describe the regional assembly at Mitau as a mere farce, for the Germans in it do not seem to have felt coerced but went along enthusiastically, supported by pro-German Latvians.
16. Linde, pp. 92ff.
17. There were urgent warnings, for Courland as well, by Gossler, Falkenhausen, and Geyl (Lewerenz, p. 146).
18. Ludendorff (2), pp. 137-161.
19. Payer, pp. 200ff., 234ff. From August 1, 1917, the military administration in Courland, headed by ex-county councilor Gossler and his deputy Brockhusen, had been under the rear-echelon command, but subsequently it achieved autonomy. A Reich commissioner for the Baltic regions was instituted only in March 1918, together with an under secretary (Falkenhausen). This system caused continual friction, in which the military usually got the upper hand.
20. I will never forget the frightful scenes of destruction and desolation seen in the fall of 1915 during the German advance through eastern Poland and Lithuania.
21. Details in Linde, pp. 57ff. Erzberger's complaints of allegedly wrong treatment of the Catholic clergy were apparently without foundation (Linde, p. 52; also Lewerenz, pp. 207ff.). A long petition of grievances submitted to the Chancellor by the Lithuanian Taryba on October 20, 1917, draws a terrible picture (Klimas, App. Doc. 19). Conditions were much better in Courland, where the well-meaning Gossler was in charge and the Baltic Germans wielded much influence–six of seven county headmen were German-speaking. "Dependable" Latvians were used there even as bureau heads and senior local officials. Gossler was often attacked because he drew on local people for local administration (personal communication from Professor Giese).
22. See the preceding Note.
23. Hoffmann, Vol. 1, p. 177.
24 It was Ludendorff, not Kühlmann, as given by Fischer, p. 605.
25. Minutes in ZA, RK II, 2, II, KR 4/^{2}, Vol. 1.
26. It is true that German was introduced in Lithuania as the official language and an obligatory subject in the schools, but this was probably in the main because there

were so few German officials and teachers who understood Lithuanian. Ludendorff agreed to the Chancellor's request that no Germanization and colonization experiments be conducted in Lithuania while the war was on (letter to Michaelis, August 17, AA, WK 15, secret, Vol. 4). It was decided at the session of November 4 not to institute compulsory Germanization, though the hope was expressed that if there were political integration, Germanization would ultimately follow of itself.

27. Stupperich, p. 348, gives an optimistic picture and is full of admiration for Ludendorff's energy. See also Lewerenz, pp. 210ff.
28. Lewerenz, p. 244.
29. Czernin, p. 309, letter of December 26, 1917.
30. The Balt Paul Rohrbach did urgently warn against a "peace of force," advocating instead a "peace of liberation for the non-Russian peoples oppressed by the Muscovites." Their joining Germany would be useful only if it were voluntary (Linde, p. 131).
31. There are many examples in the files. Thus on September 10, 1917, Ludendorff queried the foreign ministry as to what realistic guarantees in the economic, maritime, and colonial spheres could be exacted from the enemy when peace were concluded, so that German world trade could be rebuilt without let or hindrance. Germany's financial power would depend on such guarantees, and its military power would in turn depend on its financial power. Without such guarantees Germany would be at the mercy of its enemies (AA, GHQ, 232/16a, war aims). This query was taken very seriously in the foreign ministry. It was circulated through all the departments concerned, and von dem Bussche, on February 9, 1918, gave a long, careful, and shrewd reply *(ibidem)*. On October 11, 1917, Ludendorff urged that the sale of German merchant vessels to neutral nations be forbidden after the war (ZA, RK, VII, 12). The Chancellor's long reply of October 27 made it clear that this case had long been provided for. See also Ludendorff's correspondence with Bethmann Hollweg in April, on economic demobilization, in Vol. III, p. 454f.
32. Lersner to Kühlmann, December 14 (UA, Vol. 2, p. 142). See also Lersner's report to Kühlmann, August 6, 1917 (Sch&Gr, Vol. 2, No. 210). The letter of September 10, reproduced on pp. 125ff. (UA, Vol. 2), shows how seriously the General Staff viewed the disastrous lack of front-line replacements. Ludendorff wrote Wyneken on September 17 (Knesebeck, App.) that Germany's situation was better than that of the Entente since unlike the enemy Germany had lost no allies. "We must keep our nerve ten minutes longer than the enemy." War was hell, but Germany's first concern was to expand its borders, to protect German industry. Enemy airbases had to be pushed back as far as possible. "My military bias is simple and clear, and everyone is bound to find it justified." It was true that the generals ranked after the politicians, but in wartime it was the generals who set the pace (p. 162). On December 16 Ludendorff wrote, "Tension has been lifted from the western front. I think we have won victory for Germany." It was true, of course, that the western front had to be stabilized. For the typically militarist and exaggerated war aims that preoccupied Ludendorff's staff, including their concern about the next war, see UA, Vol. 2, pp. 106ff., and the remarks of Lieutenant Colonel Wetzell, chief of the operations section, made on September 30, 1917, about Belgium as a potential staging area.
33. Report by Lersner to the foreign ministry on December 16 (Zeman [1], No. 106). Ludendorff had had this directive, which embraced a very complete and sweeping political peace program, wired to the foreign ministry on December 3 with the comment that it was based (with a few changes) on an earlier directive to the eastern command, dispatched in late May with foreign ministry approval, against the possibility of peace talks with Russian delegates. After all, the Russians might now address themselves directly to the eastern command in the matter of peace negotiations! A marginal note shows that Kühlmann and

Hertling instantly rejected this—which did not keep Ludendorff from wiring his peace program to Hoffmann on December 16 in exactly the same wording, even without foreign ministry approval, in the form of a "directive" (UABL).

34. See the minutes of the Kreuznach talks, cited in Note 46, Chapter 1.

35. This assertion seems to have been based in the main on the fact that unlike the Baltic-German nobility the Latvians for the most part banked on a British rather than a German victory and that the Latvian independence movement maintained liaison with London (Lewerenz, p. 235).

36. Lewerenz, p. 130.

37. This had been already agreed to in the Berlin talks of December 7, by the way (AA, WK 15, secret, Vol. 5; see also *ibidem,* Vol. 4, Rosenberg's report to the foreign ministry, December 12; the Brest-Litovsk film of UA also contains: letter by Hertling to Hindenburg, December 12 [reply to Hindenburg's message of the preceding day]; Hindenburg's reply of December 13; Grünau to the foreign ministry, December 12 and 14). Hertling had reproached Ludendorff for meddling in political matters, and Ludendorff's rejection of this charge is quite remarkable. He said that the riots that had broken out in Livonia were threatening to spread to the occupied territories, thus endangering military security in Courland!

38. Seeckt, p. 562 (letter of late May 1917). Crown Prince Rupprecht entertained the same view (letter to Hertling, July 19, 1917, in Herzfeld, p. 393). The democratic Reichstag deputy Gothein arrived at the same judgment (Matthias-Morsey [1], II, p. 218 [December 9, 1918]). A pamphlet published by radical anti-annexationists had pointed out as early as July 1915 that every "border strip" needed still another in front of it, for "protection." Ultimately one would reach the Artic Ocean in this way! (Linde, pp. 25f.)

39. For the minutes, see UA, Vol. 12, p. 215. On the treatment of the question of Lithuania and Courland in the crown council of December 18 and the role played by the ambitions of various federal states, notably Saxony, see Janssen, pp. 174ff.

40. Tobien, pp. 226f., 235ff., and App. 2; Lewerenz, pp. 179ff. Remarkably enough, until the October Revolution the Estonian aristocracy, unlike the Livonian, was worried lest Estonia become a province of Prussia rather than an independent state.

41. On December 12, 1917, Rosenberg wrote the foreign ministry that General Hoffmann had confidentially advised the Austrian ambassador Mérey, a member of the delegation, that he would ask for the evacuation of Estonia and Livonia in the armistice negotiations. Mérey was horrified and wanted to ask his government to protest in the strongest terms. Rosenberg too had warned that such a purely political demand would have a devastating effect in Germany as in Russia. He proposed a compromise. Let the matter be postponed until the preliminary peace, in connection with the autonomy demands for the Baltic countries (AA, WK 15, secret, Vol. 4).

42. The Kaiser, influenced by Schiemann, had said as early as 1906 that he would never abandon the Baltic provinces, should there be an upheaval in Russia, but would seek to integrate them with Germany (Bülow, Vol. 2, p. 243).

43. Kühlmann, p. 523. A private letter from Czernin to Hohenlohe of January 2, 1918, shows that even the Austrian minister favored such camouflage (HHSTA, Kr. 70/1).

44. Undated foreign ministry notes (after penciled notes of December 4, UABL).

45. Minutes of December 7, 1917 (AA, WK 15, secret, Vol. 5); Lersner (for Ludendorff) to Hertling, March 14 (ZA, RK II, 2, II Kr. 4/^{2}, Vol. 1).

46. The administrative districts of Grodno and Kovno and the region west of a line from Kovno to Dvinsk were to fall to Germany as a "military border correction" and to provide direct access to Courland from East Prussia. As for the Lithuanians—if they were able at all to maintain themselves against the Russians! – they would

be left with nothing more than the area to the east of this line, which was ethnologically ambiguous. Such, at least, was what Ludendorff told Lersner, in reply to a query from the foreign ministry of November 30, 1917 (AA, WK 15, secret, Vol. 4). The following is based on correspondence and minutes (in my possession) from UABL. Some of the more important items (December 4-6, 1917) have been reproduced in Linde, pp. 246-250. Basler, pp. 287ff., based on the relevant ZA files (of which I have copies), is more accurate than Linde's account. Klimas (who was secretary to the Taryba) reproduces all the Lithuanian declarations in full, pp. 98ff. Apparently Lithuanian obduracy toward the military administration was hardened by the fact that Erzberger proffered himself to the Lithuanians as a kind of protector. During a Catholic convention in Switzerland he had established liaison with Lithuanian émigrés in Switzerland and henceforth made himself a consistent advocate of Lithuanian autonomy. By July 18 he was already writing a long letter to the Chancellor, recommending that an independent duchy be established with the German Kaiser as the duke. He insisted that such a plan could be effected within six to eight weeks, with the help of a Lithuanian "national council." This would not constitute forced annexation, opposed in the Reichstag resolution then being debated—it would serve to protect Germany's borders with the help of a friendly, allied nation (Sch&Gr, Vol. 2, No. 169). We know that later on Erzberger promoted the candidacy of the Catholic duke of Urach for the Lithuanian throne. He fails to mention in his memoirs (pp. 183ff.) that initially he himself favored *Personal-union* with Prussia (i.e., one sovereign for both countries) and recommended the duke of Urach only from 1918 on, and his biographer Epstein follows him in this (see also Linde, p. 90).

47. In a *Pro Memoria* addressed to Ludendorff on November 26 and a *Protokoll* of December 1, both from Berlin and signed by a Taryba delegation of three, headed by its president, Dr. Smetona, who was the heart and soul of the Lithuanian movement (Klimas, No. 23, p. 98; No. 26, pp. 102ff.). Legation Councilor Nadolny had a hand in formulating No. 26 for the foreign ministry.

48. Klimas, No. 29.

49. Much correspondence on this in ZA, *loc. cit.* See also Erzberger, pp. 189f., and Klimas, Nos. 20ff. Linde, pp. 139ff., simply follows Klimas, without taking into account the detailed presentation of Basler, pp. 291ff. Basler displays a certain bias, it is true, but his documentation is unexceptionable. See also Chapter 7, Note 29.

50. The negotiations at Brest-Litovsk have been described many times, the latest accounts drawing on all the German and Austrian documentation that is now available. Hence I can forego giving still another detailed account. I make specific reference to the documentation in Steglich (2), Chapters 4 and 5, and also to Wheeler-Bennett (now available in German translation), who, unfortunately, is not always reliable. I have photostat copies of the major German papers and minutes (UABL; excerpts and copies from HHSTA, Kr. 25t and Kr. 70/1). The dispatches from Brest-Litovsk published in 1917-1918 are collected in a special supplement to Wippermann-Purlitz, 1917, and also in Schulthess, 1918. John gives an account based on published sources.

51. Matthias-Morsey (1), I, pp. 381ff.

52. Trotzky, pp. 350f., treats him with respect but notes that he was something of a gambler. Wheeler-Bennett, p. 103, stresses this trait.

53. Matthias-Morsey (1), II, p. 135 (to the party leaders, January 23, 1918); Zeman (1), p. 74; Kühlmann, p. 532. A sidelight on how helpless Kühlmann was in the face of the OHL is provided by Colonel Bartenwerffer's outright refusal even to present one of Kühlmann's directives of November 20 to Ludendorff. It requested that no pressure be exerted on the Luxembourgeois during the war in favor of integration with Germany (Bartenwerffer [through Lersner] to Kühlmann, November 26; reply, November 28—AA, WK 15, secret, Vol. 4). Even

more characteristic was a directive to Grünau of December 13, asking him to sound out Ludendorff carefully on a proposal put forward by certain industrialists, to the effect that Germany should rest content with a border strip of two to three miles at Briey, since the ore deposits were so close to the border *(ibidem)*. Grünau's reply appears in UA, Vol. 2, p. 142. He said he did not dare put this question, since it might create the impression that Kühlmann was out to hand the French a bargain! On November 29, 1917, Ludendorff complained to the foreign ministry that the Belgian government general was too soft toward the Flemish, who must be shown a sharper political edge. Lancken tried to defend himself by letter and official report (December 13). He suspected that Professor Bissing, son of the late governor general, had put Ludendorff up to his protest (AA, GHQ 232, war aims, No. 16a). Particularly noteworthy is a detailed directive Ludendorff dispatched to the minister in Brest-Litovsk, via Berlin, dealing with the question of peace with Italy. It includes detailed schedules on supplying manpower to Germany; on war indemnities in cash and kind, raw silk, flax, hemp, zinc ore, and sulfur; on the disposition of Italy's colonies; on the establishment of a naval base at Vlonë; on the return of island groups to Turkey, etc.; and lastly on the fate of the German colonies (AA, WK 15, secret, Vol. 4). Evidently there was ample time at Ludendorff's staff headquarters for building castles in the air! Minister Solf, in a letter to Kühlmann on January 30, 1918, actually took an essentially approving stand. (AA, WK 15, secret, Vol. 5.)

54. Czernin said he had strict written orders from his emperor to bring back peace with Russia, no matter what happened. The Kaiser sensed that Emperor Charles was wavering in his loyalty to the alliance and had appropriate representations made to Charles through General Cramon; as a result he received vigorous assurances of undying loyalty (Cramon, p. 138; his report to the Kaiser, January 5, 1918, AA, WK 15, secret, Vol. 5).

55. Glaise-Horstenau, pp. 139f.

56. This is stressed by Steglich (2), I, p. 303, who properly calls attention to the difference between the two parts of the reply note. I cannot, however, accept the qualitative difference he finds between "conditions" (Part 1) and "remarks" (Part 2); nor do I think this distinction justifies the inference that Kühlmann regarded only the "integrity" of the Reich as an inalienable condition of peace (p. 311). Kühlmann had a minimum integration program, embracing Courland and Lithuania, which he wanted to achieve.

57. Point 6 expressly stated that this was not only not feasible but superfluous in the case of the German colonies, in view of the pro-German stand taken by the natives in the war.

58. There was no ambiguity about the assurances covering war indemnities and restoration of trade relations.

59. See Czernin, p. 306, diary entry of December 26, 1917.

60. Steglich (2), p. 299, Note 406. Ludendorff was actually apprehensive of Allied intervention in the negotiations at Brest-Litovsk (Lersner to the foreign ministry, January 1, 1918; UABL, 222).

61. Max, pp. 189ff.

62. Czernin to Kühlmann, December 27 (UA, Vol. 8, p. 223, Note 14).

63. He actually admitted it quite openly to the Austrian Baron Gautsch on December 28 (Gautsch to Czernin, December 30, 1917, HHSTA, Kr. 70/1).

64. Lersner to Kühlmann and Hertling, December 25 (UABL, 458,165). Hindenburg said that certain arbitrary "border corrections" west of Diedenhofen-Metz, in the vicinity of Liège, and (in the event of an "Austro-Polish solution") in Poland as well, would be indispensable. It is noteworthy that initially the OHL seems to have grasped the purely rhetorical character of the first part of the reply note no more than the Russians. In St. Petersburg the Bolshevists celebrated the apparently conciliatory attitude of the Central Powers as a great triumph of their

diplomacy. After December 29, however, this was no more than a deliberate ruse, expressing their mortal embarrassment (Kennan, pp. 222ff.).

65. Kühlmann knew about these internal difficulties, see his report to Hertling of January 7, published in Matthias-Morsey (1), II, p. 84, No. 20.

66. See Trotzky, pp. 354ff.; Kühlmann, pp. 523ff.

67. Kühlmann to Hertling, December 27 and 28 (UABL, 458,271 and 458,195).

68. On January 15, however, he offered, as an ultimate concession, to withdraw the troops one year after peace was concluded (Linde, p. 124).

69. Hindenburg, via Lersner, to Hertling, December 29. On December 27 Ludendorff had sent word to the Chancellor, via Colonel Winterfeldt, "that in a military sense we can maintain an attitude of complete indifference with respect to a separate peace between Austria and Russia (UABL, 458,203 and 458,180).

70. Hindenburg to Hertling, December 31, 1917 (AA, GHQ 232, war aims file No. 16a; there is no copy in UABL nor in UA, Vol. 8). On January 6 Colonel Bauer raised the crown prince's hackles against Kühlmann's "slack" policy in Brest-Litovsk, by means of a critical memorandum (BA, Bauer papers, Portfolio 2, 213ff. [fragmentary]).

71. The term used by the Pan-German Bonhard, pp. 141f., but also found in an unsigned and undated memorandum (probably dating back to February 1918) among Bauer's papers. It said that it was the Jew Trotzky who had set the goals of international upheaval. Now the Bolshevists were eager to hurl the torch of unrest into Germany (BA, Bauer papers, Portfolio 2, 207-211).

72. Hertling, p. 53. The wires were nearly all worded identically, giving a clue to their origin. On January 1, 1918, Prince Hohenlohe dispatched an interesting report on the situation to Vienna (HHSTA, Kr. 70/1).

73. On December 28 Kühlmann requested that a crown council be held on January 2, with the OHL participating (UABL, 458,195).

74. Matthias-Morsey (1),˙II, pp. 3ff., 49ff. (January 1-2, 1918).

75. Steglich (2), p. 299, Note 396.

76. Matthias-Morsey (1), I, p. 249 (compare with p. 573). The national liberals under Stresemann actually pursued an opposite course. On November 3 Stresemann promised his friend Buhl that he would instantly object if Hertling ever "engaged in intrigues against the OHL" (*ibidem*, pp. 476f.).

77. Kühlmann gave a noteworthy reply to a foolish question by Count Vitzthum, who asked whether Kühlmann's policy aimed at winning a strong Russia as an ally "for the decisive struggle that loomed with Britain." Kühlmann said he didn't believe in that kind of decisive struggle, and if it did come, Russia would not be of much use to Germany. For the time being Russia was in a process of internal upheaval, which could only serve Germany's purposes. This process, however, could scarcely go on forever and it would be important for Germany to establish good relations with the new North Russia, extending from St. Petersburg to Moscow (notes by the Bavarian chargé d'affaires Schoen on a committee meeting of January 2, 1918, GSTA, Pol. A, VII, 58; note by Vitzthum in the Dresden archive, reproduced in AF, 4, II, No. 292).

78. Letter by Hindenburg to the Kaiser, January 7, 1918 (UA, Vol. 2, p. 124, Paragraph 2). On Kühlmann's private audience and the crown council, see report by Hohenlohe, January 1, already cited, Kühlmann, pp. 525ff.; Hoffmann, Vol. 2, pp. 203ff.; Ludendorff (2), p. 438.

79. See the graphic account of the crown councils in Payer, pp. 174f.

80. Details in Matthias-Morsey (1), II, p. 77; Hertling, pp. 53ff.; Valentini, p. 190. The following is based on an exchange between Crown Prince Rupprecht's headquarters and the federated government of Bavaria and Württemberg, from January 6 to 19, 1918 (GSTA, Pol. A, VII, Series 39 and 61).

81. Report by Legation Councilor Krafft von Dellmensingen to Premier Dandl, January 10, 1918, *loc. cit.* (author not named). The memorandum was written by

Colonel Bauer, who had it sent to the crown prince on January 6, 1918, through Feldjäger (BA, Bauer papers, Portfolio 2, 213-215).

82. Crown Prince Rupprecht remarked that he could not see why large-scale annexations were needed in order to keep Germany from becoming impoverished and to maintain its status among the comity of nations.

83. Kühlmann himself thought they were satisfactory, see p. 90. At the Berlin meeting of the economic experts on January 1 many objections were raised, which Fischer, p. 649, tends to overdramatize. The German delegation (under Ministerial Director Johannes) was said not to have prepared sufficiently for integration with Germany of the marginal regions and Belgium. Kühlmann met Hindenburg's criticism by complaining that the OHL representative at the economic discussions in the foreign ministry had allowed bias to creep into his reports (UA, Vol. 2, p. 133). He pointed out that the discussions were only preliminary and not binding; but on January 5 Ludendorff wired Hoffmann that the results of the negotiations so far were "unacceptable" and demanded, among other things, "full compensation for all German property in Russia that had been damaged, liquidated, etc." (Rosenberg to the foreign ministry, January 6, UABL, 458,258). Hertling, however, immediately replaced Johannes with the seasoned privy councilor Koerner as negotiator (communication to Hindenburg, January 7, UA, Vol. 2, p. 129; Hindenburg's reply, January 9, *ibidem*, p. 134). In his memorandum of January 23 (see further on) he then gave a detailed account of the course of the trade talks, from which it is seen that the departmental meetings in Berlin had by no means been limited to criticism of Johannes (UA, Vol. 2, p. 66). In Solf's view, Johannes did get stuck in the minutiae and thus was not entirely equal to his task (Metternich-Solf, p. 101).

84. UA, Vol. 2, pp. 123ff. A somewhat different text, with an omission, is given in Ludendorff (1), pp. 452ff.

85. Ludendorff (2), p. 439; Hertling, p. 56. On January 7 Hertling had tried to reassure the general (UA, Vol. 2, p. 128). He said that no final decision had yet been taken in the matter of the Polish border strip and that a very firm stand would now be taken in Brest-Litovsk toward the Russians. Koerner had supplanted Johannes, and since the Western powers had not accepted an invitation to take part in the peace conference, Germany had a completely free hand in the matter of annexations. On January 5 a wireless message had gone from Brest-Litovsk to St. Petersburg with a reminder that the ten-day period for Western participation had elapsed. An added clause to the effect that Germany now had a free hand in the matter of annexations had been demanded by Hoffmann and bitterly opposed by Czernin, who was indeed opposed to the whole message. The phrase had been cut in the end, to avoid exacerbating leftist opposition and on the premise that the rightist parties would be satisfied without it, if only the press were properly briefed on the new situation. On January 6, Hertling, through the foreign ministry, offered a formal apology to the OHL for the omission of the phrase (Rosenberg to the foreign ministry, January 5; von dem Bussche to Lersner, January 6, both in UABL); Hindenburg's reply of January 9, UA, Vol. 2, pp. 134f., was on the whole conciliatory in tone, but expressly sided with Ludendorff in the matter of resignation. Kühlmann, p. 537, is apparently the only one to remember that.

86. Kühlmann, p. 537; Valentini, p. 192; Hertling, pp. 55f. Kühlmann was deliberately kept away from the talks, to avoid any suggestion that he had to defend himself. He was instead asked for a written opinion (Hertling to Kühlmann, January 10, ZA, RK II, Kr. 1, Adh. 5).

87. UA, Vol. 2, pp. 68f.; Ludendorff (1), pp. 455ff., 467f. The latter reference also reproduces the correspondence between Hertling and Hindenburg, January 12-14. Further exchanges on the individual alterations are in ZA, RK II, Kr 1, Adh. The final version was before the war ministry and the chief of the admiralty staff for signature on January 21. Its departures from Hertling's original draft are

noteworthy. Among the cuts were (a) the limitation to wartime of the military's voice in nonmilitary matters; (b) an express exclusion of directives by the military "which the Chancellor is obliged to follow"–he was instructed instead to give the highest priority to requests affecting strategy (see main text); (c) the phrase: "a decision by the Kaiser invariably relieves the military agencies of separate responsibility"; and finally (d) the concluding sentence providing that the Chancellor had to resign in disputes when the Kaiser decided against him. The area in which the military was to be "consulted" was much expanded–it now included changes in Germany's borders, questions of future relations with other countries, and all domestic issues "related in any way with the conduct of the present or of a future war." Expressly designated as "top military agencies" were the chief of staff, the first quartermaster general [sic], the minister of war, and the chief of the admiralty staff. Hertling's statement (p. 59) that the OHL-inspired changes were trivial formalities is scarcely in accordance with the facts.

88. Winterfeldt to Radowitz, January 14, on instructions from the OHL (UA, Vol. 2, p. 135; Ludendorff [1], p. 456).
89. UA, Vol. 2, pp. 59-68; Ludendorff (1), pp. 458ff.
90. See Note 85.
91. UA, Vol. 12, p. 216.
92. UA, Vol. 2, p. 69. For further details, see Chapter 4.
93. According to Hertling, p. 56, the Kaiser refused to accept the resignation of both Kühlmann and Valentini on January 12. On that day Ludendorff was summoned to an audience, and when he excused himself on the pretext of a cold, the Kaiser sent word to him to remain on active duty. The Kaiser's marginal notes on an article in the *Berliner Börsenzeitung* of January 9, 1918, show his indignation over the attacks in the rightist press and his complete agreement with Kühlmann's policies (UA, Vol. 2, pp. 70ff.).
94. Colonel Winterfeldt to Valentini, January 15 (Valentini, p. 192). Colonel Haeften, forever active in the foreign ministry as a mediator, reports that on January 14 he and Lieutenant Colonel Wetzell, a section head in the General Staff, urgently advised Ludendorff against resigning on political grounds (BA, Haeften papers, Portfolio 5, Sheet 4).
95. Valentini, pp. 184ff.; Müller, pp. 331f. According to Müller, the crown prince and the empress convinced the Kaiser that Valentini had pushed him step by step into relinquishing his crown rights, especially in the matter of concessions on the electoral issue. Even then the Kaiser was advised to replace Valentini with the arch-conservative Berg. The empress, however, was uncertain and anxious about this staff change. On her political role in general, see the careful study by Dorpalen, pp. 17-38. Bauer's papers include a long and very firm letter from the Kaiser to the crown prince, in which the Kaiser rejects the crown prince's importunities to dismiss Valentini (BA, fasc. 16, November 22, 1917, copy).
96. Hertling, p. 57.
97. As shown by his papers in the BA.
98. Müller, pp. 344f.
99. Contents in UA, Vol. 2, p. 174. Müller, to whom the Kaiser read the document, thought it hypocritical, mendacious, and contrived *(loc. cit.)*.
100. Matthias-Morsey (1), II, p. 103, Note 26, after a note by Berg. Kühlmann made Berg's acquaintance in Homburg on February 13 and gained an unfavorable impression of him, as a "Protestant Jesuit," an insincere courtier, and a political informer. Kühlmann calls him a "gravedigger of the monarchy" (p. 548).
101. None reacted to this disastrous event as profoundly as Bethmann Hollweg, who wrote Valentini a letter brimming with impassioned resentment. He was indignant that Valentini's achievements, "known to but a few, hence never properly appreciated," should have given way before contemptible intrigue. More than that, he sensed with dismay that a new wind was blowing "from a devilish

corner. Where will it lead us? Don't they see the forest for the trees? " Was political unreason to carry the day? "I am extremely displeased with Brest-Litovsk. Really, our total situation is not such that we can afford ambiguities, even when Trotzky is such an unreliable partner" (Valentini, pp. 253f., January 17, 1918).

102. January 13, 1918 (UABL, No. 458,408); Hindenburg to Hertling, January 16 (*ibidem*, No. 458,500). The OHL, of course, continued its campaign against Kühlmann without a letup. Ludendorff offered no protest when his military attaché in Sofia reported on January 14 that the Bulgarians were unhappy with the minister's weak stand against Trotzky. The Russians, after all, had been forced to sue for peace. Ludendorff simply passed the comment on to Hoffmann (*ibidem*, Nos. 458,470f.).

103. *Loc. cit.*, No. 458,559, January 18.

104. Fischer, pp. 642f., memorandum of October 25, 1917. Fischer's report fails to state whether this memorandum proposed permanent postwar separation of the Ukraine from Russia or in what form it envisaged "German domination" or where the document was found (the article in *Historische Zeitschrift*, Vol. 188, which he cites, is silent on the subject). When Fischer speaks of alleged plans by the governments of Germany and Prussia to "push Russia away from the Black Sea and the Straits" and to "degrade Austria to the status of a corridor for German interests in the east," he is simply confabulating. On Jagow's *Mitteleuropa* memorandum of November 13, 1915, cited in this connection, see Vol. III, p. 110f.

105. Sch&Gr, Vol. 2, No. 178 (Michaelis to the OHL, July 26), No. 181 (Stumm at the Vienna talks of August 1).

106. Thus there was some substance to the suspicions of the Austrian ambassador Mérey that the appearance of the Ukrainians was German-inspired, since the Germans wished to play off these separatists not only against Russia but also against Poland (Mérey to Czernin, from Brest, undated but probably December 14, HHSTA, Kr. 70/6). Czernin had already heard from Under Secretary Stumm on August 1 that the German-fostered Ukrainian separatists demanded Kholm and East Galicia (Czernin, p. 327).

107. Winterfeldt to Hertling, on Ludendorff's instructions, transmitted verbally on December 27, 1917; Lersner to the foreign ministry, January 1, 1918 (both in UABL, Nos. 458,180 and 458,220).

108. Grünau to the foreign ministry, February 2, 1918 (UABL, No. 458,704). The Kaiser found this so alarming that he pressed for a prompt settlement with the Ukrainians.

109. For details see Gratz-Schüller, pp. 157ff.

110. The Bolshevists habitually reviled the Rada as "bourgeois," i.e., reactionary; but while its leadership consisted in the main of petty bourgeois intellectuals, its over-all political orientation was essentially determined by the smallholders' program of the social revolutionaries. In the spring of 1918 the Rada decreed the expropriation of the estate owners without compensation, together with sweeping nationalization of natural resources. This thoroughly disrupted agricultural cultivation, elicited vigorous opposition from the propertied peasants, and soon proved totally useless in effecting the food exports, for the sake of which the Austrians and Germans had concluded peace with the Rada. Reshetar is very instructive on this entire chapter.

111. See Note 123 (Berlin meeting of February 5, 1918).

112. Gratz-Schüller, pp. 143ff.; Czernin, pp. 335f. Trotzky refused to concede the Germans a "clean bill of health," so to speak, with respect to their annexationist program, by giving his signature; but this obstacle might be overcome by formulating the treaty text in neutral terms. Trotzky persisted in refusing to recognize the peace treaty concluded with the Ukraine and to cede Riga and the islands and insisted on a less drastic eastern border for Lithuania.

113. UABL, Nos. 458,773f.
114. Directive from Hindenburg to Hoffmann, February 7, transmitted to the foreign ministry by Kühlmann. Direct petition by Hindenburg to the Kaiser on February 9, asking for a directive to Kühlmann. Grünau to Kühlmann, February 10, reporting indignation on the part of the Kaiser, whom his military entourage, including the empress, besieged to intervene immediately in Livonia-Estonia. Kühlmann to Hertling, February 10, refusing and offering resignation. Kühlmann to Grünau and Hertling, February 10, reporting that Czernin was refusing to cooperate. Two wires from Grünau to the foreign ministry and Kühlmann, February 10—all in UABL, Nos. 458,747ff. and 458,773-458,783).
115. See Note 117. Between January 3 and February 14 Freiherr von Keyserlingk, operations chief for the admiralty, sent a number of reports from St. Petersburg. Nominally, these were supposed to be military, but in reality they were pure politics, and they had much to do in firing the OHL's anti-Bolshevist mood. (Keyserlingk was a member of a commission for the settlement of the status of prisoners-of-war, as delegate plenipotentiary of the OHL and the navy). These propaganda dispatches culminated in a vague plan under which Germany would someday rule over the whole vast reaches of Russia as a colonial territory (Baumgart [2], pp. 87ff.).
116. A fragmentary set of minutes is in ZA, RK II, Kr. 1, Adh. 5, Vol. 2, of which Fischer, pp. 663ff., gives a highly colored interpretation—he roundly declares that all the participants had agreed in advance to exert military pressure on Russia and that they differed only in their views on the timing of military operations and their extent and goal. The minutes are printed in part in Matthias-Morsey (1), II, p. 241, Note 15; Müller, pp. 353ff.; Kühlmann, pp. 547f.; Hertling, pp. 73f.; Ludendorff (2), pp. 446ff. See also Ludendorff's notes for his report to the Kaiser in Homburg (Ludendorff [1], pp. 470ff.). To round out the picture, I also drew on the remarks by Kühlmann at meetings of the German delegation in Brest-Litovsk, February 10, and his letters to Hertling of February 8 and 11 (UABL, Nos. 458,792-458-804, 458,743-458,746, 458,806f.
117. According to a report by Wedel of February 16 (UABL, Nos. 458,449ff.) there was actually no sign of such opposition in the regular Austrian press. The Baltic campaign was there regarded as a purely German affair. The *Wiener Arbeiter-zeitung,* however, a left-wing paper, was extremely critical. Wheeler-Bennett, p. 233, gives an exaggerated account of Austrian indignation, which creates a wrong impression. The Vienna government did, of course, decline to take any part in the Livonian campaign (originally in the occupation of the Ukraine as well), nor was it willing to join in the new German-drafted ultimatum of February 19—but this was not to mean that the Austrians precluded participation in any further negotiations. Czernin warned against continuing occupations in Livonia and Estonia. "In my view Germany's unquenchable annexationist appetite will prevent any chance of peace in the west" (letter to Hohenlohe, February 19). Premier Seidler stated on February 19 in the house of delegates that Austria was no longer at war with Russia and that it was very unlikely that a state of war would be resumed. Baron Arz, the Austrian chief of staff, however, protested against this on February 20. On February 19 Trotsky sent a message to Vienna by wireless, inquiring whether Austria intended to engage in hostilities. After hurried consultations with Berlin, Czernin replied on February 22 that Austria was prepared to bring the peace negotiations to a conclusion in common with its allies (HHSTA, Kr. 70/1).
118. This was detailed in a memorandum by von dem Bussche of February 12. He was convinced that the German workers would not go along with any resumption of the fighting and would respond with a wave of strikes (UABL, Nos. 458,808-458,810).
119. RAW, Vol. 13, p. 364.
120. According to Müller, p. 355, Ludendorff openly admitted this in the session but

cited the "sure instinct of the field captain," already proven at Tannenberg.
121. This demand by the generals is not expressly mentioned in the Reich chancellery
     minutes, which are admittedly preliminary and which reproduce the apparently
     confused debate only in part and even so in abbreviated form. Such a demand
     must, however, have been made, for otherwise there would be no sense to
     Kühlmann's warning and Hertling's request that besides the appeals for help from
     Livonia already received there would have to be further appeals from Finland
     and the Ukraine, before there could be military action. From my study of the
     documents, moreover, it appears that after February 13 there was no further
     discussion between the Chancellor and the foreign ministry on the one hand and
     the OHL on the other, on the subject of German troops invading Finland and the
     Ukraine. The inference is that the OHL interpreted the Homburg crown council
     as having authorized these invasions even before the appeals were received.
     Müller says only (p. 353) that the reason given by the generals was that their
     action was intended to provide protection for the Germans in Livonia and
     Estonia, support to the Finns, and relief to the Ukrainians.
122. RAW, Vol. 13, p. 364. In a technical sense the General Staff had been preparing the
     expedition since February 3. In his memoirs Ludendorff (pp. 447f.) seeks to
     gloss over the excessive risks of the campaign by insisting that on account of
     Lake Peipus the line of Dvinsk, Lake Peipus, and the Gulf of Finland scarcely
     required any more troops than the line of Dvinsk and the Gulf of Riga. He claims
     to have made this argument in Homburg. Ludendorff also strongly stresses the
     need for keeping the British away from St. Petersburg by advancing to the Gulf
     of Finland, thus preventing Russia from being strengthened. (It is not clear
     whether this meant toppling or supporting the Bolshevist government!)
123. According to Müller (p. 355), Walk in Livonia was mentioned as the next goal.
     Ludendorff had already said at the big military-political conference in Berlin on
     February 5 (see Chapter 4, Note 48) that he would welcome it if the armistice
     with North Russia were discontinued. In a military sense a break with Trotzky
     would be a piece of good luck. "A government could then be installed, which
     would restore order in Russia and thus enable us to reduce our military security
     measures at the border. Another goal of ours is to protect the property of the
     Germans in Livonia and Estonia." Hertling too had said that things could not
     continue in Brest-Litovsk as they were at present. Kühlmann had merely
     carefully enumerated the advantages which a peaceful conclusion with Trotzky
     would bring, with respect to public opinion in both Germany and the Entente
     countries. "The main value of any resumed military operations would be that
     they might enhance Russian susceptibilities to peace." He did not at this juncture
     oppose another military campaign outright (AA, GHQ 16a, Vol. 1, Sheet 57).
124. Müller says so (p. 355) and his statement is corroborated by Kühlmann's press
     directive, discussed further on, and his statements to the party leaders in the
     Reichstag. The sources, in other words, lend no support to Janssen's conjecture
     (p. 199) that Hertling even then counted on integration of the northern Baltic
     regions with the Prussian crown, accepting the argument that this would
     facilitate a transition of Lithuania to the Catholic dynasty of Saxony, and
     possibly even the acquisition of Alsace-Lorraine by Bavaria. The same is true of
     Fischer's conjecture (p. 662) that the OHL urged haste mainly because it wished
     to anticipate a Latvian-Estonian anti-German democratic nationalist movement.
     This is possible, but as far as I know there is no proof. The Estonian popular
     government under Constantine Päts proclaimed Estonia's independence on
     February 24.
125. Of the numerous pieces of evidence, I cite only the report of a "trustworthy person"
     whom Czernin had sent to the Baltic in December: "Everyone is opposed to the
     Bolshevists—unless he is one himself. The entire bourgeoisie and peasantry—
     indeed, anyone who owns any property—tremble before these Red bandits and
     want to join Germany. . . . In St. Petersburg the people actually yearn for

German troops to march into the city and liberate them from the Bolshevists" (Czernin, p. 312, diary entry of December 28). Fischer seeks to create the impression (p. 664) that all the appeals were inspired and contrived, and cites a statement by the Kaiser that has a cynical ring. In the abbreviated minutes it reads: *Firma muss gemacht werden,* probably meaning that the whole project had to be realized under the auspices of the "Firma" (company), namely the aid mission.

126. German auxiliary troops landed in Finland on April 3 and on the Åland islands on March 5—not in either case, on February 21, as apparently assumed by Wheeler-Burnett, p. 252.

127. Directive from Radowitz to the foreign ministry's press bureau (Deutelmoser), on February 13. On the same date Kühlmann sent a message to the foreign ministry, asking that an effort be made to extract a request from the Ukrainians, asking to have the pressure taken off them by means of a German advance in the north. "Direct intervention in the Ukraine," he said (he had indeed warned against it in Homburg), was not intended, rather, not *yet* intended! (UABL, Nos. 458,823f. and 458,826; Kühlmann to the party leaders in the Reichstag, February 18, Matthias-Morsey [1], II, p. 255).

128. Wippermann-Purlitz, Vol. 33, II, 2, App. 150, 152. One must marvel at Kühlmann's hypocritical optimism about the prospects of the Ukrainian state and his glib talk about the "close and warm relations" with the Ukrainian leaders, and about the question of Kholm and other delicate issues.

129. Reichstag debate, February 25, 1918, Schulthess, 1918, Vol. 1, p. 88. When the Reichstag requested the text of the peace terms, von dem Bussche immediately provided it, and thus there is not the slightest reason for Wheeler-Bennett's charges (p. 262)· of subservience toward the government. Under Article 11 of the German constitution, the Reichstag had only the right of subsequently approving international treaties touching on its legislative sphere.

130. Trotzky, p. 372.

131. These regions had fallen to Russia only in 1878, and their return was not requested by the Turks until February 24, by way of the OHL, which strongly supported the Turks, to compensate them for losses and failures elsewhere, especially with respect to Bulgaria. Kühlmann and Rosenberg, on their part, thought that the Turkish demands were unconscionable and dangerous, not (as Fischer would like to make it appear, pp. 739ff.) because the foreign ministry was pursuing goals of conquest of its own in the Caucasus, but because the demands "would touch on vital Russian interests and, if realized, were bound to make a Russo-Turkish conflict inevitable in the end," while immediately the success of the whole Brest-Litovsk negotiations would be imperiled (Kühlmann to the foreign ministry, February 26). But the designs of Germany's Turkish ally could not be openly opposed at the conference, hence a compromise was adopted: Turkey would not annex regions in the Caucasus, but Russia would evacuate them! (Lersner to the foreign ministry, February 24; Privy Councilor Schüler to the foreign ministry, February 24; Kühlmann to the foreign ministry, February 26; Rosenberg to the foreign ministry, February 28 [he thought implementation unlikely]—all in AA, Russia, 97a, Vol. 11.)

132. Report by American Consul General Summers to the State Department, March 31, 1918 (FR, 1918, Russia, Vol. 1, p. 490). Rather different figures in John, p. 83; Bunyan-Fisher, p. 523.

133. Meeting of the central committee, February 18 (Bunyan-Fisher, p. 513).

134. Lersner to the foreign ministry, February 20—"after long sessions in which I was able to deter him from much more sweeping demands," Lersner has drafted peace terms with Ludendorff, which he now sends in for approval. Hertling's reply of February 21—he adds the phrase in point to Article 2 and proposes to moderate the language somewhat (UABL, Nos. 458,868-458,873). Characteristically, Hertling was afraid that the leftist parties would be dissatisfied with peace terms

that went too far. For that reason, he wished to avoid enumeration of the various points in the treaty itself.

135. Reichstag debates on February 27 (Schulthess, 1918, Vol. 1, p. 105; Matthias-Morsey [1], II, 286, 303, 307, 315ff. [Fehrenbach's protests against the military administration in the Baltic]).

136. It is true that a certain form of payment was demanded of the Russians after all. There was to be an accounting of what each side had spent on the maintenance of prisoners-of-war, which would have provided a considerable surplus for Germany. On the other hand, the value of the work performed by the prisoners was to be deducted, which would certainly have lessened the high sum the Russians insisted would have resulted, had the whole calculation ever taken place (Articles 3, 17, supplementary treaty of March 3). On the extremely conscientious work on the economic clauses at Brest-Litovsk, see Gratz-Schüller, pp. 157ff. Gratz, who personally took part in these negotiations, reports that the clauses were almost entirely based on the principle of mutuality. This was to make possible resumption of pre-1914 relations, "create a good impression with the Western powers, and serve as a good example for peace negotiations to come." This view of an expert directly concerned contrasts sharply with the opinion of Fischer (pp. 641ff.), who seeks to create the impression that ever since 1916 German policy had been trying to exploit Russia economically, in the interest of German heavy industry, and that it realized these plans only in 1918.

137. See the very restrained judgment by the American Kennan, p. 361.

138. RAW, Vol. 14, pp. 37f.

Notes to Chapter 3

1. By the fall of 1917 the author had taken the field for the seventh time.

2. Matthias-Morsey (1), II, pp. 280, 287ff. (February 22, March 11).

3. Payer, Chapter 16; UA, Vol. 8, pp. 180ff. According to Patemann, it is rather doubtful whether Roedern's report from headquarters really represented Ludendorff's precise opinion or exaggerated his supposed willingness to make concessions, for political reasons.

4. Ludendorff to Drews, November 26 and December 8, 1917 (Ludendorff [1], pp. 290ff.). Occasion for the correspondence was a rumor that the OHL was supporting the universal franchise, bowing to the popular mood. It was afraid of strikes in the munitions plants. It is noteworthy that Ludendorff was writing at the very moment when the government bill was reaching the diet. These rumors were carried back to Ludendorff by former minister of agriculture Schorlemer, an archconservative, and the leading industrialist Röchling of Saarbrücken, both of whom tried to influence Ludendorff, and of course Colonel Bauer, along their own lines. As a member of the diet, Röchling kept the OHL currently informed of the status of negotiations in that chamber (Feldman, p. 445, after Bauer's papers). Drews, by the way, himself shared responsibility for Ludendorff's meddling in political affairs. On September 11, knowing very well what he was about, Drews requested that the general receive Erzberger, in an effort to wean the centrist party away from the left and its peace policies! Erzberger was received by Ludendorff that very same day (UA, Vol. 2, pp. 45f.). More evidence of the negative attitude of the OHL on Prussian electoral reform and of the support it offered the conservative opposition is found in Patemann, pp. 100 (discussion between Hindenburg and Count Westarp, September 16, 1917), 125 (Schorlemer to Ludendorff, December 5, 1917), 133 and 147 (efforts by Hindenburg to mobilize the censorship against articles in the press favoring electoral reform, December 16, 1917, and February 21, 1918), 176 (protests from headquarters against prorogation of the diet, April-May 1918), and *passim*.

5. See Vol. III, p. 582, Note 4. On the occasion of a debate concerning the emoluments of deputies, there were provocative attacks in the upper chamber against the democratic tendencies of the day.

6. Prussian minister of the interior to Kaiser Wilhelm II, February 13, 1918 (Volkmann, pp. 291-309, reprinted without date in AF, III, pp. 1048-1066).

7. UA, Vol. 2, pp. 337ff., Radowitz to Count Limburg-Stirum (for the OHL).

8. Hertling to Hindenburg, January 11, 1918 (AF, II, No. 308).

9. Hindenburg to Michaelis, September 10, 1917 (UA, Vol. 2, pp. 125ff.); War Minister Stein to the Chancellor, December 19, replying to a query of October 28 (ZA, RK II, Kr. 1, Vol. 12).

10. Ludendorff to Michaelis, September 18 (ZA, RK II, Kr. 1, Adh. 5, Vol. 1). The military command responsible for Berlin suppressed the *Vorwärts* for several days because of an article that appeared on December 20, 1917 complaining about poor provisions for war victims. The foreign ministry press chief Deutelmoser raised serious political objections against this injunction and managed to get it revoked. The OHL thereupon, on December 22, strongly complained that political agencies were "intervening" in the jurisdiction of the military commanders, who were thus being "paralyzed" in taking decisions. On December 26, Hertling rejected the accusation politely but firmly, pointing out that he, on his part, did not respond with an injunction to every attack on his government from the right. The OHL, however, came back on January 1, insisting that political agencies were ignoring military exigencies, which should be considered on an equal basis (ZA, RK II, Kr. 10, Vol. 14). The entire RK II–Kr. 10 series of the ZA provides an abundance of evidence on the continual friction between the politicians and the generals on matters of publicity, which our account could not consider in detail. An excellent review, based on the files of the former Reich archive, is found in Vogel, p. 26, (see also Chapter 9, Note 19).

11. Ludendorff (1), Section 12, pp. 272f.

12. Characteristically, the OHL appealed to the Chancellor on January 24, 1918 on the basis that German superiority rested not least on scientific achievement. Science abroad inevitably "came out second best" (sic). Germany had generously opened its institutes and universities to foreigners, thereby materially strengthening the enemy war potential. Germany's enemies had imitated drugs, dyes, and machines formerly obtained from Germany and had improved their production methods. This would prejudice Germany's postwar competitive position. In the future, therefore, aliens must, as a rule, be kept out of German scientific institutions and industrial establishments, so that Germany would be in a stronger position in wars to come. Admission should be limited to "reliable allies." Radowitz noted in the margin: "Chinese Wall system," and had copies sent to Helfferich, the Prussian ministry of education, the war ministry, and the Reich economic office. The response was overwhelmingly negative, and Radowitz summarized the position of the two last-named agencies by stating that no further action was to be taken. In any event, the matter was one for local government (ZA, RK II, Kr. 1, Vol. 11 [actually belonging in Volume 12]).

13. Radowitz argued thus in the OHL message previously cited, by adding: "Passing moods cannot be immediately accepted as governing political decisions, often having to take second place behind calculating statesmanship based on objective facts (*vide* Bismarck in 1866)."

14. According to a report of January 25 by the Berlin chief of police (AF, III, No. 337), there were two leaflets. Oddly enough, the text is not given in the communist publication. For their content, see Herzfeld, pp. 97f. The text of these and other leaflets is given in Drahn-Leonhard, pp. 92ff. The leaflet of the independent social democratic party of January 10, given in AF, III, Nos. 953f. *Ibidem,* Nos. 312, 315, 319, 320, 324, 343, 344, provides a good deal of information from police reports (in part from Saxony) on the strike preparations of the independents and leaflet distribution, but fails to provide details on the influence wielded by the Russian Bolshevists. Herzfeld, pp. 196ff., reproduces statements and documents from the Munich "stab-in-the-back" trial of 1925 which are illuminating. On the work of the independents, see Barth and, following him, Wrisberg's Vol. 1, *Der Weg zur Revolution 1914-1918,* pp. 97ff. Prince

Hohenlohe, on February 4 and 7, provided Vienna with detailed and well-informed reports on the strike movement (HHSTA, Prussia III/174; see also Scheidemann [1], pp. 67ff. For Scheidemann's similar statements in the joint party caucus, see Matthias-Morsey [1], II, pp. 193ff.).

15. See Scheidemann's speech before the Reichstag's main committee on January 24; Schulthess, 1918, Vol. 1, p. 27. Scheidemann suspected that despite official denials there were major differences of opinion between Kühlmann and the OHL, and as we know (see Chapter 2, Part 2), he was amply justified at this time. Scheidemann was of course deeply dissatisfied with Hertling's deliberately reserved statement on the Belgian issue in his Reichstag speech of January 24.

16. See the conspicuously calm report by the Berlin chief of police, Oppeln (AF, III, No. 361); also the report by the Charlottenburg chief of police on the street riots of January 31, in which there was some bloodshed (*ibidem,* No. 373); and on the efforts by the *Vorwärts* to calm the troubled waters (*ibidem,* No. 371). The ruthless military action had much to do with the change in the political climate that had occurred since Groener had been ousted as head of the *Kreigsamt* in mid-August of the preceding year and banished to the western front by Ludendorff. Groener's fall sprang from a cabal organized by Colonel Bauer and supported by big business, notably Duisberg. Groener stood accused of not having opposed the strikes of April 1917 with sufficient vigor and with having done nothing to stop inflated wages for war workers. After his dismissal the *Kriegsamt* was placed under the war ministry. Even before then, the minister of war had called a meeting of the replacement commands, in which a policy of severity was recommended to counteract strikes and strike calls. On the consequences and on Ludendorff's occasional readiness to work with the trade unions, as well as on Bauer's baneful role, see Feldman, pp. 426ff. According to Ludendorff (1), p. 99, footnote, Colonel Bauer was dispatched to Berlin during the January strikes, for the special purpose of explaining that the OHL was afraid of weakness in the face of the strikers rather than of any reduction in war production.

17. *Loc. cit.,* report of February 4. See also the debate in the joint party caucus, Matthias-Morsey (1), II, pp. 192ff.

18. UA, Vol. 2, pp. 149, 151f.

19. BA, Bauer papers, 12 typewritten pages. On the first page, Bauer gives his reasons why Ludendorff felt justified in discussing domestic issues. These clauses are bracketed, with a marginal notation: "Not communicated to His Excellency by Berg! (Bauer)." The date may be inferred from the fact that on February 23 Bauer sent a copy to the crown prince, together with Hindenburg's letter to Hertling.

20. The OHL does not seem to have fully understood their stand. In Bauer's memorandum they are described as "closely allied" to the free trade unions, while in the OHL letter to the Chancellor they figure as anti-free enterprise (p. 150).

21. Ludendorff's confidential and often uninhibited letters to the editor Wyneken after December 16, 1917 point in the same direction. He was never afraid of a general strike. Prussian electoral reform was a grave blunder, going much too far. The OHL should indeed refrain from engaging in domestic politics, but it must keep its eyes open. Ludendorff's responsibilities gave him every right to do so! Never mind the unrest to come! An end with terror was better than terror without end! If they could only get going! To succumb was better than to act counter to one's convictions! Etc., etc. (Knesebeck, pp. 163ff.).

22. UA, Vol. 2, pp. 115f. The deputy Gothein made similar statements in the joint party caucus on February 13: "Hindenburg and Ludendorff are destroying their popularity" (Matthias-Morsey [1], II, p. 229). Naturally the *Frankfurter Zeitung* was decried as "unreliable" from a nationalist point of view. On February 23 the OHL, nettled by an article in the *Frankfurter Zeitung* on the issue of Prussian

electoral reform, asked the Chancellor for vigorous action to restrain the airing of partisan politics in the press, but the Chancellor, on March 14, rejected any such action as misguided and inadmissible (ZA, RK II, Kr. 10, Vol. 14).

23. Stresemann to Ludendorff, April 29, 1918 (Ludendorff [1], pp. 293ff.).
24. On June 7, 1918, the social democratic deputy Wendel said in the Reichstag with some hyperbole that before the war four out of every five Alsatians would have voted for Germany in any referendum, simply for reasons of common sense, while today the overwhelming majority would vote for France. They would do so, not because they were enamored of the French flag, but simply from resentment over their experiences in the war. Wendel is thus quoted in the so-called Haegy-Werk, an anthology of Alsatian autonomists, edited by Abbé J. Rossé *et al.* in commemoration of the Abbé Haegy (Vol. 1, p. 339). These illuminating four volumes, full of important documents, statistical tables, maps, etc., are sincerely devoted to an effort by Alsatian patriots to give an objective picture of how their homeland became so tragically a bone of contention between the two neighboring great powers. A parallel work on the German side is *Das Reichsland Elsass-Lothringen 1871-1918*, published by the German-Alsatian research institute at the University of Frankfurt, under G. Wolfram, in four volumes, 1931-1937. Particularly important is the contribution by R. Schwander and F. Jaffé, "Die Reichsländischen Regierungen und Ihre Verfassung," Vol. 2, Chapter 1, esp. pp. 84ff. A careful piece of work is the article by Wehler. As for volunteers, Haegy, Vol. 1, p. 296, estimates them at about 8,000. Bethmann Hollweg, at a conference of South German ministers on April 4, 1915, spoke of 5,000 (Janssen, p. 298). The piece by Schwander and Jaffé cites Roedern as writing to Valentini that there were 300 Alsatian staff officers (pp. 97f.).
25. See Vol. 2, pp. 134f.
26. Details in Haegy, Vol. 1, Section 3. See *ibidem*, pp. 248ff., for the extremely brutal treatment in France early in the war of hostages and civilian internees from Alsace. Their number is estimated at 15,000. The Germans were not the only ones to practice their militarism with political clumsiness.
27. On April 8 Bethmann Hollweg met with the leading ministers of the federated kingdoms and Baden. The minutes are given in Janssen, pp. 297ff. Janssen's book traces in detail, on the basis of documentary research, the rivalries of the federated princes to gain duchies in the Baltic and in Alsace. His account essentially supports my own.
28. Bethmann Hollweg to Weizsäcker, May 30, 1917 (Janssen, pp. 306f.).
29. Scheidemann (1), p. 85; Erzberger, p. 164.
30. Janssen, p. 137.
31. AA, WK 15, secret, Vol. 4. The letter is dated July 18 and is marked as having been presented on July 20; but it was apparently written on July 19, since it describes the Reichstag resolution of July 19 as having been already passed. It is reproduced in part in Erzberger, pp. 164ff., with a date of July 20.
32. Haegy, Vol. 1, p. 348; Vol. 4, Documents 17-18.
33. See the letter by the centrist deputy Dr. J. Pfleger to his fellow party member Ch. Hauss, August 29, 1917 (Haegy, Vol. 4, Document 22).
34. Written opinion by Payer in Schmidt, p. 232; report by David, UA, Vol. 7, Chapter 1, p. 157.
35. Erzberger, p. 166; Matthias-Morsey (1), I, p. 109.
36. Supplement to Meinecke (2), p. 192. See also Kühlmann's statement before the Reichstag investigating committee, December 17, 1926 (UA, Vol. 7, II, p. 119; and Payer, p. 268). The essay by Renouvin clearly demonstrates that Kühlmann's ideas about the French attitude toward Alsace-Lorraine after the outbreak of war were completely antiquated. Even the French radical socialists went no further, in their readiness to make concessions, than to demand some form of referendum on the part of the people of Alsace-Lorraine that would sanction *désannexion*. By October Kühlmann was still vigorously opposing any division of the

Reichsland to Hertling (Kühlmann to Treutler, October 9, 1917, Sch&Gr, Vol. 2, No. 234). On Lancken's stand, see his report of September 23 (Sch&Gr, Vol. 2, No. 265).

37. Janssen, pp. 150ff., 156f., and the sources there cited, esp. Matthias-Morsey (1), I. pp. 149f., 188; UA, Vol. 7, I, p. 285.

38. Wrisberg, Vol. 2, p. 179; Janssen, p. 130. On June 15-16, 1917, a conference was held in Bingen with representatives of the civil and military administrations, on the implementation of the expropriation and settlement programs and of the state of siege. Among other measures, this conference envisaged the establishment of a resettlement agency (Haegy, Vol. 1, pp. 381f., Vol. 4, pp. 320ff., after Schmidt, pp. 23ff.). The expropriation and settlement plans, by the way, had been formulated much earlier, and they had been recommended in part by the governor as early as 1915.

39. Statements by Wrisberg to the military plenipotentiary of Württemberg at Supreme headquarters, on April 9, see the latter's report in Janssen, pp. 305f. Ludendorff reverted to this argument later on.

40. Sch&Gr, Vol. 2, No. 207.

41. Wehler, p. 195. The agronomist Kapp also campaigned against autonomy for Alsace-Lorraine.

42. The editor of Haegy had a copy of this indictment. He names Quartermaster General Hahndorff as its author (Vol. 1, p. 381). War minister Stein, on October 1, reported to the Prussian cabinet on its reproduction and distribution (Sch&Gr, Vol. 2, No. 272). Scheidemann describes how Ludendorff tried to influence deputies who visited the front (UA, Vol. 7, I, p. 286).

43. Ludendorff to Michaelis, October 7, 1917, (Sch&Gr, Vol. 2, No. 277). At a federal council session of January 2, 1918, Ludendorff said that autonomy was a solution unacceptable to the OHL. He made the sweeping statement that Alsatian soldiers simply defected to the French, because they were confident of an amnesty, as in the case of Austria (where Emperor Charles had pardoned some convicted Czech traitors). According to a communication from Michaelis to the Prussian cabinet on September 14 (Sch&Gr, Vol. 2, No. 250), a comprehensive memorandum by Ludendorff on Alsace-Lorraine was then available, but I have not seen it.

44. It now listed exclusion of French insurance companies and share capital, German as the school language, military service by Catholic seminarians, top and middle-echelon civil servants to be exchanged for others from traditionally German regions, forestry and border personnel to be exclusively old-German, no hunting licenses for foreigners, exclusion of defectors without amnesty, Alsatians to serve only in old-German garrisons. (Memorandum by Hindenburg of December 27, Schmidt, pp. 167ff.) Hindenburg complained on January 7 to the Kaiser that Hertling still had done nothing in the matter of safeguarding Alsace-Lorraine, nor had he definitively rejected the idea of autonomy (Ludendorff [1], p. 452).

45. Schulthess, Vol. 1, p. 308, September 23. Helfferich referred to this resolution in the Prussian cabinet on October 1 (Sch&Gr, Vol. 2, No. 272).

46. Report by Helfferich to the Prussian cabinet, October 1, 1917, on the "protective clauses" of the governor (Sch&Gr, Vol. 2, No. 272).

47. Memorandum by Dallwitz of December 19 (Schmidt, pp. 129ff). Reported by Schmidt only very imperfectly, the files and memoranda were found by the French in the archive of the Alsatian government, after they marched into Strasbourg in 1918.

48. Details in Seymour, p. 286; House, Vol. 3, pp. 325ff.; Mamatey, p. 178, Note 85.

49. See Renouvin, p. 34, on what troubled the French. Renouvin also cites a report by the well-known Alsatian émigré Abbé Wetterlé to Albert Thomas, on October 20, 1917, pointing out the broad scope of the Alsatian autonomy movement even before 1914—apparently he wished to warn the socialist minister against continuing to support a referendum. In the British House of Commons a group of pacifists of the radical left on November 6, 1917, introduced a resolution that

demanded the prompt initiation of peace negotiations and "an equitable solution of the problem of Alsace-Lorraine." In support of this motion the Liberal member Lambert said there was concern "that we were fighting for imperialistic aims, and, among other things, for the purpose of restoring Alsace-Lorraine to France." Balfour and Asquith thereupon endeavored to show that the question of Alsace-Lorraine would not ultimately serve as a crucial obstacle to peace; but neither gave any details (Scott, pp. 171ff.).

50. Michaelis, in the Prussian cabinet, September 14 (Sch&Gr, Vol. 2, No. 250).
51. Haegy, Vol. 1, pp. 385f. Report by Helfferich to the Prussian cabinet, October 1, 1917 (Sch&Gr, Vol. 2, No. 272, also for the following).
52. Address to the Prussian cabinet, October 1 (Sch&Gr, Vol. 2, No. 272).
53. Janssen, p. 160, Note 612.
54. See Roedern's shrewd remarks and his letter to Valentini, August 18 and September 28, 1917. He evidently fluctuated in his stand on carving up the country, but in the end he voted for postponing the issue (Schwander-Jaffé, *loc cit.,* pp. 97f.).
55. Müller, p. 323.
56. Sch&Gr, Vol. 2, No. 275, shows that he spoke to him on the 2nd for it says that Ludendorff on that day gave the Chancellor a transcript of intercepted radio messages concerning a trip by Villalobar to Berlin.
57. Ludendorff to Michaelis, October 6, 1917 (Sch&Gr, Vol. 2, No. 277). The original letter carries a notation that it was presented only on October 9. Michaelis thought it important enough to have a copy made on that day for his private files. On October 17, Major General Bartenwerffer expressed himself similarly to the military plenipotentiary of Württemberg (Janssen, p. 162).
58. On October 7 there was a very long discussion on the Polish issue at supreme headquarters, on which Michaelis reported to the Kaiser from Berlin the following day (AA, WK 20c, secret, Vol. 18; see also Lersner to Michaelis and Kühlmann, October 9, AA, WK 15, secret, Vol. 4).
59. Erzberger to Nuncio Pacelli, October 6 (Matthias-Morsey [1], I, p. 213; Erzberger, p. 167).
60. Report by Hertling to the Bavarian house of deputies, October 9 (Erzberger, p. 168; Haegy, Vol. 1, p. 386). Communication from Hertling to the Württemberg legate (Janssen, p. 160).
61. Kühlmann thus described his own stand before the investigating committee of the Reichstag (UA, Vol. 7, II, pp. 118ff.). He gives a rather too positive account of the attitudes of Michaelis and Dr. Schwanders on the autonomy issue.
62. Diary entry by Scheidemann, September 29 (UA, Vol. 7, I, p. 286), confirmed by a report to the cabinet by Helfferich, October 1.
63. Note by Lancken, September 23 (Sch&Gr, Vol. 2, No. 265).
64. See Lancken's private letter of October 4 (Sch&Gr, Vol. 2, No. 273): "A public declaration on our part would have to allow for the interpretation that what we are prepared to do for Alsace-Lorraine represents a concession to the French."
65. Undated memorandum, Schmidt, pp. 215ff, and esp. 220, after Schwander-Jaffé, *loc. cit.,* p. 103, December 1917, where it appears in part.
66. Memorandum of January 16, 1918, cited at length in Steglich (2), p. 361, after the original in the foreign ministry. Payer's memorandum of February 21, 1918, appears in Schmidt, pp. 229ff. See also Payer, pp. 266ff.
67. Communication from Lerchenfeld to Munich, January 23, 1918 (Janssen, p. 279, Note 752). The goal of autonomy for Alsace-Lorraine continued to be maintained by the majority parties, even though more and more doubts arose as to whether it were feasible—see Fehrenbach in the joint party caucus, February 25, 1918 (Matthias-Morsey [1], II, p. 281).

Notes to Chapter 4

1. Glaise-Horstenau, pp. 100ff.; Conze, p. 285 (maximum program of Tetmajer); Zemen (2), pp. 125ff.

2. Zimmermann to Lersner (for the OHL), July 6 and 11; Wedel to the foreign ministry, July 8 and 31; Zimmermann to Wedel, July 26 (all in AA, WK 15, secret, Vol. 4).

3. Sch&Gr, Vol. 2, No. 173; see also Zeman (2), p. 150, and Conze, p. 321. When closely scrutinized, Wedel's brilliantly written report displays certain weaknesses. He draws the gloomiest picture of anti-German sentiment among the Austrians, attributing it in the main to the Polish issue, which he describes as a nightmare for Austria, poisoning all minds. In view of the fact that the Kreuznach agreement of May 18 was still being kept secret, this seems highly unlikely. And why should Wedel have expected that agreement on the "Austro-Polish solution" would immediately strengthen the alliance? Subsequent events showed that Wedel underestimated the importance of continuing close relations between the conservative Poles and Vienna society, business, and court circles.

4. Conze, pp. 303ff.

5. The text was communicated to Ludendorff only on October 12 and it did make a strong impression on him (Sch&Gr, Vol. 2, No. 173, concluding remarks).

6. Wedel to the foreign ministry, July 24 (Sch&Gr, Vol. 2, No. 176, dealing with Cramon's agreement). Hindenburg to Michaelis, July 28 (*ibidem*, No. 179). Conze is mistaken (p. 322) in believing that Beseler was not informed of the shift in Polish policy recommended by Wedel.

7. Sch&Gr, Vol. 2, No. 181. In his well-known letter to Czernin of August 17 (Sch&Gr, Vol. 2, No. 211), Michaelis reiterated the idea of returning the Polish territory to Russia, after the cession of a wide border strip. In this letter he also expressed doubts as to whether the policy of November 5, 1916 was the right one. It is characteristic of Ludendorff's attitude that he challenged Michaelis in a direct letter of August 15 to effect immediately the minimum annexations of Polish territory set in Kreuznach on April 24 and to fob off the Poles with the prospect of future eastward expansion of their borders. Michaelis, in other words, was to be committed against the "Austro-Polish solution" (AA, WK 15, secret, Vol. 4).

8. An anonymous memorandum on the papal peace effort, presumably written by Bauer, which Ludendorff had sent to the Kaiser, the Chancellor, and the foreign ministry late in August, stated that "newly created Poland is a factor that can no longer be wished away. We shall have to leave this new neighbor to its own devices, since we shall have no use for the kind of flourishing Poland the German Poles themselves yearn for. We want our Poles to be afraid of Jewish-Polish misrule" (Sch&Gr, Vol. 2, Nos. 245, 415f.).

9. Note by Kühlmann, September 2 (Sch&Gr, Vol. 2, No. 233); Ludendorff to Michaelis, September 6 (*ibidem*, No. 238).

10. Wedel to Kühlmann, September 12 and 29 (Sch&Gr, Vol. 2, Nos. 248, 271). A similar private letter to Kühlmann, October 6 (*ibidem*, No. 278).

11. The Kaiser to Michaelis, September 24. Grünau to the foreign ministry, September 27. Michaelis to Grünau (for the Kaiser), September 27. The foreign ministry (von dem Bussche) to Lersner, September 29 (Sch&Gr, Vol. 2, Nos. 266, 268, 269). The Kaiser thought he had won over the OHL to his plan by October 5—Grünau to the foreign ministry, October 5 (*ibidem*, No. 274). The manner in which he underpinned his wishes is typical: "The common man would never forgive us, if we gave up Rumania, but he obviously has little sympathy for the Poles. . . . Germany would be committing suicide, if it ever relinquished Rumania. . . . If we depart, our place would be taken by Austrian Jews rather than by Austria itself."

12. Among these supportive measures was removing all Jews from the newly acquired border strip and, as a logical consequence, an injunction against drafting Jews for military service in Austrian Poland (Sch&Gr, Vol. 2, No. 283—Lersner to the foreign ministry, October 9). This document represents the authentic version of Ludendorff's program. No part of it is the *pièce jointe* (Sch&Gr, Vol. 2, No. 280) to Prittwitz's skimpy minutes of October 7. This is a copy of a letter (minus an

introductory paragraph) in which Michaelis, on October 8, sent Grünau his notes on the meeting for the Kaiser (AA, WK 20c, secret, Vol. 18). Ludendorff, on October 11, complained about this allegedly incomplete list, explained his demand for the cession of Teschen, and added as a new item the demand that Austria must suppress any and all irredentist movements in Poland aimed at Polish-German territory (Sch&Gr, Vol. 2, No. 286). Michaelis's reply, October 12 (*ibidem,* Nos. 288, 289).

13. This formulation was set at the meeting of November 3 (AA, WK 15, secret, Vol. 4).
14. What was presumably meant was the customs border between Austria and Poland, to prevent Austrian goods from being imported into Poland duty-free, while Germany would enjoy no such privilege.
15. From a report by Cramon to Michaelis, October 10 (Sch&Gr, Vol. 2, No. 285) it would appear that Ludendorff tried to cast doubts on Czernin's loyalty to the alliance and to work for his fall, on the basis of reports he had received that Czernin had made pacifist statements.
16. Michaelis to Grünau, October 12 (Sch&Gr, Vol. 2, No. 200).
17. Wedel to Michaelis, October 20 (Sch&Gr, Vol. 2, No. 296). Wedel did not discuss the issue of Belgium and the western border, the German colonies, the future of Lithuania and Courland, and Austria's duty to fight on. He did ask that the Poles forego Vilnyus.
18. According to Fischer, p. 573, who cites two reports by Hohenlohe to Czernin which I have not seen, Kühlmann had been negotiating with Czernin on the Polish question "for weeks," possibly meaning ever since his Vienna meeting with Czernin on September 1.
19. To Fischer (pp. 573f.) this is a wild imperialist scheme (like all *Mitteleuropa* aspirations). He says that it meant that Kühlmann "stood in the tradition of Bethmann Hollweg's *Mitteleuropa* ideas." His *Mitteleuropa* was to embrace, besides the two Central Powers, "the future subsidiary countries of Belgium, Courland-Lithuania, Poland, Rumania, and Turkey, possibly even Serbia, Montenegro, and North Albania, and perhaps Greece as well." Kühlmann thus wished to "outmaneuver" the OHL. Fischer represents this whole region as a German power sphere and suggests that by giving his consent to the agreement of October 22, Czernin "virtually capitulated before the German will to rule." Oddly enough, however, Hohenlohe also agreed to the plan, after "weeks of preliminary discussion," as Fischer himself reports. Did Hohenlohe fail to discern the German "will to rule"? The exaggeration and violence done to history by this type of interpretation are too obvious to require detailed refutation. It is sufficient to establish the unequivocal trend of Kühlmann's statements during these weeks, namely that his fear of losing Austria as an ally and of heightening Austrian domestic difficulties by obstructing the Poles outweighed all his hope in the field of foreign policy.
20. The Germany copy, bearing corrections by the hands of the two monarchs, is reproduced as No. 299, in Sch&Gr, Vol. 2. The Austrian copy (HHSTA, secret, 47/13) shows neither corrections nor cuts. The same Vienna file fascicle includes an undated note by Baron Andrian (marked Ref. III/P) that speaks of an "agreement" between Czernin and Kühlmann, covering a military convention, an economic alliance, a customs union to come, the "Austro-Polish solution" subject to "absolutely essential" German border corrections, and freedom for pro-Polish Austrian propaganda after the treaties were signed. Andrian was reporting only "from memory," dating the agreement September 1, and was evidently in error since Kühlmann's note of September 2 about his talks with Czernin (Sch&Gr, Vol. 2, No. 233) says nothing on the subject.
21. The files covering preparations for the conference are in AA, WK 15, secret, Vol. 4, which also holds an important set of minutes covering the results of a special discussion on November 3. The preceding general debate appears as No. 300 of Sch&Gr, Vol. 2; *ibidem,* No. 301, minutes of a Prussian cabinet meeting of

November 4 (also in AF, II, pp. 754-757). *Ibidem,* 758-763, fragmentary notes on the crown council of November 5—details in Conze, pp. 326f.; Müller, pp. 331f.

22. There was one important statement during the special debate: "Large-scale evacuation of the territories to be ceded to us is widely held to be unfeasible." In the crown council Beseler sharply rejected expulsion and resettlement, with Hindenburg agreeing. Helfferich said in conclusion that evacuation was quite impossible.

23. Special debate on November 3-4 (AA, WK 15, secret, Vol. 4).

24. Instead there was mention only of securing the rail connection at Annaberg (Austrian summary of the Berlin talks, November 5-6, 1917, HHSTA, secret 47/3-21). The summary gives the results of the talks at much greater length than two German reports (Sch&Gr, Vol. 1, Nos. 302 [also UA, Vol. 12, pp. 210-215] and 303, the latter in rather fragmentary form).

25. According to the German minutes, in Vienna only! The Austrian minutes are more precise, mentioning that both countries had agreed that Polish *Personalunion* (a shared sovereign) with Austria would not suffice. Instead Poland would have to enter into a formal political, military, and economic union with Austria. The two empires were to agree on the precise form of this *Anschluss* before obtaining Polish consent. The Poles were then to offer their crown to Emperor Charles. After his acceptance, details were to be settled with a Polish regency council and council of state (sic). Conze wrongly places these negotiations in Vienna (p. 239).

26. Conze, pp. 328, 335f.; Hutten-Czapski, pp. 434f.

27. Czernin to Hohenlohe, November 18 (written by Baron Andrian). Czernin to Colonel General Arz, November 18. Hohenlohe to Czernin, November 26—HHSTA, secret, 47/3-21.

28. Czernin to Kühlmann, November 28, 1918 (transmitted through Hohenlohe). Hohenlohe to Czernin, December 10. Czernin to Hohenlohe, December 11, Hohenlohe's reply, December 13—all in HHSTA, secret, 47/3-21. See, *ibidem,* minutes of a meeting of leading ministers of both parts of the dual monarchy on December 7, in which Czernin is quoted as saying that he would rather forego the Austro-Polish solution, if it meant integrating a mutilated Poland with Austria. This stand was generally approved, especially by Burián, but Czernin was warned against an open break with Germany. He seemed ready, by the way, to conclude a peace without annexations with Serbia and Rumania, in order to avoid giving Germany a pretext for its annexationist demands.

29. Ministerial conference of December 7, see previous Note.

30. HHSTA, *loc. cit.,* directives dated December 16 for Governor General Count Szeptycki, Legate Ugron, and Baron Andrian. On January 10, 1918, a similar directive went to Baron Musulin in Berne, to let the Polish émigrés living in Switzerland know about Vienna's good intentions (*loc. cit.,* Kr. 56a/3).

31. Minutes in AF, II, pp. 807ff.

32. General Arz to Czernin, December 13 and 15. Czernin to Kühlmann (private letter through Hohenlohe), December 13. Arz to Hindenburg, December 16. Hohenlohe to Kühlmann, December 17 (Kühlmann very agitated and irritated)—all in HHSTA, 47/3-21.

33. Minutes in UA, Vol. 12, p. 210. According to a report by Wedel of December 14, cited by Conze (p. 330), Czernin gave Wedel Arz's map on December 13, and a sharp exchange ensued. According to Conze *(ibidem)* there were also fruitless negotiations in Katowice on January 11, 1918 between the two commands on the question of annexations.

34. Czernin to Emperor Charles, December 24. According to a communication from Mérey to Czernin of December 27, Charles had no objections to economic talks, but brusquely rejected a military convention, since it would impinge on his sovereign rights. At best, he said, the treaty of alliance might be supplemented at

a later date, to cover such matters as standardized equipment, arms, and deployment. Emperor Charles also displayed little enthusiasm for the Austro-Polish solution (HHSTA, 47, secret, 3-22).

35. See Vol. III, p. 111. After the conclusion of the new Austro-Hungarian *Ausgleich* (settlement) in February 1917, talks between the customs experts of the two allies did not resume until July 23. The decision to resume them was taken on Czernin's motion at a meeting of the joint cabinet on May 6. In this debate the worries of the Austrian ministers were clearly expressed—there must not be even a semblance that Austria-Hungary had become beholden to Prussian militarism in either a political or an economic sense, which was bound to wreck any hopes of peace with Britain! After an agenda for the negotiators had been worked out, the joint cabinet, on July 5, decided to invite the German ministers and their advisers to Vienna; it being once again stressed that on no account was Austria to relinquish its autonomy by means of a complete customs union. The only thing to be discussed was a preferential tariff, while the Polish economy was to be left out altogether. In the sessions of September 6 and 15, Premier Seidler complained that the German negotiators were trying to bring about a union beyond a mere preferential tariff. This was intolerable (HHSTA, Pol. Arch., 40, 293, Nos. 536, 538, 540; also Gratz-Schüller, pp. 59, 63, 67ff.; and for the following, *ibidem*, pp. 78ff.).

36. Gratz-Schüller, pp. 294ff. Conze, p. 330, Note 53, cites (from a Polish source) a memorandum written by Privy Councilor Williger in Katowice for the Upper Silesian Mining Association. This was intended, not merely for Kühlmann, but for all the top Reich agencies, and three printed copies were sent to the foreign ministry through the Reich chancellery on December 7 (AA, WK 15, secret, Vol. 4). On the Katowice talks, in which Bartenwerffer took part, among others, see also Fischer, pp. 699f., after Austrian sources.

37. At this time Czernin was being constantly bombarded with alarming news from Vienna (Czernin, pp. 322f.).

38. Minutes of the crown council session of January 22, 1918, are in HHSTA, Pol. Arch., 40/293, No. 545. It was the view of Chief of Staff Arz that the question of peace or war with Russia had actually become a matter of indifference, and he warned against a break with Germany over this issue. Czernin hoped to appease OHL resentment of a separate peace with an offer of Austrian troops for the western front—see also excerpts from the minutes in his memoirs, pp. 327ff. The minutes document no objection on the part of General Arz to Czernin's conciliatory attitude toward the Ukrainians, especially against the relinquishment of Kholm (Arz says so himself in his memoirs, p. 225). Indeed, according to the minutes, the question of Kholm was not discussed at all. The picture drawn by Conze (p. 340) displays ignorance of the official minutes and is therefore out of focus. Dr. Gratz, by the way, was a section chief in the Vienna foreign ministry rather than minister of finance for Hungary.

39. See the book by Landwehr, a man of great vigor who was installed by Emperor Charles as a kind of food czar, namely director of a war food office that had jurisdiction in both parts of the dual monarchy. His report is distinguished by clarity and precision. Among other things, he shows (pp. 163ff.) that while the average meat consumption was lower, meat supplies themselves were far better than in Germany, and meat rationing had to be introduced in Vienna only on July 1, 1918. Zeman (2) reproduces a report by Tschirschky of September 28, 1916, about internal Austrian difficulties, including the organization of food supplies (pp. 96ff).

40. Hohenlohe to Czernin, January 24, 1918 (HHSTA, Kr. 56a/3).

41. Ugron to the foreign ministry, January 28 and 29 (HHSTA, Kr. 56/30). See also Conze, p. 337. There had been an earlier visit to Vienna by the Polish regents in January.

42. Mérey to Czernin, January 31 (HHSTA, 47, secret, 3-22). Wedel inquired about

Austria's territorial war aims, relaying an inquiry Ludendorff had directed to the foreign ministry on January 27. Mérey's response was on the vague side—acquisition of Mt. Lovchen and minor border corrections. Oddly enough, the information Hohenlohe gave the foreign ministry (see next Note) was not passed on to Ludendorff. The foreign ministry reminded Kühlmann on March 1 (Lersner to the foreign ministry, January 27; foreign ministry to Kühlmann, March 1–AA, WK 15, secret, Vol. 5).

43. Hohenlohe to the foreign ministry, January 31 (AA, WK 15, secret, Vol. 5).
44. It had been dispatched to the Chancellor on the 24th and showed the borders originally demanded, those the Kaiser had specified on January 2, and those now conceded by the OHL. A sketch map is shown in Geiss, p. 187. Minutes of the two cabinet meetings in AF, III, 1082ff., 1087ff.
45. Details in Geiss, pp. 128ff. Geiss, however, displays palpable bias in that he minimizes civilian opposition to the expulsions. See S. H. Günther, "Keine Polenvertreibung im Ersten Weltkrieg," *Aussenpolitik*, Vol. 12, p. 603ff. (1961). No formal decision to expel the inhabitants from the border strip was ever taken. Administrator Kries calculated that even if Ludendorff's plans were put into effect, the German share in the population of the border strip could be increased to only 16.5 percent (Conze, p. 333).
46. Protection for East Prussia had formerly been the main consideration, but this was no longer mentioned, since Lithuania was now to become the border march.
47. On February 9 Hindenburg sent Hertling a new border map. He said that at the behest of the Prussian cabinet he had decided to narrow the central portion of the border strip, between Plock and Kalisz, to reduce the Polish population share by excluding these populous districts. "This concession [sic] would be rendered easier for me, if we reverted to the German-Polish [rather than the Austro-Polish] solution" (AA, GHQ 232, war aims 16a, Sheet 91).
48. Late in January he had sent for the files of March 1917, which he ordered sent to Brest-Litovsk, in the hope that they might support a mutual obligation to limit the war to the defense (Czernin to his foreign ministry, January 29, 1918, with notes by Mérey, HHSTA, secret, 47/13). There are both German and Austrian minutes of the big German conference of February 5, which supplement each other. In contrast to the Austrian version, the German text (AA, GHQ,16a, Sheets 39-68, also in part in UA, Vol. 12, pp. 217-223) underplays the disagreements. The Austrian minutes are in HHSTA, secret, 47/3-22. John, pp. 131-135, published the beginning, plus the clauses dealing with the Brest-Litovsk peace negotiations. Ludendorff (1), pp. 468f., carries a brief note on the session, probably taken down by one of the military participants. *Ibidem*, pp. 469f., the draft of a new allied agreement, which Czernin prepared during the luncheon recess. For a brief report by Hertling to the Kaiser, February 2, and Grünau's reply of February 7, stating that the Kaiser approved, see AA, WK 15, secret, Vol. 5. Hertling's report also appears in UABL, as No. 458,723, and with the Kaiser's marginal notes in AA, GHQ 16a, war aims, Vol. 1. John (pp. 136ff.) merely gives a brief Austrian summary, wrongly dated (February 6 rather than 5). See further a diary note by Czernin, p. 334.
49. It is characteristic of Kühlmann the diplomatist that he now put a different interpretation on his Alsace-Lorraine speech of October 9. He said he had meant only that there was nothing except the issue of Alsace-Lorraine that could not be settled by negotiation and compensation and not (as Hohenlohe had understood him) that there were no territorial issues except Alsace-Lorraine.
50. It is noteworthy that (unlike the agreement of March 27, 1917) there was no mention of expanded war aims in the event the war ended favorably. Even the later versions made no mention of this, but let the allies mutually pledge that they would make use of their right to withdraw from the war only when compelled to do so by "domestic exigencies." Otherwise they agreed "to carry on the war until a peace was in sight that would guarantee them better political

security and chances for economic development." The two ministers managed to agree on this last formulation.

51. Ambassador Prince Hohenlohe resented this and thought it was a sign of Hertling's senility (Hohenlohe to Czernin, February 17, 1918, HHSTA, Prussia III/174).

52. On February 18 he sent a directive to Lublin. The Poles were to be advised that since Polish public opinion had turned against the Austro-Polish solution, Vienna was no longer interested in opposing German territorial ambitions in the occupied portions of Poland (HHSTA, secret, 47/3-21, also Kr. 56/32ᵃ). On Czernin's resumption of contact with the Poles, via Count Tarnowski, on March 24, see Conze, p. 357. He used the "carrot-and-stick" method.

53. Matthias-Morsey (1), II, p. 301, Note 6, Kühlmann to the foreign ministry, March 16: "I suspect the Poles are behind it, hoping to get rid of the Austrians with our help, only then to evade German influence as well and adopt an anti-German policy, with independent support from the West."

54. Matthias-Morsey (1), II, pp. 245, 290f., 301, 315, 327, 335. See also Geiss, pp. 137f., and Conze, pp. 350f. For the agreement among the party representatives, see also Wippermann-Purlitz, 1918, Vol. 1, pp. 572f. There is a typographical error in Conze, p. 351, Note 21. Erzberger's report on 1919 is in *Die deutsche Nationalversammlung 1919,* edited by E. Heilfron, Vol. 7, pp. 302f., not Vol. 5.

55. German territorial policy in the east would have had to change radically for a reconciliation with the Poles to become possible, and this was out of the question, in view of the attitude of the Prussian diet. On April 10, 1918, the upper chamber passed a resolution proposed by Korte-Königsberg, calling for stronger military border security against the new Poland, quite along the propaganda lines Ludendorff had ordained in the eastern provinces of Prussia since March. Minister Drews warned against rebuffing the conciliatory attitude of the Poles, advising instead that they be met as much as possible. He pointed out that once electoral reform had come into force, the changed political balance of power was bound to supersede the present eastern policy. Conze misread this speech completely (pp. 351, 357f.). Eisenhardt-Rothe did support border security, but at the same time announced a softening of Polish policy (also overlooked by Conze). The debate in the upper chamber took place on April 9-10, by the way, not April 5.

56. Hindenburg, on orders from the Kaiser, to Hertling, via Lersner, April 7, 1918, Zeman (2), p. 158.

57. Grünau to the foreign minister, February 22 and 23. Von dem Bussche to Kühlmann, February 26 (AA, WK 15, secret, Vol. 5). Andrian to Czernin, February 24 (HHSTA, Kr. 56/30). The discussion between the two emperors was not without its weird features. When Charles pleaded that the border strip project be kept to a minimum, the Kaiser said that this territorial concession was being compensated for by the resettlement of the Polish population in the kingdom. In the event of an Austro-Polish solution, he insisted on the right of military inspection and influence on the organization and training of the Polish forces and their fortifications and communications. Pressing for an early peace, Charles was told that the need was for a good rather than a swift peace. Germany was well able to fight on for another two or three years, as the Bavarian minister of finance had but recently confirmed (sic). Charles on his part wished to see autonomy for West Galicia in the event of the "candidate solution," without representation in the Austrian Reichsrat, however, in return for which that region was to be enlarged by the Polish industrial district of Dombrova.

58. Grünau to Hertling, on a report by Cramon, March 7, 1918 (AA, WK 15, secret, Vol. 5). In a letter to the Kaiser of April 3, 1918 (HHSTA, Kr. 56/30), Charles pressed for a swift decision on the Polish issue along the lines of the Austro-Polish solution, for which he was willing to pay the price of strengthening the alliance as proposed by Czernin—it was to be extended for 25 years, there was to be an economic alliance as well—Section Councilor Dr. Gratz was

continuing to discuss this matter with Privy Councilor Koerner, the foreign ministry expert—and there were also to be "agreements affecting the armed forces."

59. Conze (p. 353) reports on the crown council of March 13, on the basis of a brief and manifestly inadequate report by von dem Bussche to Kühlmann of the same date. More details in notes in ZA, III GHQ 21, App. Vol. 1. Grünau reported to Hertling on March 7 on Emperor Charles's change of mind (AA, WK 15, secret, Vol. 5), on the basis of a report from Cramon; Hohenlohe to Czernin on Hertling's perplexity on March 3 and 12 (HHSTA, Kr. 56ª/3). In mid-April Burián had prepared a well-organized summary of the Austro-German negotiations on the Polish issue from early 1917 to March 1918 (HHSTA, secret, 47/3-25).

60. This is clear from a summary prepared in late April, apparently for Burián (HHSTA, secret, 47/3-22). *Ibidem,* correspondence, April 16-22, on the issue of interpreting the alliance, and various versions of the contemplated treaty.

61. In keeping with Austrian sensibilities, the German claim to restoration of its world trade position before 1914 (as suggested by Helfferich) was formulated with considerable care, in fact in negative rather than positive terms. Because of Czernin's objections, a paragraph was omitted that would have continued Bulgarian and Turkish treaty claims in support of their war aims by the Central Powers.

62. RAW, Vol. 13, pp. 180ff.

63. Bethmann Hollweg to Hindenburg, February 11, 1917, on Carp's plans for a new Rumanian constitution under a new dynasty. Beldiman, former Rumanian envoy in Berlin, to Michaelis, July 23, 1917, proposing formation of a new Rumanian government under Peter Carp. Lersner to the foreign ministry, August 2, on Mackensen's and Ludendorff's plans. Mirbach to von dem Bussche, August 8, criticizing the foregoing. Grünau to Michaelis, August 13, on the Kaiser's attitude. Lersner to the foreign ministry, August 13, on Ludendorff's objections. Michaelis to Grünau, August 14, request for postponement, approved by the Kaiser—all in Sch&Gr, Vol. 2, Nos. 7, 174, 184, 193, 196, 200, 201, 203.

64. See Gratz-Schüller, p. 180. These authors suspect that the Germans actually feared a peace offer by the Bratianu government and sought to forestall it, since they wanted a dictated rather than a negotiated peace. For a somewhat similar view, see Czernin, pp. 413ff., minutes of the Bucharest peace negotiations.

65. Lersner to the foreign ministry, December 30, 1917 (second wire). Horstmann to the foreign ministry, December 30, 1917, and January 1 and 6, 1918. Hindenburg to the Kaiser, January 9, 1918, transmitting direct report from Mackensen of January 4. The OHL to the Kaiser, January 8, 1918, transmitting a direct report by Mackensen of December 31, with comment. The Kaiser's marginal notes appear in UA, Vol. 2, p. 169. On January 31 Hertling provided a long written opinion on Mackensen's report of December 31, requested by the Kaiser, but this did not really precipitate the decision, as Fischer claims (p. 686, Note 25). It is essentially limited to what Horstmann had reported on January 1; it complains about the difficulty of finding a solution, and fails to touch on the dynastic question at all, though it reaches the conclusion that Austria holds the key to Rumania, whose favorable situation can be upset only if Austria renounces its interest by treaty, which in turn can be achieved only if Germany were prepared to make concessions on the Polish issue, in return for gaining advantages in Rumania. Undoubtedly this was in keeping with the views of Kühlmann and the foreign ministry (where Hentsch's proposals were simply filed). Fischer's notes on p. 686 all carry wrong file identifications, the items designated "WK2" all being actually filed in the "WK 2, secret" file series. As for a file designated "Rumania, polit.," there is none such. File 59, cited in Note 25, begins only in April, and the document dated February 11, ostensibly cited from that file, is not in File 57 either, which does cover that period.

66. RAW, Vol. 13, pp. 343ff.
67. Kühlmann to Hertling, February 3, 1918 (ZA, RK II, Kr. 18[1], Vol. 1).
68. Lersner to the foreign ministry, January 10 and 11, 1918 (AA, WK 15, secret, Vol. 5). Ludendorff also vigorously pressed for fulfillment by Bulgaria of the offsetting financial and economic counterobligations. He thought the German envoy Oberndorff too soft in representing Germany's interests and urged that no account be taken of the possible fall of Radoslavov (the OHL to Hertling, March 20, 1918, ZA, RK II, Kr. 18[1], Vol. 1). The quarrel between Turkey and Bulgaria over the Northern Dobrudja and the Constantsa rail line had originated in late 1916.
69. On December 29 Hindenburg and Ludendorff, in Lersner's presence, had talks with Beldiman, who promised to oust the dynasty and install a regency council, as soon as he was sure that the army would go along. Typical of Ludendorff's view of the matter is his immediate emphasis that the new government must have no military power whatever and must do nothing in the political and economic spheres against Mackensen's will (Lersner to the foreign ministry, December 30, 1917, AA, WK 2, secret, Vol. 55).
70. Details in Gratz-Schüller, Chapter 3, where the various points of the peace proposals and negotiations of all the participants are set forth at length, from the Austrian files—both authors took part themselves in the negotiations. Fischer gives an account based on German sources, especially the ZA (pp. 684ff.).
71. Tisza to Czernin, February 27, 1918 (Czernin, pp. 352ff.).
72. RAW, Vol. 13, pp. 353, 357. The agreement, however, must have been achieved at a special conference, the minutes of which I have not seen, though I have searched the AA files. There is nothing about it in the Austrian minutes cited in Note 48 nor in the German minutes of the full session of February 5.
73. ÖU, Vol. 7, p. 115, gives details of the sequence of military directives from Baden to the Kövess army command, but ignores the fact that initially Emperor Charles refused to have his troops take any part in the contemplated action.
74. On the same day, Ludendorff wired Mackensen's chief of staff, Hell, that even after the conclusion of a general peace Rumania would have to remain under German administration and continuing occupation by troops of Germany's allies! (UA, Vol. 8, p. 254.)
75. Charles to William II, February 16, with the latter's marginal note (Fischer, p. 688, Note 36; Gratz-Schüller, p. 188).
76. Martens-Triepel, pp. 856ff.
77. This was exactly what the Kaiser thought, see text to Note 4!
78. ZA, RK II, Kr. 18[1], Vol. 1 which also contains the correspondence of Kühlmann and the OHL with Hertling, cited in the following. Further items in UA, Vol. 8, pp. 290-294.
79. Kühlmann, p. 563.
80. Grünau to the foreign ministry, March 27 (ZA, *loc. cit.*).
81. Hertling to Berg, on the report to the Kaiser on April 2 (not August 15, as Fischer wrongly states, p. 697, Note 60). The distribution is noted on Hertling's letter (ZA, *loc. cit.*).
82. See his complaint forwarded to the foreign ministry through Lersner, April 8 (UA, Vol. 2, p. 187).
83. By way of proof, Hindenburg mentions only a trifling matter. A shipyard for Danube lighters in Turnu-Severin was to fall to Austria rather than Germany, to Ludendorff's discomfiture (Kühlmann, p. 561; Gratz-Schüller, p. 199). Once the treaty had been initialed, Germany prevailed in obtaining a share in the yard.
84. The noteworthy part of the report is the assertion that Kühlmann had persuaded Czernin of the impossibility of the Rumanian king returning and that Czernin in turn prevailed on Emperor Charles to reconcile himself to the candidacy of Prince Frederic Charles of Hesse. See Kühlmann's derogatory remarks on a change in dynasty (Kühlmann, pp. 562f.) made before the Reichstag committee.

He said that any king installed by Germany was bound to be transported back to that country in the baggage car of the last train, when the German army cleared out of Rumania! His real attitude is not made clear.

85. On April 15, he cited an accompanying letter from Legation Councilor Schoen of Bavaria, representing a reply to Major Kessler's letter, employed by Hindenburg.

86. An article in the *Deutsche Zeitung* of April 23 charged Kühlmann with leading a dissolute life, on the basis of such perfectly harmless incidents as visits to the ballet. Payer, as vice chancellor, joined in signing the complaint (Haussmann, pp. 189f.; Kühlmann, p. 564).

Notes to Chapter 5

1. See Newton (1), pp. 469ff. (Lord Newton was a friend of Lansdowne), and also Lansdowne, pp. 370-384 (by the Marquess of Lansdowne, Lord Lansdowne's son). Newton, among other things cites a letter from Lord Sanderson to Lord Crome of December 1917, complaining bitterly of the level of the "low class press" and the "vulgar platitudes and speeches" with which Lloyd George and his colleagues were regaling Britain. Colonel House greatly admired Lord Lansdowne as a true British nobleman of the old school (House, Vol. 3, p. 237). Lansdowne was in touch with House and had the colonel's approval.

2. December 1, 1917 (Scott, pp. 206ff.).

3. Speech to air service heads, December 14 (Schulthess, 1917, Vol. 2, p. 370; Scott, pp. 210ff.).

4. Interview with the Wolff wire service, December 17 (Schulthess, 1917, Vol. 1, p. 1035). Lloyd George, whose arrogant airs were not without critics even in the House of Commons, on December 20 sought to buttress his attacks on Prussian militarism with the most outrageous charges: "They planned and they plotted for years for this war. They were even prepared, and everybody in Germany knew it, to overthrow their own ruler in order to set up another ruler who was more in sympathy with their ambitious design" (Scott, p. 219).

5. Steglich (2), pp. 341f.

6. Dugdale, Vol. 2, pp. 254ff. (Balfour to Cecil, December 29, 1917).

7. Schulthess, 1917, Vol. 2, pp. 371ff. At this session, Lord Cecil charged the Germans with having failed to respond in any way to the Allied declaration of October 6, stating that the Allies were ready to listen to and consider any German peace offers. The Germans, he said, were merely trying to confuse the world with rumors that they were ready for peace. It is incomprehensible to me how Steglich (2) can interpret this as an invitation for new and direct soundings (pp. 269, 285, 312). Cecil was trying to show the House precisely that there was not a particle of truth in any alleged German preparedness for peace and that German peace feelers were quite pointless.

8. Lloyd George, Vol. 5, pp. 2484ff., 2505ff.; Scott, 225ff.; Schulthess, 1918, Vol. 2, 142ff.

9. This was plainly directed against Lansdowne and his followers, but Steglich (2), pp. 342ff., reads a measure of conciliation into it, indeed, a reply to an alleged new offer on Belgium made by Kühlmann late in December (which is a mere matter of conjecture). I think this is highly contrived and merely bespeaks a general tendency on the part of Steglich to overestimate British readiness for peace.

10. Telegram of congratulation, January 6 (Scott, p. 233). Pichon's defense of French government policy in the chamber on December 27, against socialist demands and criticisms, had not been very impressive (Schulthess, 1917, Vol. 2, pp. 486ff.).

11. According to Mamatey, p. 174, Wilson, in formulating these questions, seems to have been influenced by a peace feeler stretched out by the Austrian merchant and amateur diplomatist Meinl. It had come to him through the American legation in Berne.

12. Wilson to House, December 1, 1917 (FR, 1917, Supplement 2, Vol. 1, p. 331). See also Seymour, p. 282, for a detailed discussion of the background of the speech of January 8; House, Vol. 3, pp. 328ff.; Mamatey, p. 177. The latter gives detailed and interesting data on the memorandum of the Inquiry Commission, of which Wilson availed himself and of which Mamatey is highly critical, as is Kennan, p. 249.

13. Kennan, pp. 240ff.

14. Metternich-Solf, pp. 100f.

15. Max, p. 159. The author is not identified, but it could scarcely be anyone but Hahn. After the Lansdowne letter was published, Kühlmann seems to have momentarily considered repeating the secret soundings he had taken in London the preceding September (report by Hohenlohe, December 6, HHSTA, Kr, 4K), but Asquith's speech of December 11 and Lloyd George's of December 14 rendered that illusory. Steglich (1), however, offers evidence that Kühlmann did indeed repeat the soundings, late in December. He cites a talk with Conrad Haussmann of April 24, 1918 in which Kühlmann mentioned his "effort in December 1917." I am convinced that this represents a slip of memory or pen, or that September was misheard as December; for (a) in January 1918 British statesmen repeatedly complained that Berlin still had not made an unequivocal statement concerning Belgium; and (b) it is inconceivable that Kühlmann, at this time of threatening conflict with the OHL, should have secretly dared offer London total relinquishment of Belgium, especially in the wake of the crown council of December 18, in which the Kaiser declared the decisions of the crown council of September 11 to be obsolete. Steglich (2), p. 284, seeks to trivialize this, but the Kaiser actually reverted to his grotesque proposal of September 11 to have the coast of Flanders fortified against Britain.

16. Hindenburg immediately wrote Hertling on December 11, 1917, in unmistakable tones that the crown council decision held only "in the event we get peace this year and Britain quits France." Since this was not the case and Germany's military situation had improved, the Kreuznach agreement of April 23 was back in force. (For Hertling's reply, see UA, Vol. 3, pp. 265f.; further the OHL's direct report to the Kaiser of January 7, 1918, see p. 96; for Ludendorff's marginal notes on Hertling's memorandum of January 23, 1918, see UA, Vol. 2, p. 63.)

17. UA, Vol. 2, No. 6, p. 135. This was the day, by the way, when Ludendorff told Haeften that he would resign, since he was unable to bring about the fall of Kühlmann (BA, Haeften papers, Portfolio 5, Sheet 4).

18. Reproduced in the form transmitted in Ludendorff (1), pp. 473ff. For the parts that were cut in the draft, see Max, pp. 201f.

19. BA, Haeften papers, *loc. cit.*

20. Max, p. 212.

21. When verbal representations were made to Stumm, the foreign ministry got some articles into the press along the lines of the memorandum, but nothing more was done (Haeften papers, *loc. cit.*).

22. Kühlmann to Hertling, January 10, 1918. Evidence in Steglich (2), pp. 353f.

23. His attitude emerges with particular clarity from the labored statements on the Belgian issue in the memorandum of the 23rd (UA, Vol. 2, p. 63), and Radowitz's letter (*ibidem*, p. 337), already cited in Chapter 3, Note 7.

24. I do not understand how Steglich can here find "a new wrinkle in the policy of seeking an approach to Britain."

25. Mamatey, p. 192. Text of the speech in Schulthess, 1918, Vol. 1, pp. 19ff.

26. Solf, who had participated in its preparation without much success, thought it represented a step backward. Letter to Metternich, Metternich-Solf, p. 112. Haussmann (pp. 168f.) thought Hertling halfhearted (letter to his wife, January 27).

27. After Max, p. 233. The version in UA, vol. 2, pp. 136ff., mentions only Naumann,

Jäckh, and Bosch. Hahn apparently ignored Haeften's injunction against proselytizing for a Belgium declaration, that is, if this injunction was imposed on him before February 11.

28. Rosen, p. 143f., speaks of it. The Prince's own memoirs do not mention it, of course. Unfortunately they also fail to mention the date of the Berlin talks. Since there is mention of Haussmann putting in an appearance from Switzerland, they probably began during the last week of January or the first of February (Haussmann, pp. 170ff.). Rosen says, however, that he came to Berlin only in mid-February.

29. There was little concrete substance to these talks, which Haussmann describes in detail (pp. 159ff., and 170f.) and on which he reported to Hertling each time. At times there was a plan for a meeting of German and British parliamentarians of democratic convictions, and preparations were made to that end. Haussmann notably overestimated the political role of the American agent Herron, whom he also met. He was misled by Swiss friends, who shared this misapprehension. Herron's own report to the American legation in Berne on his discussion with Haussmann on February 15 (or 16), FR, 1918, Supplement 1, Vol. 1, pp. 122f., differs markedly from Haussmann's own report (pp. 177ff.). Herron's report is distinctly malicious. In it Haussmann's statements are sometimes made to look so foolish and politically unwise as to give rise to the suspicion that Herron deliberately distorted them or that there were crude misunderstandings (Haussmann neither spoke nor understood English).

30. Max, pp. 231ff. Solf too thought that the Prince's efforts were virtually hopeless. The envoy Rosen, according to his memoirs, voted for a declaration on Belgium.

31. Prince Max gained the subjective impression that Ludendorff had not spoken his final word on the issue of Belgium and might submit to a vigorous demand by Hertling, coupled with a threat of resignation; but from what we know of the events in January, it must remain doubtful whether this was anything more than wishful thinking.

32. UA, Vol. 2, pp. 92f.

33. House, Vol. 3, p. 379, Lloyd George, Vol. 5, p. 2495. In the American press it seems to have been somewhat softened by cutting (Scott, p. 262, following the *New York Times*). According to intelligence reaching House, the British government agreed only after some hesitation, and House regretted that the declaration said nothing to encourage the German socialists.

34. FR, 1918, Supplement 1, Vol. 1, p. 81, Lansing to Sharp, February 5, 1918.

35. Scott, pp. 265ff.; Schulthess, 1918, Vol. 2, pp. 563ff. For the following see Scott, pp. 271, 273, and Schulthess, p. 159.

36. Scott, pp. 271ff., 273ff. Schulthess, 1918, Vol. 2, pp. 155, 158, 159.

37. Report by Hohenlohe to Vienna on a talk with Hertling on March 3, 1918 (HHSTA, Kr. 56 a/3). For the speech, see Schulthess, 1918, Vol. 1, pp. 86ff.

38. Haussmann (pp. 172ff., 180) had come to terms with a British mathematician, Professor Young, among other things on organizing a meeting of democratically minded British and German parliamentarians in Switzerland. The liberal Runciman had taken this up in the House of Commons on February 13, proposing intimate talks rather than trans-Atlantic discussion. Hertling referred to this at the very outset of his speech. The formulation of his statement on Belgium too coincides in content approximately with what Haussmann had told Young on February 14 and 16, to Young's delight. The only difference was that Haussmann plainly spoke of freedom for Belgium, to be guaranteed on every side by international law, while Hertling carefully avoided such a thing. Hertling's remark, that he stood ready to discuss noncommittally any proposals for the future security of Belgian neutrality that might issue from the Belgian government in Le Havre, probably went back to a Vatican suggestion. In January King Albert is supposed to have pleaded with the Vatican to try to get Germany to issue a conciliatory statement on Belgium. If this were done, he would ask his allies why they were actually continuing the struggle. Of course Hertling's

subsequent declaration was not good enough for him (report by the Austrian envoy at The Hague, Széchényi, to Vienna, March 11, HHSTA, Kr. 4K). See also King Albert's statement of August 3, 1917, Sch&Gr, Vol. 2, No. 185, when he said that there could be no peace unless Germany completely forewent Belgium. Any "guarantees" would merely serve to turn Belgium into a German satellite. Belgium would resist any new invasion on its own, whether it came from Britain or France or from Germany.

39. This too may go back to a suggestion from Haussmann. The American agent Professor Herron, a political muddlehead of whom we will hear more, had told Haussmann that if Germany agreed to the four points, Mr. Wilson would challenge and indeed compel the Allies to do likewise at the outset of negotiations—"that's as certain as that Christ was nailed to the cross" (Haussmann, p. 180; Max, p. 226.).

40. Speech in the House of Commons, February 27 (Scott, p. 294). See, *ibidem,* statement on the peace treaties of Brest-Litovsk and Bucharest by a conference of Entente ministers in London, March 18.

41. Letter by Lansdowne in the *Daily Telegraph* of March 5, 1918 (Max, pp. 246ff.; *ibidem,* App. III. pp. 660ff., Hahn's memorandum).

42. Hohenlohe to Czernin, February 17, 1918 (HHSTA, Prussia III/174). Prince Max had told him about a rather colorless interview with the head of the Wolff wire service, which he had given on February 15 at the request of the foreign ministry in reply to Lansdowne's speech of January 31 (Max, pp. 217f.; Schulthess, 1918, Vol. 1, pp. 64ff.).

43. Max, p. 232.

44. The so-called "mission" of Lieutenant Colonel Haeften in May 1918 became something of a red herring before the parliamentary investigating committee of 1925. Hans Delbrück in particular believed at the time that Haeften had brought back from The Hague an American peace offer on terms that were on the whole quite favorable, but that his chief Ludendorff had rejected it and not even told the foreign ministry about it (UA, Vol. 3, see index under Haeften). When the sources available today are carefully scrutinized, this turns out to be a myth—consult Max, pp. 242ff.; Rosen, pp. 145ff.; Haeften, papers in the BA, Portfolio 5; Foerster (1), p. 256 (the first edition of this work, 1921, was used by Ludendorff, *Kriegführung und Politik* (1922), p. 293). Two sets of events must be distinguished:

(a) Early in March rumors transpired from the American legation in The Hague, through the medium of a German-American, Th. and also apparently through the Dutch foreign minister Loudon. Reaching the German envoy Rosen, they said that the American envoy Garrett sought contact with some unofficial German representative, "to explore peace possibilities." Rosen suggested that the foreign ministry send the Hamburg banker Max Warburg, who did make his appearance in The Hague, armed with personal instructions from Hertling, and met the middlemen mentioned, but departed after only a few days, since Garrett showed no signs of wanting to see him. This is the version given by Rosen and Prince Max, apparently from Hahn's report, while Haeften insisted that Rosen had learned from talks with Garrett that Wilson first of all demanded denunciation of the peace treaties of Brest-Litovsk and settlement of eastern questions at a general peace conference, which Rosen immediately rejected. It was after this that Warburg made his departure. This intelligence can scarcely be correct. Why should there be negotiations through intermediaries, when the two envoys were in direct contact? It also conflicts with Rosen's known stand on the peace question. Rosen was indignant over Haeften's attitude, discernible at the outset, that no peace effort must be permitted to interfere with Ludendorff's great impending offensive. He also resented Haeften's negotiating with a member of the American legation behind his back—he learned of this only during the parliamentary investigation in 1924.

(b) The member of the American legation was the German-American Jacob

Noeggerath, an engineer who had been in close touch with the German foreign ministry (especially its "central office of foreign service" under Rohrbach) since the beginning of the war. Noeggerath was subsequently also in touch with Haeften and Hahn, becoming particularly friendly with the latter. With America's entry into the war, he had withdrawn to Holland, where he was an adviser on German affairs to the American legation, remaining in touch with Haeften, who kept him currently supplied with information about Germany. (See Garrett's reports to Lansing, January 13 and 30, FR, 1918, Supplement 1, Vol. 1, pp. 26f., 59f.) Hahn had, among other things, explained Germany's position on Wilson's Fourteen Points and Hertling's overcautious statements on the Belgian issue of January 25, repeatedly urging that confidential talks be initiated in place of the pointless speeches by the statesmen, and that this be done before the spring offensive began. On March 4 Noeggerath had sent word to his friends in Berlin (according to Prince Max, i.e., Hahn) that it would be a good thing if Haeften came to The Hague, to inform himself of the unhappy impression made by the circumstances surrounding the treaty imposed at Brest-Litovsk. "This will probably put an end to any peaceful inclinations among the Allies." Presumably Noeggerath was trying to influence the OHL through Haeften, to prepare the ground for revision of the Treaty of Brest-Litovsk, thus making it possible for America to take on the role of mediator. This had been Noeggerath's hope and goal for years (see Max, pp. 54ff.), and he hoped it could now be effected before the offensive. Haeften thereupon went to The Hague with Hahn, without any clear mission and apparently without the knowledge of the foreign ministry, simply in his capacity as a military representative of the OHL. He and Hahn met secretly with Noeggerath at the home of Professor Lepsius, president of the German-Armenian society. Noeggerath's overtures are given in restrained form in Hahn's report (in Max), more brusquely in Haeften's report to Ludendorff (Foerster, *loc. cit.*), and lastly in Haeften's papers. Noeggerath thought it either probable or certain that public opinion in the Anglo-Saxon countries would compel their governments to make peace, if Germany made an unequivocal declaration about the relinquishment of Belgium and revised the treaties of Brest-Litovsk. The "desiderata" for any negotiations were listed as (a) uncondi-,tional evacuation of North France and Belgium; (b) payment of reparations; (c) autonomy (rather than cession!) for Alsace-Lorraine; (d) referral of eastern questions to a peace conference to be convoked by the Entente, the treaties of Brest-Litovsk being canceled; (e) introduction of a parliamentary system of government, Hertling and his government being ousted, to be replaced by a government under Prince Max of Baden, who was said to enjoy considerable prestige in the United States. Point (e), apparently put forward only wishfully, is the giveaway about this talk. It represented a foray on the part of the zealous and notably pro-German Noeggerath and not any "American peace offer."

Such an offer, in any event, would have been quite hopeless at this juncture. To Rosen's annoyance, Haeften, on March 8 talked to the military attaché Schweinitz and the banker von der Heydt, who was temporarily working at the German legation. Both these gentlemen thought that public renunciation of Belgium was essential, but that the offensive was inevitable, if only because France would never forego Alsace-Lorraine unless it were defeated (see Schweinitz, pp. 346f., with his shrewd military reports). This confirmed Haeften's own opinion and he reported to Lundendorff that no "honorable peace" could be secured prior to the offensive. Ludendorff naturally received this report with approval and did not pass it on to the Chancellor.

45. We have mentioned only a small number of these peace feelers in the course of our account and not followed them in detail. For the winter of 1917-1918, I refer to Steglich (2), pp. 220f., Kühlmann's contact with the Danish state councilor Anderson; pp. 271ff., renewed efforts by Countess Mérode; pp. 274ff., contact with Professor Herron through the Berne legation both in early and mid-

December. *Ibidem,* pp. 355ff., and Hertling, pp. 56f., mediation offer by the king of Denmark, and Halling-Kohl talks, January 1918. H. G. Nicolson compiled a list of the peace feelers that reached Britain in 1917-1918, for the Foreign Office. It includes no official overtures at all from Bulgaria, but rather serious ones from Moukhtar Bey, head of the Turkish delegation in Switzerland, in the winter of 1917-1918, with Parodi as the mediator (PRO, FO, 371/3442).

46. We cannot here dwell at length on the secret negotiations with Bulgarian and Turkish agents in Switzerland, which scarcely ceased.

47. Correspondence between Széchényi, The Hague, and Czernin, August 9 to November 25, 1917 (HHSTA, Kr. 25/27, dealt with at length in Steglich [2], pp. 222ff.).

48. Sch&Gr, Vol. 2, No. 173, see p. 146, this book.

49. Schulthess, 1917, Vol. 2, p. 214.

50. UA, Vol. 3, pp. 265f.

51. Schulthess, 1917, Vol. 2, pp. 182ff.

52. Scott, pp. 193ff.

53. Reports by the Austrian diplomats in Berne on the preliminary talks with middlemen after November 5 are in HHSTA, Kr. 25/27. They are dealt with at length in Steglich (2), pp. 224, 245ff., 249.

54. There can be no doubt that such was the intention of Lloyd George and also of General Smuts. See Smuts's report (Lloyd George, Vol. 5, p. 2462) and the prime minister's own attitude (*ibidem,* p. 2480), as well as the stand he took in the Allied council (Poincaré, Vol. 9, pp. 394f.; House, Vol. 3, p. 282). In the British war cabinet session of January 18, Smuts said unequivocally that it was his intention and his mission to discuss with Mensdorff "only the possibility of a separate peace with Austria" (PRO, Cab. 23/16, WC 325a), and this really invalidates Steglich's contrived effort (Steglich [2], pp. 261f.) to distinguish between a "separate peace" and the "isolation of Germany." Smuts was satisfied with the "result" of the talk, even though it was ultimately a failure, for he thought that the vision he painted of the future made a deep impression on Mensdorff, but to my mind this does not necessarily prove that he pursued only limited aims, but rather that the discussion afforded him invaluable insight into Austria's domestic difficulties and the uncertainties besetting its statesmen. In subsequent sessions of the war cabinet, the talks were repeatedly judged to have been valuable, in this sense. Mensdorff's demeanor is unlikely to have been as assured and steadfast as he tried to make Czernin believe in his report (Fester, BMH, Vol. 15, p. 402). At any rate, Smuts did take extremely seriously the Austrian's assurances at the end that Austria would leave nothing undone that might lead to peace, that Britain could rely on Austria gladly serving as mediator, etc.—"short of a separate peace or an act of disloyalty towards our German ally," however (*ibidem,* pp. 408f.).

55. Report by Smuts (Lloyd George, Vol. 5, pp. 2461-2480). Mensdorff's report in Fester (1), pp. 177f., and BMH, Vol. 15, pp. 401-413, 1937. Balfour's long speech in the House of Commons on November 6 went so far as to make this exaggerated statement: "Germany is more deliberately set upon universal dominion than any power I think, that has ever existed, or than any power that has existed for a couple of thousand years" (Scott, p. 181). By comparison Smuts was moderate when he compared Ludendorff's Germany with the empire of Napoleon.

56. Mamatey, p. 175.

57. Mamatey, p. 196.

58. Schulthess, 1918, Vol. 2, pp. 7ff.; Czernin, pp. 402f.

59. Report from Lammasch to Herron, FR, 1918, Supplement 1, Vol. 2, p. 88. It says that the Germans prevented its transmission. Mamatey believes (p. 196) that Czernin's statement in his speech, to the effect that the president knew quite well what he wanted to say, was mere pretense to confuse the Entente and make them believe there was a secret pipeline from Vienna to Washington. The only

thing that seems likely to me is that Czernin set great store by the effect of his speech on Wilson. Compare his attitude in the U-boat question, February 1917, Vol. 3, pp. 336ff.

60. In mid-February Kühlmann warned Czernin that Lammasch was intriguing against him and passed on certain confidential intelligence reports he had received from Switzerland. These said that Lammasch had told "an American agent" (probably Herron) among other things that Emperor Charles would have long since got rid of Czernin if he had had real freedom of action, and that he desired nothing so ardently as to shake off the German grip. He added that Switzerland was infested with Austrian plotters without any official standing, all working along lines similar to that of the official Austrian foreign service, with the result that Paris and London nourished more and more hope of Austria's imminent collapse, which explained the brusque statement by the war council in Versailles on February 3. (Undated note passed by Kühlmann to Czernin at Brest-Litovsk, and then circulated in the Vienna foreign ministry, on February 18, HHSTA, Prussia III/175.) Later in February the journalist Viktor Naumann received similar intelligence about Lammasch's talks with people in Switzerland, which he passed on to Hertling on February 22, in a background report from Vienna (UA, Vol. 2, pp. 145ff.). Czernin, of course, knew in a general way what men like Lammasch, Foerster, and Meinl were up to in Switzerland, as shown in a discussion he had with J. Baernreither, a member of the upper chamber, on April 2, 1918 (Kann, p. 424).

61. See Count Wedel's report of July 20, 1917 (Sch&Gr, Vol. 2, No. 170). Julius Meinl, a big food merchant, was among Emperor Charles's pacifist advisers. Benedikt has described the intensive political activities of this man and his associates, which he considers to have been highly promising and the failure of which he deplores. Wires to Hertling from Kühlmann on January 26 and Rosen on January 30 show that the foreign ministry in Berlin knew about the incipient Austro-American contacts (Steglich [2], p. 385, Notes 293-295).

62. Report by the American chargé d'affaires in Berne, Hugh Wilson, to Lansing, see esp. FR, 1918, Supplement 1, Vol. 1, pp. 82-105 (January 31, February 8). On Herron's character see Mamatey, pp. 138f., and on his activities as an agent from 1917 Steglich (2), pp. 272ff., with the American literature there cited, esp. Lutz, pp. 469, 580. See, further, Benedikt, pp. 144ff., based on copies of Herron's papers, among other sources. Benedikt gives a detailed account of Lammasch's talks with Herron, based on this material, having overlooked, oddly enough, that the most important part of it had already been published in FR, *loc. cit.* Lammasch-Sperl, pp. 96ff., gives notes by Lammasch on his "peace efforts with President Wilson," in which Lammasch's talks with Herron appear in a much more innocent light than in Herron's own papers. The talks took place on February 3 and 4 in the home of a former director of Krupp, Dr. Mühlon, at Gümligen near Berne, a favorite meeting-place of western agents. One reads with dismay (FR, *loc. cit.,* p. 95ff.) how this German émigré launched into the bitterest attacks against Germany before the American. Not only did he put the blame for the war on the Germans but he declared that the defeat of Germany was essential. There is reason to believe that this amateur diplomatist was mentally ill, see Payer's report on March 16, 1918, before the main committee of the Reichstag (Schulthess, 1918, Vol. 1, p. 123).

63. Mamatey, pp. 222f.

64. This time Lansing too was consulted. He evidently had a high opinion of Lammasch, whom he believed to be a sincere pacifist, and he held Herron's diplomatic skill in similarly high esteem. Through confidential channels he offered financial aid to Emperor Charles, in the event Austria should get into financial trouble on account of a separate peace! (FR, 1918, Supplement 1, Vol. 1, pp. 119, 129.)

65. Text in Fr, 1918, Supplement 1, Vol. 1, pp. 108ff.; Scott, pp. 265ff.

66. Czernin, p. 338. This passage shows Mamatey to be in error (p. 231) in believing that Czernin had a low opinion of Wilson's intelligence.

67. The British secret service intercepted the letter en route from Vienna to Madrid, decoded it, and had it transmitted to the president from London through Ambassador Page on February 20, while the Spanish ambassador in Washington presented it only on February 26. The text given in FR, *loc. cit.,* pp. 126ff., displays some major cuts from the German version, first published by Nowak, pp. 431ff. They include (a) a request to Wilson to prevail on the Allies to forego conquests and annexations, in which case Austria would endeavor to do the same with its allies; (b) the demand that all the belligerents recognize the inviolability of the status quo; and (c) Austrian assurances of irrefutable proof that not all nationalist aspirations, notably in the case of South Tyrol, were legitimate or even in the interest of the countries concerned.
68. Mamatey, p. 227, after Briggs, pp. 84f., Benedikt, pp. 243ff.
69. Balfour to House, February 27, 1918, House, Vol. 3, pp. 386f.
70. Text in FR, *loc. cit.,* p. 183 (March 5, 1918). Wilson wanted further details about the Balkan and the Slavic nations neighboring on Austria, plans for the Adriatic coast, the maximum concessions Austria was prepared to make to Italy, and methods for eliminating war-enhanced quarrels among the Balkan countries. He also wanted to know who would protect the non-Turkish peoples under Turkish rule. On Belgium and Poland common views were taken for granted, and Alsace-Lorraine was not mentioned.
71. FR, *loc. cit.,* pp. 184ff. What Nowak says about the content of this letter (p. 96) is cut from the whole cloth. I think Mamatey too (pp. 231f.) misinterprets in part both the content of the letter and Czernin's intentions.
72. Czernin, pp. 243, 297.
73. *Ibidem,* p. 230.
74. Discussion with Revertera, early October 1917, Engel-Janosi (1), p. 292.
75. *Ibidem,* p. 235.
76. Revertera, pp. 517f. To him Alsace-Lorraine was only a "border strip." See Engel-Janosi, *loc. cit.,* p. 292. On the continuing contacts between Armand's Swiss intermediaries and Vienna, see Chapter 1, Note 80.
77. Sixtus, pp. 310ff. In his public feud with Czernin in April, Clemenceau used this inquiry as proof that the initiative concerning peace talks had emanated from the Austrian rather than the French side. Evidently he had no such proof for the talks of February 2 and 3.
78. Czernin to his foreign ministry, for Revertera, January 17, 1918 (HHSTA, secret, 47/12[e]).
79. According to Armand's own report (Sixtus, pp. 321ff.), he expressed himself, on the contrary, with great brusqueness about Alsace-Lorraine. Revertera's report of February 2, 1918, appears in BMH, Vol. 15, 1937, pp. 413ff. Engel-Janosi (2), pp. 369ff., based on Revertera's papers, contributes nothing to clear up these contradictions.
80. Czernin to Musulin, Berne, for Revertera, February 22, 1918 (HHSTA, secret, 47/12e).
81. Text in Sixtus, pp. 330f. Clémenceau used the opening sentence in his feud with Czernin as proof that Austria was groveling for peace.
82. PRO, Cab. 23/16, WC 311a (January 2, 1918), WC 308a (January 8, 1918), WC 325a (January 18, 1918). Handwritten critical Foreign Office opinion, unsigned (FO, 371/3133). Text of Rumbold's report of January 12, 1918 (*ibidem,* also in Lloyd George, Vol. 5, pp. 2496ff.), stating that Skrzynski had sent word that no attention should be paid to press reaction to Lloyd George's speech in Germany and Austria, since the Austrian press was partly, the German wholly under the control of the arms industry. Czernin had had to wage a titanic struggle in Berlin to throw out annexations—evidently this refers to the Brest-Litovsk declaration of December 25. In return he had had to promise to dispatch some Austrian regiments to the western front. This was a form of blackmail, for which Austria should not be blamed. The German annexationists were furious. Following the declaration, Hertling scarcely dared leave his house, for fear of being howled

down by Berlin mobs. On the use of Austrian troops on the western front, see UA, Vol. 3, pp. 44ff. Skrzynski had had word about this setback to Anglo-Austrian relations through an informant of the British legation in Berne. He passed the information on to Czernin, through Musulin, in a wire on January 13, which demonstrates clearly that he himself was pressing for continuation of the Mensdorff-Smuts talks, through his intermediaries (HHSTA, Kr. 25/27).

83. On February 22 Rumbold reported Skrzynski as telling his middleman that he would almost certainly become a Polish minister after the war. Poland was Britain's natural ally. There was no longer any question of it becoming a third national component state in the Austrian empire. Poland would have to become an independent constitutional monarchy, preferably under a Bourbon prince (PRO, FO, 371/3133).

84. Reports from Rumbold, February 2 and 22, and March 4 (PRO, FO, 371/3133). Sessions of the war cabinet (*ibidem,* Cab. 23/16, WC 338a [February 4], WC 359a [March 5]). On March 6 Balfour recommended that Kerr's trip be postponed (*ibidem,* 360a). There was sharp, written objection by Lieutenant Colonel Hankey, the cabinet secretary, who charged that the Foreign Office was dragging its feet (letter to Lloyd George, March 21, Cab. 23/16). Foreign Office instructions to Kerr, March 6, unsigned (FO, 371/3133).

85. Report from Kerr from Switzerland, March 11, reproduced in part in Lloyd George, Vol. 5, p. 2500, March 14 and 15 (FO, 371/3133). Rumbold and Parodi at the Berne legation, were convinced beyond any doubt that Skrzynski's information was reliable. Rumbold reported his complete disillusion only on March 26, proposing that Parodi be forbidden to engage in any further talks with Skrzynski. Lloyd George's account of the whole incident is inaccurate, stating wrongly that Smuts went to Switzerland a second time, with Kerr. According to Hancock, p. 473, Smuts did not leave London between March 7 and 13.

86. House, Vol. 3, pp. 390f.

87. That was why, on March 3, he forbade the ministry to submit the British peace feeler to Emperor Charles, reserving to himself the right to communicate this information, on March 18. The correspondence on the British peace feeler between Czernin and Skrzynski, always via the Berne legation, and between him and the Vienna foreign ministry, beginning February 27, is in HHSTA, Kr, 25/27. It ends with a directive from Burián on May 10 to "cease all contact with Entente organs or middlemen for the time being." On May 15 Skrzynski prepared a final summary for Burián, showing that he regretted the rupture of these negotiations, which he thought had represented a promising "detour" to peace.

88. Details in Zeman (2), pp. 147ff.; Glaise-Horstenau, pp. 193ff.

89. House, Vol. 3, p. 384; *ibidem,* pp. 395ff., letter from André Chéradan to House.

90. He told Baernreither on April 4 (Kann, p. 424) that this provocation, cutting off further talks with France, was mainly intended to put an end to the clandestine activities of men like Lammasch, Foerster, and Meinl. The implausible element is that Lammasch was talking to the Americans rather than the French. Czernin told Revertera (Engel-Janosi [1], p. 294) that he hoped to help bring about Clémenceau's fall, but this too is implausible, since the effort was far too crude, if not hopeless. Far more plausible is the conclusion of Demblin (p. 43) that Czernin was out to give the Germans concrete proof of his loyalty to the alliance, in order to regain their confidence.

91. See Skrzynski's report of February 12 on the attitude of the Entente, in Czernin, p. 337. Text of the speech in Schulthess, 1918, Vol. 2, pp. 21ff.

92. Note by Baernreither, following statements by the mayor of Vienna, Dr. Weiskirchner (Kann, p. 427). Demblin, who was an official in the Austrian foreign ministry, defends his minister eloquently and provides a well-informed account of the crisis, from detailed knowledge and personal experience.

93. Mamatey has shown (pp. 153ff.) the error of the formerly widely held view that the change in American policy that took place in May was due to Masaryk's

influence. Whether Wilson's "Red Cross speech" of May 18, with its brusque rejection of any further peace feelers, referred only to the above-mentioned Austrian peace feeler in the winter of 1917-1918 or also to more recent German attempts to make contact will be discussed in Chapter 8.

Notes to Chapter 6

1. A most impressive account of these preparations is given by General Kuhl, who took part (UA, Vol. 3, pp. 121ff.; RAW, Vol. 14, pp. 43ff.). The account of military operations in the spring and summer of 1918 in RAW is not free of apologist bias, but the detailed data it provides are indispensable to any further research, particularly since the original sources in the army archive, on which it was based, have been lost.
2. Ludendorff (1), pp. 470f.
3. In a discussion with General Max Hoffmann, on April 17, 1917, for example (Hoffmann, Vol. 2, p. 316).
4. Rupprecht, Vol. 2, pp. 372, Note. Similarly during the preliminary talks during the winter of 1917-1918 (RAW, Vol. 14, pp. 75, 88, 169, 201, 245, 257ff; Meier-Welcker (1), pp. 162ff.). Hindenburg made similar statements, even more crudely formulated (Thaer, p. 196).
5. Crown Prince Rupprecht observed in his diary on April 5: "It is noteworthy that none of the OHL directives shows any clear-cut plan. They keep talking about this piece of ground and that, and give the impression that the OHL is living from hand to mouth, so to speak, without committing itself to any particular operational goal."
6. Such, at least, is my understanding of Meier-Welcker's criticism, p. 166.
7. Contrary to the standard criticism that Ludendorff retained too many men in the east who might have usefully supported the western offensive, Meier-Welcker insists that he kept picking over his eastern troops for men fit for combat and as a result weakened those forces to the point where they could not aid Bulgaria and Turkey when the crunch came (Meier-Welcker [2], pp. 22ff. and *passim*).
8. Thaer, pp. 196f., first used in Kaehler (2).
9. Hoffmann, Vol. 2, p. 226.
10. Lossberg, pp. 345ff.
11. To Foreign Minister Hintze in mid-July (RAW, Vol. 14, p. 514).
12. RAW. Vol. 14, p. 431; Meier-Welcker (1), p. 182, from a letter by Below, January 8, 1919.
13. Thaer, pp. 197f.
14. He advised that this be done right up to the Antwerp-Meuse position as well as in Alsace-Lorraine to the rear of areas suitable for flooding by damming, and also along the line Strasbourg-Metz-Rhine. This would make it possible, with the help of the army engineer forces, to "barricade the army territories against the homeland, and to catch and discipline the 'gold-bricks' " (Lossberg, p. 346).
15. In June he suffered a serious heart attack (Hertling, p. 144) and he must have had heart trouble long before that. Chancellor Michaelis's son told me that during the final days while his father was in office he recalled coming home to the Chancellor's residence in the Wilhelmstrasse and seeing an aged gentleman pulling himself painfully up the stairway, both hands gripping the banister, while a female relative pushed from the back. When he inquired, the doorman told him it was Count Hertling, his father's successor. Hertling is known to have been quite unfit for any further work after eight o'clock in the evening. His vision was so dim that he had his son and adjutant write the notes for his Reichstag speeches on slips of paper in a large hand. Kühlmann says (p. 577) that in one of the final talks at Spa Hertling said: "My dear Kühlmann, it seems sheer madness to me to put the burden of the chancellorship on a worn-out old philosophy professor at a time crammed with the most difficult problems."

Notes to Chapter 7

1. Discussion between Hertling and the Kaiser, April 16 (ZA. III, GHQ, 21, App. Vol. 1 [3]). About the Kaiser's initial anger, see Hertling, p. 94; Müller, p. 371.
2. Cramon, pp. 158, 161.
3. According to a report by Count Demblin to the Vienna foreign ministry, April 23, Cramon on that day brought from Avesnes the Kaiser's demand that Emperor Charles give him his oral acceptance (HHSTA, secret, 47/12e). Cramon himself reports that the demands had been toned down. There are no minutes of the talk between the two emperors.
4. For Austrian drafts, the fourth one in the handwriting of Ambassador Mércy, with a memorandum of comment, also by him, dated Vienna, May 1918, see HHSTA, secret, 47/3-23. *Ibidem,* the German counterdraft of the agreement and the final version, signed by the two emperors, Burián, and Hertling, dated May 12, 1918. *Ibidem,* the German draft for a *Waffenbund* (armed alliance), the final and virtually unchanged version of which is given in Arz, p. 251. The text of this military pact had been written by Cramon (as stated by Ludendorff at the meeting of May 11).
5. Hindenburg retained his existing disinclination, which he justified with rather crude arguments. He said he did not trust the Austrian politicians, and German officers could be scarcely expected to face the prospect, under the exchange of officers contemplated, to spend years in some backwoods garrison in Galicia. For the OHL discussions with Hertling, Kühlmann, Wedel, and Cramon on May 11 in the afternoon, see AA, GHQ 232, No. 16a, war aims. There had already been talks with the war minister and Winterfeldt on May 8 and 10, about the German draft of the pact (ZA, III, GHQ 21, App. Vol. 1).
6. The Vienna war archive contains (Portfolio Op. secret, 1579) brief notes by a Major Geyer of the Austrian general staff on the outward course of the emperor's visit at Spa on May 12; further a note by Baron Arz on the *Waffenbund,* showing that the Austrian General Staff had originally proposed only that "arms and munitions distribution shall be fixed by mutual agreement. Preliminary work by the two General Staffs for any future wars affecting the alliance is to be effected under uniform directives and the basis of discussions and again by mutual agreement." Lastly, the portfolio holds a text described as a draft for a declaration on the *Waffenbund* with Germany, reproducing Cramon's seven points with much highflown patriotic verbiage.
7. Details in Gratz-Schüller, pp. 86-106. Burián's marked reservations in the question of a customs union emerged quite clearly during the preliminary discussions he held with Hertling and Kühlmann on June 11-12 in Berlin. The Austrian minutes stress that the draft presented by Austria contains neither a demand for common legislation (especially not in the social sphere), nor the creation of common customs revenues, nor the use of common organs, nor, lastly, any common settlement of the foreign exchange question. There seems to have been much apprehension of the possibility that Austria's sovereignty might be impaired (HHSTA, secret, 47/3-23).
8. Minutes of the afternoon talks of May 11, in AA, GHQ 232, No. 16a.
9. Directive to Hohenlohe, July 15 (HHSTA, secret, 47/3-23). In the basic German discussion with Hertling and Kühlmann on June 11 he did threaten that unless there were agreement between the two powers about *Personalunion* of Poland and Austria-Hungary, no other military, economic, or political agreements could be reached; but apparently this made little impression and Burián did not act accordingly.
10. The alliance was to apply only in the event of an unprovoked attack by two or more powers, including at least one European. Article 2 of the treaty of 1879, providing for benevolent neutrality in the event of an attack by only one power, was cut (HHSTA, *loc. cit.*).

11. Burián did manage to get the German Article 5 cut: "The high contracting parties agree to conclude treaties with other states only by mutual agreement." This, of course, would have meant an express injunction against separate peace negotiations.
12. Directive to the Berlin chargé d'affaires, Count Larisch, June 20, *loc. cit.*
13. Undated, with a detailed exposition of the German viewpoint (HHSTA, *loc. cit.*).
14. For the minutes of the negotiations of September 5, see HHSTA, *loc. cit.*
15. Arz, p. 280; Cramon, p. 168.
16. Burián's correspondence about a "treaty of interpretation" begins with a directive to the Berlin embassy of June 27. Kühlmann had expressed himself as basically in favor, but when he gave his approval he was already close to the end of his tenure. After his fall von dem Bussche and Kriege said a treaty of interpretation was superfluous, and Hintze agreed (the last time on August 3). Kriege also objected to certain slight changes in the earlier German draft treaty proposed by Vienna (HHSTA, *loc. cit.*).
17. The Austrian correspondence in the HHSTA, in the secret portfolios 47/3-23, 25, 26, and Kr. 56a/7, is available only in copies. The German negotiations are documented for the most part in AA, WK 15, secret, Vol. 5, and 20c, secret, Vols. 25-26. Conze's account, pp. 366ff., is based on documents. Kühlmann made noteworthy efforts to appease the representatives of the majority parties and make them understand German policy in Poland and the East. He played down the differences both between the two allies and between the foreign ministry and the OHL (talks with the Chancellor, June 19, Matthias-Morsey [1] Vol. 2, No. 189).
18. Wedel to Hertling, June 7, 1918 (Conze, p. 367).
19. Formerly known only through a report written from memory, in Hutten-Czapski, pp. 491f. The full text has since been published in Geiss, pp. 170ff.
20. Details about the negotiations, after a set of minutes preserved at Merseburg, in Geiss, pp. 144f. Geiss seeks to weaken the favorable impression they make by reproaching the participants for their failure to overcome their obsession with the idea of a border strip and instead clinging to certain border rectifications and power positions in the east.
21. For decisions of the crown council session of July 2, 1918, see the minutes in AA, WK 15, secret, Vol. 5, partly published in UA, Vol. 2, p. 346 (also Vol. 12, p. 223). See also Geiss, p. 141, after a record of the chancellery kept in Potsdam.
22. Details in Conze, p. 372. In a directive to Hohenlohe on August 26, Burián protested vigorously against the German policy of threatening the Poles with large-scale annexations, in the event they elected Emperor Charles (HHSTA, *loc. cit.*).
23. Hintze-Ludendorff correspondence, August 28-31 (Ludendorff [1], pp. 511ff.).
24. Minutes of the Vienna talks of September 5 in HHSTA, secret, 47/3-26. On September 8 Burián asked the Austrian high command for proposals on what might still be conceded to Germany in all fairness in the event of an Austro-Polish solution. On September 15 General Arz refused to accept any subservience to Germany on Polish soil. This would be intolerable and unnecessary, besides being incompatible with Polish sovereignty. He also ruled out negotiations with Germany on the relations between the Polish and Austrian armed forces. The Polish army would of course have to be placed under the Austrian and accept Austrian direction and organization. Burián replied on September 26 rather verbosely and in some embarrassment—he said he agreed with Arz in principle, but wished to give low initial priority to military questions in negotiating with the Germans. He envisaged relations between the Polish and Austrian armed forces to be essentially those of allies with equal rights (HHSTA, Kr. 56a/7.
25. Minutes in HHSTA, Kr. 56a/7. *Ibidem,* report, October 1, by envoy Ugron, head of the Austrian delegation. Directive from Burián to Ugron, via Hohenlohe, September 20, and reports by Ugron, September 25 and 28, on fruitless

discussions with the German negotiator Prince Hatzfeldt. Main bone of contention was the question of Polish military sovereignty, claimed by Germany on the basis of the agreements of August 11-12, 1916, and June 18, 1917 (see Vol. III, pp. 217, 233; Conze, p. 291). Austria regarded these agreements as long since superseded.

26. Minutes in HHSTA, Pol. Arch. 40/293, No. 550.

27. File note by Count Wedel for the Austrian ministry, undated, but probably October 18. Directive from Burián to Hohenlohe, October 18, also direct report and draft of a handwritten letter by the Emperor to the Kaiser, October 4. All these have to do with the question of the validity of agreements concerning Polish military sovereignty of August 11-12, 1916, and June 18, 1917 (HHSTA, Kr. 56a/7).

28. On German public attitudes toward the Baltic problem see Mann. A particularly instructive example of the insistence of the majority parties on liberal eastern policies along the lines of self-determination was provided by the five-hour meeting their representatives had on June 19, 1918, with Hertling's government (Matthias-Morsey [1], Vol. 2, Nos. 189a, 189b). The minutes clearly show the government's dilemma. Kühlmann, however, was a past master at keeping the deputies under control, though there was a large residue of suspicion, if not indignation, over Hertling's weakness, as shown especially in statements Scheidemann and Ebert made to the joint party caucus on July 6 (*ibidem,* pp. 426ff., 430).

29. Ludendorff to Kühlmann, January 30, 1918, with handwritten additions and directive from Bartenwerffer to Winterfeldt to let the Chancellor know the contents. Ludendorff insisted, among other things, that Nadolny's behavior violated earlier agreements on foreign ministry-OHL cooperation. On February 2 Kühlmann said he would render a detailed report (ZA, RK 2, II, Kr. 4², Vol. 2).

30. Hoffmann, Vol. 2, p. 190.

31. Legation Secretary Wesendonck of supreme headquarters to the foreign ministry, February 9. Ludendorff to Hertling, February 10. Radowitz to Falkenhausen and Waldersee, February 11. Falkenhausen to Hertling, February 14 (ZA, *loc. cit.;* Basler, p. 293ff.)

32. On talks by Lithuanian émigrés in Switzerland with French agencies, then underway, see Linde, p. 144.

33. Linde, p. 141; Basler, p. 295.

34. Hertling to Lersner, for Ludendorff, February 17. Grünau to the foreign ministry, February 19. Von dem Bussche to Grünau, February 20, reporting on a conference presided over by Payer. Hertling to Kühlmann, February 21. Senden to the foreign ministry, March 1. Keyserlingk, Hertling's commissioner for the Baltic regions, to the eastern command, March 4 (ZA, *loc. cit.*).

35. Winterfeldt to Hertling, March 6 (ZA, *loc. cit.,* Vol. 2).

36. Ludendorff met with Count Keyserlingk, Count Limburg-Stirum, and Lersner on March 10 (ZA, RK II, Kr. 1, Adh. 5, Vol. 2). Lersner to the foreign ministry, for Hertling, March 14 (*ibidem,* RK, Courland war files, No. 2405, cíted by Basler, p. 300, No. 180).

37. On March 14 Hindenburg too had asked that he and the minister of war be consulted in drafting the reply to the Lithuanians. His wire, however, shows that he was far from sure of himself: "It goes without saying that I do not wish to influence Your Excellency's decision in any way ... [but] I cannot but make it clear that I would regard a decision [to recognize Lithuania] as disastrous, unless we manage to find a different [and harmless] approach by our reply to the Lithuanian delegation."

38. Exchanges during these weeks on the Lithuanian question are in ZA: Falkenhausen to Keyserlingk, March 5; Winterfeldt to Hertling, March 6; note by Nadolny, March 8; notes by Radowitz and Keyserlingk, March 7; eastern command to Keyserlingk, March 7; Lersner to the foreign ministry, March 7; Hertling to

Ludendorff, March 13; Keyserlingk to Hertling, March 14; two wires from Lersner to the foreign ministry, for Hertling, March 14; eastern command to Hertling, March 14–all in ZA, RK II, 2, II, Kr. 4^2 Vol. 2. Lersner to Hertling, March 14, 18, and 19 (*ibidem,* Vol. 3). Lersner, March 7, to the foreign ministry, about a kind of military instruction by Ludendorff (AA, WK 15, secret, Vol. 5). For further details see Basler, pp. 296ff., and Linde, pp. 142ff., discussing also the rather ambiguous attitude of the Taryba, which clung obstinately to the declaration of February 16.

39. Matthias-Morsey (1), II, p. 303. See the joint party caucus session of March 11 (*ibidem,* No. 168) and the talk with the Chancellor on March 12 (*ibidem,* No. 170). When the peace treaty of Brest-Litovsk was debated on March 21, the Reichstag adopted a resolution in which the hope was expressed that the principle of self-determination would be observed in Poland, Lithuania, and Courland, that immediate steps would be taken to organize local government by civilians, that existing representative bodies would be broadened, and that the agreements sought by these bodies would be promptly concluded. None of these expectations was fulfilled.

40. Schulthess, 1918, Vol. 1, p. 140.

41. Fehrenbach acted as spokesman for the joint party caucus in a discussion with Hertling on March 12 (Matthias-Morsey [1], II, p. 302). During a similar discussion on February 20, Payer had already stated that no Reichstag approval was in sight for incorporation of Livonia-Estonia (Lewerenz, p. 226).

42. Schulthess, 1918, Vol. 1, p. 88.

43. Lersner to the foreign ministry, March 7; Grünau to Hertling, March 7 (AA, WK 15, secret, Vol. 5).

44. For the upshot of the meeting of March 10, already mentioned, see ZA, RK II, Kr. 1, Adh. 5, Vol. 2.

45. Talk with Payer, February 20; Kühlmann to Hertling, March 9; Lewerenz, pp. 226ff. On March 27 Hertling strongly protested against Berg, head of the civil cabinet, responding on his own and behind the back of the foreign ministry to Baltic addresses of loyalty to the Kaiser (Baumgart [3], p. 68, Note 31.

46. According to Fischer, p. 811, the declarations of Riga and Tallin were made "at Ludendorff's behest and following his detailed stage directions." I have been unable to check the references given, but cannot offhand see how documents of December 11, 1917, and February 6, 1918, could account for the events of April 1918.

47. Details in Janssen, p. 204, including documentation. On March 18 Hertling, in the Reichstag, had expressed the cautious hope that following the organizational phase Livonia and Estonia would "enter into close and friendly relations with the German Reich."

48. Details in Basler, pp. 325f., from documents in the ZA.

49. Kühlmann made statements along these lines both before the Prussian cabinet and the foreign affairs committee of the federal council (Lewerenz, p. 233). In early May he tried to refer the joint regional council for Latvia and Estonia to the Soviet government, in pursuit of his *Anschluss* efforts (Baumgart [3], p. 261, Note 10).

50. According to a communication from Lersner to Rosenberg, the real purpose behind this was an OHL plan to gain a bridgehead beyond the Dvina at Dvinsk (Rosenberg to the foreign ministry, July 2, 1918, AA, WK 15, secret, Vol. 5). Gatzke (pp. 84ff.) gives the minutes of the meeting of July 2, insofar as they touch upon eastern questions, supplementing the OHL version with that of the foreign ministry.

51. The entire correspondence is in ZA, RK II, 1, II, Kr. 4^2, Vol. 3. Ludendorff, via Lersner, to the foreign ministry, March 19. Radowitz to Lersner, for Ludendorff, March 20. Ludendorff to Winterfeldt, March 28. Ludendorff, via Lersner, to the

foreign ministry, March 24 and 25. Hertling to Ludendorff and Keyserlingk, March 25. Ludendorff to Hertling, via Lersner, April 1. Hertling to Ludendorff, April 3. Ludendorff to Hertling, April 7 and 12. Keyserlingk to Hertling, April 16.

52. See the account by Bredt, who himself revised the more important drafts (UA, Vol. 8, pp. 338ff.); also Basler, (pp. 254ff. and App. 12, departmental meeting on May 14, with list of participants) and Fischer (pp. 813ff.).

53. Basler, p. 310, from the Potsdam files.

54. Details in Janssen, pp. 165ff., 209ff.; Linde, Chapter 7.

55. See his remarks during the conference with Payer, July 24 (Basler, p. 418).

56. The best documented account is in Linde, pp. 171ff.

57. ZA, *loc. cit.:* Ludendorff to Hertling, July 17; Hertling's agreement, July 19; see also Basler, pp. 306f.

58. Details in Fischer, pp. 817f. Soon afterward Ludendorff, shaken in his confidence ever since August 8, told Helfferich that in view of the way things were going over-all he was no longer interested in the cession of Livonia and Estonia (Helfferich, Vol. 3, p. 490).

59. Matthias-Morsey (1), II, p. 558.

60. Basler, p. 309, from ZA documents. For the following, see *ibidem,* pp. 310f. On the background of this action by Hintze, see Baumgart (3), pp. 294f., Note 152. Baumgart suggests that by early September both the Kaiser and Ludendorff had grown uncertain whether *Personalunion* could be put over. Before the foreign affairs committee of the federal council Hintze, on September 2, explicitly refused to take advantage of the supplementary treaty of August 27 for purposes of annexation in Livonia and Estonia. These two countries "had their own lives to live," he said. Under German law no special privileges could be granted to the German-speaking intellectuals and members of the nobility there. Latvians and Estonians did not desire integration with Germany. The local Germans had insisted that they would all be massacred, once German troops were withdrawn (AF, Vol. 4, p. 1517).

61. The social democratic leaders regarded him as a henchman and tool of Ludendorff and consequently loathed him. See Ebert, July 6, Matthias-Morsey (1), II, p. 430.

62. In working on this part and the next, I enjoyed the benefit of a recently published monograph by Winfried Baumgart (Baumgart [3]), which treats my subject from the same point of view. I am deeply grateful to the author and Herr K. Repken of Saarbrücken for permission to use this work in manuscript. This dissertation is based on exhaustive research among virtually all the source material accessible in West Germany, as well as on a comprehensive knowledge of the work being done abroad, especially in America and the Soviet Union. Comparison with the source material I myself have assembled confirms Baumgart's careful work. In consequence, I have been able to abbreviate my account and forego detailed references. Page references are to the printed version of Baumgart's work, which has meanwhile appeared.

63. Essential works in the study of the situation in Russia in 1918 and Allied intervention there are Kennan and Ullman, both used by Baumgart.

64. Baumgart (3), p. 73, Note 50.

65. Kühlmann himself discussed this on May 22 before the foreign affairs committee of the federal council (Baumgart [3], p. 76).

66. By Karl Staël von Holstein, submitted May 22 (Baumgart, p. 76, Note 55).

67. Document No. 1 in Baumgart's appendix. The drafter was Legation Councilor Trautmann, who held down the eastern desk, von dem Bussche merely signing the final version. Baumgart rightly stresses the contrast between certain phrases, especially concerning the economic exploitation of Russia, and Kühlmann's thinking. Fischer, p. 729, quotes this report from a mere excerpt in a popular collection of source material, also used in Groener (2), p. 403—hence the wrong date, June 14. Anyone familiar with the fact that this report was intended for

the OHL as well as with von dem Bussche's political attitudes in the war years, as revealed in the documents, must marvel that Fischer views von dem Bussche and this report as representing a policy of "complete domination of the east, from the Caucasus to the Artic Ocean."

68. Baumgart, p. 82.
69. Cited after Baumgart, p. 80, Note 66, and p. 83, Note 75. The letter of June 9 appears also in Ludendorff (1), pp. 488ff., and in AF, III, 1386ff.
70. BA, Haeften's papers, Folder 12, App. 6, also Haeften, "Erlebnisse 1918," Portfolio 5, pp. 29ff. The draft copy of this report in my possession is signed "Avesnes, June 30, 1918, Haeften, Colonel." Thus it was not written by Ludendorff himself, as claimed by Baumgart, p. 85, Note 82, who thought it merely a transcript of Ludendorff's remarks. I should scarcely describe the report as "the most important document in arriving at a true estimate of Ludendorff's views about eastern policy." On how the report came to be written, see Haeften's official report of late 1918 (UA, Vol. 2, p. 371).
71. I doubt that this somewhat dramatic theory of "blocs" really goes back to Ludendorff.
72. More intensive propaganda in the east had been called for on March 7 in a kind of political directive which Ludendorff issued to Legation Secretary Lersner. It was extremely important, he said, that Germany promptly "take hold" of the press in Finland, Estonia, Livonia, the Ukraine, and Rumania (AA, WK 15, secret, Vol. 5).
73. Documentation in Baumgart, p. 106; further details in Part 4 of this chapter.
74. Notes by Trautmann, the adviser on eastern affairs, August 2 (Baumgart, p. 243, Note 57).
75. Details in Baumgart, p. 246. According to Baumgart, Helfferich was recalled at the request of the Kaiser, and not on account of differences of opinion with Hintze. Immediately before his departure, Helfferich ordered the legation moved to St. Petersburg, which Hintze interpreted, probably rightly, as a political act. He gave the incident a different cast by ordering the legation to retire behind the line of demarcation at Pleskov, whence it returned home after some weeks.
76. Published as Document 3 in Baumgart's appendix, and in great detail by Fischer, pp. 768ff. From my observations in the Bonn archive, Fischer's file identifications in the notes on that page require correction.
77. Writing to Hintze on August 7, Ludendorff expressed agreement with the basic position Hintze had taken with Helfferich, namely that political wisdom would require Germany to take advantage of Bolshevist rule "so long as there were still anything in it for Germany," and then to sit by impassively as the Bolshevist government fell. Ludendorff said he had never intended to suggest a sharp turn in Hintze's policy toward the Bolshevists. He had merely sought to provide greater political freedom of action by holding more divisions ready. "I must say that I am afraid that the situation in Russia may not remain subject to our will. I must further make the point that we should not give the Entente more time to play the dominant role in Russia by waiting on the sidelines. I do not think that revision of the treaty of Brest-Litovsk is on, but in the long run we shall probably not be able to hold out against reunion of the Ukraine with Russia, even though, for the time being, we must uphold the fiction [sic] of a viable Ukraine. I cannot judge whether there is any chance for us to use the Ukraine for the restoration of Russia." There is already a note of resignation in all this. (AA, Germany, 131, relations with Russia, Vol. 45.)
78. This is Fischer's interpretation (pp. 768ff.). He dramatically proclaims Hintze's memorandum of August 6 to be "a key document to an understanding of German eastern policy in 1918," calling it "the culmination of German efforts at realizing sweeping political war aims in the east." German war aims came first and foremost in Hintze's mind, Fischer maintains, and there was not even an

effort to provide any "ideological embroidery." Naturally German war aims came first and foremost for any German statesman; but when Fischer says "war aims," what he actually means is "annexationist aims," of which Hintze makes no mention.

79. Minutes in Baumgart (3), App., Document 7.

80. Details in Baumgart (3), pp. 262ff., Fischer, pp. 758ff. Fischer immediately accepts the expansionist sentiments of German industrialists to characterize German foreign policy as generally imperialist in character and describes the syndicate as a private initiative enjoying a guarantee from the government. Actually the manner in which the government might give support was left quite open.

81. The Finnish envoy Hjelt initially pleaded for military assistance on his own responsibility, on the basis of a report by the Finnish delegation in Berlin of February 14, arranged for by Ludendorff! It was published in Hubatsch, pp. 56f. Hubatsch's study is based mainly on Finnish sources. For a brief account, conscientiously based on the sources, see Jutikkala-Pirinen, pp. 355ff.

82. Müller, p. 361. The date of this diary entry, March 7, may be a misreading of March 9, since Hindenburg's telegram of protest, mentioned in it, is dated March 9. (I have the relevant correspondence from ZA, RK II, 2, II, Kr. 4³, Vol. 1, and it begins with March 9). Müller's note is further inaccurate in that it mentions an alleged request by Hertling to drop the Finland project altogether, which is not what he wanted at all. Hertling merely wanted the project delayed and limited. Baumgart's account of the discussions (p. 94) is confusing in that he regards the OHL wire of March 9 as a reply to the ministerial meeting at the chancellery of March 11. At this meeting, by the way, the Reich minister of justice, Dr. Krause, did not oppose the project on the basis of international law, but on the contrary sought to disprove that there were such objections (according to the brief minutes). Hubatsch speaks of a formal auxiliary treaty (p. 63), which the OHL supposedly concluded through von der Goltz with the Finnish envoy Hjelt, adding that the foreign ministry had approved the expedition. At the time that was undoubtedly not yet 'rue, or else the above-described meetings would have made no sense.

83. He said that since the expedition was launched within the general framework of the war, it fell under already authorized blanket war credits and needed no further financial Reichstag and federal budget approval. Under international law, this was not another declaration of war on Russia, but merely a police action against Russian bandits, which the Kaiser was empowered to order without consulting the federal council. He warned against a commitment against the project. Roedern counseled letting the Finns bear the cost.

84. Apparently this was the case also at a Prussian cabinet meeting on March 9, when Hertling remarked that the difficulties could be circumvented, if arms and volunteers were made available at the expense of the Finns. He wanted the opinion of the foreign ministry and the Reich office of justice, so that the matter might be brought before the Kaiser for decision. (AF, III, pp. 1234ff.)

85. Notes in Radowitz's hand for a direct report to the Kaiser, March 13 (ZA, *loc. cit.*). Payer and the minister of war, who would have to defend the project on the floor of the Reichstag, were to be asked to take part in the crown council.

86. Wire from the OHL to the Kaiser, March 9, and the foreign ministry for the Chancellor, March 10.

87. The minutes (ZA, *loc. cit.*) mention Beseler, but this must be wrong, for his name is not listed among the participants, and then too, his participation would have made no sense. I think it is a slip of the pen and that von dem Bussche is actually meant. Mannerheim was indeed originally opposed to the participation of foreign troops in the Finnish freedom struggle and had accepted supreme command only on condition that they would not be called in. When this was ignored, he at first threatened to resign (Jutikkala-Pirinen, pp. 355ff.). A letter of thanks to Ludendorff of March 5 strikes a rather different note (Hubatsch, p. 64; ZA, *loc.*

cit.), but von dem Bussche ("Beseler") thought it was not to be taken entirely seriously. Mannerheim did request a proclamation stating that there was no intention to intervene in the internal affairs of Finland and that the auxiliary corps would be placed under his command, which Hindenburg immediately conceded on March 13. On March 20 Mannerheim did press for prompt aid, since he and his improved volunteer forces were under severe pressure (Goltz, pp. 44ff., 50). The foreign ministry was in possession of information that the former czarist general Mannerheim was more concerned with overthrowing the Bolshevist government with the aid of Finnish troops than with liberating Finland, and there was on that account a tendency to treat him rather gingerly (memorandum by Trautmann of early May, in Baumgart's appendix, Document 1). Mannerheim's quick resignation in late May was said (Jutikkala-Pirenen, p. 360) to be caused in part by his inability to win over the Finnish government to his restoration plans; but apparently there was another reason—Mannerheim did not believe in German victory and, with the Svinhufvud government ardently pro-German, was reluctant to compromise himself with the Entente.

88. Minutes in ZA, *loc. cit.*
89. A role of particular importance was played by the so-called 27th light infantry battalion, a cadre formation composed of Finnish volunteers and trained in Germany, which provided many of the officers and noncoms for the Finnish liberation struggle.
90. The German social democrat Dr. David sharply criticized this intervention on June 24 in the Reichstag.
91. Hintze to Hertling, July 28 and August 5. Hertling on his part had no hesitation to use the OHL, on July 15, to get information on the status of the monarchist movement in Finland, rather than the German envoy (wire to Winterfeldt, for Hindenburg, ZA, *loc. cit.,* repository for the entire correspondence I have here used). According to Jutikkala-Perinen (p. 358), Hjelt, on his own responsibility, told the Germans that in gratitude for the military aid requested the Finns might elect a German prince as their sovereign.
92. Ludendorff to Winterfeldt, for Hertling, July 6; and Radowitz's marginal notes about the Chancellor's decision.
93. Hertling to Grünau, July 15. Von dem Bussche to Berckheim, Grünau's deputy, and the Chancellor, August 16.
94. Hindenburg to Hertling, July 16, with handwritten marginal note: "Not for the time being L[udendorff]." This letter was probably held back but somehow got into the chancellery files after all.
95. Berckheim to the foreign ministry, July 22, repeating a wire by von der Goltz.
96. On August 24 Ludendorff was still backing the candidacy of Prince Oscar. He said he was afraid that not to do so would do military damage on the eastern front, as Berckheim wrote the foreign ministry. At an earlier stage Ludendorff was among those who respected the Kaiser's wishes and voted for another German prince.
97. Hintze to the foreign ministry, July 23. Hintze to Hertling, July 28 and August 5. Berckheim to Hertling, August 9, transmitting a written reply from the chief of staff.
98. Von dem Bussche to Berckheim, August 23, transmitting a dispatch from Brück; Hintze to Hertling, August 5; Goltz, pp. 86f.
99. Trautmann's memorandum, already mentioned in Note 87, stated the desirability of bringing Finland to the open Arctic Ocean by such an exchange of territory, and possibly even to the Archangel railway, to provide "a protective wall even at Russia's northern seaway."
100. Baumgart (p. 113) was the first to give details from German naval files.
101. Wire of Councilor Schwarzkopf to Radowitz, March 6 (AA, WK 15, secret, Vol. 5).
102. Groener (1), p. 398.
103. Groener's papers, cited by Baumgart, p. 124, Note 36.
104. Under the supplementary treaties of April 9-13, consolidated on April 24, this is

what the Rada government promised to supply to the two Central Powers by July 31: 1 million tons of grain, cereals, and fats, 400 million eggs, 50,000 tons of live stock, 27,000 tons potatoes. According to the statistics of the central purchasing cooperative this is what was actually delivered by mid-June: 50,000 tons of grain, cereals, and fats, of which only 13,000 tons were for Germany (AA file notice, according to Baumgart, p. 133, Note 78). Gratz-Schüller states (p. 174) that by the fall of 1918 a total of 40,000 carloads of foodstuffs had been delivered to the two occupation powers, but according to the rail office at Kiev, cited in UA, Vol. 3, p. 31, the number was 34,745. This careful report by General Kuhl gives detailed reasons for the failure. Overall deliveries of beef cattle and horses seem to have been substantial—Kuhl gives 105,600 head of cattle and 96,000 horses. Czernin calculated (p. 345) that there were some 15,000 smuggled carloads, over and above the figures reported.

105. Letter to Grünau, May 19, in Groener, pp. 400f.
106. Count Forgách to Burián, July 3, 1918, quoted from Vienna documents by Baumgart, p. 147, Note 152. According to Reshetar, p. 174, at least 9,000 German officers and men perished during requisitions, riots, strikes, partisan fighting, etc.
107. Groener to the eastern command, for Ludendorff, June 5, cited by Baumgart, p. 135, Note 88, from Groener's papers.
108. A detailed account, from the voluminous files in Potsdam, is given by Fischer, pp. 724ff., always with a sharp undertone of criticism of German "economic imperialism."
109. Beyer reaches the conclusion that the protracted occupation of the Ukraine was based on both economic delusions and an overestimate of the maturity attained by the Ukrainian nationalist movement.
110. Detailed letter from Groener to the Württemberg minister of war Marchthaler, July 17, from Groener's papers, Document 4 in Baumgart's appendix. In a letter to his wife of July 10 (Groener, p. 571), he was also skeptical about Russian monarchism.
111. In his memoirs (Groener, p. 404), he reluctantly admitted that from a purely objective point of view the foreign ministry had "backed the right horse" and described his own thinking about a Bolshevist overthrow at the time as "wishful." *Ibidem,* p. 402. Groener admits that his policies in Kiev were not free of contradictions.
112. Groener to his wife, June 29 (p. 570).
113. The attitude of the foreign ministry on the issue of the Don cossacks was not always consistent. At the war aims conference of July 2 in Spa, Kühlmann's representative Rosenberg (he himself was no longer in attendance) showed himself extremely complaisant with respect to Ludendorff's wishes and offered the curious proposal that the OHL might conduct its negotiations with the Don cossacks "so to speak behind the back of the government." He also favored generous disbursements of money to the Don cossacks ("every million we spend in Russia is a million saved"), and he advised the OHL on how such payments could be hidden from the Russians (Gatzke, p. 87).
114. Minutes of the session of the morning of May 13 in AA, GHQ 232, No. 16a, war aims (original in Austria, secret, 95). The Ukraine, the Caucasus, the Dobrudja, Alsace-Lorraine, the Flemish movement, and Great Russia were discussed at the same session. Kühlmann was by no means "merely a silent participant," as stated by Baumgart, p. 153. According to the excerpts from minutes cited by Baumgart on pp. 131, 181 (AA, Ukraine 1, Vol. 11; Russia 97a, Vol. 14), the Ukraine and the Caucasus region were discussed at a session on the morning of May 11. This particular session, however, is not the one I cited earlier (p. 238), which dealt exclusively with relations with Austria after the Sixtus affair.
115. Minutes published in Gatzke, pp. 90, 92.
116. Groener, pp. 401f. For documentary evidence, see Fischer, pp. 734ff., and, more recently, Baumgart (1), pp. 536ff. (from Groener's papers).

117. This demand by Kühlmann, who remarked pointedly to Ludendorff that German interests rather than emotional considerations must govern, leads Fischer to conclude, p. 735, that "in this matter the foreign ministry was certainly unwilling to settle for anything less than Ludendorff's plan." I cannot follow him.

118. Baumgart (2), p. 160, Note 20, based on the papers of Admiral Keyserlingk, shows that such notions of partition were indeed compatible with the wishful dreams about "keeping the door open to German influence" even beyond the Black and Caspian Seas to Central and Southern Asia. Baumgart unhesitatingly equates Keyserlingk's views with those of the German admiralty, but from his own account of the attitude of Admiral Hopman (p. 171, Note 77) I regard this at least as doubtful.

119. The naval minister Capelle had previously settled with Ludendorff on this compromise, nor did Rosenberg, representing the foreign ministry, offer any objections, except for expressly rejecting once again the "law of war booty."

120. Following the loss of Palestine, the Turkish army badly wanted to gain control of the Batum-Tiflis-Julfa-Mosul rail line, as a supply route for defense of Mesopotamia against the British, and this motive played an important part in the Turkish advance into the Caucasus region. See Kühlmann's report to the deputies of the majority parties on June 19 (Matthias-Morsey [1], II, p. 408).

121. AA, Russia 97a, Vol. 12. Details of the trade privileges in Fischer, p. 741. Most of the ideas in this memorandum recur in the wire to Hertling of April 26, used in Baumgart (3), p. 176, Note 13.

122. The foreign ministry to Berckheim for the OHL, April 24 (AA, Russia 97a, Vol. 13). Fischer cites (pp. 743f.), as proof of "the continuity of German war aims policy from 1914," von dem Bussche's long memorandum for the Kaiser of April 26 on German policy in the Caucasus. Like the report on eastern questions of April 1, this memorandum does mention German efforts during the war to create a Caucasian state "oriented toward Germany" and says that it would be desirable to create a friendly relationship with the trans-Caucasian state and to bring that region under German influence, economically and politically, instead of leaving it to the Turks; but there is no occasion to believe that there were goals other than economic ones behind all this. The foreign ministry was actually willing to forego a political alliance with Transcaucasia, to avoid the impression that Germany rather than Turkey desired a foothold there (Fischer, p. 745). German opposition to Turkish expansionist plans was based, not on similar German ambitions, but on the fear, put into words by von dem Bussche, that Turkey, once engaged in the Caucasus, would stop playing any significant part on other fronts. The leading men in the foreign ministry, men like Kühlmann, von dem Bussche, and Kriege, did believe that political influence was essential for the realization of economic aspirations, since in the East "paper agreements were not good enough to guarantee vital interests," as von dem Bussche wrote to Bernstorff on June 28, 1918 (Fischer, p. 752). Fischer seems unable to imagine that economic undertakings abroad could be anything but camouflage to achieve political ends.

123. On April 9 Ludendorff asked Hertling to convene a big meeting to establish guidelines for German policy toward Turkey, aimed at doing everything possible to prevent the disintegration of Turkey (AA, WK 15, secret, Vol. 5).

124. AA, Russia 97a, Vol. 14, here quoted after Baumgart (3), p. 181, Note 30. Baumgart refers to similar thoughts expressed by Seeckt in a letter to Winterfeldt of May 2, 1918 (Seeckt, p. 76).

125. Marginal note on a dispatch from Bernstorff of May 18, cited in Baumgart (3), p. 182, Note 32.

126. Highly characteristic of such military thinking is Seeckt's possibly ironic remark, in the letter to Winterfeldt already cited: "If, as I must hope, the war will still last for a long time, someone will ultimately have to knock on the door of India."

127. The important memorandum from Groener's papers in the BA is published in full by

Baumgart (3), as Document 3 of his appendix. Undated, it was transmitted on June 12 to the Kiev army command by Captain Rothkirch, on the occasion of Prince Tundutov passing through that city.

128. On June 10 Ludendorff sent word to the foreign ministry that "in Georgia as in Finland there is an opportunity to augment our power with the use of only modest forces (AA, Russia 97a, Vol. 17, cited from Baumgart [3], p. 189).

129. Bernstorff to Hertling, August 3 (AA, Russia 97a, Vol. 21, here cited from Baumgart [3], p. 194, Note 79). See also private letter to von dem Bussche, August 6 (AA, WK 2, secret, Vol. 62).

130. Fischer (particularly on p. 747, Paragraph 4) utterly ignores the sharp conflict between the Caucasus policies of the foreign ministry and Hertling on the one hand and those of the OHL and Lossow on the other. On pp. 737f. he cites the Austrian general Arz as his principal witness for his interpretation of German economic policy in the Caucasus; but Arz was the last man to qualify as an expert. Besides, the statements quoted seem quite dubious to me, particularly as they relate to Groener. Fischer mentions unidentified "secret documents" as his source, but these are unknown to me.

131. Ludendorff wired Enver Pasha via Seeckt his complete agreement with the German government that the Turkish advance without respect to Turkey's allies must be condemned. He asked once again that the lines drawn in the treaty of Brest-Litovsk be respected, "since otherwise I shall have to reserve my further decisions." He said that he could not recognize treaties concluded with the Caucasian states without the knowledge or participation of Turkey's allies. He had always warmly supported Enver's requests, but any action by Turkey in violation of treaties "will make it impossible for me to cooperate with Your Excellency." These statements were, of course, purely political (AA, Russia 97a, Caucasus, Vol. 16–Berckheim to the foreign ministry, transmitting the text of Ludendorff's wire to Enver Pasha).

132. Documents in Baumgart (3), pp. 181, 192.

133. *Ibidem*, p. 192, Note 73.

134. Fischer considerably overestimates the practical significance of these agreements (pp. 753f.).

135. On this point Kühlmann showed himself to be less worried than the punctilious jurist Kriege, who tried to persuade Ludendorff as well, setting forth his arguments in a memorandum. In this he failed, but his view did finally prevail in the foreign ministry.

136. Baumgart (3), p. 195, Note 83, from documents in Vienna.

137. At the big meeting in Spa on July 2, Ludendorff did voice serious doubts that the Russians would be able to deliver the oil they had promised (Gatzke, p. 89).

138. See Baumgart (3), p. 203, on the secret agreement, hitherto unknown, under which the Germans were to drive the British out of Baku.

139. These extraordinary facts were extracted from the naval files of the Military-Scientific Research Institute, Freiburg, by Baumgart, p. 204.

Notes to Chapter 8

1. He figures in the German documents erroneously as "Consul General," because he deputized in this vacant post in Zurich.

2. The carbon copy in the foreign ministry carries no signature, but was initialed by Envoy Haniel, holder of the American desk, who dispatched it to Switzerland. It is in the AA, WK 2, top secret, Vol. 1 file, which is the main source for my account of the Mensing-McNally and McCormick encounters that follows. My former assistant Klaus Schwabe was of great assistance to me. In preparing his study of Wilson's influence on the beginning of the Weimar Republic, he spent years combing American sources, especially the State Department files and Wilson's own papers. He was kind enough to allow me access to his excerpts and

his photostats of McCormick's letter to Wilson (see further on). I have foregone giving a detailed documentation here, in part because I did not wish to anticipate Schwabe, and also because I believe that the most important items of the Bonn archive will be published in the third volume to come of Scherer & Grunewald. Hertling's account (pp. 120ff.) of the alleged "Nathan mission," etc., is for the most part based on faulty recollection, as my account shows.

3. Harrison, head of the State Department espionage bureau, wired the Berne legation on May 17: "You must use own judgment in communication with the son-in-law, always exercising greatest discretion." On May 24 Romberg reported to the foreign ministry that McNally had been told Washington would be interested in any information obtained through his son-in-law and had agreed to treat it with discretion.

4. The Zurich chemist Professor Nathan (see further on) reported to Envoy Haniel on May 7 that McNally was back. He had initially boasted of being in possession of an important German peace document (through his daughter?), which he could easily sell for several hundred thousand dollars. Later he had said that he could do nothing with it. On McNally see also Murphy, p. 18, who sides with him.

5. From the English-language text handed by Mrs. Mensing to Consul General Simson. The German translation transmitted by Romberg was inaccurate.

6. UA, Vol. 2, p. 347, note on Hertling's direct report to the Kaiser, July 13.

7. FR, 1918, Supplement 1, Vol. 1, p. 294. Schwabe was able to find neither the alleged directive of early July nor any reference to it in the State Department files.

8. Late in August McNally said he had been informed that no reply from Wilson could be expected before mid-September, since the president would first have to sound out sentiment for the impending congressional elections in the fall (Romberg to the foreign ministry, August 25). McNally probably inferred this on his own. On October 3 Romberg quoted McNally as saying in his final discussion with Mensing that before there could be any negotiations there would have to be a complete change of government in Germany (AA, WK 2, top secret, Vol. 2).

9. Among other things, he was president of the International Harvester Company in 1919 (kindly communicated to me by Professor A. S. Link).

10. Copy in AA.

11. McCormick proposed that the delegates to the peace conference be elected by the people, i.e., the legislature. Haniel said that this was certainly a novel approach, but worth considering, if it applied to all the governments participating. Haniel further emphasized that it was not a matter of a "peace offer," and that certainly no separate peace with America was envisaged. He declined to pledge autonomy for Alsace-Lorraine. All this was in his report of April 9.

12. Berne legation to the State Department, April 27. The legation immediately added: "Stovall [the envoy] has no idea of message, doubts importance." Stovall had already discussed the "message" with McCormick in March. McCormick on his part cited "a note from Col. House"; and a copy of such a note does appear in the letter later transmitted to Wilson. All it yields, however, is that on December 5, 1917, House refused to receive McCormick in Paris and asked him "not to do anything further in the matter at the present time." He did add: "I shall be glad if you will forward me any interesting matter that may come to your attention."

13. Wilson's secretary and later biographer Ray Stannard Baker recorded numerous other visitors besides McCormick for the late afternoon of June 13 (Baker, p. 209). *Ibidem,* p. 151, Baker reports that he found the unopened letter among Wilson's papers.

14. It is marked "file," apparently in Wilson's hand (Wilson papers, Washington).

15. McCormick added to the "message" dictated by Haniel (a) a report on how he came to receive the "message," largely concealing his own part; (b) a remark that the Germans would not have been content with mere transmission of the "message"; (c) remarks by Dr. Nathan on Germany's political intentions, to explain the text;

(d) a brief "personal comment" by McCormick, pleading that the German declarations should be regarded as sincere; and (e) copies of McCormick's correspondence with House and the American legation in Berne, to justify his conduct. All this was handwritten in a most respectful and somewhat timid vein.

16. Schulthess, 1918, Vol. 2, p. 576; FR, 1918, Supplement 1, Vol. 1, p. 234; see Chapter 5, Note 93.

17. Foreign ministry to OHL, June 26, see Müller, pp. 387f. The Kaiser made the outlandish remark to Müller that McCormick had been sent by Wilson and "Wall Street" to stretch out a peace feeler to Germany.

18. On August 20 Envoy Romberg advised the foreign ministry to make inquiries through the Swiss envoy Sulzer (who happened to be in Switzerland at the time and returned to Washington only in October).

19. Rosen, pp. 172ff. Tyrrell was also the alleged source of a suggestion that responsible German and British politicians engage in "gentlemanlike" talks. It was transmitted by Captain William Blennerhassett during a Swiss holiday, through his uncle, the Bavarian major in the reserves, Count Leyden, who passed it on to the German foreign ministry (several reports by Romberg in late May, AA, WK 2, top secret, Vol. 1).

20. Schulthess, 1918, Vol. 2, p. 183. The speech was apparently aimed at Clémenceau's newspaper feud with Czernin, see Chapter 4, p. 223ff. A detailed analysis is given in Hancock, p. 477, though the most peaceable passages of the speech are omitted there.

21. Colijn to Tyrrell, June 26. Tyrrell to Colijn, July 18 (or 15), 1918, including a draft carrying the written approval of Lord Hardinge, the permanent under secretary (PRO, FO, 371/3442). In his letter Colijn says nothing about Kühlmann being the initiator and informant, but merely cites a talk he said he had on June 21 with the same person as on May 11. This, however, was undoubtedly Rosen, acting for Kühlmann (Rosen, p. 184).

22. AA, WK 2, top secret, Vol. 1. The correspondence used in the following, most of it from confidential official letters by Prince Hatzfeldt, is found *ibidem* and in AA, WK 2, top secret, Adh. 1. It has already been used in Ahlswede (2), pp. 187-197. Kühlmann's remarks (pp. 569ff.) about attempts at Anglo-German contact are not merely inaccurate but misleading. Kühlmann claims to have played a part in initiating these contacts, which is demonstrably untrue. The account by Rosen (pp. 188ff.) is also in part incorrect. Since Ahlswede has already given all the references, I refrain from doing so in every case in the following.

23. PRO, Cab. 23/6, WC 423/7, May 31, 1918.

24. See Newton (2) and also the *Dictionary of National Biography*, 1959 ed. Among other things, Lord Newton wrote a biography of Lord Lansdowne (Newton [1]), to whom he was close, both intellectually and politically. His memoirs show him to have been eminently peaceable if not pro-German. He spent part of his youth in Dresden and Vienna and spoke fluent German and French.

25. A précis on Cave prepared in the foreign ministry represented him as a second-rank political figure.

26. Kühlmann sent word to the Dutch that the foreign ministry had unfortunately learned too late that Cave was coming. Hatzfeldt was represented as being a person of great prestige.

27. Rosen's judgment was colored by a certain jealousy, which is understandable, since Kühlmann deliberately tried to keep him away from the negotiations at The Hague (Kühlmann, p. 570).

28. On June 21 Hatzfeldt expressly stated that he did not wish to receive the secret code which Kühlmann had offered him on June 19. He said that for the time being the current secret handwritten correspondence would do.

29. Hatzfeldt to Kühlmann, June 13. On June 23 Hatzfeldt proposed the minister to Lord Newton as a man negotiator. There is no mention of Middachten castle in any of Hatzfeldt's letters. There is a slip of paper in the secret file (directly

following July 29) on which von dem Bussche noted in blue pencil: "Count Bentinck Middachten castle," presumably a record following a discussion between von dem Bussche and Kühlmann.

30. PRO, FO, 371/3442, Tawnley to the Foreign Office, June 5.
31. PRO, Cab 23/6, WC 427/7, June 6, 1918. Foreign Office to Tawnley, for Cave, *ibidem*, FO, 371/4332, June 6, 1918. The directive was also instantly communicated to Paris, Washington, Tokyo, and Rome. Supplementary report by Tawnley, June 6, *ibidem*, No. 2055.
32. Private letter to Hatzfeldt of June 19, inferred solely from Hatzfeldt's reply of June 21. On that day Kühlmann sent a short telegram to von der Heydt (AA, WK 2, secret, Vol. 61), which Ahlswede (p. 191) interprets as complete approval of Hatzfeldt's report of June 17, but this cannot be its meaning. Presumably von der Heydt had inquired by wire whether Hatzfeldt was to come to Berlin to report. Kühlmann said this was unnecessary, since Hatzfeldt's report was clear enough. Tawnley reported to the Foreign Office on June 24 on an attempt by the Germans to make contact with the British embassy on the peace question, as Kühlmann wished. The attempt was brusquely rebuffed, apparently more brusquely than Hardinge thought appropriate (Tawnley to the Foreign Office, June 23 and 26, 1918, PRO, FO, 371/3342).
33. Hatzfeldt to Kühlmann, June 22 and July 5.
34. Newton's attitude is all the more astonishing, since he personally had no instructions whatever to enter into political talks with the Germans. It seems likely that he conducted his talks without Cave's knowledge, though Hatzfeldt insisted to Loudon that the opposite was true.
35. Private letter, handwritten in French, dated "Tuesday." Vredenborch uncritically reported statements by the parliamentary secretary whom Cave had brought along and who boasted that his chief was Lloyd George's successor designate and extremely powerful.
36. Wire from Kühlmann to Rosen, June 26 (AA, WK, top secret, Vol. 1). Vredenborch's private letter to von dem Bussche of June 25 reached the foreign ministry only later. To be sure, Legation Secretary von der Heydt reiterated the content in a letter on June 26.
37. Rosen, pp. 185ff., 190. When the same question was put to Newton in 1933, he replied that he had not really thought the Germans ready to negotiate peace. In his memoirs, published in 1941, he says he was greatly surprised at The Hague in 1918, not only over the unswerving steadfastness of the Germans, but also at their broad readiness to accept "reasonable" peace terms, such as the relinquishment and restoration of Belgium and the return of Alsace-Lorraine, without any reservations. Why, then, should the British fight on, merely to the advantage of the Bolshevists? He, Newton, had reported all this on July 25 to Lloyd George, who seemed most appreciative and interested and who had promised to discuss the matter with his colleagues, unfortunately without success. In any event, a negotiated peace would have been far better than the hapless peace of Versailles. These recollections of a man then eighty-five are very questionable, and quite evidently they were influenced by the events of 1941.
38. Hancock, p. 483, letters to Lloyd George, June 8, 1918. Smuts said there he thought it possible that the Germans might make a peace offer during the following winter, on the basis of their great conquests in the east and with extremely moderate terms in the west. This was perhaps a generally held view in Britain at the time.
39. Rosen to Kühlmann, June 29. The foreign ministry to Grünau, July 1—both in AA, WK, top secret, Vol. 1.
40. Hatzfeldt to Kühlmann, July 5—two letters, the first with a postscript of July 12. Vredenborch to von dem Bussche, marked "Sunday," either June 30 or July 7, reporting that Loudon was "utterly exhausted" (*loc. cit.*, Adh. 1).
41. Von dem Bussche to Hertling, July 16. Von dem Bussche to Hatzfeldt, July 11 *(ibidem)*.

42. UA, Vol. 2, p. 347 (direct report to the Kaiser by Hertling, July 13); also Hertling, pp. 126ff.
43. Hatzfeldt to von dem Bussche, July 16 (AA, WK 2, top secret, Adh. 1). Rosen was quite surprised when Loudon asked him on July 30 whether Solf might not join the talks in Holland after all, possibly to meet Tyrrell there. Rosen thought this almost absurd at this juncture, but found that Loudon was very much concerned (Rosen to the foreign ministry, July 30).
44. "The idea has not been unfavorably received, but it is thought that the case may not be dealt with without further consideration and that the present moment may not be opportune." On August 26 Loudon read two similar-sounding replies from Cave and Newton to Rosen—on the British side the contemplated meeting was not wanted "at this time." Rosen reported this to the new minister, Hintze, voicing sharp criticism of Kühlmann, who had missed the right moment for a preliminary talk between Cave and Solf and had also let an earlier opportunity for liaison between Colijn and Tyrrell get away from him. In his memoirs he describes Kühlmann as the German statesman who, by his hesitancy and continual delay, had probably done more than any other to forestall contact (p. 195). Vredenborch to von dem Bussche, August 8; Rosen to Hintze (handwritten), August 26, both *loc. cit.*
45. Kühlmann spoke in so low and tired a voice that Stresemann, who had been sitting in the front row, had to go up to the platform to hear him (Stresemann in UA, Vol. 7, II, p. 305).
46. This is shown by the extended quotations from a well-known Reichstag speech by Moltke and from a speech by Asquith on May 16 in the House of Commons (shorthand reports, Vol. 313, Col. 5610 C and D).
47. The pacifist wing of the liberal party was bitter about Poincaré's rejection of Emperor Charles's peace offers through Prince Sixtus of Parma. As leader of the moderate wing, Asquith said he hoped the British government would not balk at proposals from the enemy side, provided they had a solid basis (PD, 106 HC Deb., 5. s, pp. 585f.). Kühlmann was apparently mindful of this brief contribution by Asquith to the discussion, and even more of the speech by Smuts on May 17, already mentioned in Note 20. According to a report to Hertling on July 10 (BA, Hertling papers), he said so in his direct report to the Kaiser on July 8, 1918, as well as in discussion with Prince Hohenlohe on July 15 (report by Hohenlohe to Vienna, July 15, HHSTA, Prussia III/1174.
48. Lieutenant Colonel Nicolai wired the head of the military press office, asking that a press conference on the 25th be told that censorship would be applied to any publicity given Kühlmann's speech. The OHL, he said, was most disagreeably surprised and did not share the view that Germany's victory was in question. The foreign ministry protested to the Kaiser about this procedure and in retaliation the OHL then again protested Kühlmann's speech. The relevant correspondence between Hertling and Hindenburg is in ZA, RK II, Kr. 10 (press), Vol. 14.
49. His first reaction to Kühlmann's speech, voiced to the military men around him, was that such things "could be thought, but not said, certainly not by a German foreign minister" (Thaer, p. 210).
50. Shorthand reports of the Reichstag, Vol. 313, Col. 5709; see also Matthias-Morsey (1), Vol. 2, pp. 421ff. Distrust of Hertling's government among the majority parties had been aroused in a briefing on eastern policy on June 19 (*ibidem,* Nos. 189a, b), when Kühlmann tried his best to smooth and gloss over things. Payer too tried in the Reichstag to trivialize the differences between the politicians and the generals (shorthand reports, *loc. cit.,* Cols. 5713ff.).
51. Note 331 in Berg's papers in the BA. Berg claims that when the Kaiser once again allowed himself to be brought around by Hertling he, Berg, told him: "You are casting your crown in the dust!" Government could not be conducted that way. In another two weeks he, the Kaiser, would give ground again. The Kaiser, somewhat at a loss, asked whether Berg was willing to take the responsibility for

dismissing Hertling immediately. The cabinet chief said that he would. Berg also boasted of having engineered the dismissal of Lyncker as chief of the military cabinet. Lyncker had had the audacity to criticize OHL strategy. On Hertling's doubts about Kühlmann's ability, see Payer, p. 70; Helfferich, Vol. 3, p. 425. Haussmann is rather ambiguous in his judgment of Kühlmann (pp. 206ff.). Among other things he reproaches Kühlmann for "frivolity." On the attitude of other deputies in the joint party caucus and on the course of the Kühlmann crisis generally, see Matthias-Morsey (1), Vol. 2, No. 191, where a full list of sources is given.

52. Kühlmann, pp. 579ff.
53. Berg's papers show that the impetus for summoning Hintze to Spa came from the Kaiser himself, but that it was Berg who persuaded Hintze to take up the ministerial burden in place of the Moscow ambassadorship. Hintze was quite realistic about his capacity and prospects and resisted for a long time (details in Baumgart [3], p. 89, Note 91). The OHL had nothing to do with this appointment. Haeften was afraid of a Pan-German minister and urgently warned Ludendorff against Hintze. "Isn't he close to the Pan-Germans?" retorted Ludendorff. "He's a pure opportunist," said Haeften "He'll play it this way or that" (Haeften papers, BA, Portfolio 5, pp. 29ff.). Haeften got his information from a member of the German legation in Oslo. This man, Hilmers, drew a very unfavorable picture of his chief, first in conversation and then by letter, describing him as an unprincipled climber. Hilmers admitted, however, that he had serious differences with Hintze and did not deny that Hintze was uncommonly able and hard-working and enjoyed great prestige in Norway (*ibidem,* Portfolio 3, No. 20). The kind of expectation the Pan-Germans placed in Hintze is seen in a nasty letter Dietrich Schäfer wrote Hintze on August 12, full of denunciations of South German "defeatists" based on gossip. Erzberger was the main target, and Hintze was advised to have him arrested (AA, WK 2, secret, Vol. 63).

Notes to Chapter 9

1. Perhaps they merely welcomed the idea of intensified war propaganda. Haeften's report is included in notes headed "Experiences, 1918" (Haeften papers, BA). Apparently they were available to Schwertfeger, who quoted whole sentences literally (UA, Vol. 2, pp. 189f., 193ff.) and reprinted the memorandum of June 3 (*ibidem,* Appendix 2, pp. 339ff.–it had been originally published in Ludendorff [1], pp. 478ff.).
2. See Payer, pp. 257ff. No minutes were to be found in the AA files. Deutelmoser, the foreign ministry's press secretary, criticized Haeften's plan on June 14, stressing that effective propaganda would require real mutual confidence between government and OHL, agreement on domestic issues, notably Prussian electoral reform, and cooperation on the part of the Reichstag, in other words, restoration of the national unity front (UA, Vol. 2, pp. 197ff.).
3. This "offensive" had already been launched in early June with some articles in the *Kreuzzeitung,* signed L. H., which created quite a sensation (UA, Vol. 2, p. 199).
4. They were committed to paper only in the summer of 1921.
5. Spa, July 2-3. For detailed foreign ministry minutes and notes by Envoy Rosenberg, see AA, WK 15, secret, Vol. 5, which also includes a second set of minutes kept by the OHL. Gatzke published both (pp. 84ff.), but only for July 2. On the following day, Belgium, France, and Luxembourg were also discussed; and from the Reich chancellery files some sketchy "conclusions" were published in UA, Vol. 2, App. 4. These do not entirely coincide with Rosenberg's notes (which are not included). They were sent to Hertling on July 6 as a summary.
6. UA, Vol. 2, p. 346, repeated in Vol. 12, p. 224, as "conclusions." According to Rosenberg, there was no mention in the debate of formally dividing Belgium into

two states, only of a clear-cut administrative separation. Ludendorff, however, spoke of "minor annexations all the way to Liège," which he was willing to forego only if there were a "protracted occupation." All the fortified positions were to be razed. The Kaiser wanted only to reduce the size of the Belgian army, not to dissolve it altogether.

7. Ludendorff (1), pp. 107ff., No. 19. *Ibidem,* application to the Chancellor, June 18, and discussion with Hertling and the ministerial departments concerned, pp. 110ff. ("conclusions" in UA, Vol. 2, App. 3). The Bauer papers, Portfolios 14 and 18, include Bauer's relevant memorandum of June 10 and the war minister's reply of June 24. Once again there was rejection of the 1917 proposal for extending liability to service to all men from the age of 15 to 60, to introduce auxiliary service for women, and to intensify the employment of women in industry (see RAW, Vol. 14, pp. 519f.). Another "sifting" of workers classified as essential to war industry was also described as "unpromising." The OHL had been quarreling with the war ministry and the *Kriegsamt* over this issue since April (Ludendorff [1] pp. 103ff.; a wealth of material also in ZA, RK II, Kr. 1, Vols. 12 and 13). On plans for securing Russo-German replacements, see Chapter 7, p. 282f.

8. Hertling, pp. 139ff. Two months later Crown Prince William followed up with a very pessimistic memorandum for the Kaiser and Ludendorff. He now expressed strong opposition to annexations and even advised major concessions, if these would bring peace (Berg papers and letter to Ludendorff, July 30; Bauer papers, Nos. 15, 36–both in BA).

9. Ludendorff (1), p. 492.

10. For evidence of Ludendorff's confidence in victory as late as mid-July, directly preceding the major offensive on Rheims, see Hintze's report, UA, Vol. 2, App. 15, p. 387. Hintze said that when he pointedly asked the general whether he was certain that this offensive would result in decisive and conclusive victory, Ludendorff answered with a ringing yes. Ludendorff himself said he had merely expressed hope that the next blow would put the enemy in a mood to negotiate for peace.

11. A detailed report by Hohenlohe to Burián, July 12, 13, and 15 (HHSTA, Kr. 4 k; Matthias-Morsey [1], Vol. 2, pp. 454f., 461; Erzberger, p. 286).

12. Foerster (2), pp. 16ff. The author tries to show from his accumulated evidence that Ludendorff never lost his nerve and never suffered from paralysis of the will. I think he proves his case only partly. Major Beck (a subsequent chief of staff) is quoted on p. 35 as confirming that the OHL did lose prestige in July 1918, and to my view the rather vague excuses offered by Wetzell and von dem Bussche do not refute this.

13. The British commander-in-chief, Sir Douglas Haig, expressly confirmed this in a memorandum for the cabinet on October 19 (Lloyd George, Vol. 6, p. 3300).

14. See Radowitz's report to Payer of August 1 on the OHL's continuing confidence (UA, Vol. 2, p. 213).

15. UA, Vol. 2, App. 1, p. 363 and *passim.* Similar statements were made to Haeften (UA, Vol. 2, p. 372).

16. Niemann (1), pp. 44f. UA, Vol. 2, pp. 215ff., stresses that on July 20 Ludendorff described a memorandum presented to him on that day by Major Niemann as "good." In it Niemann argued that statesmen and generals must collaborate closely to avoid missing the point at which the war could still be used as a means for exerting "leverage" toward securing an acceptable peace, and no longer as a means of coercion. Diplomatic negotiations, in other words, had to be initiated while Germany still possessed military superiority; but when it came to the question of how diplomatic negotiations might be initiated, Niemann's practical proposals can be described only as extremely amateurish. Ludendorff's approval of this memorandum was a very general thing and does not by any means prove that he regarded the initiation of diplomatic negotiations as urgent. When he

talked to Niemann on August 3, he seemed to be saying rather the opposite (Niemann [1], pp. 29ff.).

17. UA, Vol. 2, p. 371, official report by Haeften in late 1918—see also the notes on Haeften's recollections in his papers. The detailed and precise account in UA of the negotiations from August 13-14 onward is largely based on Hintze's, given in App. 15. See also AU.

18. In his memoranda for the crown prince and Ludendorff, Colonel Bauer had been complaining bitterly ever since April of the failure of the government of "feeble old Hertling." By August he had gone so far as to demand an ultimatum to Count Hertling and the Prussian cabinet: either they were to institute a rigidly authoritarian regime or surrender their offices. "We shall not be spared the struggle, in any event." If the Reichstag deputies refused to "toe the line," the Reichstag would simply have to be dissolved. It was the home front that was exclusively responsible for poor morale at the front, not least by the failure to look after the families of servicemen and the war-disabled, who were treated with indifference. Jews were outrageously evading service, and the pay of soldiers was pathetically low, compared to what workers in the war industries got, and even women secretaries employed by the army, etc. This was the only way of accounting for the anomaly of poor army morale, at a time when the spirits of the victorious forces should be soaring. Obviously Bauer had turned into a military bureaucrat with no understanding of conditions at the front. We do not know to what extent Bauer was still exercising political influence over Ludendorff in the summer of 1918. In a memorandum written in July he concludes, after rehashing various patriotic arguments, that attempts at negotiation should after all be launched, through a reliable neutral personage, preferably a neutral sovereign. On its own the integration of Belgium with Germany was not a desirable goal, and as for the Flemish coast, it was valueless in a military sense (drafts among the Bauer papers, dated April 23, July, and August, BA, Portfolio 2). He agreed with Colonel Niemann that Germany should try to give away its (useless) armored fleet to Britain, in return for a favorable peace, and that German propaganda should stick to the truth—though in a draft dated August he says that such a change was virtually impossible, since it would undermine confidence. On August 9 Bauer told Niemann he thought Ludendorff suffered from overwork and should take a long holiday. A deputy should take his place, but peace could not be long postponed (Niemann, p. 32). On August 28, Bauer submitted still another memorandum to Colonel Wetzell, chief of operations, in which he criticized Ludendorff's style of leadership—too much backing and filling before decisions were reached, too much intervention in tactical detail, failure to prepare rearward positions in time, etc. Wetzell scribbled pointed comments in the margin; and on September 6, at Bauer's instigation, he was transferred away from the General Staff. Yet by August even Wetzell was favoring Ludendorff's relief, since "his nerves were shot and he no longer had the situation under control" (Foerster [2], pp. 66f., 71).

19. UA, Vol. 2, App. 8-10. The speeches by Solf and Payer of August 20 and September 12 are part of this propaganda framework. On August 29 the Chancellor issued a directive to all the ministers on the subject of propaganda and informational services (Ludendorff [1], pp. 288f.). On the story of this big propaganda effort, see also Vogel, pp. 56ff.

20. Hintze says (UA, Vol. 2, p. 390) that the Chancellor responded to his threat of resignation with these words: "If you do, you ought to let me go first. I'm an old man!"

21. According to Ludendorff (2), p. 553, tears stood in his eyes.

22. July 21 is the date of Romberg's first long report on the possibility of sending confidential communications to Washington via Sulzer. He first developed a program for such communications on August 20 (AA, WK 2, top secret, Vol. 1). This volume and Vol. 2 contain further correspondence on Sulzer.

23. Törring's correspondence with the foreign ministry in AA, WK 20a, secret, Belgium, Vol. 2.
24. UA, Vol. 2, App. 15, p. 389.
25. Telephone conversation, August 21, put through by Bartenwerffer to Berlin (Haeften papers, BA). Ludendorff said that on August 14 he had agreed to Haeften's plan to base further propaganda on Hertling's "declaration of appeasement" of July 12 without any reservations. It is necessary to note that Ludendorff's reservations became plainly visible on August 19 and 21.
26. According to Hintze (UA, Vol. 2, p. 389), he said on August 13 that war aims in Belgium and Poland should be revised. Ludendorff curtly replied: "Why bring up Belgium? The minutes will show that agreement was reached on that issue."
27. In response to a long memorandum on German policy in Flanders and the need for economic ties with Belgium, Hintze on September 20, 1918 wrote the governor general of Belgium, Falkenhausen, that while there had been certain changes in Germany's Belgian policy recently, these were matters of form rather than substance. "Our goals remain essentially the same" [sic], though this must not be openly admitted and caution had to be exercised. Most of the economic goals would hopefully be reached in direct negotiations with the Belgian government; and "the efforts of the Flemish nationalists will probably not be in vain" (AA, WK 20a, secret, Vol. 2, Sheet 170). Hintze is supposed to have told Westarp on August 23: "I am anxious to get as much as possible out of the Belgian issue." Unfortunately, the prospect of securing permanent guarantees had grown dim, but let the conservatives and Pan-Germans continue with their propaganda (Ludendorff [1] p. 508).
28. The initiative for these talks lay exclusively with Count Törring, who did, however, avail himself of the allegedly strongly anti-Prussian Bavarian envoy in Berne as an intermediary. The first talk between Törring and de Peltzer took place on March 27. Foreign Minister Hymans of the Belgian government-in-exile wanted badly to avoid any impression among the Entente powers that Belgium was considering a separate peace with Germany. He was skeptical of Törring's assurances that Germany was prepared to make major concessions in the Belgian question; and he kept London, Paris, Washington, Rome, and Tokyo currently informed about how the talks went. A number of reports to the Foreign Office by the British chargé d'affaires in Le Havre, Sir Francis Villiers, and the Berne envoy Rumbold, dating from April 10 to August 13, are in the PRO, FO, 371/3442. See also the report by the American envoy Whitlock to the State Department, July 15 (FR, 1918, Supplement 1, Vol. 1, pp. 288f.). On June 30 the Belgian government sent word to Törring that it had long since made its peace terms known. It was now up to the German government to offer any statements to which Belgium might respond. Törring forwarded this communication to the German foreign ministry.
29. Lancken to the foreign ministry, September 4 and 15. He said that even Foreign Minister Hymans, as elicited by one of Lancken's Belgian acquaintances, thought that a German statement on Belgium would be desirable. The Belgian people, however, thought that the government in Le Havre was too reserved in its stand. (AA, WK 2, secret, Vol. 63).
30. Whitlock's report of August 10 (FR, *loc. cit.*, p. 296). The British Foreign Office correspondence *(loc. cit.)* contains only a recommendation to the Belgians, dated July 22, "to be ready to hear any proposals German Government may have to make and to discuss them with the Allies."
31. Hintze to Treutler, Munich, for Törring, August 9. Törring was to tell de Peltzer: "Germany is mindful of Belgian military honor and the traditions of the Belgian throne. It did not propose to impose on Belgium any kind of satellite status [a phrase saying there would be no interference with internal affairs was cut]. We have no objections whatever if Belgium returns to the status of a neutral power, are prepared to leave it to Belgium whether it wishes to restore its foreign relations to the old basis, want the country to have full freedom of action, but

believe that a renewal of neutrality, to be guaranteed by all the great powers, would bring with it a great deal of intervention, especially on the part of America—in other words, would mean restriction rather than protection. Free association with Germany would probably offer the best protection for Belgian independence and for the reconstruction of the Belgian economy." Hintze noted in the margin in pencil: "This passage is reminiscent of declarations by the Belgian government, favoring some form of association with Germany." Törring no longer received this message, which reveals Hintze's reluctance to forego Belgian "integration."

32. Handwritten marginal note by Hintze on Törring's report of August 13, which the latter probably took with him to Spa. The following is also based on Hintze's marginal notes—see his report in UA, Vol. 2, p. 392.

33. AA, WK 20a, secret, Belgium, Vol. 2. It seems improbable to me that "the certain party" referred to Sulzer, who was to carry the offer to Wilson, as Hintze maintained in his defensive brief (*loc. cit.*, p. 392), rather than to Törring. Von dem Bussche immediately offered a counterproposal for Törring's instruction, not Sulzer's, and Hintze sent Romberg the above formulation only on August 19, asking whether Romberg thought it adequate. If not, he wanted to know how much time there would be to draft a better directive, "in the event it should prove possible to prevail with the desired formulation."

34. Törring, writing to Hintze on August 17, pleaded that the word *Faustpfand* (bargaining counter or hostage) be avoided. Belgium would opt out if it were to play the role of hostage to insure that German demands would be met by the Entente. The "guarantees" demanded by Hertling on July 12 would also have to be dropped. Restored neutrality and economic ties would have to serve. Some indication of German willingness to make restitution would at last have to be given. Törring met with no success. On August 21 Treutler transmitted a directive to him, which resembled Hintze's earlier one. He was to avoid becoming involved in any discussion concerning restitution!

35. As per the data in the telephone conversation referred to in Note 25.

36. Ludendorff to the foreign ministry, August 21. Solf had meanwhile already delivered his speech on August 20.

37. Romberg to the foreign ministry, August 20-24 (AA, WK 2, top secret, Vol. 1). Foreign ministry to Romberg and Romberg to the foreign ministry, August 23 (AA, WK 20a, secret, Belgium, Vol. 2). On August 23 Hintze instructed Romberg to continue avoiding a talk with Sulzer "since efforts are at present underway to prevail with the desired formulation." This directive, however, seems to have arrived only after some delay. On August 24 Romberg transmitted intelligence received from a confidential source, to the effect that the Belgian government categorically declined to enter into negotiations, so long as Germany claimed that Belgium was to play the role of a "hostage" in any form. The term was like a red rag to a bull (AA, WK 20a, secret, Vol. 2).

38. The German text (AA, WK 20a, secret, Vol. 2, Sheets 148-151) coincides in content faithfully with the British version in Whitlock's report to the State Department, September 9 (FR, 1918, Supplement 1, Vol. 1, pp. 303f.). The same text is in FO, 371/3442. Törring, in his report to the foreign ministry of August 27, explains the absence of determinations of war indemnities as the result of an accidental omission in the talks.

39. Marginal note by Hintze on Törring's report of August 27, and correspondence with Treutler, September 7. Treutler was ordered to administer a politely worded reprimand to Törring.

40. Payer's report on the trip to Avesnes and its results (UA, Vol. 2, pp. 384ff.; Payer, pp. 276ff.). Radowitz to the foreign ministry, August 25. Hintze to Hertling, August 27. Hertling to Hintze, August 28, and to Payer, August 28 (AA, WK 20a, secret, Vol. 2).

41. Lloyd George, Vol. 4, p. 3248; Balfour's reply (Schulthess, 1918, Vol. 2, p. 217).

The speech had a good effect as a statement of encouragement to the German people (Rudin, pp. 38f.; text, Schulthess, 1918, Vol. 1, p. 287).

42. He said that Törring's expressed wish for an amnesty to the Flemish activists represented an attempt to intervene in Belgium's domestic affairs; and that the proposal to revive the trade treaties of 1914 for several years would hamper Belgium in its trade with the Allies. Actually both of these issues were brought up in the form of mere proposals rather than as demands, let alone peace terms! Hymans continued that Belgian independence was apparently to be restored only conditionally, since Belgium was to agree to intercede with the Allies for the return of the German colonies—this was the last remnant of the German "hostage" approach, which had already been relinquished. Finally, Hymans said, nothing was said about reparations and indemnities (FR, 1918, Supplement 1, Vol. 1, pp. 303f.; PRO, FO, 371/3442).

43. According to a report by Lancken to the foreign ministry, September 21, *The Rotterdam Courant* carried such a denial by the Le Havre government. AA, WK 20a, secret, Vol. 2 contains much material on anti-German propaganda directed against Törring's declaration.

44. Report by Hintze in UA, Vol. 2, p. 394. The official Belgian communiqué was handed to the German legation in Berne on September 27 by the Dutch legation.

45. He says he did not wait for Ludendorff's approval but wired Berne on August 26: "Agree to status quo formula" (UA, Vol. 2, p. 393). I have been unable to find such a wire in the files.

46. Correspondence between Hintze and Romberg, August 31-September 26. Draft by Legation Secretary Schubert of a notation intended for Sulzer, with changes (AA, WK 2, top secret, Vol. 2).

47. Ludendorff (1), p. 515, official document No. 3.

48. Hohenlohe to Burián, July 27 (HHSTA, Prussia III/174).

49. Thus his own account (UA, Vol. 2, p. 395).

50. Minutes in AA, Germany 131, Vol. 47, published in Baumgart (3), App. 7.

51. Ludendorff (1), p. 508, Westarp to Ludendorff, March 18, 1919.

52. AA, WK 23, secret, peace efforts by the Central Powers, Vols. 14-15. The correspondence between Berlin and Vienna on the peace initiative is there. The Austrian counterpart is in HHSTA, 47/3-26. In the following, I have not troubled to give every single reference from these files.

53. ÖU, Vol. 7, pp. 352ff.

54. Glaise-Horstenau, p. 271.

55. Report to the foreign ministry by Oberndorff, August 27. Czar Ferdinand, on the other hand, implored the Kaiser to keep the lead in peace questions in his own hands rather than leaving it to disintegrating Austria (Lersner to the foreign ministry, August 29). On September 14 he asked him by wire for his stand on the Austrian peace note, with which he was in disagreement.

56. German minutes of the talks in AA, WK 23, secret, Vol. 14, but only incomplete, containing only the discussions of Burián's peace initiative. Published in UA, Vol. 2, App. 7. The brief handwritten notes on the peace goals of the Central Powers published in UA, Vol. 12, App. 23 (p. 224), are based on AA, WK 15, secret, Vol. 6. They show that Hintze was now asking only for the integrity of Reich territory, foregoing all annexations, while Burián sought to cling to "certain minor expansions in territory, e.g., Lovchen and a border strip against Rumania." There were similar difficulties, by the way, as in 1916 with the Bulgarian and Turkish allies, neither of whom were completely in agreement with the Austrian peace note. Detailed Austrian minutes in HHSTA, secret, 47/3-20. "Memorandum on the views of the two sides on the peace démarche," September 5, *ibidem,* secret, 47/3-26 (also in AA, WK 23, secret, Vol. 14).

57. The German ambassador in Vienna thought likewise—Wedel to the foreign ministry, September 11.

58. Austrian minutes. The German AU, p. 15, speak only of "about two weeks."

59. Foerster (2), pp. 53ff. The source material assembled by Foerster from diaries and statements by General Staff officers is invaluable, though his account tends to exculpate his subject.
60. Foerster (2), p. 61. It is not true that it remained unanswered, as Hintze asserted (UA, Vol. 2, p. 396).
61. AU, p. 16.
62. *Ibidem,* pp. 15f. General Cramon had achieved this together with the Austrian chief of staff Arz.
63. Marginal note by the Kaiser on the wire from Vienna: "Gratitude from the House of Hapsburg! Insolence! An ultimatum and an ambush. . . . Now we'll settle the Polish question even without Vienna." (Grünau to ⸺ ⸺ ministry September 14.) In his wire to Emperor Charles on Sep⸺ naive enough to express his surprise that Charles, "heedless of the field marshal's stand," had proceeded in such fashion. Charles replied that in political questions his government could not "always submit to the views of your OHL."
64. Matthias-Morsey (1), Vol. 2, Nos. 219, 221.
65. On Hertling's view, see Ludendorff (1), p. 508, discussion with Westarp. On September 16 the Kaiser demanded that Envoy Rosen let the queen of Holland know that Germany had wanted to appeal to her for a peace initiative at the conclusion of the enemy offensive. Unfortunately that had become impossible for the immediate future, because of the step the Austrians had taken (Grünau to the foreign ministry, September 16).
66. It was given, not on September 24, as asserted by Hintze (UA, Vol. 2, p. 398), but immediately, on September 18 (AA, WK 23, secret, Vol. 15).
67. On September 16 Gevers had already sought him out and expressed his amazement at Burián's note, asking whether, in view of this situation, his queen could still act usefully on behalf of peace. In AU the negotiations with Holland were omitted, at the request of the Dutch diplomats (AA, WK 23, secret, Vol. 32. correspondence of Rosen and Haniel with the foreign ministry to July 16, 1919). Ludendorff's assertion in his memoirs (Ludendorff [2], p. 584) that Hintze had admitted in Spa on September 29 that "no démarche with the queen of Holland had ever been initiated, nor any further peace step" cannot be true.
68. Correspondence between Rosen and the foreign ministry, September 21-25, Wedel and the foreign ministry, September 24–AA, WK 23, secret, Vol. 15. Rosen to the foreign ministry, September 26, *ibidem,* Vol. 16.
69. Schulthess, 1918, Vol. 2, pp. 60, 215ff., 272ff., 594; Lloyd George, Vol. 6, p. 3251; Scott, p. 405.
70. Foerster (2), pp. 83ff., also for the following. Foerster bases himself on a letter from Lersner written in 1938. This, however, does not quite coincide with Lersner's letter to Hintze of October 2, 1919 (UA, Vol. 2, pp. 400, 404), in which he insists that prior to September 25 (or even 29) Ludendorff never said the slightest word to him about the seriousness of the situation.
71. AU, No. 10dff.
72. Lersner to the foreign ministry, October 1 (AU, No. 26).
73. Thus Intendant General Eisenhart-Rothe presented it to his chief Ludendorff on September 29, who vigorously agreed (Eisenhart-Rothe, pp. 121ff., cited after Foerster [2], p. 92).
74. His report in UA, Vol. 2, p. 399.
75. Romberg reported on September 29 that proposals to Wilson would make sense only if there were assurance that the legislature would ratify them in some form. A letter from Mensing to his father-in-law McNally (see Chapter 8) reported that distrust of the government was rapidly rising within Germany. Discussions with Americans would serve no purpose, unless there were a change of system. On September 30 there was another report: Mensing said–from information provided by McNally, of course–that the president wished to award Alsace-Lorraine to the French, but disagreed with Franco-British plans for the

annihilation of Germany. If Germany were to appeal to him, he, unlike France and Britain, would be ready for a peace initiative. To this end it would be necessary to effect a change in the system at once, "preferably by the Kaiser magnanimously taking the initiative himself." Of particular importance would be indemnification of Belgium and revision of the eastern peace treaties (AA, WK 23, secret, Vol. 18). Basis for this wire was a long report by Mensing of the same date, intended for Hintze, which Romberg likewise transmitted to Berlin (*ibidem,* Vol. 20). Mensing was then nominally engaged in prisoner-of-war exchange work in Zurich and in constant touch with his father-in-law and other Americans. Hintze took his report very seriously, overestimating McNally's access to the White House, as shown in his statements to the full cabinet on October 3 (Matthias-Morsey [2], p. 68).

76. Matthias-Morsey (1), Vol. 2, Nos. 225-226.
77. Perhaps that was the reason why he had his associates Rosenberg, Bergen, and Stumm sign the document, rather than signing it himself.
78. Wilson had been considered as a possible intermediary at supreme headquarters for some time. On September 6 the Kaiser, on Ballin's advice, wired the foreign ministry to consider whether Germany should not request the queen of the Netherlands to make the first appeal to Wilson (AA, WK 2, secret, Vol. 63). On September 21 Ludendorff inquired whether Hintze was considering approaching America in the matter of peace negotiations through Prince Hohenlohe-Langenburg, who was in Switzerland as a representative of the Red Cross, eagerly playing the intermediary there (AU, no. 11f.).
79. I was unable to confirm from the AA files that these inquiries were actually made. In any event, one did go to Romberg.
80. Draft by Stumm of a wire to Romberg, September 30 (AU, No. 18. only in part). Romberg was to let Montgelas, the American expert in his legation, sound out Garrett (AA, WK 23, secret, Vol. 18). Hintze had already made this proposal on September 23, in connection with the peace program he then contemplated (see p. 330f.), in the event Sulzer should decline (AA, WK 2, top secret, Vol. 2). Garrett, however, refused to be sounded out (Romberg to the foreign ministry, September 30 and October 1, AA, WK 23, secret, Vols. 18, 19). Romberg's confidence in McNally may be gauged from the fact that he wanted to go over the text of the peace note with him before dispatching it, to get an idea of how it might be received. This was on October 1.
81. Telephone conversation between Count Wedel and the foreign ministry, October 1 (AU, No. 19).
82. It is a fact, furthermore, that Winterfeldt, the OHL liaison officer with the Chancellor, transmitted a dispatch from supreme headquarters on the morning of the 28th, to the effect that the situation was extremely serious. Because of the interaction between army and home front it was essential to calm down spirits at home and bring about the required unity front by placing the government on a broader popular basis (UA, Vol. 2, p. 253, Note; see also Payer, p. 82). Later on Ludendorff was to charge the initiators of the "revolution from above" with treason to the monarchy and denied knowing anything of the telephone conversation. It does seem to me unlikely that it emanated from Ludendorff—possibly it was Bartenwerffer. It is noteworthy that Winterfeldt's message mentioned broadening Hertling's government, but evidently said nothing about overthrowing it. Hindenburg's political naiveté is shown by his reverting at this critical juncture—to even Ludendorff's horror—to the annexation of Longwy and Briey as a condition for an armistice!
83. On his share in the prince's appointment see his notes on September 30, 1918, in Matthias-Morsey (1), Vol. 2, No. 253 (published in part also in UA, Part II, Vol. 2, p. 373). *Ibidem,* Vol. 2, pp. xviff., a detailed account of the background of the prince's chancellorship; also (pp. xxixff.) an equally detailed account of the strange chaos of "war cabinet" and "full cabinet."

84. Matthias-Morsey (2), Nos. 1-6.
85. Nor did he share the widespread criticism of Ludendorff (Max, p. 299). When Hindenburg complained to him on October 12 about rumors of Ludendorff's impending relief, adding that he would have to resign himself if that happened, he replied that he shared the field marshal's views that Ludendorff was irreplaceable, reaffirming his loyalty to Hindenburg (ZA, RK II Kr, 1, Vol. 2). Serious doubts of the prince's fitness to be Chancellor were voiced also by Hohenlohe directly after the two had met on October 4. Hohenlohe had doubts of the prince's health and stamina (HHSTA, Prussia III/174).
86. Max, pp. 331, 339. See the government program drafted for the prince by Hahn on September 6 (*ibidem,* p. 306); also the curious illusions Hahn set forth about the situation in Britain on October 2 (*ibidem,* p. 340).
87. Official report by von dem Bussche and Haeften in Ludendorff (1), pp. 535ff. The major, of course, larded his discourse with patriotic phraseology to assuage his listeners.
88. On October 5 it asked the foreign ministry for the text, through Lersner (AA, WK 23, secret, Vol. 20). When the Chancellor, on October 3, inquired of Hindenburg in writing whether the OHL appreciated that acceptance of the Fourteen Points might mean the loss of Alsace-Lorraine, of the Polish-speaking counties in the eastern provinces, and of the colonies, Hindenburg replied evasively (AU, No. 73). When the new war minister, Scheüch, put the same question to Ludendorff on October 11, Ludendorff declared that he was convinced acceptance of the Fourteen Points would not mean the surrender of even an inch of German soil. It would be up to the German negotiators at the peace talks to represent this German position successfully. (Matthias-Morsey [2], p. 140, Note 16). Ludendorff expressed himself similarly to Thaer on October 1 (Thaer, p. 236). Erzberger suffered from similar illusions (Matthias-Morsey [2], p. 141).
89. Matthias-Morsey (2), pp. 72ff., consultation of October 4.
90. The detailed account in Prince Max's memoirs seems essentially the work of his assistant Hahn. Matthias-Morsey (2), pp. liiiff., gives a highly critical evaluation of Hahn's methods. The memoirs, nevertheless, contain a wealth of invaluable source material, including important documents, offering an interpretation of the Chancellor's political thinking that is unquestionably authentic. I went through Haeften's papers in the BA and had them photocopied, but the important items have been meanwhile published in Matthias-Morsey (2), together with an almost complete set of cabinet minutes, the originals of which are in the ZA. I had copies of only some of these.
91. Haeften has criticized the prince's account (Max, pp. 354ff.) in his papers, published in Matthias-Morsey (2), No. 23; but this does not alter the fact that Haeften originally approved Simon's draft speech and raised objections in the name of the OHL only afterward, when he realized that the speech would impair the effect of the peace offer.
92. See Snell (2), p. 199. Oddly enough, McNally was not at all upset when the prince's earlier views (which he no longer held) became known; and he said so to Washington (Romberg to the foreign ministry, October 13 and 14, AA, WK 23, secret, Vol. 22). According to Schwabe, this earned him a reprimand from the State Department.
93. Among them a leading role was played by Attorney General Davis, Page's successor designate as ambassador.
94. Romberg to the foreign ministry, October 10, 13, and 14; the foreign ministry to Romberg, October 13. Switzerland refused to make the verbal representations for which it had originally offered itself. According to a marginal note, Solf thereupon forewent the whole action (AA, WK 23, secret, Vols. 12, 22).
95. McNally had urgently warned of the possibility of such a mishap on the 11th (Romberg to the foreign ministry, October 11; AU, No. 68).
96. Discussion with Sir William Wiseman, October 16, published in Snell (1), pp. 366ff.,

a very important document. See also House, Vol. 4, p. 83 (discussion with House, October 15).

97. Discussion with Maurice Janin, September, cited in Snell (2), p. 198.

98. Scott, pp. 399ff.

99. House, Vol. 4, pp. 76ff.; see also Snell (2), pp. 198ff., an interesting study based in part on important original American documentary material. See further Rudin, pp. 89ff., for the following. This is a carefully researched basic study, even though it is based only on published material. Schwabe's study, already cited in Chapter 8, Note 2, will present an exhaustive evaluation of the American source material with respect to Wilson's German policy in 1918-1919; and in the following I occasionally base myself on his data.

100. He also showed Wiseman a wireless message from Solf to a German commander in Russia, intercepted by the British Secret Service. It instructed the commander to stage popular demonstrations against premature evacuation of the country. Wilson took this very seriously, apparently without understanding the context of Solf's directive.

101. Professors and publicists, joined in part in the well-known "inquiry commission," organized in September 1917 to study problems of peace.

102. According to Schwabe, Wilson seems to have been impressed by a long letter from Herron in September 1918. The letter was brought to him by Lansing with a warm endorsement. It implored the president to make one last effort to convert Germany to democracy, before the decision was left to the arbitrament of arms.

103. For the following see Lloyd George, Vol. 6, pp. 3278ff.; Foch, Chapter 14; L'Hôpital, who presents the text of Foch's memorandum and part of his correspondence with Clémenceau; Mordacq, not too fruitful a source; Deist; Mermeix; Keit; Tardieu.

104. Lloyd George, Vol. 6, pp. 3255, 3285.

105. "It was pointed out that President Wilson's demands for the reform of the German constitution were not of a very practical character, inasmuch as even in states with a liberal constitution such as Great Britain or the United States of America, there was no very secure safeguard against a hasty rushing into war" (PRO, Cab. 23/14, WC 489 A [19], session of October 21, 1918; and *ibidem,* 489 B [2], session of October 22). See also Lloyd George, Vol. 6, p. 3305. On Haig's stand, see Rudin, p. 138.

106. According to Seymour (House, Vol. 4, p. 112), this was the only instruction issued to House. Seymour published it incompletely in the deciphered version he found among House's papers. The complete text of Wilson's original text, in a slightly different version, is in Baker, p. 523. Further details in W. Stull Holt, AHR, Vol. 65 (1960), p. 569.

107. Baker, p. 520. I am indebted to Schwabe for calling my attention to this passage.

108. PRO, Cab. 23/14, WC 491 B (3), October 26. Wilson's talk with Wiseman was already referred to in Note 96.

109. Bliss to Secretary of War Baker (Baker, p. 508, cited after Rudin, p. 176).

110. Foch, p. 285.

111. House, Vol. 4, p. 120.

112. House, Vol. 4, pp. 118f.

113. AU, undated draft of October 23, No. 76a.

114. William II to Prince Max, ZA, RK II, Kr. 15, Vol. 17.

115. Matthias-Morsey (2), No. 62.

116. At the war cabinet session on October 16, Haeften read a long wire from the OHL, expressing concern about "pusillanimity" on the home front and pleading for more patriotic propaganda (AU, No. 112). He appended two questions, which he represented as coming from the OHL, but which were evidently his own. They were formulated in such a way as to be viewed rightly as an attempt to blame deficient homefront morale for military defeat. This was furiously resented, and Haeften had to try to calm the anger—see Matthias-Morsey (2), pp. 205ff., 209.

117. Hindenburg to Prince Max, October 24 (ZA, RK II, 2, II, Kr. 10, Vol. 15). One reads with mounting surprise about the vast quantity of subjects that were still being discussed and embodied in papers in the OHL in October. On October 21 Ludendorff sent the Chancellor a lengthy memorandum on how best to combat unemployment after the war. It maintained that agriculture needed to be strengthened by "sound land reform" and the establishment of veterans' settlements. This would result in vigorous progeny, which was essential to replace war losses and strengthen Germany's position. Ludendorff requested that these questions be promptly solved. "Easiest thing in the world," Wahnschaffe penciled in the margin (ZA, RK II, Kr. 1, Vol. 13).

118. On October 1 Hintze had already made it clear to Admiral Scheer of the naval command that during the armistice and peace negotiations, the U-boat campaign would have to be halted (Deist [1], pp. 349f.).

119. Matthias-Morsey (2), Nos. 71-74; Max, pp. 458ff. Romberg too on October 15 urgently advised the foreign ministry to halt U-boat warfare immediately, since advices from McNally indicated that otherwise armistice negotiations would fail (AA, WK 23, secret, Vol. 23).

120. AU, No. 66; Max, p. 471; Matthias-Morsey (2), pp. 289, 295, 299.

121. Matthias-Morsey (2), No. 86.

122. Thaer, p. 243.

123. Lersner to the foreign ministry, October 26 (AA, WK 27, secret; Ludendorff [2], p. 615; Niemann, p. 178; AU, pp. 235f–Hindenburg to Prince Max, November 1). From Hindenburg's letter of apology it would seem that Heye informed himself on October 15 at the foreign ministry or the chancellery about the government's stand.

124. Max, p. 466.

125. AU, No. 79, telephone conversation of October 25.

126. Deuerlein (1), p. 319. Solf is supposed to have made similar statements before the war cabinet on October 24 (Matthias-Morsey [2] p. 339). On that occasion Solf remarked that Ludendorff's resignation would make a good impression in America.

127. *Ibidem,* pp. 333f.

128. Matthias-Morsey (2), No. 360 (report by Haeften). Prince Max's account shows that he did not fully appreciate the extent of Haeften's political activities, directed against his government.

129. Plessen's diary, Foerster (2), p. 116. For this and the following see Kaehler (1), pp. 439ff., reprinted in *Studien zur Geschichte des 19. und 20. Jahrhunderts,* ed. by W. Bussmann (1961), pp. 259ff.

130. Payer, pp. 141ff. Payer to Hintze, March 4, 1919 (Foerster [2], p. 119). Report by Lewetzow (Niemann, pp. 411f.).

131. Niemann, pp. 183f.

132. Report by Ludendorff to Thaer, *loc. cit.,* p. 247. In an audience of the Kaiser on October 20, Count Lerchenfeld had drawn the Kaiser's attention to the fact that while a Chancellor could constitutionally submit his resignation, a general could not (Matthias-Morsey [2], pp. 287f.). Ludendorff had actually threatened to resign on October 17, if the government polled any other generals. The cabinet was furious but did not dare risk his resignation (Max, p. 417).

133. Thaer, pp. 247f.; Matthias-Morsey (2), p. 363–Haeften's notes on a report Ludendorff gave him directly following the audience. Kaehler has given a highly detailed account of these events, even evaluating the sources, but he had not yet seen Haeften's papers.

134. Snell (2), p. 217.

135. The German soldiers in the front lines were basically apolitical, see Groener (1), p. 376. Groener's discerning observations entirely coincide with my own.

136. Among them Meinecke (Meinecke [1], p. 328). Max Weber had even before this, on October 11, written a letter to voice his concern that the Hohenzollern dynasty

could be spared a shameful end only by the voluntary abdication of William II. Details in Stutzenberger, pp. 37f. In the following, I have foregone enumerating and evaluating the immensely abundant memoirs and monographs on the history of the German November Revolution. I refer readers to the bibliographical notes in Snell (2) and Matthias-Morsey (2).

137. Max, pp. 497, 512, Note 1; Matthias-Morsey (2), pp. 357, 427. On October 25, the *Frankfurter Zeitung* opened the discussion with a simple reference to the concluding sentence of Wilson's note, which it represented as a very dangerous demand.

138. Matthias-Morsey (2), pp. 212, 264, 333, 338.

139. Cabinet session of October 31 (Matthias-Morsey [2], p. 446). Report by Lerchenfeld (*ibidem*, p. 449).

140. As contained in two reports, dispatched to the State Department on October 17 and 18 (according to Schwabe).

141. Hague legation to the foreign ministry, October 16 and 17 (AA, WK 23, secret, Vol. 23). Prince Max published an alleged round-robin directive from Hindenburg to the various army commands, based on information from Hahn, but this coincides only in part with the two reports and in respect of Britain is actually contradicted by them.

142. FR, 1918, Supplement 1, Vol. 1, p. 459, Lansing to Chargé d'Affaires Bliss at The Hague, November 4. See also Snell (2), p. 209.

143. Rosen to the foreign ministry, October 27 (two wires, AA, WK 23, secret, Vol. 27).

144. I suspect it was Noeggerath (see Chapter 5, Note 44). In Rosen's wire he figures under the cover name of "Melchior's friend." On the same day Prince Max had charged Rosen with asking him whether Wilson would regard Ludendorff's dismissal and the latest constitutional changes as adequate guarantees (the Chancellor to Rosen, October 27, AA, WK 23, secret, Vol. 27). On October 28 Rosen reported that Ludendorff's dismissal would be regarded in America as drawing a good deal of the blame away from the Kaiser (AU, No. 86d).

145. Solf to Romberg, October 27. In addition to the much corrected German draft, there is an English translation (AA, WK 23, secret, Vol. 27). Romberg to the foreign ministry, October 28 (*ibidem*, Vol. 28). The intention was to see to it that the memorandum also reached House in Paris.

146. FR, 1918, Supplement 1, Vol. 1, pp. 457ff., 459.

147. Foreign ministry to Copenhagen legation, October 25 (AA, WK 23, secret, Vol. 26). Brockdorff-Rantzau to the foreign ministry, October 26 (*ibidem*, Vol. 27).

148. Osborne's report was transmitted to the State department on October 29 through the chargé d'affaires Grant-Smith (FR, 1918, Supplement 1, Vol. 1, pp. 416ff.). It also reflects Hahn's statements exclusively and is silent on the discussion of the question of the Kaiser, as are the American reports from The Hague of October 17 and 18 (see Hahn's report, referred to before)—Max, pp. 517, 532f. For Envoy Brockdorff-Rantzau's stand and report to the foreign ministry, October 29, see AA, WK 23, secret, Vol. 28. According to Osborne's report Hahn tried to make clear to the other participants in the discussion the deep disappointment of the German liberals with Wilson's third note and to convince them that the democratic reformist intentions of Prince Max's government were genuine. According to a simultaneous report by Grant-Smith to Lansing (FR, *loc. cit.,* p. 415), Hahn also said that the Kaiser, who did not fit into the new system, was about to abdicate and the crown prince would renounce the succession, though the monarchial system was to be retained. If this is true—and Grant-Smith does not actually name Hahn—it would seem that Prince Max charged Hahn with confirming that abdication was inevitable rather than with rounding up arguments against it. Presumably the letter from Prince Hohenlohe-Langenburg, which reached him on October 27 (Max, pp. 513ff.), had in the meantime convinced the Chancellor that the Kaiser would have to go. Hahn's own views are shown in his letter to Prince Max of October 30 (Matthias-Morsey [2], pp. 427f.).

149. Solf apparently shared this esteem, since on October 22 he asked McNally through Romberg to explain the German note of reply to Wilson and describe the swift democratization of Germany (AA WK 23, secret, Vol. 25).

150. Mensing to Hintze, September 30. Lancken to the foreign ministry, October 17. Mensing to Solf, October 12. Mensing to the foreign ministry, October 17. Lersner to the foreign ministry, October 18 (British advise by wireless to depose the Kaiser). Note by von dem Bussche, October 21 (on advice given by McNally). Hintze from headquarters to the foreign ministry, October 21. Replacement General Staff, Berlin, Department IIIb, October 21 (information forwarded by the International Red Cross on Wilson's demands). Romberg to the foreign ministry, October 25 (on McNally's views). Lancken to the foreign ministry, October 25. Romberg to the foreign ministry, October 28. Hintze to Romberg, October 29. Romberg to the foreign ministry, October 30–all in AA, WK 23, secret, Vols. 20-29. Note also the mission of General Chelius, who appeared on October 28 at Lancken's behest (Max, pp. 518ff.; AU, Nos. 78, 94, 95).

151. A glaring example of his embroidered reports is the wire he sent Lansing on October 26 (FR, *loc. cit.,* p. 418). Herron, the apostle of democratic conversion (see Chapter 5, Note 62), seems to have cast a spell over the German politicians of the left, affecting even Scheidemann (Matthias-Morsey [2], p. 398). His German liaison man was the Bavarian (formerly Austrian) journalist Roberto de Fiori, a political mountebank who pretended to Herron that he was a confidant of the Bavarian royal family and government and offered late in October to stage a popular rebellion in Germany, if that was what Wilson wanted (Snell [2], p. 209). A voluminous handwritten report of his talks with Herron on June 15, 1918 is in AA, WK 2, secret, Vol. 61. The American legation in Berne reported to Washington on de Fiori's outlandish efforts to negotiate peace with Herron, as did the British legation to London (Rumbold to the Foreign Office, July 30, 1918, PRO, FO, 371/3442). A report of August 11, from a Mr. Erskine in Rome, described de Fiori as a seasoned spy and warned against entering into any dealings with him *(ibidem).*

152. Schwabe, in his forthcoming work, already mentioned, will present further details from the State Department archive.

153. Max, p. 516. Letter from Prince Hohenlohe-Langenberg *(ibidem,* pp. 513ff.). See also Romberg to the foreign ministry, October 25 and 26 (AA, WK 23, secret, Vol. 26).

154. Premier Dandl to Lerchenfeld, October 28 (Matthias-Morsey [2], pp. 411f.). He wrote that in Munich the Kaiser's abdication was regarded as an urgent necessity. More than that, a Prussian regent as a successor would be regarded as intolerable. Openly separatist statements by Deputy Held were represented by Dandl to the war cabinet on November 3 as harmless *(ibidem,* pp. 477ff.). See also reports by Treutler, October 25 and November 2 (AU, Nos. 77, 97), and by Romberg, November 3 *(ibidem,* No. 98; also Max, pp. 659f.). At the federal council meeting on November 1, when Prince Max reported on the abdication issue, Lerchenfeld was the first to report the assent of his king *(ibidem,* p. 556).

155. There is a brief unsigned statement (possibly by Haniel) dated October 24, in AA, WK 23, secret, Vol. 26, stating that German democratization would become credible in Britain and America only if the Kaiser abdicated, which might well push public opinion in the direction of favoring a prompt peace. On October 30, in a handwritten note, Solf requested the foreign ministry to get up a memorandum on the abdication issue, solely from the viewpoint of foreign policy and treated in such a fashion that it could be submitted to the cabinet. The American desk promptly provided such a document, mentioning the American elections of November 5, in which Wilson would be greatly helped by so dramatic an action as the Kaiser's abdication *(ibidem,* Vol. 28).

156. Max, p. 467.

157. Hindenburg always denied that he was responsible for this unfortunate journey

(Groener [2], p. 441), but Haeften insisted that the impetus had come from a telephone conversation he held with Hindenburg (Matthias-Morsey [2], p. 429, Note 4). The Berg papers show that Berg, in concert with the empress, pressed the Kaiser to depart for Spa. Although he had been dismissed, Berg was still active as a political adviser to the Kaiser and his consort. Both of them, however, implored the Kaiser again and again not to abdicate at any cost (Dorpalen, pp. 33ff.).

158. The Kaiser's thinking, stated in his customary brash and baroque style, is summarized in a letter of November 3 to an unnamed confidant (Schiffer, pp. 135-137). He would "write my answer on the pavement with machine guns, even if it means shooting up my own palace. There is going to be order. . . . I wouldn't dream of abandoning the throne on account of a few hundred Jews and a few thousand workers."

159. Matthias-Morsey (2), p. 531.

160. Ludendorff told his first wife and Breucker (Breucker, p. 61) that the Kaiser even said when he was taking leave: "I shall try to build up a new Reich with the help of the social democrats." Ludendorff thought this rather absurd.

161. Matthias-Morsey (2), p. 516.

162. Max, p. 600.

163. This charge is leveled with special severity in Snell (2).

164. Not only Erzberger but Stresemann as well suspected at the time that the Kaiser's abdication was quite unlikely to result in any mitigation of the armistice and peace terms (Matthias-Morsey [2], p. 521, joint party caucus of November 5). When members of the Swiss federal council recommended that the Kaiser should sacrifice himself, with a view to "sympathies abroad" (AU, No. 94, October 28), Hintze, representing the foreign ministry at headquarters, wrote Romberg that such a step could not possibly be taken on the basis of mere sentiment (AA, WK, secret, Vol. 28, October 29).

165. Among the Kaiser's sons the only one to have been considered seems to have been Prince Augustus William (on account of his more "civilian" education), besides the son of Prince Albrecht, Frederic William of Oels, who had once been a county councilor but was totally unknown to the public.

166. See the plans by Colonel Bauer and Niemann to achieve a reconciliation with Britain by surrendering Germany's armored vessels (Chapter 9, Note 18). My account is based essentially on Deist (1), pp. 341ff., a very conscientious study using the files of the German naval archive at the Freiburg Institute of Military History (Deist is a former student of mine). The work updates all the older literature cited in it.

167. This same motivation, built around the concept of honor, is found in Levetzow's later report (Niemann, p. 409). A remarkable fact, characteristic of German military thinking at the time, is that even the otherwise self-possessed Groener says (Groener [1], p. 442) that had he known of the German navy's battle plan, he should have approved of it, even though he realized that it would have been, in effect, a pointless "heroic gesture. . . . I should have preferred to see our ships go down fighting rather than come to rest in British hands."

168. The evacuation began on September 29.

169. Report by Levetzow (Niemann, p. 404).

170. Discussing the matter much later (Max, pp. 575f.), the Chancellor said that had he been advised of the navy plan, he should have unconditionally affirmed its military-political utility; for whether the navy had won victory or went down to "glorious defeat," the event would have boosted the country's morale, thus making possible a saving final struggle. His approval, however, would have been linked to timing the naval battle only after Foch's peace terms had become known. The passage is typical of Prince Max's fuzzy and unrealistic idealism. He would almost certainly not have succeeded in gaining cabinet approval of such a plan, had he put the issue to it. On October 24 the centrist party in the Reichstag

had unanimously voted against the idea of a "national uprising" (Matthias-Morsey [2], p. 340). Conrad Haussmann, who was especially close to the Chancellor, did in late October draft a proclamation, calling on the German people to fight on, but in a matter of days he concluded that such an undertaking was senseless (Haussmann, p. 264).

171. According to Levetzow's own report (Niemann, p. 409). The order was unmistakably offensive in character, even though Levetzow and Trotha subsequently tried to represent it as purely defensive (Deist [1], p. 367).

172. The most recent account from the communist side (Zeisler) is based on published sources long since familiar.

173. Asked by Levetzow whether he "personally and materially estimated the situation of the fleet to be such as to permit a major operation at this time," Trotha, on October 16, answered in the affirmative without reservation. In view of the unhappy experiences of the German navy ever since August 1917, the answer seems either ignorant or frivolous.

174. According to Neu (p. 67, citing Popp and Artelt, *Ursprung und Entwicklung der Novemberrevolution* [1918], and statements by Artelt in UA, Vol. 9, p. 580), the Kiel torpedo division put forward a program with but two political demands (in addition to many nonpolitical ones): the Hohenzollern dynasty to abdicate; and introduction of the universal franchise for both sexes. Noske gives the same two points in his memoirs (Noske, p. 12). The confusion in Kiel, when Noske arrived there, was so complete, however, that it would have been virtually impossible to establish the degree to which this program was accepted by the sailors. Noske had been among the first in the Reichstag to call for the Kaiser's abdication; and perhaps that was the reason why he took the program seriously and reported it to Berlin (Max, pp. 491, 497).

175. The best account is given by Mitchell.

176. See the statements by Ebert and Gröber before the joint party caucus on November 4 (Matthias-Morsey [2], p. 499; also Groener, p. 448). On November 6, Groener put an end to conscription.

177. Groener, p. 441; Max, p. 590. Prince Max states that Groener was still clinging to this notion on November 6. "If necessary, he would have been willing to fight on behind the Rhine."

178. Lloyd George, Vol. 6, pp. 3299, 3309. See also Rudin, pp. 397f.

179. In the meantime, however, an American breakthrough at Verdun had created a very dangerous situation on the western front.

180. The content of the note became known by wireless in the afternoon, and Erzberger was told about it just before his departure for headquarters. The cabinet had decided on capitulation even before Wilson's fourth note containing the formal Allied commitment to the Fourteen Points had been transmitted, and this suggests that the minutes of the cabinet session of November 6 were removed from the files of the Reich chancellery and destroyed (Matthias-Morsey [2], p. 547, Note 1, pp. xlvff.). The secretary of the Chancellor, Arnold Brecht (Brecht, p. 175), insists, however, that no minutes were taken, since he was ill with the grippe.

181. There has been controversy about Erzberger's appointment and his initial reaction to it. The most recent and highly competent account is given in Matthias-Morsey (2), Introduction, pp. lviiff. and No. 131. Apparently the delegates never had a formal order to sign anything that was placed before them. Such subservience followed only when the great mutiny made such swift progress. Epstein is wrong when he says (pp. 311ff.) that Erzberger was named head of the armistice commission on Hintze's advice. Poll's well-documented study shows (p. 43) that Lersner was the real instigator, because he regarded General Gündell, previously appointed by Ludendorff, as unqualified. Erzberger was rightly considered the man most familiar with the preliminary negotiations with Wilson. It is inconceivable that a man like Lersner should have in this fashion wished to

relieve the OHL of responsibility for a bad armistice and blame the government instead. Not unnaturally, however, Groener and Gündell did feel a certain sense of relief that the OHL would not have to carry the blame alone. I cannot follow Epstein in attributing such vast importance to the manifestly foolish intelligence of October 15 (AU, No. 230), which claimed that Foch was refusing to negotiate with any German from headquarters. Brecht has now published, from his private papers (pp. 176ff.), the minutes of the cabinet session of November 2, missing from the foreign ministry files. This was the session at which Erzberger proposed that a minister should take part in the armistice negotiations (see also Matthias-Morsey [2], No. 117, identical with UA, No. 96b). There is no indication, however, that Erzberger at this session expressed the view that the military would be too obstinate.

182. Crown Prince William departed Spa before a final decision on the future of the monarchy had been taken, leaving all further action on his behalf to his chief of staff Schulenburg. This action seems to me to demonstrate his incapacity to represent his dynasty with any dignity. I rather think that his subsequent flight to Holland is less excusable than his father's. Prince Max, in Note 553, mentions a letter from the crown prince to the Chancellor, originally intended for publication. This handwritten letter was found among Prince Max's papers at Salem, and the administrators kindly made a photocopy available to me. At the suggestion of the chancellery, the crown prince endeavored to dispel public doubts of his political integrity by giving assurances that he, like his father, represented no obstacle or danger to "the continued development of democratic institutions." It was true that in the past he had repeatedly expressed support for firm political leadership; but as a soldier he was not essentially concerned with the government's political complexion. "I firmly declare that I am thoroughly convinced of the necessity for basic constitutional change in the Reich and constitutional reorganization in Prussia, involving electoral reform, and that I accept the new system unreservedly. The immense wartime achievements of the German people as well as the issue of the war itself preclude any return to the old situation." But while obsolete institutions should be discarded, care should be taken to retain those that were viable. "Even had the war ended less unfavorably for our side—indeed, had it ended well for us—the present developments, whose importance I was not initially able to appreciate, could scarcely have failed to eventuate. . . . As early as 1917 I went on record as stating that Germany could consider itself fortunate, if it were able to conclude peace on the basis of the status quo." Since then he had repeatedly pressed for a swift conclusion to the war, as evidenced in a number of written statements to leading government figures (see pp. 49f. and William, pp. 156f., 161ff.).

183. For eyewitness testimony to the events at Spa on November 9, see Westarp; also Baumont, p. 130.

184. Details in Kaehler (1), pp. 452ff.; Michaelis (4), pp. 695ff.

185. See Haussmann's minutes of the first session of Ebert's "cabinet" on November 10 (Haussmann, pp. 272f.). The ZA contains a partial set of the minutes of this same session (II, 2, II, Kr. 33, Vol. 1). Evidently the OHL stated that if necessary it was prepared to conclude an armistice in place of the "irregular" government of Ebert, "since the army was already threatening to fall apart." The wireless message that was subsequently dispatched from the OHL to Compiègne was simply signed "Reich Chancellor."

Index

Adenauer, Konrad, lord mayor of Cologne, 125

Adolph Frederic, Prince of Mecklenburg: suggested for Finnish throne, 273

Aland islands (Ahvenamaa): in treaty of Brest-Litovsk, 112; German claims to, 250, 266; Germans land on, 269, 272

Albert I of Belgium, and papal peace initiative, 20

Alexander, Prince of Hohenlohe-Schillingsfürst: indiscreet letter of Prince Max to, 348-9, 353

Alexeyev, General, Cossack commander, 258, 264

Alfonso XIII of Spain, suggested as mediator (Aug. 1918), 324

Alsace: regiments from, 130; Kaiser and Hertling plan future of, 144, 249

Alsace-Lorraine: return of, to France, as French war aim, 8, 9, 31; suggestion of plebiscite in, 8, 61, 138; German social democrats and, 8, 30; Pope and, 19; Britain and future of, 32, 207; Lloyd George on, 10, 11, 64, 138, 194; Asquith on, 49, 67; Balfour on, 64; OHL and, 33, 93; as prime obstacle to negotiated peace, 35, 317; Austria, and German attitude toward, 35, 36, 50, 149, 170, 207, 210, 214, 216; in French Fribourg terms, 37, 38, 87, 132, 202; in Belgian peace feeler, 61; Kühlmann's speech on (Oct. 1917), 66-7; effect of military regime in, and prospects for autonomy of, under Germany, 128-44; Wilson and, 137-8, 348, 358; Hertling

argues Germany's historic right to, 201; Emperor Charles on, 224; Hertling and Kühlmann not willing to negotiate over, 300, 303, 310; question of, evaded in Swiss talks (Aug. 1918), 328; to be surrendered (armistice terms), 357; French postwar treatment of, 131

Anatolia: eastern part of, returned to Turkey by treaty of Brest-Litovsk, 112

annexationism: of Italy, 9, 198, 215, 220; of Pan-Germans and Fatherland Party, 16, 119, 185; of OHL, 30, 53, 75, 89, 92, 152, 161, 222; of France, 215, 220

arbitration, Wilson's idea of international court for: included in papal peace proposals, 19, 41; supported by Czernin, 208, and Hertling, 300

Archangel, bombarded by British, 275

Armand, Major Count: as representative of Painlevé, meets Austrian envoy in Switzerland, (Aug. 1917) 35, 37, (Feb. 1918) 216, 217, 223

Armenia: in papal peace proposals, 42; included in temporary Trans-Caucasian Republic, 286; Turks and, 287, 288

armistice: proposed by Pope for Christmas Day (1914), 17; with Rumania (1917), 175; with Bulgaria (1918), 340; with Germany (1918), 356-60, 383, 384, 385

army, German: political indoctrination of, 16; on eastern front, 107, 116; advances on St. Petersburg (Feb. 1918), 111, 112, 204, 214; western offensive by (Mar.) 215, 229-35; offensive fails,